ALUMINIUMVILLE

Government
Global Business
and the Scottish Highlands

with a Foreword by Rt Hon. Charles Kennedy MP

ANDREW PERCHARD

Crucible Books

Aluminiumville: Government, Global Business and the Scottish Highlands

Copyright © Andrew Perchard, 2012

First published in 2012 by
Crucible Books

Crucible Books is an imprint of
Carnegie Publishing Ltd,
Carnegie House,
Chatsworth Road,
Lancaster LA1 4SL
www.cruciblebooks.com

British Library Cataloguing-in-Publication data
A catalogue record for this book is available from the British Library

ISBN 978-1-905472-15-4

Designed, typeset and originated by Carnegie Book Production, Lancaster
Printed and bound in the UK by Short Run Press, Exeter

ALUMINIUMVILLE

Construction of pipelines to Kinlochleven. © RTA/GUA.

*Dedicated to the memory
of a dearly missed friend
Rick Payne (1944–2006),
and
for Angela, Orla, Jess and Emily*

Dr Andrew Perchard is Lecturer in Business History & Strategy at the University of Strathclyde Business School. He is also a Research Associate of the Centre for Business History in Scotland and the Scottish Oral History Centre. Formerly he was post-doctoral research fellow on the history of aluminium project at the Centre for History, University of the Highlands and Islands. He is the author of *The Mine Management Professions in the Twentieth-century Scottish Coal Mining Industry* (Lampeter, 2007).

Contents

Tables and figures

Figures:

Tables:

Abbreviations

AAC	Alliance Aluminium Company
AAUK	Alcan Aluminium UK
Al. Corp.	Aluminium Corporation Ltd
ADM	Admiralty
AEU	Amalgamated Engineering Union
AF	L'Aluminium français
AFC	Alais, Froges et Camargue
AGR	Advanced Gas-cooled Reactor
AIAG	Aluminium Industrie Aktiengesellschaft
Alcan	Aluminum Company of Canada (Previously the Northern Aluminum Company)
Alcoa	Aluminum Company of America (Previously the Pittsburgh Reduction Company)
AlFed	Aluminium Federation
AM	Air Ministry
AP	Aluminium Pechiney
BACo	British Aluminium Company Ltd
BMRB	British Market Research Board Ltd
BNFMRA	British non-ferrous metals research association
CBA	Canadian British Aluminium Company Ltd
CHA	*Cahiers d'histoire de l'aluminium*
BH	*Business History*
BHR	*Business History Review*
DNN	Det Norske Nitridaktieselskap
DSIR	Department of Scientific and Industrial Research
EEF	Engineering Employers Federation
EHR	*Economic History Review*
ETU	Electrical Trades Union
GUA	Glasgow University Archives
HIDB	Highlands and Islands Development Board
HIE	Highlands and Islands Enterprise

HSE	Health and Safety Executive (Formerly HM Inspectorate of Factories)
HMIPI	HM Industrial Pollution Inspectorate
IHA	Institut pour l'Histoire de l'Aluminium
IVS	Inverlochy Village Society
JICH	*Journal of Imperial and Commonwealth History*
KVIS	Kinlochleven Village Improvement Society
LAC	Lochaber Archives Centre (Fort William)
MAP	Ministry of Aircraft Production
MoD	Ministry of Defence
MoM	Ministry of Munitions
MoR	Ministry of Reconstruction
MoS	Ministry of Supply
NACO	Norsk Aluminium Company (Now Norsk Hydro)
NAS	National Archives of Scotland
NBACo	North British Aluminium Company Ltd
NFMC	Non-Ferrous Metals Committee (Min. of Munitions)
NS	*Northern Scotland*
NSHEB	North of Scotland Hydro-Electric Board
PCAC	Compagnie de produits chimiques d'Alais et de la Camargue
RAE	Royal Aircraft Establishment (Before 1918, Royal Aircraft Factory, and after 1988 – Royal Aerospace Establishment)
RAF	Royal Air Force
RTAIC	Rio Tinto Alcan Information Centre
RTAlcan	Rio Tinto Alcan (previously RTZ)
RTZ	Rio Tinto Zinc
SCDI	Scottish Council Development and Industry
SDD	Scottish Office Development Department
SEC	Scottish Economic Committee
SLH	*Scottish Labour History*
SLF	Scottish Landowners' Federation
STUC	Scottish Trades Union Congress
TGWU	Transport and General Workers Union
TNA	The National Archives
TUC	Trades Union Congress (GB)
UKAEA	United Kingdom Atomic Energy Authority

Glossary

Throughout this book, I have endeavoured to provide readers with contemporary values for historical prices and costs. These have been calculated using the invaluable tool developed by a transatlantic initiative, Measuring Worth, accessible at http://www.measuringworth.com/. By and large, most have been calculated using the GDP deflator against 2009 prices inserted in brackets adjoining the original cost. Where possible, all weights have been calculated in metric tonnes (mts) to save readers from unnecessary conversion calculations. Prices in Canadian and US dollars are expressed respectively as CAD or USD. For the purposes of this book, the European spelling, Aluminium, has been used as opposed to the North American, Aluminum. A discussion of the etymology of the word is available on the website of the International Aluminium Association: http://www.world-aluminium.org/About+Aluminium/Story+of

(Primary) aluminium reduction: Although a substance called 'alun' was used in ancient China, it would be nearly four thousand years before aluminium was isolated. The discovery of aluminium owed much to the early work of an English chemist, Humphrey Davy (1778–1829) who identified the metal in 1809, and initially called it alumium. Knowledge of the metal was further advanced by the work of Danish chemist Christian Oersted (1777–1851) and his German contemporary Friedrich Wöhler (1800–82). These chemical processes helped to separate aluminium from oxygen, with Wöhler producing aluminium powder in 1827. Crucially, this confirmed the properties of lightness and malleability for the metal. A further important stage in the emergence of the metal came with French chemist Henri Sainte-Claire Deville's production of globules of aluminium in 1854. His display of ingots of the metal at the Paris Exhibition of 1855 attracted the attention of Napoleon III, who saw its great potential, as did the French chemical producer Compagnie des produits chimiques d'Alais et de la Camargue (PCAC). This led directly to the major breakthrough some twenty-six years later. While chemical production of aluminium continued, the watershed came in 1886 with the discovery concurrently by French and American chemists Paul Louis Héroult and Charles Martin Hall (in a twist of fate both men were born and died in the same years, 1863–1914) of an effective electro-chemical means of aluminium reduction. This transformed aluminium production from a metal produced in small quantities for luxury products to one that could be produced on a mass industrial-scale. The Hall-Héroult process continues to be the principal method of aluminium reduction to this day. In this process, aluminium oxide (alumina) is added to a carbon-lined steel bath (furnaces/cells/pots) of molten cryolite heated to 960–1000° Celsius. Electricity is passed through the bath between carbon-lined anodes, suspended on steel prongs, and the cathode lining of the bath, separating the aluminium from the oxygen and leaving the metal to sink to the bottom of the furnace from whence it can be tapped. After testing for purity, it is then cast into ingots and blocks. This is then transported to downstream extrusion works and rolling mills.

Bauxite: The mineral prevalent in the earth's crust from which alumina is extracted, through the Bayer process. It is named after the southern French town of Les Baux where the principal supplies of the mineral first came. Austrian chemist Karl Josef Bayer (1847–1904) discovered the means in 1887, through distillation, filtering and calcination, of producing alumina. It requires four tonnes of bauxite to produce the two tonnes of alumina necessary for obtaining one tonne of aluminium. Current global supplies of the mineral are principally drawn from Guinea, Australia, Vietnam, Brazil, Guyana and Jamaica.[1]

Cryolite: Unlike bauxite, cryolite is a rare mineral, with Greenland the principal supplier throughout much of the late nineteenth and twentieth centuries.

Duralmin: Discovered and patented by German metallurgist Alfred Wilm, and named after the Rhineish-Westphalian village of Düren where he worked, this aluminium alloy (containing 3.5 per cent copper, and 0.5 per cent magnesium) improved the tensile strength and durability of aluminium. As Wilm noted at the time, 'this alloy will offer multiple applications for military equipment and aerial developments.'[2] The full significance of this discovery would dawn in the impending global conflict of 1914–1918.

Extrusion: The production of cross-sectional items (e.g. piping, railway tracks and rails) through a cold or hot process.

Acknowledgements

I T IS A GREAT PLEASURE to be able finally to thank the many people who have aided and contributed in one way or another to this book and the project upon which it was based. The sheer numbers involved preclude me mentioning everyone by name but my heartfelt thanks to them is every bit as sincerely intended.

Archivists and librarians, as well as funders, provide the very life-blood upon which historians survive. I would like to thank the staff of the Bodleian Library, University of Oxford, and the family of the estate of Lord Addison (for permission to use the latter's personal papers), General Registers of Scotland, Highland Council Archives and Libraries, the Lochaber Archives Centre, the National Archives of Scotland, the National Archives at Kew, the National Library of Scotland, and Joan Ross and her colleagues at the Alness Civic & Heritage Centre. In addition, Carole McCallum of the STUC archive at Glasgow Caledonian University as always provided unstinting help. Particular thanks are due to the staff at Glasgow University Archives Service – whose professionalism and friendliness made the considerable amount of time spent pouring over the company archives all the more enjoyable – and Nicole Hébert at Rio Tinto's (formerly Maison Alcan) Montréal information centre. Funding from Rio Tinto (formerly Alcan), HIE Lochaber, HI-hopes (ESF), and the Institut pour l'Histoire de l'Aluminium (IHA) made this project (and book) possible. I am grateful also to a number of colleagues for their comments on drafts of this book and helpful pointers: Simon Ball, Ewen Cameron, Mark Freeman, Matthias Kipping, George Peden, Ray Stokes, and Geoff Tweedale. John Wilson, Alistair Hodge, Rachel Clarke, Penny Hayashi, as well as Alasdair Robertson, all played important roles in helping to realise this book. My thanks also go to the Rt Hon. Charles Kennedy MP for agreeing to write the preface to this work.

There are a number of other groups of people and individuals who deserve particular mention for their parts. Without the expertise and support of the staff (past and present) of the IHA, in particular, Ivan Grinberg, Mauve Carbonell, Hélène Frouard, Maurice Laparra, and Jenny Piquet, this would not have been the book it is. Similarly, the discussions of scholars surrounding the IHA and the Comparative Aluminium Research Project (CARP) provided critical intellectual stimulus to the formulation of this text. Hans Otto Frøland, Mats Ingulstad, Pål Thonstad Sandvik and Espen Storli deserve especial mention for insightful comments and good company during this process. At the UHI Centre for History, James Hunter, Steven MacKay and Rob MacPherson were all very supportive. In Fort William and Kinlochleven, I owe considerable thanks to the many oral history respondents and members of the community who showed a considerable interest in this project. In particular, I would like to single out John Blair, Cynthia Cassidy, Robert Cairns, Jimmy Dunlevy, Liz Grieve, Iain Grainger, George Haggart OBE, Bob Herbert, Margaret Mathieson, Bill Maxwell, Douglas MacDiarmid, Eleanor MacDonald, Mary MacPherson, Brian Murphy, Jack Silver and Sandy Walker. I have also benefited enormously from the friendship, intellectual insights and general good counsel of Niall MacKenzie, Arthur McIvor and Jim Phillips. Any errors are my own. To my mother and sister, for their support over the years. Above all, my thanks and love go to my partner and colleague, Angela, and daughter Orla, for their love and support.

Andrew Perchard
Glasgow, September 2010

Foreword

by Rt Hon. Charles Kennedy MP

T HE HISTORY of larger-scale industry within the Highlands is, to say the least, chequered. The course of my fifty-year lifetime has seen the establishment and extinguishing of fast breeder nuclear technology at Dounreay, aluminium smelting at Invergordon and pulp and paper manufacturing at Corpach.

Yet the visionaries of a further two generations earlier did succeed in establishing something truly remarkable. Their version of aluminium production, one which harnessed the endless supply of West Highland precipitation as its source of power, has stood the test of time. Its presence today may be, given technological advance, somewhat diminished in employment terms, but its fundamental economic and social importance remains. As such it is a fitting subject for this study conducted under the auspices of the UHI Centre for History, a key component of the University of the Highlands and Islands, with financial support from Alcan Aluminium (now Rio Tinto Alcan), Highlands and Islands Enterprise, and Hi-Hopes, a social development initiative funded by the European Union.

While West Highland developments are at the core of Andrew Perchard's book, those developments are explored in ways that link them with the global trade in aluminium and with the metal's strategic importance – an importance reflected in the nature of the industry's relationship with the UK government. There is much else here of wider significance – not least in relation to debates about land use and about industry's environmental impacts. But above all else, this is a compelling human story – one brought to life on following pages in the oral testimony of the many people interviewed in the course of the study from which this arises.

For myself, the aluminium story – the story of 'the BA' as the original British Aluminium Company was known to Highlanders – could hardly be closer to home. The Lochaber smelter stands less than one mile from our family crofts just across the River Lochy; upon his return from the First World War my grandfather was engaged as a foreman on the teams who built the extraordinary tunnels through the hills which carry the water supply to this day; during the Second World War his brother farmed the land which today houses the facility's sports and recreational club, narrowly surviving enemy bombs intended for the factory. These associations are both long and strong.

Currently, the great turbines which drive the Lochaber plant are in the process of being replaced. It is a major task, one which stretches over a number of years. Gazing down from the gantry above the powerhouse is like observing a great archaeological excavation under way. The fact that the operation tests today's engineering skills and technology to the utmost renders all the more remarkable the original construction feat itself. And that feat, like the pipeline constructions, all too often came at a heavy price in terms of fatalities at the time. It acts as a sobering reminder of the legacy left by the countless and all too often nameless navvies who were lost as the work progressed. Let today's refurbishments – and the vote of confidence which they represent in an enduring future – stand as testament to their memories. And let this book stand as testament to one of the most remarkable stories of the developed world across the course of two centuries.

Charles Kennedy
October 2010

Introduction

IN THE COURSE of a summer field trip to the Scottish Highlands in 1907 – which passed by Loch Leven, straddling the counties of Argyll and Inverness – the veteran American geographer Ralph Stockman Tarr noted of the region that it was 'unproductive' and lacking in the 'basis for development of a high degree of enterprise'.[1] Had Tarr journeyed up Loch Leven during his travels, he would have seen a large factory complex, hydro-electric scheme and industrial settlement taking shape. The artificers of this industrial village in the Highlands originally toyed with the idea of calling it 'Aluminiumville', but settled instead on the name of Kinlochleven.[2]

Three years earlier, in 1904, the quiet of the then sleepy enclave of four cottages and two hunting lodges at Kinlochbeg and Kinlochmore in northern Argyllshire awoke to a new sound. The sharp hillsides enveloping this isolated settlement at the head of Loch Leven came alive to the shouts and labour of a teeming army of some 2,000–3,000 navvies engaged in constructing the British Aluminium Company's second Highland aluminium smelter and hydro-electric scheme. One of these 'pioneers of civilisation', the Donegal labourer and writer Patrick MacGill, was later to provide the following vivid description of the work at Kinlochleven in his semi-autobiographical work, *Children of the Dead End*:

> We turned the Highlands into a cinderheap ... Only when we had completed the job, and returned to the town, did we learn from the newspapers that we had been employed on the construction of the biggest aluminium factory in the kingdom. All that we knew was that we had gutted whole mountains and hills in the operations.[3]

In the space of five years, British Aluminium's subsidiary, the Loch Leven Water Power Company, and its contractors constructed the Blackwater Dam, which held the largest volume of water of any dam in the UK until the 1950s, and a reinforced concrete conduit of nearly four miles long driven through solid rock by the skill and grist of this army of human labour. They had laid six mile-and-a-quarter long iron pipes through which the 20 million gallons of the Blackwater Dam descended 935 feet to a power house producing 33,000 horse-power to satisfy the energy requirements of

'Turning the Highlands into a cinderheap': Blackwater Dam under construction, view from the south west. Image provided courtesy of Robert Cairns.

an industrial complex that included an aluminium reduction works, carbon electrode factory, laboratory and offices. On the eve of the First World War this factory produced nearly 90 per cent of the company's primary aluminium output and 12 per cent of the global total. Meanwhile, another British Aluminium subsidiary, the Loch Leven Pier Company, oversaw the development of a deep-water harbour for importing supplies of raw materials and goods, and exporting the precious ingots of aluminium. Finally, to accommodate its employees, British Aluminium constructed a township of 166 two- and three-bedroom houses, hostels, schools, shops, churches and leisure amenities.[4] Reflecting on this industrial experiment after nearly half a century, the authors of the company's official history declared: 'the building of the dam, power-house and works at Kinlochleven in the early years of this century caused a stir in the western Highlands something like that caused by a gold rush in the United States or Australia.'[5]

Inside the wall of the Blackwater Dam in construction phase (n.d.). Image provided courtesy of Robert Cairns.

British Aluminium's claims of having opened up the district and extended prospects in a depressed region were apparently borne out by the flood of labourers and trades into the area from surrounding local areas, as well as from the Hebridean Islands, lowland Scotland, Ireland and England.[6] The scheme became something of a *cause célèbre*, acclaimed by Highland émigrés as far afield away as New Zealand; the *Otago Witness* declared in 1908: 'Of the many schemes which have from time to time been projected for the establishment of industries in the West Highlands none has been on so large a scale, or had such a prospect of success, as the gigantic scheme now in course of development at the head of Lochleven in Argyllshire.'[7]

The developments at Kinlochleven would be dwarfed by the company's Lochaber scheme constructed near Fort William in Inverness-shire. This was constructed in three arduous stages between 1929 and 1943. The first stage alone had cost the company £2.5 million by 1929 (£128 m), and included driving the longest tunnel in the world at the time (15 miles in length) through the solid granite of the Nevis range, most of this being achieved using explosives and pneumatic and hand-held picks. When completed this conduit was to carry 860 million gallons of water daily from a catchment area of 303 square miles. This was then channelled down two steel pipelines falling nearly 600 feet to the hydro-station, where ten giant generating units produced 10,000 horse-power each to supply the factory. At the height of the first stage, the project employed around 3,000 navvies and tradesmen, involved in constructing the factory and hydro-electric scheme, as well as a 21-mile-long network of railways. A second stage, completed in 1938, to enhance the productive capacity of the Lochaber plant by increasing the water catchment area resulted in the construction of two large dams, across Loch Laggan (700 feet long × 130 feet in height) and Loch Treig (400 feet spanning the loch), connected by a two-mile tunnel. This was extended in 1943 by the 1st Tunnelling company of the Canadian army with the addition of a tunnel channelling the headwaters of the River Spey, via Loch Crunachan, into Loch Laggan. Here also, in the nearby small settlement of Inverlochy, they constructed another company village for their employees.[8]

Blackwater Dam being flooded. Image provided courtesy of Robert Cairns.

'The magical hand of modern science?' The temporary factory at Kinlochleven *c.* 1908. Image provided courtesy of Robert Cairns.

Formed in 1894, by the 1920s the British Aluminium Company (BACo) had operations and subsidiaries in the UK, France and across the British Empire, as well as being the largest single foreign investor in the Norwegian aluminium industry; this expansion was part of the dramatic growth in global aluminium production in response to the exponential rise in demand for this versatile and cheap alternative to other more established non-ferrous metals. By 1948 the company had risen to become one of the UK's fifty largest companies, although in the decades following the Second World War British Aluminium became an increasingly peripheral player in the global market for aluminium. Nevertheless, despite being taken over by a partnership of the UK firm Tube Investment and the American aluminium producer Reynolds Metals in 1959, British Aluminium remained a highly respected and recognised household name

Constructing Aluminiumville: Kinlochleven, 1908. Image provided courtesy of Robert Cairns.

in Britain as late as 1967. BACo disappeared in name in 1982, after its merger with the UK subsidiary of Canadian multinational the Aluminium Company of Canada (Alcan), to form British Alcan. The Kinlochleven works continued in operation until 2000, followed by the closure of most of Alcan's remaining Scottish assets between 2001 and 2004. Yet, in spite of the contraction of the native Scottish aluminium industry in a vastly changed and far more competitive global market, the Lochaber smelter continues to produce around one per cent of the primary aluminium output of the second largest producing region in the world, western Europe. In 2007 Alcan were themselves taken over by the British-based global metal miner Rio Tinto Zinc (RTZ).[9]

In his contribution to an edited collection of essays reviewing the economic development of modern Scotland – published four years after the high-profile and premature closure of that 'grandest of all the greatest industrial cathedrals of the north', British Aluminium's short-lived Invergordon smelter (1971–81) – the former chairman of Scotland's Highlands and Islands Development Board (HIDB), Sir Kenneth Alexander, issued a rebuke to the wholesale and prevailing pessimism following the closure: 'The long history of aluminium smelting in the Highlands at Foyers (1895), Kinlochleven (1909), and Fort William (1929) itself, suggests that it

Interior of temporary factory at Kinlochleven, 1908. © RTA/ GUA

Lord Kelvin, British Aluminium's scientific adviser, inspecting No. 3 intake at Kinlochleven c. 1906. Image provided courtesy of Robert Cairns.

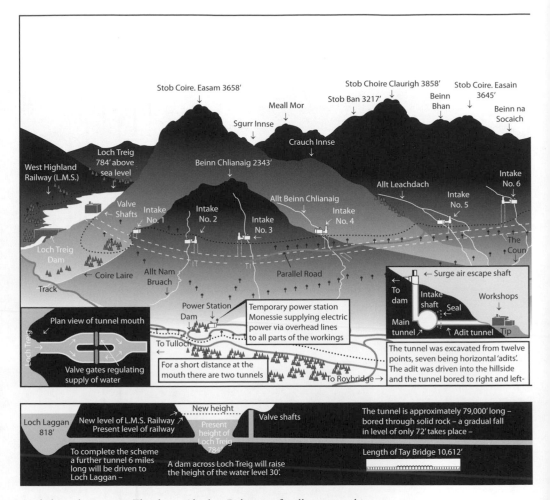

Lochaber scheme 1929. Thanks to Alasdair Robertson for illustrating this.

would be mistaken to allow a particular failure to condemn this form of employment for the area under all circumstances.'[10] Alexander's role as chairman of the HIDB, the social and economic generation agency for the region established in 1965, gave him a prime insight into the intractable problems of attracting industry to locate (and remain) in the Scottish Highlands. His observations were not directed primarily at the industry's historical provenance but rather the future of the economy in this geographically diverse and neglected part of the British Isles. As an eminent Keynesian economist – with practical experience, before the HIDB, as chairman of Govan Shipbuilders and on the National Coal Board's Industrial Relations Tribunal – Alexander would have been only too acutely aware, at the time of writing, of the

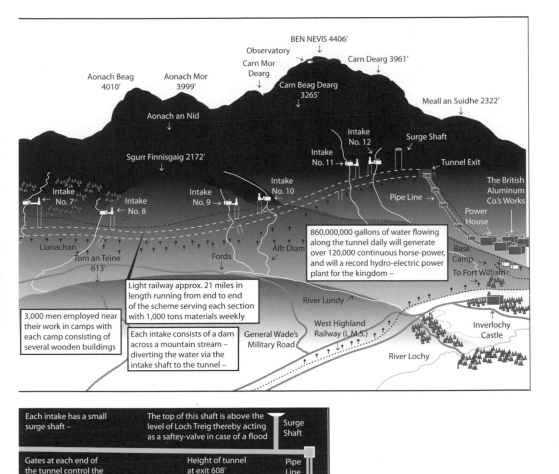

BEN NEVIS 4406'
Observatory
Carn Mor Dearg
Carn Dearg 3961'
Carn Beag Dearg 3265'
Meall an Suidhe 2322'
Aonach Beag 4010'
Aonach Mor 3999'
Aonach an Nid
Sgurr Finnisgaig 2172'
Intake No. 12
Surge Shaft
Intake No. 11
Tunnel Exit
Intake No. 10
The British Aluminum Co.'s Works
Intake No. 7
Intake No. 8
Intake No. 9
Pipe Line →
Power House
Lianachan
Tom an Teine 613'
Fords
Allt Diam
Base Camp
To Fort William

860,000,000 gallons of water flowing along the tunnel daily will generate over 120,000 continuous horse-power, and will a record hydro-electric power plant for the kingdom –

Light railway approx. 21 miles in length running from end to end of the scheme serving each section with 1,000 tons materials weekly

River Lundy

3,000 men employed near their work in camps with each camp consisting of several wooden buildings

Each intake consists of a dam across a mountain stream – diverting the water via the intake shaft to the tunnel –

General Wade's Military Road

West Highland Railway (L.M.S.)

Inverlochy Castle

River Lochy

Each intake has a small surge shaft –

The top of this shaft is above the level of Loch Treig thereby acting as a saftey-valve in case of a flood

Surge Shaft

Gates at each end of the tunnel control the water supply –

Height of tunnel at exit 608'
Pipelines falls 600'

Pipe Line

fragility of Scotland's post-war economy with its emphasis on heavy industry, and of the dependency of the UK on certain costly imports. As such, he also recognised the broader desirability, both socially and economically, of being fiercely protective of manufacturing jobs of this nature in the generally gloomy outlook of the Scottish economic landscape of the 1980s. Moreover, as Alexander was only too aware, the Highlands and Islands of Scotland were long seen as a 'problem' area.

Writing seven years after Tarr's damning observations, in a report for the Department of Agriculture for Scotland in 1914, the St Andrews University economist W. R. Scott observed: 'For some reason, which may be either racial or geographical, or perhaps both, it is necessary to discard largely from hopeful anticipations of industrial

Loch Treig tunnel before lining 1930. © RTA/GUA.

progress from the Highlands.'[11] Despite a fundamental shift in government policy towards the Highlands and Islands, especially with the establishment the HIDB, this pessimistic view of the Highlands persisted. Economists Donald Mackay and Neil Buxton, writing in the same year as the HIDB was born, further propagated the view that had for many years formed orthodox and official opinion on the best policy to be adopted to the region when they stated: 'what evidence there is available suggests that there is no economic case for the development of the Highland area ... the economic solution to the "Highland Problem" is to induce the movement of labour out of, and not the movement of capital into, the area.'[12]

Perhaps even more damaging for confidence in the region were the remarks of one of Alexander's predecessors at the HIDB. Professor Sir Robert Grieve – the eminent Scottish post-war planner and first chairman of HIDB (1965–70) – famously declared in a television interview in April 1978 that: 'Glasgow is one joker in the Scottish pack; the Highlands are the other.'[13] Underlining the significance of the aluminium industry to the Highlands, at the time Alexander penned his piece in the early 1980s, British Alcan's two remaining Highland primary aluminium smelters, at

View up the pipeline, Lochaber, 1930. © RTA/GUA.

Kinlochleven and Lochaber, employed around 7 per cent of the economically active population in the Lochaber District on permanent contracts within the smelters, and contributed very substantially to the local economy. This was set against the backdrop of the high-profile closure of a number of large government-sponsored plants in the locale between 1971 and 1983, leading to a dramatic rise in unemployment in the area of 14 per cent, from significantly below to uncomfortably over the regional and Scottish averages.[14] Around sixty years earlier, Colin Young, a former Provost of Fort William and local tenant farmer, giving evidence to the House of Commons sub-committee considering the Lochaber Water Power Bill of 1921 – the statutory instrument for the establishment of BACo's third Highland aluminium smelter and hydro-electric power scheme – declared: 'I am a whole hearted supporter of this scheme for in it I see the salvation of this district and far beyond.'[15] Young had good reason to express so forthright and optimistic a view in a region that had lost 17 per cent of its population to emigration between 1861 and 1911, most of them from the most economically active age brackets.[16]

The importance of the scheme to the area was further underlined by the fact

Figure 1.1 *Global production of primary aluminium production (mts) by selected years (1900–2000)*

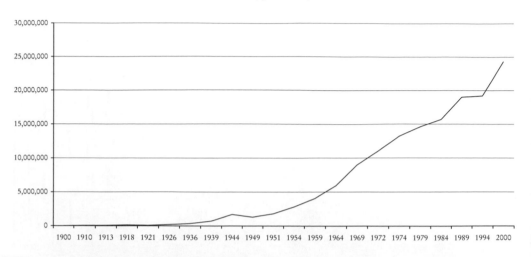

Source: D. A. Buckingham and P. A. Plunkert, 'Aluminum statistics: US Geological Survey' in T. D. Kelly and G. R. Matos, Historical Statistics for mineral and material commodities in the United States, U.S. Geological Survey Data Series 140, (2005), http://pubs.usgs.gov/ds/2005/140, accessed 14 May 2007.

that the Highlands and Islands experienced a further 13.8 per cent fall in their population between 1921 and 1930 alone. British Aluminium's Highland aluminium works contributed much needed permanent and temporary employment not only to those in the vicinity of the schemes, but also to crofters and crofter-fishermen from the Hebridean Islands, such as Lewis, which continued to be plagued into the 1920s by considerable privations, failed harvests, poor housing and disease.[17] Moreover, the company's provision of 'crofting leave' – allowing for employees who were also crofters and fishermen to return respectively to their crofts and boats during the fishing season and at harvest time – was sympathetic to existing traditions of seasonal migration.[18] It was precisely these sentiments that British Aluminium was to marshal effectively in its support.

The development of the primary aluminium industry in the west Highlands of Scotland was of great significance. For not only was it to be one of the largest employers and one of the largest single rate-payers in the region, its investment also showed confidence in the opportunities for economic diversification in the Highlands. Quite aside from the initial benefits that attracted British Aluminium to the area, namely the potential for hydro-electric power (the driver behind the growth of aluminium), the Highlands became integral to the company's public image, projecting itself as a

Figure 1.2 *Global consumption of aluminium by selected years (1903–1990) (mts)*

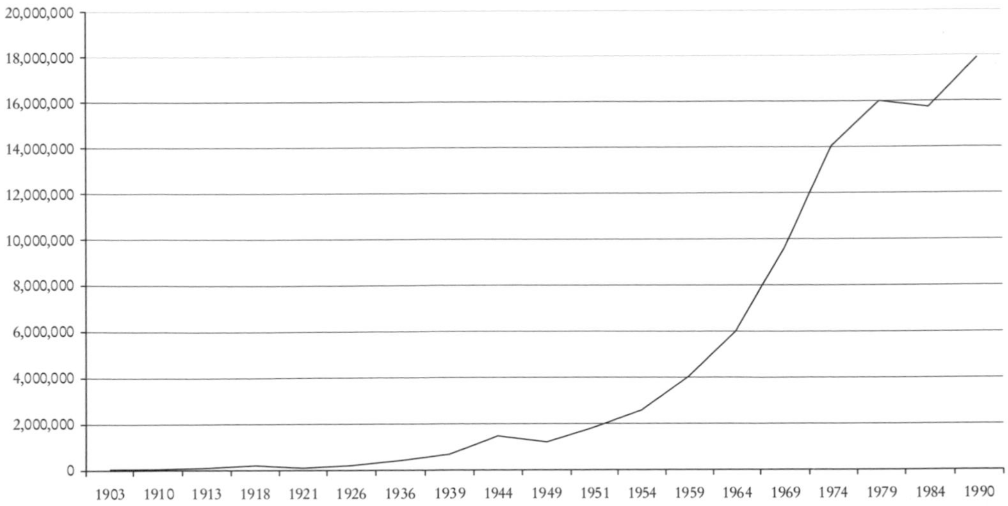

Source: Metal Statistics employed in I. Grinberg and F. Hachez-Leroy (eds), *Industrialisation et sociétés*, annexes 2.1, 2.2.

benefactor and civilising agent. This was at the core of the organisational culture of the company, and linked to its ambitions for itself as a national enterprise. Moving beyond their local and regional significance, British Aluminium's Scottish smelters were, until the early 1970s, the only significant territorial producer of the virgin metal within the UK. Moreover, their combined Scottish operations accounted for no less than 24 per cent of jobs in the (admittedly small) Scottish non-ferrous metal industry between 1935 and 1950.[19]

However, the significance and legacy of the development of this native industry extends far beyond the Highlands. The survival of a native aluminium industry in Britian has been remarkable in itself. The absence of adequate water-power resources and access to domestic resources of other raw materials of sufficient quality for aluminium production meant that direct and indirect state support for the industry was critical to its endurance. The growing significance of aluminium as a metal of strategic importance, and Britain's increasing reliance on imports of the primary metal, cemented a long-term association between the industry and the state. As the executive director of the US Public Affairs Institute Dr Dewey Anderson observed in 1951: 'Aluminium has become the most important single bulk material of modern warfare. No fighting is possible, and no war can be carried to a successful conclusion

THE LOCHABER HYDRO-ELECTRIC POWER UNDERTAKING

British Aluminium Lochaber Works 1930. © RTA/GUA.

today, without using and destroying large quantities of aluminium.'[20] If aluminium were not quite the material of 'national independence' for Britain that it was for France and Germany, then it certainly fostered interdependence between the state and native producers.[21] As such, aluminium provides another important example, beyond the traditional preoccupation with defence contractors, of raw materials stockpiling, the defence economy and British strategic priorities, raising questions about the existence of a military-industrial complex in Britain, a *Warfare State,* during the twentieth century.[22]

The contemporary significance of this historical case study is underlined by recent developments in relation to geopolitical tensions over national sovereignty and raw materials stockpiling – such as over mineral assets in Australia – which have once again seen business–government relations taking centre-stage. Whether in relation to the incarceration of Rio Tinto executives in China, the subsequent heated debate about the Deep Water Horizon oil spill in the Gulf of Mexico, or revelations about the relationship between Whitehall departments and defence contractor BAE Systems, all set against the backdrop of the global financial crisis, this subject is as pertinent as ever. More broadly, it begs questions about the validity of overly prescriptive descriptions of distinctions between private and public sectors in the UK. This illusion of sharply defined 'boundaries of the state' in Britain belies the long history of business–government relations and state intervention, especially across

Figure 1.3 *Global prices for selected non-ferrous metals and years (1900–2005), ($98/mts)*

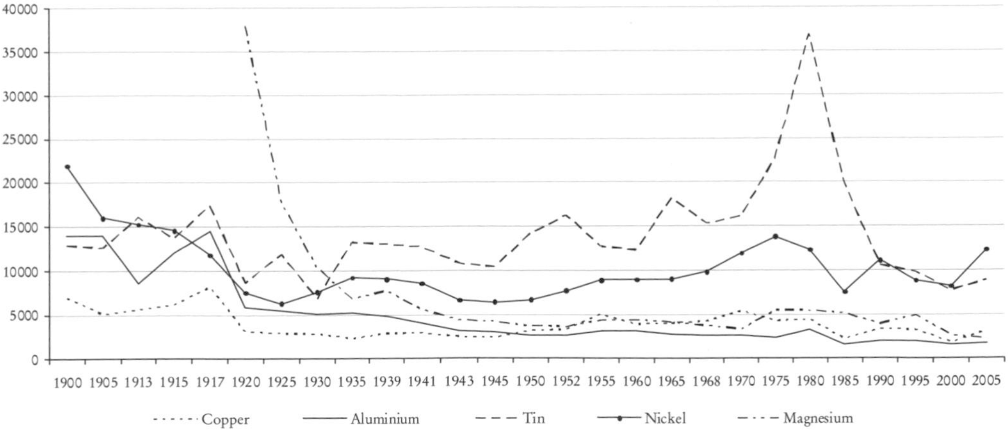

Source: United States Geological Service.

the twentieth century, as well as the movement of senior figures between public and private sectors.[23]

British Aluminium was also closely tied to a range of imperial interests, with this study therefore engaging with important questions about the existence of a 'gentlemanly capitalist' order. Almost inevitably, this leads to discussion of whether the British Empire and metropolitan Britain were guided by the conjoined interests of capital and the state. This relationship between the industry and the state was also to have a profound impact on the strategic outlook, organisational culture, staffing, and consequently the fortunes, of the company. Yet the story of 'Aluminiumville' is more than the global shifts within the industry, and of the politics of development and business–government relations within the defence economy; it is also one of human ecology, capturing a chapter in what one Canadian historian has referred to as the 'aluminium civilization'.[24]

The impact of the industry on ecosystems, and on the social structures within the company settlements and in the Highlands, is integral to this study, as are questions over 'progress' versus aesthetic-conservationist arguments, environmental impact and the cultural construction of the Highland landscape. Similar debates to those over the construction of BACo's Foyers first reduction works and hydro scheme at Foyers have been resurrected in recent debates over the controversial upgrade of the Beauly–Denny power line. Equally profound, in terms of the anthropology and sociology of industrial communities – in view of the organisational culture and traditions within the industry, alongside dominant narratives of Highland history – have been the effect on collective and individual memory in the region. What follows underlines the importance of the global to the local, and vice versa.

The history of aluminium in the UK

It is remarkable, given the significance of native aluminium production to the global industry, national defence and the Highlands, that over 110 years after the commencement of operations at the first Foyers reduction works, historians have given scant attention to the development of the aluminium industry in the UK. Moreover, this relative dearth of literature on the native UK industry is in marked contrast to the fairly extensive literature on the industry worldwide, and, in particular, on that of France, Norway and North America.[25] An official company history of British Aluminium was published in 1955 and subsequently distributed to all employees. Like most company histories of this vintage and genre, it was a prestige publication, largely devoid of analysis, and was primarily concerned with preserving the company's legacy, untarnished, for posterity, and as a tool for promoting company values. However, it is precisely this that makes it so valuable, providing, along with other company publications, another telling insight into organisational culture and narrative. Duncan Campbell's official history of Alcan devotes considerable attention to Alcan's British subsidiary, the Northern Aluminium Company, Ltd, to historical developments within British markets, as well as to the merger between Alcan UK and BACo in 1982 and subsequently to the conjoined concern. As typical for a work of this genre, the study has limitations in terms of its analysis.[26] The one close academic analysis of the British aluminium industry is brief, confined to the period between 1945 and the 1980s, and, as the ensuing chapters reveal, crucially lacks a detailed examination of the company's relationship with the state.[27] In this, Ludovic Cailluet deploys British Aluminium, in particular, as a motif for wider 'British economic "failure"', citing the environmental (cultural, regulatory and competitive) constraints on the industry and failings in strategic management. In the main, histories of the global industry have stressed Britain's weak position in the market for primary metal and its strong semi-fabricated sector.[28] From a neo-marxist perspective, Ronald Graham explores British Aluminium and Alcan's assets and role in the British Empire, and subsequently in the politics of decolonisation and the majority world.[29]

Where other historians have acknowledged the existence of the industry, it has tended to be as an aside. Scottish historian Ewen Cameron has characterised these developments, *en passant*, as 'the disappointed retreat by electro-metallurgical concerns stimulated by the lack of cheap power for their industrial process'.[30] Cameron's view echoes that of the leading historian of the electricity supply industry in Britain who acknowledges that, by the 1930s, political opposition to further hydro-electric development and limited water supplies ensured that this particular source of energy was not commercially viable for supporting further industrial developments.[31] A number of histories of the Highlands have acknowledged the developments in relation to their civil engineering prowess and their legacy. Of these, James Hunter's *Last of the Free* recognises one of the more significant factors arising from the placement of primary aluminium reduction works in the Highlands – as an exemplar of the potential for industrial development in the region.[32] As is often the case, the first drafts of the history of British Aluminium's Highland operations were written not by an historian but by a leading human geographer, David Turnock.[33] Meanwhile the official histories of the British electricity generating councils (and their predecessors) and the North of Scotland Hydro-Electric Board (NSHEB) have illustrated the significance of BACo's Highland hydro-electric to the development of that industry in the British Isles.[34]

The most compelling reason for the native British industry's relative ignominy has been its peripheral role globally and domestically in recent years. Curiously until recently the role of the state in the industry's history had been little referred to.[35] This is all the more pointed given the strategic importance of the metal and questions that it raises more broadly about business–government relations, and the firm in society. As far as the Highlands are concerned the limited coverage of the aluminium industry from much of the historical literature has arisen primarily because of the dominance of the *causes célèbres* of land reform and agitation on the one hand, and government-sponsored initiatives for Highland regeneration on the other, as the chief principal areas of study. Equally, Scottish economic and business historians have been far more preoccupied with the heavy industrial mainstays and the financial sectors in the lowlands, with industry in the Highlands chiefly being associated with state-sponsored failure and the oil boom. At first sight, the story of the indigenous aluminium industry may appear insignificant from a global perspective. If that is the case, it is because its importance has not been recognised fully.

British Aluminium's forays into national and regional politics illustrate the significance of looking at the firm as a socially embedded organisation, subject to a variety of competing social and political, as well as economic, forces. Important as economies of scale and scope, strategising and maintaining 'competitive advantage' are, the performance and outlook of any business are also determined by specific national and historical contingencies.[36] Businesses, indeed economic activity, rarely operate within the straightened, 'rational' and uncomplicated scenario that many orthodox economists persist in promoting.[37] This history is also a contested 'site of memory'. While the industry was undoubtedly a benefactor to the Highlands in some respects, workplace effluents also damaged the health of some employees and of flora and fauna in the vicinity. This is all important in attempting to measure the impact of the business, given that environmental and occupational health are all too often overlooked in business and economic histories.[38] The collective memories of the opponents and proponents of BACo's various Highland schemes form just as strong a legacy as the physical signs of the pipelines, dams and company villages. Equally, this study considers labour struggles and the conflicting feelings amongst some former employees of the degradation of work, but also of pride in workplace and occupational identity. The ultimate expression of these complex sentiments is captured in the sense of loss experienced by others at the closure of some of the plants.

During the course of this book, the development of the industry and its impact are explored using a thematic approach and deploying a broad theoretical framework. The archival research informing this work was conducted in archives spread over two continents and in four countries, based around the main company archive for British Aluminium and British Alcan held at Glasgow University but encompassing also the records of major competitors, the relevant UK and Scottish territorial government departments, trade unions, as well as private papers. This examination of archival collections has also been complemented by the use of oral testimony and questionnaires. For these purposes two cohorts of respondents – one of former employees, the other residents of the two company settlements – were recruited through appeals in the media, as well as through 'gatekeepers' in the local area. All the interviews for this book – with men and women aged between the ages of 56 and 93 – were conducted by the author and Angela Bartie between 2006 and 2008. Although oral testimony, and the practice of oral history, have become strongly embedded among historians both in the academy and beyond as a source, partially informed critiques of it persist occasionally, with Niall Ferguson observing in a recent interview: 'Oral history is a recipe for complete misrepresentation because almost no one tells the truth, even when they intend to.'[39] Aside from the evident implications that this throws up more generally in relation to the provenance and reliability of historical sources, as oral historian Alessandro Portelli has observed:

> The importance of oral testimony may lie not in its adherence to fact, but rather in its departure from it, as imagination, symbolism, and desire emerge. Therefore there are no 'false' oral sources. Once we have checked their factual credibility with all the established criteria of philological criticism and factual verification which are required of all types of sources anyway, the diversity of oral history consists in the fact that 'wrong' statements are still psychologically 'true', and that this truth may be equally as important as factually reliable accounts.[40]

Thus elucidates Portelli further: 'Oral sources tell us not just what people did, but what they wanted to do, what they believed they were doing, and what they now think they did.'[41]

Moreover the use of oral history, particularly in interpretive form, provides a valuable insight into the impact and legacy of corporate narratives. Of particular relevance here are the observations of oral historian Alistair Thomson's interviews with Australian Anzac (Australian and New Zealand Army Corps) veterans of the First

World War, later published in his 1994 book *Anzac Memories: Living with the Legend*. Focusing on the interaction between 'private' and 'public' memories, Thomson observed that: 'we compose our memories to make sense of our past and present lives … In one sense we "compose" or construct memories using the public language and meanings of our culture. In another sense we "compose" memories which help us to feel relatively comfortable with our lives.' What he had discovered in the course of his interviews was that, 'how we remember and articulate will change over time, and how this can be related to shifts in public perception'.[42] Similarly Portelli has observed from his interviews that individual memories develop and compete alongside those of various communities of interest, with public memories representing the different authorised accounts of different agencies such as company, government, trade unions, party, and 'communities'.[43]

This same approach is also instructive in exploring company publications, as this work does, showing their 'interpretive', as well as their 'reconstructive', value; something often ignored in reviews of company literature. Thus textual analysis of BACo and Alcan's publications for employees has provided a window into the companies' autobiographies; their carefully constructed narrative imbued with the image they wished to project of themselves and values they wanted to impart. Identifiable in the 'BA' version (British Aluminium's historical narrative) – the corpus of the collected speeches of directors, and subsequently the company's organ, *The B.A. News*, and official company history – are the autobiographical traditions so prevalent in the writings of Western Europe and the white narrators of the British Dominions:

> Life is an odyssey, a journey through many trials and tests, which the hero must surmount alone through courage, endurance, cunning and moral strength … His achievement comes about through his own agency, and his successful rite of passage leaves him master of his fortunes, though, of course, still subject to the whims of the gods or the turning of the wheel of destiny.[44]

This heroic epic was to be abundantly evident in the lives of BACo's engineers and their endeavours, laced with emblematic episodes in Highland history. The company's use of these 'sites of memory' in company literature, as well as in the street names of the company towns, was designed to cultivate 'loyalty'; the legacy of which is seen today, reproduced in personal testimonies contained within this book. British Aluminium's fetishistic account was not isolated but, as befitted an industry of the second industrial revolution with the perceived philosophical debt for advances in science and technology attributed to the enlightenment, was endemic in an industry which heralded aluminium as the *leitmotif* of modernity, and the twentieth century as the 'light metal age'.[45] Moreover the cult of the engineer is one that continues to pervade writing about business and economic development in the 'long nineteenth century' (when BACo took its first steps), with one recent history of British technology declaring: 'Engineers are empire-builders: active agents of political and economic empire.'[46]

What follows traverses the 'high politics' of national and imperial defence, global corporate capitalism, as well as the nuances and complexities of regional politicking, every bit as pertinent to the global as the local. It holds a microscope to social relations in company board rooms, workplace and village life alike, and delves into contests over landscape, health and the environment. The pages usher forth the experiences of individuals and organisations alike, reflecting the importance of 'the smallest aspect of daily life' in elucidating the 'impact of the whole of culture'.[47]

1

Aluminium in the UK

IN A LECTURE to the Royal Economic Society in December 1948 Siegfried Moos outlined the dilemma facing the native UK aluminium industry in the post-war period. His paper posed a number of crucial questions: was the survival of native primary production of aluminium desirable, or should Britain focus on its semi-fabricated production supplied by imports of cheaper ingot from Canada? If the former, how was the native industry to be sustained, by nationalising it or offering preferential contracts to 'enterprising' companies?[1] Moos' comments were hardly prophetic given the following observation of the leading international authority on the global industry in 1937: 'it is very questionable whether aluminium reduction in the United Kingdom was economically justifiable.'[2] Although Donald Wallace also noted in the same essay that few countries in the world had the natural resources to host such primary aluminium production, the British industry's survival remains a notable case of a triumph in the face of considerable adversity.

Introduction

The main emphases of this chapter are to place the British Aluminium Company, and its successors, within the contexts of the UK and global aluminium industries, and to analyse the historical development and performance of these firms. Evidently this needs to be reviewed alongside evidence in the following chapters to establish a full picture of the history of the native industry, particularly its relationship with the state. In order to be able to understand both how and why native British aluminium enterprises, and indeed the global industry, developed and performed in the way they did, this is located within a broader discussion of the expansion and behaviour of industrial capitalism. At the same time as exhibiting similar characteristics to other industrial enterprises of the second industrial revolution – which occurred between 1870 and 1914, and saw the growth of capital-intensive, high-technology industries – aluminium retained some features that were highly specific and determined by geographical location, alongside social and political forces.

Aluminium, as an industrial sector, has much to offer in exploring dominant themes around the nature of British industrial capitalism and its much-vaunted failings, especially with British Aluminium emerging as one of the UK's largest and most established firms by 1945. As one of the doyens of business history Alfred D. Chandler Jnr famously argued, it was the failure of British industry in those sectors of the second industrial revolution to develop sophisticated management structures – 'managerial hierarchies' – that had the most profound effect on Britain's economic growth and industrial competitiveness. Yet Chandler – in his seminal, comparative study of industrial capitalism in Britain, Germany and the US, through a survey of the 200 largest manufacturing concerns in these three economies – judged British Aluminium to be a comparatively proficient player. Chandler noted that in comparison with other British non-ferrous metal concerns, BACo made the necessary investment in plant (both domestically and overseas), as well as in sales organisation and professional managers. This, he opined, along with wartime demand and government subsidy enabled British Aluminium 'to maintain its secondary position in the industry's global oligopoly'.[3] Ludovic Cailluet's study of British Aluminium attributes the company's survival to the safe haven offered by the international aluminium cartels, two world wars, and insatiable post-war demand for the metal. Cailluet further concludes that the role of Britain's state was far less 'positive' than in other continental European countries. While concurring with industry judgements of poor management of the company until the 1970s, he judges that the industrial enterprise ostensibly suffered as a consequence of the national competitive environment. However Cailluet's judgement of poor management predominantly stems from his acceptance of the views of British Aluminium's former chairman and managing director Ronny Utiger, who blamed the company's post-war decline on significant managerial failings and missed commercial opportunities.[4] As this history reveals, Utiger had a vested interest in promoting the image of a failing company saved by new blood, in an account that ignored the historical context to British Aluminium's post-war performance.

Market structure and the economics of aluminium production

Aluminium is very capital-intensive, with new entrants required to inject a substantial outlay into sunk costs. Consequently 'pioneers' in the industry exercised considerable control. Historically this was characterised by a pronounced tendency to vertical integration of its products, national monopolies and international oligopolies. As a result, independent 'latecomers' to the industry, without state subsidy, were rare, and frequently foundered. The modern aluminium industry owed much to a 'burst' of entrepreneurial activity, on both sides of the Atlantic. Had the Swiss Neuhausen company not invested in French chemist Paul Héroult's process – something that the latter's erstwhile French employer and successful chemical entrepreneur declined to do – and the Mellon brothers not offered financial support to the fledgling Pittsburgh Reduction Company, the growth of the global industry at that time would have been in doubt. However, it was only with the necessary 'pre-conditions' (the development of electricity and scientific knowledge) that the 'trigger' of the Hall-Héroult process emerged. Aluminium therefore offers an excellent opportunity to interrogate the impacts of innovation over invention on economic growth.[5]

The legacy of an initial burst of activity by these early entrepreneurs and their dominance thereafter is evident from the market share held by 'pioneers' and their 'price leadership' in this industry throughout the course of the twentieth century. This has been particularly pronounced in the industry's upstream activity from bauxite mining to primary aluminium production. Throughout much of the century it was an industry characterised by rapid backward vertical integration, oligopolies and powerful cartels, as well as by a pronounced incidence of state involvement. In 1913 seven companies controlled 94 per cent of the global share of aluminium production. Over sixty-five years later, in 1979, six firms controlled respectively: 54 per cent of bauxite mining; 74 per cent of alumina production; and 62 per cent of primary aluminium production. Although the majors had seen a sizeable decrease in their dominance of their share of the market for the primary metal and a smaller drop-off in their position within alumina production, they still controlled 36 per cent and 62 per cent respectively of these activities by 1994. In comparison eight producers controlled 48 per cent of the global market for copper in 1912. Although a relatively small number of firms (around twenty-one) continued to exercise considerable influence in global markets for other non-ferrous metals (such as copper, tin and zinc) by 1980, the trend was moving towards greater proliferation of locally owned small and medium sized enterprises (SMEs).[6] The next twenty years saw a return to the concentration of control into the hands of a small number of global conglomerates with metals and minerals portfolios.

Because of the monopolies exercised by aluminium companies over a raw material of growing strategic importance, and the metal's military importance, not surprisingly it attracted government scrutiny; the subject of discussion in the following chapter. The industry was historically characterised by a high degree of international cooperation among the 'first movers' and cartelisation. The first sustained, global aluminium cartel (1901–08) attempted to eliminate competitors after the expiry of the original Hall-Héroult patents by reserving national markets for territorial producers and apportioning the remaining competitive markets to members.[7]

The efficiency of aluminium enterprises historically has been affected by a number of key factors: access to cheap raw materials, the economic location of plants, and the extent of vertical integration. The balance of high *fixed costs* (natural energy resources, capital and plant) to *variable costs* (raw materials and labour) brought with it associated risks and a market advantage. On the one hand, insufficient capital funds could bring financial ruin on the enterprise. On the other, the high capital costs made it difficult for new entrants to move into the market. The commercial viability of primary aluminium production is reliant on two key factors: access to a cheap and plentiful source of power, and reasonably priced bauxite (the mineral from which aluminium is derived). The significance of these is illustrated through the breakdown of costs for aluminium production at the historical intervals of 1948 and 1970. In 1948, between 72 per cent and 75 per cent of the total cost of manufacturing aluminium was attributable to alumina (in particular, the cost of bauxite) and electricity. By 1970, the costs linked to alumina production had fallen by 20 per cent, but electricity costs had remained constant. By the 1990s alumina production and power costs accounted respectively for 30–33 per cent and 24–26 per cent of full operating costs. Moreover the testing power demands of aluminium production – requiring a constant high load factor – for an industry which remains predominantly supplied by the source best placed to provide that, hydro-electricity, demands large water reserves and land. Thus the industrial location of aluminium reduction works has been critical to the success of enterprises in this industry.

There has been an equally visible tendency in the industry towards rapid backward integration of upstream activities (bauxite mining, alumina and aluminium production). The sizeable gains to be realised – and conversely the penalties for plants not working at minimum efficient scale – from improved furnace technology and high quality raw materials, sustained investment in research and development as well as plant for those wishing to remain significant players. As an illustration of this, at the beginning of the century most reduction works required 30,000 kilowatt hours of electricity per tonne of aluminium produced (kWh/t). By the mid-1990s, most smelters consumed between 13–16,000 kWh/t.[8] Increasingly efficiency arising from technical innovation and investment in plant over plant scale has proved critical, with cost gains arising from modernisation of aluminium reduction furnaces (cells, pots) highest in Europe where savings of 15 per cent on average have been achieved. It is also worth noting that after a period of investment in nuclear power generating capacity to supply aluminium smelters between the 1960s and 1980s (invariably with government assistance), nearly 60 per cent of global primary production continued to receive its power from hydro-electricity in the last decade of the twentieth century because of the significantly lower cost of this energy source for the industry. Britain's limited access to extensive water-power reserves would severely constrain the development of its native aluminium industry.[9] The degree to which British Aluminium was largely debilitated by 'factor' and 'demand conditions' – such as the limitations of natural resources (for example, the limited water reserves of the Highlands and access to bauxite), ready sources of capital, and an absence of domestic markets for their finished and unfinished products – or whether it can be attributed to the strategies and governance of the firm, is the subject of scrutiny here.[10] It has been popular to inculpate the shortcomings of British firms in the twentieth century on underdeveloped domestic markets as well as to managerial failings (alongside the perceived fraught industrial relations). What was of absolutely central importance to the development of this industry (in Britain, as elsewhere), were broader social and political forces, especially the state. Equally critical – and so often lacking in much business literature – is the subsequent analysis in this book of the political environment, and social and environmental impacts, which cannot simply be dismissed as 'externalities'.[11] Also of paramount importance is the culture of the time and the behaviours and role of employees as social actors in shaping this.

The uneasy infancy of Britain's 'light metal age', 1894–1915

Although a number of British enterprises had attempted chemical manufacture of aluminium on a commercial scale before British Aluminium, they were unable to compete on a commercially viable basis with those producers using the Hall-Héroult process.[12] The modern aluminium industry was born in the UK with the registration of the British Aluminium Company Ltd on 5 May 1894; starting out as a limited liability company with an initial capital of £100,000. In the two months preceding, the company's managing director acquired the exclusive British and Colonial rights to the Héroult process from the Neuhausen Company of Switzerland (Aluminium Industrie Aktiengesellschaft (AIAG) Neuhausen) who held the global rights for the process. Between 1894 and 1895 British Aluminium developed into a vertically integrated aluminium concern acquiring the necessary upstream and downstream activities: two bauxite mines near Larne in Northern Ireland; an existing rolling mill in the midlands of England; a carbon factory in Greenock on the Firth of Clyde for making the electrodes necessary for the process; and the water rights to their first aluminium reduction works at Foyers on the banks of Loch Ness in the Scottish Highlands. The first board of directors included among their number three industrialists – one copper smelter, an iron master and a cotton spinner. The initiator behind the project though was an Italian engineer Emmanuel Ristori (1857 – 1911), who had previously been Head of Ammunition at Nordenfeldt Guns. It was Ristori's understanding of the military potential of the metal – through his contact with the military arsenals and work conducted with Alfred Nobel on explosives – that provided the impetus. Another director, Alfred Bolton, a copper smelter, who had combined with Callender's Cables, invested partly because of the possibilities presented by aluminium in the electricity market, and in part because of the threat it posed to copper. British Aluminium also enlisted the scientific services of the eminent British scientist, Lord Kelvin – first as the company's scientific adviser and then as a director. Without doubt one of their most astute appointments was that of an able ex-student of Lord Kelvin's and engineer (at Kelvin's behest), William Murray Morrison (1873 – 1948), who joined the company first as the manager of their Foyers works. In time Morrison would become the managing-director, and *pater familias*, of British Aluminium.[13]

The company started producing primary metal at their Foyers works in 1896, completing the expansion and modernisation of their plants by March 1898 at a cost

FOYERS. 5TH SEPTEMBER, 1895.

Benefactors to the Highlands: BACo directors at Foyers, 1895 (Emmanuel Ristori, Roger Wallace and Charles Innes, the company's Highland solicitor). © RTA/GUA.

of around £141,000 (£14.8m) in the process.[14] They acquired a controlling share of French bauxite producer Union des Bauxites, in 1902, and in 1906 constructed a modest smelter in Stangfjorden in Norway. To further meet the rate of expansion in this rapidly growing market, the company started work on their scheme at Kinlochleven in 1904 at an estimated cost of £500,000 (£51m), funding this through the raising of additional share options. Concurrently British Aluminium acquired water reserves in the Swiss Alpine region of Orsières, with the intention of expanding their primary reduction operations in 1906. However, their plans were thwarted when AIAG Neuhausen was able to argue successfully that the British producer only held the patent for aluminium production in Britain and the colonies, and that it AIAG had the exclusive rights for Switzerland. By this time, BACo had already successfully applied for a licence for and embarked upon the construction of a costly railway to run through the St Bernard Pass connecting Switzerland with Italy. It was a major coup for the Swiss and Italian governments, who had long desired a railway link but baulked at the price, but a disastrous error on the part of the BACo board. Had this bold strategic move succeeded it would have given BACo manufacturing

Lord Kelvin 1903. © RTA/GUA.

capacity close to their bauxite reserves in the south of France, and a foothold in the lucrative continental European markets. An attempt during the First World War to gain a share in the Swiss industry also ended in disappointment. Eventually British Aluminium was forced to sell its Swiss water rights and retain the railway. As BACo finally admitted in 1954, it had been a 'bad decision', strategically ill-conceived and legally questionable.[15]

British Aluminium's problems multiplied with their failed attempt at a takeover of the Aluminium Corporation Ltd (Al. Corp.) in 1908. By then, Al. Corp., the only other native producer of primary aluminium, had operated a small reduction works and hydro station at Dalgarrog in North Wales since 1907, but was in receivership. Nevertheless, Al. Corp.'s creditors rejected BACo's offer (of £50,000 in cash, £50,000 worth of fully paid and £24,000 partially paid preference shares), stating that they would prefer to restructure the firm rather than be subsumed into British Aluminium. To make matters worse for BACo, their Kinlochleven scheme had suffered serious delays and did not come on-stream fully until 1909, while bad floods that caused considerable damage at Foyers in 1902 delayed important development work there. Concurrently the global market for the metal, which had seen a dramatic expansion with an associated fall in prices of 30 per cent since 1894, was experiencing a downturn. Prospects looked particularly bleak for BACo in 1909–10. The company

BACo, Stangfjorden, *c.*1920. Image courtesy of Fylkesarkivet I Sogn Og Fjordane (the Paul Stang collection)

faced demands for liquidation and were only saved by financial restructuring. They were over-extended and, like a good many English-registered limited liability companies of the day, had raised most of their capital to fund this expansion from calls to shareholders. Moreover investors had been expressing anxieties about the capital structure of the company from an early stage; British Aluminium's first chairman Roger Wallace was repeatedly called on by shareholders to recognise the sheer scale of fixed capital costs associated with this industry. While the entrepreneurial drive of British Aluminium's early directors, in the face of adversity, consumer scepticism and risk-averseness among shareholders, was crucial in advancing the position of the company in the emerging global market for aluminium, the lack of commercial acumen among BACo's directors was glaring evident, as revelations about Wallace and Ristori's personal business transactions later revealed.[16]

The company also complained from the outset of conservatism among domestic users of metal, in particular singling out the engineering and armaments sectors. Though there was some substance to these complaints, the following chapter questions BACo's claims against government armaments factories. Indeed this later subterfuge owed more to attempts by the company to cajole the government into offering contracts. Nevertheless, unlike France and the United States lucrative markets such

Pater familias: William
(later Sir William) Murray
Morrison, 1920. © RTA/GUA.

as those for components for cars and buses were slow to emerge in Britain. This characteristic absence of general opportunities in domestic markets that affected so many British industries, particularly of those of the 'second' industrial revolution, partly explains why British Aluminium was one of the few early global aluminium producers who integrated forward (as well as backward into upstream activities) into semi-manufactured aluminium products in order to create markets for the emerging metal.[17]

In contrast to Britain, by 1914 around 80 per cent of US cars used aluminium components extensively. The French automobile industry was also active in promoting the use of aluminium, with an estimated one-seventh to one-fifth of France's domestic consumption of the metal used in that industry. Britain's car industry did not really take-off until 1909 (after the beginning of the recession in global aluminium markets), and prior to First World War only used aluminium in cylinders. By 1911 twenty-six omnibus companies across Western Europe, mostly in France and Germany, were testing aluminium wire for bus engines while none of their British counterparts was. The British electricity industry was more willing to use aluminium for wire and junction boxes, but still lagged behind competitors in the USA and France. In the US, a method for strengthening aluminium using a steel core for overhead cables was developed in 1908, and by 1912 consumed around 20 per cent of the annual output of the US industry. By 1914 France was using 2,000 kilometres of aluminium cables. Between 1913 and 1914, manufacturers of electricity cables in Britain used between 11 and 13 per cent of the total output of native aluminium in cables, although its uses were limited. The slow growth of its use in the native electricity industry does not appear to have been for lack of enthusiasm among electrical engineers, but owed more to small-scale and municipal provision of electricity, as well as Britain's access to copper.[18] For all British Aluminium's protestations, as remarks made by customers in the 1930s appear to indicate, the company's marketing of their products and customer relations reveal real weaknesses in their commercial strategy.

British Aluminium and Al. Corp. were not alone in being faced with the threat of liquidation around this time; two French producers l'Aluminium du Sud-Ouest (ASO) and La Société Electro-Métallurgie du Sud-Est (EMSE) were also victims. However Al. Corp., ASO and EMSE were all 'latecomers', with the latter two having been formed in 1906. BACo, in contrast, was a 'first mover'. However she did not enjoy all the advantages that other 'pioneers' in the industry did. The Pittsburgh Reduction Company (subsequently Alcoa) and the AIAG enjoyed the distinction of market leadership, having acquired the global patents and experience of working with Hall and Héroult respectively. The Pittsburgh company also had the financial backing and business acumen of venture capitalists, the Mellons. Andrew and Richard Mellon sat on Pittsburgh's board (remaining major shareholders in the company) and were under no illusions about a speedy return on their capital investment. It was they who engineered the company's highly successful move to their larger factory at Niagara Falls. Moreover, as US Treasury Secretary, Andrew Mellon did not hesitate to use his influence to promote the business. AIAG Neuhausen emerged out of negotiations between I. G. Neher Sons – iron masters keen to diversify, using their water-power resources on the Falls of the Rhine, into more secure new markets and interested by Héroult's process – and Héroult (whose former employer, the French producer Produits chimiques d'Alais et de la Camargue (PCAC), had flatly refused to adopt his technique) establishing themselves as the Swiss Metallurgical Society. In late 1888 they joined forces with the German Edison Company to form AIAG. As such they were early leaders with considerable established expertise, fixed assets and combined acumen. Héroult's erstwhile employer, PCAC, was established in the mid-nineteenth century as producers of chlorine and soda, as well as other chemical products. It was their expertise in this area that attracted the grandfather of the modern aluminium industry, Henri Sainte-Claire Deville, to set up his first industrial process for aluminium manufacture at their works in Salindres. Despite the early disinterest in Héroult's process, their lengthy experience of working with aluminium, considerable fixed assets and their ability to effect economies of scope afforded them a strong market position and competitive advantage.[19]

British Aluminium had undertaken major capital investment, vertically integrating backwards, as well as forwards into the market for semi-finished and finished products. However their costly Swiss foray revealed very real weaknesses in the strategic management of the firm. Similarly the Loch Leven development showed critical failings in tactical and operational arenas too. The civil engineering contractors, Messrs Sir John Jackson Ltd, had assured the board of the Loch Leven Water & Electric Power Company (in effect, the BACo board) that they would be able to complete the construction of the dam, upper works, pipelines and the reduction factory at Kinlochleven by Autumn 1907. Their repeated failure to meet deadlines – largely as a result of employing insufficient labour, and the difficulties in retaining labourers willing to endure the hard and dangerous working conditions on the scheme – meant that it was not completed until November 1908. Some of the delays can be attributed to objections raised by local vested interests and their subsequent investigations by the UK Board of Trade, along with the inevitable need to seek amendments to the legislation to extend the time allowed for the construction. However both the board of directors and their managing agents, Thomas Meik & Sons, repeatedly failed to bring the project back on schedule. As a result their scheme was delayed, incurring considerable additional costs, not least in Parliamentary expenses. To make matters worse, it also appeared that the contractors had used inferior quality cement in the dam and there were problems with the foundations of the carbon factory.[20] Yet, as their conduct during the passage of the legislation for their next major scheme (the Loch Leven Water Power Bill 1918) showed, BACo had failed to learn some of the important lessons from the previous passage of legislation through the House of Commons.

Despite these setbacks, on the eve of the First World War, British Aluminium had firmly established itself as the dominant native producer of the metal, and as a significant player in global industry. Between 1911 and 1912, BACo expanded its operations in Norway and the UK, acquiring another small reduction works, Vigelands Brug, and a rolling mill at Warrington in England, and installing the first extrusion plant in the UK (the latter in order to diversify their product range for important new markets). In the following two years they invested in new mills at Warrington, purchased land to construct a large new alumina works at Burntisland in Fife, and extended their Kinlochleven works to include a carbon factory for the manufacture of electrodes on site. By 1913 BACo's Scottish reduction works were making a major contribution to global output and produced 92 per cent of the UK's aluminium.

On the outbreak of war, the board of directors of BACo was completely changed from that of 1894, although the company retained the skills of William Murray

Morrison as general manager. Of this board it was to be Morrison, and the chairman for nearly twenty years, Andrew Tait, who would most influence the direction of the company.[21] The entrepreneurial dynamism, coupled with the scientific and technical acumen, of a number of the leading lights in British Aluminium in the early years – notably Ristori, Wallace, Morrison and Lord Kelvin – prevailed in the face of adverse factor and demand conditions. The picture that emerges from these early years is of a company dominated by scientists, engineers and enthusiasts with poor strategic judgement. This was exemplified at a personal level by the fates of Emmanuel Ristori and Roger Wallace. Ristori, BACo's founder who had collaborated with Alfred Nobel and excelled in his field, spent his last few years in ignominy and was declared bankrupt the same year he died, 1911. His wife and daughter would have been left destitute were it not for a public appeal launched by prominent friends in the metal trade.[22] BACo's first chairman Roger William Wallace KC (appointed as a barrister in 1882 and becoming Queen's Counsel in 1896) was an inveterate investor in new enterprises. By 1913 he had run up debts of £150,000 (£14.1m), and was declared personally bankrupt in 1919.[23] Their successors John Bonner and Henry Wolfenden scarcely improved upon their stewardship. Upon taking over, Bonner and Wolfenden accepted no responsibility for failings in the company, evaded questions about the financial position of the concern (especially in relation to delays in the Kinlochleven scheme), and were unable to explain why the company's accounts had been withheld from shareholders.[24] It was Andrew Tait who managed to salvage the company from financial ruin. Tait already had an enviable reputation in corporate rescues, notably as the chairman of the electrical engineering company Ferranti, where he was attributed with the successful restructuring of the firm after it almost went bankrupt in 1903. He was one of the founders of the Federation of British Industries (FBI) and prominent in the British Electrical and Allied Manufacturers' Association. According to his biographer, had it not been for a financial scandal in 1925 and his premature death five years later, Tait 'seemed destined to become one of the country's leading businessmen'. Aside from his business acumen, he was also immensely politically savvy.[25] However this period was also to mark the start of BACo's long and chequered relationship with the state.

From the metal of Mars to a filigree of the modern age, 1915–1936

War was to transform both the fortunes of the metal, and the future of national aluminium companies. The detail of, and implications for, British and Canadian producers of aluminium of the relationship with government that developed during the course of the First and Second World Wars are explored in detail in the next chapter. The economic and technological effects of the First World War on aluminium were profound. Demand for and supplies of the metal increased dramatically, while research into both the properties and the practical applications of aluminium expanded. This, and the growing familiarity with the metal among manufacturers exposed to it during the conflict, greatly extended its applications, notably in the field of transport.[26]

Some comparison with other European aluminium industries further illustrates war's role as a stimulant to the national aluminium enterprises, and the increasing strategic significance of the metal. The effective naval blockade of Germany (and the Central Powers), limiting supplies of certain non-ferrous metals like copper, and the controls imposed by the allies on imports from their main supplier, Switzerland, from early 1915 forced Germany to develop its own domestic industry under the Reich Ministry's *Kriegsmetall AG* (which became *Vereinigte Aluminium Werke AG* (VAW) in 1917). Between 1915 and the end of 1918, four new reductions works were completed in Germany. The absence of copper permanently shifted the balance in aluminium's favour (and against copper's) in the non-ferrous markets of central Europe.[27]

Initially in 1914 the productive capacity of much of France's aluminium industry (and its hydro-electricity) was given over to other chemical processes that were deemed to be far more crucial to national defence, especially with the German advance cutting off their access to their northern and eastern coalfields with the loss of 40 per cent of their coal production. As far as the French war effort was concerned, the use of aluminium was largely confined to buttons in the early years. Thereafter demand grew in two markets – for weaponry and helmets (exclusively marshal-uses); and those that were easily converted to civilian 'spin-offs' after the conflict (aluminium and aluminium alloy sheets for cars and planes). In October 1914 PCAC managed to persuade local authorities in the Rhone that all of Swiss group AIAG's alumina was destined for central Europe (even though some was exclusively for use in Switzerland), and at the beginning of 1915, the French government declared the AIAG's subsidiary in France and its works 'enemy assets' and sequestrated them, ceding control to Aluminium Français. The government also pressed French captains of industry to select market leaders to coordinate efforts in their discrete sectors – with PCAC and Badin respectively leading the electro-chemical and electro-metallurgical industries. The tripling of the world price of aluminium ingot at the end of 1915 panicked the allied powers into recognising the strategic importance of aluminium.[28]

In the case of both global conflicts, the main beneficiaries, in terms of a growth in their share of the global aluminium market, were Alcoa and their Canadian subsidiary (subsequently Alcan). War in Europe, as Alcoa's historian observed, 'was good to Alcoa', as it effectively stopped foreign imports into the US and it became a mass exporter to the British, French and Italians during the conflict; the bulk of this going from the Northern Aluminium Co. Ltd's smelter at Shawinigan Falls, in Canada, to Britain.[29]

At the outbreak of war in August 1914, native British production of primary aluminium stood at 7,500 mts (just over 90 per cent of which was produced at Foyers and Kinlochleven). Britain could also rely on a further 3,000 mts from British

Aluminium's Norwegian subsidiaries.[30] Current estimates of the rise in consumption of the metal in Britain between 1914 and 1919 grossly underestimate wartime purchases of the metal, not just for British territorial forces but also as the armoury for imperial forces and on behalf of Allies.[31] By August 1916, 70 per cent of aluminium for the British (and Allied) war effort (24,385 mts) was sourced from Canada. The crisis arising from shortages of the metal in 1916 was narrowly averted through a variety of measures, including expansion of native productive capacity, economising on the use of aluminium and imports chiefly from Canada. In addition, by the last year of the war, around 510 mts of metal were being collected from scrap per month. By the armistice in November 1918, Britain was able to meet all its requirements for aluminium.[32]

Prior to the outbreak of war, the native aluminium industry's chief domestic markets had been for finished aluminium and aluminium alloyed products (such as cooking utensils, motor vehicle and machinery parts) and other products such as paint and chemical products. By 1916, aluminium alloy castings were used in military motor vehicles, submarines and increasingly aeroplanes (largely in aero-engines but elsewhere too). Aluminium itself was being used in the manufacture of ammunition and machine guns. Some indication of the impact of the war economy on the demand for aluminium is evident from the increase in production for those munitions that used the metal. Between 1914 and 1917, the number of shells produced in British munitions factories increased from 500,000 to 76,200,000. The production of powder and explosives reached its peak of 188,985 mts in 1917, from a figure of 5080 mts in 1914. Most significantly, aircraft and aero-engine output rose from 2,000 aircraft and 1,000 engines in 1914 to 32,000 and 22,100 respectively in 1918. Upon the outbreak of hostilities, the industry had experienced a dropping-off of its export trade and a concurrent rise in military orders. Under the Munitions of War Act of August 1915, the aluminium industry was brought under the direction of the Ministry of Munitions, and all sales were subject to government scrutiny and approval. After this date all supplies of aluminium ingot and semi-fabricates were destined for the war economy with prices fixed by the ministry.[33]

Increasing martial demand for the metal and the growing realisation of its strategic importance prompted the extension of Kinlochleven. It played a crucial role in ensuring Board of Trade support for the company's legislative attempts to extend its domestic smelting capacity after 1918, culminating in the Lochaber reduction works. However the crisis had also set the government to work looking for colonial and dominion suppliers of aluminium ingot and reserves of the raw materials necessary for its production. While production at domestic reduction works and latterly rolling mills was kept busy, the financial burden on the industry of wartime prices (for purchasing raw materials and selling metal) and the fatigue on plant (added to a lack of investment in fixed capital) were to take their toll on the native industry. On the other hand, wartime research undertaken at government facilities, such as the National Physical Laboratory, led to an expansion in the uses of aluminium alloys, particularly in aircraft. In the longer term this would be one of the positive contributions that government-industry collaboration would make.[34] The First World War then had a profound effect more generally in promoting the use of the metal in alloy form, showing both its existing deficiencies and encouraging further critical research into alloys, and in illustrating its potential civilian 'spin-off' for transport. As Andrew Tait observed in 1920: 'the application of the metal during the war has stimulated the utilisation of the metal for a considerable variety of new purposes.'[35] Crucially British Aluminium was also able to have its status as a 'key industry' (of national strategic importance) acknowledged, and exact assurances from government over support for its future projects.

However BACo's global market position had been compromised. In the decades following the Great War, it became an increasingly marginal player in the international scene. With the silencing of the guns, the global aluminium industry almost immediately saw a dramatic drop in demand with international consumption reaching its post-war nadir by 1921. This was coupled with the dumping of stockpiles of aluminium ingot and aluminium scrap on global markets. In Britain, this was not

Figure 1.4 *UK domestic production and consumption of virgin aluminium, 1896–2005*

Note: Differences in the consumption figures for 1915 from those obtained by Grinberg and Hachez-Leroy occur because this uses Ministry of Munitions figures, whilst the Grinberg and Hachez-Leroy figures are based on those collected by the German Metallgesellschaft which would not have access to these wartime British figures.

Sources: Chilton to Hardie, 21 January 1955; Bremner to Llewelyn, 31 August 1916; Postan, *British War Production*; Grinberg and Hachez-Leroy, *Industrialisation et sociétés*; AlFed, 2008 and 2010.

Flight of Sopwith Camels with Bentley Aluminum pistons. © Imperial War Museum (IWM).

aided by the government's hasty sale of strategic stocks of the metal. Between April and June 1920 alone, the government sold £725,000 (£25.3m) worth of aluminium.[36] Between 1923 and 1929 the market for aluminium recovered with global orders for the metal nearly doubled. The most dramatic growth was experienced in Great Britain (where consumption almost quadrupled), the United States and Germany, although BACo's share of the global market declined further.

The impact of the worldwide depression and the accompanying loss of consumer confidence saw sales fall, to recover again in 1933. Thereafter, and particularly from 1935–36, global consumption of the metal grew exponentially (particularly in Europe) to meet the demands of rearmament. Between 1936 and 1939, global primary aluminium production had more than doubled, with German output trebled. The most important characteristics of the market for primary aluminium during the inter-war period were the gradual shift in production and consumption away from North America to Europe, the impact of cartelisation in the latter, and anti-trust actions in the former. In 1929, Europe and the North America enjoyed a joint share of the world market. By 1935, Europe accounted for 70 per cent, with North America producing around 25 per cent. By 1938, Germany had become the largest global producer of the metal. By way of contrast, British production had grown by two-thirds on its 1933 figure, a much more modest expansion.[37]

The market for aluminium in the inter-war period of 1918–39 was characterised

Table 1.1 *Global market share of leading aluminium producers (%), 1913–1929*

Country/national producers	1913	1919	1929
AIAG Neuhausen	14%	6%	7.5%
Alcoa (incl. Canadian assets)	42%	66%	49%
BACo	11%	6%	5%
French producers	24%	8.5%	12.2%
German producers	2%	11%	12.2%

Notes:

Alcoa: Formerly the Pittsburgh Reduction Company, and including output from assets of its Canadian subsidiary Northern (subsequently Alcan).

French producers: Chiefly PCAC and SEMF, after 1921 these merged to form AFC.

German producers: Prior to 1917, largely AIAG assets. After 1917 VAW, as well as AIAG.

Source: Lesclous, *Histoire des sites producteurs d'aluminium*, diagrams 16 and 17, tables 24, 25 and 27.

by four distinct phases. Between 1918 and 1923 the aluminium industry operated arbitrary agreements. Almost immediately after the silencing of the guns, Andrew Tait, Louis Marlio of Alais, Froges et Camargue (AFC) and Arthur Vining Davis of Alcoa, and separately Jacques Level of Aluminium Français, met to discuss how to carve up global markets in the *postbellum* world; apportioning Alcoa North American markets, and AFC and BACo, Germany and Scandinavia as spheres of influence.[38] Initially international agreement was complicated by the vicissitudes that had emerged between producers over wartime alliances. Though the peace between the doyens of global aluminium, particularly BACo, AFC and Alcoa, was periodically rocked and the formal agreements sharply severed by German producers with Nazi rearmament, the fraternal ties and country club atmosphere would remain until the bitter fallout after BACo's takeover in 1959. In 1926 price and quota fixing arrangements were formalised in the establishing of the Aluminium Association (AA). This built on price-fixing arrangements agreed upon by the main European producers in 1923 and 1924. However, these proved fragile. Hence, at the behest of AIAG, the formation of a formal cartel, in the form of the Association. It was principally charged with regulating sales, expanding market opportunities and coordinating transport. Transnational relations in the industry between 1927 and 1931 teetered on the edge. Only restraint and careful and lengthy transatlantic diplomacy on the part of all the main players prevented 'economic strife' breaking out. On the whole though, aluminium was spared the far more volatile internal relations of some other cartels, not least because of the oligopolisation of the global industry assuming almost the air of an exclusive country club.[39]

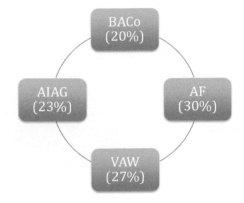

Figure 1.5 *Alliance Aluminium Company:*
shares of the European majors, 1931

The Aluminium Association was superseded in 1931 by the formation of the Alliance Aluminium Company (AAC) . The move to a more comprehensive cartel in the aluminium industry (as in the other non-ferrous metal and chemicals industries) was given added impetus by the rejection of proposals submitted to the World Economic Conference of 1927 for transnational mechanisms for controlling global raw material supplies by fifty of the national representatives present. Subsequent allocations of sales quotas were largely based on market share (including that of subsidiaries), with any extra needing dispensation requiring the authority of the 90% support or more of the first division of shareholders: Aluminium Français (AF, representing French producers), AIAG, BACo, VAW and the Aluminium Company of Canada (Alcan) (through their major shareholdings in the Norwegian firms Det Norske Nirtidaktieselkap (DNN) and the Norsk Aluminium Company (NACO)). In addition, the AAC purchased controlling shares in two small, independent British companies, Al. Corp. and the International Aluminium Company. The Alliance had three main constitutional aims: (1) the regulation of the output and reserves of its members; (2) the division of and control of the markets; and (3) to coordinate marketing and research in the industry. The organisation did not however devise prices centrally. Price controls were reliant on member companies faithfully adhering to their pledge not to undercut the prices of the main plants. This system operated fairly effectively, with most quotas adhered to, until 1935 when VAW – to meet Germany's re-armament programme – started to buy more concessions to increase her output beyond her quota. The cartel also encouraged a more prudent distribution of fixed capital investment to demand, by coordinating efforts on marketing, and research and development. Nevertheless, the British aluminium industry, in particular, suffered during the inter-war period as a result of higher imports, resulting from the UK's lower tariffs than many of its competitor nations. Certainly contemporary economists considered the non-ferrous metal industries in general – and aluminium, in particular – to have been far more successful in regulating their own industry and making the organisational changes prudent under the economic circumstances of the period.[40] Indeed, the inter-war aluminium cartels illustrate moth the complexities and successes of cartelisation.

Despite BACo's loss of global market share, it played a central role in the cartels as one of the doyens of international aluminium circles. British Aluminium also expanded both their upstream and downstream activities during this period. They completed their Burntisland works in 1918, and purchased William Mills who operated a foundry in Birmingham. Most significantly, by 1929 they had added their larger smelter and hydro-scheme at Lochaber. As the major partner in a consortium of British producers, including Al. Corp., BACo provided much of the initial finance and administration for the British and Colonial Bauxite Company Ltd (B&C), registered in 1927 with bauxite mining assets in British Guiana (later Guyana) next to those of Alcan's subsidiary, the Demerara Bauxite Company Ltd (DBC); with the latter taking over mining of the British and Colonial's leases on their behalf in 1936. British Aluminium also acquired mining rights in Awaso in the then British Gold Coast (present-day Ghana) in 1928, and in 1933 established a subsidiary, the Gold Coast Bauxite Company Ltd, but made little attempt to exploit these bauxite reserves until pressed to do so by the Ministry of Aircraft Production during the Second World War. The politics of imperial bauxite deposits, and British Aluminium's involvement, were inextricably bound up in the company's relations with government and is discussed elsewhere. However it is pertinent to point out that British Aluminium continued to experience problems with bauxite from Guyana, if not Ghana (which became one of its most valuable sources of bauxite), and that the purchases were tokenistic to some degree. BACo also expanded their primary metal production by purchasing one-third share from Aluminium français of DNN that operated two smelters at Eydehavn and Tyssedal in 1923, and in 1932 invested in Haugvik Smeltewerk; becoming by the early 1920s the largest foreign direct investor in the Norwegian industry.[41]

Between 1928 and 1929 BACo acquired further holdings in a number of other valuable concerns both domestically and abroad, notably shares in James Booth, the former Vickers subsidiary and alloy producer for specialist defence procurement markets, who for years had dominated the duralmin market in Britain. The importance of alloys also encouraged BACo to expand scope of their operations – in a joint venture with Imperial Chemical Industries (ICI), the Imperial Smelting Company (in which they held a share), and Murex and Johnson-Mattley – by investing in magnesium production, forming the Imperial Magnesium Corporation Ltd (IMC) in 1935. Once again this and other imperial ventures, were linked to their relationship with government. In addition, BACo acquired shares in another vital alloy material, the Electrolytic Zinc Company. This was matched by sustained capital investment programme in plant technology. IMC's assets were later increased when ICI, Imperial Smelting and BACo bought cable manufacturing, and brass rolling and extrusion plants in Australia. The horizontal integration into these markets made sense for producers like ICI and BACo who had a significant share in the burgeoning aircraft business (which heavily relied on aluminium-magnesium alloys) and electricity markets.[42]

However, this expansion had required considerable capital outlay coinciding with less than buoyant sales, and there were rumblings of disquiet among shareholders.[43] In particular, the expansion of British Aluminium's Highland smelter capacity had been protracted and expensive. From initiation of its original incarnation in 1918 it took until 1929 to complete the first stage of the Lochaber scheme, and a further thirteen years for the second and third stages of the project to be fully completed. In part, British Aluminium was a hostage to fortune. When the company proposed a Provisional Order to extend their Kinlochleven Scheme in 1918, they were forced to withdraw it, despite government support, in the face of considerable opposition. To some degree this stemmed from a more widespread, and longer running, distrust among some Parliamentarians of private hydro-electric schemes. However opponents also drew attention to the fact that the proposed scheme planned to divert water from one river, the Lochy, in the County of Inverness, to that of the Leven in Argyllshire. The company was required to reconsider its plans and submitted the Lochaber Water Power Bill before Parliament (once again with government support) in 1920, with it becoming law in 1921 and operations commencing in 1924. The delay proved costly both to its market position, and in Parliamentary time and lobbying. William Murray Morrison admitted that he estimated that the cost of the two statutory applications in themselves had cost the company £40,000 (£1.96m). Given its experience in the original development of the Kinlochleven scheme, British Aluminium's assumption that evocation of wartime service, and government support, would allow for the smooth passage of the 1918 Order was cavalier to say the least.[44] Around the same time, BACo's attempts to extend the capacity at Vigelands Brug fell victim to local politics and, partly, historical forces beyond control. However, like the failed Orsières scheme before, these incidents also revealed lapses in strategic judgement and political management.

In preparing for the passage of the Lochaber Water Power Bill, BACo was decidedly more cautious. Sensing the mood for change in government, and Parliament towards some form of central organisation of electricity generation, British Aluminium's lawyers counselled them to place a far more opaque bill before the House. In addition, the bill sought permission to use the water resources to supply a third aluminium reduction works to be established near Fort William within the boundaries of Inverness-shire. This ensured widespread local support for the bill within the county, which was critical in ensuring success. In preparing its supporting evidence to Parliament for the bill, the company again deployed its wartime service and the strategic importance of the metal to great effect. Andrew Tait stressed the strategic significance of expanding native aluminium production for Britain:

If this power is not available to the Company, there are, I understand, no other powers in this Country of sufficient size with suitable location to warrant their development for the aluminium industry, and if the necessary powers for its development are not granted the Company will be obliged to develop water powers in the Colonies or elsewhere to meet the necessity for increase in production, and several favourable propositions have been submitted to the Company for consideration. Should this course unavoidably become necessary, it would be regrettable in the National interest, and would be distinctly against the expressed desire of the Government that the increased need for production should be met by the manufacture of the metal in this country.[45]

For good measure a number of influential Highland spokesmen gave evidence to the Commons select committee, heaping fulsome praise on the impact of company's existing works at Foyers and Kinlochleven, and of the labour market benefits to the depressed Highlands of the proposed scheme. Even with the support of the Board of Trade and approval of the electricity commissioners, opposition to the bill was significant. Moreover government support for the bill had been exacted at some cost to British Aluminium, in terms of commitments to concede the potential of compulsory government purchase of the water rights and/or accept charges.[46] Nevertheless British Aluminium was more fortunate than the British Oxygen Company whose repeated attempts to develop a calcium carbide factory near the Lochaber smelter (powered also by hydro-electricity) had foundered in the face of opposition from landed and coal owner interests.

The North British Aluminium Company Ltd was incorporated with inter-locking directorships with the parent company, and, in January 1925, the Treasury guaranteed under the Trade Facilities Act, the interest on BACo's £2.5 million (£123m) Debenture Stock.[47] However, as at Kinlochleven, the Lochaber development was beset by delays. Problems with contractors on the tunnel set back progress, and in June 1929 the company was forced to apply for a Provisional Order to extend the time needed for the scheme. Lochaber started producing metal on 30 December 1929, and Parliamentary approval for work to start on the second stage – expanding generating capacity by building the Laggan and Treig Dams and the conduit connecting the two – was granted in 1930. The latter necessitated the raising of a further £5 million (£257m) through the raising of ordinary shares, subsequently approved at an extraordinary general meeting in October of the same year. Despite the completion of the second stage of the scheme in 1935, the plant was not able to operate at full capacity until rearmament brought a brisk upturn in trade after 1936. By 1938, British Aluminium had expended £7.5 million (£383m) on its Highland schemes.[48]

The protracted Parliamentary process (and political brinkmanship), and substantially higher capital costs of BACo's west Highland schemes relative to the costs of schemes in Norway and Canada, such as the Isle de Maligne in Québec

British Aluminium
UK operations 1937.
© RTA/Rio Tinto
Alcan Information
Centre, Montreal
(RTAIC).

– an estimated £20/kW as opposed to around £56/kW at Lochaber – effectively
signalled an end to further construction of native, peace-time, hydro-electrically
powered aluminium reduction works (and other cluster industries) on the British
mainland. Norway and Canada offered the potential of considerable competitive
advantage in such an energy-intensive industry. BACo's experience domestically,
its long association with Norway and the knowledge that only a tiny fraction
of Norwegian water resources had been developed (16 per cent before the early
1950s), attracted BACo to expand their interests there.[49] In addition, the transport

infrastructure in the west Highlands of Scotland remained poor. From the outset the company had busied themselves attempting to press for improved rail and water borne freight services, but high carriage charges in the area were sustained by the monopolies enjoyed by both the railway and shipping companies. As the 1938 report of one government inquiry into the economic conditions of the Highlands and Islands (on which William Murray Morrison served) observed: 'the freights charged by Railway Companies for the carriage of goods and live-stock may, as in the case of the shipping freights, be held to be largely responsible for the high living costs and lack of industrial development ...'[50] And of roads in the region, the committee reported them to be either 'inadequate' or non-existent.[51] To compound matters, in 1937 the company saw a dramatic rise in their local government rates in the area from £5,800 to £23,010, or an increase of 297 per cent.[52]

The inter-war years also provided an ominous indication of what lay ahead for British primary aluminium producers, and particularly British Aluminium. Competition intensified in domestic primary aluminium markets with an increase in imports of Norwegian, and increasingly Canadian, aluminium ingot, and in semi-manufactured and finished aluminium products, especially after 1933, from Germany. The British government's reluctance to impose protective tariffs for aluminium (as for other products) was in marked contrast to other nations. Between 1930 and 1936 the United

Figure 1.6 *Imports of aluminium to the UK, 1924–1934. The temporary fall-off of imports from Canada and Norway in 1926 and 1929 respectively are explained by a diversion of exports to the United States (in the case of Alcoa's subsidiary, Northern) and Germany (for Norwegian producers)*

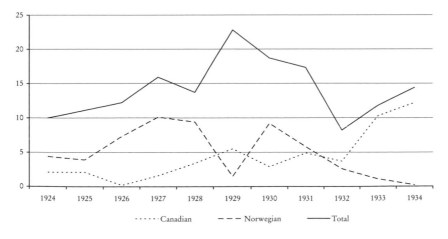

Sources: *Statistical Abstracts for the UK, 1924–1934.* My thanks also to Espen Storli for figures derived from *Norges offisielle statistikk, 1908–1939.*

States, who had imposed stringent duties on aluminium imports since 1903, was operating tariffs of between 13 and 20 per cent on all aluminium products. France raised their tariffs on aluminium products to 30 per cent in 1936. After the withdrawal of a system of government import licences, Germany imposed a tariff of 11.5 per cent in 1930. With the ascension of the Nazis to power German exports were also heavily subsidised by the state. The Swiss and Italians imposed tariffs of 26 per cent in 1930 and 1931 respectively.[53] When the British government finally did impose a general tariff of 30 per cent on aluminium ingot, after the Ottawa Agreements of 1932, Alcan, as a British Empire producer and one of two biggest importers of the metal to the UK, was exempted from duties. Furthermore, the other major competitors for the British domestic market for ingot, the Norwegians, enjoyed a concessionary duty of 10 per cent under the Anglo-Norwegian trade agreement of 1933. The change in duties dramatically altered foreign imports of aluminium ingot, with Alcan's share of the import market increasing from 45 to 85 per cent between 1932 and 1934, while Norwegian importers' income from exports to the UK fell from £878,000 in 1930 to £266,000 in 1932.[54] In 1934, UK customs and excise duties increased to 15 and 20 per cent for aluminium rolled products and foil respectively, which did little to stem imports of semi-manufactured aluminium goods from heavily subsidised German producers. However BACo's commercial strategy in the market for sheet metal scarcely aided sales.[55]

To compound BACo's misery, Alcan acquired a UK subsidiary, the Northern Aluminium Company Ltd, and by 1931 had an aluminium castings foundry, a hollowware plant and a rolling mill around Birmingham and Oxfordshire to take advantage of the expanding car and aircraft factories nearby. Thus Alcan was in a prime position to exploit British markets particularly after 1932. This, and developments in imperial defence stockpiling plans after October 1930 (examined in the next chapter), provided Alcan with a strong base from which to expand in the UK and within the British Empire after the Second World War, as it had been Aloca founder Arthur Vining Davis' original aspiration that they do. In a number of these ventures, such as the Aluminium Products Company of India Ltd and their Australian operations, they collaborated with BACo.[56]

The outlook for British Aluminium was not wholly dismal though. Research conducted during the First World War and thereafter by government, university and industry laboratories, much of it on behalf of the Air Ministry, expanded the uses of the metal especially that of transport. As well as a growth in military and civil transport markets, the establishment of the Central Electricity Board in 1926 and the ensuing development of a National Grid in Britain brought in large orders for the native aluminium industry. Between 1929 and 1933, 12,000 mts of aluminium were used in the Grid's pylons with much of the metal supplied from BACo's Highland smelters. In addition, the British Non-Ferrous Metals Research Association (BNFMRA) set up with industry finance and some government subvention, made important advances that brought real benefits in improvements to the aluminium reduction process and opened up lucrative new markets, such as that for colour coated aluminium and aluminium alloys.[57] By 1934 British Aluminium commanded 22 per cent of the market for alloys in the UK, and by 1936 the growing market for semi-manufactured aluminium products contributed over 50 per cent of BACo's sales, with the company's Milton works alone experiencing a 75 per cent growth on 1933.

And yet these concealed fundamental weaknesses in BACo sales strategies and worrying signs for their future position in the domestic semis markets; their investment in technology was not matched by marketing expertise and sales infrastructure.[58] The company's experience as a producer of primary aluminium had affected its approach to the far more competitive and customer-orientated market for downstream products. British Aluminium had adopted a 'cost focus' strategy to sales of sheet metal (one of their largest in the semis market): offering customers a limited range of stock sizes at low prices. However buyers were increasingly expressing a wish to see a better quality of metal and in a form better matching their specifications. Remarkably, in the face of falling sales of stock sizes – 8 per cent between 1933 and 1934 alone – general manager George Steel (a former career civil servant) proposed, at the company's annual meeting of managers in June 1934, that BACo's rolling mills managers impose 'penalties' on those customers who wanted special specifications. Critically, they failed to attract increasingly important, newer entrants to the British car industry, such as Ford (who controlled around 23 per cent of the market by the mid-1930s) because they could not offer aluminium-copper alloys.[59] One large transport contractor, present at a lecture given in May 1933 by BACo director George Boex, was reported as stating that he 'hoped … that the author and the manufacturers of aluminium more generally did not imagine that aluminium would sell itself. The Edinburgh Corporation Transport Department had found that when they specifically called for aluminium alloys in their specifications they were never supplied.'[60] In addition to this, in 1932 British Aluminium's largest rolling mill at Warrington had been experiencing problems that led to nearly 39 per cent of soft sheets being rejected because of blisters in the metal; the problem being rectified over the next few years using methods developed by the BNFMRA, the NPL and BACo scientists. Nevertheless knowledge of and interest in using aluminium among British manufacturers – with the notable exception of the armed services – continued to be presenting BACo with problems, although as end-users were quick to point out aluminium producers could have substantially improved their promotion of their portfolio. In his May 1933 lecture, George Boex can scarcely have won friends when he urged end-users to curb the inappropriate use of the metal by 'enthusiasts', remarking that this had 'often retarded for years a development which was found satisfactory when proper care was taken of materials and methods'.[61]

Much of the expansion in the semis trade from 1936 onwards was accounted for by sheet aluminium, also aided by its share in James Booth who operated a virtual

monopoly in the duralmin market. Of this, most arose from the expansion of the
Royal Air Force (RAF) with the Air Ministry requesting an increased effort and
increasingly absorbing much of British Aluminium's output by the late 1930s. The
growth in demand prompted the company to join Alcan's Northern Aluminium and
AIAG Neuhausen in opening a short-lived reduction works in South Wales under
the auspices of the South Wales Aluminium Co. Ltd. BACo also froze prices for
semi-manufactured metal going to ICI and Booth's Duralmin rolling mills, and,
through an IMC subsidiary the Magnesium Metal Company, erected a magnesium
plant in Swansea. By 1938, 50 per cent of aluminium produced in the UK was being
employed in aircraft production, although some of the demand for sheet derived from
civilian transport and housing.[62]

During this period British Aluminium had integrated further both vertically
and horizontally by expanding operations in upstream and downstream activities,
and diversified into related fields. Investment in plant and processes was also
paying dividends – in terms of economies of scale and scope – at both the primary
aluminium reduction works and their semi-manufacturing units. Yet senior managers
within the British Aluminium were expressing their concern at the company's
poor market share in lucrative, newer semis markets, while paradoxically failing to
invest in an effective sales infrastructure and alter their sales strategy. Despite their
capital investment programmes, British Aluminium's profitability was consistently
behind that of Alcoa. Compared against British manufacturing averages of 16 per
cent in 1937, British Aluminium's rate of 6 per cent (even lower than the 10.4–10.6
per cent of troubled British heavy steel and steel sheet producers) looked even more
disappointing.[63] Admittedly there were few industries that had such high sunk costs as
aluminium producers. A further indication of British Aluminium's financial position
was provided by the response of Treasury officials to the request by the company for
a further government assured loan. In September 1936, Sir Frederick Phillips, then
Under-Secretary at the Treasury, opposed a loan to BACo on the grounds that their
'capital structure is already overloaded with debentures', and as such were a risk for
the government to underwrite.[64] Though the Chancellor of the Exchequer finally
approved the loan, the grave concerns expressed by senior Treasury officials paint a
bleak picture of the company's financial health at the time. In the end BACo gathered
the necessary capital for the extension of Lochaber by raising more share options that
caused disquiet among some of its shareholders. By the late 1930s it was evident to
British Aluminium that any dramatic expansion of primary aluminium capacity in
the UK on a commercially viable basis was inconceivable in the foreseeable future.
This was confirmed by the company's deputy general manager, the Hon. Geoffrey
Cunliffe, to officials in June 1940, while serving as the government's wartime
aluminium controller.[65] Thus BACo was faced with the option of either relying on
imports of ingots (largely from Canada), or contemplating developments outside of
the UK.

One possibility was the Gold Coast where British Aluminium held bauxite reserves. The British government geologist who had brought the reserves to the attention of the metropolitan government had also highlighted the great water-power potential of the Volta River in discussion with the Colonial Office. British Aluminium was luke-warm to the suggestion of constructing an integrated smelting complex in west Africa because the company's main markets and fabricating capacity were in western Europe and transport costs would have been crippling. Its operations in both Australia and India were in their infancy. Quite aside from these questions, British Aluminium was chronically financially over-extended, and could not seriously entertain the prospect of investment on this scale.[66] The resignation of Andrew Tait in 1928 had robbed them of a supremely able, and commercially and politically astute chairman. Tait was replaced in the first instance as chair by his vice-chairman and former military officer, Lt Col. Stephen Pollen, a figure chiefly chosen for his civil and military connections, rather than commercial experience.[67] Pollen relinquished the chair to Major Robert Cooper in 1930, and remained as vice chair until ill-health prompted him to retire in 1934. Aside from his career as a solicitor and distinguished service during the First World War (winning the Military Cross), Cooper was a businessman of some repute. So well respected was he that Andrew Tait brought him onto the board of Ferranti in 1913; a decision which was judged by Ferranti's chairman Vincent de Ferranti, and subsequently the leading historian of the company, to be immensely prudent given Cooper's connections in the City of London and financial knowledge.[68] If BACo were, to some extent, the victim of historical contingencies – caught up in events that they were not fully equipped to adapt or respond to – it was aided by government contracts and finances. However, it was a company that was becoming 'locked-in' to its relationship with the state and the behaviours this cultivated within the organisation. This increasingly determined its strategic outlook.

'Let slip the dogs of war': aluminium and the war economy, 1939–1945

As the dark clouds of war gathered over the world by the late 1930s, the AAC was suspended, as German producer VAW acquired as much of the aluminium quotas as possible, while dumping cheap (and heavily subsidised) metal on other national markets. The AAC also faced problems trying to regulate the Italian industry, especially given the political patronage enjoyed by Montecatini through the chairman and MD, Guido Donegani. Global production of aluminium increased from 589,100 mts in the last full year of peace (1938) to 1,949,000 mts in 1943, with consumption growing from 505,400 mts to 1,682,000 mts over the same period. Despite a lull in the two years immediately following the War (arising from the surplus of aluminium, including aluminium scrap), the conflict was to prompt a dramatic expansion in both markets and productive capacity.[69]

Figure 1.7 *Return on capital expenditure (ROCE) for BACo and Alcoa by selected years 1928–1987*

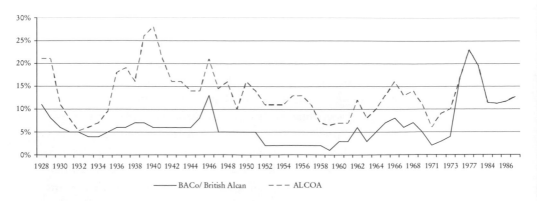

Calculated by Perchard using formula in B. and J. Elliott, *Financial accounting and reporting* (Prentice Hall: London, 2007).

Sources: BACo, Annual reports, 1928–1978; Memo from J. S. Potten, Alcan Aluminium UK (AAUK) Mill Products Division, to D. Morton, AAUK Banbury, 'The British Aluminium Company Ltd', 25 June 1979, UGD 347/10/3/4; British Alcan, Presentation to bankers on post-merger achievements, 1111 Smith, *From Monopoly to Competition*, Appendix B.

(a) Between 1940–1945 BACo was subject to the wartime Excess Profits Tax, and aluminium production was controlled by the Ministry of Supply and then the Ministry of Aircraft Production. Until 1 January 1953, supplies of aluminium remained controlled by the Ministry of Supply.

(b) Net profit for the Group for 1962 include profits for the Canadian British Aluminium Company, but assets for that year do not include CBA's. The calculation for years 1963–38 includes both the profits and assets of CBA.

After Hitler's ascension to the German Chancellorship in 1933, and particularly after the establishment of the Luftwaffe as an independent branch of the armed forces in 1935, expansion of aluminium production in Germany once again grew dramatically, principally for aircraft production. Between 1934 and 1939 alone, aluminium output in Germany rose from 30,000 to 200,000 mts. In addition, the German industry rapidly expanded semi-fabrication during the war. Germany had gone from being almost entirely reliant on Swiss production in 1915 to being the largest single global producer of the metal in 1939, when it alone produced nearly 30 per cent of the world output of ingot. By 1944, the Third Reich was consuming 267,000 mts of the metal, most of which went into the 4,000 military aircraft produced that year.[70] Less dramatic, but significant nonetheless, Italian aluminium production grew from 1931 onwards, particularly after fascist Italy's invasion of Ethiopia in 1935. Over the next four years, the quantity of alumina and aluminium produced in foreign-owned concerns had overtaken that of the main Italian producer, Montecatini. Initially fascist

Italy, like Nazi Germany, relied heavily on the contribution of the Swiss company, AIAG Neuhausen, whose Italian subsidiary la Società Alluminio Veneto Anonima (SAVA), supplied 44 per cent of Italy's aluminium and 69 per cent of its alumina by 1939. Alcoa's subsidiary, Aluminium Ltd, provided much smaller quantities (6.2 per cent by 1939). By 1942–43, the Italian industry – dependent as it was on supplies of German coal – was severely affected by the Nazi authority's decision to dramatically reduce imports to Italy; and by 1943, Italy's primary smelting capacity reached its peak production of 47,000 mts. France's aluminium producers received a boost from rearmament again from 1936 until 1941. After the fall of France in May 1940, French bauxite, alumina and aluminium production – even though produced within Vichy jurisdiction – came directly under German control, as did Norway's valuable industry. French wartime aluminium production peaked in 1941 but technological developments continued. By 1945, it had a modern smelting capacity of 70,000 tons, but its finishing and semi-fabricating capacity was less well developed.[71]

It was, however, to be the North American industry that received the greatest boost during the Second World War. The US and Canadian producers, with their vast energy resources, generous loans from US and British governments and their plants unaffected by aerial bombardment – not to mention an accommodating domestic tax regime in Alcan's case – expanded their production of ingot and semi-manufactured aluminium and alloys dramatically. By 1945 the European aluminium industry was completely overshadowed by its North American counterparts, who had built much larger and more technologically advanced smelters and rolling mills. At the peak year of wartime production in 1943, the USA alone produced 835,000 mts of aluminium ingot (representing 43 per cent of the global total) largely to satiate the appetite for aircraft production, reaching 83,000 military aircraft that year.[72] North American producers also played a crucial role in meeting Britain's wartime demand and immediate post-war demand for aluminium. Moreover the financial and trade support lent to the Canadian industry by the British government throughout this period was to have a dramatic effect both on Alcan and on British Aluminium.

Between 24 August 1939 and 22 May 1940 statutory measures were introduced in Britain to control domestic and foreign sales, prices, production initially, and then the industry, under the direction of the Ministry of Supply: the aluminium control being one of fourteen sections set up within the ministry. In August 1940, the aluminium control was transferred (reflecting where its primary uses lay) to the Ministry of Aircraft Production (MAP).[73] As in the First World War, senior BACo executives were drafted in to work within the control, with BACo's Geoffrey Cunliffe initially serving as aluminium controller, along with other staff such as George Boex. As in the other combatant nations UK aluminium consumption expanded exponentially, from 66,000 mts in 1938 to 322,000 mts by 1943. At the outbreak of war the native industry was producing around 25,400 mts of ingot and 40,600 mts of aluminium alloy. Despite planning measures put in place since 1927 by the government, the slippery

The Managing Directors

The Hon. Geoffrey Cunliffe joined the Company in 1932 and became Deputy General Manager in 1937 and was appointed a Director in 1938. During the war he was seconded to the Ministry of Supply and later to the Ministry of Aircraft Production as Aluminium Controller. He went to the Board of Trade as a whole-time member of the Industrial and Export Council in 1941. He later returned to the Company as Depute General Manager and became General Manager in 1944. He was appointed Joint Managing Director in 1945 and Deputy Chairman of the Company in 1947.

Mr. George Boex, B.Sc.(Eng.), M.I.C.E., M.I.E.E. joined the Company as Assistant Manager at Foyers in 1914 and moved to Kinlochleven as Assistant Manager in 1920. In 1925 he was transferred to Head Office as Assistant Technical Manager with particular reference to Lochaber which was then being designed. In 1940 he became a Director and also Technical Manager of the Company. In 1945 he was appointed Joint Managing Director with Mr. Cunliffe

The Old Guard: Geoffrey Cunliffe and George Boex, 1949. © RTA/GUA.

Lancaster bombers under construction at AV Roe Bristol factory, 1943. © IWM.

problem for service departments of producing accurate or even meaningful estimates meant that a shortfall quickly developed.[74] Increasing demand prompted by the growth in aircraft production, losses in the Battle of Britain, water shortages at BACo's Highland works (a recurrent problem) saw a worrying shortfall emerging by January 1940. By July, the government concluded that as there was no new primary smelting capacity at home and extensions to Canadian capacity would take a further twelve months, demand must be met by making economies, stepping up measures to acquire scrap metal, increasing secondary (and short-term primary) smelting capacity and acquiring further supplies of North American metal.[75] To meet this immediate deficit, Geoffrey Cunliffe was dispatched to Canada to negotiate further supplies of the metal in August 1941. Concurrently MAP invested in the construction of secondary and primary smelters, fabrication plants (notably rolling mills), as well as primary smelting capacity in Canada. Throughout the period 1941–44, no less than 60 per cent of the aluminium consumed by the British war effort came from Canada. During the course of the war the capacity for primary ingot production was expanded by 45 per cent, reaching 57,000 mts by 1943 (largely through temporary non-commercial reduction works that operated for part of the war), and semi-fabricating capacity by 75 per cent. This investment by the British government in upstream and downstream activities

Aluminium being poured into a mould for a Merlin engine 1942. © IWM.

came at the cost of £53.5 million, with a further CAD55 million in loans advanced to Alcan to develop smelting capacity in Canada.[76] By 1945, British Aluminium was at a crossroads; still under government control, it was also constrained by a weak capital structure, lack of domestic opportunities and poor commercial leadership. In contrast Alcan, its major competitor in UK markets, was a picture of rude health.

Losing 'an empire' and searching for a role: 1945–1958

The post-war years continued to see a dramatic growth in demand for and output of aluminium. World consumption of primary aluminium rose by an annual average of 9 per cent between 1950 and 1970, while global production grew by 577 per cent from 1,509,000 mts to 10,214,000 mts over the same period. Europe, and particularly the UK, was forced to rely heavily on imports of Canadian ingot; British consumption alone grew from 116,000 mts to 224,000 mts between 1946 and 1952. Of the aluminium consumed in the UK over the same period around 76 per cent was in the form of Canadian ingots imported under government contracts. This set against the backdrop of Britain's ongoing foreign exchange crisis, and net Dollar drain, throughout the period 1946–1961.[78] In 1949 alone, four-fifths of UK imports of aluminium had to be financed from the Marshall Aid programme. Moreover Britain was committed to 'lend' the United States 10,160 mts in aluminium in 1951, and a further 15,240 mts in 1952.[79] The impact of the Dollar deficit from this trade was not only critical for Britain but, as the largest producer of semi-fabricated aluminium in the immediate post-war period (with an output of around double that of the next largest producer, France), for Western Europe too. In their report of February 1949, the Non-Ferrous Metals Committee of the Organisation for European Economic Co-operation outlined the crux of the problem:

> Increases in aluminium consumption were most marked in the highly industrialised countries (USA, UK, Switzerland, France and Belgium), and this is still true when consumption in armaments is ignored ... the whole question, in fact, is one of supplying the United Kingdom, to which Canada is the main supplier.[80]

However, as the committee noted, with the spiked prices of other non-ferrous metals like copper, nickel and zinc, it was also incumbent upon the member states to promote the use of aluminium as an alternative. Thus they concluded in their October 1949 report: 'for these reasons it has to be recognized that Canada cannot be entirely eliminated as a source of supply to the participating countries concerned.'[81]

Government control of the UK aluminium industry continued until 1953, with the pricing, supply and export of the metal strictly managed by firstly by the Ministry of Supply and then the Ministry of Materials. The government's procurement of practically all native production of ingot – save for a small proportion allowed for export in order to secure valuable dollars – and control of sales meant that British Aluminium (as the sole integrated native producer) was particularly disadvantaged as a result of having to sell most of her ingot to the ministry at cost price, and then having to buy back the primary metal from them (as a semi-fabricator) at government prices. In contrast, domestic producers of semi-fabricates benefited from a degree of subsidy from the Ministry of imported metal. Meanwhile the secondary aluminium industry (expanded significantly during the war) supplemented shortfalls in primary aluminium reaching 74,272 mts by 1952, with the quality improved by the use of virgin ingot.[82] Crucially, as Moos had observed, these years of control were a time for government and the industry to take stock of the situation. The following chapter shows that government was doubtful whether Britain should retain native primary aluminium production, and if BACo's smelters would survive. Nevertheless material shortages (and dollar exchange) prompted the UK government and British Aluminium alike to sustain existing native production and look further afield to develop upstream activities, particularly in the Sterling area. The voracious demand for the metal, along with the changed domestic social and political environment for many European and North American producers, prompted a 'worldwide scramble' for mineral reserves and water power rights. In particular the attention of European and North American producers was focused on West Africa, Australia, and to a lesser extent Latin America and the South East Asia.[83]

Although British Aluminium was registered as one of Britain's largest fifty companies in 1948, the company was in a precarious position: the war had extended its semi-fabricating capacity with the addition of the large (and valuable) Falkirk rolling mill (which came on-stream in 1944) and Newport, but left it (and the UK) dependent on supplies of Canadian ingot. In his address to British Aluminium shareholders at the annual general meeting in 1946 the company's chairman Robert Cooper acknowledged BACo's changed circumstances and set out the way forward: 'The Company's pre-war position as an ingot producer primarily, with semi-fabrication as a secondary consideration, has changed. Our primary interest now rests in semi-fabrication ...'[84]

BACo had indeed primarily become a semi-fabricator, controlling just over 37 per cent and 10 per cent respectively of the domestic markets for aluminium sheet and strip, and extrusions, in 1946. By 1948, it held 15 per cent of the UK market in strong alloys, and accounted for around 39 per cent of the rolled aluminium sold. This growth was sustained to some extent by demand for aluminium houses (and the shortage of wood and steel) fuelled by the Labour government's post-war housing programme, expansion of the nation's transport and electricity distribution infrastructure, and ongoing aircraft production. Between July 1945 and December 1951, 19289 permanent aluminium houses were constructed and installed in Britain, with this market alone absorbing 24 per cent of BACo's output in 1946 and 16 per cent in 1947. The newly formed British Transport Commission also stimulated demand for the metal, with its replacement of large numbers of their older railway carriages with aluminium alloy cars.[85] Furthermore, the substantial rearmament programme for the Korean War saw demand for aluminium soar. Between 1951 and 1953 expenditure on metal goods alone for defence purposes in Britain totalled £1,285,000 (£28m). With shortages in many ferrous and non-ferrous metals, aluminium was vital to rearmament. Aluminium and aluminium alloys were used extensively in military aircraft, such as RAF Bomber Command's new longer-range V-class bombers and the Canberra (growing in popularity with Commonwealth air forces also) as well as a new generation of jet fighters, providing large orders both to BACo and to Alcan's UK subsidiary Northern Aluminium. BACo's extension of their Falkirk strip mill – and Northern's at Rogerstone in south Wales – were in no small measure a response to the rise in demand from the RAF and the Admiralty, with the company offering a number of official and semi-official aluminium and alloy specifications by the 1950s for the Ministry of Supply and Admiralty.[86]

Though defence requirements were met from existing metal supplies it did result in a shortage for other users. This was particularly pronounced given the number of other industries seeking to replace costly materials (such as copper), and those in short

Interior of BACo's
Falkirk rolling mill
1957. © RTA/GUA.

supply (steel and wood), with aluminium. With the price of copper – traditionally
the electricity industry's metal of preference because of its higher conductivity
than aluminium – reaching around £370/ton in 1955 (more than double the price
of aluminium ingot) the British Electricity Authority and its area boards eagerly
sought to replace copper in both low and high voltage power lines with aluminium
and its alloys. Similarly the UK Atomic Energy Authority (UKAEA) started to
experiment with aluminium alloys, with a view to replacing expensive Zirconium
alloys for the casing of uranium fuels with 'Aereal' alloys (combining aluminium
with iron, nickel silicon or titanium) in their DIDO class reactors. Britain's first
generation of Magnox nuclear power stations were constructed using magnesium-
aluminium alloys. Here British Aluminium's diversification into magnesium, as a
major shareholder in the Magnesium Elektron Company, paid dividends. As well as
alloys for the Magnox programme, Magnesium Elektron Company also led the way in

Falkirk rolling mill 1957. © RTA/GUA.

magnesium-zirconium alloys for aircraft production. Increasingly British Aluminium and Northern Aluminium, came to see great potential in the use of aluminium in the UK nuclear programme both in its direct applications within reactors and also as a niche market opportunity for export.[87]

Despite their problems, BACo pressed ahead with investigating potential schemes both within and outside the British Commonwealth and Empire. Between 1947 and 1953 BACo sent fact-finding missions to Australia, Iceland, New Zealand and North Borneo. In part, this was prompted by recurring concerns that the French government would impose export duties on bauxite from their French subsidiary. In anticipation British Aluminium doubled supplies of bauxite from their Gold Coast subsidiary between 1948 and 1953, and acquired mining leases in North Borneo (Sabah and Sarawak) in 1951, even briefly entertaining the idea of expanding operations in what was to become part of Malaysia. However any plans for developments in Sarawak were abandoned after surveys were made between 1950 and 1952. In the lingering twilight years of the country-club atmosphere of the first rank global aluminium producers, British Aluminium collaborated with Alcan and Alcoa, AIAG (later Alusuisse), Pechiney and VAW on a number of international projects. In part, the closer working with the North American majors was engineered in the hope that they could benefit

Inside BACo Falkirk 1957. © RTA/GUA.

from knowledge transfer from the former whose technology was understood to have advanced during the Second World War. In this connection, BACo directors visited Alcan plants at Arvida in Québec and Rogerstone in Wales. Alcan, BACo and AIAG entered into a short-lived partnership in China in 1949 (with BACo and Alcan later selling their shares to the Swiss firm), while Alcan and British Aluminium cemented their existing working relationship in British Guiana by forming a joint company. By the mid-1950s, British Aluminium held a 10 per cent in the speculative FRIA development in the then French colony of Guinea – alongside AIAG, VAW and US firm Olin Mathieson Chemical Corporation, under the project leadership of Pechiney (formerly AFC) – to construct an integrated bauxite mine and 480,000 mts alumina refinery complex. Having secured further deposits of bauxite at Awaso in the Gold Coast from the Ministry of Supply, British Aluminium was also reluctant participants, along with Alcan, in the Volta River Scheme to establish a vast hydro-electric project and aluminium smelter sharing the cost with the British and Gold Coast governments. The project, however, was mired in BACo's complex and chequered relationship with government, and the company withdrew from the project in 1956 much to annoyance of the Board of Trade. They were also 50 per cent shareholders and partners with the Australian Government and Consolidated Zinc in COMALCO in the development of rich bauxite deposits of Weipa in North Queensland, investing £400,000 in their associate the Australian Aluminium Company Ltd in 1950.[88] However the most fruitful overseas development of these years was to be their 66 per cent stake in the construction of the Baie Comeau smelter with 80,000 mts capacity in Québec (on the shores of the St Lawrence River), initially in partnership with the Quebec North Shore Paper Company (part of the Chicago Tribune Group). The costs of this project alone were estimated at CAD72 million, with the actual price rising to CAD$78 million. Yet its Canadian subsidiary, the Canadian British Aluminium Company (CBA), was to pay rich dividends in the long run.[89]

Closer to home, between 1947 and 1954, BACo converted its small works at Foyers and Vgielands into 'super purity' aluminium refineries and undertook major capital investment projects to modernise the Kinlochleven and Lochaber smelters, their Avonmouth aluminium sulphate works (damaged during the war), and their important Falkirk rolling mill (sinking £1.5m alone into the latter). In addition, British Aluminium took an equal share with one of the other largest semi-fabricators in the UK, Tube Investments, and the defence group Hawker Siddley, in forming the Aluminium Wire and Cable Company in 1946. British Aluminium continued to experience water shortages at its Highland smelters, causing stoppages, and spent much of the next decade in fraught negotiations with government and the publicly owned electricity board for the North of Scotland to prevent their hydro-electric assets being taken into public ownership and then arriving at a viable price for peak-load electricity. The ongoing problems with accessing cheap power in the Highlands underpinned their decision to increase their share of DNN to 50 per cent in 1958.[90]

All of these were to be critical to BACo's attempts to reassert itself among the premier rung of aluminium producers and establish itself as a major exporter again, especially in lieu of the fact that lucrative orders for semi-fabricated products such as specialist sheet for aircraft manufacture were diminishing. By the late 1950s, for example, 75–80 per cent of the output of BACo's Falkirk rolling mill (the largest at the time in Europe) was for the domestic market.[91] In an admittedly jaundiced account, BACo's future MD, Ronny Utiger, judged of this period that the partnerships and prospecting looked set to bear fruit and that the company seemed 'poised for a major breakthrough, which would have put it back among the leaders'. Critically though he observed that the technical proficiency and 'foresight' of the British Aluminium directors and engineers, who worked to set up these partnerships, was not 'matched by similar foresight in financial and commercial management'.[92] René Lesclous judges that though British Aluminium undertook a thorough search for new global reserves for bauxite, ultimately they 'had no long-term vision', while Cailluet asserts that 'From 1945 to 1958, BACo's management failed (or was too slow) to define and apply a proactive industrial strategy'.[93] Utiger, Lesclous and Cailluet are undoubtedly right to highlight the shortcomings of the BACo board, although they were not entirely masters of their own destiny.

In the event British Aluminium was chronically under-capitalised, and once again forced to raise £7 million in capital from shareholders to cover its 66 per cent share in the Canadian project, as well as issuing CAD10 million worth of shares in Canada and 'a complicated debt structure'. Aside from Baie Comeau, British Aluminium's estimated financial commitments on the Fria project and the Volta River project alone totalled a further £15 million. Canadian British Aluminium (CBA) was to provide the British Aluminium group with half of its pre-tax profits between 1962 and 1968. However, under its contract with the Canadian subsidiary, it was bound to buy all of the output from Baie Comeau and had little room for manoeuvre, with 44 per cent of the shares in CBA held by the Canadian public and the Tribune Group. Domestic taxation in Canada also diminished returns to BACo. British Aluminium's attempts to form a consortium to spread their share of the burden on the Volta River Project failed to interest other British private sector investors, and the company were forced to withdraw from the integrated scheme. Their role in the negotiations and withdrawal had further sullied their reputation in government circles, and their financial position was well known to their main competitors. Both undermined their strategic position. As director William J. Thomas was later to note, 'we were sitting ducks'. In fact, BACo had attracted the attention of banker Siegmund Warburg, who had been looking to mount a US takeover of the company since 1956.[94]

The 'Great Aluminium War', 1958–1959

By 1958 the company's attention was drawn to the fact that an undisclosed buyer was purchasing increasing numbers of British Aluminium's shares. The opening offensive of the 'Great Aluminium War' had begun. The controversial takeover of British Aluminium was widely reported in the domestic and international media, embroiling the British government, the City of London, and prompting heated discussions in Parliament. It also sent shock waves through British industry, and the comfortable country club atmosphere of the established order of the global aluminium seniors. It was subsequently played out in the press on both sides of the Atlantic as a broader battle between the established order of 'Old Freddies' in the City, and the arrivistes represented by the raiders.[95]

The raiders were UK semi-manufacturer Tube Investments (TI) and US Reynolds Metals (RM). The Reynolds Metals Company members were veterans, battle-hardened from their attempts to break Alcoa's monopoly of US markets, having moved into aluminium production from cigarette manufacturing via a rapidly assembled semi-fabrication business built up during the Second World War. They were also powerful political operators, holding considerable influence within the US Democratic Party. Despite some successes, Reynolds, and the other US 'latecomer' Kaiser, had been unsuccessful in breaking Alcoa's monopoly. Therefore they were keen to expand their operations elsewhere. Reynolds had already attracted BACo's ire for their role in counselling one of the largest holders of bauxite reserves in the Gold Coast to hold out against British Aluminium's paltry offers for his mining concessions. Reynolds had also clashed with both Alcan and the British government over bauxite rights in Jamaica. Tube Investments was made up primarily of iron and steel manufacturers and bicycle frame makers who had moved horizontally into aluminium semi-fabrication during the Second World War. In 1948 they were ranked 27th, against BACo's 48th polling, in the register of Britain top fifty companies in 1948, with a market value of almost double that of BACo. Allegedly the former's chairman, Sir Ivan Stedeford, and BACo's Geoffrey Cunliffe were also at odds over another business interest. Both companies had net assets and profits that dwarfed those of British Aluminium.[96]

Reynolds Metals' interest in British Aluminium commenced in early 1957, with the former struggling to find a way of expanding its operations in North America and attracted by British Aluminium's Canadian assets. Reynolds had also long wanted a stake in the Volta River Project but did not have bauxite reserves in the Gold Coast. As a party with a close interest in the West African development, the company was also acutely aware of British Aluminium's vulnerability, as was TI from its partnership with BACo in the Aluminium Wire and Cable Company. In May 1957 Reynolds signed a $15 million contract with TI to become partners in UK aluminium semi-fabrication operations (Reynolds-Tube Investments Aluminium (RTIA), and by September had enlisted Stedeford's support for a takeover bid of BACo.[97]

Reynolds pursued its quarry through the unconventional bankers, SG Warburgs, and the relatively youthful City of London legal firm Allen and Overy, with a tenacity that was a taste of future hostile takeovers. This was matched by the BACo board's inept handling of the struggle. Stedeford indicated his willingness to buy BACo stock, as part of the partnership, but initially found the prosecution of the takeover distasteful. By October 1958, RTIA had acquired 10 per cent of British Aluminium's shares but felt it was time to approach BACo openly with a deal. At the beginning of November 1958, Stedeford and Joseph McConnell (Reynolds' representative) along with their banker Siegmund Warburg met with Viscount (Lord) Portal of Hungerford – the former Chief of Britain's wartime air staff, who had become the BACo chairman in 1953 – Cunliffe, and BACo's bankers Hambros Bank and Lazard Brothers (two of the most established City firms). Portal and Cunliffe dismissed the RTIA deal, allegedly in a derisory fashion that offended McConnell, Stedeford, and Warburg, and strengthened their resolve to pursue BACo aggressively. Learning that Portal was about to depart for Canada, the TI chairman subsequently wrote to the BACo chairman stating that RTIA wanted to purchase all the BACo shares at well over the market price. During the course of his visit to north America, Portal fashioned a deal with Alcoa for the US giant to purchase £4.5m worth of British Aluminium shares (or 40 per cent) over the following three to four years, which they submitted for Treasury approval upon Portal's return. Yet the board failed to submit RTIA's earlier offer – 18 shillings more per share than that agreed with Alcoa – to its shareholders.[98]

RTIA retaliated by making public all of its correspondence with BACo. At a second meeting with Stedeford, McConnell and Warburg later that month, Portal and Cunliffe declared the latter's offer to be inadequate and walked out of the meeting. In the aftermath, RTIA released details of its offer to the press with the intention of letting the shareholders decide for themselves on 29 and 30 November. There was a backlash against the British Aluminium management in the press for keeping details of the RTIA offer from its shareholders. BACo's board responded publicly, stating that the Alcoa deal was the best for the company allowing it to grow rapidly with a partner. In another public slip, Portal's suggestion that RTIA was trying to 'acquire a powerful empire at the price of a small kingdom' was quickly picked up by *The Economist* who responded by questioning the BACo board's intent to sell off the same assets to Alcoa, 'for the price of a small municipality'.[99]

As the next chapter explains, as well as misleading their shareholders, Portal and Cunliffe's further miscalculation was to assume that they could expect the government to intervene on their behalf. On 19 December 1958 a consortium of Britain's most august financial institutions led by Lazards and Hambros offered to buy shareholders' stock for 82 shillings – 4s. more than RTIA's offer, but subject to the condition that they could only collect half of this before 31 March 1959 and the rest thereafter – to save British Aluminium in the 'national interest'. That same day the BACo board also fought back with the offer of a 5 per cent increase on the dividend to be paid to shareholders for 1958. Shareholders held fast until after the New Year but the banking consortium's offer prompted Richard Reynolds to authorise McConnell to buy all the BACo shares. This initiated a dumping of stock by shareholders within the first two days of 1959. Crucially this included large shareholders like the Church of England (also shareholders in TI), who had hitherto held fast. However, the allure of selling at this time was too great, netting the Church Commissioners around £0.5m (£8.86m).[100]

By 9 January 1959 RTIA held 80 per cent of British Aluminium's stock, and by July of that year 94 per cent. At the close of the affair, the Bank of England had been forced to bring both sides around the table to defuse the divisions within the City but to no avail. The Treasury approved the RTIA merger with BACo on the understanding that the majority of the capital and board remain British, with TI retaining 51 per cent of the shares. Portal and Cunliffe resigned their positions on the board of the company, respectively recompensed with £30,000 and £58,000 (£532k and £1.03m) in tax-free payments. Cunliffe complained bitterly that 'he had under-estimated one fact; in every public company there is a fifth column: the shareholders'. Portal's biographer notes that he continued to bear a grudge against the shareholders for the rest of his days. A spokesman for RTIA asked for his opinion on the shortcomings of the BACo boards' conduct during the takeover battle noted acidly: 'If you ask me what mistake they made, I'd reply in one word: arrogance. Their kind applauds the rules and practices of capitalism only when it suits them.'[101]

The battle has been judged to represent a contest between the 'new' and 'old' orders, and, in some cases, between a stereotype of ossified British capitalism and more aggressive unconventional US interests. In reality both sets of opponents were socially well connected, including with political elites. Reynolds was, however, far more battle hardened from its own struggles in North America. British Aluminium's board, particularly Portal and Cunliffe, exhibited glaring naïveté at times and were woefully out-of-step with the changing world of global business. Critically though it was the patrician style of leadership within British Aluminium that explains their behaviour in part; Portal and Cunliffe feeling that they alone should take the strategic decisions within the company without deferring to other executive directors or to shareholders.

Sir Ivan Stedeford and G. W. Lacey, a fellow board member of Portal's at the time of the takeover, both separately suggested to Portal's biographer that Portal was out of his depth and advised very poorly; Lacey going as far as to say that the former Chief of the Air Staff was 'not much more than Cunliffe's mouthpiece'. A fellow director of Portal's on the board of British bank Barclay's DCO inferred that Portal was out of his depth in the world of commerce, remarking that the Viscount provided reports on his visits to UK and overseas assets that were 'superficial and felt that he lacked any real financial knowledge'. Another Barclay's director observed that Portal was not greatly interested by the 'business of banking ... he always picked up *The Field* [a field sports magazine targeted at the hunting, shooting and fishing fraternity] rather than *The Economist* in the directors' dining room after lunch.'[102] His lack of acumen and his tendency to defer to advice from Cunliffe, to limit discussion and to use the board to rubber stamp the papers put before them, can have helped little. Cunliffe, for his part, was the caricature of the 'ornamental' director. Siegmund Warburg's initial impressions of him – as 'remarkably slow in grasping anything unusual' – were confirmed over time. Reflecting on BACo's MD years later, he observed, 'Cunliffe was upper class, received his job through good connections, but was not up to it although he was in no way conscious of his limitations'. If Warburg's judgement of Cunliffe were tempered by a personal distaste for the BACo MD, as well as an ideological antipathy for what he represented, it was all the same well-founded. In his actions, both on the BACo board and briefly as the aluminium controller during the first year of the war, he gave ample evidence to sustain Warburg's observations.[103]

In particular, Cunliffe and Portal lost the confidence both of their shareholders and the public jury. This was all the more remarkable given the strength of opposition among much of the British public – if not policymakers, and some sections of the financial press – to aggressive 'Americanisation' of British companies, with US affiliates controlling between 30 and 50 per cent of a large number of markets for consumables in Britain. After the war there had been an upsurge in US takeovers of

British companies: 64 per cent over the period 1951–66, against 23 per cent and 31 per cent respectively for the 1930s and 1940s. Public indignation over US raiders reached a peak after the hostile takeover of the Trinidad Oil Company by US firm Texaco in 1956.[104] By failing to discuss either the RTIA package, or the tentative agreement with Alcoa, with the BACo shareholders until after the raiders had publicly disclosed details of their (more attractive) offer, British Aluminium lost public support. In fact British Aluminium's main shareholders had remained remarkably loyal to the board throughout the struggle. The board was also mistaken in expecting the government to support its interests, anticipating that the Treasury would step in to authorise the Alcoa deal. In reality, as the next chapter shows, policy makers were divided over the deal and cautious about intervening, especially in the run up to an election with the opposition making successful political capital out of their management of the economy.

The takeover was to leave a bitter legacy in the industry, and the City of London. If BACo shareholders, Warburgs and Allen and Overy immediately prospered from the takeover, it benefited none of the other main belligerents in the long run. Paul Thompson has described the bitter legacy of the takeover in the city – based on interviews conducted with City traders in the 1980s – as 'an epic struggle, a turning-point ... to the old City order, Warburg's victory was as welcome as King Billy's on the Boyne to the Ulster Catholics.'[105] Warburg, 'ridiculed as a "squirt, an upstart"' in the City, was seen after the BACo takeover as an, 'upsetter of the establishment'.[106] Within the global aluminium industry, the takeover was met with dismay and disbelief. At a meeting in January 1959, the board of Aluminium Pechiney lamented the loss of one of the 'doyens' of the industry, but expressed incredulity at British Aluminium's 'lamentable' strategy in ignoring shareholders and underestimating its opposition. Of more pressing concern to the French was that they would have to cooperate with Reynolds in the Fria project, and that Commonwealth and European markets would now be open to Reynolds.[107] The country club atmosphere of the of the old guard meant that, while outwardly the industry could appear closed, there was a considerable exchange of sensitive commercial and technological information between European producers. BACo appears to have enjoyed a particularly close relationship with Aluminium Pechiney including visits between employees (and children of BACo and Pechiney staff) at both companies. As the spring 1956 editorial of The B.A. News remarked, in relation to a recent visit by Company staff to Pechiney's St Jean de Maurienne factory: 'Pechiney, as many readers will know, is our "opposite number" in France, with whom we have maintained very close and cordial relations over the past 30 years.'[108] Moreover Pechiney's concerns about Britain as a Trojan horse were hardly misplaced, given that US firms had traditionally used Britain and Canada as staging points from which to mount assaults on European markets.[109] The takeover was also an embarrassment for Alcoa chairman Irving Wilson (the 'Chief') who was, 'chagrined by the entire ungentlemanly business'. Alcoa's historian, David

Smith argues that had the US giant been more aggressive in the struggle and had a 'coherent strategy' it could have gained British Aluminium.[110] However Smith overlooks the fact that there were considerable obstacles in the way of the Alcoa deal, not least the British government. In addition it is questionable whether an elder statesman of the industry, like Alcoa, wished to become embroiled in what was, to the *ancien régime* within world aluminium, fast becoming a sordid affair.

British Aluminium found itself stuck in the middle after 1945; increasingly peripheralised as an international player the company struggled to position its strategy and yet sought (despite depleted finances) to maintain a role as a primary producer of global stature. It was locked into a relationship with government that was turning increasingly sour. It was also guided latterly by a chairman and managing director with scant business acumen, and out of touch with political and commercial realities of the post-war world. All of which was glaringly exposed in the takeover battle of late 1958 to early 1959.

Into the wilderness: 1959–1982

The takeover was a hollow victory for Reynolds and TI who paid a vastly inflated price for British Aluminium stock. Moreover, as Ronny Utiger observed as a new employee joining BACo in 1961, it left a legacy of bitterness in the company still present 'well into the 1960s'. He judged the merger to have been 'little short of a disaster', with British Aluminium changing in the space of a few years, 'from an international aluminium company looking for major expansion overseas to an inward looking British company trying unsuccessfully to defend its home base'.[111] Having paid an unrealistic price for BACo, the new owners were unwilling to countenance major expenditure, while saddling British Aluminium with new debts, and receiving a cold reception from British Aluminium's former partners in its joint overseas projects. The partnership with Consolidated Zinc (CZ) crumbled in autumn 1960 after the Australian Government offered COMALCo (the BACo–CZ joint concern) full control of the Bell Bay smelter and alumina refinery. CZ was keen, but British Aluminium refused, its new owners baulking at the cost. In the event CZ kept one of the most lucrative bauxite deposits in the world at Weipa, while BACo kept deposits at Gove that they lost two years later after failing to develop them. COMALCo took Kaiser into the partnership after BACo's departure, and became a major player with profits after tax in 1979 nearly double those of British Aluminium. By 1978 Australia had become the largest miner and exporter of bauxite, with COMALCo operating the largest bauxite mining, alumina and aluminium operations. In addition, with a proliferation of semi-fabricating plants in the UK after the merger – four rolling mills and three rolling mills – British Aluminium was forced to sell its 50 per cent share in the Australian Aluminium Company. Forfeiting the Gove deposits and Australian Aluminium, BACo lost out on a potentially very lucrative market.[112]

The new owners' policies within the UK had more mixed results, although they represented a period of stagnation for the primary smelting division. Over the next eight years the company focused mainly on its downstream activities in the UK, including major developments at Falkirk, modernisation programmes at Rheola rolling mill and Burntisland, and pursuing a low-cost model. Accompanying this was a drive to increase efficiency and productivity, improve financial reporting, and expand British Aluminium's sales force and marketing. As later discussions in the book make clear, the RTIA takeover also brought with it a change in company culture, with a far greater emphasis on meritocracy, as well as an expansion of vocational education opportunities and professional development pathways for all staff. In spite of external criticisms of the firm as being poorly managed at a strategic level, the very real culture shift during this time that was to bear some dividends in the long term. In addition, research and development activities in finished and semi-fabricated products were strengthened with the addition of TI's research facilities and staff. However, the primary aluminium arm (including the Highland smelter group) received little in the way of funding, at a time when many other aluminium producers were making heavy investments in their aluminium reduction plant to increase output and improve efficiency, and research and development into semi-fabricated products was not matched for primary aluminium production. This was all the more critical for the survival of the Highland smelters by the 1960s, given their small size and the high cost of their electricity relative to other producers, with the construction of new smelters of over 100,000 mts with the economies of scale that these brought.[113]

Moreover the strategy of concentrating on the semi-fabrication market brought with it far more risks and lower potential returns on investment. In 1958 British Aluminium and Tube Investments controlled 45 per cent of the market for rolled aluminium, and 27.5 per cent for extruded products alone. By 1962 their combined share of the market as a group had fallen to 37.1 and 20.6 per cent respectively for aluminium sheet and extrusions. Two years later, in 1964, British Aluminium shared 73 per cent of the UK market with Alcan Industries, James Booth, and the Imperial Aluminium Company. However Alcoa and Kaiser had also joined Reynolds in purchasing UK semi-fabricators. By 1967, the UK National Board for Prices and Incomes (NBPI) was reporting that the native industry had invested too heavily in expanding semi-fabricating capacity, and that as a consequence there was considerable over-capacity in the industry resulting in an over-proliferation of unprofitable product lines.[114] While industry insiders conceded that TI had little experience as an aluminium producer, they were baffled by Reynolds' behaviour, as one of the largest global producers of aluminium. An internal Pechiney memo of September 1964 commented: 'it is increasingly difficult to understand the logic [of Reynolds' strategy]. Prudence does not appear to be a dominant characteristic. The business is heavily committed in doubtful and difficult countries ... It is true that financial analysts have attributed Reynolds with an "incurable optimism".'[115] When

Reynolds sold its stock in British Aluminium in 1978, it made little return on its 1959 investment. In addition, critics argued that RTIA had done little to modernise the management structures and culture of the company after the former's own advisers had counselled that British Aluminium's senior management echelons were ill-suited to the realities of modern, competitive commercial markets. In fact the change in the structure, from fairly dispersed share-ownership, and malleable share owners, who deferred to the BACo board – fatally providing Cunliffe and Portal with considerable powers – to one in which the board's major strategies were more closely scrutinised and controlled by the new major shareholders was also to have a pronounced effect on the structure and managerial hierarchies within the company.[116] The criticisms of Reynolds equally revealed much about the division between more traditional producers (like Alcoa and Pechiney) and integrated producers like Reynolds, and were certainly not entirely justifiable.

Reynolds' approach to British Aluminium may be explained by a number of factors, aside from the purchase price, and shareholder reluctance to countenance considerable investment programmes in upstream activities. Reynolds had built its domestic reputation and market share on semi-manufactured and finished aluminium products with a powerful marketing strategy tapping into the burgeoning demand for consumables (household appliances, toys, golf clubs and leisure boats among other things) in the growing US markets for these products of the 1950s. It had also led the way in recycling in the States. Throughout the 1940s, 1950s and 1960s, it had integrated upstream, as well as downstream, very rapidly with operations across the globe, including in Canada, Cuba, Guyana, Jamaica, Japan, Panama, and Philippines. However, by the mid-1960s it was experiencing considerable difficulties. Its interests in Cuba had been nationalised after the revolution, and there was a backlash against aluminium multinationals in Jamaica and Guyana. It had also experienced major delays in its US domestic expansion plans, and by the mid-1960s had expended $650 million on these. Its acquisition of British Aluminium in fact made perfect sense strategically, securing not only a foothold and integrated operations in the UK (with the potential for access to European continental markets too) but also a smelter in Canada (to supply its North American semi-fabrication operations). It added bauxite reserves (as an alternative supply to the Caribbean but not as far away as Australia), and a stronger negotiating position in the Volta River Project.[117]

With their experience of recycling in the US, Reynolds clearly felt that to establish themselves in the UK semis market they could rely on output from limited investment in modernised plant at British Aluminium's secondary aluminium foundries at Latchford Locks and Williams Mills rather than investing heavily in the infinitely more expensive option of the primary reduction works. With the decline of markets like defence – which required metal of a higher purity that had to be supplied from primary ingot – in the UK by the late 1960s, the cheaper cost of producing semis from secondary metal was attractive. While RTIA's planned £10 million (eventually

£6 million) investment in Falkirk may have appeared to outsiders to have been ill-advised in view of the progressive contraction of civil and military aviation markets in the UK by the 1960s, this was designed to aid the plant – whose business in the late 1940s and 1950s had relied heavily on these markets –to diversify. Nevertheless defence and civil aviation markets remained important to UK aluminium producers in the decades ahead.[118]

In key areas such as the marketing and sales, RTIA's stewardship undoubtedly had a beneficial effect. For example, in promoting the use of aluminium in the construction trade, identified by the NBPI report of 1967 as an under-developed market in the UK. Though British Aluminium had an interest in this market, after the end of the aluminium house building phase BACo supplies to the building trade had levelled off to around 10 per cent of semi-manufactured output by 1956. Under RTIA control BACo launched the BA Building Service to offer advice to architects and builders about the potential benefits to be accrued from aluminium uses within construction; with the company rewarded by a 'substantial increase' in the use of the metal in the building trade by 1964. Similarly Reynolds, with expertise accrued from US markets, encouraged BACo into aluminium trims market (e.g., for car wheels) in which British Aluminium was later judged by its competitors to be a 'strong' player.[119]

Between 1963 and 1965, other factors aside, British Aluminium's export trade rose from 20 to 35 per cent, and the group's trading profit increased from £1.2 to £5.4 million over the same period, with much of this attributed to improvements to BACo's sales force and marketing. However by 1966 CBA provided the group with 63 per cent of their profits, even allowing for the large minority shareholding in CBA and after paying 55 per cent tax in Canada. The group's other assets did not look like an attractive prospect for investors.[120] Moreover competition in the UK semis market was intensifying. The proportion of UK rolled and extruded aluminium markets accounted for by imports almost doubled between 1969 and 1970 alone. BACo lost around 11 per cent of its share of the sheet market between 1967 and 1971 (most of it in 1971), with Alcoa the main beneficiary. Alcan Aluminium UK (AUK) also saw its share of the UK market squeezed. This was part of a wider trend of greater penetration of UK markets, resulting from the Kennedy Round of the General Agreement on Tariffs and Trade (GATT), which came into effect in 1971 and saw most sectors of British manufacturing affected. This, and the prospect of enlarged European markets with Britain's entry to the European Economic Community (EEC) in 1973 (removing the tariffs of 12 per cent paid by UK exporters to the EEC), prompted AUK to entertain the prospect of a merger with BACo.[121] Furthermore, in a submission to the DTI in June 1972 Alcan had stressed, what the government already knew, that TI 'is neither able nor willing to provide the large sums of money that would be required to build up BA into a much larger unit'.[122]

TI's chairman Lord Plowden had approached the Department of Trade and Industry (DTI) in November 1971, asking whether the government would be willing to countenance a shift in ownership of BACo giving their US partner Reynolds the majority share on the basis that:

> Tube Investments for their part, have felt for some time that their interest in aluminium, which is somewhat distinct from the remainder of their activities, was placing a disproportionate burden upon their investment resources in relation to the return on capital received from the investment and would be glad to reduce their commitments in this field.[123]

In the event, as the ensuing chapter shows, the then Conservative Prime Minister Edward Heath was sensitive about a proposal that would hand a US company majority control of a native British concern that accounted for 40 per cent and 30 per cent respectively of the UK's primary aluminium and semis markets. In reality TI's general caution about the primary arm of the business, in particular, meant that Reynolds was afforded ample opportunity for direction. As well as being well represented on the board, one of Reynolds' former engineering directors, Jake Hedgecock, had been appointed as BACo's engineering director.[124]

During the summer of 1972 Alcan UK's managing director John Elton held discussions with the DTI about a possible merger with British Aluminium. AUK's proposal promised both initiatives for improving efficiency and the potential of a greater share of European markets for the merged companies. They also stressed the importance of the union to compete against larger continental competitors, especially given the recent merger between Pechiney and Produits Chimiques Ugine Kuhlmann to form Pechiney Ugine Kuhlmann. The deal ultimately foundered on a number of factors. Firstly senior figures within Alcan UK were sceptical about a merger with British Aluminium. In a report for John Elton, AUK's senior sales director Denniss Pinn painted an unremittingly dismal picture of British Aluminium.

> Baco's record of performance is uninspiring, their management reputation and market attitudes are generally considered to be archaic, their equipment is more repetitive than complementary with our own (certainly not as complementary as was James Booth's) and it is thought that they are considerably behind us in their approach to labour relations.[125]

Pinn considered Alcan to be in a strong position in the UK, and on the cusp of a further break through. In contrast, he could see little benefit to AUK of absorbing BACo, with its capital commitments and debts, as well as 'the burden of finding markets for Baco's spare capacity'. He considered that a merger would require further rationalisation and would demoralise Alcan staff, while imposing 'new problems (not necessarily insuperable) in the field of co-operation with associated companies in Europe and elsewhere'.[126] Addressing concerns about the effects on AUK of a possible alliance between British Aluminium and Rio Tinto Zinc (RTZ), Pinn judged that this would not pose a threat as they would not be 'so expert as to solve rapidly the problems which face Baco', perceiving that the only possible risk would be if Shell invested substantial capital necessary in BACo's operations.[127] Pinn's generally poor view of BACo was a little unbalanced, given that his detailed evaluation of the company in 1971 suggested that in half of the semis markets BACo was a 'strong' player.[128] However his opinion was particularly significant in explaining why the proposed merger was shelved, as he succeeded Elton as managing director between 1974 and 1979.[129]

The second major factor in the negotiations with government was that Alcan wanted a major review of the power contract between electricity generators and BACo over the latter's Invergordon smelter, which came on stream in 1971 and closed in controversy in 1981.[130] As this episode in British Aluminium's history is inextricably linked to its relations with, and bound up in the historical legacy of their proximity to, government, this is explored in detail in the following chapter. The smelter programme also introduced greater competition to the domestic market for aluminium ingot, with the construction of RTZ's smelter on Anglesey and Alcan's at Lynemouth.

The UK was not alone in its experimentation with nuclear power and aluminium production. Between 1970 and 1974 six European smelters received some or all of their electricity from nuclear power stations: three in Germany, one in the Netherlands, and two in Britain. Alcoa also briefly experimented with supplying its Massena smelter with electricity generated by nuclear power. What initially attracted European producers, quite aside from promises about cost, was the fact that if successful smelters would no longer have to be located near natural sources of power. Moreover in the epoch of decolonisation, for European producers operating in former colonies the idea of relocating production close to downstream markets, with an apparently endless supply of cheap power, was attractive. Among European primary aluminium producers the energy mix varied. German smelters operated with a coal-nuclear mix, with electricity provided by regional generators. Pechiney's Vlissingen smelter was built with extensive Dutch government support, with the nuclear reactor built next to the reduction works and located near a harbour area. Admittedly most French smelters derive much of their electricity from nuclear power, in a country that in 1990 relied on 80 per cent of its electricity coming from nuclear reactors; the last being Pechiney's construction of a 215,000 mts smelter at Dunkirk (completed in 1995) that drew its electricity entirely from the nuclear power station at Gravelines. However, further afield most aluminium producers turned away from their flirtation with nuclear energy. Increasingly nuclear power became far less attractive to aluminium producers globally because of the costs of reprocessing fuels, safety concerns, and the necessity of ensuring an alternative source of power (in the event of a partial or full shut down). Only state support made nuclear power a viable option. By 1990 just over 5 per cent of the energy needs of aluminium production were met from nuclear power. In comparison, around 57 per cent were still provided by hydro-electricity, and 32.5 per cent by coal.[131] In addition, the operating costs of hydro-electricity, even for smaller schemes like Kinlochleven and Lochaber, fell.

With electricity costs at their Highland works almost three times those of their chief Canadian and Norwegian competitors, and the heavy taxation on dividends from CBA, the prospect of establishing a 120,000 mts smelter close to their main markets looked highly attractive to British Aluminium. Moreover there was the allure of cheap and abundant electricity from the new, and much vaunted, generation of Advanced Gas-cooled Reactors (AGR)that the UK Atomic Energy Authority (UKAEA) had been devising.[132] A further inducement was the Special Electricity Contracts offered to aluminium producers when the competition to tender for the two 120,000 mts smelters was announced by the Prime Minister Harold Wilson at the Labour Party conference in October 1967.[133]

Invergordon, which came on stream in 1971, was plagued from its inception; The much vaunted potential of nuclear power never materialised and British Aluminium was saddled with crippling power costs, while being committed to investing £30m into the construction of the delayed Hunterston B AGR nuclear power station. In addition, in the face of criticisms from Norway under the European Free Trade Agreement, the original economies of scale to be accrued from the construction of a new generation of 120,000 mts smelters was lost when these had to be reduced in capacity to 100,000 mts. The project was beset by a shortage of skilled labour (on the back of the oil bonanza in the north of Scotland), problems with the Reynolds 'cell' (furnace) technology, strikes, and acts of nature. With debilitating losses from the smelter, and the refusal of the then Conservative government to countenance further subsidy to rescue the plant, British Aluminium was forced to close Invergordon in December 1981.

By the late 1970s British Aluminium's share of domestic semis markets was also suffering with sales of aluminium sheet and extrusions (formerly their two largest semis markets) decreasing by 46 and 27 per cent respectively between 1967 and 1978. Alcan's share of the semis market was also being squeezed. In 1978 BACo announced that it was going to invest £30 million in a modernisation programme for its chemicals, semis, and primary smelting divisions; with £20 million of this alone going into reconstructing the Lochaber smelter and modernising Kinlochleven (in the end the project cost £45m).[134] However BACo's hand, as chapter four shows, was forced by the intervention of the UK's Health and Safety Executive (HSE). The modernisation was financed by a medium term loan with the European Investment Bank of £17 million, and other mid-term loans, all totalling £55 million. This capital expenditure on the Highland smelters was intended both to improve efficiency, and reduce emissions within and from the plant (resulting from RTIA's neglect of the west Highland assets). The decision to invest in French (rather than North American) prototype furnace technology and new fume extraction systems proved a good one. The reconstruction of Lochaber took practically four years to complete and saw the workforce reduced to one-third of its former size, expanding output by only 5,000 mts, but making it one of the most efficient (and with one of the best environmental records) smelters in Europe. British Aluminium also committed to reorganising its operations.

Between 1977 and 1980, the company almost quadrupled its annual capital expenditure from £8 to £29 million. It had also acquired a number of specialised producers, and significant shareholdings in others, including Alcoa's lucrative UK foil operations, with expenditure totalling £18.3 million over 1978–79. In addition BACo's sales force had opened up lucrative markets with car manufacturers, as well as continuing to profit from existing markets such as specialised sheet metal for the aircraft and defence industries.[135] In 1978 Reynolds finally pulled out of British Aluminium selling some of its 48 per cent share to TI and the rest to private investors.[136]

In spite of British Aluminium's ongoing problems with Invergordon, Alcan UK was sufficiently interested to consider acquiring BACo by the late 1970s. What appealed most to Alcan was the British group's increase in capital investment in its operations, their success in a leasing (as opposed to purchase) policy, and its 'strong balance sheet and borrowing capacity'. However in most other respects Alcan's evaluation reports on British Aluminium were less favourable. The specialised downstream activities, on which so much had been spent during RTIA's reign, were viewed by Alcan as 'a bit of a lame-duck set-up'. Its semi-manufacturing, smelting, and chemicals divisions were all suffering from a legacy of under-investment. Curiously Alcan was little concerned by Invergordon's power contract, and viewed the smelter as a good prospect. Alcan ultimately abandoned an approach to BACo at this stage because of the high price of the latter's shares. By February 1982, however, with forecasted losses of £26 and £12 million respectively for 1981 and 1982 for Alcan UK, the board decided – despite their parent company's opposition to invest any more capital in the UK – that they should evaluate the benefits of a merger with British Aluminium in advance of approaching the board in Montréal. The Canadian board delayed their decision but eventually authorised AUK to set up a working group to consider the proposal. Concurrently AUK's managing director George Russell approached his opposite number at BACo, John Ford, who confirmed that British Aluminium board was amenable to a merger. In the meantime, Alcan staff visited BACo plants to evaluate the state of the business. This was particularly important given both companies' view that a merger would strengthen them but that it had to be accompanied by dramatic rationalisation especially of the downstream activities.[137]

Seen alongside Alcan's June 1979 report about the dilapidated state of BACo's Highland smelters – which they attributed to a lack of major capital of investment and 'a fairly hard nosed policy on purchasing possibly with smelter materials which must account for a large part of their costs,' – these evaluation reports delivered a damning indictment of the RTIA legacy of selective investment. However Alcan did admire what they saw as BACo's forward looking attitude to the hire of plant and their sales force.[138] Alcan's evaluation of BACo's Falkirk rolling mill in July 1982 drew highly unfavourable comparisons with Alcan's operations at Rogerstone (Wales), Oswego and Norf (Germany). Of the 25 task areas evaluated, the central Scotland plant was judged to be seriously inferior to Rogerstone, Oswego and Norf. In 22 of the 25 areas, Falkirk scored either 'very bad' or 'bad'. Among other areas, the report identified the huge pay discrepancy between that paid to shopfloor employees and staff at Falkirk (in comparison to much more equitable levels at the other plants), ageing and inefficient plant, and little evidence of investment in new technology.[139] Reports of visits to British Aluminium's Silvertown (London) and Glasgow foil works were equally damning about the legacy of chronic under-investment, stating that at a bare minimum both sites needed an immediate injection of between £3 and £4.5 million in buildings and plant. Of the plant that was not antiquated at Silvertown, the report observed, much was of a comparatively 'cheap base', with no 'pollution control equipment' in a building that was 'not built for foil conversion … very old … and [with] building height an absolute minimum'. Of the Glasgow works, the report noted that two of the three mills were built in 1965 with 'no shielding around … nor a fume filter system', and 'the hydraulic system is a problem' requiring £1.5–2 million worth of investment alone; much of the converting and cutting machinery was at least twenty years old; and there was 'no incinerator or pollution control'. The report concluded that though the local management at both plants had done their best, they had been starved of capital, and that the foil operations would be better off 'as an independent operation … than with a bad managed integrated system'. What made these all the more damning was that the comments were also informed by discussions with the managers of the two works, along with the director of BACo's Alu-fabrication and the managing director of British Aluminium's foil division (Baco-foil), suggesting considerable disquiet among staff.[140] Another report to Alcan's vice president, research and operations technology, Ihor Suchoversky about British Aluminium's raw materials operations was generally more optimistic stressing the BACo's success in producing specialised products like specialised hydrates for toothpastes and plastics, as well as zirconium chemicals. However it highlighted problems with the company's Ghanian operations, notably transport between the mine and port.[141]

Both the AUK and BACo boards estimated that a merger of the two companies would require 4,000 redundancies across the two groups and payments of £49 million (£21 million of that in redundancy payments). In secretive discussions with Utiger, Alcan revealed that they might be prepared to offer BACo double the market value for a complete buyout. Later that month, at a covert, evening meeting at BACo's London residence – as both Alcan and BACo were public limited companies they did not want anyone finding out about the discussions – Alcan's Patrick Rich assured Utiger that Alcan was serious but could not move until problems with Alcan's investments in Spain were rectified.[142] In reality all aluminium producers were facing tightened circumstances, with the price of aluminium on the London Metals Exchange falling by 40 per cent between 1980 and 1982, chiefly because of the global recession. By September AUK's own losses of around £2–3 million per month hastened Patrick Rich, VP of Alcan's European operations and chairman of AUK, (who had been undecided) to support the merger wholeheartedly. After fraught negotiations in early October 1982, BACo's representatives agreed to approach the boards of TI and British Aluminium with Alcan's offer, of double the market value of £13 million (which was later accepted). In advance of Rich and Russell's presentation of the deal to Alcan's board in Montreal on 28 October, Ford and Russell drew up contingency plans for managing the public relations and administrative details of the merger. 'Bullfinch' and 'Auk' (the codenames adopted for BACo and AUK respectively) wished to reduce the time until the announcement to nine weeks to limit the risk of leaks. Alcan Montreal and TI ('Papa' and 'Tern' respectively) had been kept apprised of developments. Though they could count on government support for the venture, they recognised the desirability of 'Bullfinch', as the British company (and for reasons of political presentation), approaching the government first about the merger before a joint advance was made, not least because of the scale of redundancies involved. Among the main obstacles they foresaw were the integration of two fundamentally different: company structures (Alcan's was more decentralised); management strategies (Alcan's more long-term); and personnel and industrial relations policies. For this purpose it was felt important to take senior managers, trade unionists, and politicians into their confidence in advance of any public announcement of the deal, and to ensure adequate British Aluminium representation on the joint board. Particular attention was to be devoted by both companies to managing the political fallout – if not the real misery – that would be caused by the closures, in particular Falkirk. Alcan's Montreal Board authorised a £29 million loan to its UK operation. The preparations and Elton's close political contacts enabled the acquisition of BACo (for £30 million) to be cleared by the office of fair trading (OFT) without reference to the monopolies and mergers commission (MMC), as well as the EEC and German cartel authorities, on 29 November 1982. Eighty-eight years, seven months, and twenty-five days after its registration as a British company, British Aluminium merged with AUK. The joint press release issued by the companies stressed the difficult trading conditions that both Alcan and BACo had been experiencing, and that together they could survive as a strong and unified concern. The Board of the new company, British Alcan Aluminium Limited, met in December.[143]

British Aluminium's surrender to RTIA effected more profound changes to the company culturally than has hitherto been accepted. With the benefit of historical hindsight the new strategic direction was flawed; the company chose to compete in the far more competitive marketplace of downstream activities and neglected its upstream assets. It also failed to cast off the legacy of its cultural ties with government, so brutally exposed over the Invergordon episode. Yet organisationally, under RTIA's stewardship, BACo moved to a multi-divisional structure with integrated professional development schemes and improved its sales and marketing teams and its accounting processes. The merger with the stronger, but nevertheless exposed and struggling, AUK, was inevitable and was part of a global trend towards concentration of global producers in far more competitive, and crucially consumer-orientated, international markets.

Rationalisation and survival in hostile waters: 1982–2008

As chapter three shows merging the two very different company cultures was an uphill struggle. Rich was able to report to a meeting of major Canadian bankers in December 1985 that the companies who had jointly posted pre-tax losses of £36 million in 1982 were recording net profits of £57 million for 1985. He also confirmed that despite increasing capital expenditure from £6.1 to £18.3 million between 1983 and 1985 and taking on additional debts of £68 million, over the same period their profitability had increased by 27 and 54 per cent respectively for their primary and speciality semis divisions, and improved on their debt: equity ratio from 64: 30 per cent in 1983 to 51:49 in 1985. Moreover with a UK government Finance for Industry loan they had managed to repay the parent company.[144] British Alcan emerged as a leader in niche markets such as aerospace and defence, and more general commercial markets like foil, with sales increasing exponentially by the late 1980s. It was the UK and European leader in recycling. The company also saw a considerable increase in valuable export sales (chiefly to EEC countries), and in UK markets. Between 1983 and 1989 their capital expenditure rose from £6.6 to £73 million per annum (totalling £253.1 million), with £11 million or 20 per cent of capital expenditure being spent on R & D by 1988. British Alcan – prompted by the Conservative Government's privatisation of electricity – also briefly considered reopening the Invergordon smelter (to be supplied from coal-fired power stations) but this was eventually abandoned given uncertainty in the electricity markets. By the millennium Alcan Aluminium Ltd (UK), as it had become once again, was one of the most efficient producers in Europe, with a good reputation on both the continent and in the UK for rigorous environmental and safety management before the introduction of the Environmental Protection Act of 1990. Alcan Aluminium had, like many aluminium producers, chosen to sell off non-core activities to sustain its smelting and speciality alloys businesses.[145]

In 1994, Alcan indicated its intention to close the Kinlochleven works towards the end of the century. This announcement was predictable given the smelter's small-scale output and aged plant, and was carried out gradually, with the plant finally closing in June 2000. Downstream parts of the business – in Banbury and

Latchford, rebranded as British Aluminium, were sold to Alcoa in 2000. Between 2001 and 2004, Alcan closed the Burntisland, Falkirk and Glasgow works. In 2007 Alcan was itself taken over by the British-based global metal miner RTZ, who in turn was the target of an increasingly hostile takeover bid by BHP Billiton. This was part of an increasing trend towards the creation of minerals, metals and power clusters, with global 'miners' moving horizontally into aluminium production, or aluminium producers divesting themselves of all but their upstream operations and acquiring further power assets. In January 2008 Rio Tinto Alcan announced a further £45m investment in the Lochaber smelter chiefly to install new generators in the power station, with the intention of increasing output there from 43,000 mts/annum to 50,000 mts.[146] Questions have persisted over whether the $38.1 billion RTZ paid for Alcan was wise, in view of the heavy debts inherited from the latter contributing the lion's share of Rio Tinto's $38.9 bn (£27.1 bn) deficit, especially in light of the fact that it may force them to sell off some of their most valuable assets to compensate. In the midst of a worsening global recession, with a correlating downturn in metal markets, BHP abandoned its ambitions, but the Aluminium Corporation of China (Chinalco), which had acquired a 12 per cent share in the global miner in February 2008, was increasing its share.[147]

Conclusion

In common with counterparts of the second industrial revolution (like chemicals), from the outset British Aluminium was plagued by the twin disadvantages of the requirement of the absence of domestic markets for its products – in marked contrast to aluminium producers in France and the United States – concurrent with contending with mounting sunk costs. This forced BACo at an early stage to become, unusually among the European entrants, a fully integrated upstream and downstream producer of aluminium. Though judged to be a 'pioneer' in the industry, it enjoyed neither the advantages of the leading French producer nor those of Alcoa. Remarkably in the face of these odds it embarked upon a programme of major capital investment – sustained by a reluctant shareholder base – and managed to cultivate markets for its products.

The first decades of growth for British Aluminium, in the face of considerable adversity, say much for the technical prowess and entrepreneurial dynamism of these early directors. However, British Aluminium's infancy exhibited chronic failings both in corporate governance – such as transparent financial reporting and accountability to shareholders – and operational management, notably in the oversight of large capital projects like Kinlochleven. As the *Financial Times* observed in 1904, of the company's 'far from prosperous ... early career ... the recent history of this Company thus forms a valuable object lesson in regard to the importance of the management factor in all industrial ventures which might well be taken to heart in other quarters'.[148] This somewhat calls into question Chandler's appraisal of British

Aluminium, while sustaining his critique of British firms' shortcomings in key managerial functions.

Like many of its European and North American counterparts British Aluminium was buttressed, for the period 1914 to 1955, to a greater or lesser degree by its ties to the state. However, as the next chapter shows, if this were a blessing in the short term, it bred in BACo a dependency on state procurement and moulded the outlook of the company's management cadre. Certainly it was also responsible for sustaining the recruitment of 'gentlemen' amateurs – lacking commercial acumen, if not important civil and military knowledge and connections – to strategic positions within the company. Even as the company became increasingly staffed by professional managers, their experise predominantly lay in science and engineering. More significantly, as the following chapters illustrate, the firm was debilitated by a path dependent on strategy and and behaviourally to its relationship with government. The loss of Andrew Tait, the man who might have provided an alternative future for BACo, upset the balance of the board, allowing it to be dominated by enthusiastic engineers, and retired senior civil servants and military officers, who were either too close to government or lacked a head for business. However, as the discussion that follows shows, the problem by the interwar years lay in the culture and norms that were beginning to bed down in the company. After the First World War, though to a lesser degree than in most other countries with tighter tariff regimes and thus less exposed to foreign competition, to some extent like all aluminium firms they were also sustained by the international cartels, and by the gentleman's accord between the leading global producers. Crucially their financial position after 1945, along with government controls on prices and exports, prevented them committing fully or as speedily as they might have done to overseas opportunities that might have born fruit in the long term. The weakness was exposed when they lost out on important international developments and their debt structure forced them to take on disadvantageous terms over the Baie Comeau smelter. Alongside the VRP incident, it also left them exposed to a takeover. Moreover the high price paid by its new parents, who themselves were contending with pressures in other parts of their portfolios, precluded any substantial investment in any of the remaining major international projects they had been working on.

While the RTIA takeover prospered the company in some quarters – strengthening its management structures with the move to a multi-divisional organisation, and its commitment to building an efficient and effective sales team as well as to developing talent within the organisation – its focus on certain downstream markets and comparative neglect of key upstream activities undermined the company still further in the long term. The company's determination to re-enter the ranks of international aluminium producers, as well as its strategic shortcomings, provided the backdrop to the subsequent Invergordon affair; myopic in its dealings with government and hyperopic in its projections. Like all aluminium producers the floating of aluminium on the LME exposed the company to far more volatile market conditions. Alongside this producers faced intensified competition from alternative materials, such as new metal alloys and plastics.[149] Lochaber and Kinlochleven survived because of the collapse of Invergordon and the subsequent investment that came their way. The merging of the by now two of the struggling major UK aluminium producers, British Aluminium and Alcan UK, into British Alcan was a painful episode but one which probably ensured both firms' survival. It brought together two companies, as chapter three shows, with a markedly different outlook, even though British Aluminium was not by the late 1970s the organisation that it was sometimes portrayed as being.

That an integrated native aluminium industry has survived in the UK against all predictions is testimony to some achievements. Within just over three decades of the flotation of aluminium as a commodity on the LME, most of the grandee, 'first-movers' of the European aluminium industry had ceased to exist as separate entities, with Alusuisse (formerly AIAG) and Pechiney succumbing to Alcan takeovers in 1999 and 2003 respectively, only to be subsumed into Rio Tinto Alcan in 2007. Indeed throughout the twentieth century Donald Wallace's original prognosis that Britain lacked the basic natural resources to sustain primary aluminium production if anything gathered more weight, albeit climate change priorities and energy efficiency nearing the close of the millennium providing sustenance to small efficient plants like Lochaber that rely on hydro-electricity.

2

Aluminium and the British government

A s in the rest of Europe and North America, aluminium's growing strategic importance during and after the First World War – especially with the expansion of aerial warfare – ensured that there was no avoiding growing state interest in the industry in Britain. Aluminium's importance as a strategic raw material was underlined in 1940, between the evacuation from Dunkirk and the height of the Battle of Britain when, as one historian of military aircraft production points out, shortages of the metal had a profound effect on meeting aircraft production targets.[1] Britain's reliance on imports of North American metal, and questions over bauxite reserves within the British Empire, ensured that the metropolitan government in Whitehall also played an important part in the histories of Alcan, and to a lesser degree, Alcoa. As James Foreman-Peck and Giovanni Federico have observed of European industrial policy in the twentieth century, 'the most important historical motivation for promoting industry' has been 'the desire to enhance military capabilities'.[2] Even after the end of Britain's 'great power' period – with the development of the hydrogen bomb, and the diminishing importance for the UK of raw material stockpiling for military purposes – aluminium remained a vital strategic material.[3] Involvement with the state both benefited and debilitated British Aluminium. On the one hand, it received vital orders, and political, financial and scientific and technical support from government, which aided the expansion of the industry. On the other, this proximity to the state – including around 17 years under direct government controls – fostered a culture of dependency within BACo, increasing myopia in its dealings with ministers and officials, and was compounded by the recruitment of former senior military staff and civil servants.[4] It also tied British Aluminium in with a number of other networks linked to imperial concerns. Moreover, the company's ties to the British Empire reflected the social milieu of many of the directors and their personal, and sometimes political, convictions. BACo's shortcomings were to be starkly exposed in a number of incidents. At a local level, British Aluminium's role in the Scottish Highlands was to involve it further with officialdom both in Edinburgh and Whitehall. The company was to deploy both its role as a 'key industry' and as 'saviour of the highlands' as political capital. A further arena, which brought the industry into close contact with the state, was over the environment, and occupational and public health, the subject of chapter four.

Business–government relations in the UK

The history of aluminium in the UK reveals the deeply ambiguous relationship that could prevail between business and government, reflecting the fundamentally different corporate identities and the complexions of political administrations. In so doing it suggests that a far less prescriptive, and more nuanced, view of the interaction between the firm and British government is needed than that those of Michael Porter, who has asserted that the sum total of state policy to British industry can be characterised as, 'inappropriate and rarely sustained' attempts at failed intervention.[5] Equally the case of aluminium illustrates the limitations of overly deterministic explanations of the state as necessarily subordinated to the interests of capital in Britain. More nuanced work has shown that this relationship was very much more complex and mediated by competing interests within business as well as the state.[6] All too frequently the exchanges between business and government in Britain have either been sidelined or assumed to be extraordinary.[7] As one leading business historian has pointed out, existing detailed studies of business-government relations in Britain have on the contrary, 'revealed a high degree of interaction between representatives of government, public administration, businesses, and their representatives, as well as a range of semi-public, semi-private institutions. It also has demonstrated that in many instances alliances and coalitions, in favour of or against particular policies, were formed not within but across the divide.'[8]

Work on the British coal, chemicals, steel and ship-building industries, has provided detailed illustrations of this, highlighting divisions among employers over the best interests of British capitalism and society placing them at odds with the state, as well as contusions between government departments.[9] Rejecting corporatist arguments about the emergence of a consensual alliance between employers, trade unions and the state especially after the First World War, John Turner has observed of business–government relations in Britain during the first half of the twentieth century: 'business interests did not capture the apparatus of the state, though it was often possible for industrial or financial interests to exercise a veto over policies.' Rather, Turner suggests, 'one can say that businessmen got much of what they wanted in Britain in the first half of the twentieth century. They were able to do so because the "business interest" constituted a loose coalition of groups.'[10] This could also be a double-edged sword, as became evident here. Aluminium companies' relationship with the British state was mediated by competing priorities, with the industry inextricably bound to the strategic concerns of the British metropolitan government for half a century.

Absolutely central to understanding the native aluminium industry's relationship with government was the growing military uses for the metal and thus its position within Britain's military-industrial structures. As military historian Greg Kennedy observes of procurement for Imperial defence – notably for the RAF and the Royal Navy – it was 'big business ... tied to a web of industrial and economic interests'.[11] David Edgerton's highly significant work *Warfare State: Britain, 1920–1970* has renewed debate about Britain's military-industrial complex (MIC), illustrating in detail the interaction between business and government, during both war and peacetime, and the diffusion of scientific and technological knowledge that this allowed for. This study also shows the personal links between industrial laboratories, university and government departments.[12] Highlighting the continuing, if admittedly diminished, importance of defence procurement to the aluminium industry, half of the members of the first Review Board for Government Contracts (appointed in 1971) – the body chiefly charged with appraising defence contracts – were connected with the aluminium industry.[13]

Although the aluminium industry, as manufacturers of a raw material, did not closely follow the pattern of turbulent trade cycles identified for 'the ring' of 'approved' armaments manufacturers, it was subject to periodic volatility between 1915 and 1960.[14] There is also much similarity between the descriptions of defence contractors' relationship with British government – one in which the state dominated and obliged 'companies to tailor themselves to its demands' – and that experienced by British Aluminium. Here the descriptions of the effects of proximity to government on armament manufacturer, Armstrong-Whitworth, bear more than a passing resemblance to British Aluminium's story:

> There arose an intimacy between Armstrong's company and the British state, a complex relationship of mutual dependency, acrimony and cooperation. It was a period of contradictions: the company lost much of its entrepreneurial independence in exchange for tremendous growth in the service of the state ... The border between national interests and business profits blurred, the distinction between foreign policy and strategy on the one hand and the economics of the armaments industry on the other melted away.[15]

As such, aluminium offers an illustration of the way in which firms supplying other strategic raw materials – such as optical glass, rubber, steel, dyestuffs, to name a few – may well have been profoundly affected by their relationship with state. This deserves further research. As well as defence procurement, the fortunes of the British and Canadian industries were also closely bound up with colonial and trade policy. Although many of British Aluminium's directors were 'imperially steeped' – in terms of their background, career pathways and personal views – drawn from precisely the sort of 'gentlemanly capitalist' order (landed aristocrats and the new bourgeoisie of the City of London, as well as senior military officers and metropolitan civil servants), the experiences of the company suggest that the case for conjoined interests between British capitalism and colonial policy of an 'imperial system' are only identifiable for specific periods. British Aluminium's relationship with the metropolitan government reflects that described by one recent study of British mining interests in Africa: 'it may, rather, be more accurate to speak of temporary convergences of interest.'[16]

The relationship with government profoundly affected the culture of British Aluminium, nurtured by close contact with supply and service departments, as well as the movement of personnel between the company, government and the armed forces (as the ensuing pages and following chapter show). If this was not quite akin to the French experience of *pantouflage* or Japanese *amakudari* (the 'revolving door' between public and private sectors in North American parlance), nonetheless it still had a profound impact on the strategic outlook of the firm.[17] For their part, Alcan's UK subsidiary and its Canadian parent outwardly exhibited some of the same features of this trade, such as recruiting retired, senior military personnel and politicians to the board of the company. However, theirs was a *realpolitik*, which never inured in the firm the same organisational culture as in BACo and did not deflect them from their 'Global Mission'.[18]

Sowing the seeds

As early as 1862, the Royal Gun Factory experimented with aluminium bronze. By the early 1890s it was using aluminium bronzes in artillery pieces, rifles and shells. Similarly the Royal Naval Dockyards were experimenting with aluminium bronzes by 1890. More extensive military uses for aluminium in Britain were primarily stunted by the small quantities of the metal available, its prohibitive cost prior to the development of the Hall-Héroult process, and by an absence of laboratories in government facilities to test the properties of the metal. Emmanuel Ristori's tenure at Nordenfeldt had familiarised him with the metal and built up contacts within the Royal Gun Factory at Woolwich. British Aluminium was therefore being a little disingenuous when they claimed that the British government was not making the most of the opportunities that aluminium offered for military purposes.[19] BACo's board was further aided in its attempts to increase military procurement of the metal by a report from the imperial journalist, future Unionist Member of Parliament for Davenport and Chairman of the Naval and Dockyards Committee in the Commons, Clement Cooke, later Sir Clement (who later changed his name to Kinloch-Cooke in 1905). Cooke pointed to the growth in uses of the metal by the French, German and Russian military, citing also Hiram Maxim's experimenting with 'his machine and quick firing guns which have proved so useful in native warfare'.[20] BACo's public campaign admonishing the War Office and Admiralty was all part of a strategy calculated to pressurise the armed services into greater usage of aluminium; a tactic pursued by other aluminium producers and armaments manufacturers.[21] BACo set about capitalising on concerns about the shortcomings of British Army supplies after the Second Anglo-Boer War (1899–1902), and general paranoia about the military preparedness of other European powers, notably Germany, especially after the defeat of Russia in the Russo-Japanese War (1904–05), to apply pressure to the government through pronouncements at shareholder meetings and trade association meetings, as well as the trade press. In a 1908 sales brochure, BACo proclaimed 'Aluminium: The Soldier's Friend' and sought to link the metal to imperatives of national security and identify themselves as a patriotic concern:

> The advent of aluminium now places a cheaper and a lighter material at the service of the War Office ... It is not surprising, therefore, to learn that Germany has already adopted aluminium for military purposes ... sooner or later the British War Office will follow the example [of the Germans and Swiss], and Tommy Atkins will then have cause to thank the light, bright, clean, rustless metal for its share in diminishing the burden (if not the heat) of the day.[22]

In fact by 1908, both the British Army and the Royal Navy were using aluminium in reasonable quantities, not least on basis of its performance in the field during the Boer War (which had stimulated further military interest in and demand for the metal). The newly established government funded National Physical Laboratory (NPL) had also started conducting more extensive tests into the properties and potential uses of the metal, and investigating the potential of aluminium alloys and powder for uses in airships, airframes, aero-engines, and proofing for balloons for the nascent air force.[23]

In years preceding the First World War, BACo's connections with the defence industrial base and colonial economic interests – as well as cultural sentimentality and loyalty to empire – were further cemented with the addition of Cooper, Pollen, as well as Albert Sharwood (who had mining interests in Rhodesia, and joined in 1907) to the BACo board. As well as his military and imperial connections, explored in the following chapter, Pollen was the brother of the famous Arthur Hungerford Pollen, a director of the Birmingham Small Arms Company, renowned for his part in introducing new methods of naval gunnery. In addition to his city connections, Cooper was also 'imperially steeped' and remained intensely interested in land stewardship, which would prove important in the Highlands.[24] Yet the watershed for the industry was to come with the upheaval of the First World War.

The dance macabre: war, metal and the British state, 1914–1919

British military strategy on the outbreak of war in August 1914 assumed 'business as usual' for the economy. This was predicated on the belief that Britain could limit itself to committing five divisions of territorials to support the French 'left wing' in a short continental military campaign, using its naval supremacy to blockade the Central Powers into submission and bombard Baltic ports. The shortcomings of this policy – predicted well before the outbreak of war – were soon brought sharply into focus with the so-called 'shells crisis' of May 1915 and subsequent Allied shortages in manpower, military equipment and raw materials, not least because of reliance on imports. The crisis prompted unprecedented levels of state involvement in the British metropolitan and imperial economy, not least with Britain as the armoury and financier of the British Empire and the Allied powers.[25] As all the combatant powers were to find out, this war, pursued with new technology and a voracious appetite for human life, raw materials and finance, was a conflict of economic, as well as social and military, attrition.

The direct controls imposed on the sale and purchase of aluminium, bauxite and cryolite between August 1915 and January 1917 – which remained in force until 1 March 1919 – were testament to the wider drive to reorganise Britain's war economy.[26] More profound still as a legacy than prescription of raw materials was to be the significant changes in the conduct of business-government relations and the level of state intervention in industry. The state was to become actively involved in labour relations, using both legislative tools and negotiation to mediate and enforce production imperatives. Equally significant was the widespread practice of drafting businessmen and trade union leaders into government – after David Lloyd-George's appointment as Minister of Munitions in 1915, and Prime Minister in 1917 – to aid reorganisation of the war economy. Culturally the experience of wartime control was to cast a long shadow over those essential industries and raw materials brought under government control. As Chris Wrigley has observed of the legacy of 1914–18 war:

> The experience of the Ministry of Munitions left a lasting impression on people's thinking, and not just on that of politicians and civil servants. After the First World War many industrialists, bankers, politicians and trade unionists became disillusioned with free market competition at home and abroad and favoured co-operation in industry, mergers and large-scale organisation.[27]

In addition, Lloyd-George's direction of this powerful wartime ministry was used as a template by Lord Beaverbrook – newspaper magnate and one of Churchill's warlords – in 'consciously modelling' the Ministry of Aircraft Production during the Second World War.[28]

As the chairman and general manager respectively of the largest native concern,

Andrew Tait and William Murray Morrison served in various capacities within the Ministries of Munitions and then Reconstruction during the conflict. Both Tait and Morrison used their positions to further BACo's middle and long-term goals. Tait's political skills on the national stage, as a prominent supporter of a 'Business Parliament' and a founder of the Federation of British Industries (FBI) in 1916, were deployed to considerable effect during the course. The relationship between British aluminium producers and government during the First World War was similar to that between their French counterparts and the Third Republic, one of 'serving the immediate public interests of national defence, and the medium term post-war interests of private sector business'.[29] It signalled a period of convergence between industry-government priorities that would determine the tenor of British Aluminium's subsequent entreaties to the British state after the end of hostilities.

Along with controls, initially the government had attempted to make up the shortfall in domestic supplies, by supporting the expansion of the native industry. The Treasury advanced £200,000 in 4½ per cent loans to British Aluminium to extend their water reserves at Kinlochleven, with the work being carried out, in part, by German prisoners of war.[30] It quickly became clear that supplies could not be sourced domestically or from among allies. With demand for aluminium growing dramatically, what increasingly worried officials within the Ministry of Munitions was the growing reliance on costly imports of ingot from North America, accounting for 70 per cent of their supplies by 1916. Between January and December 1915 alone, prices for imported ingot rose from £81 to £220 per tonne. This was set against the wider increase of 68 per cent in the volume of US imports (as well as prices) to Britain between 1913 and 1915, and the depreciation of sterling against the dollar. By summer 1916, the issue had reached crisis point. In a minute to the Ministry of Munitions' Director of Materials Sir Leonard Llewelyn in August 1916, the leading munitions official with responsibility for aluminium, D. A. Bremner, set out both the Ministry's concerns and the suggested approach to be taken. Bremner stressed the necessity of locating aluminium production within the UK, or less preferably the Empire. Similarly the raw materials necessary for producing it (in particular, bauxite) should be sought in Britain or its Commonwealth. The comparatively greater expense of native production of ingot was to be justified by its strategic importance:

> It must be said, however, that in spite of the relatively high cost of hydro-electric power in this country, as compared with Scandinavia, Switzerland, Canada and America, the British Aluminium Co. Ltd, and the Aluminium Corporation Ltd, have been able to justify their existence, and have rendered invaluable service during the war ... Although the cost of power is an important factor in the commercial production of aluminium, the results achieved by the British Aluminium Co. Ltd, and the Aluminium Corporation Ltd, shew that even in this country, it is not prohibitive, and it would be unwise to assume that the

economic possibilities of aluminium manufacture in the United Kingdom have been exhausted.[31]

Significantly for British Aluminium's future developments at Lochaber, Bremner continued by advocating:

In view of the necessity of increasing our home production, not only of aluminium, but of certain essential ferro-alloys for which we are now dependent on America and Scandinavia, it would appear to be highly advisable that the potential sources of hydro-electric power in the United Kingdom should be thoroughly investigated. It may be that vested interests and legal difficulties have hitherto prevented the development of certain water powers, and that these obstacles may have to be swept aside in the national interests.[32]

Bremner duly considered other potential locations for secure aluminium production and supplies of raw materials within the Empire, acknowledging that the evident and considerable shortfall had to be met from outside the UK. Yet it was clear that the only serious contender was the Canadian aluminium industry:

Unfortunately, however, none of these countries, with the exception of Canada, is favourably situated geographically to become the seat of any indispensable portion of the Empire's Aluminium manufacture. The United Kingdom being not only the largest British consumer of aluminium, but also the Arsenal of the Empire, it is essential that as large a proportion of as possible of her military requirements should be covered by home production. Supplementary supplies might be drawn from Canada with the minimum risk …[33]

One thing about the Canadian industry vexed Bremner though. In order that it could be counted on as a secure supplier, 'it would be necessary to render the Dominion independent of the United States for her Alumina'. Bremner continued in a similar vein expressing concern that:

At the present time, the whole of the aluminium industry of the United States of America and Canada is practically under the autocratic control of Mr A. V. Davis, who is President of the Aluminium Co. of America, and the Northern Aluminium Co. Ltd. of Canada, the only producer in that country.[34]

Bremner's concerns about US control of Britain's major source of ingot stemmed from growing tensions between the Ministry of Munitions and Inter-Allied Munitions Board (IAMB), on the one hand, and Alcoa, on the other, over the sharp rise in prices of imported ingots. Negotiations with Alcoa over imports, conducted through the British government's intermediary, the banking house Morgan Grenfell & Co., worsened during 1916–17, with one ton of imported aluminium ingot reaching £300 by November 1916. The wider significance of this ongoing conflict between Alcoa and the British government is underlined by the financial position British found itself in by this stage of the war. Even with Woodrow Wilson's agreement of further advances in July 1917, 'the Treasury continued on a knife edge for the rest of the war'. With Britain acting as financial intermediary for the Allies to US banking houses, and as the Allied and imperial arsenal, the very ability of the Allies to prosecute the war hung in the balance.[35] The tensions culminated with the ministry authorising the Governor of British Guiana to use his right to halt exports of bauxite to the United States from the colony, where Alcoa had purchased mining leases in 1913. The ransom note to Alcoa from the Inter Allied Munitions Board (IAMB) stated the British government's intent, 'to continue to make use of the export prohibition clause until the Company are prepared to be reasonable' over the 'excessive price of aluminium to be supplied in 1918'.[36]

Though economy measures, encouraged from November 1916, were highly effective in reducing the consumption of aluminium in certain areas, the growth of the aircraft programme in the last two years of the war more than compensated for these. For example, motor transport, which accounted for 3,000 tons in 1916, had been reduced to around 2,100 tons by 1918. However the combined Admiralty and War Office air requirements increased more than five-fold from 2,000 tons in 1916 to the 10,840 tons required by the Admiralty for airships and by the Air Board for aircraft in 1918.[37] Furthermore, the supply crisis was further exacerbated when it became apparent that the IAMB and ministry had wrongly assumed that they could include French shares of the output from the their Tyssedal works in Norway for joint allied supplies.[38] French representatives on the IAMB confirmed that because of the growing military aircraft programme they could not afford to spare any metal. Within the ministry, these events reinforced Bremner's suggestions that security of supply necessitated support for domestic producers, and imperial supplies if they could be wrestled from foreign (and possibly hostile) control, while re-affirming suspicion of Britain's allies and of neutral powers.[39] It also prompted inter-departmental criticisms of the perceived lack of vigilance exercised over the control of imperial minerals reserves and of the absence of a policy on this.[40]

In the midst of the crisis, on the premise of sourcing other supplies of metal, Andrew Tait drew munitions official Captain Walter Broadbridge's attention to the fact that shares were becoming available on the board of fellow aluminium producer, AIAG Neuhausen. In all likelihood, another BACo director, Ernest Sawyer, seconded to the Ministry and operating in France, Italy and Switzerland, provided Tait's intelligence on this matter. Tait suggested that if the British government could gain financial control (which British Aluminium could take over after the war) of AIAG then they might secure additional supplies of metal from Switzerland. Though a

Swiss company, AIAG was largely German owned, and, until 1916, counted Dr Walter Rathenau (the German industrialist and wartime 'commissar' of Kriegsmetall AG) as one of its directors. In 1914, the French authorities had sequestrated AIAG's French assets, with the Allies restricting their exports to the Central Powers in 1915. Nevertheless, as late as 1916 AIAG Neuhausen was still providing the Central Powers with a considerable quantity of aluminium, and receiving supplies of bauxite from Hungary and Austria.[41] For good measure, Tait also pointed out that his suggestion could not only have the effect of denying the German war effort of a valuable supply of metal, but it could deprive of Germany of this source post-war too. In effect, Tait sought in this move to aid British Aluminium to gain control of one of the 'pioneers' of global aluminium and their central European markets, and allow BACo finally to develop their existing assets in the Martigny-Orssières region purchased in 1906 (which had been restricted by contractual agreements with AIAG). Tait's bold move found favour with ministry officials, not least Sir Budd Cecil, the chief adviser on metals. However, it foundered on French refusal, in the event, to supply alumina to the works (on the grounds of diminished capacity to do so), and strategic concerns that with French alumina redirected to Neuhausen, and the Norwegian works standing idle, ingot from neutral Norway might be used to supply Germany. Evidently French producers privately could also hardly have been encouraged by the idea of British Aluminium gaining control of the Swiss industry and trying to encroach on central and west European markets after the war. Nevertheless, an attempt, this time for control of AIAG shared between BACo, Alcoa and Aluminium Français, was made again after a meeting between aluminium producers of the victorious Allied nations in Geneva in December 1918. With the endorsement of the French Government, BACo subsequently approached AIAG. Ultimately despite the failure of this attempt, as Espen Storli has insightfully observed, '… the plan was important, since it served to cement the co-operation between BACo, AF and Alcoa'. This was a relationship that was to survive until the RTIA takeover. It also prefaced the bad blood between AIAG and AF for years to come.[42]

Tait's choice of allies and his timing were impeccable. He knew that his proposals would find particular favour with ministry officials, notably Budd (a former leading figure in the London Metals Exchange), as well as Lloyd George's successor as Minister of Munitions, Christopher Addison. Both Budd and Addison were dredging up considerable xenophobic feeling against the Henry R. Merton company – infamously pursued through the Non-Ferrous Metal Industry Act 1918, directed at preventing the ownership of British smelting concerns falling into 'alien control' – and promoting an agenda for an imperial metals policy. This imperials metals policy subsequently took shape in the form of the Imperial Mineral Resources Bureau and a public-private corporation (the British Metal Corporation), which encouraged British capital to invest in and develop imperial resources and preventing foreign companies taking over control of strategic reserves.[43]

The convergence of Budd's imperial minerals agenda with the strategic interests of native aluminium producers, seen especially through the tactics of Tait and Morrison, was visible in the conduct of affairs in the Board of Trade's Departmental Committee on the Non-Ferrous Metals Trades (DC-NFMT), appointed by the President of the Board of Trade in October 1916 to consider the immediate post-war position of this group of industries, and the Minister of Reconstruction's own advisory committee on aluminium. Budd served both as a member of the DC-NFMT and chair of the sub-committee on aluminium. He was joined on the committee by Andrew Tait and on the sub-committee by William Murray Morrison, who also served, alongside Budd, on the advisory committee to the Minister for Reconstruction. Tait, Morrison and Walter Broadbridge (who was also supportive of Budd's agenda) appeared as expert witnesses before the committee.[44] Tait and Morrison used their appearance to appeal on the grounds of patriotism and the industry's wartime service for financial support and protective trade tariffs postbellum, as well as specific support from the government to enable the smooth passage of their proposed private water power bill (the Loch Leven Water Power Bill 1918) to extend their Highland smelting capacity. Both resurrected the spectre of Arthur Vining Davis and Alcoa, finding a sympathetic audience in Cecil Budd.[45] In his subsequent evidence to the committee, on behalf of the Minister of Reconstruction, Broadbridge had already lamented the cost incurred by the Exchequer from reliance on Alcoa-owned supplies, and urged the expansion of indigenous production notably promoting British Aluminium's forthcoming scheme with vocal support from Andrew Tait who was receiving evidence on the day.[46] The committee's final report recommended that aluminium be considered a 'key industry'; attempts to block water power developments by the industry be overcome with government support; French proposals over control of bauxite mines in France and export taxes on bauxite be carefully monitored by the UK government; that substantial duties be imposed upon cheap foreign imports undercutting native producers; and that support be given to imperial producers. In connection with the last point it raised misgivings about US financial control of Canadian production.[47]

The Ministry of Reconstruction's sub-committee which reported to Addison in June 1918, made almost identical recommendations, with impetus added by the withdrawal of BACo's original Loch Leven Water Power Bill of 1918 in the face of stiff opposition and despite support from President of the Board of Trade, Minister of Munitions and the Minister of Reconstruction.[48] Budd continued both to pursue the chance of British representation on AIAG's board, and advocate support for the native British industry, lobbying the British Mission to the Versailles peace conference.[49] It was a coup for BACo, and further bolstered the ambitions of Budd, Addison (and his successor Winston Churchill) for the establishment of the IMRB.[50] It was also essentially Bremner's memo of August 1916. Politically then – not least as a result of Tait's adept brinkmanship in the context of the opening presented by the emerging imperial minerals strategy – the war had afforded British Aluminium the opportunity to secure its position. This continued immediately post-war on the coat tails of the agenda pursued by the 'social imperialists', such as Lord Milner, Secretary of State for the Colonies (1918–21) and his under secretary, Leo Amery, as well as Lloyd-George and Churchill. However, what BACo could not possibly have envisaged was that the favourable climate in which its relationship with government prospered in the late war years and early 1920s would change so dramatically by the end of that decade, as the Treasury reasserted itself. BACo also could not have fully anticipated the future repercussions over the government's insistence that Alcoa expand its primary smelting capacity within Canada (as a British dominion), as a proviso for Alcoa obtaining rights to bauxite reserves in British Guiana (Guyana), especially after Alcoa's legal separation from Alcan, which was to remove any residual concerns from the First World War that officials in Whitehall had about relying on Canada for future strategic supplies of the metal. This new factory, Arvida, was to play a significant role in supplying Britain with aluminium in the next conflict.[51] At the same time, British Aluminium was becoming more locked-in to its relationship with government, financially and culturally.

British Aluminium, along with the Consolidated Zinc Company (CZC) (later Rio Tino Zinc) and a number of other British mining concerns and merchant banks, acquired interests in Budd's BMC, formed in 1918 with government support. BACo's activities with this network of operators became far more widespread over the next decades, such as in their interest in CZC's subsidiary, the Imperial Smelting Company (ISC). Through these activities, they had access to William Sydney Robinson (1876 – 1963), the CZC and ISC chairman, of whom Oliver Lyttelton – later BMC's general manager, for a time the non-ferrous metals controller during the Second World War, and later Cabinet Minister – noted, 'no less than ourselves, [Robinson] was pursuing the theme of a self-contained British Empire in metals'.[52] In April 1935, Robinson's son and protégé, Lyell Robinson – who succeeded his as father as managing director of the Zinc Corporation in 1947, and Consolidated Zinc in 1956 – joined the BACo board.[53] However, as negotiations over the Lochaber Water Power Bill and the company's mining concessions in British Guiana and the Gold Coast (Ghana) illustrate, British Aluminium's portrayal of itself as an imperial concern and its directors' professions of patriotism were also governed by ulterior domestic motives. In this Tait and Morrison were no different from some of their contemporaries whose service had been enlisted in the war economy. As one leading industrialist remarked forty years after the end of the First World War, in 1959: 'The businessmen who had helped Lloyd George to organize production during the war intended to see to it if they could that post-war governments helped industry intelligently.'[54] However the use of patriotic rhetoric would not assure them of state support permanently.

'National' industry, 1919–1939

In the years immediately following the end of the First World War the British government, spurred by the experiences of wartime and adopting Budd's avowedly imperialist mineral resources policy, pursued the search for and securing of bauxite within the Empire, through the IMRB. Lord Milner announced that further bauxite concessions should be granted to British interests. In June 1920 Lloyd George, issued a despatch pressing British colonies and protectorates to step up their efforts to secure mineral resources within the Empire supporting this with grant-in-aid funding for colonial minerals research.[55] British Aluminium had been approached in 1915 by a British mining engineer, Donald Campbell, operating in Guyana who attempted to interest BACo in purchasing bauxite mining rights in the colony. Since August 1914, the Admiralty and the Board of Trade had urged caution against attempts by German conglomerates to purchase mining rights within the Empire. In early 1915, the Admiralty insisted that British interests control any syndicates wishing to purchase bauxite reserves within the British Empire. Campbell reported the outcome of his meeting with British Aluminium's William Murray Morrison to the Colonial Office in April 1915, noting, 'Mr. Morrison … expressed the opinion that the properties [in Guyana] cannot be profitably be exploited for shipment to England, and that his company would not undertake the expense of exploration or development.'[56] Morrison had apparently indicated that BACo would be more amenable to Indian reserves of the mineral because of abundant supplies of coal nearby to produce alumina, which would be infinitely cheaper to ship. British Aluminium, for its part, did not register an interest with the Colonial Office in leases in Guyana until March 1920.

BACo's ulterior motives became abundantly clear in the ensuing negotiations over mineral rights in the Empire. In this they were aided by a series of events. In late 1919 the Colonial Office wrote to British Aluminium reminding them that prospecting licences for British Guiana were still available. Following discussions with the IMRB and Colonial Office, a British consortium led by William Murray Morrison and including BACo, Al. Corp., the Australian Aluminium Company Ltd, and R. and J. Garraway, submitted a proposal to purchase bauxite reserves in British Guiana to the Colonial Office in March 1920. In reality the consortium was largely underwritten by BACo capital and dominated by the company's personnel. Morrison stated that the main motivation for the group's interest arose from the threat that French authorities would refuse export licences for French bauxite or impose a heavy export duty. A month later in a letter to Leo Amery, the IMRB's John Evans recommended that any agreement on imperial mineral rights should include the following clause:

> Not only should the refining of the metal be carried out on British territory but by means of British capital. It might also be desirable to stipulate that a certain proportion at least, say one third of the product should be employed

for the preparation of metallic aluminium and that this should be carried out by British companies with British capital.[57]

This all served to further reinforce the recommendations of the DC-NFMT and MoR sub-committee reports. Although an agreement with the consortium was drafted in 1920, nothing was signed until 1927. Conveniently the Colonial Office attributed this hesitation on the part of the consortium to a poor global market outlook, and protracted negotiations with the armed services over their requirements. After the registration of the British and Colonial Bauxite Company Ltd (B&C) in September 1927, little effort was to taken to exploit the reserves until 1936, after the signing of their agreement with DBC to act as *de jure* managing agents.[58]

In reality British Aluminium had little intention of exploiting the reserves when it took them out, given that French reserves were located much closer to its smelting operations and main markets. Moreover the Guyanan bauxite was ill-suited to produce the type of alumina required for most European reduction works (and was better suited to North American smelters). Given their agreement with the DBC in 1936, their acquisition of the Guyanese assets cannot be claimed to simply have been an action motivated by patriotic duty. Rather British Aluminium was primarily motivated by its need to enlist both financial and political support from the British government for their Lochaber Scheme, both of which they got. This eventually secured the passage of the bill through the commons and a Treasury loan. It was a measure of government support that the loan under the Trade Facilities Act – originally intended by government as a measure to encourage concentration and rationalisation, as well as alleviating high unemployment (criteria which the aluminium industry did not fit) – was granted. This was justified by the Treasury on the grounds that the BACo scheme was essential to national defence requirements rather than because the industry needed reorganising or to alleviate unemployment.[59] Tait's appeal to the House of Commons select committee on the grounds of national defence was undoubtedly opportune. However government support for the bill had been won at some expense, both in terms of the capital investment overseas and riparian rights. More profoundly it further sustained members of BACo's senior management in the view that they were indispensable to government.

By the end of the First World War therefore, and in spite of their loss of global market share, British Aluminium had assured itself of government financial and legal support for expansion. The war had also introduced aluminium and aluminium alloys to a large number of manufacturers who had no prior experience of the metal. Moreover the amount of research undertaken at the NPL, Royal Aircraft Establishment (RAE), as well as university laboratories and factories, brought very real dividends in improvements to technology, processes and in diversifying product ranges. The bulk of the 360 separate reports submitted to government committees on light alloys and aero-engines between 1917 and 1930 related to new aluminium alloys, greatly extending knowledge of these alloys and increasing applications for them. Specifically this work greatly improved the efficiency of aero-engines with the replacement of iron and steel with aluminium alloys, while work on anti-corrosive and colour coated aluminium alloys resulted in an explosion in patents as its uses in the civilian consumer markets became apparent. Part of the work was financed by donations from the industry itself, but most funding came from the state.[60]

In addition, a network of thirty-two scientific and professional societies had been set up, with government subventions, and working in conjunction with both military and civil laboratories and the newly established Department of Scientific and Industrial Research (DSIR), including the British Non-Ferrous Metals Research Association (BNFMRA) formed in December 1919.[61] Work into aluminium alloys continued unabated throughout the 1920s and 1930s, not least given the impetus to replace wood with light alloys in aircraft structures. By the late 1930s, earlier misgivings of aero-engineers and the Air Ministry had been overcome by extensive research and resulting improvements in alloys. In 1934 senior Air Ministry officials confirmed that in the expansion of the RAF's fighter squadrons that had taken place since 1925 at least 23 per cent of the metal used in new planes had been aluminium or aluminium alloys. By the late 1930s RAF expansion was dependent on aluminium alloys. In 1937 the Secretary of State for Air declared that:

> The problem of securing the greatest possible operational efficiency for defence purposes of the matériel of the Royal Air Force has involved an intensive programme of research and development ... Improvements in the performance of present day aircraft have also resulted from intensive research on aluminium materials. In particular, the aluminium alloys, used to a considerable extent in the structure of aircraft, now shew a notable improvement in mechanical properties.[62]

Nevertheless, government contracts also brought with them inherent complications. Aside from the small-scale and technical conservatism of the native airframe industry, a major obstacle to meeting the supply demands of aircraft production in the first few years of the Second World War would be the inherent difficulties for the Air Ministry and RAF of estimating demand in the event of a future conflict. By the 1930s the Royal Navy too was using aluminium extensively, with success.[63]

Other research undertaken on behalf of DSIR and BNFMRA at government establishments and laboratories had both military and civil uses. Notable discoveries included solutions to extracting nitrogen from reduction furnaces to improve the quality of metal and aluminium-brass condenser tubes being used extensively in both civil maritime and naval vessels.[64] Critically these developments also aided civilian 'spin-off' such as BACo's growing civil transport markets. The government's establishment of the Central Electricity Board in 1926 and the ensuing development of a National Grid in Britain also brought great dividends for the aluminium industry.[65] These collaborative R&D activities also brought the industry, the armed services, civil servants and government scientists into regular and close contact.

In spite of the cartel provisions, British Aluminium experienced considerable competition in inter-war domestic markets. The situation was compounded by the reluctance of the British government to introduce import tariffs on aluminium products, and exacerbated by the high value of sterling under the Gold Standard. Prior to the introduction of the first wave of tariffs in 1931, the company reported to their shareholders that 13,000 tons (or 67 per cent of the British market share) of relatively cheap ingot, along with 6,000 tons of semi-fabricated products and £370,000 of finished goods were being imported into the country.[66] This was not aided by the exemption of Canadian imports of primary metal from import duties under Ottawa agreements. Here the native aluminium industry was another victim of the political concessions for, as the Secretary for the Colonies Jimmy Thomas put it, the primacy of 'the maintenance of imperial unity'.[67] In response to this predicament, British Aluminium again attempted to marshal the political capital associated with their role as a 'key industry', with chairman Robert Cooper declaring to shareholders in 1934:

> The British Government is directly concerned with the position of this company by reason of their guarantee, as to principal and interest, of the £2,500,000 loan of our subsidiary company, the North British Aluminium Company, Limited. Indirectly also our Government is concerned in consideration of home supplies of an essential metal, together with employment of British labour, revenue derived from taxation of profits, and other considerations ... We, on our part, have entered into onerous to our Government so as to ensure a national supply of aluminium, but under existing conditions it is increasingly difficult for us to fulfil those obligations ... I cannot refrain from observing that a greater measure of support and encouragement from our Government is what our national industries await and require.[68]

Despite BACo's repeated attempts at political blackmail, arguments about national defence requirements proved less effective muted by the alternative sources of metal available to government.[69]

In the decades that followed the First World War, British Aluminium did not simply confine their political activities to the high politics of national defence and Empire but also to building alliances in Scotland and in the Highlands, in order to raise their profile and to resist rate increases. The addition of Gerald Steel – who until 1925 had been assistant secretary at Scottish Office (the government department with responsibility for overseeing the introduction of district policies for Scotland), after equally notable service at the Admiralty and Ministry of Transport – to the company's board as general manager in 1931, where he was to remain until his retirement in 1954, was undoubtedly of help in the pursuit of these interests.[70] BACo's position as one of the major rate-payers, employers, and landowners, made it a significant political player in the Highlands. This was something that the company was keen to capitalise on in its approaches to government and in its contact with Highland political lobbyists and groups, by promoting itself as 'saviours of the Highlands'. British Aluminium's public profile was further aided by William Murray Morrison's membership of a government committee of inquiry into economic conditions in the Highlands and Islands (hereafter the Hilleary Committee). In the aftermath of the government's disappointing response to the committee's 1938 report, the company's reputation was, in contrast to the Scottish Office, further enhanced by its continued commitment to the area. This won the company a number of regional allies who felt maligned by policymakers in Edinburgh, who appeared willing to abandon the Highlands, while offering assistance to the industrialised Special Areas of the lowlands.[71] The significance of British Aluminium's Highland developments was also not lost on the committee appointed to enquire into hydro-electric development opportunities in Scotland (hereafter the Cooper Committee), who reported in 1942, and upon whose recommendations the North of Scotland Hydro-Electric Board (NSHEB) was established. In its report the Cooper Committee concluded that: 'We do not think that we are overstating the position when we say that the existing electro-metallurgical industries could not have been established in this country except by the use of water power.'[72] Similarly in a memo to the Cabinet about the British Oxygen Company's attempts to establish calcium carbide and ferro-alloys production in February 1937, the Minister for the Coordination of Defence, Sir Thomas Inskip observed, 'The value of such proposals to the Highlands is demonstrated by the British Aluminium Company's works at Fort William which employ several hundred men of whom 75% are Highlanders.'[73]

More ominous for British producers were the discussions that were taking place by the late 1920s between the British government and Canadian producers over long-term strategic supplies. With Alcan established as being legally independent of Alcoa in 1928, the British government had begun to put aside previous concerns it had with relying on Canadian supplies of the metal. Concurrently the British government had started planning in earnest for the next major global conflict by putting in place the necessary infrastructure for directing a war economy. In 1927 officials representing the major supply departments were brought together with staff officers from the three branches of the armed services in the Principal Supply Officers' Committee (PSO), reporting to the Committee of Imperial Defence (CID). This shift in the government's position was indicated at the meeting of the PSO in December 1928 when it was agreed:

That in view of the Aluminium requirements of the fighting services, it is desirable that bauxite prospecting and mining in British Guiana should be thrown open to the world at large, in order to secure the maximum development of the bauxite resources of the Colony ... That in the Regulations there should be no differentiation between the rates of royalty charged to British and foreign companies.[74]

The significance of this decision lay in the state's determination to source secure supplies of aluminium from elsewhere, thereby diluting British Aluminium's purchase power with ministers. This was further cemented when the PSO approached Alcan and the Canadian government about possible arrangements for the supply of metal in the event of war. At a meeting of Canadian and British government representatives in October 1930, Board of Trade officials serving on the CID floated the suggestion that in the event of war Canada would become the main supplier of aluminium for Britain and that supply of the metal for the Empire should reside there also.[75] The urgency for identifying stockpiles of essential raw materials only intensified following the British cabinet's overturning of the so-called 'ten year rule' – which had hitherto placed a moratorium on rearmament unless a war appeared imminent within a decade – following the Japanese invasion of Manchuria in September 1931. For aluminium, as for certain other strategic raw materials and finished munitions, increasingly Canada was looked upon as the 'Arsenal of the British Empire'.[76]

From this moment on British Aluminium, and other smaller producers, were in a much weaker bargaining position with government. While BACo's George Boex acted as the PSO adviser on aluminium prior to the outbreak of war, and director Geoffrey Cunliffe (the son of Lord Cunliffe, Governor of the Bank of England 1913–18) served as the wartime aluminium controller for both the Ministries of Supply (MoS) and then Aircraft Production (MAP) between 1939 and 1941 – with other managers working in other roles within the wartime supply administration – the company would never again have the same influence within government circles that it had once had, and continued to think it enjoyed.[77] Nevertheless it continued to pursue government contracts and support, not least with the strategic deployment of staff in negotiations. British Aluminium attempted to further strengthen its position in procurement negotiations by recruiting senior staff officers now retired from the services. These figures and the company's deployment of them in negotiations with government provide an insight into BACo's outlook, *modus operandi*, and ultimately what would become their shortcomings.

With increases in demand prompted by rearmament and particularly the aircraft production programme, one of British Aluminium's newest directors, Lt Gen. Sir Ronald Charles, despatched a memo to the Supply Board of CID-PSO reiterating the company's commitment to aiding rearmament in April 1935. The memo also pressed British Aluminium's case for government contracts and finance for expanding smelting capacity. Unlike other committees in the PSO, this was heavily composed of senior staff officers from all the branches of the armed services. Here Charles's credentials were intended to come into play. In his last nine years before retiring and being offered a place on British Aluminium's board (which he took up in 1934), Charles had served consecutively as the Commandant of the military arsenal at Woolwich (1924–26), the Director of Military Operations and Intelligence (1926–31), and finally as the Master-General of Ordnance (1931–34). Charles's length of tenure in these posts was highly unusual. In addition, from 1931 until his retirement from the Army, Charles had served in an *ex-officio* capacity on the Army Council. He was also a highly decorated and respected staff officer – having proved himself a highly effective military commander during the First World War – and was socially very well connected.[78] Most important though were Charles's last three military posts; for he was among a small number with practically unrivalled access to and knowledge of the arms procurement process and staff involved in it. Charles's role in this was most probably also influenced by his personal views, as a prominent member of the Army, Home and Empire Defence League – formed in 1937 to lobby for rearmament – and a vocal public advocate of their aims.[79] His memo was followed up by discussions and correspondence between officials at the Board of Trade and the Air Ministry with William Murray Morrison during 1936. BACo's ulterior motives were made clear when, on the pretext of establishing the supply requirements for the government rearmament programme, the company probed officials on the possibilities of another government guaranteed loan for £2 million at a 3 per cent interest rate for expanding their capacity at Lochaber. With the end of the Trade Facilities Act, this would have required a discrete Parliamentary order, and was fairly unusual.

The changed bargaining position of the company was starkly highlighted by the response of Treasury officials in a series of Treasury memos in late 1936. These memos also illustrated the divisions within government on the subject of support to industry, in particular the Treasury's guiding principle in the inter-war years of attempting to 'assist industry' by 'lightening the burden of debt by prudent financial administration', and challenges advanced by other government departments.[80] In September of 1936, Sir Frederick Phillips, the Under-Secretary at the Treasury, opposed the proposal, suggesting that British Aluminium was a financial liability that the government should not shoulder. Edward Bridges, at the time Head of Defence Materials within the Treasury, was more sanguine about British Aluminium's potential and proffered a deal by which a loan would be amortised against all the company's assets and subject to a clause under which the company promised to provide aluminium to the government at 'reasonable prices'. In this view, Montagu Norman, governor of the Bank of England, supported him. In the end, although the Chancellor of the Exchequer sanctioned a guaranteed loan, the offer was withdrawn when Alcan and Norwegian suppliers came forward with stockpiles of metal. BACo was obliged to fund the extension to Lochaber itself.[81] BACo's relationship with government was starting to sour, as Britain looked towards Canadian shores to meet its defence requirements.

Total war and building the 'New Jerusalem', 1939–1953

As the official historian of raw materials planning in Britain during the Second World War noted: 'Aluminium occupied a unique position. No commodity, with the exception of magnesium, bore comparison with it in its complete or virtually complete diversion to service needs.'[82] Britain was absolutely reliant on Canadian supplies of the metal. Against this context, the altered relationship between the British government and native producers, on the one hand, and Canadian producers on the other, was illustrated by a number of incidents, neatly summed up in the comments made by Treasury official, Burke Trend, in 1944. In correspondence referring to the investigation of criticisms of the far more preferential loan terms offered to Alcan than to BACo between 1940 and 1941, Trend noted:

> I can appreciate the force of Sir Murray Morrison's argument that a British aluminium producer should not be expected to operate on terms less favourable than those accorded to a Canadian aluminium producer. But let us forget for a moment the aluminium aspect of the question, especially since in dealing with A.C.O.C. [Alcan] we were dealing with a Company not under our own jurisdiction and not, therefore, amenable to the influences that we can frequently bring to bear upon one of our own contractors.[83]

The background to Trend's memo illustrates the shifting attitude to native and Canadian producers in UK government circles, against the backdrop of strategic demands. Between 1940 and 1941 the Ministry of Supply agreed to advance loans to both BACo and Alcan. On Treasury advice, the terms advanced to BACo were considerably less favourable than those for Alcan. British Aluminium sought a government loan of £450,000 (£20.2m) to further develop the water resources at Lochaber so that production could be expanded. The Treasury agreed to the loan at a recommended rate of five per cent interest, and further suggested that it be stipulated that in the event of nil output repayments still be made. The Ministry of Supply, with whom the original negotiations were conducted, offered BACo the loan at 4 per cent but with the Treasury's suggested repayment stipulation left standing. In contrast, Alcan was loaned CAD55 million (£14,360,313 at 1940 prices, or £644m) for capital projects in Canada at three per cent interest, and with the infinitely more favourable condition that repayment be suspended in any year where production fell below 60,000 tons.[84] When the board members at British Aluminium discovered this from Cunliffe in 1944, they were incensed, and demanded a reduction on the interest offered to them and a review of conditions in their contract. The broader significance of this lies also in the fact that by mid-1942, 84 per cent of MAP's external investment was committed to expanding the Canadian aluminium industry.[85]

In the investigation that followed, it was revealed that the logic behind the conditions stipulated by the Treasury official involved, Frank Lee, was because he mistakenly believed the two companies (BACo and Alcan) were connected due to their joint involvement in a small wartime smelter project, the South Wales Aluminium Company. Despite the vocal support of MAP and the Board of Trade for British Aluminium, the Treasury refused to reconsider the conditions of the loan maintaining that BACo should be treated like any other UK defence contractor, although privately the Treasury conceded that the original terms of the loan to Alcan were very lax.[86] In his reply to the Treasury in June 1944, Sir William Palmer at the Board of Trade summed up the situation pointedly: 'The British Aluminium Co. say it is impossible for them to compete with Canadians who get better terms from the UK Government than they do. As Canada is really the main importer in this market, this is a difficult one to answer.'[87] If the Board of Trade, and BACo, anticipated some sympathy for this point of view, they were to get little from the Treasury. In his response to Palmer, Treasury official Arthur Fforde said that he felt little sympathy for BACo, and that in his opinion they had been 'treated very favourably'.[88]

The same double standards and laxity where dealings with Alcan were concerned were also evident in the government's negotiations with the Canadians over aluminium prices. Claims of profiteering and sensitivities to it were uppermost in officials' minds when it came to the British industry. Conversely, despite repeated criticisms raised by the UK High Commissioner to Canada, the Sub-Committee on Air Services and the Parliamentary Select Committee of Public Accounts, the fixing of Canadian prices for aluminium were never thoroughly investigated. Under arrangements within the PSO, all negotiations over the price of ingot were to be negotiated between the Canadian government and Alcan, with reference to UK government. In the early years of the war the UK's negotiator was the aluminium controller, ironically BACo's own Geoffrey Cunliffe (a further telling sign of his limitations which would manifest themselves with disastrous effects for the company in 1958–59). In a report to Winston Churchill on 17 May 1940, the Sub-Committee on Air Services issued a stinging attack at the way this aluminium control was being operated. One of the more benevolent comments they made – in an otherwise blistering assault – was in gently criticising the ineffectiveness with which Cunliffe had pursued the price question with the Canadian government. Around the same time, the UK High Commissioner to Canada had complained that Cunliffe had failed to consult with him prior to negotiations with the Canadian government about conditions on the ground, notably over the domestic waste of aluminium in Canada and its continued sales in civil markets. Subsequent investigations suggested that Alcan was making sizeable returns on its sales to the UK: a matter which was raised by the Parliamentary Select Committee on Public Accounts and refuted by MAP officials in their evidence.[89] Although Alcan's company historian questioned the validity of the charges levelled at Alcan as well as the Canadian Minister of Munitions and Supply, he did acknowledge that Alcan's Vice President, R. E. Powell and the Minister, the Hon. Clarence Decatur

(C. D.) Howe, 'conducted a regular person-to-person liaison which cleared away red tape and expedited the company's efforts ...'[90] If Howe's subsequent negotiations on behalf of Alcan with the US Government are anything to go by, then Campbell's defence rings hollow. Commenting on US loans to Alcan's Shipshaw factory one of Howe's political opponents, Major M. J. Coldwell, President of Canada's left-centrist party, the Cooperative Commonwealth Federation (which supported the war effort), ventured that he found Howe's denial of the involvement of the Canadian Legation of negotiating on behalf of Alcan, 'very difficult to believe'. During the Second World War Alcan had benefited not just from the British contracts, but also from US Government advances and additional finances that allowed it to make handsome profits on sales to the United States. As well as the British and US advances and loans, Howe negotiated tax breaks for Alcan, which were not extended to all Canadian defence contractors.[91] Howe, the 'Minister of Everything' (who served as Minister of Reconstruction and then Trade and Commerce after the War) was certainly lobbying on behalf of Alcan for defence contracts to supply the US during the Korean War in January 1951 before joining the Alcan board, upon retiring from public office in 1958.[92] Nevertheless, despite a chequered record as a minister for succumbing to lobbying by private interest groups, Howe's actions may have had more to do with his ambitions for the creation of an integrated national economy for Canada, with aluminium a mainstay of post-war Canadian economic growth. Moreover Howe's proximity to Powell was characteristic of his *modus operandi*, as opposed to being motivated by naked self-interest.[93]

The experience of the war economy further convinced officials that they could not rely on adequate supplies from native production; a view apparently confirmed by Cunliffe to the then young wartime civil servant Alec Cairncross (later a prominent economist and Head of the Government Economic Service).[94] Cunliffe's remarks certainly cannot have helped to instil any confidence in government about the future potential of the indigenous primary aluminium industry, although it is questionable whether any major smelter development using water power could have been undertaken in Britain after the war. Moos' neat assessment of the position that the native aluminium industry and the state found themselves in, and options open to them, post-war, was informed by his study of the supply issues Britain in his wartime service at the Institute of Statistics at Oxford. He recognised that British producers could neither compete with the price of secondary metal swamping the market nor with the highly advantageous position of Canadian producers exporting to Britain.[95] Between the 1944 and the end of post-war control of the industry in 1953, there had been discussions within British government circles about the future shape of the industry in the UK, with some officials questioning whether there was any benefit in sustaining a native primary industry if favourable contracts with Canadian and other producers could be secured to sustain domestic market.[96] Despite the compliance with a number of the criteria set down for nationalisation by the first post-war Labour government, the aluminium industry was not considered as a candidate for socialisation. It is wholly questionable whether it could have been politically achievable or desirable, and it is also doubtful whether in the medium or long term it would have benefited either Britain or the industry.[97] By 1953 the strategic realities of the post-war period (not least the balance of trade and dollar-exchange rate) had called into question the prudence of running down the domestic industry, particularly since defence requirements accounted for one-third of the output of British Aluminium's fabricating plants by 1951–52.[98] However British government officials were not optimistic about any potential for further development of primary smelting capacity in the UK (or indeed of the survival of the existing reduction works) in the near future, with an official at the Board of Trade's Office for Scotland declaring as late as 1962 that: 'personally I should doubt whether the Highland plants will last very long. I have never seen any sensible explanation of why they should be kept going.'[99] Ironically, what these officials were overlooking was the importance of the Highlands works to the company's public image and their political capital.

As the Ministry of Supply acknowledged after the war, the continued control of aluminium prices in the UK until 1953 and Alcan's natural competitive advantages, as well as British, Canadian and US government wartime investment, left British Aluminium in a vulnerable position. The company's Highland reduction works faced another brake on expansion. It was one that was to be highlighted during the Invergordon debacle. With the periodic problem of droughts in the west Highlands, the works were in time forced to buy additional peak-load power from the newly established statutory electricity body for the region, the NSHEB. The problems of purchasing peak-load power from the board lay in the conflicting aims of the NSHEB's mission, present since its constitution. When the NSHEB was formed in 1943, it was the intention of the then Secretary of State for Scotland Tom Johnston that the Board would be 'an instrument for the rehabilitation of the Highlands'.[100] Johnston had made it clear that he saw any future development of hydro-electricity in the Highlands as being the territory of state, rather than 'conferring valuable natural resources upon a private corporation'.[101] From the outset the new board was to have a social, as well as an economic, function. This was to become a major bone of contention. On the one hand, Johnston and sections of the Labour movement did not wish to see the Highlands' water resources fall into private hands. In their report *Highland Power* published in 1944, the Scottish Area Committee of the Association of Scientific Workers (AScW) recommended that:

> The best method of ensuring that the Highlands region attains its own level of prosperity by its own resources and efforts is to insist that the larger industrial enterprises, namely the magnesium, carbide, plastics and synthetic rubber industries must be run as public concerns, the initial capital coming from the State.[102]

Labour's MP for the Western Isles, declared, in support of the social clause to the House of Commons, that: 'It will be a blessing when we can supply the domestic user with electricity.' Yet he also wished for the new board to bring 'full employment, a sure livelihood, and a decent standard of living to the regions'.[103] The Cooper Committee, for its part, had recommended that the development be used to attract businesses in the electro-chemical and metallurgical industries, and help expand existing ones, as had the Hilleary Committee four years previously, although admittedly both of these bodies were more influenced by private and commercial interests (among them BACo's own Morrison).[104]

In addition, BACo felt it was being penalised by property rates in the Highlands on assets into which it had sunk considerable capital investment. Reporting, the Parliamentary committee examining Scottish valuation and rating systems recognised the fine balance to be struck, both in terms of retaining existing concerns and attracting new investors. Observing the high capital costs of developing hydro-electric and smelting capacity – and the problems, for concerns like BACo, of maintaining competitiveness against Canadian and Norwegian producers with far more extensive water reserves – and the economic and social importance of such industries to the Highlands, they counselled against imposing rates that were too high:

> We recognise that for the Highland local authorities it must be a question of balancing advantages, but after attempting to visualise the alternatives from their point of view we are satisfied that their interest lies in making some concession to modify the rating burden borne by hydro-electric undertakings ... The direct benefits are obvious. Even if the rate of contribution of the undertakers is reduced it will remain a substantial addition to the local authorities' funds; and a supply of electricity will be provided for more rate-payers at a cheaper price ... most important of all, the introduction of electro-metallurgical and electro-chemical industries would add greatly to the income of the local authorities.[105]

In support of this point, the committee cited the example of British Aluminium's contribution to the Highlands through the high rateable value of their schemes and the £500,000 channelled into the local economy through employees' wages alone. Equally significant was the fact that after the introduction of the Local Government (Scotland) Act 1929, large ratepayers like British Aluminium played a significant role in the financing of Public Assistance in the Highlands, not least given the low rateable value of much property in the region. Moreover under the terms of the Lochaber Water Power Bill, BACo had agreed to set aside 3000 horsepower of electricity for local industry.

The NSHEB's 'social clause' immediately caused frictions in the wartime coalition government between Johnston and the Conservative Minister of Fuel and Power (the latter of whom had responsibility for Central Electricity Board), Major Gwilym

Lloyd-George.[106] However, the matter was left unresolved between the two and would continue to present a problem that successive governments tried to confront.[107] It is all too easy with the benefit of hindsight to pour scorn on decisions made some time previously. In many ways, all parties appear to have been dazzled by the possibilities of hydro-electricity – as politicians and public commentators would be by nuclear power a decade and more later – rather than carrying out a realistic appraisal of the water power potential of the Highlands and the substantial energy requirements of business and domestic consumers. *Ceteris paribus*, the only way in which such energy-intensive industries could have been adequately supplied with power at a commercially viable rate, at the same time as meeting obligations to domestic consumers, would have been to import heavily subsidised electricity through an integrated network from the southerly generating boards. Given the type of 'high load' power required by such industries and the difficulties and cost of transmitting (transporting) electricity for peak periods, it is highly questionable whether this would ever have been practical immediately. However with a better-integrated network it may well have been.

As far as British Aluminium was concerned, in real terms the cost for the company by the 1950s of having occasionally to rely on purchasing peak load electricity from NSHEB precluded any reconsideration of the position stated by Cunliffe in 1940. The NSHEB's rates were 22 per cent higher than those paid by industrial customers in the central industrial belt of Scotland, and of the UK national average. British Aluminium required electricity at a maximum of 0.15*d.* per unit, while NSHEB was selling to industrial customers at 1.40*d.* per unit.[108] Fraught negotiations with the NSHEB ensued from the late 1950s until an agreement was reached in the early 1960s for NSHEB to provide up to 10 per cent of the British Aluminium works' power in the event of water shortages or as peak load at 0.75*d.* (0.25*d.* more than BACo's own unit costs for power generation). During the course of these discussions NSHEB attempted to wrestle control of BACo's water resources.[109] Even so these rates were substantially higher than power costs at Canadian and Norwegian plants, so that British Aluminium was operating at a substantial comparative disadvantage to its main competitors. Moreover, in Alcan's case, it was able to benefit from changes in federal legislation introduced in the late 1940s, which allowed the provincial government in British Columbia to sell water rights to the company at bargain prices for the development of its Kitimat smelter and Kemano scheme.[110]

The problems faced by British Aluminium in the Highlands reflected deeper flaws in the industrial planning mechanisms for Scotland despite wartime and post-war improvements (such as the formation of the Scottish Council (Development and Industry) and the NSHEB. The Highlands, in particular, remained poorly served by government.[111] The continued efforts of the Scottish Trades Union Congress (STUC) and other campaigners to establish a strategic development authority for the Highlands largely fell on deaf ears, although under the auspices of the Distribution of Industry Act 1945 (extended to cover the Highlands in 1948) – designed to stimulate industrial developments in designated Development Areas of high unemployment – a number of high profile industrial schemes was brought to the region in the 1950s and 1960s. Moreover, prior to the establishment of the Scottish Development Department (SDD) in 1964, coordination of industrial planning for Scotland was still largely determined from Whitehall.[112] It was not until 1972 that a Chief Economic Adviser was appointed to the Scottish Office – with economists poorly represented in the department – and 1973 that the Scottish Economic Planning Department was formed. So that even after the creation of the SDD in 1964, decision-making on the Scottish economy was largely determined by Whitehall economists who, as one economic historian points out, 'saw Scotland's problems from a UK, macroeconomic perspective', while 'allocation of funds tended to be decided by the hunch of administrative civil servants and the political concerns of ministers'.[113] The establishment of the Advisory Panel on the Highlands and Islands in 1946 – to advise the Secretary of State on the coordination of planning in the Highlands by central and local Government, and other public bodies – signalled greater coordination of policy towards the Highlands. Nevertheless until 1965 (and the establishment of the HIDB) economic diversification and growth in the region owed more to the ongoing programmes of the NSHEB, and the efforts of entrepreneurs such as through the Highland Fund (established and bankrolled by industrialist John Rollo and businessman Herbert Ross).[114] This failure to attend to the pressing matter of the Highland economy in part resulted from the rejection of proposals for an authority, but also from a deeply held view that attempts at economic diversification in the region were pointless. The Scottish Office thus remained above all keen to retain the favour of companies like British Aluminium. It is therefore unsurprising that BACo retained a central role in the Highland communities in which it was based and was able to exact favours from the Scottish Office. Aluminium had also become a major employer in post-war Scotland from its Highland reduction works to its sheet and foil works in Falkirk and Glasgow, as well as being, like iron and steel, a critical link industry in the chain of supply in the Scottish economy.[115]

The end of the affair, 1953–1959

Even after the devaluation of sterling and the rise in Canadian ingot prices in 1949, British Aluminium's capital structure was further weakened when it emerged from government controls in 1953.[116] Equally the government's cajoling of the company to engage in Commonwealth projects ignored its own role in weakening British Aluminium's market position and strengthening its chief competitor in UK markets.[117] However, like sections among Britain's white colonial settlers, some senior figures within British Aluminium do not appear to have appreciated the changed climate. This was compounded post-war by the continuing practice of selecting board members from among the higher echelons of the armed services and the senior civil service. Among those who joined Sir Ronald Charles was Viscount Portal, the former

The Old Guard: Viscount Lord Portal,
Marshall of the Royal Air Force, 1943.
© RTA/GUA.

head of the wartime air staff, and the man attributed with persuading Clement Attlee
that Britain needed to be a nuclear power. Crucially, he was also the first post-war
controller of the UK's nuclear programme from 1947 until 1951. Also appointed
to the BACo board was Lord Plowden, who had served as the chief executive of
the government's Aircraft Supply Council between 1945 and 1946, later becoming
chief planning officer and chairman of the Economic Planning Board (1953–54)
and subsequently the first chairman of UK Atomic Energy Authority (1954–59).
Crucially Plowden also served as chairman of committees on public expenditure and
on the aircraft and electricity industries, as well as on NATO's temporary council
committee (1951–52).[118] As with Charles, these men were not simply selected for
their social milieu but also because of their intimate knowledge of defence and civil
procurement procedures, and policy development. British Aluminium's continued
reliance on government civil and defence contracts for the first two decades after the
war required those skills to service a core part of its business.[119] As one of the largest
and most important non-ferrous metals producers, the company continued to work
closely, through their main laboratory at Warrington and through the BNFMRA,
with the Admiralty, the DSIR, the UK Atomic Energy Authority, and the Society of
British Aircraft Constructors.[120] Even though defence procurement declined relatively
as a proportion of sales after the Korean War, profitable new markets such as civil
aviation and metals production for civil nuclear programmes expanded. Moreover,

as one history of British industrial policy between 1951 and 1964 has noted of civil research and development, it was hard to distinguish between civilian and military programmes.[121] This collaboration can only have further reassured BACo that it had government approval. What British Aluminium was apparently oblivious to was just how profoundly the relationship with government had shifted. This was brutally exposed by three incidents over the next 30 years, in which it chronically misjudged official opinion and exhibited a misplaced optimism in government's guarding of the company's interests. The first related to British Aluminium's involvement in the Volta River project in the British colony of the Gold Coast (late Ghana), where it already had bauxite mines.

The Volta River Project

On the back of a report published by consulting engineers who had explored the option of constructing a hydro-scheme and 210,000 mts capacity smelter in the colony, a meeting was held between the major participant aluminium producers, the metropolitan and Gold Coast government in 1951 to discuss the proposals and a potential commercial agreement. The scheme was initiated by the Colonial Office and the Gold Coast government in response to the rise of the nationalist movement in the country. Crucially, the report, that employed BACo's expertise, as well as that of its long-time civil engineering associate William Halcrow partnership and the subsidiary of major British firm Vickers Metropolitan, stressed that the scheme could not go ahead without the backing of the aluminium companies. British Aluminium initially dropped out of discussions claiming that the third of shares offered in other valuable reserves – held by a company set up by a mining engineer, with whom British Aluminium had a long animosity – were too rich for its tastes, and because Alcan dominated the partnership holding 60 per cent of the reserves. In addition to this and its financial state BACo's eyes were firmly fixed on the possibilities presented by Borneo at this time. British Aluminium rejoined discussions in 1952, but requested assurances from the government about subsidies and a ceiling on unit costs for power and shipping. In the meantime, discussions were also affected by the changing political scene and specifically the ascendant nationalist leader Dr Nkrumah's dissatisfaction (encouraged by Reynolds Metals) with the deal for the Gold Coast. The metropolitan government went ahead with the publication of a White Paper setting out plans for the Volta River Project in 1952 but developments were held up by negotiations over the power contracts, freight and the Gold Coast government's share in the scheme. With the nationalists by now in power, BACo and Alcan were also tainted by their association with the colonial power.[122]

In the meantime BACo had attempted to interest other British fabricators, such as Tube Investments, Imperial Chemical Industries (ICI) and the Hawker Siddley Group, to invest in the scheme but to no avail. By 1956 BACo was forced to drop out (this time for good) because of capital overstretch – the British government estimating that British Aluminium would have had to invest £11 million in the scheme – with outlay on a new smelter at Baie Comeau and involvement in Fria in Guinea. More important though for BACo was the change in reaction to the company within government circles that its dallying, and eventual withdrawal, provoked. In January 1956 Board of Trade official, G. T. Field, declared that though 'we have always been doubtful whether, when the decision came, B.A.C. would be willing to share in the risks of the Volta development ... politically and in other ways, HMG [Her Majesty's Government] would welcome B.A.C. participation – and, perhaps, even more welcome the participation of a group of U.K. fabricators including B.A.C.' [123] Clearly it was politically desirable to have British producers involved if the government were to be able to justify public investment in the scheme to Parliament and the public, as well as the currency exchange benefits to be accrued. However government frustration with British Aluminium was mounting. A few days after Field's initial memo, in advance of a meeting between BACo and the Board of Trade the same month, he noted bitterly: 'Frankly I would not shed any tears if the British Aluminium Company decided not to participate in the Volta River Scheme, and I certainly would not feel disposed to offer them any money to do so.' [124] After the meeting with BACo, the government felt even more wary (rightly as it turned out) of counting on the company's support for the project, questioning whether government should assume the risks involved with providing guarantees for the project, and concluded that: 'we ought to consider whether we feel participation by U.K. industry to be so important that we must make some special arrangements to bring it about (I myself am completely sceptical on the point).' [125] Thus officials had reached the stage where they were less insistent on securing support from British industrialists, and more in finding a partner with the capital to advance the project and reduce the financial risks to the exchequer.

Alcan, for its part, was also heavily committed in Canada, Jamaica and Australia, and, as the government acknowledged, was questioning involvement unless it was the largest stakeholders in the project. [126] Alcan duly pulled out, committed to a project with Reynolds Metals in the Congo (subsequently Zaire), but returned to participate in the scheme. In 1957, the Gold Coast gained independence from Britain as the new state of Ghana. In the end the Volta River Project went ahead with Alcan (through a subsidiary), Reynolds, Kaiser and Alcoa forming the Volta Aluminium Company in September 1959, after US President Dwight Eisenhower authorised a loan to the Ghanaian government in 1957 to support the project. [127] British Aluminium continued to exploit its bauxite reserves in Ghana, having discovered more in 1957. As over the issue of primary aluminium production, where the British government settled into a status quo until the late 1960s of relying on Canadian (and Norwegian imports of ingot), in the end it was forced over the issue of Ghanaian bauxite to resign itself to the fact that British producers could not be relied on to support the Volta River project. The changed political environment also forced the government to beat a hasty retreat from involvement with the scheme.

BACo's falling share price, its weak capital structure and both Tube Investments and Reynolds Metals' close knowledge of this through the Volta River negotiations (as well as Reynolds' interest in acquiring BACo's mining rights in Ghana) was instrumental in contributing to the duo's decision to mount an aggressive takeover bid in 1958/9. British Aluminium was desperate in a changed policy environment, and forced to involve itself in a scheme not of its making, to attempt unsuccessfully to retain government support. The disfavour that British Aluminium had fallen into within government circles rendered any personal connections between individual board members and ministers or officials redundant, as the government's behaviour during the RTIA takeover revealed.

The takeover, 1958–1959

British Aluminium's continued, misplaced faith in government support was to be further exposed in the RTIA takeover.[128] The then Conservative government of Harold Macmillan was keen to encourage takeovers by US firms of British counterparts who were deemed to be under-performing in the hope that it would improve their, and the country's, fortunes, especially given the political criticisms being levelled at the administration for ineffectiveness. Nonetheless British Aluminium could be forgiven for expecting Conservative ministers to protect its interests as a British company. Senior Conservatives continued to stress the importance of Imperial and Commonwealth preference over free trade. At the 1956 Conservative Party conference, Alec Douglas-Home – the then Secretary of State for Commonwealth Relations, an ally of the PM and a future Conservative Prime Minister – clamoured for a policy that placed 'UK producer first, Commonwealth producer second, and foreigner last'.[129]

In the event, Ministers and officials remained divided over the competing offers on the table for British Aluminium over the winter war of 1958–59; the briefing paper for the cabinet's meeting to conclude their decision on the offers for British Aluminium acknowledged that, 'political and commercial factors had made it hard to adjudicate expressly in favour of one or other of the proposals', especially in light of the forthcoming election.[130] Over two years previously, in 1956, the Conservative government of Anthony Eden had faced a public outcry over the government's perceived indecisiveness in the face of a hostile takeover of British company Trinidad Oil Company by the Texas Fuel Company (Texaco). The government, especially then Chancellor Harold Macmillan, received a mauling from the Labour Party opposition, and all quarters of the press, over the handling of the affair. Around eight months later the government was forced into the humiliating withdrawal from Suez – lambasted at home and abroad, and shunned as international pariahs – and Eden resigned. In the year leading up to the 1959 election, an ebullient Labour Party had launched its *Plan for Progress* (1958), an original appraisal of comparative economic performance. The Labour opposition, led by Hugh Gaitskell and Shadow Chancellor Harold Wilson, took the Conservatives to task for their failure to grow the economy and modernise

Britain.[131] In addition to these political factors, ministerial deliberations were further complicated by the fact that the Chancellor of the Exchequer, Derek Heathcoat Amory, held a substantial number of shares in Tube Investments (and for this reason did not take a leading role in the government's final decision), while the Treasury had a $1.8 million shareholding in Alcoa and an indirect share in BACo.[132]

Both Heathcoat-Amory and Douglas-Home supported the Alcoa deal citing the latter's expertise and position as a more seasoned global aluminium producer (than Reynolds Metals) with the capital to invest heavily both in domestic and Commonwealth schemes, urging immediate acceptance of the offer. Heathcoat-Amory also argued that the Alcoa deal would be advantageous from 'a broad economic standpoint' because it would make capital available from non-sterling sources.[133] In his reply to his Chancellor and Douglas-Home, Macmillan, by then PM, declared himself to be doubtful about BACo's Alcoa proposal, offering as his misgivings, 'it seems in effect American control – and not only of the company but of all the ancillary services, shipping, etc.'. In so doing he was expressing British and Canadian ship owners' concerns that Alcoa's control of Baie Comeau, for example, would result in the considerable loss of business for Commonwealth shipping, a major invisible export.[134] Contrary to the assertions of Portal's biographer, Dennis Richards, from the outset British Aluminium (ironically given their proposed deal with Alcoa) attempted to whip up of economic nationalism among Ministers by stressing the hostile and foreign nature of the RTIA bid. Reporting to the Prime Minister on 1 January 1959 about that day's meeting with Portal and Cunliffe, the President of the Board of Trade, Frank Erroll, reported the BACo chairman as declaring that '... The whole Reynolds/ Tube Investments manoeuvre had now been exposed for what it really was, namely an American "smash and grab" with a British front (which might soon become an unnecessary adjunct)'.[135] In an imperious fashion, Portal then 'urged the Government to adopt the only course of action which in his view would ensure the retention of British control, namely the immediate grant of consent to Alcoa'. Portal also requested a meeting with the Prime Minister.[136]

Neither the Treasury nor the Stock Exchange was keen to intervene on behalf of the Alcoa deal, despite pleas from the Bank of England to prevent the increasingly bitter battle affecting the reputation of the City, especially since they had no assurances from Alcoa about British control of the company and British shipping interests. On 2 January the Financial Secretary to the Treasury met with all the main parties involved separately, to exact their assurances on both of the government's main points of contention, namely British control of the company and shipping interests.[137] All parties were able to give the assurances required. Events in the meantime had progressed apace, and RTIA was able to claim sufficient control to expect Treasury agreement to its acquisition of BACo. In a desperate last-ditch attempt to urge the government to intervene, Portal wrote to the PM on 6 January 1959, declaring:

... I have always appreciated that it was the wish of Ministers to adopt a neutral position in order to allow our Shareholders an opportunity to make known their views on the rival plans submitted to them ... Since early December, however, an entirely different situation has developed through the 'neutrality' of the Government, in that a single Shareholder, a foreigner with a vested interest in the decision, is buying the shares and therefore the votes of the rest ...[138]

In contrast to BACo's hysterical misrepresentation of events, TI's Chairman Sir Ivan Stedeford comported himself with dignity and presented the RTIA case dispassionately.[139] The government waited until the 9 January deadline and issued a statement approving the merger, and acknowledging Alcoa's withdrawal; Portal was shell-shocked. In what appears to have been an emotional meeting with Harold Macmillan that morning, the BACo Chairman was in 'a rather excited and depressed state' – apparently uncharacteristic of his usual stoicism and quiet demeanour – declaring in pungent terms to the PM that he 'regarded the T.I. people with great distaste and thought that they would ruin British Aluminium'. In his note of the meeting Macmillan added that Portal 'obviously regards T.I. and Reynolds as a set of crooks'. Portal expressed disappointment at the government's role, while acknowledging that the British Aluminium board had not 'managed the affair very well'.[140] In true classical style the former Chief of the Air Staff then declared that he and most of the rest of the Board would fall upon their swords, before ending their meeting. Portal's loss of composure was probably a measure of the fact that, as his biographer notes, it was one of only two major defeats he experienced during his lifetime, as well as the fact that until recently he had still held great sway in Whitehall among Ministers, officials and the Chiefs of Staff. It is not clear what he expected to gain from this meeting with Macmillan. Portal had already approached the PM at a shooting party in November about the takeover, with Macmillan claiming that he had told the BACo chairman that the government could not intervene. However this may well have been a subterfuge on the PM's part.[141] As one of Macmillan's oldest and closest friends remarked of him: '[he] really should have been a Cardinal Archbishop in the Middle Ages, where absolution from irregularity over the facts could always be obtained by a shot visit to the Vatican.'[142] Furthermore, just how restrained Macmillan was under the circumstances may be masked by the image of 'non-chalance and indifference' he was attempting to project to set him apart from his predecessor. As his private secretary, John Wyndham, observed of an audience with 'Super-Mac': 'Anyone who got excited got short shrift.'[143] British Aluminium's negotiations with the government during the takeover exhibited poor strategic judgment, combined with blind faith in ministers accepting their perspective. Portal and Cunliffe grossly inflated their own importance in thinking that they could direct the hands of ministers, in particular, underestimating the political wile of the PM.

However, this was not to be last time that British Aluminium misread the political environment and placed unquestioning faith in ministers. Given the nature of BACo's deal with Alcoa – effectively ceding control of most of the company's shareholding to the largest US aluminium multinational – it seems remarkable that the company had the impudence to argue for government intervention to protect the industry in the national interest. Although the government was keen on retaining national control, serving ministers would have struggled politically to defend such action, even with British public opinion (and that within its own party) so opposed to the US takeovers of British companies. As the takeover proceeded and British Aluminium fell into public disfavour, it would have been suicidal for a serving government to intervene (as the ensuing political battles illustrated), quite aside from the desirability of such a move as far as Conservative policy was concerned.

While the Opposition chose to support the government's decision at the time, the matter was raised some six months later (in the run up to the October election) after the payouts to Portal and Cunliffe were disclosed. Harold Wilson drew on popular rhetoric to great effect, identifying Portal and Cunliffe as examples of the, 'hereditary squirearchy … honest chaps, whispering, all of them, the sweet enchantments of a bygone age, good husbands and fathers, no doubt, but entirely out of touch with modern industrial society', to highlight the government's failure to modernise British industry, and to stop 'golden handshakes' to failing boards of directors. During the debate Wilson used the examples of Portal and Cunliffe to expose what he suggested was the hollowness of remarks by the President of the Board of Trade encouraging the threat of bids to keep 'directors on their toes'.[144] At the 1959 Trades Union Congress, delegates mirrored Wilson's critique, contrasting rewards paid to Portal and Cunliffe, as incompetent business leaders who had exposed British industries to foreign takeover, with the workforce facing job insecurity.[145] In the ongoing political battle of Britain at the time, over who was in step with modernity, it was a timely stick with which to beat a Conservative Party portrayed as being out-of-step with popular opinion and led by Edwardians. Macmillan was well aware that the Conservative Party could ill-afford to lose the support of its sizeable working-class vote, including many trade unionists.[146]

'Industrial cathedral': the Invergordon debacle

Once again the proximity of senior board members to government departments – in the case of Invergordon smelter project, the UKAEA, and their familiarity with British civil nuclear programmes – would unduly colour their judgements. It was this close relationship with ministers and officials to which BACo's failure to adequately assess the risks of the project, and accept the gentleman's agreement, can be ascribed. The contrast with Alcan – unfettered by a debilitating relationship with government – could not be more pointed. BACo's belief in government to act in the best interests of British Aluminium percolated down; The manager of the company's largest rolling mill at Falkirk declared to Board of Trade officials as late as 1963

BACo Invergordon smelter site, March 1969. © RTA/Invergordon smelter site, courtesy of Malcolm Dunley.

that he felt it unlikely that the Highland reduction works would be closed because: 'even if for strategic reasons, he did not think the Government would permit them to be shut down.'[147] British Aluminium's principal negotiators were no less blinded by the potential presented by Britain's programme for the new generation of civil nuclear power reactors (the advanced gas cooled reaction (AGR) than were ministers. Invergordon also serves as an example of the mismatch between short-term political goals and necessity of long-term planning required in capital-intensive industries. Personalities and informal networks among key players in this saga are crucial to an understanding of how this played out.

It is unsurprising, given British Aluminium's links to defence, and the recruitment of directors with connections to the highest levels of the military procurement process and civil and military nuclear programmes, that BACo was closely linked to the UKAEA. The company collaborated with the NPL and the Atomic Energy Authority over the use of both magnesium and aluminium alloys for fuel casings. More importantly though, senior figures within British Aluminium had been intimately involved with the development of the UK's post-war nuclear programme, and in wider policy circles, starting with Lord Portal. The principal figures within TI and BACo certainly had an intimate knowledge of Britain's civil (and military) nuclear programmes. Sir Edwin Plowden – who was a British Aluminium director between 1946 and 1954, albeit *in absentia* much of the time – served as chairman of the UKAEA between 1954 and 1960. He was joined a year later as a member of UKAEA until 1959 by another former Treasury official, Sir William Strath. Plowden

BACo Invergordon smelter, December 1970. © RTA, courtesy of Malcolm Dunley.

had played the crucial role in the substantial expansion of Britain's civil nuclear programme during the mid-late 1950s. In the aftermath of Suez, with fears running high of secure supplies of energy, it had been Plowden who lobbied successfully for a substantial increase in the civil nuclear programme, with an estimated two-thirds of new generating capacity in the 1960s to be nuclear.[148] Equally significant was Plowden's role in helping to secure the role of the new chairmanship of the Central Electricity Generating Board (CEGB) for the former MD of the UKAEA's industrial group, Sir Christopher Hinton. It was Hinton who would go on, with the support of Plowden, to argue for a scaling back of the Magnox programme and to gain more funding for the prototype AGR programme. Plowden joined the TI board in 1959, to become chairman in 1961. Strath became managing director of BACo the same year, and then chairman.[149] Sir Ivan Stedeford, who stepped down as TI chairman in 1963 (to become a life president), had also served as a part-time member of the UKAEA board, as well as being on the advisory panel for DSIR. Stedeford – who chaired the committee reviewing Britain's railway network in the early 1960s, and clashed with Dr Beeching over his vision – represented, 'something of an "Establishment" figure', who, 'epitomised the British policy style [to] construct a consensus and avoid policy imposition'.[150] While he was responsible for reforming the organisational structure of British Aluminium and introducing a more transparent and meritocratic culture into the company, his sense of public duty and proximity to government (like Strath and Plowden) did little to dispel the historic reliance on the state. By the time Plowden and Strath joined the BACo and TI boards, they were both supporters of nuclear energy, with the former an enthusiast for the potential represented by the AGR.

In his review of the Invergordon contract, Ronny Utiger claimed that though Plowden and Strath 'knew the leading figures in atomic energy', 'they did not themselves have the expertise to judge how realistic the estimates were, but placed a great deal of reliance on people who did have the expertise, and whose judgement and integrity they relied on'. Utiger further claims that 'experience with Magnox and the AGR prototype gave a sound basis for operating performance'.[151] In fact Plowden was party, ten years before the Special Electricity Contracts for Invergordon were signed, to Hinton's damning appraisal of the Magnox stations. In evidence to the Parliamentary Select Committee on Estimates in 1959, Hinton judged that the cost of generating power from Magnox stations was 40 per cent above those of conventional steam generation. Even with improvements in design, the official historian of the electricity industry Leslie Hannah noted that: 'By early 1963 Hinton felt that economic nuclear power might be as far away as the later 1970s, but everyone recognised that such prognostications were speculative. What was already clear was that nuclear power could not make the serious contribution to Britain's energy economy that had been expected.'[152] The first AGR prototype was constructed at Windscale in 1958 and operational by late 1962. This formed the basis of the next generation reactors programme proposed by the Wilson government in 1964, of which Hunterston B was one, that was to provide the cheap power to the new generation aluminium smelters announced in 1967. Historians' retrospective judgments of the AGR programme have damned it as 'one of the major blunders of British industrial policy'. Never realising the potential expected for them, they have been described as 'enormously expensive and led to a net loss to Britain'.[153] Yet, as early as October 1967, and despite their support for the AGR programme, the UK Parliamentary Select Committee on Science and Technology (which was investigating Britain's nuclear reactor programme) observed that though, 'from a technological standpoint, the results [from the gas/graphite system] had been outstandingly successful', they recognised that 'there may be room for argument about the economics of gas-cooled reactors'.[154] It seems highly unlikely given Plowden and Strath's continued standing in government circles that they would not have been aware of these concerns.

For their part, Labour ministers vaunting the smelter and AGR schemes were primarily concerned with the political capital and economic benefits to be exacted

BACo Invergordon smelter, March 1975. © RTA, image courtesy of Malcolm Dunley.

from concluding speedy contracts with the aluminium concerns. Encouraging a new generation of aluminium smelters supplied by nuclear energy offered the attraction of reducing the UK's dependency on costly imports of ingot; the government assessed that this potentially would aid the balance of trade deficit by as much as £50–60m per annum, with the bulk of Britain's aluminium ingot imports coming from Canada which was in the Dollar Zone. They also reasoned that it could also promote British nuclear technology. Crucially, the development of this technology – along with other trans-European work UKAEA was involved in to develop a gas centrifuge to enrich uranium – had the potential to make Europe and Britain independent of the US for supplies of uranium and to open up a potentially valuable export market. Moreover Ministers saw the work as an entrée to British membership of the European Common Market, and of toppling France from its dominant position in the continent.[155] Quite aside from other potential economic benefits and political objectives, it fitted

with Labour's trumpeting of its modern image. Ironically, the smelter programme also illustrated the shortcomings of what passed for British planning mechanisms and the endurance of short-termism, and, after 1967, 'on reducing unemployment by nationally determined measures'.[156]

The choice of locations was given added political impetus – hence the location of two of smelters for north Wales and the Scottish Highlands – by the rising support for nationalist parties in Scotland and Wales.[157] Negotiations over Invergordon illustrated on the one hand the determination of the then Secretary of State for Scotland, Willie Ross (1964–70, 1974–76), and Scottish Office civil servants to attract one of the smelters to Scotland, and on the other the greatly strengthened planning mechanisms north of the border by the 1960s. Moreover the Scottish Office's determination was given added weight by the earlier report of the Scottish Council Development and Industry (SCDI)-sponsored inquiry into the Scottish economy (hereafter the Toothill

Report, 1961), which called for greater state investment to stimulate the Scottish economy, in particular the growth of new high technology sectors. Unfortunately the Invergordon smelter was to serve as a monument to the failings of government to heed another crucial recommendation in the Toothill report, that the growth of new industries be based on their commercial sustainability.[158] However the possibilities presented by this opportunity, for government and company alike, seemed too good to miss, especially as concerns had been mounting about the long-term survival of BACo's existing assets in the region. Only a few years before, in 1964, the Board of Trade's Highland study observed that if emerging cheap power sources were ever to make aluminium smelting commercially viable in the UK then the 'company are assuming ... this would almost certainly mean siting new production near the source of power rather than taking the power to the Highlands to expand production there'.[159] The year before the smelter announcement, on the back of the closure of BACo's Foyers works, the company had called on the Scottish Office to intervene after Inverness and Argyll County Councils moved to increase rates paid on their assets at Lochaber by 31.6 per cent (an increase of around £22,000 over 12 months, and nearly three per cent more than the 28.7 per cent increase proposed for Inverness-shire as a whole) in line with that paid by industry in Scotland as a whole. The SDD was quick to spot the looming threat posed by the county councils' proposals, observing that given the 'financial state' of BACo's Highland assets, a rise of this magnitude 'might cause the Company to take stock and review its continuation in the Highlands'.[160] In this case the Scottish Office was able to successfully intervene and propose rate increases in line with the respective county averages for Inverness and Argyll.[161] In the unravelling tragedy of the Invergordon smelter, the Scottish Office was to play a less auspicious role. Though little of the blame for shortcomings in the planning of the scheme can be laid at the door of the Scottish Office, as much of the detail of the development was determined by Whitehall departments, it was to be leading Scottish officials who would drive the nails into the smelter's coffin.

The negotiations over Invergordon were also mired in growing tensions between the Scottish Office and the HIDB. Initially economic growth in the Highlands was to be achieved through projects in identified 'growth points' one of them was around the Cromarty and Moray Firths. Encouraging industry to invest in the region was an important strand of the HIDB's mission.[162] In reality, Scottish Office officials became concerned that the first board, in particular, was moving forward without consulting their political masters in Edinburgh. Neither the Scottish Office nor the Board of Trade was all that willing to concede real decision-making power to the HIDB. Disagreements between Scottish Office ministers and officials and the HIDB were not so easily resolved. Increasingly tensions arose over where responsibility lay for inviting and initiating large industrial developments to the Highlands. In addition questions were being raised by the press and in the House of Commons about the personal integrity and financial probity of individual board members. It was to be this conflict that Alcan was to become unwittingly embroiled in, for it was to them that the HIDB first turned to develop the Invergordon site. In February 1967 Sir Robert Grieve, the then HIDB chairman, had outlined the board's plans for developments on the Cromarty Firth to the Inverness Chamber of Commerce. Included in these plans were the establishment of Invergordon Chemical Enterprises, who, it was planned, would operate a petrochemical complex on the site. In the meantime, a part time board member, Phillip Durham, leaked documents to the press, which chiefly appeared in *The Scottish Daily Express* newspaper as a dossier, suggesting that other board members, notably Frank Thomson, who had founded Invergordon Chemicals and devised the idea of the complex, were using public funds to advance their own personal business activities. In the aftermath Thomson was forced to resign, as did the planning department of the local council (Ross and Cromarty), while others on the board notably Grieve were tempted to follow and Willie Ross was put under considerable pressure in the Commons and the press.[163] In a meeting at palace of Westminster ten days after the Durham dossier had been published, Ross – of whom one former Scottish Office minister remarked upon hearing of his appointment, 'how will the Scottish Office cope with the wrath of God?' – stamped his personal authority on a situation that he declared 'seemed to be getting out of hand'. He made it clear that: 'it was not the purpose of the Board to deal with projects of this size which affected the national investment programme. Any proposals would have to be seen in a United Kingdom context …'[164] One interested party, US petroleum concern Occidental, with whom the HIDB had been in discussions, pulled out. However the board did not abandon its plans for the area. John Robertson, the board member given responsibility for the developments, revived discussions with Alcan over the possibilities of establishing a smelter at Invergordon. Though Ross declared his faith in the HIDB at the meeting in March, he had made it clear to them both collectively and individually that he expected no repeat of the crisis. He also arranged for reports to be sent back about them. In one of these reports, in April 1967, Bobby Fasken, a Scottish Office secondee to the HIDB, noted the serious rifts between the 'civil servants' and 'commercials' fed by Grieve and Robertson, providing a damning impression of Robertson's undertakings to businesses, including Alcan.[165]

In the meantime Robertson had been progressing discussions with Alcan, and in June allowed them sight of his confidential proposals on Invergordon to go to Willie Ross. This bold plan, which Robertson misleadingly claimed had been developed in conjunction with the Scottish Office, UKAEA, and NSHEB, proposed a complex of 430 Acres employing 1570, jointly owned by a number of enterprises including Alcan. The plan echoed those proposed in the 1930s and 1940s to establish electro-chemical and electro-metallurgical clusters in the Highlands (then around hydro-electricity). Robertson's plan urged the construction of two phosphorus and four ferro-alloy furnaces, as well as a caustic chlorine electrolyser, alongside the aluminium smelter; the power requirements to be met by the construction of a 600–625 megawatt AGR station on site, with peak load to be supplied by electricity produced by the NSHEB's hydro-electricity plants (transmitted down the Beauly Gridline), and after 1973 from the UKAEA's Prototype Fast breeder Reactor at Dounreay (the latter at 0.25*d*. per unit. Robertson projected that it could be completed by May 1973, and would work alongside the separate petro-chemical terminal. Robertson acknowledged that to secure the cheap electricity the proposal would need the support of Ross. On the basis of these plans, a proposal was made to the UK Government in May 1967. In a letter to Nathanael Vining Davis in June 1967, John Elton revealed that he was party to a HIDB document to be submitted to the Secretary of State for Scotland, assuming 'that the Alcan smelter alone will be in operation [at Invergordon]'. Elton also indicated that RTZ was still trying to interest British Aluminium and another semis producer Birmetal in their Anglesey plans.[166] At the same time both the Board of Trade and the HIDB were continually pressing Alcan to commit to the project. Yet if Alcan were being given 'some confidence' by the HIDB that the power could be delivered at commercially viable prices, Scotland's most senior civil servant, Sir Douglas Haddow, informed the Board of Trade that he was 'doubtful'.[167] It was an ominous portent of things to come.

Robertson's plans were shelved with his resignation after a clash with the Scottish Office in July, although they resurfaced again in an altered form in proposals submitted by the third HIDB Chairman Admiral Dunbar-Nasmith after the closure of Invergordon smelter in an attempt to revive the project.[168] The HIDB, and local opinion, favoured Alcan over BACo – fuelled by the anger over the closure of British Aluminium's Foyers works announced in January of that year – was overruled in the struggle of wills with the Scottish Office. The board had been party to the plans for closing Foyers since May of the previous year, and was frustrated by BACo's refusal to hand over plans of the layout of Foyers or to facilitate visits to allow prospective employers to look over the facilities. However BACo did not want its closure plans made public until it had taken all the necessary steps to negotiate severance packages and transfers. The Scottish Office who, along with the Board of Trade, had been alive to the possibility of the plant's closure since the early 1960s, was keen to retain British Aluminium in the area, and reasoned that if BACo were unsuccessful at Invergordon it might call into question its entire Scottish operations not just in the Highlands but at Burntisland, Falkirk and Glasgow.[169] Moreover with support for Scottish home rule growing among business leaders and the labour movement – as well as the electoral successes of the SNP – retaining jobs like those at British Aluminium's Scottish works were critical to unionist politicians' defensive strategy. In addition, British Aluminium was able to draw on their long history in Scotland to shore up political and business support for their claim on Invergordon; Gus Margraf, BACo's MD, declaring in a piece in *The Scotsman* only the year before the smelter contracts were launched:

Scotland was the cradle of the aluminium industry ... British Aluminium's faith in Scotland and the future of the aluminium industry is exemplified by the 6½ million modernisation programme under way at the Falkirk rolling mills, and the recently completed extension of capacity at its Burntisland alumina plant ... For many years B.A. has been the largest industrial employer in the Highlands.[170]

Margraf perhaps also had his eye on Scottish business leaders' ambitions for greater devolution of decision-making over the economy, including creating new sectors and renewing existing ones. During the next decade in Scotland prestige jobs in manufacturing, like those offered by British Aluminium, would became all the more valuable in an economy that shed over 100,000 of them in the 1970s. In addition the urgency of re-affirming the commitment of BACo to Scotland, as a London-headquartered and English and US owned concern, was pressing in view of debates over the Scottish economy's increasing dependency on outside investment, and especially after the closure of Foyers.[171]

BACo had set up an internal working group led by Ronny Utiger to prepare proposals to government on a smelter development that had consulted Reynolds engineers on plant, as well sunk and running costs. In August BACo held discussions with the Central Electricity Generating Board (CEGB) and the Scottish electricity boards – the South of Scotland Electricity Board, and the NSHEB. Aware of the quickening 'scramble', Elton wrote to Davis again towards the end of August seeking the latter's views. Elton expressed his consternation at the confusion among government officials and power generators about the detail of any prospective scheme, declaring: 'It is difficult to be concise about the whole position of smelting in the U.K., as Government and Civil Servant views are still being formulated. I think it is now clear that the Government wishes to have aluminium smelting but that the means of achieving it are still muddled, particularly in relation to power.'[172] Significantly, in terms of the deal that BACo would sign in due course, Elton also outlined his opposition to any scheme requiring Alcan to make a capital contribution to a public power scheme, stating that:

I have argued, so far, that the method that they are proposing concerning a capital contribution really does not make sense, since it is moving against the trend of State-supplied power in different parts of the world for aluminium, quite aside from the needs of companies to concentrate their capital directly on aluminium operations. Furthermore, if a proportionate capital contribution were required, it would probably be preferable for the aluminium company to build its own power in an appropriate part of the world so that at the end of the amortization period he owned his asset.[173]

On this basis Elton suggested it might even be worth Alcan constructing its own oil or coal fired power station on site. Nevertheless Alcan submitted a proposal for a smelter at Invergordon supplied by nuclear power and a planning application in early November 1967.[174] Both Alcan and BACo had secured sites near Invergordon, at Inverbreakie and Ord farms. The day after Wilson's announcement at the 1967 Labour Party conference, it was Alcan (not BACo) who met with Scottish Office officials, the NSHEB and HIDB at St Andrew's House in Edinburgh to discuss their proposal.[175]

Further problems with the smelter programme ensued when discussions with the generating boards over power costs subsequently had to be recalculated and reconsidered after the devaluation of sterling later that month. In December, the government informed the aluminium companies that coal proposals would also be considered. Alcan submitted its revised nuclear proposals to government just before Christmas 1967.[176] However in January, after negotiating a more advantageous deal with the National Coal Board's (NCB) chairman, Lord Robens, Alcan submitted an alternative proposal for Invergordon, to be supplied by coal-fired power station, and then announced details of both to the press. In an interview with BBC Scotland Home Service in late January 1968 Elton defended Alcan's preference for the coal-fired option on the basis that 'the original North of Scotland Hydro-Electric Board proposal was not just nuclear versus coal, it included transmission charges, system reinforcement charges and cost of power pending the nuclear station coming in'. This was a message that BACo would have done well to listen to. The agreement between Alcan and the NCB embroiled them in a political furore between the government and the coal board, whose chairman (a former Labour minister) was becoming an increasingly vocal critic of ministerial energy policy and a particularly enthusiastic and ebullient champion of coal. Alcan also angered the SNP and the Scottish Area of the National Union of Mineworkers when it was revealed that the coal to be used at Invergordon would come not from the Scottish coalfields – which had been decimated in the preceding decade – but from the North East of England.[177] Alcan who had started off as the preferred choice of both the HIDB and with some considerable public support, was caught in the crossfire. The company had also done little to curry favour with the Scottish Office. Nevertheless by June 1968 Terry Hyland, Alcan's press secretary, reported to Elton that the Scottish National Party had collected 'a "vast number" of signed petitions … backed by approximately a quarter of a million people throughout the Invergordon area to demand a reversal of the government's decision to 'send Alcan to the North East Coast' [a reference to their planned smelter at Lynemouth in Northumberland, England] and allow Alcan to continue with their original plan at Invergordon'. Hyland responded to the SNP informing them that the decision was irreversible, and consoling him with the news that the BACo plant would provide jobs in the area. Alcan was being more than a little disinguous as it preferred the coal option, and had managed to negotiate this with the UK government on the basis of a deal centred around repayments against wartime loans advanced to the company that were due.[178]

Concurrently British Aluminium launched a concerted local, regional and national publicity campaign from St James' House and its caravan on the Inverbreakie farm site: with the press taken on visit around BACo's sites at Kinlochleven, Lochaber and Falkirk; delegations of senior executives visiting the HIDB, Cromarty County Council, and Invergordon Burgh Council; and the various presentations given and leaflets distributed to the local community. This was unsurprising given that Alcan's claim on Invergordon posed a real challenge to BACo which saw Scotland as its territory, with the core of its upstream and downstream UK operations there. As chair of the working group charged with overseeing the project it is perhaps his sense of achievement from this aspect that led Utiger to claim that Alcan was incensed that BACo received government assent to construct Invergordon. His claims would appear unfounded given that building at Lynemouth, with an on-site power station connected by conveyors to the supplying collieries – rather than incurring the cost of coal transported by ship to the north of Scotland, or having electricity supplied via the Grid from a far greater distance – meant that Alcan received the deal they had long preferred. In addition Alcan was becoming frustrated with the pace of progress being held up by the disagreements between the HIDB and the Scottish Office.[179]

Unsurprisingly – given government recognition of their other substantial Scottish interests and the inter-connectedness of those interests – British Aluminium was awarded its preferred site of Invergordon. Invergordon had been selected because of the proximity to the company's other Highland plants. This was important in so far as they were familiar with working with local agencies, politicians, and workforces. Also, some of the key materials for constructing and maintaining the smelter were to be produced at their Lochaber works. Reynolds had already agreed with British Aluminium that if the smelter bid were successful they would buy BACo's share of CBA (having already purchased a 36 per cent in the company), providing the former with the capital for the project. The other consortium Anglesey Aluminium Metals Ltd (AAM) – involving RTZ, alongside British Insulated Callender's Cables (BICC) and James Booth (in whom Alcan had a share, and were eventually replaced by US producer Kaiser) – got their selected site at Anglesey. The BACo and RTZ proposals submitted that the impact on balance of payments would save the Government an estimated £45.5 million p.a. The contracts for these were however negotiated separately.[180]

Initially the British government had proposed, in agreement with the aluminium producers, that the smelters be designed to produce 120,000 mts per annum. However the British government was faced with an outcry from the Canadian and Norwegian governments, on behalf of their producers about the impact on their exports. Crucially the Norwegian government also questioned whether these contracts and subsidies broke with European Free Trade agreements. Without consulting the companies affected, the UK government announced that the smelters would now be limited to a capacity of 100,000 mts per annum. This initial setback affected the producers' economies of scale from these smelters, pushing up the costs by some 2.5 per cent. The government also had to make it appear as though the companies were not receiving any subsidy. British Aluminium's power contract was further complicated by the fact that it had to negotiate with two power boards: NSHEB, who were to provide electricity in the intervening period before Hunterston B AGR station came on stream, and South of Scotland Electricity Board (SSEB) who were to operate the AGR station. In addition, it had to deal with both Whitehall departments and the Scottish Office. AAM in contrast only had to negotiate with the CEGB and Whitehall. Moreover the CEGB was not constrained by the same 'social clause' that NSHEB was. With British Aluminium's power costs for the west Highlands standing at 40 per cent of the total cost of aluminium ingot production, the detail of the power contract was absolutely critical. In the end the Company agreed on a price of 5 per cent over their preferred cost (0.263p/kWh as opposed to 0.25), and over double the unit costs of their main competitors, the Norwegians and Canadians. As the key minister involved in discussions acknowledged, the only way for the electricity contract to be competitive with Norwegian hydro-electricity was with a 40 per cent government investment grant. The detail of the agreement was that British Aluminium make a capital contribution to the construction of the Hunterston B AGR station of £30m (advanced to them in the form of a government loan). Further that they would contribute proportionately to the costs of a coal-fired power station run by NSHEB or SSEB until 31 March 1974, after which time the same terms would apply to Hunterston B, and that the annual costs from each (in terms of interest charges and capital repayments) be spread over the 28 years of the contract. BACo was also committed to paying the additional costs for increasing power from coal-fired power stations before the aforementioned date, and then the AGR after that date. The company and the generating boards further agreed to have charges fixed on the basis of actual operating costs by March 1973. In addition NSHEB required that a further £1.5m be provided in case of the escalation of electricity prices.[181] In contrast AAM's negotiations with CEGB and the government were simpler, although it was required to contribute £33m to the construction of an AGR station. Moreover its size and relative proximity to large generating centres also meant that it was better able to meet the smelter's supply demands, while the amount being supplied to the Anglesey smelter were relatively small.

In July 1968 British Aluminium reluctantly agreed to all the provisions. Despite lobbying for a contractual clause to protect them, BACo received no commitment against incurring extra costs in the event of delays. This assurance was only made in a gentleman's agreement between Strath and the President of the Board of Trade, Edmund Dell, who inserted a 'fair clause' in a letter to the former confirming that the government would instigate a review of proceedings in the event that the project was delayed and they were incurring additional costs. Strath accepted this.

Concurrently Conservative MPs were questioning the viability of the contracts on the basis of free trade, the eventuality of what would happen if prices rose, and whether the import savings were worth the public investment. Within two years the government saw a marked improvement to the balance of payments, the chief reason for its worryingly hurried approach to the negotiations. Even accepting British Aluminium's weak position and 'their enthusiasm for new technology', the acceptance by both the BACo and TI chairs of the terms of the electricity contract and Dell's extra-contractual assurances suggests that the extant relationship between Plowden and Strath, and the other players played a significant role in persuading them to accept the terms offered by NSHEB and the government. Added to this, former TI executive Fred Catherwood was the Chief Industrial Adviser to the Wilson government within the Department of Economic Affairs, charged with taking forward the government's National Plan for economic growth.[182] These personal contacts and assurances also explain why Plowden and Strath were willing to accept the clause in the contracts with government, making British Aluminium liable for the rise in capital costs (with Hunterston B running over its projected deadline) and 'derating' (lowering the original output specifications of the station, resulting in a higher unit cost for the electricity for the consumer) of the reactor. This added expense to BACo, that AAM was not required to shoulder in their contract with the CEGB, was bound up in the exercise of NSHEB's 'social clause'.[183]

That something was awry with BACo's agreements was acknowledged by officials by the early 1970s; A Treasury memo to Edmund Dell (by then Paymaster General) in December 1974 conceded that: 'Very provisionally the indications are that the BACO claim that they are receiving much less favourable treatment than Anglesey Aluminium is justified.' Dell had by this time assured Plowden that 'the Government were looking sympathetically at BACo's claim in relation to the derating of Hunterston'.[184] Negotiations were not aided by the 'incredibly complicated arrangements' surrounding Invergordon, as one Treasury official described to them in May 1973. The situation was made all the more difficult by the NSHEB's lack of sympathy, at this stage, for British Aluminium's concerns about the escalating costs of the construction of Hunterston B and electricity costs, commenting dismissively:

BACo are well aware that the price of fuel is outwith the control of the Electricity Boards and that any forecasts could be no more than speculative. Similarly, the effect of inflation and design changes on Hunterston 'B' could hardly have been anticipated. No doubt the BACo took the best possible advice from all sources before opting for a 100% nuclear supply tranche from 1974/75 onwards.[185]

The smelter contracts had become a morass for all concerned. Tellingly in a report to Parliament the year previously, 1972, the DTI declared: 'the criteria applied in judging the cost to Her Majesty's Government of generating foreign currency have been more stringent than with the computer industry or the aluminium smelters.'[186] By July 1973 officials within the DTI accepted that: 'In practice, the smelter contracts have worked to the disadvantage of all parties, largely because of the slippage in the nuclear power programme, which has raised the Boards' costs and charges and slowed the flow of plutonium.'[187] By this time, as well as claims being lodged by BACo, and the NSHEB and Scottish Office (on NSHEB's behalf), the CEGB was making discontented noises, and Alcan was attempting to secure a regional development grant (unlike BACo and AAM, Alcan had not been beneficiaries of a grant because they chose to negotiate a private generation deal with the National Coal Board).[188] The matter was further complicated by the politics between the government and the generating boards, and over negotiations between the former and the chemical industry, which had been lobbying for special electricity rates for large industrial consumers. In addition, there were also divisions of interest within government between the various departments involved.[189] Eight days after the DTI review of BACo's case, they concluded in a letter to their Treasury counterparts that:

> We have reached the conclusion that BACo have established a valid case for a revision of the arrangements. We are clear that the Government cannot refuse to respond to the situation. We are satisfied that the amount, form and means by which assistance is given will be matters for complicated negotiation and take a considerable time to determine.[190]

In the meantime they urged that assurances be given to the company. The delay also arose because the ministers of Edward Heath's government (June 1970–March 1974) had no wish to sully their hands with what they saw as the errors of their predecessor, and chose instead to defer the matter.[191]

In February 1974 Labour was returned to office with a slim majority, committed to a programme of renewed change in industry, planning agreements with industry in the national interest, improving the balance-of-trade, and a commitment to regional planning. The growing dissatisfaction over the power contracts would not sit comfortably with the proposals set out in their White Paper *The Regeneration of British Industry* (subsequently included in the Industry Act 1975), or the assurances given in the manifesto for the general election of October 1974, *Britain Will Win With Labour*, especially with an disgruntled electorate more than a little disillusioned with political rhetoric. Thus when BACo, NSHEB, and the Scottish Office (on NSHEB's behalf) approached the new Minister for Industry, Tony Benn, and Dell invoking the clause in the latter's letter, Dell was keen to resolve the matter, with the least political fallout possible. Willie Ross, re-appointed as Secretary of State for Scotland, immediately took up NSHEB's corner, advocating that 'the Government must accept responsibility for the deficit accruing to the NSHEB ...'[192] It is clear from correspondence between Dell and Tony Benn at the end of April that Dell was attempting to extricate himself from assurances given to BACo and pressure them into accepting the electricity at full economic cost (followed to its logical conclusion would have forced the closure of Invergordon in the mid-1970s). It became abundantly clear that Dell had little understanding of the economics of aluminium production.[193] By mid-December 1974, agreement had been reached between Tony Benn, Eric Varley (the Secretary of State for Energy), and Peter Shore (the Secretary of State for Trade) to follow Dell's suggested plan to extend a loan to BACo for the additional capital costs for Hunterston B, to cover NSHEB's deficit in the smelter account and relieve BACo of charges arising from de-rating of the reactor. Dell suggested that this be channelled through NSHEB and the smelter account, set up initially to distinguish between BACo and its other customers. This approach met with Shore's particular approval as it avoided the threat of the UK government being questioned by the Norwegians and Canadians under the General Agreements on Tariffs and Trade (GATT) as 'unjustifiable subsidy', although Varley was concerned that this did not give extra ammunition to CEGB to make a claim over Anglesey.[194] The one major objection came from Willie Ross. Ross was content to agree to the extension of the loan to BACo and to the proposal that the company be relieved of the effects of derating, but was opposed to the relief being channelled through NSHEB. The Treasury and Departments of Trade and of Industry were not keen on having to fund the deficit through the other route available to them, a grant under the Industry Act, both because of technical difficulties in doing this and the potential political embarrassment. Fortunately for Dell and the government, officials from the Scottish Economic Planning Department proposed that SEPD write to the NSHEB proposing that they (NSHEB) cover interest relief and capital payments to British Aluminium in advance of the government loan to the company. As one Department of Industry official admitted privately: 'We are grateful for and support this suggestion, which would extract the Government from a potentially very embarrassing situation.'[195] In the meantime Benn's officials had informed a relieved Lord Plowden. By April 1975, the Scottish Office had confirmed that both the NSHEB and Willie Ross were content with the suggestion, with one important proviso, that British Aluminium relinquish its right (as set out in the gentleman's agreement), to increased electricity 'on the same principles', if they sought to expand production. On this point NSHEB and SEPD were immovable.[196] The Treasury's opinion was equally firm. In a briefing note for Dell's meeting with Plowden to discuss the government assistance, they declared:

The Government have gone a long way in providing additional assistance to BACO. What we are prepared to say ought to reassure their auditors about the contingent liability they would otherwise face. They for their part should, and we believe do, appreciate that in return the Government cannot be expected to meet further bills if the smelters capacity is expanded. Since there is no intention to give additional subsidies to NSHEB to reimburse them for supplying any additional power to BACO the question whether a special rate should apply will be for NSHEB to decide, and the Paymaster General may wish to make this point.[197]

Plowden was understandably unwilling to accept this and lobbied for the clause to be retained in some form allowing for equal negotiations. This was once again refused by the Scottish Office who suggested the following form of words (clearly favourable to NSHEB but not to BACo): 'It is not intended to preclude the negotiation within the framework of the electricity statutes of special terms for the supply of power which are commercially acceptable to NSHEB.'[198] In view of the fact that BACo had been forced to limit the size of the smelter initially in order that the government could avoid any challenge under EFTA regulations, this felt like an added injustice. Moreover the £7 million loan granted to BACo came with an interest rate of 14½ per cent (more than double the original loan rate of 7 per cent, and 45 per cent above the minimum lending rate of the Bank of England at the time).[199] Subsequently Parliament approved, under the Electricity (Financial Provisions) (Scotland) Act 1976, two payments to NSHEB totalling £170 million by March 1977. Hunterston B's cheap power never materialised. British Aluminium was left paying nearly five times the original estimated unit cost for their power. By 1981–82, they posted losses of around £19 million, and were embroiled in legal action with NSHEB over disputed power charges.[200]

Margaret Thatcher's Conservative government came to power in May 1979, and pledged to sort out Britain's 'lame duck' industries. Among neo-liberal economists, criticisms of the AGR programme had been gathering momentum throughout the 1970s. This culminated in the publication in 1977 of 'a devastating cost-benefit analysis of Concorde and the AGR' by a former economist at the Ministry of Aviation, as well as 'a scathing study of the AGR programme, and of British nuclear policy more generally' (including 'its poor nuclear technology') by the right-wing Institute of Economic Affairs in 1978.[201] Core to the new Conservative government's economic thinking was that both the supply of money and public sector borrowing requirements needed to be reduced. It should be pointed out though that contrary to assumptions made about the administration, economic policy in these early years of the Thatcher administration was decided by a small cabal of ministers, most of whom with the exception of the new Financial Secretary to the Treasury, Nigel Lawson, had 'little economic knowledge' but many politically motivated, predetermined ideas.[202] In spite of their pledges on 'lame duck' industries, the Conservatives pursued an essentially pragmatic approach in Scotland, especially before the 1983 election. Moreover, 'in his Scottish fiefdom', Thatcher's first Secretary of State for Scotland, George Younger, 'made no pretences to Thatcherite rigour and portrayed himself as a supporter of interventionist old-style Keynesianism'.[203] That said the claims of 'many "lame ducks"' owing their survival to Younger, expounded in the pages of that bastion of the New Right, the *Daily Telegraph*, clearly had not surveyed the Scottish industrial landscape of the early 1980s.

With losses of £2 million/month by 1981, British Aluminium was forced to approach the Government with the options they had on the table, which SEPD was charged with investigating. On the basis of initial investigations, George Younger argued that it would be cheaper to keep the smelter open. He was aware of the more favourable conditions enjoyed by AAM under their contract with CEGB (which was not public knowledge), and was keen to retain the jobs especially in a political environment in Scotland in which the Conservatives were haemorrhaging support. Even Margaret Thatcher – who 'failed to appreciate or failed to accept the need for a distinct Scottish dimension' [204] – 'was extremely concerned at the possible closure of the smelter, with its financial and other implications'. She duly instructed officials to use terms of reference that would allow the administration to publicly justify continued financial support to BACo:

> Her off-the-cuff view, however, was that the £20m gap between the closure and the continuation of the smelter was too big and that it would be easier to make a case for continuation of the smelter if the gap could be narrowed. She suggested that it might be possible to do this by taking more account of the consequential effects of closure on local communities, local businesses etc.[205]

This suggests a strategy of political pragmatism on her part, which was primarily determined by timing, rather than concerns over job losses, despite the assertion that they 'did not aim deliberately to create mass unemployment (they believed such mass unemployment to be politically fatal)'.[206] As the subsequent BACo–Alcan merger illustrates – and the impact of the government's policies towards the public sector revealed – sections of the administration were impassive in the face of large numbers of job losses. Taking place as this decision did in Thatcher's first adminis-tration – before the Falklands War and second electoral success in the 1983 – the Conservatives were cautiously testing the limits of their policies. Moreover in the early years of the administration, it remained predominantly a 'non-monetarist Cabinet' including many senior Conservatives who 'remained entirely unconvinced about the direction of government policy'. And while Thatcher apparently remained ebullient, she was by early 1982 the most unpopular British Prime Minister since polling began, with murmurs in the party about replacing her.[207] Equally, as over the precarious future of the British Steel Corporation's Scottish strip mill at Ravenscraig, Thatcher was aware of the uneasiness of senior Scottish Conservatives, including George Younger (who threatened to resign over the proposed closure of Ravenscraig in the 1980s), over large-scale closures of Scotland's manufacturing base.[208] This view of a more selective, and politically pragmatic, approach to industrial policy under the Thatcher administrations was also illustrated by the Prime Minister's later insistence on protecting collieries dominated by the Union of Democratic Mineworkers (irrespective of their viability under the new criteria applied to the coal industry) who had supported the government against the National Union of Mineworkers in the 1984–85 miners' strike.[209]

Simultaneously the then HIDB Chairman Rear Admiral Dunbar-Naismith was also lobbying George Younger to invoke the NSHEB's economic clause.[210] However it was Younger's own officials who were most convinced that 'arguments against any concession to BACo are very strong and it would be extremely difficult for the Secretary of State to convince other Ministers that further assistance was justified'. In this scenario they also felt that the continued operation of Alcan's Lynemouth smelter would be 'indefensible' if propped up by 'an unrealistic price for its coal supplies at the taxpayer's expense' from the NCB, and 'embarrassing' if the Anglesey smelter survived 'with continuing heavy losses for the CEGB'.[211] The Chief Economist to SEPD, Dr Gavin McCrone, tasked with evaluating the options found himself unable to recommend support for Invergordon:

> I am bound to point out that although we have done the best we can with the paper I do not find its arguments all that convincing myself. I fully recognise the scale of the tragedy which will be brought about by the closure of Invergordon but the size of annual subsidy required in relation to the jobs provided is quite disproportionate. £20m a year to subsidise electricity supply for this project would be equivalent to the whole of the budget of the HIDB and it would be likely to be a continuing subsidy beyond the 4 years shown in the table unless the trends in electricity prices turn out to be very favourable.[212]

When British Aluminium ventured to the Department of Industry that the closure of Invergordon would force them to close a number of other operations, including Falkirk (with the potential loss of over 1,000 jobs), one of McCrone's colleagues in a minute to the Minister declared: 'there may be an element of bluff in this claim and even if there is not, £30m is a large sum to spend to safeguard 1,000 jobs at Falkirk and an unspecified number, probably not exceeding 2,000, elsewhere in the Company.'[213]

Refused further support, British Aluminium was left with little choice but to close Invergordon to protect the rest of the group.[214] BACo gave assurances under their deal with government that they would keep the plant in a serviceable state while attempts were made to find another buyer. Ironically the government's proposal was for power to be provided to the smelter by the Scottish electricity boards, with a five-year power subsidy in the form of a direct grant through the HIDB. In declining the offer, the newly merged British Alcan outlined the cost of such a deal, which would see the unit cost of electricity rising to around 45 mills (double those of their Lynemouth smelter, and over treble that for Canadian and Norwegian works) and require a subsidy of £30 million.²¹⁵ Concurrently British Alcan had been lobbying Ministers about the future of Lynemouth. Despite a clause in the original contract with Alcan allowing them to raise prices, with an increase in the price of coal and a government scheme offering a 25 per cent discount to industrial customers of switching from oil- or gas-fired to coal plant, the NCB was keen to renegotiate. George Russell and John Peyton, British Alcan's MD and chairman, wrote to Ministers indicating their serious consideration of closing the plant if the power costs rose substantially. They further pointed out that if Lynemouth were to close the NCB would struggle to find a customer for the 9 per cent of the total output of the Northumberland and Durham coalfields that the smelter consumed. The response that Peyton elicited from the then Secretary of State for Industry, Patrick Jenkin, was less sympathetic than that struck in relation to Invergordon. It also left British Alcan in little doubt as to the change in government attitudes to long-term viability of the UK aluminium industry, and large-scale industrial producers in general:

> You posed the question of the extent to which the Government regards the existence of an aluminium industry in this country as desirable or necessary … In the main this will be determined not by Government but by market forces … The Government feels under no obligation and sees no necessity to maintain primary aluminium smelting capacity regardless of economic realities … There is undeniably a question mark over the viability of the primary smelters at present, but I would not go so far as to assert that there is no prospect of viability in the future.²¹⁶

Both Jenkin and Nigel Lawson, at the time Minister for Energy, felt that British Alcan was attempting to call their bluff, with the latter rejecting Russell's claim that the NCB would be unable to export the unused coal from the smelter. Jenkin also rebutted Peyton and Russell's claims that Alcan's downstream activities would become 'commercially unattractive' if its upstream activities had to be closed, using British Aluminium as an example of a 'long-established' company convinced that 'their position will be strengthened now that the group has become a net buyer of the metal'.²¹⁷ Aside from the negotiations being played out, it further reveals the selective nature of the policy, notably given that the seat covering Invergordon at the time had been occupied by a serving Conservative minister, Hamish Gray, whereas Lynemouth sat in solid Labour heartlands.²¹⁸ Fortunately for Alcan's Lynemouth employees, the 3500 miners employed at the NCB's Ellington and Lynemouth collieries that supplied the smelter, and the local communities, the Northumberland works did not go the way of Invergordon.

Aside from the impact on unemployment in the Invergordon area – which leapt from 10 per cent in 1971 to nearly 20 per cent in 1982 – the HIDB had to be subsidised to pay £10 million into the local economy between 1981 and 1984. It also cost Hamish Gray the constituency of Ross, Cromarty and Skye, with it being taken by Social Democratic Party candidate Charles Kennedy. Afterwards, the serving HIDB Chairman Rear Admiral David Dunbar-Naismith, in an article to *The Times*, posed the question that he had privately asked of George Younger in September 1981, namely what had happened to the NSHEB's obligations under its original ordinances to develop the local economy and support industry. Privately, in a memo to George Younger, Dunbar-Naismith declared that the closure had been 'extremely destructive to the strategy of the Highlands and Islands Development Board, which has been laboriously built up over 15 years'.[219] After the collapse of attempts to revive Invergordon in 1982, further discussions were held between generators and British Alcan in 1984 and the late 1980s to re-open the smelter but both foundered over the price of power.[220] Ultimately the withdrawal of the lifeline of public finance for the smelter hinged on the advice of Scottish Office officials, particularly Gavin McCrone.[221]

The failure of Invergordon was symptomatic of British Aluminium's historical proximity to government, and the cultural dependency nurtured within the company. Added to this was the very significant part played by key personalities, such as Plowden and Strath. Their acceptance of Ministerial assurances, and the tendency to approach negotiations with government as insiders, undermined BACo's bargaining position from the outset. As Lord Armstrong, the one-time Cabinet secretary, observed of Plowden in his obituary in February 2001: 'He consciously set himself to diminish mistrust, and to bridge and narrow the divide, between the private sector and the world of public service.'[222] Both Plowden and Strath were aware of the shortcomings of Britain's civil nuclear programme but nevertheless, albeit after lengthy discussions, conceded to the government's demands. Perversely Dell declared in his last book (published posthumously in 2000) that Plowden 'had always thought the idea of aluminium smelting in Britain was absurd', and, 'he took some pleasure in emphasizing that his past experience with the AEA justified his doubts about all its calculations'.[223] Admittedly British Aluminium was not in such a favourable market position as either RTZ or Alcan, but it was the company's close relationship to, and faith in government that provided a weakness in negotiations that should have been in its favour. Neither RTZ nor Alcan was burdened by this legacy. In particular, the contract signed by Alcan with the NCB reflected their independence of outlook, unhindered by proximity to the state.[224] In establishing the original agreement, the Wilson government acted partly out of what they saw as being the best national interests, and in part because it fitted with their political mantle. The hastiness with which the contracts were drawn up was characteristic of the speed at which political imperatives move and change. Indeed this was the legacy of ill-conceived technological policies – that of the shortcomings of the UK nuclear power programmes – conceived under successive Conservative and Labour administrations. Niall MacKenzie is undoubtedly right, in his detailed study of the smelter contracts, to state that without Dell's intervention in 1974, 'the company would have been left to deal with the problems it was facing alone'. However his suggestion that 'Sir Edmund was proving a good friend to the project' is questionable.[225] As negotiations over the costs of escalation displayed Dell was initially keen to explore whether he could extricate himself from his commitments, and was then primarily (and understandably) concerned with limiting the potential for political damage. Increasingly he sought to distance himself from the decisions taken over the smelter contract as another of the 'technological extravagances of the Wilson government'. Dell also blamed the administration's tendency to accept the word of businessmen on the Industrial Reorganisation Corporation as being at the root of the failure of the smelter contracts (for it was they who had decided on the viability of the projects).[226] Seen alongside the collapse of other post-war industrial schemes in Scotland, such as the Rothes Colliery in Fife and Glenochil Mine at Clackmannan, Ravenscraig strip mill, the Rootes car plant, the British Motor Corporation at Bathgate, the Wiggins Teape Pulp and Paper Mill at Corpach (all admittedly with different origins), Invergordon was symptomatic of the shortcomings of British economic planning, suffering as it did from the very 'lack of concerted actions, cooperation and consultation that planning was designed to attack'.[227] It also reflected planners' oversight of the prescriptions of the Toothill report for the Scottish economy. Weaknesses in post-war British industrial policy and economic planning stemmed from the lack of consensus among the parties involved and inadequate state machinery, leading to the 'final tragedy of planning' in ushering in 'a Thatcherite reaction that rejected not only planning, but the idea of state intervention itself'.[228] As it happened Conservative ministers, including the 'Iron Lady', showed themselves to be more hesitant about allowing the closure of Invergordon, as part of a pragmatic strategy in the early years of the administration.[229] It was their officials who proved to be more forthright in that respect. In fact the advice of leading officials like Gavin McCrone was of considerably more import than they have hitherto been given credit for.[230] Yet all of this should not detract from the very real weaknesses inherent in the type of relationship between British Aluminium and government Ministers and officials. It would appear that instead of strengthening their position, it made key personalities within the company more vulnerable in their negotiations with government. They failed to accept the disjuncture between the far more short-term political aims and gains required by the politicians concerned, and the long-term requirements of their industry. While the agility of John Elton's AUK was evident from their subsequent negotiations, claims of foresight in recognising the limitations of the nuclear option and resorting to coal are not born out by the historical evidence; it was Alcan's good fortune, rather than their planning and resolve, that they were not shouldered with the burden of Invergordon. However, it is questionable whether AUK would have settled for BACo's 'gentleman's agreement'.[231]

National or international concern?

With British Aluminium's merger with Alcan – who, as a multinational company with UK operations, had more of an arms-length relationship with the British government – contact with departments of state was managed generally in far more formal terms. However, Alcan's chairman John Peyton – a former government minister (including at the Ministry of Power), Conservative MP and then Peer – enjoyed a closer relationship with some ministers, which was in use, for example, in land valuations for Lochaber. Moreover, Alcan Inc was a sophisticated and experienced political player in North America. On the whole, Alcan preferred engagement with policy networks through industry and employer bodies. Thus in preparing the merger in 1982, it was decided that British Aluminium as the UK company would approach government first and that for reasons of presentation the company be called British Alcan and include directors from both boards.[232]

In the event Margaret Thatcher's administration took a very different view of the merger than Edward Heath's government had in the early 1970s. TI's proposal in the early 1970s, that Reynolds take a greater share in BACo, had provoked considerable alarm in some quarters of government. Despite DTI and Treasury support for the move, Secretary of State for Trade and Industry John Davies acknowledged that: 'Parliamentary and public opinion has shown some sensitivity about multi-national companies, their ownership and their behaviour, and memories of the immense battle over British Aluminium in the late 1950s are by no means forgotten.'[233] Similarly a year later, despite AUK's cautious handling of proposals for a takeover of BACo with Whitehall – from whom they were seeking support for a move that would be referred to the Monopolies and Mergers Commission (MMC) – the government was understandably cautious about a deal that have given Alcan a major share of all the market with job losses estimated at 2000.[234] In a well-judged memo to the DTI, Alcan set out its rationale for the merger:

> In recent years the industry, while still young and growing, has been suffering from over-capacity, low returns, and areas of ageing plant and inadequate productivity. These trends, if left unchecked, could eventually lead to an essential industry requiring to be subsidised or nationalised. Rationalisation and reorganisation within the private sector could provide the answer to these problems.[235]

The memo also played on the traditional aversion of Conservative governments to nationalisation, as well as on their political vulnerability in the aftermath of the Cabinet's climb down over the future of the Upper Clydeside Shipbuilders (UCS), in which the Heath government had been forced to continue subsidy to UCS in the face of mass protests and a work-in.[236] In addition, by 1973 the tide had turned significantly against mergers, both with the aftershock of the oil crisis of that year (with its impact on manufacturing) and changes to the regulatory system with the enactment of The Fair Trading Act 1973 and the establishment of the Office of Fair Trading. From 1974 onwards there was an upsurge in the number of mergers referred to the MMC, and an increase in the numbers of mergers that were ruled against because of a perceived threat to competition and consumer interests.[237] In contrast by 1981, as negotiations over government subventions for the expansion of British Alcan's capacity reveal, the company represented a possible *cause célèbre* for the Thatcher administration as DTI official John Allen observed:

> The Department was strongly in favour of the Alcan/ BACo merger as the means of strengthening the UK aluminium industry against competition primarily from Europe. The merger was carried out without assistance, and it would seem unfortunate if BAA's [British Alcan] progress towards further improvements in competitiveness was delayed now by its inability to build on the benefits of rationalisation. There appears to be all the elements in terms of additionality, viability, and benefits to the UK, to justify assistance to the UK to justify assistance to maintain the BAA momentum.[238]

As far as the DTI was concerned, British Alcan represented just the sort of industrial role model that ministers were keen to see being emulated across British industry. Ironically for those at the sharp end of the redundancies across the UK (particularly those at Invergordon) given the recent closures, British Alcan was already in discussions with DTI over government finance to support modernisation of some of its key assets, most of it for Lynemouth and Rogerstone, through Regional Development Grants and industrial finance initiatives. Government support for the amalgamated company was visible from the accommodating approach adopted by DTI in discussions with British Alcan, although the Scottish Office remained far more cautious and doubtful.[239]

The survival of the merged concern can have been of little consolation to the 3,600 employees of both companies who had already lost their jobs: some 2907 between December 1982 and the end of 1983, with the rest over the next year. This, against the backdrop of long-term unemployment figures in the UK that had risen to levels not seen since the 1930s. In Scotland, the loss of most of the Falkirk workforce, leaving a small number to continue the plants' lucrative aircraft sheet (and other speciality products) business for customers like British Aerospace and Airbus, was met with outright anger. In the House of Commons, and speaking for all the areas affected by the closures, Harry Ewing, the Labour MP for Stirling, Falkirk and Grangemouth, declared that: 'the Government – through the Secretary of State for Scotland – have been deeply involved in all the events leading to this industrial and human disaster [Falkirk and Invergordon].' The indignation arising mounted with this coming so soon after the closure of Invergordon, with Scottish unemployment standing at a fifty-year high, and at a time when primary and manufacturing industries were experiencing what one Scottish social historian has called an economic 'holocaust', and with foreign direct investors particularly singled out for criticism. Similarly other closures at Latchford Locks and Skelmersdale in the north-west of England, and Redditch in the West Midlands, would have been particularly hard-felt with unemployment in both areas either more than or almost doubling the national average between the mid-1970s and mid-1980s.[240]

British Alcan continued to have close links with government establishments through the defence industry, notably continuing work on lightweight armoured vehicles and aircraft. Even after the controversy over the use of aluminium alloy in the superstructure of the Royal Navy's Type 21 frigates – and the metal's apparent failure to withstand intense heats after the warships *HMS Ardent* and *Antelope* received direct hits and were sunk during the Falklands War in 1982 – the government argued for the continued use of aluminium in naval construction, although all remaining Type 21s were sold by the Royal Navy in the early 1990s. The continued importance of the defence sector, as well as public confidence in their products, prompted the industry to deploy its formidable public relations machine, and lobby ministers to refute the claims of detractors in the aftermath of the furore. Despite the ongoing controversy over this issue, the industry's rebutting of assertions linking the sinking of the Type 42 destroyers *HMS Sheffield* and *Conventry* (both steel structure ships) to aluminium, was justified. In the last two decades of the twentieth century Alcan continued to collaborate with the Royal Aircraft (later Aerospace) Establishment on the development of aluminium-lithium alloys for greater strength in aircraft construction, the European Armaments' Agencies' new European armoured utility vehicle, and the Ministry of Defence's EH101 helicopter programme. The industry was to be mired in one last whiff of controversy towards the end of the century when Alcan's armoured plate division was caught up in the Arms to Iraq affair in the mid-1990s.[241]

After the collapse of a number of government-sponsored large industrial-scale development in the Highlands, as well as the bursting of the North Sea bubble (with the loss of an estimated 30,000 valuable support jobs in that industry), the continued presence of operations such as the Lochaber and Kinlochleven smelters once again assumed significance as one of only a clutch of major employers in the region. The HIDB was unfairly attributed with much of the blame for the failure of some schemes not of their making. In the Lochaber area, with the closure of the Wiggins and Teape pulp and paper mill (an initiative under the DoI Act), and Yvette Cosmetics (attracted by HIDB), and the contraction of both the Lochaber and Kinlochleven smelters in the early 1980s, retaining the remaining prestige jobs at Lochaber gained added impetus, especially with the marginal slowdown and decline in population between the 1980s and the turn of the century. The direct and indirect contribution of the remaining Lochaber smelter to the local economy and labour market is still highly significant.[242] It was the continued significance culturally to the company of these sites, and their political symbolism, that prompted a more measured timetable for closing the Kinlochleven works. In contrast, Alcan faced considerable public criticism over the closure of its plants at Burntisland, Falkirk and Glasgow, with the loss of 655 jobs, between 2001 and 2004.[243]

Conclusion

Alcan MD John Elton's observation of apparent opaqueness among policymakers as to the future aluminium industry in the UK lies at the heart of business-government relations. It represents the competing and, at times, converging priorities of businesses with those of the state and the complexities of business-government relations. This was all the more acute in the case of aluminium, as soon as it became a raw material vital first for national defence and subsequently for civil and currency exchange purposes. It was a double edged sword: for without doubt the support of the state for the native industry sustained it early on, while at the same time constraining and at times undermining it. Periodically British Aluminium wrapped itself in the Union Jack sitting at the feet of the warlike Britannia. At others it harked to its role as the benefactor of the Highlands. In British Aluminium's case this relationship reached into the heart of the organisation helping to nurture the culture of the 'service' – perpetuated for much of its history by the company's choice of retired senior military personnel and civil servants; as well as its part in the infrastructure of Britain's *Warfare State* – rather than that primarily of a business. This bred a familiarity with government procedure that acclimatised it to the way of transacting with departments and officials, but also had the effect of making it less cautious than it should have been in these dealings and 'locked' it in to a marriage of convenience of sorts. This bred a strategic 'path dependence' within the company to devastating effect. The examples of the Volta River project and Invergordon, as well as the battle for British Aluminium, illustrate the follies of such myopia and the persistent trust in their enjoyment of a special relationship with government. It was one in which the company's presentation of its role in the Highlands and as a 'key' industry of national importance were central motifs in their negotiations. As aluminium was of increasing strategic importance to Britain both militarily but also financially, so British Aluminium became a significant employer in Scotland and of particular importance (especially in advance of government measures) in the Highlands as an example of the potential of economic diversification for the region and of hydro-electric power. Ultimately the story of British Aluminium offers a cautionary tale about business interaction with government, and the profound effects that this can have on the culture of the firm. In contrast, Alcan as a concern unfettered by these ties was able to operate with considerably more autonomy, although like all businesses having to negotiate the social and political environment in which it operated.

3

Manufacturing Consent:
From BACo's 'Service' to Alcan's
'good corporate citizens'[1]

Rath le rian is neart nan dul.[2]
(Prosperity with good order by the strength of the elements.)
Inscription on first commemorative coin cast
at British Aluminium's Lochaber reduction works, 1929.

I N   A   P R I V A T E   L E T T E R to Alexander Fraser, a foreman at British Aluminium's Kinlochleven smelter, to thank him as one of the signatories and contributors to the book presented (along with a piano) by BACo employees to him on completion of 25 years' service with the company in February 1920, William Murray Morrison declared:

> I am deeply touched by the affectionate appreciation extended to me by my fellow workers, many of whom have long and honourable records in the Same Service. To have been so closely identified with a great British Industry, to have struggled through its pioneer stages and to have seen it grow to be a vital 'Key' Industry in the country is a record I am exceedingly proud of. Without the loyal co-operation of everyone employed by the Company its advancement to the position it now occupies would not have been possible. Community of interest has been an outstanding feature in our organisation and no man could have had more whole hearted help and support than it has been my good fortune to experience. The relationship that has existed between my colleagues and myself has always been of the most friendly nature which has made our work together a very real pleasure to me … I desire to express my pleasure in having your signature along with that of so many other friends and to assure you of my heartfelt thanks for your participation in this most kindly recognition of the work of a quarter of a century.[3]

Morrison figured alongside his former teacher, Lord Kelvin, in British Aluminium's corporate literature as a figure of heroic stature and the epitome of BACo's company values; the 'Father of the Company', as his posthumous appreciation in the British Aluminium organ *The B.A. News* crowned him.[4] Though not a founder of the company, Morrison was a potent *pater familias*, replicated in the relationship between British Aluminium and its employees until after the RTIA takeover of 1959.

Morrison was born into an affluent middle-class family in Inverness in 1873, and studied natural philosophy at the University of Edinburgh before training as an engineer at the Royal Technical College in Glasgow, subsequently under the tutelage of Lord Kelvin.[5] The architect of the company's Kinlochleven and Lochaber schemes indubitably believed and took pride in the fact that British Aluminium was not simply a business but was a national enterprise with social and moral responsibilities. At the same time Morrison had become a seasoned player in national, regional and local politics. As the later chapters illustrate, he was also able to use family connections through his uncle Charles Innes, BACo's first Highland solicitor and Conservative and Unionist agent for Inverness-shire, to great effect, in his contacts with leading Highland landowners. His evocation of British Aluminium as a 'service' sustained by a 'community of interest', bound by 'loyal cooperation', was to be a common feature of the image that the company cultivated for itself, set against its patriotic duty as a 'key industry' to the nation and to empire. These were themes to which senior BACo managers returned; British Aluminium, as chairman Robert Cooper observed in 1934, was as befitted 'a great British industry', bound by the 'traditions and enthusiasm of the service', and a 'vital "Key" Industry in the country'.[6] Morrison's reference to the company's 'pioneer stages', an allusion to the portrayal of the company as a progressive force saving the Highlands, was similarly a central and recurrent theme in the company's narrative. The highly prized character of this 'service' was made clear in the inscription on the commemorative coin struck at Lochaber in 1929 reflecting that other tenet in the company's culture, 'order'. This same culture of the 'service' was evoked by Geoffrey Cunliffe and Lord Portal in their parting message to BACo employees in the Spring 1959 edition of *The B.A. News*: 'We are both deeply conscious of the "B.A. Spirit" which has pervaded the whole Company and it is this spirit of good will and unselfish devotion which, more than anything else, has made it a pleasure and a privilege to work with you all.'[7]

Over half a century after Morrison's correspondence with Alexander Fraser, Alcan's John Elton declared to the then Secretary of State for Trade and Industry, Peter Thornton, of the proposed merger between BACo and AUK that: 'it would be Alcan's intention that the company operate as "a good corporate citizen" in the United Kingdom and that the interests of the company would not be subordinated to other external interests or Alcan interests elsewhere.'[8] In part, this reflected Alcan's historical evolution as a firm that was 'born global' – because of its forced separation from its parent, Alcoa – without 'a strong nationality'.[9] Partly, Elton was being

For King and Company: BACo Roll of Honour, displayed in the company's offices. Courtesy of Robert Cairns.

purposefully vague given public concerns over, and therefore political presentation of, foreign takeovers of British firms. As becomes apparent in this chapter and part two of the book, many of the former employees from the Highland smelters and residents of the company villages interviewed for this book, identified British Aluminium's merger with Alcan, when it finally came, as the great disruption; an historical event that fundamentally changed the nature of the workplace and the settlements.

The firm and society

The importance of examining the sociology and memory of the firm and of workplaces, aside from revealing the adaptability and awareness of management within an organisation in the shifting economic, social and political conditions, lies in recognising it as a social organism; part of, rather than distinct from, its social context. If the preceding chapters illustrated the historical processes that forged British Aluminium and British Alcan, and the effects, then this chapter and those which follow provide greater detail about the role of social actors in shaping the organisation and responses to it.[10] Invoking American sociologist Charles Perrow, a recent article surveying memory and organisational culture observed that: 'large bureaucratic organisations [such as public limited companies] have absorbed society ... constructing "societies in themselves, providing, on their own terms, the cradle-to-grave services ...".'[11] These structures evolve alongside corporate cultures, described by one management theorist, Edgar Schein, as: 'a pattern of shared basic assumptions ... learned by a group as it solved its problems of external adaption and internal integration, that has worked well enough to be considered valid and, therefore, to be taught to new members as the correct way to perceive, think, and feel in relation to those problems.'[12] In explaining the provenance of this 'culture', Schein suggests that it frequently emerges from the 'founder' (the 'entrepreneur' or 'convenor of a new group') who 'imposes' 'certain personal visions, goals, beliefs, values, and assumptions about how things should be done' on 'the group and/or select members on the basis of their similarity of thoughts and values'. Schein maintains that this culture will only be 'recognized as *shared*' if it is successful – 'in the sense that the group accomplishes its task and the members feel good about their relationship to one another'.[13] How successful and stable this culture is depends on how it is 'transmitted to' and 'perceived by' the group and how the leadership responds to crises.[14] These crises, or 'social dramas' as Andrew Pettigrew has referred to them, are, according to Schein, immensely important:

> Crises are especially significant in culture creation and transmission because the heightened emotional involvement during such periods increases the intensity of learning. Crises heighten anxiety, and the need to reduce anxiety is a powerful motivator of new learning. If people share intense emotional

experiences and collectively learn how to reduce anxiety, they are more likely to remember what they have learned and to ritually repeat that behavior in order to avoid disruption.[15]

'Social dramas' might include the retiral of key personnel or the death of the founder. Corporate regime change also typically has the effect that 'members who continue to cling to the old ways are either forced out or leave voluntarily because they no longer feel comfortable with where the organization is headed and how it does things'.[16] The limitations of such explanations are that they understate the confluence of two further forces (of particular relevance to British Aluminium, if to a lesser extent to Alcan), that of 'behavioural lock-in' as a result of proximity to other organisations (for example, government) – arising from 'habit, organizational learning' and 'culture' – and the 'feedback process', such as local pressures and sensitivities prompting change.[17] For explanations of the former, it is also important to emphasise the influence of the social milieu, career pathways and personal views of senior managers. Alternatively expressed, the latter process exhibits the very importance of the 'moral economy' (one in which local networks and shared moral customs and norms can affect economic activities) in which firms operate, and in which transgressions can provoke action by individuals and groups to remind the transgressor of the error of their ways.[18] Viewed another way, the economic should not be considered without the social and cultural dimensions. Neither were they historically divisible. As one study of business behaviour in Britain between 1880 and 1939 observed: 'Frequently, even continuously, public opinion and government also exhorted voluntary action in diverse fields: national economic defence, commercial truthfulness, restraint in the exercise of market power, philanthropy, industrial safety, conciliation in industrial disputes, and job maintenance in depressed areas.'[19] Equally important is the fact that by its very nature much management literature chooses to assume the legitimacy of corporate culture – and ignore the unequal power held by capital in its relations with labour and local communities – so that although aspects of their methodology are instructive in explaining models of organisational culture to a certain degree, they are often consciously limited in their perspective in avoiding the legitimate role of workplace struggle. These avoid questions over 'coercion', as well as more radical interpretations of 'consent' (explaining labour effort, beyond compulsion), critical to explaining the growth and shape of company and workplace culture. At the same time, an overly deterministic assumption that 'consent' is forged at the 'point of production' – and that 'monopoly capitalism has managed to shape our very character in accordance with its rationality' – can overlook broader human agency in this process.[20] In essence, the approach adopted in this book refutes the view of the firm as a black box impervious to the national and local context; businesses are products of the social, as well economic and geographical, environments in which they operate. Concurrently, this is also a story about socially embedded workplace culture, and threats thereto.

Forging British Aluminium, 1890–1936

That British Aluminium was profoundly shaped by its long relationship with government is already abundantly clear, as were the effects of this on strategising, and the recruitment of retired military staff officers and senior civil servants. BACo's company culture was also shaped by the 'social crises' in the company's history – most significantly the 1910 and 1936 strikes at the Kinlochleven and Lochaber works, and the RTIA takeover – and by broader industrial politics in Britain. What follows explores how internal and exogenous factors shaped the culture and organisation of British Aluminium, and British Alcan, over time.

Morrison's description of British Aluminium as the 'service' – though determined by his portrayal of it as a 'key industry' for national defence – captured the essence of a company that was patrician in nature, propagated in part by the close and sustained proximity to the state, but also by the social milieu of those recruits to the board that dominated BACo until the 1960s. For it was this, as well as their former career paths in the military, civil and colonial service, that exercised considerable influence on their personal views and had much import into the corporate culture. This was evident too in the French firm AFC, which employed many ex-military officers as managers. However, in France the practice of *pantouflage* (movement between the public and private sectors) in the late nineteenth and twentieth centuries was well established, not least as a reflection of France's conscript military. The quality of the technical education and training possessed, and the technocratic ideals espoused, by many army engineers meant that their transition to French industry was a well-trodden path.[21]

BACo's board exuded social privilege from the outset, with a number of the leading figures steeped in imperial service and drawn from land-owning families. Stephen Pollen, British Aluminium's vice-chairman from 1910–28, and chairman for two years, for example, had apparently effortlessly acquired a post as the aide-de-camp (ADC) of Viceroy of India, Lord Landsdowne – 'a patrician to his fingertips', and 'the very model of the well-meaning representative of the aristocracy' – at the tender age of twenty-one, within two years of graduating from the Royal Military Academy. Following service under Landsdowne's successor, the Earl of Elgin (who later headed the Royal Commission enquiring into Britain's military preparedness during the Boer War, in which BACo had an interest), Pollen joined the staff of Sir Redvers Buller – the epitome of the 'patrician officer', who had few qualms about using his connections to promote his friends – in the Boer War, before retiring in 1902. Pollen volunteered again for war service during the First World War, as military secretary to the Commander-in-Chief of British forces in the Mediterranean, Sir Ian Hamilton, during the Gallipoli campaign and then to the Commander-in-Chief of British forces in Egypt, and was made a Companion of the Order of St Michael and St George and the French Croix d'Officier. At the coronations of King Edward VII and George V, Pollen acted as the captain of both monarchs' ceremonial

CALENDAR
1917

"*I have implicit confidence in you, my soldiers.
Duty is your watchword, and I know
your duty will be nobly done.*"
—H.M. THE KING.

THE DAM, KINLOCHLEVEN.

For King and Company:
BACo calendar, 1917.
Courtesy of Robert
Cairns.

bodyguard. His funeral was well attended by many figures in the military and civil elite, including the then Admiral of the Fleet and the chief whip in the House of Lords. Tellingly Pollen's obituary writer singled out the chief attributes of the former BACo chairman as being 'a good shot, having had much big game shooting, and was also an angler and a golfer'.[22] Lt Col. Pollen was thus both imperially steeped and immensely well connected. Robert Cooper, Pollen's successor and company chairman for twenty-three years, was from a Anglo-Irish military and land-owning family. Trained as a solicitor and well connected in the City of London, Cooper appears to have been the epitome of the 'gentlemanly elite' linked to imperial interests. During the First World War, Cooper was awarded the Military Cross for valour serving as an officer in the Brigade of Rifles – one of the few parts of the British Army of this period, like the Brigade of Guards, still judged to be a bastion of the 'vestigial gentry life-style' – and then served as an ADC. In his personal life, he maintained a strong interest in land-owning and stock-breeding. Though clearly immersed in the world of commerce unlike Pollen, Cooper's perspective was nonetheless a patrician one, coloured by a world view of an empire on which the 'sun would never set' and a gentrified sense of *noblesse oblige*.[23] The imperialist sense of a 'Greater Britain' – as advocated by 'social imperialists' from Sir Charles Dilke, J. R. Seeley to Lord Milner who had some bearing on BACo's history – were no better captured then in the personage of the company's first scientific adviser and pre-eminent man of Victorian science, Lord Kelvin (Sir William Thomson), whose views are explored in more detail in the subsequent chapter. Indeed it was Thomson's political, rather than scientific, activities – in campaigning against Irish Home Rule, he was one of a number Liberals who split with the party over the issue to become Liberal Unionists – that led to him being recommended for a peerage, by an approving and grateful Conservative administration.[24] Thomson would come, like Morrison for the Highlands, to occupy a special place in BACo's literature, embodying a progressive future within empire. The continuity of these ideas was also sustained by the promotion of military service within the company. During the First World War, the company took great pride in the fact that a high proportion of its male employees had rallied to the colours before conscription was introduced, with much being made of the military honours bestowed (including one Victoria and two Military Crosses; one to a future manager of the Highland smelters) and sacrifices made, as well as the service of Morrison, Sawyer and Tait in wartime ministeries.[25] This was a theme to which the company would return time and again during its history. Service, loyalty and empire were further sustained and promoted by the inclusion of Sir Ronald Charles on to the BACo board. Born in British India in 1875 to the Deputy Surgeon-General and physician to Queen Victoria, Charles was immersed in empire and was quickly marked out in his service career for rapid promotion, on account of his abilities and heroism (he won the Sword of Honour at the Royal Military Academy, Sandhurst, the Distinguished Service Order in the Second Anglo-Boer War, and passed out top of the Army Staff College), as well as his social connections. Between 1904 and 1914, Charles served in India, involved initially in campaigns against tribes on the north-west frontier and subsequently as a staff officer, a role which led him to the western front in 1914 on the staff of the Indian Corps. Charles proved himself also as an effective commander during the First World War, and one who showed concern for those under his command. In December 1915, he was appointed as Chief of Staff to XVII Corps, and his leadership saw the 17th as the only corps of the British Army on the western front able to repel the German spring offensive of 1918. His aptitude for 'tactical innovation' and 'military efficiency' was illustrated again by his ability to turn the shattered and demoralised 25th Division, whose command he was given in 1918, into a highly effective force. Charles's personal commitment to empire, as well as to the tenets of 'muscular Christianity' – the redefining of manhood 'marrying physicality to spirituality', with 'militaristic' and 'patriotic overtones' – were embodied in his prominent position within the Young Men's Christian Association, an organisation which embraced these ideas in the 1930s.[26] The personal convictions and connections of Tait, Morrison, and Gerald Steel – a public school and Oxbridge educated career civil servant, and a director for over a quarter of a century, and general manager for most – were also to be immensely important.[27]

A company culture of loyalty and social order linked to patriotism was also sustained by the background of many of British Aluminium's managers at a tactical and operational level, many sharing a similar education, upbringing and code to Morrison. A survey of British Aluminium's works managers who joined the company between 1920 and 1957 revealed that three had attended either an English public school or Scottish private school; six were educated in English grammar schools and Scottish high schools; thirteen were confirmed as graduates (most in metallurgy, engineering, and natural and applied sciences). Of the graduates, three held Oxbridge science tripos, three studied at the University of Birmingham, and a further trio at one of the Scottish ancient universities (in these cases, Edinburgh, Glasgow and St Andrew's), one received his degree from the Royal School of Mines, with the remnants from other well-established English or Welsh institutions. Unsurprisingly, given the period this covers, many had seen active, and in some cases distinguished, service in the armed forces, a number of them having been officers in the Territorial Army (TA) or naval reserve prior to both world conflicts.[28] Compared with surveys of managers in British industry undertaken for the period between 1920 and 1950, British Aluminium's managers were particularly well qualified technically. However their quota of relatively highly qualified staff was far more common in the chemicals sector.[29]

Like many in British industry few, if any, of British Aluminium's managers at operational, tactical or strategic (middle or senior) levels had undergone any formal management education before 1949, when the first senior managers attended the Administrative Staff College at Henley. This remained the norm across much of British industry until the 1960s, not least because of the dearth of formal management education programmes, courses and business schools in Britain before then.[30] That many of BACo's managers were drawn from English grammar schools or Scottish high schools, should not however lead to the assumption that their attitudes on such subjects as empire or labour management were diametrically different from those of the board. English grammar schools, such as the renowned King Edward VII school in Birmingham (attended by a number of BACo managers) were transformed in the early decades of the twentieth century to produce Oxbridge candidates. At such schools, students were taught to modify their accents, assuming the 'received standard English of the BBC', allowing for the 'easy social interchange among prosperous middle-class people from different regions' imbued with an 'automatic political Conservatism'.[31] Despite the 'softening' of middle-class attitudes in the aftermath of the Second World War, including a sense that 'post-war levelling had not altogether been a bad thing', bourgeois 'interpretations' in this period remained, as Ross McKibbin has pointed out,

> Largely shaped by an ideological hostility to the organized working class, which forged a strong sense both of middle-class unity and loss, and exaggerated the cultural differences between the middle-class and working-class way of life. Such hostility was ideological because its origin was ideological: an intense fear of loss of social esteem and relative status.[32]

Although clearly attitudes and responses differed among the works managers, the social outlook prevalent among the middle class was to be evident in the remarks and behaviour of BACo's managers. Even allowing for distinctions between the educational and cultural background of those British Aluminium managers who were Scots, some of the same social attitudes were evident.[33] If Morrison's hand were visible in forging the company's culture, then it was cultivated within this social milieu.

Aside from links with the state, and British imperial concerns, and the social composition of the company's management, two 'dramas' most profoundly affected the company's culture before 1945. These were those of the 1910 strike at Kinlochleven, and even more so that at Lochaber in 1936. To a company, in which familiarity was much fêted, these sent shock waves to the very top of the company, not least as Morrison, as a Highlander who prided himself on having a feel for the area, had been at the centre of them. The character of the historical narrative that emerged after the Second World War from these experiences reflected the recognition that the company had been punished for transgressing the rules of the 'moral economy', and that a semblance of trust needed to be reestablished. In part, this shock, particularly after the latter strike, stemmed from the fact that BACo recruited from many generations of the same family at the Highland smelters, with a good number of long service managers who established roots in the area. Like the Glasgow engineering firm Mavor & Coulson who recruited through 'durable family networks', British Aluminium recognised the value of kinship as 'cheap and efficient screening mechanism' that 'underwrote a powerful paternalist ideology', as 'the basis for consensual labour relations'.[34] And yet, it was precisely these local links, as the following discussions over industrial pollution exhibit, which brought operational managers in the Highlands and Norway into conflict with their senior managers. In this sense, BACo's strategies were 'emergent', rather than defined, informed by these 'social crises', the 'feedback' from workers and community members, and by broader social, economic and political circumstances. Like many British businesses, the company over time developed a 'sophisticated paternalism'; one that was a conscious mixture of attempts at 'control' characterised by, 'a more complex relationship not only between employer and employee, but also between parent and child, elder and younger siblings, officer and private', nurturing 'consent'.[35] With the social stratification of the company villages

– mimicking structures within the workplace – BACo's strategy echoed that of other aluminium producers like AFC in the Alps, and Alcoa/ Alcan at Shawnigan Falls and Arvida, as well as that of other British welfarist employers, such as Lever Brothers at Port Sunlight.[36] The widespread adoption of industrial welfarism in the aluminium, like the chemical, industry was born of pragmatism, in a capital-intensive industry in which stoppages could be particularly costly, in terms of energy lost and the potential for aluminium furnaces to 'freeze' over.

Discord in the 'Garden of Eden': Kinlochleven 1910 and Lochaber 1936

In the aftermath of the eight-day strike at BACo's Kinlochleven works in October 1910, the secretary of the union representing the striking workers denounced British Aluminium for its misrepresentation of the Highland mission. Gas Workers and General Labourers' Union Secretary Lynds repudiated the company's representation of Kinlochleven as a 'Garden of Eden' in the making, contrasting it with the 'real picture' of 'misery and degradation' endured by workers in the village. The strike had been prompted by the dismissal of a worker, low wages and rising prices for goods (due to tariffs charged by BACo's subsidiary the Loch Leven Pier Company Ltd for discharging provisions) and at the absence of a company canteen.[37] The company for its part, in the personage of Morrison, refused to recognise the union's right to bargain on behalf of the strikers or to meet the strike committee, informing the union secretary that: 'we were always ready to meet men in our service but that the men having left the work I had nothing to discuss with them but that if they made application and were re-engaged we should meet them at any time.'[38] The strike ended with the remaining 200 strikers agreeing to return to work on British Aluminium's terms, after BACo issued notices of cessation of employment (on 29 August) and of eviction from company housing for those who had not returned to work on 3 September.[39] Morrison concluded that the resolve of the strikers was weakened by the lack of strike pay, and pressure being placed on some of the strikers by their wives. This was a view shared by Lynds, along with at least one of strikers writing into the Glasgow Independent Labour Party paper, *Forward*, who confirmed that the strikers' resolve had been weakened by the lack of strike pay.

In the immediate aftermath of the strike, a number of points became clear both to the company and the strikers. While the company had been able to defeat the strike by refusing to recognise the strikers' demands or the union's right to negotiate on behalf of the men – aided by the fact that a significant proportion of the workforce, largely tradesmen, had continued to work, that BACo had been able to supply the works from their Foyers and Greenock factories, and that community support for the strike was not entirely forthcoming – and ultimately with the threat to evict strikers, this had come at a cost. With the company in a precarious financial position, the strike had delayed production while the market for the metal was growing rapidly, and provoked considerable adverse publicity, tainting their image as benefactors to the region. The board's hardline attitude and Morrison's attribution of the dispute to 'rabid agitators', the '"red hot" addresses of the union secretary' and the 'intimidation of the ring leaders', were a gross misrepresentation: Though the company was worried by an outbreak of violence, none of its fears was realised and BACo managers were able to freely move about the village, as Morrison privately admitted and the chief constable of Argyllshire was quick to point out. As far as the strikers and union were concerned, the outcome of the strike was mixed. Although the strikers' other demands were conceded by the union, the company ultimately acquiesced to recognise union representation at the plant.[40] The strike illustrated to the workforce the importance of community support and the settling of sectional differences. In the long term, the strike represented a significant milestone in the social history of the company, forcing the company, albeit reluctantly, to acknowledge union representation. By 1916 workers at British Aluminium's Warrington works were also unionised; while between 1918 and 1920 the Workers' Union at Kinlochleven was able to pursue successful wage claims and resist the company's attempts to reorganise shift patterns.[41]

The seven-week dispute at BACo's Lochaber reduction works, which started on 14 June 1936, was to have an even more marked effect on the company's approach to labour management. Though the 1910 strike at its sister smelter marked the beginning of the growth of trade unionism within many of the company's larger works, the depth of bad feeling at Lochaber signalled by the length of the strike and the mobilisation of community support in Inverlochy made a far more profound impression. The strike had its origins in longer running attempts by the company to impose flexible shift working, and attempts by employees to overturn wage cuts imposed since 1932 by the company, as well as over recognition of the Transport and General Workers' Union (TGWU) and holiday entitlement.[42] However, where this differed from the earlier dispute at Kinlochleven was in the strategy adopted by the trade unions and their ability to harness community disquiet in Inverlochy over rents and the cost of living into solidaristic action, underlining the importance of the 'moral economy' to disputes and recognising the sensitivity of the company locally, regionally and nationally to public accusations of the neglect of their social responsibility.

In 1932, general manager Gerald Steel announced to that year's managers' conference that in the commercial climate the wage bill had to be reduced and greater uniformity of rates introduced across the company. Within three years of entering operation the Lochaber smelter had some of the highest wages in the group, and was therefore to be an immediate target for wage cuts. By 1934, managers from all of BACo's rolling mills were able to report that they had reduced shifts and weekend working.[43] In the 18 months leading up to the strike, Morrison resisted claims for flat increases in wages, introducing instead increases for selected foremen and workmen based on loyalty and productivity. BACo's subsidiary had also raised rents in the company village of Inverlochy, which served the plant. In June 1936 the Lochaber workforce's frustration boiled over. Unlike the earlier strike at Kinlochleven the strikers were ready, well organised and skilfully led by Dr Isaac Maciver. Maciver, a local physician who stood as the Labour Party candidate for Argyllshire, had already proved a vocal critic of the company at the Scottish Trades Union Congress (STUC), highlighting injuries and fatalities during the civil engineering work on the Lochaber scheme. It is quite possible that Maciver – who acquired the moniker of the 'Lewis Democrat' among some of the navvies working on the scheme – like some of the strikers, also brought to this struggle some of the experiences and traditions of radical land agitation in the west Highlands and Hebridean islands. In addition, the nearby town of Fort William had a strong tradition of radical trade unionism on the railways, while incoming tradesmen to the Lochaber smelter from eastern and lowland Scotland brought with them experiences of industrial politics from the shipyards of Dundee and Glasgow, as well as the central Scottish coalfields. Recognising the tactical value of publicity, the Lochaber Vigilance Committee – set up by the strikers, with Maciver as secretary – staged a march through Fort William led by the Inverlochy Pipe Band followed by 250 workers from the plant. In a letter to Scottish MPs the committee pitted the company's refusal to restore wages cut in 1932 against the BACo's profit of almost half a million pounds for 1935, and astutely pointed out to parliamentarians that as the government was guaranteeing the interest on the debenture stock they would be concerned with a prompt settlement and should intervene. Though admittedly BACo's profits were largely committed to the extension of the Lochaber scheme and the company was considered a financial risk by some within the Treasury, this was a shrewd move on the part of the strike committee.[44] The committee was also extremely effective in ensuring that the Scottish, as well as local, press ran with the story, with *The Scotsman* carrying the content of a letter from Sir Murdoch Macdonald (the MP for Inverness-shire) to Maciver in which the former declared that though it was not in the locus of the President of the Board of Trade to intervene, the Minister of Labour may well involve himself. The pressure mounted on British Aluminium to negotiate a settlement; the longer the strike continued the greater likelihood of its reputation being tarnished both nationally and locally, as well as the greater loss in output. British Aluminium was also only too aware of the opposition of certain leading landowners to the Lochaber scheme, and of retaining the support of others. The Perthshire landowner, the Duke of Atholl, having declared of the Lochaber scheme over a decade before: 'I can imagine the effect of this new Bolshivist [sic] population of the Radical minds of the average Fort William democrat, which will spread north and cast. While poaching fish and game will become worse than it is at the present moment.'[45]

A few days after Sir Murdoch Macdonald's letter was published, Sir Donald Cameron of Lochiel – chieftain of the Clan Cameron, and a highly influential figure locally and across Scotland, and one of BACo's land-owning allies – intervened by writing to the strike committee offering to mediate between the strikers and the company. Concurrently a delegation of strikers from Lochaber led by the General

Secretary of the Scottish TGWU, J. C. McLean, visited Kinlochleven urging the men there to come out on strike in sympathy with their colleagues at the neighbouring works. Fearing stoppages spreading throughout their works, BACo announced wage increases and holidays with pay to all of their other works in England, Scotland and Northern Ireland. The TGWU, sensing a complete victory, refused to concede on its demands. Ending on 29 July 1936 with the offer of wage increases to all employees and with a week's paid holiday, the strikers triumphantly marched back to work. In addition, at the behest of the Inverlochy Village Society (IVS), rent on company housing in Inverlochy was reduced significantly from January 1937.[46] Meanwhile BACo was faced with the task of repairing its besmirched image, representing itself once again as an honest broker and social benefactor in the region at the annual general meeting of shareholders the following March:

> We have always maintained the most friendly relations with our employees, settling amicably any differences which arose from time to time, but I regret to say that an ill-advised "lightning" strike occurred at our Lochaber works in June of last year. This was a regrettable happening without precedent in the history of our Company since its reconstruction in 1910.[47]

The directors went on to declare that it had always been their 'desire to grant them [the workforce] a week's holiday per annum with full pay', inferring through their surprised tone and the identification of it as a 'lightning strike' that it was caused by militants as opposed to profound discontent among Lochaber employees and residents of Inverlochy village.[48] The company's true motives were betrayed by its actions behind the scenes. Less than five months after the end of the strike, Morrison was once again attempting to implement a similar wages strategy to that of 1935 at the Lochaber works. This time, with increased orders for aluminium arising from rearmament, the company could not risk another confrontation. Added to this, after the defeat of the engineering employers during a strike of apprentices the next year, BACo was ill-placed to adopt such a tactic in the foreseeable future. However, this did not stop the company's then manager at their Milton works, W. A. Fowler, successfully launching an assault on the relatively weaker position of clerical workers at that plant, replacing a good number with machinery to undertake the payroll. This attack on the soft underbelly of the workforce at the company's plants preceded Fowler's (and other managers') ambitions at tackling process workers and the trades.[49]

Seen against these strikes, the development of British Aluminium's corporate culture and industrial welfarism over the following decades takes on an added significance. BACo's directors recognised that they could neither afford another strike of the duration and magnitude of this dispute, nor could they risk the adverse publicity. The response of the company before, during and after the strike reveals its willingness to deploy a range of strategies, incorporating coercion and consent. It also attempted to use the power of the *ancien régime* by enlisting Cameron of Lochiel to intervene to bring the strike to a close. What the strikers had recognised both in 1910 and 1936 – and the Lochaber Vigilance Committee had quickly exploited – was the significance to British Aluminium of its self-constructed image as benefactors to the Highlands and, given its relationship with government as well as regional elites, the imperative for upholding its reputation as a reliable supplier and social entrepreneur. These events, as well as the increased capital of the labour movement in the aftermath of the Second World War, would determine the labour management strategies, as well as the content and tone of company literature in the decades ahead. The language and tone of the Lochaber strikers' campaign was not one suffused with the rhetoric of class warfare but couched in terms of morality and what they viewed as the company's breach of the social contract. The 1936 strike represented a 'crisis' to which the company was compelled, albeit reluctantly, to respond by reviewing their labour management strategies, with additional compulsion being added during and immediately after the Second World War by greater incorporation of the trade unions within workplace bargaining. Both disputes and the events leading up to them equally represented broader trends in British industrial politics; the former took place during the heightened period of labour unrest occurring between 1910 and 1914 accompanied by expansion of trade union membership, and the latter against the backdrop of attempts by employers nationally to use the inter-war depression to impose managerial prerogatives and exact concessions from labour.[50] Like much of British industry, BACo was affected by the changes in capital-labour relations ushered in during both world wars. Thus BACo's post-war strategy needs to be viewed within the context of a cyclical pattern of capital-labour relations. These strikes also exercised a profound effect – alongside other factors explored in the following chapters – on the central place that the company's 'Highland story' came to occupy in the company's narrative, as a key tool in 'manufacturing consent'.

By 1945, BACo was a company whose culture had been forged by two generations of directors steeped in empire and the 'vestigial gentry life-style'. It was a culture sustained by the close relationship with the state, as well as proximity with elites within the Highlands. The culture was also one born both of pragmatism and the personal values of the leaders. The historical narrative, which would become such a recognisable feature of the corporate culture in the post-war period, was already starting to take form, with Lord Kelvin and William Murray Morrison the cult heroes.

Constructing consensus, 1945–1959

British Aluminium's corporate culture from 1945 until the RTIA takeover was determined by two factors: labour management and 'behavioural lock-in'. After 1945 the company adopted a more complex, if not entirely sophisticated, range of labour management strategies, designed chiefly to incorporate trade unions into bargaining mechanisms nationally and locally through endorsing informal agreements. It was also to formulate a comprehensive means of communicating with employees. In itself, the creation of a new general establishments office led by a director – to oversee personnel policy and employee communications – reflected the importance of these changes. This was in direct response to a number of factors: full employment and labour shortages; continuing government control of sales of aluminium; and the incorporation of the trade unions within British industry and society, not least given their efforts in leading production initiatives during the war and immediately afterwards.[51] As the Austrian political scientist and economist Joseph Schumpeter observed of the impact of the Second World War on business in 1942: 'The business class has accepted "gadgets of regulation" and "new financial burdens", a mere fraction of which it would have felt to be unbearable fifty years ago'.[52] Though this, Schumpeter's most controversial work has not stood the test of time well, his observation of the Second World War as a watershed was certainly well placed.[53] BACo's essentially pragmatic, 'emergent' strategy to labour management was exhibited through their approach to a variety of industry bodies.

Though the only firm in the aluminium industry not federated to the Engineering Employers' Federation (EEF), British Aluminium was not alone in not wishing to be constrained by confederation agreements and collective approaches; a survey of 970 British manufacturing premises in 1977 revealed that in nearly 53 per cent of industrial workplaces (covering around 68 per cent of employees), wage bargaining was conducted through single employer agreements. Nevertheless, BACo had contact with the EEF and monitored the outcome of its negotiations with the trade unions. Like much of the rest of the British chemicals and metalworking industry sectors, British Aluminium was attempting to grapple with the proliferation of payment systems at their various works (wage drift), and to negotiate a national framework with the trade unions.[54] Clearly this varied according to a variety of conditions, and depended on individual firms. While BACo subscribed to the services of the Industrial Welfare Society – an organisation espousing 'mutually agreed goals and the interest of successful and efficient production' – this was on the firm understanding that worker participation was to conform to its organisation and values. Thus the formal mechanics of participation were intended as a means of responding to cyclical challenges; as a consequence, in some plants, the machinery fell into disrepair and significant negotiation was conducted informally.[55] For all the appearance, the tenor of this strategy was intensely patrician and was primarily determined by the expediency for industrial accord. Equally evident in BACo's entreaties to its employees after the Second World War was the harnessing of the language of 'social citizenship', based around a discourse of 'rights and responsibilities'.[56] The operation of the machinery of industrial relations within British Aluminium met, like the experience across British industry, with mixed results, not least because it was a policy determined by expediency rather than being founded on trust. It was also a policy that from the outset exposed differences among individual managers and different layers of management, and equally trade unions. In contrast, the enduring legacy of these years, especially in the west Highlands, was the historical narrative that the company developed. The success of this was a direct result of the company's decision to integrate popular 'sites of memory', specifically those from Highland history, with the well-tried male hero at the centre, in the forms of Lord Kelvin and William Murray Morrison.[57]

Esprit de corps

The continuity in BACo's outlook and corporate culture after 1945 was also sustained by the wartime service of the company's staff, and the recruitment of figures like Lord Portal, Sir Edwin Plowden, and perhaps most significantly in this respect, Commodore Robert Gordon Hood Linzee, the career naval officer who became British Aluminium's general establishment manager, responsible for personnel policy. So that despite BACo's rhetoric and outward signs of reforming recruitment of managers and professional development among staff, 'service' culture in the senior echelons of the company persisted. As one of Britain's top fifty companies by 1948 – wishing to be seen to be responding to the Labour government's initiatives for modernising British management, while also recognising increased competitiveness in the market for high quality graduates against newer foreign entrants and larger UK employers (e.g. Imperial Chemicals Industries (ICI) and the Anglo-Dutch Unilever) – BACo recognised the importance of embracing organisational reform. Noting the shortcomings in management within the company, BACo's personnel officer, Alfred Smith, proposed a committee to consider options to report in 1949 but added (anticipating objections): 'It was very important to recognise that Management was something for which people had to train, and was not something that men happened to be born to.'[58] In response to concerns about career stagnation and narrow specialisation across the company, BACo's management committee suggested adopting two programmes – one for young technicians joining the company, and the other made up of marginally older engineers joining from outside – both essentially aimed at developing knowledge of the business and creating generalists. These ideas were enthusiastically embraced by the management conference. Though described as management programmes, these related far more to the specifics of the company's product range and businesses than to equipping managers with general management skills. This was scarcely surprising, given the professional development pathway adopted for the future leaders of the company. As in other areas, the prescription for the patient was to be a characteristically 'BA' approach, reflecting the armed and civil service backgrounds of key senior managers.

That British Aluminium had started to enrol a number of senior management trainees at the newly formed Administrative Staff College (ASC) at Henley-on-Thames – a former RAF staff college that primarily trained senior civil servants and strategic-

Commodore Robert Gordon Hood
Linzee, RN. © RTA/GUA.

level managers from among the newly nationalised industries – was unsurprising.
Admittedly there were few business schools and limited business courses in Britain
and companies were often forced to draw up blueprints for internal management
training programmes or approach university departments to develop bespoke courses
for them. However crucially for BACo, great emphasis was placed in the Henley
curriculum on public service:

> Although concerned with techniques and practicalities, the Henley programme
> stresses more than do most courses in this country the importance of
> public policy, the public interest, the idea of a growing political economy,
> the importance of character, the values of civilisation – and perhaps this is
> a necessary consequence of the above – the College pays less attention to
> manipulation and personality as determiners of administrative results ... A
> special virtue of Henley is its recognition that government and business leaders
> must be trained in common problems of policy and administration if they
> are to understand one each other and take independent but consistent action
> designed to further the common interest of the nation.[59]

These had been the aspirations wished for the ASC by its midwives as 'a meeting place of the two main categories of administrators – the officers of the private and of the public services', in which they should learn that, 'they must work together' and 'acquire, so far as may be, the characteristic virtues of the other, and know its own characteristic defects'. All of this knowledge was to be 'directed to the fuller service of the public interest'.[60] This ethos fitted perfectly with British Aluminium. Although some criticisms of ASC were forthcoming, British Aluminium's internal committee on training and selection, reporting in 1949, recommended maintaining links. In supporting this recommendation the managers conference that year averred: 'that the A.S.C. course was not claimed to be of use in itself as a training for management, but only as a supplement to basic experience and training'.[61] In arriving at this decision, they were also swayed by the continued commitment of Unilever to the College. The embracing of just such an ethos of management education also reflected BACo's wish to associate of itself with the group of leading 'progressive' concerns that included Unilever, ICI, Cadbury, Imperial Tobacco, as well as many British subsidiaries of American firms. These firms also enthusiastically endorsed the modernisation of management methods in Britain, including the use of work-study and formal education management programmes as recommended by the 1945 committee on education and management chaired by the 'doyen of British management' Lyndall Urwick, and promoted post-war through the newly founded British Institute of Management (BIM), which had set down standards for Henley and contributed to its establishment.[62] British Aluminium's attachment to Henley as a staff training establishment continued well into the 1960s.[63]

The character of management within the company was further compounded by fault lines between the 'practical man' and the new generation of managers – for whom the former often exhibited contempt – more broadly reflected in British industry.[64] By the mid-1950s, but especially after the RTIA takeover, engineers and scientists increasingly replaced the former military officers. That the military tradition endured so long within the company is indicative of the dominance of the senior echelons of British Aluminium by retired staff officers, but also reflected the belief in some influential quarters that military leadership had something to offer within industry. It was these survivors of the bygone era that assured the persistence of patrician overtones, deference and dependence long after the RTIA takeover. BACo was not alone, with similarly patrician concerns like Lever Brothers facing similar divisions in their attempts at a company makeover in the 1960s. However, with a few exceptions, these attitudes were prevalent among many government ministers and industry leaders alike.[65]

'Estate of the Realm'? BACo and labour[66]
The shift in approach over labour management was hotly debated at the company's annual managers conferences immediately post-war, with the contributions of various

MANAGERS' CONFERENCE. CHALFONT PARK, APRIL, 1950.

Back Row :   left to right—T. E. Mills (Chief Accountant), H. E. Russell (Staff Accountant), H. W. L. Phillips (Research), J. E. Hatton (Milton), J. G. Bullen (Gen. Manager, Highland Reduction Works), J. Salter (Head Office), H. A. R. Jubb (Legal Adviser). H. H. Cundell (Sales Manager), F. E. Laughton (Lochaber), N. Fyfe (Architect, Scotland), E. E. Spillett (Development Manager), A. W. Langham (Sales Planning Manager), W. B. C. Perrycoste (Production Manager, Overseas), Dr. W. L. Kent (Warrington).

Second Row :—J. Ritchie (Deputy Secretary), J. H. Dickin (Latchford), W. A. Robertson (Head Office). D. A. Murray (Construction Manager, Head Office), A. Smith (Personnel Manager), Dr. T. G. Pearson (Deputy Director, Research), W. Henkel (Kinlochleven), Miss E. Hay. R. McDonald (Purchases & Supplies Manager), H. A. Woodroffe (Assistant Secretary), G. A. Anderson (Deputy Gen. Sales Manager), L. V. Chilton (Intelligence Manager), C. G. McAuliffe (Publicity & Sales Research Manager), W. R. Thomas (Burntisland).

Front row : .W. A. Fowler (Production Manager Manufactured Materials), Dr. H. Mastin (Newport), Dr. C. J. Smithells (Director of Research), R. Linzee (Gen. Establishment Manager), W. J. Thomas (Asst. Managing Director), Sir Ronald Charles (Director), Hon. G. Cunliffe (Managing Director), G. Boex (Managing Director), G. W. Lacey (Gen. Sales Manager), D. Menzies Fraser (Foyers), A. J. Field (Falkirk), A. G. Chalmers (Factor, Highland Estates).

BACo Managers' Conference April 1950. © RTA/GUA.

participants reflecting wider public debates, not least about the role of trade unions within British society. Broadly speaking two strategies emerged from these meetings. First, the spring 1948 conference proposed the development of a more sophisticated and systematic approach to communicate with employees in order to gain their 'loyalty'. Second, moves were made to incorporate trade unions into the machinery of bargaining and arbitration, and isolate Communists (and militants) within the workplace. As the agenda for the discussion of this at the same conference in April 1948 put it, the priority was for the: 'Establishment of closer relations with the Unions with a view to influencing or ensuring the election or appointment of the right type of official in the interests of the Nation, the Company, and the body of employees.'[67] There was, however, to be some considerable disagreement over how this was to be achieved.

Some managers, such as W. A. Fowler, by then manager of BACo's rolling mill at Falkirk, advocated that the company press the trade unions to establish a system of secret workplace ballots to elect union officials and operate a 'service qualification', ruling out candidates from standing who had not been employed by the firm for long. This Fowler judged would improve discussions between management and shop stewards, as the former would feel that 'the shop stewards were fully representative of the employees'.[68] Fowler was not alone in this. John Bullen, the general manager for the Highland smelter group railed against a local branch secretary at Lochaber – 'the man was quite incapable of discussing anything with the management' – and asked: 'could anything be done by the Company to avoid such a position.'[69] The Bullen-Fowler position was rejected by most present at the meeting, including Cunliffe and Linzee. Fowler and Bullen's responses reflected a strand in post-war British middle-class opinion which attributed Britain's productivity lag to 'a working class made "uppity" by full employment'.[70] As Fowler acknowledged, his response was affected by his objection to the chairman of local branch of the TGWU being a 'well-known Communist', though he 'could not point to anything very seriously objectionable having arisen in the past as a result of this political connection'.[71]

In place of this confrontational stance, Cunliffe and Linzee proposed a more insidious strategy aimed at using their influence with the senior echelons of the trade unions, and the anti-Communist stance of the leaders of certain unions like the TGWU, to lever for self-regulation. Thus, in spite of the company's theoretical antipathy to the principle of the 'closed shop', as Linzee pointed out:

> The Company did recognise to some extent it was convenient if all employees were properly organised in a Trade Union. The basic objection to the principle [the 'closed shop'], however, remained, namely, that it was not for an employer to dictate to a man whether or not he should join a Union, and it was for the Union to persuade a man to join. Should 100% membership of a particular Trade Union develop at any factory, then he thought in the case of new employees they should be told of the position and encouraged to join the Union, otherwise there would be trouble.[72]

In contrast to Fowler's response, Cunliffe and Linzee from their strategic vantage points were well aware of the potential political sensitivities of confronting labour. They clearly recognised the importance of courting the trade unions and exercising more caution, against the backdrop of fuller employment after the Second World War. In the rather different political climate of the late 1940s, the company was also trying to repair its public image after parliamentarians' wartime claims of profiteering, as well as calls for anti-trust action similar to that taken by the US government against Alcoa, what the leader of Chemical Workers' Union Bob Edwards referred to in 1944 as, the 'modern brigands' and 'freebooters' of the aluminium industry.[73]

The 1948 managers' conference signposted a change in the company's strategies in response to the post-war environment, as well as reflecting on the lessons of the Lochaber strike; senior managers recognised that the power of managerial prerogative exercised through absolute patrician authority combined with welfarist measures had been waning in recent years and that pragmatism about, if not enthusiasm for, the realities of shifting social relations in the workplace demanded a more sophisticated approach. Moreover as Cunliffe and William Thomas both recognised in their comments to the previous year's conference – when they 'stressed that the aim of our welfare policy should be to make our working conditions as attractive as possible' – there was fierce competition for skilled labour in post-war Britain, while a number of British Aluminium's plants were plagued by high labour turnover rates.[74] Henceforth managerial authority would have to be tempered, at the very least, by recognition of workplace consultation with employees and trade unions, through the Joint Works Councils (JWCs) and the Shop Stewards Committees (SSCs). At the same time BACo was equally determined to assert managerial prerogative and control the work process as far as possible. Nevertheless its continued commitment to joint consultation was certainly at odds with the route that other engineering employers were adopting, although some of other sectors undoubtedly had easier access to reserve labour than BACo did, especially in the Highlands. Yet, this was significant, given that a contemporary survey of joint production committees in post-war British manufacturing revealed that joint consultation was more likely to survive and work where employers were supportive.[75] For BACo's strategy to work to its advantage, it meant attempting to influence the terms of these negotiations by exerting pressure on unions at a national level to exercise control over the behaviour and selection of local union officials (and assuming that they could in turn be assured of bringing rank and file members behind them). It would also require a doubling of effort to strengthen employee loyalty, service to and identification with the company through investment in publications, social activities, and benefits; in order, as George Boex put it in May 1947, to maintain 'close personal contacts with employees'.[76]

The implementation of an agreed framework for conciliation and arbitration, incorporating the trade unions, was made all the more pressing for the company by government attempts to control wages through a national incomes policy immediately post-war. BACo pursued national agreements with all of the manual trade unions, to contain wage drift arising from the proliferation of localised and sectional settlements across the business. Rising inflation and government controls also added to the sense of urgency. This was set against a greater levelling of pay that had started immediately pre-war and continued post-war, alongside a further reduction of working hours. Metals, along with chemicals, also saw a greater degree of the levelling of gender pay inequalities than most sections of British industry. Equally union membership grew substantially and was strengthened by legal reform, and, more questionably, by their participation in institutional arbitration and conciliation mechanisms.[77] Moreover at British Aluminium's large rolling plants at Falkirk and Warrington, as well as Lochaber, the SSCs held more sway than the JWCs over work organisation and general production matters.[78]

British Aluminium had been negotiating with the main unions since 1947 to achieve 'a General Agreement with a view to bringing all works and employees under one set of conditions'.[79] Given the proliferation of local agreements across the business, BACo's strategy in these discussions was to put the onus on the unions to undertake the, at times, difficult task of convincing rank and file members to agree to a general agreement – effectively ceding much of the control for wage negotiations to national officials – and enforce the discipline of those agreements. Revealing BACo's thinking on this matter BACo's personnel manager declared in April 1948 that 'it would be felt that we were not making much progress in this matter [the General Agreement]. It was however, our deliberate policy not to force the pace but rather to leave the pressure to the Unions themselves.' The Amalgamated Engineering Union (AEU) was already locked into discussions with the company.[80] By 1948 the company could feel far more secure in the knowledge that at national level it would find a sympathetic ear among some of the larger trade unions to attempts at negotiating national agreements and regulating rank and file activity; the general secretary of Britain's largest union, the TGWU, Arthur Deakin, for example, having shifted from being an opponent of wages policy to being far more amenable, albeit on the basis that it was regulated by the trade unions rather than by government.[81] BACo encountered more difficulties with the smaller local unions, such as the Federation of Building Trades Operatives in Scotland, who were not as susceptible as members of the large federated unions to pressure from senior officials. Similarly, any national deal was unenforceable at their Newport works because of the separate agreement covered by the Welsh Engineers and Foundries' Association.[82]

At a local level BACo conceded to voluntarism, especially where agreements were strongly embedded. This essentially pragmatic approach, belying a barely concealed mistrust of trade unionism, was illustrated by the parameters to the accommodation of the unions; BACo initially flatly refused, for example, to recognise white-collar trade unionism at their plants, despite the Association of Supervisory Staffs, Executives and Technicians (ASSET) having significant membership numbers at the company's Falkirk and Milton plants and furthermore specifically targeted certain welfarist measures at professional and managerial employees to undermine support for white-collar trade unionism. BACo's attitude to Communists in the workplace was one of barely concealed animosity, as epitomised by the title of an apparently innocuous article about fire engines that appeared in *The B.A. News* in Spring 1954: 'A Red that May be Missed'. However, it was tempered by pragmatism in the immediate post-war years given the popularity of Communist shop stewards among rank and file trade unionists (arising from CP shop stewards' lead in wartime and immediate post-war productivity drives), with one government estimate of Communist Party of Great Britain membership among 1948 TUC delegates being as high as one in thirteen. As if to underline the expediency of this strategy as far as BACo was concerned, CP shop stewards held considerable sway among rank and file TGWU members – a union that was vociferously anti-communist at national executive level – at Falkirk, British Aluminium's most modern rolling mill responsible for producing much sheet metal for military aircraft.[83]

Meanwhile BACo assiduously expounded its rhetoric of loyalty and service to the company, bound up with political appeals for wage restraint during the national economic crisis made during the Labour government's spring 1947 'Work or Want' campaign – exhorting greater productivity and restraint on the part of British industry and workers.[84] The message was carefully contrived by the general establishment's staff in the employee magazine, to sit alongside the company's historical narrative of it as a social benefactor to the Highlands, reminders of BACo's munificence in its provision of company welfare schemes, and the benefits of wider social reform. This combination is well illustrated by articles featured in the two summer editions of *The B.A. News* of 1949. The May–June edition carried a comprehensive summary of the company's welfare and leisure schemes, and an article on British Aluminium's long service society, the 'Thirty Year Club'.[85] The following edition hastened to remind its readership of the new social benefits it was reaping, but reminded them of the precarious position, the 'economic Dunkirk', that Britain was faced with, and therefore of employees' responsibilities to the company and the nation:

> Briefly, the main justification for longer holidays, welfare schemes and other amenities at this time of stress should be that they enable us to work harder and increase our productivity. This country is engaged in a battle to maintain its present standard of living and this battle will only be won when the battle of productivity has been won ... We hope all employees have thoroughly enjoyed their longer holiday and have returned feeling fit and ready for the great dollar earning tasks that lie ahead.[86]

As the paper was also quick to remind readers, if trade unions had indeed become a 'fourth estate of the Realm' this brought with it responsibilities:

> When one considers the extremely favourable shift-work conditions, and the retirement allowance scheme, one recognises the kind of steady effort that is required to pay for all these things. For the Company, and the Country, there will be no lasting prosperity unless there is a willingness to earn what we receive.[87]

During the course of the article, the author cited the Labour government's 1948 White Paper, *Statement on Personal Incomes, Costs and Prices,* which sought collective agreements, taking account of the national economic climate and the exercise of restraint against the further proliferation of individual claims. That year a majority at the TUC had voted to support the government's policy, with some reluctance, to aid the Labour administration through the economic straits and because of government assurances to retain food subsidies. The TUC, like its federated unions, sought to raise wages through active engagement and leadership with productivity drives.[88] Increasingly, both within British Aluminium's works and the country more broadly, inflation was testing the patience of the labour force over wage restraint.

By April 1948 Alcan's subsidiary Northern Aluminium was preparing to reject a major claim, as was the EEF, and British Aluminium followed suit. The matter was referred to the National Arbitration Tribunal which ruled in favour of wage rises for male and female workers in the National Union of General and Municipal Workers (NUGMW) and the TGWU, as well extending the paid holiday allowance from one to two weeks.[89] The main bone of contention for NUGMW and the TGWU, and a key theme in their advocacy for this claim, had been the demands of shift work in British Aluminium's works. These long and antisocial hours had led to high labour turnover especially at two of their largest works, Lochaber (where environmental conditions in the furnace rooms were in part responsible for rising wage claims) and Warrington, which they increasingly sought to counteract with special shift payments. At BACo's rolling mills labour turnover was standing at 20–25 per cent, and was as high as 50 per cent at the Warrington works with the company forced to rely on shift workers drawn from elsewhere.[90] In attempting to retain skilled labour in the west Highland smelters, particularly Lochaber, BACo was also plagued by the perennial problem of a shortage of housing in the area, and by the periodic lay-offs as a result of water shortages that prompted a scaling back of production. By July 1948 labour turnover at Kinlochleven and Lochaber stood respectively at 61.8 and 64.3 per cent.[91]

With the implementation of the machinery of industrial relations, from 1948 onwards the company sought concurrently to roll out method study and a bonus scheme – designed to increase individual productivity and reduce the size of the workforce – across the business over the next few years. To support this foremen and junior managers were instructed in the use of work-study by consultants such as Associated Industrial Consultants (AIC).[92] However uptake was patchy, with managers reporting by 1950 that, in the main, employees rejected the bonus schemes, continuing to prefer working on lower wages than receiving supplementary shift payments. At smaller plants such as Kinlochleven and Latchford Locks, the company was able to gain the support both of the shopfloor and the unions to support reorganisation of work processes. At Kinlochleven, for example, AIC reported that: 'the men were performing more units of work for the basic pay they were receiving than we were entitled to expect from them.'[93] On the back of this, at AIC's recommendation, Bullen and Henkel (the Kinlochleven plant manager) sought to increase the functions undertaken with bonuses – implementing 80 minutes of work per hour. British Aluminium also attempted to strengthen and resurrect (at plants such as Falkirk, Lochaber and Warrington, where they had fallen into disuse) the JWCs, and to assert their primacy in productivity matters.

By 1950 all of the works, bar the smallest and oldest at Larne and Foyers, had resurrected the JWCs. Once again, the company was quick to remind members of JWCs of their obligations to 'help the company in its task of maximum efficient production', 'consider the welfare of all those who work in the factory', and 'to promote a close understanding between management and work employees'. Setting out desirable qualities for a prospective JWC representative, it identified: 'loyalty to his colleagues in the works, to the company and management', enjoy 'good relations with his foreman' and show an, 'understanding of the rules of the works' (including lines of authority), and 'he should have a keenness to co-operate with the Company to promote efficiency'. Councillors should also comprehend 'the need for discipline' as 'one enthusiastic team with unity of purpose', understanding 'what is meant by an interest in the job and a fair day's work'. Though presented as guidance for management and employee representatives alike, they appear to have been very much directed at the shopfloor. The company's guidance concluded by stating: 'We have printed the above notes believing that they will be appreciated by all our own Councillors – Management and Worker – in the job they are trying to do for the benefit of us all. The Councils fail in their purpose if they exist merely as a Complaints Committee.'[94] In addition to JWCs, the company introduced a 'suggestion scheme' system (retained into the 1970s) primarily as a means of encouraging limited worker participation – as well as a sense of participation and responsibility – underpinned by guidance from the Industrial Welfare Society.[95]

By early 1950 the company had experienced a stoppage at Warrington, and was fully anticipating a 'show-down' over wages across the industry.[96] Against rising prices prompted by the devaluation of sterling – between 18 September 1949 and June 1950 food prices rose by 7 per cent against male wage rises of 1 per cent – and the Korean War, opponents of wage restraint defeated the General Council of the TUC in the vote over wage restraint at the Congress of September 1950. The General Council for its part urged the incumbent Labour government to clamp down on illegal strikes, acknowledging that it was unable to control its members. The incoming Conservative government of Winston Churchill was keen to revive the cooperation of wartime with the trade unions, with Churchill telling his Minister of Labour, Walter Monckton, 'to preserve industrial peace', although opposition within the Conservative Party was starting to grow to those in the administration perceived as the 'arch-appeasers'. The Conservatives' withdrawal from the 'commanding heights of the economy' – industrial intervention, controls, and subsidies – also had the effect of decentralising 'collective bargaining as workers looked more to money wages rather than the social wage'.[97]

Though JWCs were functioning to a greater or lesser degree at some of the smaller plants, by 1953 the company was forced to confront criticisms that they were not effective, accompanied by a suitably patrician rebuke:

Joint Works Councils are something our fathers did not have. They lived in an age of 'deputations' (often they were only 'disputations') and they had no say at all in the running of the factory. Such is no longer the case. The Councils exist to give workers an opportunity of having their say and to make their contribution to the success of their factory and the Company at large. It would be a great pity if workers through apathy towards the conditions in which they are employed allowed this opportunity to pass unseized. It is to be hoped that 1953 will see not only continuance of all the good work being done by the Councils, but a great increase in their activities in response to reasonable and well-considered requests from the Workers.[98]

The editor further encouraged employees to listen to the BBC's 'Just the Job' programme broadcasting the views of leading industrialists extolling the value of joint consultation in industry, remarking, 'many of our readers will have heard these men declare their sincere belief in the value of Joint Consultation in industry'.[99] If the formal machinery, such as the JWCs, were subject to scepticism, especially in the large plants, and had been overtaken by 'triviality', this probably owed much to the workforce recognising the real intent behind them.[100] The company continued to make appeals on the basis of the social wage. In an article published in the Spring edition of *The B.A. News* entitled 'what productivity really means', the editorial team highlighted the growing productivity gap between Britain and the US and Germany, stating:

> There are two conclusions to be drawn from all this. The first is that as a nation we shall all either sink or swim together. If as a nation we go under, then as individuals we are bound to go short and hungry, whether we are managers or employees. No political arguments, no rights or wrongs of industrial disputes can possibly obscure the hard facts of this situation. The Second conclusion is that our national tendency to rest on past laurels or to be satisfied with modest achievements is not enough to ensure economic survival. The truth is we have been lulled into drifting with the tide of events. And the things which have lulled us – American aid, artificial high prices, a seller's market – no longer apply. So that we are left with nothing but our own genius, our own strength of heart and mind, and our own will to co-operate for the common good ...[101]

British Aluminium might have been forced to adopt the mechanisms of joint consultation, but it struggled to relinquish the tone of the patriarch. The company's 1956 *A Plan for your Retirement* was no less redolent with the language of loyalty: 'This Company has already recognised that it has a moral obligation to supplement the State pension for employees who have served it long and faithfully, and the existing scheme for retiring allowances was instituted for this purpose.'[102]

In addition, to support control over the labour process, the company also sought to improve the status of foremen in their works, in response to disquiet about their pay and conditions falling behind in the face of rising minimum wages on the shopfloor and productivity agreements.[103] Equally important, as Linzee pointed out to his fellow managers in April 1948, was the fear that with the centralisation of labour management functions and the growth of the personnel department and system of welfare officers, foremen 'may tend to feel they are being deprived of some of their functions'.[104] By 1950 the company had improved wages and conditions for foremen, concurrently introducing structured selection procedures and training for them. However more comprehensive training programmes from apprenticeship through to different levels of management (ladder schemes) were not properly initiated until after the RTIA takeover. In contrast to BACo's belated schemes, AFC started to establish its training programme for supervisory grades over two decades earlier. As with recruitment for the expanding work-study branch, in selecting candidates for supervisory grades, the company sought to reinforce loyalty and discipline by recruiting, 'returned ex-service men who would be suitable for training on the production side'.[105]

Industrial relations, with the company's complicity, continued to be characterised throughout the 1950s (and the 1960s) by the parallel existence of the 'formal' mechanism of arbitration and conciliation (as represented by the structures of JWCs and SSCs) and the 'informal' bargaining at local level, affected by the micro-politics of the plants. Though method study had been introduced at BACo works in the early 1950s, standard costings and control systems did not start to be introduced across the group until the late 1950s. These were accompanied by incentive schemes for the trades – electricians, mechanics and building trades – and bonuses for process workers.[106] To all intents and purposes it mirrored the general picture of contemporary industrial relations within private-sector industry in Britain, as highlighted by the significant report of the Royal Commission on Trade Unions and Employers' Associations (the Donovan Commission) published in June 1968.[107]

Composing the BA Version

Yet the decision with the most profound long-term impact to be reached at the 1948 conference, especially in the Highlands, was that of producing a comprehensive strategy for communicating with the workforce, local residents around BACo works and the public at large, in order to 'stimulate the interests and loyalty of employees'. These publications were to be produced by the Establishment Division – which also oversaw the management of BACo's estates, alongside personnel policy – and were compiled by Hugh Woodhouse, a former Fleet Street journalist, RAF officer and then welfare officer at the Highland reduction works. Woodhouse worked under the watchful eye of the manager of general establishments, Commodore Linzee.[108] The announcement of the death the following month of Sir William Murray Morrison sharpened the attentions of the company's narrators; the *pater familias* was to be enshrined as a legend in the company narrative, a role in which he had long been cast.[109]

In part, the growth of the business by the late 1940s called for an improved means of communicating with employees. However British Aluminium's publications were explicitly designed to cultivate certain core values among its employees; coupled with the 'sculpting' of the 'Garden of Eden' in the Highland company settlements, these aimed to create a 'landscape of the mind', forging a 'disciplinary power' over the workforce to modulate both behaviour and outlook.[110] They were also intended as a charm offensive to shore up wider public support for the company. This marked a more systematic approach bringing together the narrative developed in earlier, company publications, along with the public and private utterances of senior figures in British Aluminium's history, above all William Murray Morrison and Lord Kelvin. Morrison's projected 'personal vision, goals, beliefs, values, and assumptions about how things should be done' was to be shared.[111] In a similar vein, the social historian of the French company Aluminium Pechiney, and its predecessor AFC, observed the latter's 'modelling' of the 'landscape' around their Alpine works, both physically but also socially.[112] As the ensuing chapters illustrate, BACo also invoked of bonds of kinship through cultural attachment to the clan system, while using social structures to modulate behaviour in the company villages of Kinlochleven and Inverlochy. These deliberate attempts to 'sculpt' cultural attitudes – complimentary and intrinsic to their managing of social relations in their works and by extension the company villages – have left an enduring legacy in the memories of individuals in the Scottish Highlands every bit as evident as the physical manifestations of the industry seen in the vast pipelines hugging the steep sides of *Meall an t-Suidhe* leading to the Lochaber smelter.[113]

This synthesis of existing accounts – in the pages of the company's magazine, *The B.A. News* (arising out of BACo's *Highland News* started in 1947), the BACo employee handbook published in 1948, and British Aluminium's company history completed in the mid-1950s – of the company's first half century into a compelling historical narrative and deploy this to great effect in its publications. At the centre of the BA version was the story of its Highland ventures: a tale of daring human endeavour against adversity, of salvation, and social mission set against the common *motifs* of modern Highland history. This was combined with BACo's wartime service to the nation at large (at company and individual level). Though the form may have changed over time, until the RTIA takeover the predominating message – observance of duty, loyalty and service – did not. BACo's employee handbook, issued in 1948, reminded the reader, after a dramatic preamble explaining BACo's early history, that

> Those of you who have read so far will now understand that you have become part of an important concern with very large resources but also with very heavy responsibilities. There are several thousand people in the Company's employ,

and it is the Company's aim to provide regular employment for them, a fair wage in return for a fair day's work, a comfortable place to work, reasonable conditions and above all reasonable security of employment.[114]

Their historical narrative embedded a formulaic 'heroic' storyline with several popular *motifs*. Whether it was a conscious decision on the part of the company to present it as such, simply the imaginings of the enthusiastic editor, or a mixture of both, BACo tapped into the country's persisting and voracious appetite for adventure stories and historical fiction. One of these *motifs*, that of British male character in the face of adversity, as epitomised by imperial endeavours, was redolent within contemporary literary evocations and cinematic representations, such as in *Scott of the Antarctic* (1948). It also attempted to draw on the popular collective narrative of the 'blitz spirit', the British nation pulling together in the face of adversity (in this case the economic, as opposed to the military, Dunkirk).[115] This call to national pride was vividly evoked by the editorial of *The B.A. News* in the winter of 1948, with Britain in the throws of economic crisis, but with a new age heralded by the launch of the National Health Service and the continuation of Labour's national-isation programme:

Through the ages the good customs have lived: the bad have been allowed to die. So let it be with Industry. The bad old customs of child labour and sweated labour, and the indifference to mutilation by unguarded machinery are all dead. The over-long working week, the fear of unjust dismissal and the complete absence of joint consultation are all being hastened to their graves. No one will mourn their passing. But in our energetic killing-off of the bad traditions of Industry, let us take great care that we do not destroy also the good traditions. It is still a fine tradition to work hard, to take a pride in craftsmanship and quality of work, to be a willing and helpful member of a team, to expect wise discipline and to see service to one's fellows and to the community, as well as to oneself, in every day's work well done. Let us guard these traditions zealously for it is these that have made us free citizens of a great nation.[116]

Another tradition rehearsed in this narrative to great dramatic effect was that embodied in literary and film representations of the Scotland of 'tartanry, kailyard and faery', combining romantic depictions of the 1745 Jacobite rebellion and the Highlands, with 'domesticated village Scotland'. This drew on the popularity, around the late 1940s and early 1950s, of films like *I Know Where I'm Going* (1945), *Bonnie Prince Charlie* (1948), *Whisky Galore* (1949), *Rob Roy – the Highland Rogue* (1953), and Warner Bros' adaptation of Stevenson's classic, *The Master of Ballantrae* (1953). In essence this developed out of the company's earlier championing of their role in the Highlands, and depiction of themselves as 'saviours' of the Highlands.

The B.A. News launched the first of series of articles on the history of the company in their autumn 1948 edition. Four more articles followed between September 1948 and June 1949 (all of them with the Highlands at the centre), and in summer 1952 the magazine carried 'Our Highland Story'. By 1950 the company was printing 4,000–5,000 copies of *The B.A. News* to be distributed not only at the works but also in the surrounding communities. Evoking the spirit of Lord Kelvin, the second episode of the serialised history, appearing in the winter 1948 edition, declared:

> Starting at a time when water power in this country conjured up visions of a water well at the end of a mill race, the Company has blazed a trail in Scotland with three fine hydro-electric plants which have brought industry to the Highlands. We have accomplished this against obstacles, natural, legal and financial, which producers in lands more favoured with great rivers and falls can scarcely comprehend. The Company can take great pride in the history of its Reduction Works.[117]

This representation of the heroic pioneering role was not restricted to the Highlands, but equally to BACo's Norwegian works; an article by the Vgielands manager J. Mørch carried in the same edition stated that: 'The British Aluminium Company have been the pioneers and have played a very prominent part in the development of the Norwegian aluminium industry.'[118] The concluding article in the company's magazine on BACo's history once again reiterated the centrality of the Highland and Norwegian endeavours to display its pioneering, as well as its welfarist, credentials:

> From the commencement of operations at Foyers and Kinlochleven the management has taken a close interest in the lives of employees and their families ... permanently expressed in the building of workers villages both in Scotland and in Norway ... By 1908 in the wilderness that was Kinlochleven, a neat and orderly village had already been established ...[119]

The motive for the reference to British Aluminium's 'Garden of Eden' is evident from the references to its 'neat and orderly' nature, but was explicitly spelt out in the following paragraph:

> The mutual interest between employer and employed in such closely knit communities became the basis of relations between management and operatives in factories subsequently developed by the Company. From the beginning there has been knowledgeable appreciation of the needs of workers, and a general desire to do everything practicable to ensure their health and contentment.[120]

This was of critical importance in nurturing the sense of the familiar and of the company as the benign parent – and shaping consensus, loyalty and service – in a large and growing modern firm. As the second part of the book shows the apogee of the company's attempts to cultivate or 'sculpt' a sense of togetherness was to be seen in the village of Kinlochleven.

The company's long tenure in the Highlands, and its experience of the persuasiveness of this narrative with policy makers, lobbyists, and key luminaries alike, taught it the value of deploying popular features of recent Highland history that could be readily associated with by the local communities. Thus, in 'Our Highland Story', the idylls of the company villages of Kinlochleven and Inverlochy and 'prosperity' brought by British Aluminium were preceded by a dramatic preamble of the heroic but failed 1745 Jacobite rebellion, the Highland clearances, and the demise of the big sporting estates. These themes were subsequently reinforced in other articles in *The B.A. News*.[121] Cataloguing the tide of emigration from the region, the piece again revived the spirit of Kelvin noting: 'With the electricity generated aluminium was produced, employment found for many Highlanders and a new metal was supplied for the use of mankind.'[122] This theme was returned to in British Aluminium's company history, published in the mid-1950s and distributed to its entire workforce: 'Though the language is lofty, the British Aluminium Company can claim to have played an important part in staying "the devastating tide of emigration" and preventing depopulation and decay, both here [Foyers] and elsewhere in the Highlands.'[123] Readers of the corporate literature were left in little doubt as to the hero of the piece, Morrison: 'Most of our developments in the Highlands were planned by a man who for obvious reasons had the interests of the Highlands at heart – he was himself a Highlander who loved his native country.'[124] Reinforcing his role as *pater familias* the author assured readers that, 'those who have succeeded Sir Murray in his high office are equally mindful to areas where we have set up factories'.[125] Similarly the other significant public luminary of the company's pioneering years, Lord Kelvin, was oft evoked.[126]

The magazine's editor also attempted to maintain the sense of familiarity between BACo and its employees by featuring stories about its long service employees and multi-generational employment with the company, not just in the Highlands but also in some of the English plants, such as the Willotts of Staffordshire who had 400 years of service between the three generations of family members who had worked at BACo's Milton factory.[127] Stories like this, aside from the long family connections, helped keep alive this close relationship with the company for decades. The sense of family was further moulded in the company magazine by features such as 'Round the Factories', 'The Other Chap's Job', 'The Other Girl's Job', and 'Meet the Boys'. For most effect, connections with Morrison himself were identified, especially in cases where they referred to the camaraderie and pluck of the 'pioneering' years. The autumn 1949 edition, for example, featured Donald MacLellan, an elderly commissionaire at the Lochaber smelter who had worked in Morrison's household for many years. These were intended, as the managers' conference had directed, to develop a culture of loyalty and service within the company. This cultivation of a sense of familiarity and common endeavour was further promoted by inter-factory visits between the various UK plants to encourage 'a family feeling between the factories of Scotland and Wales, and England and Ireland'.[128]

Older employees were also encouraged – mimicking the parental role of British Aluminium with its employees – to nurture this sort of spirit in the young as both parents and workplace guardians, such as in this *B.A. News* editorial from 1951:

> ... With well over half the entire population dependent on Industry, the major responsibility for the well-being of our country must rest on the shoulders of those 13 million ... we maintain that the first responsibility of Industry is to continue the work which should have been started at home and school to produce good citizens. It takes very little effort to announce that Industry should be manned by 13 million good citizens ... To make good citizens the accepted standards of a the groups in which they [young apprentices] live, work or play must be raised to such a level that the wrong-doer finds that he is rejected, not acclaimed every time he behaves in a way which is not the way of a good citizen. We, in all the ranks of Industry, can help to raise the standards. Don't allow this chance to pass.[129]

The sense of duty and order were also linked to individual employees' military service, mirroring the company's wartime and continuing service to national defence. This was underpinned by the active nurturing – not least due to the dominance of the company general establishments department by former service personnel – of links with the Territorial Army (TA), as well as to pre-national service training and youth programmes. Above all, Sir Ronald Charles's role was visible here, mirroring his public utterances as part of the Army, Home and Empire Defence League – an organisation 'for all men and women who care for their liberty and for the ideals for which the British Empire stands' – in calling for patriotism and an interest in military service by youth, as well as his close involvement in the YMCA.[130] These activities were often organised by former military officers, and embodied both Armed Service and public school traditions. Under the 'Spare Time for Britain Scheme' British Aluminium sought former servicemen among its workforce to volunteer for TA camps to train young men before National Service, offering them another week away from the workplace and £3 on top of their TA pay. Juvenile employees attending these camps were also offered additional time off. By 1950 the company had also secured places on the Outward Bound Sea School and the Mountain School at Eskdale in Cumberland. Promoting these places for young employees, the editor of *The B.A. News* extolled the values of 'leadership', 'team playing', and 'Christian fellowship', concluding that: 'All who attend the course should be prepared to live up to the motto of Outward Bound: To Strive, To Serve, And Not To Yield.'[131] In addition the sons of BACo employees at all levels were offered the opportunity to compete for scholarships to Bryanston School (a minor English public school established in 1928). By mid-1950 twelve children of employees were attending the school, among them the sons of shopfloor workers.[132] The choice of these organisations was not inconsequential, they all promoted 'shared values' to those of BACo's directors were familiar and that they wanted to impart to their employees: loyalty, service, and patriotism. The first edition of BACo's *Highland News* in December 1947 carried a cover piece on National Service, juxtaposed with a story about a canteen attendant at the Lochaber smelter attending honours ceremonies at Buckingham Palace to pick up her son's posthumous medal and being entertained by the company, underlining the duty, patriotism, and ultimately sacrifice made by this former employee as a lesson to others.[133] If British Aluminium were less enthusiastic about trumpeting its role as a leading supplier of aluminium to the defence industry than its competitor Northern, then it did not miss the opportunity to mention this as an aside to its patriotic duty when it arose. Commenting on the use of BACo alloys in Britain's new ground-to-air missile defence system, the Bristol 'Bloodhound', in 1957, *The B.A. News* noted with due solemnity: 'Guided missiles are naturally distasteful objects to any right-minded person. Such things must remain with us, however, so long as we have to maintain force to defend our way of life.'[134]

The B.A. News also gave an insight into the prevailing attitudes within the company on gender and race, while providing another opportunity to press home the themes of loyalty and order. An article on the Gold Coast Bauxite Company Ltd in summer 1948, for example, described the stratification of company housing, with the names of the white staff housing immediately identifiable to anyone familiar with BACo's heritage in the UK, while inferring the assumed superiority of the white British staff:

> Most of the Africans [employees] live in the two villages built by the Company for the mine. They are brick-built with corrugated iron roofs. The African clerks and craftsmen have individual huts built with verandahs. Others, who live in African villages nearby, have mud huts thatched with straw, a common form of habitation in many parts of Africa. The British, of whom there are about fifteen, have their bungalows on the top of the hill, each with its own garden. The bungalow names soon make visitors feel at home, for one sees such names as 'Leven', 'Lochaber' and 'Shrewsbury'.[135]

The following January, covering the strike of miners at British Aluminium's Awaso mine, the paper seemed to embody the most trenchant views of some white settlers:

> A strike throughout the Gold Coast Colony of African cooks and stewards – i.e., all domestic servants – meant the sweeping of all festivities overboard.

Everyone was too busy "doing" for themselves ... Trade unionism among the Africans is very strong and obedience to the decisions of the Union is enforced by methods we might consider rather brutal. In view of this the strike was complete and even our faithful old 'boys' left us – many of them with tears in their eyes.[136]

While E. A. Langham, British Aluminium's senior representative in India, covering Burma and Ceylon too, writing in *The B.A. News* in spring 1949 also epitomised these remnants of colonial administration struggling to contend with the changed world around them:

Indian labour is not difficult to train and can become highly skilled, but supervision needs to be much more extensive ... the tendency on the part of the office 'babu' (Indian Clerk) to errors of omission or commission has been known to develop tendencies on the part of European staff to throw inkpots at him. At such times, the only cure is to send the European concerned to the hills for a few days' local holiday ... In the good old days, when beer was a reasonable price, the senior old Indian hands used to take great delight in seeing how much beer could be drunk by the English "sahibs" at one sitting, the Indians providing the beer.[137]

If the social imperialism of the pioneering years had, to some extent, been displaced by the changed geo-political climate of the post-war world, then some of the unsavoury remnants of empire lingered on. Nevertheless these sorts of attitudes appear to have been reasonably prevalent among expatriate British businessmen operating in colonies or commonwealth countries immediately after the Second World War.[138]

Similarly prevalent attitudes to gender were evident with the company's publications. While female employment increased within British Aluminium after 1945, if anything the types of jobs available to women became that much more restricted outside works like Warrington, where female employment in the manufacturing processes was historically much more commonplace. At other BACo plants small numbers of women worked in process engineering (usually confined to quality control) immediately after the war, but most female employees were segregated into areas of the business deemed to be appropriate for their sex namely personnel (including female welfare officers), secretarial, laboratories (usually as lab assistants), canteens and nursing. Moreover those women remaining after wartime service in production areas gradually left or were expected to leave. During the 1940s and 1950s, the majority of female employees in the company works – with the exception of canteen staff (many of whom increasingly worked for subcontractors) and nurses – appear to have been predominantly young and single. This was in line with national trends in post-war female employment in Britain with around half concentrated around distributive, professional, scientific, and 'other' job classifications; the biggest increases post-war being in insurance, banking, business services, public administration, local government, teaching, nursing, and retail work. Once again, outside the former textile hubs of Lancashire and Dundee, as well as fishing villages, this was typical of the national trends in Scotland, and England and Wales, where by 1951 69 and 52 per cent respectively of women employed were single, with 55 per cent of female employees in Great Britain in 1951 under the age of 35.[139]

In the early years of *The B.A. News*, the inherent assumptions about women's roles in the business were evident from those articles featuring female employees, such as the short-lived series 'The Other Girl's Job' which ran twice in 1949 and was then discontinued. Examples included that on Miss Margaret Ball, an assistant at BACo's central research laboratories at Chalfont Park, who, according to the stereotypes played out in this piece, was mystified by science:

> Miss Ball tells us that when she first saw the instrument on which she was to work she was rather awed, as spectroscopy was a new subject to her. However, she soon learnt how to use the instrument and how to produce from it the analysis of various aluminium alloys. But while learning she made several mistakes and on one occasion startled her seniors by informing them that in one sample of aluminium she had discovered platinum.[140]

In marked contrast, features on male employees stressed their skills, military service and physical prowess – whether through sport or work – to underline their masculinity; furnacemen's jobs, for example, were declared as 'no job for a weakling'.[141] Increasingly where female employees appeared in the magazine, the features focused on them in traditional jobs that involved 'servicing men' – such as those on canteen staff, 'The Cup That Cheers' – or on the wives of BACo employees involved in the village improvement societies and local groups, for example 'Highland Wives are Busy'. For much of the 1940s through to the 1960s, *The B.A. News* did not, as a rule, feature the smutty sexist jokes and pictures that appeared in Northern's *Noral News*, although there were exceptions; The 1950 Christmas edition, for example, featured a number of this genre of cartoons, including one with a secretary sitting on Santa Claus knee uttering the line: 'And does my 'ittle "sugar daddy" have any nylons.'[142]

By the late 1940s British Aluminium had laid the foundations of a 'shared culture' and a framework for industrial relations that was to prevail in some form for the next two decades. This was cultivated out of the vision, principles and shared values of its board and managers, articulated in the preceding decades by senior figures within the company, not least the *pater familias* Sir William Murray Morrison whose stature grew with his death. Crucially it was also shaped by the careful deployment of BACo's public identity, and its sensitivity to adverse publicity, which was used to great effect;

the lessons of the 'social drama' of 1936 had to some extent been learnt. Equally the company's reliance on government meant that it had been decidedly more politically sensitive to the potential for controversy than those sections of private industry who were not as close to the state. In this respect it sought to mimic the public corporations and select private sector employers, such as ICI, by incorporating trade unions into the mechanisms of formal bargaining and arbitration and through the professionalisation of management. This half-way house between public and private sector was also used by BACo's senior management to further enforce the sense among employees that the company was a national enterprise, a 'key' industry, with the principles of loyalty, order and service to British Aluminium being indivisible from patriotism. It was also promoted by the *esprit de corps* nurtured among its managerial cadre.

An end to patronage? The path between takeovers, 1959–1982

Nothing better contrasted the break with the past, and signposted the future in BACo than the two consecutive editions of *The B.A. News* immediately after the 'Aluminium War'. In the first of these was featured Portal and Cunliffe's patrician *adieu* to employees. The following edition, published in the spring of 1959, provided an overview of TI's business, and a focus on Sir Ivan Stedeford, the TI chairman. Stedeford's own rise from grammar school dropout to successful entrepreneur could not have contrasted more sharply with the backgrounds of Portal and Cunliffe. Yet Stedeford was no renegade. He attended the same King Edward VII grammar school in Birmingham, came from a modestly well-to-do middle-class family, served as a Fleet Air Arm pilot during the First World War, and had been knighted for his lengthy public service during the Second World War and after. Equally crucial to the strategic outlook of the firm (as the negotiations over the Invergordon smelter suggested) a retinue of the old 'service' class was visible on the boards of both BACo and its majority shareholder, TI. Among this number were Plowden – who after departing BACo's board and further public service, joined the TI board – Sir William Strath, and Field Marshal Montgomery's former Chief of Staff and Director of Military Intelligence, General Sir Francis ('Freddie') de Guingand.[143]

De Guingand, a career army officer who was also imperially steeped, had not formed a favourable impression with those who had experience of the man. In a damning report on the leadership of the British Army in the 1940s – in which their 'man management' style was described as lacking, incidences of 'high living' and 'plunder' while in combat arenas were highlighted (in contrast to the privations faced by the ranks and local communities), and 'buckpassing' and 'lack of enthusiasm for paperwork' was observed as commonplace – Lt Col. Standford identified General de Guingand as particularly representative of these failings.[144] More controversy surrounded the General with the publication of his memoirs – which betrayed similar attitudes to colonial subjects to those articulated by *The B.A. News* in its reports on

The Old Guard:
General Sir Francis
('Freddie') de
Guingand (right)
with Field Marshall
Montgomery, *c.*1943.
Image courtesy of
Tim Challis.

the Gold Coast and India – in 1954. As one reviewer of de Guingand's reminiscences
of his stint as a young officer in the King's African Rifles in Nyasaland observed:

> If one is curious as to the reasons for the smouldering resentment of Africans
> against the attitude of white superiority, this author unconsciously supplies
> some of the answers. One needs little imagination when reading of the
> adolescent amusements indulged in by army officers at the expense of African
> servants, the cold-blooded floggings, the arbitrary firing of huts, to recognize
> the seeds of present unhappy relations.[145]

Cultural change
Nevertheless there was a significant change in tone and tempo after the RTIA takeover,
denoted by Stedeford's address to BACo employees – identified also in the personal
narrative of his meteoric rise as an entrepreneur. This was not simply intended to

stamp his mark on the company but also to appeal to those sections of the workforce on the shopfloor and in management who had felt constrained by the previous administration. As the editorial proclaimed: 'There is no element of paternalism in his attitude. Every employee is expected to make his own effort, but, if he does, then he will find every encouragement to develop himself – from comprehensive education and training schemes, up to free university degree courses.'[146] Opportunities for promotion on the basis of ability, duty to work, and all-round diligence replaced those of fealty previously impressed upon employees. In essence the social contract in British Aluminium's message remained but the language shifted from one of *noblesse oblige* to being steadfastly based on rights and responsibilities. This was to be supported by a comprehensive programme of continuing professional development, largely funded by the company. These new values were actively promoted through *The B.A. News*, as epitomised by the following report about young technical apprentices run in the summer of 1964: 'Industry in Britain can give opportunities to young people, opportunities for adventure as well as personal achievement. Giving chances is one thing, but taking advantage of them is another. The fact that these chances are accepted and made good use of proves that things are not as bad as they sometimes sound in the headlines.'[147]

Professional development programmes complemented the strengthening of the sales team during this period and the drive towards a streamlined multi-divisional structure by the late 1960s. The longer-term drift of former military officers out of strategic and middle management positions accelerated – especially with the removal of a layer of tactical management – and more opportunities were offered for mobility within the organisation. By the mid-1960s the company was funding fully accredited courses in a range of management subjects, and providing financial support for apprentices undertaking degree programmes. Eventually, in October 1969, the company instituted an accredited taught course and qualification in supervision.[148] One such example of mobility under the new regime was George Haggart, who commenced as an apprentice at Lochaber straight from school in 1943. Within nine years of being appointed as a work-study superintendent at Lochaber in February 1958, Haggart had been appointed as Chief Industrial Engineer for control systems at head office and managing director of BACo's Primary Aluminium Division by January 1980. By the time Haggart retired in 1990 he was assistant managing-director of British Alcan.[149] Asked about his observations on changes that he had observed in a career spanning over half a century in the industry, he responded: 'There was probably more of a levelling in Alcan than there was in BA, but I think I've got to say that BA from the early BA that I knew to the BA at the end in 1980s time, there had been a lot of levelling.' Explaining this further, he noted: 'In the early days of Geoffrey Cunliffe and so on, it was very much a hierarchy [...] Naval and army, very much so, and in other words the top of the house tended to be those kind of people.'[150]

Among the dozen former British Aluminium (and Alcan) managers from their Highland reduction works, as well as a couple of senior managers (ranging in ages from 56 to 81) interviewed or surveyed for this book, 82 per cent entered as graduates (nine holding pure or applied science degrees from Scottish or provincial English universities, and one Scottish graduate of accounting); one had attended a Scottish private school, while all of the rest had attended Scottish high schools or English grammar/secondary modern schools. Admittedly only three had undertaken a graduate-level qualification in general management at a business or recognised engineering management school, or British Aluminium's own in-house training programme (of these three, two went on to become directors of British Aluminium or British Alcan).[151]

Change at the shopfloor?
BACo, and TI, continued to accept the voluntary conduct of industrial relations at a local level, while also recognising the imperative of further incorporating trade unions into the formal mechanisms of collective bargaining, with union membership rising by 30 per cent to the 13 million mark, and union density rising from 44 to 55.4 per cent of the UK workforce between 1964 and 1979. Furthermore like government, the company saw the benefits to be accrued from using the trade unions and shop stewards as tools of 'economic management' in pursuing wage restraint, managing redundancies and renegotiating working practices.[152] While BACo certainly continued to offer reasonably generous benefit packages, the wage discrepancy between shopfloor and managerial employees remained markedly more pronounced than at Alcan's works. Pay and conditions in the Highland reduction work group were structured around two parallel systems that for shift workers (mostly located in the main and carbon factories, power houses and the upper works), and day workers (offices and laboratories). Reflecting the continuous nature of the aluminium reduction process, employees in the former group were required to work three sets of seven consecutive shifts, working on average a forty-two hour week.[153] Arbitration over wages and conditions were negotiated through the formal structures as pursued by SSCs and JWCs, as well as more informal negotiations between union representatives for the various trades in different parts of the works and foreman and managers. In addition, union officials, supervisors and managers often continued negotiations outside the works. Despite the removal of a level of tactical management between the 1960s and 1970s, and the centralisation of management functions, the conduct of industrial relations remained largely unchanged from the preceding decades in the west Highland smelters combining both formal structures and informal negotiations. Moreover the tone in management style evolved as an older generation of the patrician officer class of manager retired between the 1950s and 1960s. For example, Norman Goss, a graduate of the Royal School of Mines, replaced Col. F. E. Laughton MC, the Lochaber manager. In due course, the general manager of the Highland smelters,

John Bullen, also retired. Like the departures of Cunliffe and Portal, as *The B.A. News* noted with unintentional prescience, it marked the 'end of an era'.[154]

Reflecting on these changes, nearly two decades on, one chief industrial engineer – himself a beneficiary of the more meritocratic system under RTIA control – remarked: 'things are much better nowadays. There is much more participation in plant affairs by all employees. In the past, as in all industry, orders were simply passed down.'[155] Even allowing for the familiar company rhetoric of 'rights and responsibilities' so evident in the paper at the time, this was a view shared by trade unionists reflecting on the period, albeit from the vantage point of the twenty-first century and with their own narratives to promote. One AEU member, Sandy Walker, characterised the conduct of industrial relations at the Lochaber works during the 1960s and 1970s as follows:

> We had disputes with management and we always resolved them, because there was never any danger of us going [...] too far, which I don't think management at the time appreciated, because it wasn't a job, it was a community [...] although we were really in dispute with management, we could go and we could sit down with them afterwards and have a drink. That was the way, with Alex Fairley. He was personnel manager up there for years and years and years. Norman Goss was the manager. He was, you could go and talk to him [...] Regardless of what the dispute was about, you could always sit down at the end of the day and talk to these people.[156]

Sandy Walker emphasised the persistence of the informal nature of negotiations and the importance of the local networks in the workplace. Retired AEU area branch secretary, Jimmy Dunlevy – a BACo tradesman who had moved to the area by way of work as an engineer in the shipyards of Dundee and Greenock – covered negotiations for all of the BACo west Highland plants and the Wiggins Teape Pulp and Paper Mill, described industrial relations as being 'not bad, not perfect, but amicable enough to resolve through negotiation and discussion'. Like Walker, he attributed the relatively cordial relations to BACo's place within the community, as well as noting British Aluminium's image as a good employer in the area. Similarly he suggested that as far as possible 'informal negotiations' allowed local officials and managers to arrive at a settlement rather than referring it on through the formal machinery, especially in the precarious position that the older west Highland smelters felt they were in by the 1960s and 1970s 'because it was a means of resolving things before they got out of hand, and to the credit again of the foremen and the officials and workshop and senior management in the plant, things were dealt with on a strict basis, although there was obviously certain things on the shop floor where it would be dealt with quietly'.[157] The informality of negotiations was even more pronounced at the smaller Foyers and Kinlochleven plants where both union and managerial employees acknowledged negotiations were also subject to a good deal of deference.[158]

The informal nature of negotiations was aided to a certain extent in the west Highlands by the fact that managers, like trade union officials, remained in post for long periods and resided within the local communities. Norman Goss, mentioned in Walker's testimony, served as manager from 1950 until his untimely death in 1971, having previously been Assistant General Manager under John Bullen of the Highland Reduction Works group since its formation in 1944. One visiting Board of Trade official similarly described Goss as 'approachable'.[159] If the same could not necessarily be said of his predecessor John Bullen, then all the same his long service at the west Highland smelters as a manager from 1920 until his retirement in 1958 meant that he had a loyalty to the locality, as his role in discussions over pollution controls would show. W. H. Weston, who retired as manager at Kinlochleven in 1963, had served in managerial capacities in the west Highland smelters since 1925.[160] Similarly there was also little mobility among the trade unions, with branch secretaries, such as A. MacLean at Lochaber, often remaining in post for the best part of thirty years at Lochaber. As well as illustrating the characteristics of Britain's post-war industrial relations, the local negotiations at British Aluminium's Highland plants embodied what sociologists have referred to as the distinction between 'public issues' and 'private struggles' between the generic practice of management and the specifics of the process of making aluminium and local conditions at plants.[161]

What was increasingly preoccupying the Highland workforce, including local managers, was the precarious position of these plants in the long term, and the dearth of suitable alternative employment. Since the 1930s there had been considerable unease at the plants due to the periodic lay-offs and short-time working as a result of the relatively frequent droughts in the area, before agreement was reached with the NSHEB over emergency supplies of electricity. As early as May 1964, BACo had indicated in evidence to the Board of Trade that it envisaged that efficiency gains would allow a cut of the west Highland workforce by 150–200 (or 15–20 per cent) by the 1980s; reports purporting to have evidence of plans to close the works surfaced periodically in the local area and the regional press from then on.[162] Further concern for the Highland reduction works followed BACo's announcement in February 1962 that 150 workers at the rolling mill in Falkirk, who had already been reduced to a four day week the month before, were to be made redundant. In the two years preceding this, Falkirk had been bolstered by news that the company was intending on investing a further £10 million in the plant, accompanied by speculation that a further 600 jobs would be made available at the works. In fact, more than 400 workers had left (in search of better pay and overtime) or been paid-off from the Falkirk plant by June 1961. While murmurings continued in government circles and around the group about the future of the Highland reduction works, BACo announced the closure of its Milton works in September 1962, with most of the 1000 jobs to be transferred to Falkirk or Resolven in South Wales. In February 1966, Falkirk experienced a one-day walk out of three-quarters of its workforce over the employment of non-union labour in the laboratory.[163] After 'technological improvements' at Lochaber, British Aluminium reduced the size of the workforce by 80.[164] The sense of insecurity only further increased with the closure of BACo's historic Foyers works in 1967 – an ill-omen calling into question, in the minds of many in the locale, the long-term viability of all of the west Highland plants – while a further 1000 job cuts were identified across the group in 1971, 100 of them at Falkirk.[165] Pessimism can scarcely have been dispelled by the under-investment in the plants. Adding to the palpable fear of closure was the fact that the loss of manufacturing jobs in Scotland accelerated in the 1970s, with a further 100,000 going during the decade adding to the 40,000 already lost between 1954 and 1970.[166] Despite the influx of other large employers to the Lochaber area, not least the Wiggins Teape Pulp and Paper Mill as well as concerns like Yvette Cosmetics, British Aluminium was still considered the best employer in the area; so much so that the Lochaber manager Norman Goss felt confident enough to boast about it to visiting Board of Trade officials in 1963: 'he has stated, perhaps with his tongue in his cheek, that he would welcome another sizeable project in Fort William, as he thinks that the conditions for his company's workers would compare favourably with those of any other concern.'[167]

As far as the Highlands and the Lochaber district were concerned the efforts of trade unionists continued to be primarily directed towards attracting industry to the region, and lobbying for trade union recognition, with British Aluminium one of the few employers in the area who formally recognised trade unions. The added significance of this is underlined by a letter to the general secretary of the STUC in September 1975 enclosing a copy of a recent letter written by the Lochaber Trades Council (LTC) – on which BACo trade unionists were heavily represented – to local paper *The Fort William Free Press*. William Mood of the Council observed of the situation in the area: 'This article shows how concerned we are at the way public money is being used to induce firms to set up in this area. We particularly resent the fact that every firm so far induced has never been amenable to Trade Union representations indeed their main reason for coming here is to get cheap labour.'[168]

The article had appeared in the paper the very same day and catalogued the number of firms introduced into the area with HIDB support, on the back of the unceremonious withdrawal of Yvette Comestics, which had refused to recognise the TGWU, representing a number of Yvette's female employees and had given their workforce half an hour notice before the end of their shift.[169] In a letter written by the LTC's secretary D. F. Hunter to Jimmy Milne, the new General Secretary of the STUC, Hunter requested that Milne write to trade unionists in the Highlands asking for a meeting to discuss what he considered to be 'foremost in all our minds namely unemployment'.[170] Milne's reply expressed sympathy with the position of Highland trade unionists, given their 'small numbers, vast distances and generally operating in what can certainly be rarely described as a friendly atmosphere'.[171] As labour market opportunities in the area contracted further the LTC's efforts remained squarely focused on pressing the HIDB to attract jobs to the area and the local council to provide vocational education to the unemployed.[172]

As with the negotiations over the construction of the Invergordon smelter, the conduct of industrial relations at the plant and the subsequent closure did much to sour the air in the company as a whole. Relations at the Invergordon smelter represented an attempt to make a break with BACo's traditional company values, and to address the company's historic problem with wage drift. At the same time, BACo aimed to increase productivity through joint production agreements and closer supervision.[173] Shortages in council housing – and a lack of foresight on the company's part in ensuring provision of accommodation – left many of the employees living on a caravan site to face a chilling Ross-shire winter. A far greater proportion of the Invergordon workforce had no 'hereditary' link with the company. As well as increasing competition for employers in the labour market, the North Sea oil bonanza that followed shortly afterwards created additional pressure on houses and services in the area, with an early strike among AEU members at the Invergordon site directly resulting from demands for increased subsidies for lodging and subsistence allowance.[174] Having invested considerable time and effort into courting the local population, the cumulative effect, as Ronny Utiger observed was that: 'Within two years the whole industrial relations climate changed from one of co-operation and goodwill to one which was a fertile breeding ground for dispute.'[175] The plant experienced two go-slows followed by a short strike at the end of 1973 and a major strike in May 1974 (during which output was reduced by 60 per cent), and yet more discontent among the employee-residents of 'Caravanville'.[176] The impact of the job losses on the area and the suddenness of the closure of the plant – coming during the Christmas period and with workers on the night-shift discovering by listening to the local news when they woke – left an even more bitter taste among many within the company and locally. As the manager tasked with announcing the closure observed: 'I think that's one of the most traumatic things in my life, from having to go and tell people in the first place and then actually the shutting down. And even after that, we felt there was a lot of feeling that in actual fact it would re-start again.'[177] The difference between the Invergordon system and the company's traditional conduct of industrial relations in the west Highland smelters also prompted a clash of cultures between the new arrivals and the existing workforces at Kinlochleven and Lochaber.[178]

Sensitive enough to its image in the Highlands and the centrality of the smelters to BACo's public profile, when faced with the prospect of either closing the west Highland smelters or modernising them, the company exhibited a great degree of care, not least in the choice of George Haggart – as a local man who had risen from the shop-floor to seniority within British Aluminium – to take over the management of the group and oversee the working party on their futures. Despite having roving briefs within the company since the early 1960s, Haggart had always kept his base in Fort William and indicated his preference for the assignment. The modernisation of both plants required a 30 per cent reduction of both workforces, with the payroll at Lochaber having been reduced to 50 per cent of its 1978 size by 1983. Negotiations over the modernisation and redundancies were conducted through a working group that deliberated options and alternatives. In some respects, the Fort William plant was the beneficiary of the demise of Invergordon. Had a satisfactory contract been negotiated at Invergordon, and the plant continued in operation, then it is entirely plausible that the finance for the Lochaber reconstruction and Kinlochleven would not have been made available, and both plants would likely have been deactivated.[179] Moreover it is questionable whether any other international global aluminium producer would have even contemplated such a reconstruction at this time given that the economic threshold for smelters being constructed during the late 1970s and early 1980s was around 250,000 mts, compared to the modernised Lochaber's more modest 40,000 mts.[180] However as Gus Margraf had stated, 'Scotland was the cradle of the aluminium industry' and had been a major employer in the Highlands for 'many years'; in essence these west Highland plants remained absolutely central to the company's public image and were the barometer by which its sense of corporate social responsibility would be judged.[181]

The plants also represented a familiar reference for many employees, against a backdrop of organisational change. If the corporate ethos changed after 1959, then its new parents still recognised the value of the 'BA' version. The pages of *The B.A. News* continued to mimic this successful recipe. In an article celebrating British Aluminium's seventy-fifth anniversary, the editor B. W. McDonald declared:

> The early days of BA were characterised by pioneer work in every sense of the word. This was particularly the case with Foyers, the first of three factories that were to make such an economic and social impact on the Highlands of Scotland. When construction began at Foyers, a year after the registration of the company, it meant work for some 300 people in an area which was hard hit by depopulation and emigration. When one considers the work involved in the construction of Foyers and the largely unmechanised construction methods it was remarkable that the first ingot was produced at the plant a year after the start of the scheme ... The building of the dam, power-house and factory at Kinlochleven between the years 1905 and 1909 has often been compared with the Gold Rush days in the United States and Australia.[182]

Individual vignettes were also used to sustain this, such as the 1975 feature on Jimmie Batchen – a powerhouse worker, and one of three generation of Batchens to have served in the Highland plants – upon his retirement from the Lochaber works, including a story about his father working alongside Morrison in the early days at Foyers.[183] As the 1978 president of BACo's long service club, the 30 year club, observed of that organisation, but as easily applied to the editorial logic of maintaining stories emphasising the familial connections within the firm: 'An organisation such as this is a very good thing in any firm. It helps to promote a sense of stability, of having roots – a very good thing in such a rapidly changing world.'[184]

The same themes of tradition, service and loyalty were evident in British Aluminium's promotional films, such as *Metal in Harmony* – released in 1962, scripted by the eminent Scottish poet Norman MacCaig (1910–96) and narrated by his compatriot Tom Fleming, who also provided commentaries for Royal weddings and the Queen's Silver Jubilee, as well as appearing in the 1971 film *Mary, Queen of Scots* – a combination of the epic pioneer tale set against the dramatic background of Highland scenery. Through the medium of that quintessential ingredient to the aluminium reduction process, water power, the film stressed the 'harmony' with its natural surroundings (ironically given descriptions of the impact on the landscape of the major civil engineering work and footage of smoke billowing from the factories). BACo's 1972 short film, *The Invergordon Smelter*, reflected the company and the era's emphasis on modernity and scale, stressing the enormity of the undertaking, its newness and the clean lines of the plant, while implicitly continuing to portray BACo as a pioneer again, this time of a different age.[185]

Changes in company ethos, and broader social change, were reflected after 1959 in pieces about rights and responsibilities, and ultimately social conformity. As the article about young apprentices from 1964 had praised the values of hard work and conformity – against the background of clashes between Mods and Rockers, those seen as deviating from mainstream social values – so a later piece, set to the backdrop of the student sit-ins of 1969, stressed how order and diligence was rewarded through praise in the company:

> Once again though we all tend to fall into the trap of lumping everyone together – there are students and students. 'Stop their grants', 'sack the lot' – these are calls that have gone out after the riots and sit-ins. For many of those involved this is a fair comment and for some they would be lucky if that was all they received. But what about the rest? Those who want to work and those who work very hard – those who can't spare the time to sit –in, on, up or down rather than work.[186]

Articles of this type were a direct response to the challenges to traditional vestiges of authority emerging during 'the long sixties' (1956–74) – a time when, 'various counter-cultural movements and subcultures … did not *confront* society but *permeated* and *transformed* it' – representing an inter-generational shift.[187] It reflected broader inter-generational gulfs, and ruptures, between the different generations of men who had served in both world wars (and lived through the inter-war depression) – events that had profoundly affected their outlook, both in increasing familiarity with those who had experienced the same and in isolating them from wider society – and the 'baby boomers'.[188]

Conservatism still permeated the company over gender attitudes. If women remained the 'other', confined to the peripheries of the company magazine between 1949 and the late 1950s – as secretaries, wives and mothers (either biologically or as surrogates within the hostels) – *The B.A. News*, (as did its competitor, Alcan's *Noral News*), reinforced these stereotypes even more into the 1960s and 1970s. This was accompanied by increased sexual commodification of women in cartoons and features. The May/June 1963 edition featured female workers at the Fort William plant on its front cover as 'The Lochaber Lovelies', while the 1970 Christmas edition carried as its front cover three female workers from their Warrington works sporting mini-skirts standing on a bridge with the caption: 'Who wants to look at anything else but Susan Carter, Deborah Shale and Ida Jones? But that is Baco Guardrailing, now going on sites all over Britain.'[189] In 1972, the magazine ran a 'Miss BA' competition featuring female employees. The autumn edition emblazoned the back cover with 'Miss Burntisland'. After providing Una Watt's 'vital statistics', the company organ stated: 'No, Una does not work for BA, so you may ask why put her photograph in *The BA News*? Well, if we do need a reason, and quite honestly we didn't need much of an excuse, we have a factory at Burntisland.'[190] This was then qualified by pointing out that one of the judges of Miss Burntisland had been the manager of the BACo works. By the late 1970s *The B.A. News* discontinued articles of this nature, although they did include a regular cooking feature by a housewife promoting BACo foil and other products. While *The B.A. News* carried a two-page spread explaining the work of the Race Relations Boards in the workplace, no such explanations or features appeared following the Sex Discrimination Act of 1975. Whether the change in *The B.A. News* was initiated as a result of pressure from female employees through the trade unions, shareholders, customers, or simply on the basis of an internal decision completely unrelated is unclear. Certainly since the late 1950s female trade union membership had grown and was exerting pressure on the TUC, government, and businesses in the campaign for equal pay, alongside women's groups. Moreover by the late 1960s and early 1970s the rise of the women's liberation movement also placed pressure on businesses and the trade union movement to effect change.[191] If BACo's publication procedures had changed in this respect then Alcan's had very certainly not. As late as February 1978 *Newspak* – the in-house journal for Alcan Foils at Wembley – carried a marketing and productivity campaign featuring a semi-clad model with a prominent chest wearing a t-shirt emblazoned with the slogan 'consider it delivered – Alcan', and with the model depicted as saying: 'When I make a date, I keep it – how about you?' *Newspak* continued to carry a 'page 3 girl' into the 1980s. This was in spite of apparent indifference among its employees to the feature, with it receiving one of the least enthusiastic responses in a survey conducted about the journal among employees in 1978.[192] The persistence of these sorts of misogynistic attitudes was captured in a letter from one of the former senior sales managers for Alcan's UK sales subsidiary, Aluminium Union Ltd, to the then Secretary of Alcan Canada, Tom Brock: 'I think everyone enjoyed the annual dances, as there were some quite nice bits of stuff in the office.'[193]

The period between the RTIA takeover and the merger with Alcan saw a change in company culture, strategic outlook, as well as recruitment processes and professional development pathways. This was epitomised by BACo's last MD, Dr John Ford, who, alongside AUK's George Russell, steered the merger of two companies through. The product of a grammar school followed by undergraduate and postgraduate study at University College Swansea, Ford had coupled the demands of his various managerial roles within the company with membership of the Scottish and Welsh councils of the Confederation of British Industry (CBI), as well as being a rugby referee, coach and a member of the Sports Council for Wales. In what was a clear indication of the work culture being encouraged within BACo just before the merger, as well as the embodiment of what the new British Aluminium man should aspire to, one of Ford's colleagues observed of him: 'his idea of a good holiday is to come to work in a sports jacket for two weeks.' Ford promoted the cultivation of a new identity for BACo, with an implicit assertion here of what distinguished 'productive' and 'non productive' work cultures.[194] Similarly the official mechanisms for and corporate messages about the conduct of industrial relations were different. Nevertheless, their continued to be a greater discrepancy in pay between managers and the shopfloor in BACo and Alcan. However even the removal of a layer of tactical management could not change the unofficial conduct of industrial relations at the west Highland reduction works, and explains the later clash of cultures when staff from the Invergordon smelter were redeployed at Kinlochleven and Lochaber. Despite the change in emphasis of the organisation, seen also through its staged withdrawal from its community commitments, TI's recognition of the potency of and its deployment of the 'BA' version was reflected in the goodwill it generated; Among those canvassed for a large British Marketing Research Board survey, conducted on behalf of Alcan in 1967 to explore their public profile alongside that of BACo and a number of other prominent large companies (including IBM), British Aluminium was deemed to be the most public-spirited company and the one most respondents stated they would like to work for.[195]

The great disruption? The birth of British Alcan

If the merger of British Aluminium and Alcan Aluminium UK were viewed as a success in boardrooms in London and Montréal, as well as in Whitehall, it was met with concern among the ranks of both organisations and in the Highlands.[196] It was not difficult for anyone with more than a passing knowledge of the two companies to judge that there was good cause for this, especially in the political and economic climate of 1980s Britain. In spite of the secretive way in which negotiations were conducted, there was a leak prompting an earlier release. An indication of the alarm in some quarters was visible from a letter, in advance of the announcement, from the former Invergordon manager Gordon Drummond, by then working for the HIDB, to the Scottish Office expressing his concerns at the rumours he had heard of the merger and of what he saw as the possible threat to the Kinlochleven and Lochaber smelters.[197] Though a question mark was raised over the future of Kinlochleven during the negotiations, this was dropped, most probably due to the symbolic importance of Kinlochleven to British Aluminium and the heritage of the UK industry, as well as material concerns about what to do with water-power assets there. Newly modernised, Lochaber was a highly efficient plant even though comparatively small by modern standards. Nevertheless although further job cuts took place in the early 1990s reducing the workforce by around one third.[198]

Quite aside from the immediate impact of the substantial job losses and uncertainty, the two company cultures were not easily wedded and clear divisions were evident from the outset. However, while Denniss Pinn's minute a decade before had identified strong opposition within AUK to a merger with BACo, Alcan's worsening trading position, and their Canadian parent's increasing anxieties with their subsidiaries position in UK markets, over-rode these concerns. Nevertheless, as a manager at Alcan's UK head office admitted privately to Alcan's biographer Duncan Campbell in December 1982, even if Alcan staff at HQ 'accept that the merger was necessary, and they appreciate philosophically that rationalisation and redundancy are inevitable ... the Alcan-Baco development is indeed traumatic.'[199] The sense of trepidation from the BACo-end was no less marked. George Haggart, at the time of the merger managing director of BACo's Primary Aluminium Division, recalled the hurdles to be overcome: 'It was a merger, it wasn't a takeover but we had to stop calling it BA. It was British Alcan right? But in practice that never happened because it just took [...] so many years and they still talk about BA, right? So that was one of the things, but things that we weren't sure of was this question of [...] British Aluminium were very socially minded. We knew what they'd done for the area right? And we wondered.'[200] Capturing the gulf between the two corporate cultures, Douglas MacDiarmid – who had joined British Aluminium at Lochaber in 1974 as a trainee graduate accountant, and at the time of the merger held a management position in BACo's primary aluminium division – observed of the merger and its aftermath:

> In the first year or two if you looked at the room of a hundred and fifty managers and directors you could immediately see, it was as though some were red and some were green: there were British Aluminium Company, and there were Alcan people, and you knew them by not just by their faces, but by their style of management. But I would say within five years that had completely gone and there was a new cadre of British Alcan Aluminium managers who were of a different mould and cut to the old BA style altogether.[201]

As an avowed admirer of Margaret Thatcher, MacDiarmid underlined his testimony about his experiences as manager within British Aluminium and Alcan within the narrative of perceived British decline; deploying BACo as a motif of what he saw as the inherent 'industrial malaise' of Britain in the late twentieth century and Alcan as the remedy:

> So all of that from my point of view gave me I suppose not just an affection for the old company British Aluminium Company which is right in there. I can still see the BACo logo, and if you open me up I'm sure it would be deep down in there. But I also formed a really great respect for Alcan as a company: utterly different in its culture from the British Aluminium Company. It was not, I mean it was billed as a merger, but it was absolutely a takeover. And anyone who had been lulled into a false sense of security that the world would continue that you know that the post-Imperial world would continue forever was in for a big surprise and the biggest manifestation of that was you've got to get your act together and you have to perform. We're not necessarily going to tell you how to run your works although there are certain standards that you have to meet for, you know, a respectable multinational company around the way you treat people, around the way you deal with communities, around the way you manage your finances, but the main thing, the main job, for you is to make this place work, and to make it sing.[202]

In fact MacDiarmid's view of the 'takeover' and the 'malaise' undermining British industry bore close resemblance to thinking among Conservative ministers and DTI officials as well as that of British Alcan's chairman, Lord Peyton.[203] MacDiarmid further identified two of those culprits commonly assigned by Conservative politicians and commentators at the time – and more broadly by historians of the 'declinist' school – for British Aluminium's inherent failings, namely weak and indecisive management, on the one hand, and recalcitrant trade unions, on the other:

> I suppose if I was to characterise that period, late seventies/early eighties, there was a bit of a malaise around the whole company which really only cleared away probably in the mid–late eighties/early nineties. There was a bit of a malaise. I suppose a sort of an end of empire. The paternalistic company feel had induced a laziness in senior management; a lack of decisiveness and clarity of direction in senior management. Probably a lack of good and capable influencing and communication skills with the men and women that worked in the company. That had induced in the company on the other side, as part of the general British industrial scene, strong and very proactive unions. Or perhaps proactive isn't the right word, they seemed to oppose and object to everything that was suggested as a change, or a development, or an improvement.[204]

Others saw the merger with Alcan in a far less favourable light. Like most of the trade unionists and shop floor workers interviewed, Sandy Walker contrasted what he saw as the praiseworthy priority that Alcan placed on employees' health and safety, with a much more confrontational management style and a loss of interest in the community:

> That's when the divide came and it was a massive divide, massive. I don't blame the people who Alcan employed as managers, it's probably just what they were told to do as the ethos of managing a plant, but however, it destroyed the whole community, aspect, of being employed there [...] whether that was being dictated to from Canada I don't know, but any thoughts of, I hate using that word, paternalism that was all gone [...] you were just literally a number then. Of course they had a job with the new smelter and old timers like me who would refuse to change their ways. That did not begin well I can assure you [...] They would bring in these guys that would shove you off to a place like [...] the Grand Hotel [in Fort William] or somewhere and go through all this, and of course I was totally negative and all this [...] teamwork and all, because we were natural team workers prior to that. We could – we couldn't think any other way, this is – that's the way we thought. It's just like being a soldier: I've got to look after you, you've got to look after me, but they couldn't understand that.[205]

Walker's testimony, illustrating the clash between the two cultures, reflects in equal measure a sense of bereavement at the disappearance of BACo and a feeling of alienation from Alcan's process of change. While Ford and Russell had acknowledged the immediate fallout from the merger, it was questionable whether either had fully appreciated the full magnitude of the long-term task of assimilating both cultures, or the legacy of BACo's traditions and narrative.

Alcan's global structure meant that historically its national subsidiaries operated with considerable autonomy. In part, this was a strategy, which stemmed from the need to be seen as both national and international to maximise the commercial benefits. This was particularly the case within the British Empire, as Arthur Vining Davis had surmised, with Alcan marketing itself as British by the 1930s.[206] Nevertheless AUK had operated a far less patrician culture, although a good many of their directors, such as John Elton and John Peyton, were socially well connected. Where – as in the case of Earl Alexander of Tunis and the Hon C. D. Howe – AUK's parent Alcan Inc. recruited public servants to the board, they were the usual individuals with broad political skills and connections that did not interfere with the commercial management of the business but were principally employed as sales and political ambassadors for the company.[207]

In particular, attempts by Alcan to reorganise working practices provoked growing resentment. For the first time in over half a century, Lochaber experienced a strike in 1990 over working practices.[208] At Alcan's Lynemouth smelter, industrial relations were tense up until 1990, with workers complaining of 'assertive and autocratic management styles during the 1980s'.[209] Furthermore this was taking place against a general assault on trade unions after Margaret Thatcher's victory in the 1983 election – and subsequently the defeats of the miners and other groups of workers – with further legal infringements imposed on trade union rights and new statutory tools to allow employers to reject voluntary negotiations. In the face of sustained managerial assaults on extant workplace mechanisms of negotiation, and the marginalising of trade unions and shop stewards, union density by 1990 fell by 23.4 per cent on its 1979 figure, and membership to its lowest figure since 1961. Moreover between 1979 and 1987 job losses in Scottish manufacturing reached almost 20,000 per annum, with unemployment rising to level not seen since 1939, at over 13 per cent by the mid-1980s.[210] Other former employees at the west Highland smelters, such as James Ross who retired from the cell room in 2004 – having worked as a fitter in the plant and thereafter as a cell room worker before spending his last two years as a team leader – were more ambivalent about their experiences of the changed work systems under Alcan. Bob Herbert, a former career soldier, started at British Alcan's Kinlochleven smelter in 1987, where he worked as a cleaner before starting in the cell room. On joining, Herbert observed that people still referred to 'Alcan' as the 'BA', and was struck by what he perceived as the continued delineation of tasks, and the persistence of two cultures:

> I think the best way to sort of explain it is [...] you've got sort of two different societies within the factory. You've got people who grew up with the BA, and they still regard it as the BA, and they've still got a BA ethos. You've got the younger element coming through that had joined it as Alcan and have got the Alcan ethos, and there is this sort of very marked line, and it's the same in the village [...] You know, because Alcan were a multinational company, and BA was really a sort of local company, and therefore had the workforce at heart.[211]

In part, Herbert's observations reflect the absence of an emotional tie to the old company. It can also partly be explained by his immersion, as a former serviceman, in a work culture that was quite distinct from some of the strong craft traditions that existed within the Highland works. The strike at Lochaber in 1990, and discontent at Lynemouth, underlined the need for a different approach. Like 1910 and 1936 before it, this moral outrage served as a sharp reminder to Alcan that they would need to restore 'trust', especially within the Highlands (in the community, as in the workplace). Alcan recognised the need not only to give greater autonomy back to the shopfloor, albeit in a very different fashion to the workplace relations under BACo, but also the value of appropriating some of BACo's robes, in the form of the 'BA' version.[212]

Revision of work organisation had some immediate effects for those working at the Lochaber and Kinlochleven plants, and one longitudinal study of Alcan's Lynemouth smelter found dramatic improvements in industrial relations within the workplace almost immediately after the introduction of autonomous work teams between 1991 and 1994. This was more complementary to traditional methods of working within aluminium cell rooms. In particular, the study noted that employees identified the 'elimination of supervisors' – replaced by team leaders drawn from among existing shopfloor workers, as at Lochaber and Kinlochleven – with 'improved job satisfaction', 'increased interest in their work, and greater decision-making autonomy'. This had led to a fall in accidents and absence, with management-union relations becoming 'more open and consensual'.[213] At Lochaber, changes in work organisation saw a significant contraction of the workforce so that by 2007 it numbered a little over one hundred employees from around 600 in the early 1980s. Nevertheless, while the staged closure of Kinlochleven was managed in a model fashion, Alcan's hasty withdrawal from Burntisland, Falkirk, and Glasgow, around the same time, provoked public outrage, not least because Burntisland and Falkirk were still reeling from other closures in the area. Seen against the importance for Alcan's public profile of continuing BACo's legacy of deploying the Highlands as an important motif in their corporate identity, this decision appears all the more calculated; the sensitivities around Alcan's Highland plants were neatly alluded to in a comparative study of corporate social responsibility (CSR) and aluminium companies within Europe produced for the European Aluminium Association (EAA) in 2003: 'At Lochaber, the group discussions returned to the question of the responsibility of Alcan, an international company, in providing employment and developing the skills of the local community, especially the younger generation. When the Kinlochleven smelter was closed in June 2000, it was seen as a duty for Alcan to participate actively in regeneration projects.'[214]

Conclusion

When the 1948 British Aluminium managers' conference commissioned *The B.A. News* and the company history against the changed backdrop of the post-war world, with the 1936 Lochaber strike a fresh memory, they recognised the potency of the wealth of material that their predecessors had left in inuring 'loyalty' and cultivating further Morrison's vision of 'a community of interest'. The relaying of this narrative still almost approaches a catechism among former employees and residents in the Highland village of Kinlochleven and in Fort William. This is the enduring legacy of the reforms of 1948 that captivated employees into seeing themselves within this great 'pioneering' endeavour. It carried the company through the crises of 1958–59, and 1982. RTIA, and Alcan in time, recognised the value of the brand and the caution with which they would have to approach the Highland smelters. It is doubtful whether the organisational change and the functioning of both the formal mechanisms and informal system of workplace negotiation would have functioned so comparatively smoothly without the firmament of this compelling story.

Hostility to the Highland schemes among conservationists and other opponents, the early struggles of 1910 and 1936, the nature of aluminium production, and the company's place in the defence economy impressed upon BACo's senior managers that cultivating a robust and pristine public image was an absolute imperative. The 'behavioural lock-in' arising from proximity to the state was sustained by the characteristics of the culture adopted by the company, arising from the social milieu and also career backgrounds of a number of its leading figures. While leading figures within the company undoubtedly approved of welfarist measures, British Aluminium's self-appointed role as social benefactors and the cultivation of a 'service' culture could scarcely have proceeded unaccompanied by the workplace reforms. Equally they should be firmly placed within the context of enduring power struggles between employers and labour. The patrician tone of BACo's relations within employees until the 1960s was only to be expected given the social milieu of its board members, and its managerial echelons. After 1936, and the watershed of the 1939–45 war, the progenitors of the company's labour management strategies essentially recognised the importance of adopting a pragmatic approach to the subject, irrespective of their natural discomfort with trade unions. Thus these welfarist measures and mechanisms for incorporation of trade unions and shopfloor workers were intended, like British Alcan's later initiatives on team work, as much as to respond to the periodic increased power of labour and achieve managerial control of the labour process. Yet, while workplace relations within the smaller west Highland works of Foyers and Kinlochleven could be characterised as deferential – something that owed much to their small size and, as the pursuant chapters show, the 'capture' of the individual in the villages – with this fealty came an expectation of responsibility on the part of the company. However, as the state exerted considerable influence on the company's culture, so too did pressure from local communities and employees, as part of the 'feedback process'. The Lochaber strikers had reminded the BACo board in July 1936 that the company had a moral obligation to fulfil its side of the social contract, and had transgressed the rules of the 'moral economy'. As the foundering of the JWCs at larger plants like Falkirk, Lochaber and Warrington illustrated, the formal machinery was disregarded where it became apparent that this was simply intended as a mechanism for promoting managerial prerogatives. That industrial relations at Lochaber remained relatively peaceable after 1945 owed much to the low turnover of managers and union officials and the close contact that workforce and managers were in outside the plants.

Even with the diminishing role of the company in the locality after 1959, the prevailing cultural legacy of the 'BA' meant that Alcan struggled to be accepted. As a multinational which understood social engagement within the parameters of corporate social responsibility, Alcan found it hard acclimatise, to a wholly different cultural outlook. Ultimately it reflected, on the one hand, the success of BACo in cultivating a binding culture built around a compelling, almost beguiling, company narrative. The corollary to this was that it was deployed by employees to remind their employers of their 'responsibility' and 'duty'. While RTIA recognised that the obstacles to supplant this, and indeed the desirability of harnessing it to their ends, Alcan faced a struggle in attempting to introduce its culture especially with long service employees at the Highland works; the 1990 feedback serving once again to remind the employer of his or her moral duty. These clashes were also about a fundamental breach between a more public service orientated model of management with that of Alcan, as the highly competitive global player. It also represented the sense amongst some BACo employees – reflecting experiences of globalisation more broadly – of what sociologist Richard Sennett referred to as 'the corrosion of character' and the denigration of their skills and workplace identity, overtaken by targets.[215] Belatedly Alcan recognised the benefits of maintaining aspects of it, not least the historical narrative, for their own standing within the local communities and the plants.

4

Health and environment: 'contested' terrain

That magnificent piece of work of the Aluminium Company was the beginning of something that would yet transform the whole social economy of countries such as the Highlands, where water abounded. He looked forward to the time when the Highlands would be re-peopled to some degree with cultivators of the soil, but re-peopled also with industrious artizans doing the work which that utilization of the water would provide for them. The British Aluminium works were very popular in the locality … He thought when the time came that every drop of water that now fell over the Falls of Foyers was used for the benefit of mankind, no wise man, no man who ever thought of the good of the people, would regret that the power in the waterfall was developed for the benefit of mankind.[1]

Report of Lord Kelvin's speech at the opening of the British Aluminium Company's carbon factory at Greenock, 4 August 1897

J UST under a century before British Aluminium started work on its development on the banks of Loch Ness at Foyers (in 1895), Scotland's national bard Robert Burns opened a poem describing the falls and its immediate environs:

> Among the healthy hills and ragged woods
> The roaring Fyers pours his mossy floods;
> Till full he dashes on the rocky mounds,
> Where, thro' a shapeless breach, his stream resounds.[2]

The fame of the falls grew, with the English poet Samuel Coleridge, who visited them in 1803 in the company of William and Dorothy Wordsworth, describing them as 'one of the five finest things in Scotland'.[3] By the late nineteenth century, the Inverness-shire beauty spot had become popular with those Victorian urbanites able to holiday in the Scottish Highlands, as part of tours operated by shipping company MacBrayne's, as well as for budding poets and artists.[4]

In contrast to Lord Kelvin's grand vision, some Victorians were outraged by British Aluminium's development on the shores of Loch Ness. The campaign against the scheme was spearheaded in the letters pages of the London *Times* by the National Trust for Places of Historic Interest and Natural Beauty (formed that same year, 1895), and supported by a number of important benefactors to the organisation. The newly founded Trust, formed by Canon Hardwicke Rawnsley, and his friends and fellow campaigners Miss Octavia Hill and Sir Robert Hunter, came fresh from a campaign against civil engineering developments affecting the English Lake District. Among its chief benefactors were the Duke of Westminster, and the poet, artist and critic, John Ruskin, both of whom were also linked to the National Health Society (founded in 1873, and a precursor of the Smoke Abatement Society) and the Kryle Society, which sought 'to bring beauty home to people'.[5] They were joined in the public outcry over Foyers by the Conservative Baron Sir William Augustus Fraser who pledged to donate £100 to any organisation willing to oppose 'this act of barbarism', while the editor of Britain's popular Victorian travel companion, *Thorough Guide Series*, J. B. Baddeley referred to British Aluminium's development as 'the greatest outrage on Nature perpetrated in the present century ...'[6] Brother Oswald Hunter-Blair, a monk at the nearby abbey in Fort Augustus, warned locals against trading the, 'secluded straths and peaceful glens which they love,' for, 'the guilt and grime, the smoke and squalor, and sin of a busy manufacturing district', all for the promise of employment and prosperity, evoking the transformation of the English town of Middlesbrough (once a village) and Chicago. Brother Hunter-Blair was not alone among critics in stressing the threat of moral decline, notably, as they saw it, with the influx of 'alien labour' who would 'drink, fight, desecrate the land, and disappear when the work is done'. Ironically the monks of Fort Augustus had instigated the construction of one of the earliest hydro-electric schemes in Britain. Some posited this as a battle between 'science' and 'religion'. As one correspondent put it: 'Shall we without speech or protest, let this display to the glory of the Lord be done away with or even suspended?'[7] Rawnsley and his compatriots set about organising a petition to Inverness-shire County Council (ICC) in an attempt to block the development at Foyers and sought to broaden their campaign through the press, to no avail. Meanwhile the Duke of Westminster was engaged in increasingly bitter correspondence with British Aluminium; the company maintaining that through the Neuhausen Company – who had supplied it with technical advice, as well as the Héroult patent – it had been instructed as to how to substantially reduce fluorine emissions from the factory. However they did not directly address the concerns of campaigners about the alterations to the falls themselves and the impact of the substantial civil engineering work involved, including driving a tunnel of half a mile in length through the rock above the falls, and building dams at Lochs Garth

Loch Killin seen from Garrogy, 1894. © RTA/GUA.

and Killin. By late September the company followed through with its threat to Westminster of publishing details of their correspondence with the Duke along with a riposte in the *Times*.[8]

The company had also been busying itself with ironing out any obstacles in the planning permission for the scheme. British Aluminium avoided the need to introduce a bill to Parliament to seek permission by purchasing the entire estates covering the water catchment area (7729 acres) thereby, their detractors maintained, effectively eliminating any potential local protest. In April 1895 British Aluminium submitted a report to the ICC in which the company highlighted the substantial public works that would be undertaken as a result of the scheme (as it would mean also diverting public roads) – having first garnered support among local landowners and tenants, as well as securing the approval of district committees – and made a pledge to considerable temporary and long-term employment in the district, as well as the construction of company housing. The report made reference to this development being the first commercial one of its kind planned in the UK, of the growing market for aluminium, and to the possibility of attracting other related industries to the area. BACo was also at pains to present its development as complementary to the pastoral idyll of the area, including assuring them that any emissions from the factory would be negligible.[9] In addition, BACo paid for the County Medical Officer for Inverness-shire, Dr Ogilvie

The roaring Foyers: Upper falls of Foyers, 1894. © RTA/GUA.

The roaring Foyers: Lower falls of Foyers, 1894. © RTA/GUA.

Grant, to travel to Neuhausen to inspect the premises and see the methods in place for reducing effluents, winning his praise for provision of accommodation for employees, paying for medical cover, and a building a small hospital.[10] In the months preceding, the company had received the endorsement of a large number of local residents, the local councillor, and clerics from all of the main denominations, who had met in the Parish of Boleskine and passed a number of resolutions applauding the scheme and calling for the introduction of more manufacturing into the area. Moving the motion in support of these developments, local Free Church of Scotland minister, the Reverend Macleod, spoke with gravity about the outward flow of young people of employable age from the district noting that:

> The country was depressed in agriculture and in other ways, and many questions were agitating the Highlands; without going into these questions, he might say that the great question for them in the Highlands was how to provide employment for the people. The resolution alluded to the introduction of manufacturing or other industries calculated to develop local resources. They undoubtedly had local resources in the Highlands which, he might say, were at present lying waste, without doing any good whatsoever. Especially had they resources in water which had not been utilized for any purpose. The Aluminium Company proposed not only to establish works for the using of water power in the district, but at the same time they would improve the present aspect of the country ... It was not good for them to be idle; the Almighty did not create man to be idle. He gave man work in the garden of Eden. Work meant moral progress and physical comfort; want of work meant poverty and depopulation. Those with whom he had come in contact for many years – the wisest people he had met with – were all desirous to see some industry established to keep the people in their native Strath, and enable them to live happy and comfortable lives.[11]

Macleod's endorsement of British Aluminium's proposals was enthusiastically reproduced by the editor of the *Northern Chronicle*, Duncan Campbell. The paper was explicitly Conservative in outlook, and subscribed to by prominent landowners and clan chieftains, such as Donald Cameron of Lochiel, as well as William Murray Morrison's uncle, BACo's Highland solicitor and Conservative Party agent, Charles Innes.[12] Enlisting the backing of leading Highland landowners was critical to the success of these schemes and was also bound up in the politics of regional development. The apparent local enthusiasm for the scheme was joined by support regionally and among engineers further afield; one Inverness-based engineer proposing that it signalled the 'inauguration of a new era for the Highlands' contributing 'its share to the uses of man, and light, heat, and power may be carried from distant glens to homes of rich and poor alike'.[13] British Aluminium's considerable groundwork

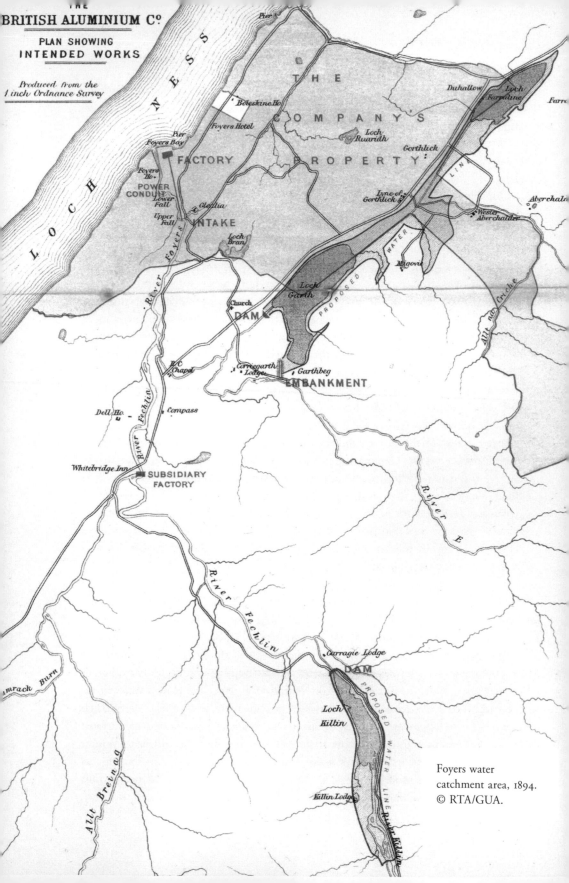

THE
BRITISH ALUMINIUM C?

PLAN SHOWING
INTENDED WORKS

*Produced from the
1 inch Ordnance Survey*

L O C H   N E S S

T H E

C O M P A N Y ' S

P R O P E R T Y

Pier

Boleskine Ho.

Foyers Hotel

*Loch
Ruaidh*

Duhallow

*Loch
Farraline*

Farr

Gorthlick

Pier
Foyers Bay

FACTORY

*Foyers
Ho.*
POWER
CONDUIT
*Lower
Fall*

*Upper
Fall*

Cleitia

INTAKE

*Loch
Bran*

*Lyne of
Gorthlick*

*Wester
Aberchalder*

Aberchald.

LINE

W A T E R

*Loch
Garth*

Migovie

P R O P O S E D

Allt an Criche

Church

DAM

River Foyers

*R.C.
Chapel*

*Carriegarth
Lodge*

Garthbeg

EMBANKMENT

Dell Ho.

Compass

River Fechin

Whitebridge Inn

**SUBSIDIARY
FACTORY**

River E

River Fechin

Carragie Lodge

DAM

*Loch
Killin*

P R O P O S E D   W A T E R   L I N E

River Killin

Killin Lodge

Allt Breinag

mrack Burn

Foyers water
catchment area, 1894.
© RTA/GUA.

paid dividends with the ICC, who accepted their proposals in the face of no less than 281 objections.[14] In defeat, Baddeley excoriated the 'local press' for their 'reticence, if not absolute silence', while Ruskin lamented the 'imminent destruction of one of the most lovely and poetic scenes in Scotland … in the face of the apparent utter apathy of the countrymen of Burns and Scott'.[15]

Seen from Lord Kelvin's perspective, as his biographers observe, though his views on harnessing the power of the falls for human progress 'could scarcely fail to provoke the anger of late-twentieth-century critics of industrialization':

> His remarks did have a powerful logic of their own. The pestilence, poverty and over-population accompanying the industrial development of his beloved Glasgow had as their counterpart the depopulation and decline of the Highland economy. Now the advancement of science, and especially science-based industry, which was transforming Glasgow into a healthier, more spacious and very prestigious Second City of Empire, would equally bring economic and human salvation to the vast Highland regions, for so long, like Ireland, the mere reservoirs for Glasgow's labour.[16]

This 'logic' was apparent in Lord Kelvin's 1897 speech at Greenock, in which he explicitly linked these scientific developments with social progress and Britain's role as an imperial power.[17] This reflected the view among such quarters that: 'the fruits of the Baconian and Newtonian Revolutions were a resolve not to accept nature as an unalterable given, a *fait accompli*, but as an enormous unrealised opportunity, the material from which man could fashion his worldly improvement if he were daring and knowledgeable enough.'[18] As the conservative philosopher Thomas Carlyle put it, rather more belligerently than Kelvin: 'we war with rude nature and by our restless engines, come off always victorious; and loaded with spoils.'[19] The impassioned debate around Foyers was to be repeated over and again with British Aluminium's Highland developments, and while arguments changed in their tone over time they remained remarkably redolent; with those supporting British Aluminium's, and other such schemes, deploying variants of the moral and material arguments advanced by Lord Kelvin and others, while those opposing the schemes did so primarily on the basis of 'aesthetic' arguments.[20] Opponents were not immediately aware of the impact of the disruption of water flow and alteration of aquatic ecology that the hydro-schemes themselves involved. Only latterly were provisions added to the Lochaber Water Power Scheme to protect salmon and to make some acknowledgement of the need to be mindful of potential impact on the aesthetic appearance of landscape. However, even here, as with later legislation to regulate environmental conditions within the plant, and effluents from it, these were only as effective as the transparency and rigour with which these were applied. Moreover, as in the case of salmon fishing rights, objections tended to stem from economic arguments about the value of these riparian rights.[21]

Among the opponents of the Foyers scheme were the early vestiges of the environmental movement, whose stirrings have been attributed to William Wordsworth. For the emerging conservation movement in Britain:

The countryside was a haven of tranquil timelessness wherein a contented peasantry pursued its quotidian life in meditative communion with soil and season. To many, this romantic vision carried transcendental qualities whereby the contemplation of nature offered insight into God's purpose. Man living in accord with his natural environment would come to understand the Creator's workings, a notion secularized by modern ecocentrics.[22]

While the opposition to these schemes would become very much more diverse overtime – incorporating questions over land ownership, the perceived threat posed by hydro-electricity to coal, and industrial effluents on flora and fauna – as Jill Payne has observed more generally of opposition to hydro-electric schemes in the region: 'Romantic perceptions of Scotland shaped the origins of agitation for landscape protection, as well as the form subsequently taken by this protection in the twentieth century ... projected some way into the last century and even by the 1980s was far from extinguished.'[23] Indeed, recent opposition to and the tone of debate about the controversial Beauly–Denny power line in the Highlands have been very reminiscent, deploying language that would have been all too familiar to John Ruskin and his contemporaries.[24] It was also those aesthetic remarks to which Colin Russell's history of the British chemical industry returned when discussing the environmental impact of the aluminium industry on the Highlands, while unproblematically labelling the landscape as 'unspoilt'.[25] Crucially for British Aluminium, opposition in Scotland to such schemes was not coordinated by any umbrella organisations until the formation of the Association for the Preservation of Rural Scotland (APRS) in April 1927, and after 1931 by the National Trust for Scotland (NTS). In addition, the former was plagued by a lack of real power and divisions, notably with the Scottish Landowners' Federation. Concerted action against major engineering projects affecting the landscape did not act as an effective lobby until the mid-1930s – after most of British Aluminium's developments had been completed – with groups such as APRS keen to strike a balance between industrial development and conservation. This allowed BACo to make overtures to such groups, with one of APRS' leading lights, Sir John Sutherland, serving as chairman of BACo's village (improvement) societies for Foyers, Kinlochleven and Inverlochy.[25]

As opposition to Foyers and Kinlochleven illustrated, there was no shortage of vociferous critics of the schemes, though many of these objections were raised from outside of the region, further aiding proponents of industrialisation to characterise their nemeses as wealthy urbanites more intent on waxing lyrically about the grandeur of the Highlands landscape than caring for the plight of its human population.

Certainly a good proportion of the opponents of electro-chemical and metallurgical schemes in the region continued to lobby along the same cultural and aesthetic lines – suffused with the iconography of imagined Scottish nationhood and racial undertones – as their environmental progenitors. One such opponent, voicing his concerns about the Caledonian Power Scheme in *The Scotsman* in 1935, declared:

> The great natural beauties of the Scottish Highlands are a heritage of the whole nation, and the exploitation of the water-power inevitably involves the destruction of something that no money could buy – that never could be restored, that belongs to everyone of us; and this terrible destruction is planned for the advantage financially of a very few people, and those not even mainly Highland natives ... To the business man, weary of the often depressing struggle, the terrible rush of cities, the Highlands are the finest of all mental tonics, and even those much-maligned fellows whose souls, if they have any, are never supposed to rise above the Bank rate, need the Highland solitudes more than most people ...[26]

Not all opponents were 'outsiders'. However local opposition was fairly easily overcome. For example, Sir John Stirling Maxwell – whose sporting estate bordered the Loch Leven scheme, and who was later to become a leading light in both the APRS and NTS – raised objections to the Kinlochleven development, these were largely lodged on the basis of delays in the project and over minor disagreements. Crucially these were settled with generous compensation payments to Maxwell of £3,500 (£345k) between 1906 and 1908.[27] As ever, British Aluminium, as veteran political operators nationally, regionally and locally – with support among some leading landowners, Highland development campaigners, and the local populations, as well as Whitehall departments – was sensitive to its carefully cultivated self-image as a 'benefactor to the Highlands'. This they used great effect to counter opposition and in negotiations with government, while continuing to use a system of generous compensation to buy the silence of critics.

Supporters of such hydro-electric schemes pointed out that the allure of one person's imagined Highlands masked an altogether different reality for the settled residents living on the land. As a report by the think-tank Political and Economic Planning declared bluntly in 1936:

> The romance, history, and scenery of the Highlands, which are among the region's greatest potential assets, are also, perhaps, the greatest obstacle to a recognition of the desperateness of their case. In Jarrow or the Rhondda grim and derelict buildings and works force the most unimaginative onlooker to appreciate the economic tragedy of the place. In the Highlands it is not so. Bracken spreading over hundreds of acres of once cultivated fields looks

pleasing enough to the casual eye. Even ruined buildings may appear merely picturesque if one does not inquire about the fate of their former inhabitants.[28]

In his *Plan for the Highlands,* also published in 1936 – which advocated a solution for the region along the lines of the New Deal Tennessee Valley Authority – the Highland development campaigner, Hugh Quigley, was equally unequivocal about opponents of these schemes. He railed against those 'more enthusiastic lovers of the past, imbued with a nostalgic longing for sentimental aesthetics', whose 'evocation of a poetical past may fire the imagination and warm the blood, but it is not sufficient in itself to bring prosperity to any single part of the Highlands'.[29] Reporting some seven years later, the Cooper Committee was no more restrained in its view:

> The final issue of this matter must be faced once and for all realistically. If it is desired to preserve the natural features of the Highlands unchanged in all time coming for the benefit of those holiday-makers who wish to contemplate them in their natural state during the comparatively brief season imposed by climatic conditions, then the logical outcome of such an aesthetic policy would be to convert the greater part of the area into a national park and to sterilise it in perpetuity, providing a few 'reservations' in which the dwindling remnants of the native population could for a time continue to reside until they eventually became extinct.[30]

Environmental concerns remained secondary, or sidelined, in planners' prioritisation of economic regeneration and job creation until the 1970s, especially in the Highlands. Moreover it was not until the 1970s that an effective and recognisable modern environmental, as distinct from the conservationist, movement started to take shape globally, although notable ecological critics were evident before this time (not least domestically, the veteran ecologist Frank Fraser Darling). After the publication of former US government biologist Rachel Carson's *Silent Spring,* an exposé of the dangers of chemical effluents, in 1962, public awareness of the risks posed by industrial pollution grew. In Britain, the grounding of one of the world's first supertankers, the *Torrey Canyon,* off the Cornish coast represented a watershed in environmental politics in the UK, prompting the Wilson government to form a Royal Commission on Environmental Pollution (of which Frank Fraser Darling was a member) and the setting up a Central Scientific Unit on Environmental Pollution, with his Conservative successor establishing the first Department for the Environment. The success of greater scrutiny and regulation of industrial pollution is brought into sharp focus in what follows.[31]

Contested 'terrains': Industry, health and the environment:

This chapter explores the oft-neglected subject of the environmental and health impacts of, and debates concerning, the construction of British Aluminium's Highland smelters and the hazards generated by the industrial processes, as well as at their Norwegian plants. In the Scottish Highlands, as in many other similar resource-rich but historically impoverished regions of the world, the politics of development often framed the responses to environmental damage and industrial hazards locally, regionally and nationally. As Peter Dorman has noted: 'when it comes down to the public issues surrounding life and death such as environmental and safety regulation ... such a judgment is more than the sum of our individual preferences as inferred by market behavior; it is fundamentally *social* and demands public discussion and decision-making.'[32] The response of those directly affected is determined in equal measure by what economist Amartya Sen refers to as 'moral choice', where individuals weigh their interests in broader terms, reflecting on cultural customs, shared material experiences and localised values and networks as well as the immediate material future.[33]

'Social choices' affected the responses of policymakers, local communities, trade unionists, and operational managers in and around BACo's Highland works. For policymakers, the industry was a boon to the perennial 'Highland problem'. This directly affected their response to environmental and health issues. Similarly many trade unionists and residents in the localities offset the concerns they had with the gratitude they felt to an industry willing to provide jobs in a region largely overlooked, and with the potential to attract other businesses. As a recent examination of the planning process for the nearby Wiggins Teape Pulp and Paper mill at Corpach, which opened in 1962, has revealed, government ministers and officials contented themselves with the knowledge that 'although there would be some environmental damage, it was containable within the political equation of Highland development'.[34] Potential risks were calculated alongside the perceived greater social good, frequently not too dissimilar in tone to that of Lord Kelvin, not least as a result of the company's skilful propagation of these ideas through company publications. The company's strategic level management was not unaffected by social considerations, even if their actions were motivated by the priority to reduce adverse publicity given their high public standing. British Aluminium's strategic management attempted to control knowledge of the risks to human and animal health and the environment represented by processes within and industrial effluents from their plants, in the face of objections raised by some local medics and a dentist, the factory inspectorate (and their successor the Health and Safety Executive (HSE), and 'lay' epidemiological knowledge emerging from the trade unions and communities.[35] Thus the capacity of the individual to evaluate and respond to risks needs also to be understood in terms of the knowledge available to them – what psychologists have referred to as 'bounded rationality' – and the control and filtering of epidemiological knowledge by interested parties, particularly the company. British Aluminium, like other industries, connived, with the explicit support of other medics, vets, scientists, and some regulators, as well as the tacit complicity of government, to create a smokescreen under the auspices of science to refute counter claims.[36] In addition, through private compensation schemes and political alliances, British Aluminium sought to eliminate complaints and outmanoeuvre regulators, pursuing a policy of conducting regulation 'behind closed doors'.[37]

Regulating and policing industrial pollution in Britain

Legislative responses for improving workplace atmospheric conditions, and reducing emissions from industry, were late in developing in Britain.[38] Real progress in the field did not start to be made until after the Dangerous Trades Committees, with the Workmen's Compensation Acts (holding employers responsible for the safety of their employees) of 1897 and 1906. However even the latter only identified six prescribed occupational diseases. the First World War provided greater impetus for work in this field, linking the productivity of workers to their health. Further research and developments in the fields of occupational health and policing of health and safety in the workplace throughout the 1930s were nevertheless held back by a general reluctance on the part of the state to intervene. The Departmental Committee of the Factory Inspectorate, for example, reporting in 1930 noted that the numbers of factory inspectors was quite inadequate for the task at hand. Moreover there was a general lack of interest among many doctors to pursue industrial medicine. The introduction of the 1937 Factories Act, which stipulated that workplaces with more than fifty people employed on the premises should have a trained first aider with necessary equipment – as well as prescription of a maximum working week of 48 hours and rest breaks – and gave the Home Secretary the power to insist that companies form occupational health services, was largely ineffective as the powers were never properly enforced. Despite the introduction of the Industrial Injuries Act of 1946, which substantially extended both the coverage of and benefits for those injured at work from the 1906 Act, compensation could be patchy. Some firms, British Aluminium included, did engage the services of local doctors as part-time industrial or consulting medical officers. However they were not compelled to do so. Many of the medical officers and nurses engaged by companies were not specialists in their fields. As Arthur McIvor has observed of British workplace conditions and their regulation into the 1950s, 'there was still a discernible tendency not to prioritise occupational health and well-being'.[39]

Crucially both the Factory Inspectorate and the Medical Factory Inspectorate – responsible for informing and policing health and safety practice, and penalising infringements – remained chronically understaffed. The Medical Factory Inspectorate numbered only fifteen inspectors by the 1940s – these being required, on top of their inspection duties, to keep pace with developments in the discipline of occupational health, as well as liaising with other government departments such as the Department of Health in Scotland – with their numbers being supplemented by 1800 Appointed Factory Doctors (AFDs), supported by 175 full-time occupational health doctors, 700 doctors with a part-time involvement in occupational health, as well as 2500 State Registered Nurses and 1400 other nursing staff employed in factories. After 1948 most AFDs were limited to a district and also worked as GPs, operating their own medical practices. One year later it was estimated that these demands meant that 78 per cent of AFDs were only able to devote three hours a week to undertaking factory work. Moreover some identified more with the factory employers than the shopfloor.[40] The government missed a number of opportunities to establish a dedicated occupational health service in Britain after the Second World War – as recommended by a number of Parliamentary and professional medical committees, and the International Labour Organisation – and coverage remained patchy. As late as 1959, the Trades Union Congress (TUC) – from which the Scottish Trades Union Congress (STUC) took its lead on health and safety matters – noted that factory inspectors were still not able to meet the guidelines for frequency of inspections set down in 1930. That same year, the Factory Inspectorate reported that even in large factories with a workforce of over 1000 only some employed a full-time doctor. Three years later the TUC reported that the Inspectorate was working on an average of four years between inspections, as against the 1930 recommendations of yearly visits for key factories and bi-annual for lesser factories. One detailed study of the role of the factory inspectorate in the south of England in the 1960s observed that inspectors frequently enforced health and safety regulations more through means of frequent advice and notifications, rarely with recourse to legal action even with negligent employers: 'Inspectors were attempting to steer a middle course between the conflicting interests of workers' health and safety and the unbridled pursuit of profit.' The Society of Occupational Medicine (who represented the thousand or so occupational health medics in the UK) was still complaining of the poor coverage of occupational health provision as late as 1970.[41] The scale of the problem in Scotland can be seen by the fact that by 1971 50 factory inspectors were responsible for reviewing conditions in 25,000 industrial workplaces leading to four year inspection gaps between each establishment. The major change to health and safety practice within the British workplace came with the introduction of the Health and Safety at Work Act 1974, holding both employers and workers responsible for workplace health and safety, and establishing two new bodies the HSE and the Health and Safety Commission. The latter was charged with enforcing the 1974 Act, and the latter to bring together employers, labour and Government to advise on and oversee health and safety matters. The year before the Employment Medical Advisory Service (EMAS) was set up to bring together AFDs into an advisory network. Nevertheless an EMAS survey of nearly 3,500 firms in 1976, revealed that the only medical provision for 85 per cent of these firms was first-aiders. In 1977 the introduction of the Safety Representative Committees Regulations –

informed by the same Robens Committee on health and safety at work that had led to all of these developments – was intended to require employers to consult their workforce about health and safety matters. After 1979, the legislation was diluted further so that this only applied to unionised workers, against a decline in trade union membership. At the same time the fall in the number of inspectors in the UK meant that by the mid-1980s 10,000 workplaces were overdue visits. Some seventeen years later, in 1993, a similar survey revealed that little had improved.[42] Added to this was the fact that in the Scottish Highlands medical services were thinly spread. Even after the establishment of the Highlands and Islands Medical Service in 1913, the Scottish Board of Health in 1919, and the National Health Service (NHS) in 1948, Highland medical staff were often isolated and unable to get cover to pursue professional development opportunities.[43]

Regulation of smoke emissions from factories in Britain prior to 1956 was characterised by 'hot air but little action'. Although legislation in 1863, 1875, 1891, and 1907 sought to enforce reduction of airborne effluents from factories to be regulated by the Alkali Inspectorate (established under the Alkali, etc., Works Regulation Act, 1863), and interest was growing among the medical profession, regulation of pollution from workplaces was ineffective except in cases where it could be proved by prosecutors to be of a black hue or a 'nuisance'. Moreover industrial polluters could avoid penalties under legislation if they were able to prove that they were taking 'the best practicable means' to eliminate the 'nuisance'. Inter-war developments in the form of the recommendations of the Newton Report of 1921, and the following Public Health (Smoke Abatement) Act, 1926, made some advances not least in extending definitions of fumes and smoke beyond its hue. However the act was watered down, in part by lobbying on behalf of the Federation of British Industries, and lacked sufficient powers of compulsion, retained the 'best practicable means' circumvention for industry, and imposed a paltry increase in fines. Little was done to improve the situation until after the public outcry arising from the London smog of winter 1952, which saw a pronounced increase in deaths from bronchitis and pneumonia in particular. Churchill's post-war Conservative government appointed a committee under Sir Hugh Beaver to examine the problems of smoke pollution nationally in 1953, resulting in the introduction of the Clean Air Bill to Parliament in 1955. The final act of 1956 was much watered down. Notably it did not apply to industrial premises covered by the Alkali Inspectorate. The Act did see some improvements over time with the National Society for Clean Air reporting in 1960 that businesses were enthused by better fuel efficiency, and that contraventions of the Act by factories were being more readily reported. Provisions were extended for industry (as well as to domestic consumers) under the Clean Air Act, 1968, making it an offence to emit any dark smoke from industrial or trade premises. Partly as a result of better reporting mechanisms, the government's Programme Analysis Unit estimated that air pollution was still costing the UK economy £1.2 billion (including £510 million for the health costs of pollution), with 38 per cent of this attributable to industry, and the rest to domestic fuel consumers.[44] However, testing of carbon and other industrial emissions found in sediment showed that, having risen dramatically in the early twentieth century, these fell by 40 per cent after 1970, indicating some degree of success on the part of clean air legislation.[45]

The politics of health and safety in the aluminium industry

The international aluminium industry has continued to pride itself on the safety of its products, its workplaces, and on its monitoring of and procedures for addressing associated occupational and environmental health risks. As the joint editors of a compendium of papers from an international industry-sponsored symposium on *Health in the aluminium industry* stated in 1997: 'It [the aluminium industry] has been vigilant concerning health issues relevant to its production workforce and of health concerns raised from within the community at large.'[46] The same view was expressed in one of the leading histories of the British chemical industry; Colin Russell declaring that 'few branches of the modern chemical industry can claim such an enviable record of environmental probity'.[47] However, this confidence in occupational and environmental health safeguards in the industry has long been the subject of vigorous debate in international arenas.[48] Most recently, research conducted in the United States has highlighted Alcoa's attempt to reshape the regulatory environment rather than seriously tackle emissions from the industry under the spotlight.[49]

As evidence over occupational health and safety, as well as over the environment illustrates, British Aluminium was less concerned with the risks posed than with the appearance of tackling them. In this, once again, the 'social choices' of all the key players, not least weighing up the risks of losing a source of employment over those of a dangerous working environment or exposure to potentially harmful effluents, was paramount. The prioritisation of opportunities for economic growth and employment opportunities over safety, as well as health, was illustrated early on by the conditions endured by navvies constructing the company's hydro-electric schemes. The leading historian of hydro-electricity in the region has described the conditions experienced by those labourers working on the developments at Foyers, Kinlochleven and Fort William (the Lochaber scheme) as 'appalling – almost suicidal', and as little different from those experienced by navvies in the building of the Caledonian Canal a century before.[50] While detailed records of conditions are limited, some picture can be gleaned from those that do exist. The perilous nature of the work at Kinlochleven was vividly evoked in MacGill's *Children of the Dead End*, and can be seen from the numbers of isolated gravestones in the navvies' graveyard high above Kinlochleven. Certainly the work was so dangerous that frequently those living in impoverishment in the Scotland's cities dispatched by Poor Law commissioners to the scheme frequently left in haste unwilling and unable to persevere working under such hazardous conditions.[51] Around 30 years after MacGill and his comrades had packed up and headed back to Glasgow, Dr Isaac McIver, the 'Democrat from Lewis' at the centre of the Lochaber strike in 1936, introduced an emergency motion to the 29th STUC congress calling for a government enquiry into the carbon monoxide gassing of navvies employed in the construction of the Lochaber scheme.[52] Between 1925 and 1929 a catalogue of serious injuries and fatalities was reported on this scheme. Admission records for the local Belford Hospital reveal that there were 78 (with 28 fatalities) from the scheme in 1925–26 alone. Of these, 60 per cent were caused by direct trauma (explosions, rock falls or from machinery). In his retirement address, one of the doctors, Dr Shay Connachie, employed to cover the scheme recalled that in the tunnel development alone there were 48 fatalities.[53] Connachie's colleague, Dr Cameron Miller, the Medical Superintendent for the Belford Hospital formed a different impression. In his serialised account of the medical work on the Lochaber scheme, Miller mentioned in passing that 'unhappily, but perhaps inevitably in a work of such magnitude, several fatal accidents occurred, including misadventures not due to the work', while suppressing any hint of casualties of this scale.[54] As a postscript to the series, Miller acknowledged the verdict of a fatal accident enquiry recognising carbon monoxide poisoning of a worker on the scheme. Much of the series of articles was given over to lauding the company for its adequate provision of housing on the scheme, and blaming casualties on other factors, not least the behaviour of the workforce. Crucially, Miller made much of his admiration of British Aluminium's efforts in introducing this form of employment to the Highlands, couching it in language similar to that of Kelvin and identifying as the hero of the piece, William Murray Morrison:

> It is a matter of common knowledge that the fountain and origin of the present scheme has been the determination in the general public interest to utilise the waste water-power of the Highlands so as to provide profitable employment, both in the immediate and in the permanent sense, for the indigenous people, and to enrich the producing capacity of the nation as a whole. That enormous Electrical Energy lay latent in the lakes and rivers of the Highlands was known as a truism, but the difficulty of tackling the problem on a massive scale with the above double object in view seems to have baffled the minds and the means of enterprising men; until, finally, the British Aluminium Company under the direction of a master Highland brain resolved to make essay.[55]

Miller's explanation is a familiar one of portraying deaths and serious injuries as the regrettable but unavoidable price of progress, while abrogating the company and contractors of any responsibility. His language and message also illustrate the potency that BACo's publicity and Morrison's personality could have on determining responses to such subjects, as correspondence between the latter and Lachlan Grant and Cameron of Lochiel further testifies to in the next chapter.

Integral to this was British Aluminium's promotion of itself as a welfarist employer, as illustrated by its provision of a contributory health insurance scheme for their employees, in advance of the National Insurance (NI) Act of 1911. Like a good many British employers of this era, this was also used as a means of counteracting the effects of the NI Act, which it was feared would fundamentally affect the workplace bargaining power with employees.[56] British Aluminium also employed two consulting medical officers, Dr Ronald Cadell Macdonald covering Foyers and Dr Lachlan Grant for Kinlochleven. Both were experienced physicians of some standing. Their emolument was received from the weekly payments of 2 pence (*d*.) from single and married workmen, and 3*d*. for family men, to the scheme (roughly £1 per annum for married workmen or around £90 at 2007 prices). British Aluminium also constructed a hospital at Foyers but this was little used apart from accidents, and had a car at hand in the absence of any ambulance to take critical cases to Inverness.[57] Certainly Cameron Miller judged British Aluminium to be the type of employer 'only too willing to fulfil the moral claim that lies before them'.[58]

While none of the accident books for the works survived and disaggregated figures for accidents – excepting specific incidents – collected by the inspectorate were grouped by sector, rather than industry or company, some insight from inspectorate reports, alongside other sources, is possible. In the metal refining and extraction sectors the most common cause of both fatal and non-fatal accidents well into the late 1950s was gassing or profound burns from molten metal, while in metal conversion (rolling and extruding) injuries and the fatalities in the main arose from power or machinery accidents. HMFI's reports made frequent reference to the loss of eyes by furnace workers in aluminium smelters because they were not wearing goggles and were hit by molten metal. Though both fatal and non-fatal accidents involving molten metal and explosions declined by the late 1950s, the non-ferrous metals industries continued to have a consistently poor comparative safety record. Although accident incident rates in the aluminium industry were lower than those for the iron and steel sector by the mid-1970s, they were still nearly double the national average for manufacturing and had increased since 1970.[59] Evidence from interviews with former employees, and reports from Inspectors suggests a lax safety regime under British Aluminium, although Alcan showed itself to be far more committed to health and safety.

It is one of the great ironies that while British Aluminium's post-war health and safety campaigns attributed high accident rates to worker negligence – mainly from falling objects, falls and walking into stationary objects – it failed to tackle the atmosphere in these workplaces. As well as the long-term effect on workers' health, the fact that visibility was negligible in the furnace rooms at the Highland works meant that it was altogether more likely that accidents of this nature might occur.

An editorial for *The B.A. News* for September–October 1950, for example, showed itself more interested in criticising furnace workers for the 'unwanted "decoration" of furnaces though, in general, of a more harmless nature', while the previous year's new year editorial carried the following sage advice: 'cleanliness – when applied to the paint on walls and machinery – is not only next only next to godliness but is also a great aid to reducing the possibility of accidents.'[60] A further indication of the company's attitude towards workers' long term health is evident from comments made by John Bullen, while discussing plans for employing full time works doctors, rather than relying on panel doctors, in 1948: 'Mr. Bullen thought that with a Doctor available at a Works, absenteeism would be greatly reduced'. Bullen also 'visualised such a Doctor being a regular member of the staff working through the factory organisation'. The company's production director, W. J. Thomas, felt that 'a Works Doctor would, to some extent, operate as a check on Panel Doctors certificates'.[61] Yet this was indicative, alongside the strategy of deploying professional opinion to re-frame the parameters of debates about hazards, of the company's preoccupation with its public image and of its attempts to deflect attention from its own shortcomings in tackling unhealthy working conditions. In the absence of a sufficient body of medical opinion on the health of aluminium workers, British Aluminium was easily able to rebut criticisms made on the basis of lay observation. The underlying principles behind BACo's health and safety strategies where they existed were those of maintaining the image of being responsible employers in this as in other areas (hence membership of Royal Society for the Prevention of Accidents (ROSPA), but also to limit claims under the Workmen's Compensation Act 1897 and subsequently the Industrial Injuries Act 1946.

'Death in the pot'? Aluminium production, health and environment

Both the alumina refining and aluminium reduction process include procedures that produce harmful effluents, although it is the latter that is most associated with environmental damage and health hazards. However some of the earliest, and most enduring, concerns about the effects on human health of aluminium related not to the industrial process but to questions about its safety in cooking utensils. As early as 1913, these prompted a Ministry of Health enquiry, in light of the evidence that 'many people have banished aluminium ware altogether from their kitchens'. One text from 1937, *Death in the Pot*, claimed a link between the onset of cancer and traces of aluminium.[62] Responding to growing disquiet, BACo's chairman, Robert Cooper, declared confidently in March 1931 that: 'The evidence of scientists is overwhelmingly in favour of the absolute non-toxicity of aluminium.'[63] In this he was supported by the British Aluminium's medical officer, and land campaigner, Lachlan Grant, who issued a strongly worded rebuke to critics of aluminium in the *British Medical Journal*, in which he stated assuredly that: 'There appear to be no grounds whatsoever for the campaign against aluminium.'[64] In contrast, the potential effects on flora, fauna and human beings, of the various stages of the manufacture of aluminium appear to have excited little interest among medical practitioners in Britain, or indeed elsewhere in continental Europe or North America, throughout much of the first half of the twentieth century. The first clinical case of an occupational illness related to aluminium in the UK was reported by a north London GP in *The Lancet* in June 1921.[65]

Prior to establishing the Foyers reduction works, British Aluminium had received details of investigations conducted by a Swiss factory inspector between 1892 and 1894 into emissions from the Neuhausen aluminium reduction works. Local residents in the locality of these works had complained that vegetation around the factory was being destroyed, and speculated that these same gases were responsible for affecting the yield of a vineyard two kilometres from the factory and for the chest pains suffered by a man staying in nearby hotel. After his investigations, a Swiss government inspector concluded that though there was no evidence to support the latter two claims, there was ample substance to locals' complaints that the emissions from the works were affecting the vegetation in its vicinity. The cantonal government subsequently charged the factory owner with finding a remedy or closing the works. The damage was discovered as having been caused by hydrogen-flouride and 'fluoride-silicon' fumes escaping from the factory chimneys at the extent of 0.101 to 0.121 per cubic metre. Using a variety of sprays and fans, the factory proprietors managed to reduce 97 per cent of the fluorine gas emissions from the furnace room. Significantly the Swiss report was cited by the British Aluminium Company's secretary, Charles Jones, in his letter to the Duke of Westminster – to counter the latter's conjecture that the fumes from the plant would destroy vegetation in the district – as evidence that, at the company's works, 'no such destructive effect will occur'.[66] Thus BACo was aware from the outset about the potentially damaging effects of effluents from the aluminium reduction process.

'Dante's inferno': workplace conditions and emissions

[...] Hell on earth, hell on earth, hell on earth. My father-in-law worked in there and my brother-in-law, in the furnace room, and it was unbelievable. How these men, big, huge, strapping men, six foot six, and yet some never reached the age of fifty, fifty-five. I've seen 'Big Camera'. It was his nickname. McDonald was his name [...] He was named after the Italian boxer. He was huge [...] and he worked in a job called the stubbing ... breaking up the crust, and sometimes it would go up in a sulphurous plume and the flames would go up [...] I've seen him and he was – before they built a bridge over the railway line here, that was a short cut to work from the village [Inverlochy] here – putting [...] his leg over the fence and bang. When you think back, a lot of big, big men: Big Sandy MacKenzie, big Jock MacKenzie. They had the habit of employing big men for that type of work in here, but these men were very, very lucky. Very few reached retirement, very few.[67]

Around the time that Sandy Walker, as a young boy, observed 'Big Camera' dropping dead after he scaled the fence into Inverlochy village, Lord Malcolm Douglas-Hamilton, the sitting MP for Inverness, asked the then Minister of National Insurance, Dr Edith Summerskill, in a debate in the House of Commons in November 1950 if she was aware that around four hundred workers had left British Aluminium's Highland smelters in the past year as a result of ill-health.[68] Two years later, in early 1953, Dr Barnett Stross – Socialist GP and Labour MP – quizzed Minister of Labour Sir Walter Monckton about the incidences of carcinomas of the skin among furnace workers melting aluminium at British Aluminium's Milton works (in Stross' constituency) stating: 'The fact that the warts appear so quickly on the skin of the worker and are pre-cancerous might well suggest that the inhalation of such dangerous materials into the lungs might later cause rapid and widespread outbreaks of carcinoma of the lungs and bronchi.'[69] Some months after, Stross instigated a debate on the effects of fluorosis in his constituency urging the government to invite the Medical Research Council to investigate the effects on cattle and workers.[70] In 1969, the Chief Inspector of Factories reported on the case of a 64-year-old whose sudden death he attributed to chronic pulmonary fibrosis and fluorosis arising from twenty-four years service in the furnace room of an aluminium factory.[71] These separate events, though divided by geography and time, were connected to a set of health risks arising from the industrial processes related to the production of aluminium that were fast becoming obvious to those working in the industry, building up a 'lay' epidemiology, as well as to some local doctors, dentists and vets.

Primary aluminium production poses a number of health risks arising from the industrial process and specific technologies. Within aluminium reduction works the most serious of these related to the preparation of the carbon anodes, and the fumes emitted from the aluminium reduction furnaces themselves. In the case of the latter, this was particularly associated with a particular type of furnace technology, which proliferated in the industry until the 1970s. The Söderberg self-baking furnace – in which carbon expended on the exposed face of the anode was replaced by adding carbon paste (a mixture of ground coke and coal tar pitch) to the top of the anode casing, and the fumes (including large quantities of pitch and tar volatiles) were released into the furnace room atmosphere – was identified as being the main contributors to occupational health problems in the industry. Designed by, and named after, a Norwegian steel engineer, Söderberg furnaces were introduced into the aluminium industry from the mid-1920s onwards. The technology increased the profits of Carl Willhelm Söderberg's employer, the engineering firm, Elkem, by over 500 per cent between 1932 and 1938, and made it one of the most internationally renowned and successful Norwegian companies; hence from Elkem's, as well as aluminium producers' perspective, there was a vested interest in over-riding concerns.[72] French producer AFC acquired a licence for Söderbergs in 1924, and started to experiment with the new technology first at their La Praz works, and then at Chedde and St. Jean de Maurienne. From the outset there were a number of problems to be overcome with the anodes in the new furnaces and the consumption of energy. AFC, and subsequently Pechiney, started to observe after 1929 that self-bake Södebergs emitted plentiful and noxious gases, not aided by the rudimentary and ineffective ventilation systems in reduction works of the time.[73] In 1960, Pechiney built its last smelter with Söderberg furnace lines at Noguères. By the early 1960s it had become clear that the Söderberg technology had failed to live up to expectations, and was being superseded by other 'pre-bake' furnaces, although as late 1960 60 per cent of global aluminium production continued to use the technology.[74] The problem was particularly pronounced in the Söderbergs because of the method of replenishing the carbon in the anode and the lack of hoods (to contain the fumes) on the furnaces. In addition, in a good many furnace rooms in first (up until 1952) and second (1952–63) generation smelters, the buildings were low lying and extraction units woefully inadequate.[75]

Workers in coke production, gas industries and aluminium reduction works exposed to polynuclear aromatic hydrocarbons (PAHs) derived from carbon and hydrogen – specifically benzoαpyrene – over a prolonged period have been observed as having noticeably higher rates of cancers.[76] Equally aluminium furnace room workers have been identified as having pronounced levels of occupational asthma.[77] Although coal tar pitch, and in particular the causative carcinogen, benzoαpyrene, was recognised as early as 1775 as the cause of occupationally related skin cancer among chimney sweeps and identified for some time as the cause of skin cancer among workers in the aluminium industry, it was only in the 1950s that a growing body of medical literature began to draw a link between ingestion of carcinogens and skin, bladder and lung cancers.[78] Initial recognition of compensation for ill-health arising from aluminium production emerged in Britain from the body of knowledge about respiratory diseases contracted by coal miners and others working with carbon dust. It was not until 1978 that the Royal Commission on Civil Liability and Compensation for Personal Injury recommended that 'any occupation in or incidental to the manufacture of carbon electrodes for use in the electrolytic extraction of aluminium from aluminium oxide' be included among the list of prescribed diseases.[79] This recommendation was extended in 1981, with the Industrial Injuries Advisory Council advising that broncho-pulmonary diseases caused by dust or fumes from the manufacture of aluminium or its products be recognised by the parent department, the Department of Health and Social Security.[80] By 1995 the International Agency for Research on Cancer (IARC), reporting on its review of research into the links between metals, chemicals, and various carcinomas conducted between 1971 and 1995, reported that the fumes in aluminium smelting were a category 1 carcinogen (the greatest potential threat on

IARC's scale), with sufficient evidence in studies among human subjects that these could cause lung, skin and bladder cancers among aluminium smelter workers.[81] More recent developments in biomarkers have made an even clearer link between PAHs and bladder and lung cancers.[82] In 1992 the UK's Industrial Injuries Advisory Council reporting on behalf of the Secretary of State for Social Security recommended that bladder, but not lung, cancer associated with the Söderberg process be added to the list of industrial diseases for which disablement benefit could be claimed. This finding against lung cancer, in the face of IARC's findings, reflected the very great difficulties for epidemiologists of attributing lung cancer to specific industrial process, the significance here of interpretation and thus the greater ease with which prescription could be blocked by vested interests.[83] More recently lymphatic leukemia among smelter workers has also been attributed to electro-magnetic fields in the industry.[84]

Other noxious fumes emitted in the furnace room that were also to have an adverse on human health and the environment, included alumina, cryolite, and carbon dusts, as well as airborne fluorides, sulphur dioxide (SO^2), and carbon monoxide.[85] Of these emissions airborne fluorides (both within the furnace room and from the factory) have given much cause for concern. If ingested in large quantities whether through the air and water, this can lead to bone deformities among animals and human, and can kill flora. Two other tasks in the factory historically represented a threat to workers' health: preparation of carbon anodes in the carbon factory; and renovating furnaces (chipping out the carbon lining of the cathode). Curiously one emission that has been overlooked has been that of sulphur dioxide, that was emitted in substantial quantities within and from the factories. Untreated, this is responsible not only for 'acid rain' but also for childhood and mature asthma, with high dosages of sulphur dioxide even resulting in death.[86]

Workers in the carbon factory were also traditionally exposed, working as they were with both anthracite and American petroleum coke, to carcinogens and ingestion of substantial levels of carbon dust; the latter of which could result in asthma and in the most pronounced form, chronic dyspnea, leading to disability and heart conditions. The obstacle for environmental, as indeed for medical, epidemiologists (and thus for historians in this area) attempting to establish links between industrial hazards and ill-health and environmental damage is often being able to attribute the effects to a specific process or effluents.[87] Nevertheless, local medics at BACo's Highland works had long since started to identify coincidental patterns emerging among cohorts of certain age groups of furnace workers. Local dentists had picked up on the mottling of children's teeth (a sign of excessive levels of fluorine) and local vets, bone deformities among cattle and sheep, while the lay public in the village of Kinlochleven could scarcely miss the evident bio-markers presented by the thin covering of dust which pitted rooves, the fluorides that turned windows blue, and the numbers of furnacemen who did not make it past retirement age.

The first major epidemiological survey into the UK aluminium industry was conducted during the mid-1930s by the Industrial Pulmonary Diseases Committee (IPDC) of the Medical Research Council (MRC), at the behest of English pottery owners. They were keen to establish whether alumina would be a safe substitute for flint, and to determine if there was a potential link between alumina and pneumoconiosis. This study conducted among a sample of 50 workers (out of a cohort of 145) at BACo's Kinlochleven and Lochaber works reported in 1936.[88] It concluded at the time that 'the committee was unable to find, within the limits of the material included in this investigation, any evidence that the inhalation of alumina dust had caused fibrosis of the lungs'.[89] The investigation of links between alumina dust and pneumoconiosis continued to dominate the scant literature relating to occupational health and aluminium subsequently. This was possibly a reflection of the greater and growing awareness of occupationally related pneumoconiosis among clinicians and medical scientists at this time.[90] In contrast to the IPDC's findings, a larger German wartime study of workers in a factory that used alumina dust in their processes noted an alarmingly high incidence of pulmonary fibrosis among the cohort.[91] As far as the UK aluminium industry and the medical profession were concerned, the link between pneumoconiosis and processes involving alumina continued to be the main arena for debate and the subject of a number of studies during the 1950s and 1960s.[92]

Critically it was not within the MRC team's remit to report more generally on other hazards, although one of their number, factory inspector J. K. Goodall provided a telling observation of effects of the fumes that came off the uncovered Söderbergs: 'Digressing for a moment, in connection with the discussion of the materials present, as dust and gases in the furnace room, it may be stated, that none of the workers to whom I spoke, complained at all of the dust, but they objected to the fumes which they had to stand on the furnace crust during the process of removing and fixing the anodes, in the process of "blocking".' Further Goodall commented that the concentration of dust present in the furnacerooms would not have been tolerated had it been in the Black Country potteries.[93] The fumes that Goodall noticed would have included PAHs and SO^2. Significantly Professor E. L. Cummins of the IPDC suggested that the team's report would have been well served by examining pathological, as well as clinical and radiological evidence that might have detected future risks.[94] While team member Dr Bradford Hill concluded that, 'operatives in the reduction works appear to have rather a low incidence of respiratory complaints', radiological examination found abnormalities in the lungs of fourteen workers. Of these, the report observed that the results for three furnace workers showed indications of abnormal levels of fibrosis, and a further four from slight emphysema.[95]

If the IPDC report was inconclusive and the MRC's remit precluded them investigating further, British Aluminium's attention was already being drawn to health problems arising from the reduction process at its Norwegian subsidiary. In November 1937, at the annual general meeting of British Aluminium managers, J. Mørch, the manager of BACo's Vigeland works, reported that the works had

Lochaber furnace room, 1950. © RTA/GUA.

received a complaint from the Norwegian factory inspectorate that 'asthma troubles occur more frequently among men working in the furnace room than in any other factory in the district', and they were in negotiations with the inspectorate to improve ventilation in the furnace rooms. William Murray Morrison, who was chairing the session, cast doubt on the Norwegian 'claim' adding that it was 'contrary to the experience in this country'.[96] British Aluminium had only just started to experiment with Söderbergs in 1934 at Lochaber and Kinlochleven. In 1938 BACo introduced a further 140 of the furnaces to Lochaber, adding 72 more in 1942. Of the 140 new Söderbergs adequate extraction and scrubbing towers were only provided for 70.[97] Between 1948 and 1952, a further 56 100,000 amp vertical stud Söderbergs were added at Lochaber, although only 40 were in operation by July 1951. By 1951, Kinlochleven had 96 Söderberg furnaces. Of Kinlochleven's two furnace rooms, one housed the older type of uncovered self-bake Söderbergs; and the other newer furnaces with a fume cowl (hood) and integrated fume duct.[98] Another MRC team which undertook research at both Kinlochleven and Lochaber in the late 1940s – responding to local concerns about the effects of fluorine emissions on human beings, cattle and flora

Tapping in progress in Lochaber furnace room, 1950. © RTA/GUA.

in the area – noted that the atmosphere was far from conducive to the employees' health. In furnace room A of the Lochaber works (housing furnaces from 1929) they found no fume extraction system, with the only ventilation provided by doors and windows, with workers here complaining of having sore eyes and skin.[99] These first generation pre-baked furnaces were being phased out by this time, although these were not the most hazardous in terms of pitch fumes.[100] In furnace room B (active since 1938) they noted 'a considerable fog of pitch fumes produced by the baking of the "green paste" from the Söderberg furnaces'.[101] Furnace room C contained the most modern furnaces with hoods and apparently effective fume extraction units. However the team noted with concern that fumes extracted from furnace rooms B and C were 'not treated or scrubbed in any way, but were allowed to escape from vents … the dense white cloud of smoke which forms drifts across the surrounding countryside.'[102]

Further insights were provided by a group of visiting engineers from Pechiney, which toured the Kinlochleven and Lochaber smelters between July and August 1951. At both works they were particularly struck by the regularity with which the anodes were raised for cleaning and topping up. Each of the 384 anodes at Kinlochleven was

Crust breaking, Kinlochleven furnace room, c.1962. © RTA/GUA.

lifted for the carbon paste to be added every week, with the same form being followed at Lochaber (although the new furnaces allowed them to raise 22 anodes at one time). This was an inherent problem with many self-bake Söderberg furnaces with anodes of this type using 4–5 per cent more pitch and thus emitting more hazardous fumes.[103] However the Pechiney engineers observed that at their French works they did not use anything like the amounts of carbon that BACo did and chose instead to remove their anodes entirely after about two years.[104] Although fascinated in this from the point of view of efficiency – as they felt the BACo methods were highly labour intensive and wasteful of carbon – they also noted that the Kinlochleven furnace room workers involved in this operation were exposed to 'terrible fumes' in the 6½ minutes devoted to each anode. Whereas the new furnaces at Lochaber operated a fume extraction unit (although this was quite inadequate) around the anodes when they were raised to eliminate the 'abundant yellow fumes it gave off', at Kinlochleven no such system existed.[105] They also noted – both visually and from the smell – that the anode paste used at both suggested high levels of sulphur in the coal used (German coke and American petroleum coke).[106]

The year previously at the BACo annual managers' meeting Dr T. G. Pearson of British Aluminium's laboratories at Chalfont Park, who had recently visited the works, refuted both works managers' view that the fumes would always be present from these furnaces, judging that with the right ventilation and technical mastery of the furnaces these could be eliminated. This was ruled out for Kinlochleven on the basis of cost, and respirators were suggested despite the company personnel managers' advice that the factory inspectorate as well as the furnacemen would object to this suggestion. The assertion of local works managers that the increase in costs arising from augmented payments to furnacemen to cover the discomfort of working under these conditions would more than justify investment in new ventilation and treatment plant apparently went unheeded.[107] Fitters, electricians and funacemen at both Kinlochleven and Lochaber – like their counterparts at Alcan's Arvida works – remarked that working above the furnaces and on the anodes, in particular, was deemed to be one of the worst tasks to be employed on in the furnace rooms, that involved inhaling a considerable quantity of noxious fumes. By the mid-1950s, the risks to workers at the Kinlochleven plant were sufficient to prompt the contributors for the area to the *Third Statistical Account for Scotland* to comment on incidences of pneumoconiosis and an increased risk of occupational carcinomas among aluminium workers. Depite numerous visits from Reynolds' engineers after the RTIA takeover, the west Highland works saw little in the way of improvements.[108] Certainly, the task of working above the anodes or replacing them on Söderbergs would be the most likely to expose employees to high levels of both fluorine gases and PAHs. The type of vertical stud Söderberg with steel apron used at both Kinlochleven and Lochaber reduced the effectiveness of the skirting and exposed the manual crust breakers in particular to these same fumes.[109] Thus while epidemiological evidence was not being systematically collected, there was ample awareness of risks associated with particular jobs within the factory.

Until the fitting of plant to the carbon factory in the late 1930s the Kinlochleven works was emitting 80 tons of tar into the atmosphere per annum.[110] The regularity with which anode paste was topped up and the exposure to conditions in the carbon works at Kinlochleven were not particularly favourable either, with workers finishing their shift, 'black with carbon'.[111] Significantly, the carbon factory – where the work of employees included grinding anthracite coal for anode blocks, and American petroleum coke, as well as working with large consignments of pitch tar re-heated in the factory, to make carbon tar paste – was also not included in the IPDC's 1936 study. At Lochaber's carbon factory too, workers were exposed to the same risks.[112] All of these activities would have exposed workers both to high levels of dusts associated among coal miners and coal trimmers in the docks with pneumoconiosis, and to highly carcinogenic benzoapyrene. The one legal occupational health case from a Highland smelter brought against the industry was one brought by coal dust pneumoconiosis ascribed to his job grinding anthracite at Kinlochleven's carbon

View from the Mamore Estate onto the BACo Kinlochleven, *c.*1962. © RTA/GUA.

factory.[113] Moreover the highly flammable nature of the materials being used meant it could also be immediately risky, with Lochaber's carbon factory having two major fires (in December 1950, and January 1962) in just over eleven years.[114]

The effects of fluorine gas emissions from aluminium reduction works – the subject of the Swiss reports on the Neuhausen factory – most notably identified as the cause of skeletal and dental deformities found among livestock grazing next to aluminium smelters, has also raised concerns about hazards associated with the industry. BACo's response to the risks posed by fluorine emissions provides further evidence of its approach to occupational and environmental health. British Aluminium had engaged in extensive correspondence with the manager of the plant belonging to their subsidiary A/S Stangfjorden Elektrokemiske Fabriker (SEF) in Norway about damage to local farmers' crops from fluorine emissions. In October 1932 the manager of the Stangfjorden smelter Maurice Turner wrote to Gerald Steel at BACo HQ, expressing concern about the emissions from the factory and detailed claims made by local farmers to a Norwegian court. At Steel's behest, Turner sought quotes from a Bergen builder for constructing a fume extraction and washing system at the factory, as well as improving ventilation for the furnace room workers who had been complaining for some years about the atmosphere in the furnace room. Some idea of the parent company's attitude to this matter can be gleaned from two telegrams to

BACo Stangfjorden factory, *c.*1920. © RTA/GUA.

the Stangfjorden manager from Steel sent in February and April 1933. They are also important in view of the conduct of the company in relation to subsequent complaints raised against them around their Highland works, and the differences in approach of the local managers and British Aluminium's senior echelons of management. In his reply to Turner of 10 February 1933, Steel barely disguised his scepticism about the former's principled stance in the economic climate of the time.[115] Turner was astonished by his superior's judgment. However he persevered, re-emphasising the importance of the work on the grounds of the well-being of the workforce, the likelihood of farmers' crops being affected again in the new season, and the savings to be made from avoiding costly litigation. He also impressed upon Steel the importance of at least introducing some of the renovations as a matter of urgency, not least given the spate of strikes in Norway between the 1920s and 1930s, with the metals sector especially affected. An anxious Turner wrote again in the second week in April, having heard nothing from Steel and with local crops starting to sprout.[116] Steel's response 10 days later was to refuse capital for the project, noting:

> Capital expenditure and purchases have to be kept to the absolute minimum, and in the circumstances it is considered preferable to incur the risk of possibly having to pay some compensation rather than the capital expenditure on the

Stangfjorden furnace room, *c.*1920. © Hydro.

proposed scheme. The fact that certain compensation has been paid to Gjerde farmers does not mean that other claims will be accepted without question, and in any case it should take many years' compensation to equal the cost of the proposed scheme.[117]

Turner and SEF were told to re-apply the following year, when it was once again rejected. Each time Turner's disappointment was tangible; his frustration, in part, no doubt stemming from his frequent thwarted attempts to have the parent company invest in the Stangfjorden plant. Despite Turner's persistence, the critical renovations to improve conditions and reduce effluents had still not been carried out by October 1936, and one of SEF's Norwegian directors Mr H. F. Blom, who had visited the plant that month, sought a meeting while he was due to be in London with Steel to advocate the case in person.[118] The legacy of BACo's under-investment in SEF was indicated in a report by the Nazi occupying authorities which considered the plant technically outmoded. Turner, like his counterparts at Lochaber, Kinlochleven and Vigelands, advocated these changes not just on the basis of avoiding costly payouts by the company but also on principle. An Englishman, Maurice Russell Turner was part of the Stangfjorden community. Having married and raised a family locally, he

Maurice Russell Turner with his family, Stangfjorden. © Fylkesarkivet i Sogn og Fjordane.

resided there for over thirty years until he was forced to flee the Gestapo with his family in 1940. As a sign of his commitment to the village, during the downturn in trade in 1921–22 Turner and his brother-in-law paid for the construction of a boatyard in the town to provide additional employment out of their own finances. A measure of his relations with the workforce and local residents is indicated by the fact that while other Norwegian industries were subject to charged industrial politics during this period, Stangfjorden maintained very cordial industrial relations.[119] At BACo's Vigelands works, Mørch, though driven by more material considerations than Turner, namely to save the company 'meaningless compensation for supposed smoke damage', reported in 1937 that they had been settling claims from local farmers for three years. Steel's response was once again characteristic of the company's continuing approach – as later examples from Lochaber and Invergordon show – in referring the manager to compensation agreements and seeking to buy the silence of local residents rather than sink capital into rectifying the situation, even when made aware of environmental damage and risks to the health of workforces, local communities and livestock.[120]

Like Turner's objections, the disquiet of operational managers in the Highlands in pursuing this line – with its implicit transgression of the 'moral economy' – balanced against the interests of local communities in which they were often long-term residents brought them into conflict with senior managers. By December 1938 a Divisional Officer for the Forestry Commission in the Inverness area had filed a report noting 'marked discolouration' and damage to Norwegian Spruce trees in Glen Nevis three-quarters of a mile from the Lochaber smelter. The Forestry Commission reported damage to their plantations and nursery to British Aluminium. This had to be followed up by a letter from the Head of the Commission Sir Roy Robinson to Steel in July 1939. At that stage Steel asked for more details of the 'alleged "harmful fumes"', and questioned why, given that the Lochaber smelter had been in existence since 1929, no damage had been noticed before. What Steel knew privately was that from June 1932 the company had been adding aluminium fluoride to the furnaces at Kinlochleven and Lochaber – thus increasing the levels of fluorine present in both the furnaces and emissions – to counteract the high levels of sodium oxide in Burntisland alumina. Moreover John Bullen, the Lochaber manager, had been complaining about pollution from the plant more generally to the annual managers' conferences since November 1936, while the Highland estates manager (William Murray Morrison's brother), had also repeatedly highlighted the effects of pollution from both plants on the housing stock in Kinlochleven and Inverlochy in his reports to the annual meetings.

By March 1941 Forestry Commission inspections revealed that the damage had become more 'pronounced' – 90 per cent of the Norwegian spruces originally surveyed were now affected and most 'were almost completely defoliated' – and had extended beyond the areas previously damaged, including other species of tree like Douglas fir and Scots pine. The damage worsened progressively, and the local conservator called for an investigation.[121] Between October 1943 and the Spring of 1944, farmers at Nevis Bridge Farm and Achintree Farm in the vicinity of the Lochaber smelter complained about the debilitation of their livestock. Resulting examination of both farms' stock of sheep and cattle in 1943–44 showed skeletal abnormalities (including fractured ribs and pelvises) in 111 of the 201 sheep (or 55 per cent of the flock) at Achintree Farm, and pronounced dental deformities among both sheep and cows at Nevis Bridge Farm, attributed to high levels of fluorine ingested during grazing in areas polluted by the factory. A subsequent post-mortem of three sheep from Achintree conducted in October 1945 showed dental deformities. In August 1946 Joseph Hobbs of Torlundy Farm (around 1¾ miles north of the factory) registered concerns about the uncommonly 'poor condition' of and deteriorating milk yield from his prized dairy herd. Investigations revealed that thirteen out of the seventeen cows examined showed signs of dental fluorosis, while further examinations found that 32 out of the 35 inspected were suffering from dental fluorosis. One of these cows was in an 'awful condition' by September 1946, and was slaughtered. In the subsequent examination it was discovered that chronic fluorosis had deformed its teeth and resulted in the creature having 11 cracked ribs. Hobbs promptly filed proceedings against the company.[122] Significantly Hobbs had established for a good reputation for himself in the locale, as an enterprising businessman who had transformed a previously infertile 'bog' into 'a smiling arable and pasture land' with a 'large and thriving herd'.[123] Crucially, as well as public health concerns, this was now also affecting the business conducted by the Forestry Commission and farmers like Hobbs. The effects of emissions from the factory on the village of Kinlochleven was also immediately apparent to visitors around this time:

> As some of the houses are far too close to the factory, their occupants complain of the smoke, carbon dust, and fumes that blow across … A common grievance throughout the village is the curious effect of the fumes on window glass, causing a bluish film that is very difficult to clean.[124]

This bluish film on the windows of local houses was caused by traces of fluorine. Public criticism of Kinlochleven, including the town's pollution had been gathering momentum – as opponents and proponents of industrialisation battled it out over whether it was an example to be emulated – citing among other things the pollution from the factory wafting over the town.[125] Concurrently local dentists noted the mottling of children's teeth. Interested by these observations, the Chief Dental Officer for Scotland visited Kinlochleven and confirmed that the state of youngsters' teeth was exceptionally good.[126] The Chief Dentist for Scotland's investigations did not assuage local concerns or those of the Scottish Office.[127] In March 1945 the MRC's Fluorosis Committee appointed a team to investigate concerns about the effects of fluorine emissions from Lochaber on the local population, flora and fauna.[128]

Reporting in 1949, the main conclusions of the team – composed of experts from the medical, veterinary, dental, and biological sciences – were that the effects of fluorine emissions on human beings in the area were generally 'small' and the amounts of fluorine ingested negligible. Among the human population, they concluded that despite above average levels of mottling of children's teeth from those examined at local schools, this was not particularly pronounced and gave little cause for immediate concern. Of the four test groups only one, those working in the furnace room at Lochaber, showed particularly accentuated levels of fluorine in their urine and blood. Of the first group of furnace workers, bone deformities were found to be fairly prevalent (although not debilitating) among those who were fully exposed to the fumes in the furnace rooms. This was especially visible among those who had served in the furnace room for five years or more.[129] In contrast the team discovered further and extensive evidence of acute fluorosis among cattle and sheep resulting often in emaciation and death, attributed to high levels of fluorine in the grazing pastures near the factory. In particular, they noted wasting of cattle and sheep caused by inability to feed because of the distortion and deformity in the livestock's teeth attributed to the contamination of grass with fluorine in the vicinity of the works.[130] The team's report concluded by noting that 'workers inhale considerable quantities of fluorine', and warning that: 'the conditions under which these men [in the furnace rooms] work are such as to call for constant vigilance and for determined efforts to reduce the amount of fluorine to which they are exposed.' They also recommended that though they saw little effect on the wider human population, it was probably wise to keep residents 'out of the zone known to be most liable to contamination', while concluding that 'effects on animal husbandry … obviously constitute a serious impediment to economic methods of sheep and cattle farming in the area'.[131] Subsequent evidence given by Dr Donald Hunter, part of the MRC fluorosis team at Lochaber, in a case on the impact of ingestion of fluorides around an aluminium smelter in Oregon against Reynolds Metals three years later, illustrates that though members of the team did not have sufficient evidence of links between ill-effects on human beings, they were still convinced of the potential risk:

Q. Why, Doctor, are both cattle and animals, as well as men, humans, affected by effluents from an aluminium factory?

A. Because fluorides – fluorine compounds are deadly poisonous to mammalian tissues, and man is a mammal just as much as a cow or sheep.[132]

Evidence provided in the case brought by Hobbs against NBACo at the High Court in Edinburgh revealed that by the late 1940s the Lochaber factory was emitting 1016 mts (1000tons) of fluorine per annum from its chimneys or the equivalent of 41.45 kgs of fluorine (F) to every tonne (t) of aluminium(Al) produced. Of this, 750 tons, or 2 tons every twenty-four hours, was hydrofluoric acid – a particularly toxic compound and one of the most acidic gases known – that attacks glass, concrete, metals and all organic compounds. This represented some 0.09 per cent of the total smoke production of British industry (which stood at 1.1 million tons, or 55 per cent of total smoke emissions in the UK) in 1948. By way of comparison with the Lochaber figure of 41.45kgs F/t Al, untreated emissions from French smelters immediately post-war stood at an estimated 14kgsF/t Al and 12kgsF/tAl for new Söderberg lines at Saint-Jean de Maurienne. Quite aside from the environmental impact, this loss of so much fluorine was also very inefficient.[133] The emissions almost certainly, given the evidence from the visiting Pechiney engineers, included high levels of sulphur dioxide.[134] What also became evident from the deliberations of the presiding judge, Lord Birnam, was that British Aluminium had been made aware of the damage to flora and fauna in the area both by John Bullen, and were conversant with international research into airborne fluorine hazards from other aluminium smelters and engineering methods for considerably reducing emissions from the mid-1940s onwards. Not noted in the judge's ruling, and possibly unbeknownst to him, was that the company had long been apprised of the effects of fluorine damage and methods for the containment of airborne effluents as the Neuhausen advice and the Stangfjorden and Vigelands cases show.

For his part, the general manager of the Highland smelters, John Bullen had written to Head Office in August 1946, after a visit to Hobbs' estate, expressing sympathy for the latter's plight and offering a vivid account of the damage:

> It is undoubtedly true that by far the larger number of fir trees surrounding the Castle [Inverlochy Castle, a site of considerable historic importance] are suffering severely from what appears to be leaf scorching. The general impression from the Castle is most disheartening as all these trees show large areas of brown, while some have been killed altogether. The damage is not confined to the immediate surrounds of the Castle, but extends as far as the eye can reach in all directions.[135]

The company's research department attempted to deploy expert opinion to discount fluorine as the cause of the damage blaming parasitic fungi and hard frosts, but this was rejected in evidence provided both by the Senior Research Officer from the Ministry of Agriculture, Dr Hamilton-Green, and the Head of the Department of Forest Mycology (the study of woodland fungi) at Oxford University in separate advice provided between 1946–48. Both Hamilton-Green and Day found high levels of fluorine in the affected trees and grass, and concluded that the parasitic fungi only appeared once the trees were dying. Another expert hired by the company, Dr. Malcolm Wilson, admitted that the fumes could damage the trees to a 'small extent', although both Wilson and a practical forester (with little knowledge of mycology) attributed much of the destruction to the fungi. Lord Birnam was convinced by Hamilton-Green and Day's evidence, judging that factory fumes from the factory had been 'at least an important contributory cause of the damage complained of' and that they constituted 'a serious interference' with Hobbs' property. Moreover he established that plants both in Britain and abroad had been far more effective in reducing fluoride emissions. In arriving at his conclusion Birnam was also affected by company correspondence showing that, despite Bullen's repeated requests in correspondence with head office from 1944 onwards to provide capital investment for the necessary fume treatment solutions to be installed, the senior management of the firm had failed to act. In one of his later letters sent in the summer of 1946 after Hobbs had lodged his complaint, Bullen and British Aluminium's land factor Gordon Chalmers – no doubt keen to maintain the generally good relationships that British Aluminium had built up with landowners in the area over the years – 'warned' their superiors that even though Hobbs appeared to be 'averse from creating a fuss he had very real ground of complaint which it would be desirable to deal with in a friendly spirit rather than at a later period when tempers may be somewhat frayed'. Further evidence, in the form of a brochure from head office of November 1946, outlining the company's reason for delaying renovation – 'heavy capital charges which would be incurred if treatment of the fumes from the present furnaces had to be undertaken' –

incensed Lord Birnam.[136] He would, perhaps, have been even less favourably disposed to the company than he already was, had he realised that other works managers had complained at their 1948 conference that modernisation at BACo's works were being 'impeded' by 'centralised' procurement policies.[137] Birnam commended the actions of local managers in attempting to remind senior managers of the company's responsibilities in the area but noted: 'unfortunately this excellent advice was ignored at Head Quarters whose attitude appears to have been that they were entitled to take their own time to re-construct their factory provided they were prepared to pay for any damage that the petitioners might suffer in the meantime.' The Lord of Session's evident indignation mattered little as political machinations behind the scene (in the form of submissions from the Ministry of Supply) citing the importance of the factory both to national interests and to the local economy) forced his hand in postponing a decree of interdict 'with considerable reluctance'. This after BACo pledged to rectify the problem promptly with 'remedial action' and compensate the petitioners.[138] In light of the continued reliance of Britain on domestic aluminium supplies and safe in the knowledge that the government would intervene, Commodore Linzee had confidently declared to the annual meeting almost a year before Lord Birnam's ruling that: 'The Judge had ordered Proof Before Answer, calling for expert witnesses and so on. The case would not go to proof for some considerable time, but if it ever did, Commodore Linzee felt certain it would not be successful.'[139] By January 1950 Hobbs and the distillery were again submitting their petition for an interdict claiming that there had been no improvement. BACo claimed the work was ongoing, and the Ministry of Supply intervened again on their behalf. The petition was later withdrawn when the Distillery became satisfied that the work was being undertaken.[140] This, in spite of the admission at the BACo managers' conference four months later, that half of the fluorine emitted 'could not be accounted for'.[141] By this time, with Britain rearming to meet the Korean War, the company could once again be assured of government intervention in the case. BACo's case bears some resemblance to Alcan's deployment of Cold War defence priorities with the federal and provincial governments, and US State Department, to silence critics of their proposed developments in British Columbia in the late 1940s.[142] By the time the Pechiney engineers visited at the start of August the next year, fume extraction had been fitted to the new Söderbergs, and BACo revealed that the pre-baked furnace lines were being phased out.[143] What is clear from the examples preceding and those that follow, is that British Aluminium's senior management was forced reluctantly and only very belatedly into action to reduce emissions to save itself from further adverse publicity and legal action. It illustrates the powerlessness of legal mechanisms when faced with interventions by government departments on behalf of business. It also shows the powerlessness of operational and tactical management to undertake necessary development work at their plants in the face of retrenchment by strategic management; an example of what one management historian, talking of the mismatch between the myth and realities of management, described as 'how powerless managers can feel, and be, away from the "rhetorical illusion and myth" of the worlds of the "business guru", the "executive summary" and "manager as hero"'.[144] British Aluminium was not alone among its international counterparts. Historically aluminium producers considered environmental concerns to be secondary to those of the contribution of the industry to the nation and its material contribution to local communities. Even though the first attempts to treat emissions were made by Neuhausen at the end of the nineteenth century and attempts had been made as early as 1905 at PCAC's La Saussaz works to collect noxious gases, the strategy of producers for a long time was limited to the political expedient of generous compensation paid to farmers.[145]

Any changes that had been made within the Lochaber smelter had little apparent effect on the workplace environment by the 1960s. Unfortunately a study into the health of furnacemen at Lochaber, proposed by British Aluminium's then consulting medical officer Dr E. Sweeney in 1963, never reached fruition due the latter's cavalier proposal, despite the enthusiasm of the MRC for the potential of the study in principle. Of note, especially given the recognition of pulmonary obstruction among some furnace room workers by trade unionists, later local general practitioners and staff at the Belford Hospital alike, was Sweeney's assertion that despite the 'considerable fume at work' the furnacemen at Lochaber were (in contrast to other industrial locations) lucky 'to live in a very clean environment on the shores of a Highland loch'.[146] Sweeney's confidence in the furnacemen's good health was not to be shared by all local doctors. In particular, one local GP, Dr Allison, was alarmed by the high incidence of respiratory obstruction and chest complaints that he observed among his patients who had worked in the furnace room. By 1973, Allison, trade union representatives at the works and their own medical advisor, had become increasingly convinced that this was being caused by the inhalation of the coal tar pitch fumes, particularly during the changeover of anodes. They pressed the company for an investigation and a team from the University of Dundee's Institute for Occupational Health (IOH) – with support from the Environmental Health Service, as well as specialists in community and cardio-respiratory medicine from the Universities of Edinburgh and Glasgow, and the NCB's Respiratory Centre – were appointed to investigate.[147] What they found in the furnace room at Lochaber was described by one medic from the IOH team as, 'Dickensian'.[148] Another local GP newly arrived to the area, who visited the works in the early 1970s, was similarly taken aback by conditions noting that 'you couldn't see from one furnace to perhaps two or three down the row'. He recalled being called out to administer injections to a cohort of older furnace workers suffering from 'chronic obstructed airways disease [...] not infrequently with marked bronchospasm, difficulty breathing, breathlessness [...] with bad chest did come heart failure'.[149] These victims of what locals referred to as the 'BA [British Aluminium] chest' or 'BA lung' – known more universally as 'pot room asthma' –

were similarly treated by the current medical adviser to the Lochaber smelter when he started practicing as a GP in the area in 1979.[150]

Concurrently the Health and Safety Executive and HM Industrial Pollution Inspectorate had also been called into investigate conditions. By the mid-1970s, results collected by the HSE's industrial hygiene laboratory had established that levels of the carcinogenic PAHs were 'several times the threshold limit', and the HSE was pressing for British Aluminium to invest in the modernisation of both plants. Though the later findings of the IOH study – which carried out tests on around half of the Lochaber workforce, and 94 per cent of furnacemen, against a sample of local residents – was inconclusive, the HSE remained firmly convinced of the threat posed to employees' health. At a meeting with trade unions and senior BACo managers at the Lochaber works in April 1975, the HSE warned the company that unless an assurance was given to completely modernise the processes and dramatically reduce emissions they would close the factories down. British Aluminium stalled by claiming that existing market conditions would not allow for a modernisation, which they estimated would cost £5 million (in fact it would cost many times more than that), and that they may have to close the plant. At this threat, the local trade union branches withdrew their objections, concerned by the spectre of job losses.[151] In fact an internal minute from the company a few days after the HSE-BACo meeting revealed that modernisation of the cell rooms had been recommended two years previously by their own engineers but ignored. The group's engineering director, and former Reynolds' engineer Jake Hedgecock, was forced grudgingly to accept that the modernisation might have to be contemplated:

> In view of the growing pressure from shop floor employees for improved conditions, the limits now being imposed on fluoride and tar levels in the working areas by the Factory Inspector and the Employment Medical Service; also the Company's declared Policy to create and maintain a healthy working environment to ensure the health and safety of their employees, may justify a fresh look at the proposals.[152]

During the course of these discussions the Pollution Inspectorate attempted, with the support of the Scottish Economic Planning Department, to block the HSE's attempts to pressurise the firm into modernising the plant. Concerned that the company might close these plants and pull out of the west Highlands, the deputy senior inspector for Scotland, Bill McCamley declared that this 'would have a serious impact on the district both in terms of loss of jobs and loss of opportunity for young people to receive an apprenticeship training'.[153] Yet, clearly recognising what he was advocating, McCamley was careful to counsel his Scottish Office colleagues to caution:

Lochaber furnace room prior to modernisation, 1975. © RTA/GUA.

Until the outcome of the current discussions between the firm and the Health and Safety Executive is known, there is little that the Scottish Office can do without appearing to interfere with the responsibility for industrial health and safety of the Health and Safety Commission and Executive. I suggest therefore that the Scottish Office should take no positive action meantime but I will keep in touch with the situation.[154]

These negotiations provide an invaluable insight into the tactics and bargaining behind the policing of occupational health and safety, revealing the degree to which the response of officials in Edinburgh, Inverness and London was determined by the politics of regional development, with retention of the manufacturing base and defence of jobs in this sector (especially in the Highlands taking precedence over public health and environmental concerns. Unnerved by BACo's threats to close the plant, trade unionists were also left with 'Hobson's choice'. The company consciously used this bargaining to defer a decision on the subject, and delay investing the inevitable capital. Ultimately the company conceded reluctantly to demands, and with the securing of the necessary investment, and was able to undertake the reconstruction of Lochaber and modernisation of Kinlochleven, while using this as leverage to exact government loans and support for European investment.

Regional development and the limits of regulation: Invergordon
The shining 'industrial cathedral' of Invergordon, as befitting its status as a 'white heat' project, benefited from all the features of a modern aluminium plant, including a wet scrubbing plant to treat fumes. Secretary of State for Scotland Willie Ross confidently declared himself 'satisfied' that there would be 'efficient control over effluent from any industrial plant and that if there are ever any harmful effects, they will be occasional and effect a very limited area'.[155] Once again the debate over the construction of the smelter was mired in the politics of regional development, with battle lines between supporters and opponents once again advancing familiar arguments. Opposition to the smelter, and other industrial developments, was led by the local branch of the National Farmers' Union (NFU) – angered by what they saw as the requisitioning of fertile agrarian land for industry – along with conservationists and environmentalists. The case made by supporters followed similar lines to those of their predecessors, citing emigration of the young from the region and unemployment levels above the UK and Scottish averages.[156] With a commitment among Ministers to regional planning and industrial placement as answers to the Highland problem, combined with the rhetoric of the 'white heat' of technical progress – alongside the balance of trade benefits to be accrued – STUC support, and against a background of unemployment levels in the area of more than three times the UK and double the Scottish average, as well as rising support for the SNP in the area, it is scarcely surprising that there was overwhelming support in both St Andrew's House and Whitehall for the scheme, irrespective of the environmental cost.[157] Yet quite aside from its significant footprint on the Ross and Cromarty landscape, within a few years of opening, local farmers started to observe cases of fluorosis among their livestock too. True to form, British Aluminium's meticulous preparations ensured that it had already managed the situation and established mechanisms for mollifying critics. Moreover, they could be assured of the tacit support of government in Edinburgh and London, mindful of the contribution that BACo made to the Highland and Scottish economies. British Aluminium quickly recognised that in order to neutralise opposition to the scheme, it had to reach out to specific groups to mollify them. In this connection, and anticipating compensation claims, British Aluminium signed a compensation agreement with the NFU of Scotland that required any claimants to comply with procedures set down by BACo and NFU (on terms favourable to the company), and absolved the company of any public culpability. The joint NFU–BACo committee to consider claims allowed for a nature conservancy representative but one that held no vote. Any farmers making a claim through the scheme were bound to the process. Two opinions were given, one on behalf of the claimant, and the other from a veterinarian on behalf of the company. The arbitration process – should the two vets not agree – required the Committee to consult the Veterinary Investigation Officer of the North of Scotland College of Agriculture (NOSCA), with samples being sent to the Central Veterinary Laboratory at Weybridge in Surrey, England.

If, after this advice, the two vets disagreed, the claimant or the company could seek further expert advice from an arbitrator appointed and selected by the President of the British Veterinary Association. Until the judgment was pronounced, claimants had to cover all their own legal and veterinary costs. As well as dissuading complainants, this tactic also diluted the effectiveness of collective action on the part of farmers, such as through the Easter Ross Land Use Committee (ERLUC), and pushed persistent critics among them on to the periphery. Coincidentally the National Farmers Union Mutual Insurance Society Ltd was a major shareholder in BACo.[158] In addition, as an internal memo from the Scottish Development Department (SDD) to HM Industrial Pollution Inspectorate (HMIPI) and the Animal Health Branch of the Department for Agriculture and Fisheries Scotland (DAFS) revealed, the government was keen to absolve itself of any role in these negotiations. The lead official at DAFS made it clear that the government had no locus in these discussions – having devolved responsibility to the local planning authority, Ross and Cromarty County Council – and had 'no powers under agricultural or planning legislation for action to be taken against the Company because of the effects of their operations on neighbouring farmers'.[159] Critically Ross and Cromarty County Council had ceded responsibility and complete authority to British Aluminium over the location and form that sampling of fluorine levels took as early as November 1967.[160] As one keen eyed historian of Alcan's negotiations over their Nechako project in British Columbia has observed: 'the politics of development sometimes turn on small clauses.'[161] Combined with its advertising campaign and general local charm offensive, this proved highly effective in eliminating any existing opposition.

Even before the plant entered operation, problems had started to arise. By May 1970, a local farmer (Mr Forsyth) whose property bordered the Ross and Cromarty smelter raised concerns about fluorine emissions damaging his livestock, noting that he had already received compensation of £7,000 from BACo. In their reply to the farmer, the Scottish Office – who viewed him as a nuisance – directed Forsyth to the NFU–BACo agreement (once again abrogating any direct responsibility) and revealed that HMIPI and NOSCA were monitoring the situation.[162] Little had improved by 1978 when Forsyth's daughter wrote again to the Scottish Office calling for an enquiry into pollution from the smelter. She also mentioned that a sample of bone from one of the family's cattle sent to Weybridge had confirmed that fluorosis was the cause of the animal's lameness. Privately Scottish officials were growing concerned, for while Weybridge had no evidence of a recent sample being sent, they did not to dismiss her claims, 'since there have undoubtedly been animals which have had to be slaughtered because of broken bones owing to fluorosis'.[163] Around the same time the Chief Inspector of Industrial Pollution had visited the Forsyth's farm at Balintraid in September 1978, and assured them that BACo had launched an investigation into the lameness among livestock in the area to examine whether other mineral deficiencies were responsible rather than fluorine. The SDD wrote to the

Forsyths again in November 1978 stating: 'if you consider that the fluorosis problem is such that livestock farming at Balintraid is no longer feasible it is, of course, open to you and Mr. Forsyth to seek expert support for that view ... and to take such action as you see fit with British Aluminium Company.'[164] The Scottish Office sought additional advice from NOSCA in 1978 – in addition to the study being undertaken by HMIPI and Weybridge – who replied in January 1979. The Principal of NOSCA, Professor Lewis Littlejohn, objected to the fact that NOSCA (the designated first-stage arbitrators in the claims process) had effectively been by-passed at all of the initial stages of process, with the terms of reference of the research being determined by BACo. Under these investigations, led by their local vet, C. Sutherland, and advised by their veterinary consultant, Bristol University's Professor C. Gunsell, attention was focused on examining the high levels of molybdenum occurring naturally in the area – that caused mineral deficiencies in the local livestock – alongside fluorine levels. BACo's conjecture being that it was this, as much as fluorine emissions from the factory, responsible for the high number of pedal bone fractures among cattle. Littlejohn acknowledged the widespread problem of fluorosis at Invergordon. He further judged the BACo led investigations to be a smokescreen:

> The term 'red herring' was certainly not introduced but if BACO are using the fact that they have initiated this experiment as an argument to dissuade farmers from pursuing claims against them ... I would tend to agree that 'red herring' is a not inappropriate term to apply.[165]

At a meeting at the smelter – chaired by Grunsell, and attended by Sutherland, along with Scottish Office representatives – in April 1979, it was admitted that 'fluorosis will be a continuing problem in this district', and that despite the HMIPI's efforts, 95–96 per cent efficiency at the plant 'is the best that can be done'.[166] By July 1979, high traces of both fluorine and molybdenum were reported at Inverbreakie and Broomhill farms in the area, with 25 per cent of cattle showing pedal bone fractures as well evidence of dental fluorosis.[167] However evidence that British Aluminium had been dumping toxic 'red mud' or 'aluminium sludge' into the Moray Firth was not considered to be serious by the pollution inspectorate because it had only affected areas immediately around the smelter.[168] In January 1980, the inspectorate received further complaints from a croft close to the smelter. At a meeting in October of that year, BACo revealed that all the animals at Inverbreakie, Ord and Broomhill farms were showing signs of dental fluorosis. British Aluminium, like other aluminium producers, grazed cattle and sheep around smelters to increase public confidence.[169] Tensions between the Forsyths, on the one hand, and the Scottish Office, BACo and the smelter's supporters had their roots in the ERLUC's campaign against arable land being acquired for industrial uses. Forsyth's daughter, Jean, had proved a thorn in the side of local government planners, the Scottish Office and BACo, in attempting to block permission to have the land around Ord and Inverbreakie farms re-zoned for the smelter.[170] Given the financial pressures on the company – and the numbers employed at the smelter – there was little appetite among government and regulators to pursue the matter with vigour. Just over a year later, the smelter closed. British Aluminium's strategy at Invergordon was directed at controlling the volume and size of claims, as well as attempting as far as possible to eliminate adverse publicity. Aided by complicity from central and local government – for whom the growth of the regional economy and labour market was the priority – they were able to exercise considerable control over the gathering of data on effluents and therefore establish hegemony over the process.

Aluminium slumps, oil shocks and environmentalism

With a slump in demand for aluminium prices between 1970 and 1974, followed by an increase in global aluminium prices, and then the advent of a buyers market after the metal was launched on the LME, improvements in energy efficiency and economising on raw materials became all the more pressing. This also coincided with greater pressure on the state to introduce measures to reduce industrial emissions, especially airborne effluents, and energy consumption among manufacturers. The rate of industrialisation and urbanisation during the nineteenth and twentieth centuries was built on access to cheap energy and water. By the latter part of the twentieth century, this gamble 'with the planet, without knowing all the rules of the game' was starting to accumulate very tangible, if contested impacts, while political uncertainties and legislative responses made a strategic response from within the industry all the more pressing.[171] By the late 1970s, aluminium producers globally were scrutinising developments in the United States, both in terms of emissions and recycling of aluminium. The US Environmental Protection Agency having set a standard for fluorine emissions of 1kgF/tAl, European producers started to use this as a benchmark.[172]

As at their other plants, further evidence of BACo's reluctance to respond to potential hazards to health, safety and the environment, where this was deemed to be too costly, was revealed through Alcan's review of the company's plants in the years leading up to the merger. Reinhold Wagner's visits to BACo's sites at Silvertown in London and Glasgow revealed dilapidated plant and buildings, with much machinery without exhaust filters and with fumes and pollution as a problem; while an internal report compiled by Alcan staff in 1979 cited the 'environmental problems' at BACo's 'older smelters' as a potential obstacle to a takeover, although by this stage BACo's modernisation of their west Highland plants was under way.[173] The project to reconstruct Lochaber led by George Haggart was to see a profound improvement in the workplace environment and efficiency, and a dramatic reduction in emissions.[174] With the support of all the main trade unions at the works, including trips to smelters in North America, Australia, and France, the working group opted for the installation of new AP-18-2 furnace technology, along with a new and extensive fume extraction system, from Aluminium Pechiney. The working group was able to persuade the board of the efficiency gains to be effected from this improvement. George Haggart had much interest in persuading the directors of the virtues of the scheme and improving the workplace environment. Brought up in Inverlochy, Haggart's father and brother had both worked in the furnace room, and he had been promoted from the shopfloor. Moreover having previously been landed with the unenviable task of announcing the closure of the Invergordon smelter, here was a far more positive challenge. The AP-18-2 furnaces were covered and with integrated fume extraction systems and pre-baked anodes. The feed of alumina to the furnaces was also automated and controlled from a computer bank, immediately significantly reducing many of the health and safety risks traditionally present in the furnace room, and emissions from the factory. Returning to undertake further studies of workplace conditions in Lochaber smelter, the member of the IOH team who had conducted the studies over a decade before was struck by the changes: 'When the company revamped the Fort William smelter there couldn't have been a bigger contrast because you walked into this beautiful area where everything was enclosed ... whereas you could barely see from one end of the smelting room to the other in the early days, in the new plant you didn't know you were in a smelter.'[175] Concurrently the modernisation expanded the output of the smelter, vastly improved efficiency, and secured its future.[176] Opinion was also split among employees in the smelter because of the job cuts that it meant. What is abundantly evident was the reluctance of the company to undertake this work, except under pressure and in the face of a potential takeover (thereby making BACo's fixed capital assets more attractive).[177]

If Alcan already had a *prima facie* reputation for greater commitment to the environment and to more rigorous occupational health and safety regimes, then conditions at their Canadian smelters had not always inspired confidence, with the famous 1941 strike at their Arvida works, for example, attributed to the terrible working conditions in the plant. Alcan continued to be mired in controversy in British Columbia surrounding their Nechako scheme and the extension to this, the Kemano project, supplying their Kitimat smelter.[178] Nevertheless by the late 1970s, Alcan appeared to be showing a greater degree of genuine commitment to these priorities than BACo, albeit chiefly motivated by the changing context of access to global resources, especially for an energy-intensive industry like aluminium, with its reliance on hydro-electric power.

Over the following decades, recycling and energy efficiency were to become business imperatives. In 1985, British Alcan established as its three main priorities: reducing energy costs, tackling acid rain, and focusing on recycling cans.[179] Britain was Europe's biggest market for drinks cans, but recycled about 10 per cent, in contrast to estimated recycling of 66 per cent of cans in the United States. Opening in December 1991, British Alcan's new 50,000 mts recycling plant at Warrington cost £28 million to contribute to the industry's pledge to recycle 50 per cent of cans by 1995.[180] As well as cans, recycling of aluminium from the transport and construction sectors also increased. Between 1989 and 1993, recycling of aluminium in the UK rose from 2 to 20 per cent, rising to 34 per cent in 1998 when it was producing 250,000 mts of recycled metal.[181] Undoubtedly the fact that recycling only required 5 per cent of the energy needed in primary production encouraged the industry's penchant for it. That the figures for recycled metal were not higher may have owed more to insufficient collections points and centres (as well as a culture of disposal rather than recycling) than to the industry's commitment to recycling. In contrast, recycling of aluminium employed in sectors such as transport and construction had risen to 90 and 70 per cent respectively by 1998.[182] The number of collection points at supermarkets for aluminium cans increased from 660 to 1100, but recycling of municipal waste remained low with figures of only 5 per cent for England and Wales in 1996–97. Scottish figures for 1999–2000 suggest only 5.1 per cent of all household waste was recycled, with a Scottish Households Survey of 2004 noting that only 9 per cent of adults in Scotland who responded acknowledging that they had recycled metal cans in the 2000. European Union figures for 2003 revealed that the UK came close behind Greece and Portugal, proportionately recycling less than any of the then other EU15, choosing to dump most of its household waste in landfill sites. Figures for recycling of aluminium (and steel) cans fluctuated due both to increased sales and the commitment of local government to provide recycling collection points. By 2004, 20 per cent of Scottish households surveyed claimed to have recycled metals cans, while the quantity of steel and aluminium cans recycled in England and Wales increased by 55 per cent between 2002–3 and 2003–4.[183] However the importance of recycling of metal cans, especially aluminium, was not just in reducing waste in landfill sites but also in terms of the reduction of carbon emissions in the process. By 1999–2000 recycling of aluminium was saving 1,500,000 mts in carbon emissions (or around 1 per cent of the UK total for that year), seeing the greatest impact of any industrial sector.[184] Concurrently, with the primary aluminium industry the sole industrial producer of tetrafluoride and hexafluoroethane (two of the major perfluoro-carbons (PFCs) or climate change gases) in the UK, Alcan sought to reduce outputs of these, both to avoid penalties as well as because of its public commitments. By the early 1990s in three out of the four UK smelters, Alcan and AAM had worked with the pollution inspectorate to reduce these emissions. By 1993, according to the Department of the Environment's rough calculations, emissions of these two had both been reduced to 29 per cent of their 1990 figures.[185]

Inspections by the HSE of both the Lochaber and Kinlochleven smelters in 1998, revealed that while at the former, with its covered cells (furnaces), 98 per cent of the fumes were captured and treated, only 60 per cent of emissions could be captured at the latter because of the retention of the original Söderberg furnaces. This was

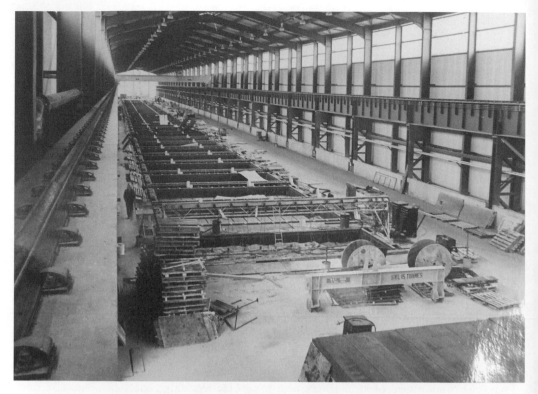

Modernising the Lochaber smelter: new cell room. © RTA/GUA.

proffered as one of the reasons for Alcan's closure of Kinlochleven because it could not meet with the standards set out by the Scottish Environmental Protection Agency (SEPA).[186] Of course this is a moot point for had Alcan felt that Kinlochleven could operate on a commercially viable basis then they would have been ready to reconstruct the plant. Instead electricity generated in Kinlochleven's power station was, with the installation of a £2.3 million, 10 megawatt alternator, by the late 1990s supplying the Lochaber smelter with additional power.[187] Asked about his initial impression of the state of the Kinlochleven furnace room when he started there (four years after the merger between BACo and Alcan) Bob Herbert observed:

> Not having worked in heavy industry before, I've always had an outside job in the forces and you know the papers and things [...] I walked in and it was a bit like Dante's inferno [...] sort of the environment and health and safety weren't at the top of the agenda then, and [...] people worked in jeans and t-shirts and sort of had wet hankies over their face to stop the fumes getting in and it was quite sort of basic.[188]

Modernising the Lochaber smelter: fume extraction plant. © RTA/GUA.

Herbert recalled improvements to safety procedures in the plant with the arrival of a new manager, Jim Bruce, not long after he joined. Certainly HSE inspection reports indicated that Bruce introduced far more rigorous health and safety procedures from 1988 onwards, and by 1998 the plant had experienced no accidents in the previous four years, winning Alcan's health and safety award. According to the HSE inspector's discussions with a number of workers at the plant, all employees and subcontracted labour onsite were provided with and required to wear air-fed respirators, molten metal protective clothing, prescription eye protection, ear defenders, and hard hats. They also confirmed that the respirators were maintained at the end of the shift by staff other than themselves and the filters replaced for each shift.[189] The importance of this lies in the fact that by way of contrast when prototypes of these masks were introduced in coal mines in the mid-1970s, neither the regulating government department nor the NCB enforced the wearing of the masks or provided training in their use.[190] Critically Herbert confirms that the health and safety regime under Bruce was very strictly enforced, in contrast to earlier laxity. An indication of this increased vigilance to occupational health risks is provided by a case against the company in the Court of Session in 1994. A furnace room stubber sued British Alcan for loss of earnings incurred due to his departure from the industry caused by low grade dermatitis attributed to the barrier creams that the company 'demanded' that he wore to prevent skin melanomas.[191] Although the case infers inflexibility and certainly grounds for unfair discrimination on the part of the employers as far as the plantiffs' terms of employment were concerned, it does suggest paradoxically alertness to occupational carcinomas. This was most probably also driven by the growing literature linking aluminium smelting and cancers, and the threat of future legislation.[192] The HSE visit to Lochaber too had revealed a strong safety culture there too, with the same health and safety attire required. Concurrently inspectors held separate meetings with both the plant managers and union representatives to congratulate them on what the HSE saw as the company's good performance in health and safety; the leading inspector observing that the fact that the company had gone without an accident for a year was 'creditable in a molten metal environment'. Alcan was also attempting to achieve best performer benchmarking against the chemical industry.[193] The HSE's sanguine observations about progress achieved under Alcan were reflected in the report of the Pollution Inspectorate after their visits to both Kinlochleven and Fort William in June 1993:

The influence of the Canadian Parent company is evident in the increasingly formalized approach to staff training which encompasses environmental protection as well as occupational safety. In addition to the missions statements which appear on every noticeboard, there have been seminars for key personnel for the purpose of discussing what can be done to improve environmental performance. These have been followed by one-to-one interviews for all staff who must sign to say that they understand what is required of them individually. Despite my cynicism I have to say that the state of affairs in the Kinlochleven cell room suggests that the policy is paying dividends; the conditions are many times better than they were 10 years [ago] despite the dramatic fall in the staff complement.[194]

Even allowing for the unusual circumstances surrounding an inspection, the testimony provided by Herbert, Walker and other former employees certainly seems to bear out considerable improvements in environmental conditions within the smelters. Six years later HSE inspectors reported that the works had experienced one incident of time lost to an accident in that period. They also confirmed strict compliance with wearing of protective clothing and breathing apparatus.[195] At both plants all employees apparently underwent annual audiometric, lung function, and urine tests, with all prospective employees undergoing medical screening in advance. In addition, furnace room workers were provided with salt tablets to counteract the effects of dehydration and heat. In the anode maintenance ('break out') area the operator

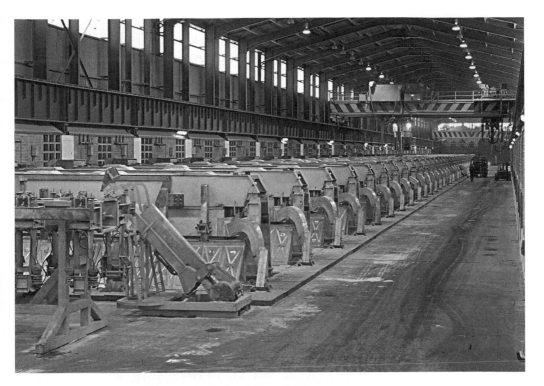

Modernised cell room, Lochaber, 2005. © Alex Gillespie/RTA.

sat in an acoustically protected booth eliminating most of the dust, although this was being redesigned. The Lochaber report did reveal a 10–15 per cent absence rate attributed to musculoskeletal problems, and the HSE inspector Christina Woodrow also recommended that the plant carry out a risk assessment on vibration from pneumatic tools used to remove slag from ladles in the plant's casting shop where metal was made into billets for customers.[196] Two months later a further inspection was carried out by an HSE and a medical inspector to investigate a complaint made by an employee about whole body vibration, with the inspection team recommending that the cell room manager improve vibration control in one aspect of the cell room operations.[197] In July 1999 the HSE was called to Lochaber after some employees in the casting shop were exposed to chlorine gas and taken to hospital for check-ups. A follow-up in May 2000 insisted that the plant have breathing apparatus in the casting shop as well as their planned automatic alarm and shutdown system.[198] A comparative 2003 CSR study, on behalf of the EAA, of six European aluminium plants – including two smelters, Saint-Jean de Maurienne and Lochaber – revealed that the factory had surpassed both national and international environmental emissions requirements for aluminium smelters. Lochaber's fume treatment programme had reduced emissions of CO_2 from around 2.8 mts per tonne of aluminium to 1.68 mts, and PFCs from 0.17 kgs per tonne of aluminium to 0.018 kgs between 1990 and 2005, although sulphur dioxide emissions from the plant were steadily being reduced it still remained Scotland's seventh largest industrial contributor of SO_2 to the atmosphere.[199] Studies of PAH concentrations in shellfish and sediment in the waters around the Kinlochleven and Lochaber smelters also noted high levels of these – including the carcinogenic, benzoαpyrene – seeping into Lochs Leven and Linnhe emanating from discharge from the smelters fume treatment systems. Mussels collected in a fish farm in Loch Leven between July 1999 and February 2000, were deemed 'unsuitable for human consumption' due to the pronounced levels of PAHs within them, causing a temporary closure of the farm, although much of this stemmed from problems in pollution control from the aged Kinlochleven smelter, which was close to closure.[200]

The native aluminium industry's modernisation of processes and attempts to reduce energy consumption were, at the turn of the twenty-first century, also being driven by the new UK Labour government's attempts to introduce a Climate Change Levy (CCL). The DTI's own report on the subject, chaired by Lord Marshall, then head of the CBI, had earlier concluded that even though aluminium producers had done much to reduce emissions (and had led industry in targeting emissions and making efficiencies) more could be done by them. The aluminium industry mobilised opposition, along with other energy-intensive industries, like steel and chemicals, to the proposals through the Aluminium Federation (Al. Fed.) and the International Federation of Industrial Energy Users. Al. Fed.'s chief objections to the plans to put in place a system of tariffs to tax industrial users on the basis of carbon consumption was that the projected bill of £40 million (of which £28 million would be shouldered by the primary reduction works) would make the industry uncompetitive, and that as such UK aluminium producers would be forced to close their operation. Although this was a familiar call, it was not entirely unsubstantiated. Producers like Alcan did initially have reasonable grounds to contest the government's proposals, where it was suggested that they would impose the levy on those producers using hydro-electricity to supply their combined heat and power, such as at Lochaber and Kinlochleven, as well. In the end the then Chancellor of the Exchequer, the Rt Hon. Gordon Brown MP, went even further than conceding to this demand. Not only were industrial producers using renewable energy, such as Alcan's operations at the Highland smelters, exempted but so was the entire aluminium smelting sector (as well as chlor-akali production). In addition, Gordon Brown conceded lower CCL rates, and offered some £50–150 million to aid energy efficiency schemes. Al. Fed. continued to lobby the DTI for exemptions from emissions generated by recycling operations and energy consumption related to pollution abatement measures.[201]

The legacy: health and environment

Undoubtedly health and safety practice in modern smelters has improved beyond recognition. Similarly as a recent independent study has shown the non-ferrous metals industry, aluminium included, has expended more than many other sections of UK industry in pollution abatement schemes.[202] However certain technologies left a legacy of ill-health among a cohort of workers, mostly a generation passed. The full impact on health among those workers, in terms of complications contributing to partial disability and premature mortality, are not quantifiable because of other contributing factors. This should not detract from the recognition among employees, local communities, and local medical practitioners and occupational health professionals that conditions such as 'BA Chest' were debilitating and chronic, and due in part to the working conditions which furnaceroom and carbon factory workers endured until the reconstruction of Lochaber, and even later at Kinlochleven. Certainly perusal of the pages of *The B.A. News* shows a high number of furnacemen, in particular, who appeared to be dying prematurely (either before or soon after retirement). Yet, as an examination of a sample of the death certificates for some of these workers reveals, though many shared similar causes of death, such as cardiac failure caused by myocardial infarction as well chronic bronchitis emphysema (identified by local GPs as being common among this group), attributing these incidences to the processes in furnaceroom rather than other social factors (such as diet and smoking) is problematic.[203] In the case of occupational carcinogens, links between occupation and specific cancers have been even more difficult to attribute. A 1999 study into the incidence of cancer in Kinlochleven and Invergordon between 1975 and 1996 carried out by the National Health Service Cancer Surveillance Unit concluded that the levels of lung and bladder cancer were on the whole lower than expected, although the incidence of cancer were marginally higher for males and females alike in Kinlochleven, taking into account other factors. The report concluded by stating that 'on the basis of the data examined, there is no evidence of an increased risk of cancers associated with PAHs in populations in Scotland with potentially high residential exposures to these substances'.[204] However this population study did not isolate former furnace or carbon factory workers from among this number who were the groups most exposed to high levels of PAHs. Equally fluorine emissions, and other airborne pollutants, periodically had a devastating effect on local flora and fauna as the examples of Lochaber and Invergordon show. What is more it is clear from the evidence provided here that strategic management at British Aluminium was aware of these problems, and chose at times to disregard local concerns and the advice of its plant management in order to avoid the expense of investing in the necessary engineering solutions to reduce emissions. When head office was moved to action it was by the threat of poor publicity from high profile litigation and statutory environmental measures. As the case of Invergordon shows legislation can be ineffective in the face of weak enforcement.

The response of British Aluminium prior to 1978 was clearly inadequate and medical opinion divided. To a large degree, the response of all of these parties, including policy makers, was ultimately framed by the recent economic and social history of the Highlands, and particularly the areas experience of depopulation and migration. The complexity of, and at times diverging priorities to, this issue were illustrated by the example of Cameron Miller and Lachlan Grant. Though Grant was a progressive reformer, his passion for Highland regeneration prompted him to be an uncritical advocate for British Aluminium. Whether it was Grant's political inclinations or, in his mind, a dispassionate clinical logic, which led him to rally sometimes uncritically to the industry's side is debatable. Yet Grant was neither alone among Highland opinion nor was he immune to BACo's carefully composed public relations messages. Grant's defence was swift and his loyalty to the company unquestioned. In an open letter to the *Lancet* in 1931, he declared that 'numerous [British Aluminium] workers who have spent the greater part of their working lives, some for thirty years, are in 'excellent health'. Similarly he judged the health of local residents to be 'exceptionally good'.[205] Tellingly, he made a point of emphasising the size of the dependent population in Kinlochleven in the course of his letter. His belief in aluminium's properties even led him to furnish the Labour Prime Minister, Ramsay MacDonald, an acquaintance of his, with aluminium spoons, and to develop and patent a throat swab made of the metal.[206]

The response of trade unionists and shopfloor workers, while at times critical, was framed by the context of regional development; their priority continued to be that of attracting responsible businesses to the region, and expanding and retaining employment opportunities.[207] To policymakers, the priorities of full employment and regional development remain paramount in the post-war period. These concerns were pointedly illustrated by the response of trade unionists, and policymakers, over occupational health issues and environmental damage at the west Highland smelters and Invergordon. The contraction of the workforce at Lochaber was met with ambivalence, with some stifled rancour over job losses but equally a recognition that environmental conditions had to change in the plant. The only union-inspired class actions brought against BACo/Alcan were those brought by employees at the company's Burntisland, Falkirk and Glasgow plants over industrial deafness.[208] Interestingly, all the testimony provided by former employees at the Highland smelters acknowledges the poor environmental conditions at the work and is peppered with anecdotal evidence of colleagues who had succumbed to cancers or the 'BA lung', but posited this against this public narrative of BACo as a 'saviour of the highlands', in some cases linking this to the clearances.[209] Their views of their former employers may also have been coloured by the generally more cordial industrial relations at the west Highland smelters, at any rate, and the fact that the company offered attractive pension plans and housing sell-offs.

Conclusion

While humankind's footprint has been visible on the planet for some four million years, the pace and extent of change in the twentieth century was unprecedented in its impact on ecosystems.[210] Yet critics of that impact largely confined themselves, until the late twentieth century, to arguments about the aesthetic impact of industrialisation and urbanisation. Landscape in the Highlands, as elsewhere, was a 'contested' terrain. The perpetuation of the notion of the Highlands as Britain's last pristine wilderness lay, as Jill Payne points out, in 'the outsider perception of the region as "unspoiled" developed as a response to obviously more discernible changes in the south of Britain. Even on the grounds of this simplified example, the quest for, and the appreciation of, "unspoiled" landscape must surely be viewed as the pursuit of a cultural contest rather than a precise environmental condition.'[211]

As in the arena of industrial relations, occupational and environmental health and safety was leavened by the context of the politics of regional development. Contrary to Priest and O'Donnell's remarks, BACo's board did not listen to 'lay' or expert opinion that warned of risks to health and the environment. Instead, as in other industries, such as chemicals, coal-mining and asbestos, British Aluminium utilised a variety of devices to circumvent costly investment in major plant, especially under RTIA's stewardship, notably deploying familiar motifs of itself as a 'saviour' and as a 'key industry' with policy makers, as well as using professional knowledge to delay judgments and manage compensation payouts. In this, British Aluminium was not distinct from its counterparts, with wealth generation and secure employment considered the priorities to consecutive generations, traded often at the expense of good health and the natural environment. Where British Aluminium's board was forced into action, it was under pressure from potentially damaging adverse publicity and latterly the HSE. These politics of development profoundly affected the policing of industrial hazards, with the 'social choices' of shopfloor workers, policymakers, trade unionists, and communities shaped by this paradigm; measuring the potential health hazards of working against the risks of not working, especially for a generation with living memories of times of the interwar depression, was for many Highland employees a case of 'Hobson's choice'. At an individual level, this is vividly illustrated in the ambiguities and contradictions present in the personal testimonies of former employees.[212] It could also, as the preceding examples at British Aluminium's Norwegian, as well as its Highland, works show, reflect the contusions between local management and directors, with the former looking beyond the purely materialist transaction, and making a 'social choice' based on their position within the community. As the public contests and negotiations over pollution from the various Highland works, and the workplace environment, illustrate, BACo held the trump card by threatening to withdraw from the region. Moreover the fact that many of these discussions took place 'behind closed doors,' negated the effectiveness of the statutory tools that regulators had at their disposal. Ultimately for British Aluminium, as for other global aluminium producers, change was forced more by the changing economic and political contexts, and the need for energy and other resource economies. In this Alcan led the way, proving itself acutely aware of the benefits to be reaped from greater energy efficiency, as well as the need to be seen to carefully manage environmental concerns. It did not want to be caught depicted as an industrial behemoth belching fumes into the atmosphere, but as a responsible 'corporate citizen' whose processes were to seem as clean as the gleaming metal that they produced and the modern corporation that they projected. As evidence in this chapter illustrates, contrary to the chimera of a clean industry, the aluminium industry in the UK had a chequered past. British Aluminium, in particular, knowingly exposed its workforce and local communities to dangerous emissions, while seeking to evade responsibility.

5

'Practical and lasting good':
Aluminium and community
in the Highlands

W RITING to British Aluminium's medical officer, and Highland development campaigner, Dr Lachlan Grant in January 1935, William Murray Morrison declared: 'It is a most pleasing recollection in my career that I have also been able to do some practical and lasting good to my beloved Highlands.'[1] If the Scottish Highlands were central to British Aluminium's business activities and its public image, then stewardship in the region, and popular perceptions of that, were also core to their mission. In 1949 the company owned a total of 150,000 acres of land in the Highlands, and managed four sheep and a dairy farm. By 1977, despite the sale of around 22 per cent of their landholdings in the intervening years – symbolically the bulk to the other major employers in the region, the NSHEB and the Forestry Commission – they were the largest landowner in Inverness-shire (with more modest estates of 6,300 acres in Argyll), and the eighth largest in Scotland. Alcan's Highland property made it the fifth largest landowner in Scotland by 2001 with 135,000 acres of estates. The 'practical and lasting good' of British Aluminium's operations for the region, as they were quick to point out, were apparent; by 1920 the company employed between 250 and 300 in the west Highland area, paying out £170,000 in wages (£5.93m), and by 1937 British Aluminium was the largest single employer in Argyll-shire and one of the largest across the whole of the Highlands. In addition, the company contributed one-fifth and one-twentieth of the rates to Inverness-shire and Argyllshire respectively. Running costs aside, the Highland land holdings also brought valuable income in rent; the rental from estates acquired around Foyers promised to net the company £3,054 11s. 4d. (£1.46m) in its first full year of ownership alone (1895). By the mid-twentieth century, aside from its large estates, the company also owned a significant proportion of property in the town of Fort William, including the forty bedroom Grand Hotel, as well as Inverlochy Castle built in the thirteenth century.[2] Between January 1925 and the purchase of the latter in 1945, BACo's subsidiary the North British Aluminium Company spent no less than £71,202 – 80 per cent of that between 1924 and 1937 – acquiring property in and around the town of Fort William, excepting the cost of Inverlochy Village. In addition until the Electricity Act of 1947, the company supplied all of the town's electricity.[3]

Cultivating consent: BACo's Highland Mission

Nowhere did the cultural legacy of the industry make more of an impression than in the Highland villages of Kinlochleven and Inverlochy, and Foyers to a lesser extent, which were unmistakable as company settlements. In these, British Aluminium sought to 'sculpt' the social geography through their physical layout, and social organisations and networks. This was most in evidence in the 'BA' company village of Kinlochleven, which represented a 'panoptican', in which time, space, behaviour, and discipline were modulated by an extension of the factory and company regimes; the physical embodiment of Morrison's 'community of interest'.[4] As with Patrick Joyce's observation of the character of nineteenth-century factory owners' 'paternalism', in their exercise of planning and control over towns, British Aluminium sought to engineer the 'entire reality' of Inverlochy and Kinlochleven.[5] In Kinlochleven, and to a lesser extent Inverlochy, the lines between factory and communities blurred to create one ecosystem.[6] The success of this policy was variable: in Kinlochleven the company's 'cultural hegemony' was to become deeply entrenched; while in Inverlochy the power relationship was subject to some mediation. As Diane Drummond has observed of her own study of the railway company town of Crewe 'company paternalism *did not* produce an outright deference on the part of the townspeople … a whole spectrum of deferential to non-deferential responses were held by the people of Crewe. Some even *acted* deferentially out of expediency.'[7] Similarly Alcoa, and later Alcan, discovered when attempting to orchestrate the social 'rhythm' of the town of Arvida in Québec, that their 'Yankee values' had to accommodate existing social norms and cultural forms of the rural Saguenay.[8]

Harnessing the politics of Highland Development
That British Aluminium managed to maintain a high visibility in the west Highlands, despite the growth in public services, the contraction of the workforces at the Highland smelters and openings offered by alternative employment opportunities, as well as BACo's retreat under RTIA from previous social commitments after the Second World War, owed much to their deep entrenchment in local civic society and the collective memory of the region.[9] The endurance of the deep-seated loyalty to British Aluminium – and in equal measure the hostility felt towards Alcan for its perceived breach of the social contract – evident in the testimonies of respondents from Kinlochleven and Inverlochy bear witness to the effectiveness of the company's inculcation of its role as a social benefactor, interwoven with symbols of the collective narrative. This strategy was also to serve the purpose of ingratiating BACo in the

localities in which it operated and the region as a whole, in the face of periodic public criticism of their schemes. As part of this strategy, BACo also sponsored cultural events which symbolised the ideal of Gaelic Scotland, such as that foremost of celebrations of Scottish Gaelic song, arts and culture, the Mòd, financially, as well as symbolically with aluminium crowns and maces. As with the provision of 'crofting leave', this stressed its commitment to assimilate. Equally, the planning of the company settlements, stressing order and respectability, was aimed at rebutting criticisms and allaying the fears of allies of the sort of nightmarish, chaotic industrial tableau painted by Brother Oswald Hunter-Blair in 1895. Underlining this was also BACo's attempts to negotiate the waters of regional politics building alliances with key landowners and other figures within the civic elite – epitomising what sociologist Ian Carter characterised as the embodiment of the forces of 'conservative modernisation'; those who 'used political and social levers to hold down a labour force on the land' – by utilising the practically extinct, but culturally symbolic, vestiges of the clan system, which conveniently conformed closely with BACo's own values of 'loyalty and service'.[10] The company's self-appointed role as a regional benefactor also lent it support from Highland development campaigners.

The politics of the region required careful negotiating. Whatever Carter's characterisation suggests, as private correspondence between Highland landowners and from within the Scottish Land and Property Federation (SLPF) and the Scottish Landowners' Federation (SLF), the lobbying bodies representing Scottish landowners reveals, this was an elite whose views diverged on the means of maintaining a workforce on the land, but who organised collectively to great effect, in particular over the perceived threat of nationalisation of the land and taxation.[11] Thus, in spite of the abject opposition of some of the members of these bodies to industrialisation in the Highlands, British Aluminium was able to garner support among those influential Highland landowners committed to economic diversification for the region. They were aided by the fact that some of their directors moved in similar social circles and shared values in common with these landowners. The senior managers at a tactical and operational level in the area also regularly fulfilled this function. British Aluminium's conduct in regional and local politics was as important as its attempts to master the 'high politics' of Whitehall and Edinburgh; something which the strategic level managers sometimes forgot over time, as over the issue of atmospheric pollution. Equally the unwillingness of some staff to mix with those they deemed to be their social inferiors undermined their social strategies.

Across the western Highlands, against the backdrop of the recent history and politics of development in that region, BACo's activities were critical to maintaining their standing, as social benefactors and responsible stewards of their estates. Moreover, Allan MacInnes' observation that the clan system – in particular, the apparently long abandoned notion of *duthchas*, 'heritable trusteeship' – left a legacy of the 'cultural baggage of clanship' that 'even incomers felt obliged to exercise paternalism to offset periodic economic distress among their tenantry', was to be evident in their transactions with local communities. This was made all the more potent given the poignant representation of the Highland emigrant, and the endurance of the clearances in the collective memory of the region.[12] *Duthchas*, or *noblesse oblige*, was as central to BACo's image, as that of it as a patriotic key industry, in its representations to politicians, lobbyists, and policymakers. In this respect British Aluminium's pursuit of cordial relations with clan chieftains such Sir Donald Walter Cameron of Lochiel (after BACo, the second largest landowner in Inverness-shire), and the fourteenth Lord Lovat, as well as Mackintosh of Mackintosh – all from powerful land-owning families with, equally important, colourful and influential places in Highland history – alongside their courting of elements of the Highland development lobby (notably Lachlan Grant) take on an added significance.

Courting Lairds and Activists

Morrison cultivated a sound working relationship with Lochiel, in particular, doing much of the necessary lobbying on local committees to ensure the support of district and county councillors for the amended Lochaber scheme. Mirroring the language in his correspondence with Lachlan Grant and his evidence to the Royal Commission on Canals and Waterways in 1907 – when Grant stated, 'it is a matter of great gratification to me that I happen to be connected with companies who have done something towards that part of the country' – Morrison was at pains to impress upon the Chieftain of the Clan Cameron the degree of personal commitment he had to the developments, declaring in a letter to Lochiel during the passage of the Lochaber Water Power Bill in May 1921: 'I have the enormous personal reward of knowing that the foundation has been laid for a lasting and far-reaching benefit to the Highlands of Scotland.'[13] Both Lochiel and Lovat submitted evidence in support of the Lochaber Water Power Bill, and acted as public advocates on other occasions. The value of Lochiel's support was evident from his campaign as convenor of Inverness-shire County Council after the Local Government (Scotland) Act of 1929 to draw attention to what he perceived to be the disproportionate burden of subsidy on landward non-agricultural ratepayers. Though driven by Lochiel's desire to support economic diversification for the region, and therefore recognising the potential obstacle that this might present to enterprises prospecting the area, this served British Aluminium's interests.[14] Lochiel was clearly infuriated by what he saw as the further abrogation of duty by central government, as epitomised by changes under the 1929 Local Government Act and the perceived shift in burden from central government to landward Highland ratepayers, commenting in correspondence with the Provost of Inverness, and prominent Highland development campaigner, Sir Alexander MacEwen: 'By putting the Islands in with the Mainland the Government made a very astute move, as all applications for Grants have to go through the County Council, and as the County Council are expected to make a contribution of the

Mainland Non-Agricultural Ratepayers, the Treasury are perfectly safe in assuming they will have very few calls made upon them.'[15] Furthermore this took place against the backdrop of a region in which these rates subsidised Public Assistance payments to impoverished areas like the Hebrides, which as late as 1924, relied on a public appeal for relief in the face of potato crop failure.[16] This resentment compounded the distrust that members of the Highland political elite harboured for their counterparts in lowland Scotland; Lochiel declaring in a letter to Sir Alexander McEwen in 1935: 'I heartily distrust Glasgow and the Lowlands far more than I do London.'[17] As with their alliance with Sir Cecil Budd, BACo recognised that the frustrations of Lochiel and others with the Scottish Office could be exploited to the company's advantage. It also all served to underline the importance of British Aluminium to the region.

The connection between sections of the Highland landed elite and the company was cemented by close personal links, such as those through Morrison's uncle Charles Innes and the Conservative and Unionist Party machinery in the area. Lochiel and Lovat in their separate ways were not simply retrenched reactionaries but showed themselves to be more prescient, and pragmatic reformers. as well as being politically well connected.[18] As well as being a large landowner in the area, Simon Joseph Fraser, the fourteenth Lord Lovat, was the first chairman (1919–27) of the other large employer in the region, the Forestry Commission, the first convenor of Inverness County Council after 1929, and served between 1927–28 as Under-Secretary of State for the Dominions, chairman of the Overseas Settlement Committee (1928–29), and the first chairman of the Highland Reconstruction Association.[19] Lochiel was an important figure in the region and locality – politically as convenor of Inverness-shire County Council and Lord Lieutenant of the County, and symbolically as twenty-fifth chieftain of the Clan Cameron – and highly influential in Scottish public life; when deliberating who would best represent Highland landowners' interests in responding to the findings of the Hilleary Committee, one senior member of the Scottish Landowners' Federation (SLF) suggested to the secretary, Erskine Jackson, 'The publicity value of Lochiel's name on this H & I subcommittee would be very great should its actions get into daylight. He ought to be on it even if he can't attend.'[20] As late as 1964 the influence of, and apparent affection for, the Camerons of Lochiel – by now the clan had a new sitting chieftain, Donald Hamish Cameron of Lochiel who was passed the seat in 1951 after his father's death – were mooted as the reason for the poor performance of the Labour Party in Fort William after a local Labour candidate remarked that 'A Wilson government will sort out Lochiel'.[21]

Informal alliances between figures such as Lochiel and Lovat and British Aluminium also aided in sustaining large landowners' social and political influence in a climate in which the real political power of the landed gentry and aristocracy was waning in Scotland, and they felt increasingly threatened especially after Lloyd George's 'People's Budget' of 1909 (and the associated increase in taxation). By 1918 with the rise in death duties, many Scottish landowners were struggling to retain their estates, although Lovat was the notable exception of an aristocrat whose rationalisation of his estates made the 1920s 'the most prosperous [decade] in his life'. Meanwhile, 'actual or threatened' land raids – the occupation of land by local residents (including ex-servicemen) – after the First World War was responsible in Argyll at least, according to Leah Leneman, for 'most of the land settlement schemes'.[22] In addition, after the collapse of the Liberal Party in the early twentieth century, the Conservatives were keen to encourage former Liberal voters into their ranks with the retention of land-owning Tories felt to be more socially liberal than the businessmen gaining increasing importance in the party. The political complexion and shared social outlook of senior figures within British Aluminium – for example, Lord Kelvin's Liberal Unionism, and the predominantly military and land-owning backgrounds of subsequent senior directors until the 1960s – can only have helped to recommend them to these Conservative constituencies, as would BACo's much feted position as a key industry with an essentially imperial outlook. Thus the relationship was mutually beneficial. In addition, many of BACo's senior managers in the region – such as Colonel F. E. Laughton MC, John (formerly Major) Gris Bullen, and W. Henkel – up until the regime change under RTIA, shared similar values and had contact with the 'county set' through social and sporting events, political and territorial army or naval reserve activities. Nevertheless, this did not stop some landowners being vociferous opponents of BACo's developments. The Duke of Atholl – though not a west Highland landowner, Atholl represented the interests of the seventh Baron Abinger, who was primarily an English landowner with inherited estates at Inverlochy – accused Mackintosh and Lochiel of pursuing sectional interests in their support for the Lochaber Water Power Bill.[23]

In a similar vein to his entreaties to Lochiel, Morrison's careful choice of message to figures like Lachlan Grant played to the latter's commitment to Highland development and his appreciation of what he perceived to be the socially ameliorative effects of 'paternalism'. As Grant explained in an article to the *Caledonian Medical Journal* of January 1930:

> Voltaire said that labour rids us of three great evils – irksomeness, vice, poverty. But to do this effectually the labour must be on a moralized basis, and in proportion to man's needs and capacities. Man's whole sphere of manifestation has been divided into thinking and acting … Enlightened captains of industry like the Leverhulmes, the Fords, and the Cadburys have rediscovered the fact that man is not a machine, and that his capacity for work has a psychological side. They have found from experience that sufficient leisure not only conduces to the workers' health and happiness but to loyal service, augmented output, and a higher quality of work. The new 'paternalism' in industry pays, and also makes for stability and social progress.[24]

Like his colleague Cameron Miller, as Grant made clear in his public utterances, British Aluminium fitted the model of the social enterprise, and was worthy of his support and indeed participation in their mission. This included the physician also providing public lectures on social improvement in Kinlochleven.[25]

Grant, the forthright advocate of British Aluminium, had himself been at the centre of industrial strife in the nearby Ballachulish slate quarries, when the slate quarriers went out on strike in sympathy with him, after his dismissal as the works physician by the local company manager. Grant was a man of political and social complexity – having in his career been a Liberal imperialist (and unionist), a social democrat, and eventually a prominent supporter of the Scottish National Party – but was above all dedicated to the adopted Highlands. Grant campaigned for the regeneration of the region from the early decades of the twentieth century, writing a number of tracts on the subject, as well as being a prolific correspondent to the newspapers about the region. Crucially he was also one of the founders of the Highland Development League (HDL), a lobby group, which advocated a New Deal-style settlement for the region. Underlining the significance of this group, and despite characterising them as mostly 'enthusiasts, including extremists', the SLF acknowledge the HDL's influence: 'It is in touch with clan societies and it engineered the deputation to Parliament some 2 months ago.'[26] Despite his reputation as a progressive physician and social reformer, his political devotion to Highland regeneration could compromise his judgment; in a letter to *The Scotsman* in October 1936, for example, Grant declared: 'I have no doubt that if Hitler took the Highland problem in hand, we should have a transformation bordering on miraculous within a few years.'[27]

The 'advantages' of personal contact with Grant were certainly not lost on Morrison, as his New Year's Day epistle of 1935 indicates. Grant corresponded with Morrison over a number of years, and became wholly uncritical counsel for British Aluminium publicly. He made speeches in support of BACo's first unsuccessful Lochaber Water Power Bill at meetings around the locality (Onich, Glencoe, and Ballachulish) in February 1918 and for the resubmitted successful 1921 Bill. He publicly admonished critics of housing conditions in Kinlochleven and roundly dismissed suggestions that the manufacture of aluminium was affecting the health of workers involved in the processes.[28] Yet his guiding principle in all of this was undoubtedly well intentioned: that of supporting a company who had showed themselves committed to the Highlands, at a time when the government was, for advocates of Highland regeneration, guilty of neglect. As with the sentiments expressed in his letter to Alexander Fraser, Morrison was undoubtedly sincere to some degree in his correspondence with Grant, if tempered by pragmatic considerations. Given Grant's prominence as a long-standing and vocal advocate of Highland development, it is highly unlikely that Morrison was not carefully composing his message (to ensure the continued support of Grant for BACo's Highland mission) when he wrote in the same 1935 letter:

My feeling is that as more and more attention is drawn to these matters and development in other directions, we shall gradually restore better conditions in our native land, and you are doing your best in this that connection.[29]

The recompense for Morrison's efforts are evident from a piece published by Grant in the *Caledonian Medical Journal* later that year:

The enterprise of the British Aluminium Company, and the very great benefit to the Highland communities of Kinlochleven, Foyers, and Inverlochy, resulting from their operations, might well be repeated in other parts of the Highlands. To a far seeing Gael – Mr. W. Murray Morrison of the Aluminium Company – is mainly due the credit for the development of this hitherto neglected, great national asset – water power.[30]

That Grant had been busy extolling the company's virtues at other public engagements is clear from this warm letter from Morrison from December 1936:

I am obliged to you for your letter of the 10th instant and for having sent me the paper containing a report on your recent speech in London, which as a matter of fact I had seen in another paper. I was very pleased to observe the clean bill of health which you give to our employees as a result of your long experience of the health of our community at Kinlochleven. As a layman I can speak to the same effect from my own experience going still further back – namely for the 40 odd years during which the Foyers works have been in operation. You will be interested to hear that a recent census of our 1,100 employees in the Highlands shows that 74% of these are Highlanders and 93% are natives of Scotland, and this is a fact of which I am very proud. With kindest regards and wishing Mrs. Grant and yourself and your family all the compliments of the season.[31]

Conversely the support of British Aluminium, and Morrison personally, for the Caledonian Power Bill, greatly served Grant's political ends.

In the final analysis it was British Aluminium's ability to garner support overtime among such apparently incongruous bedfellows as Lochiel, Mackintosh, Lovat, Sir John Sutherland (of the APRS and a chair of the village improvement societies) and Lachlan Grant, and spanning the political spectrum from land-owning Conservatives to the Labour Party and trades unions, which set them apart from those who failed to understand the subtleties of the politics of the region.[32] British Aluminium was also careful to court the various religious denominations – while the clergy, for its part, appears to have been largely supportive of the company's aims for the same reasons as other local opinion – with care taken to either provide space and support to construct new places of worship or affordable rents for properties that came under BACo's jurisdiction. This was equally critical in reassuring key constituencies and support existing social structures. Nevertheless in Kinlochleven, as the following chapter makes clear, certain denominations would become associated with social distinctions.

Building order

Aside from these devices, the company's construction of accommodation and investment in other social infrastructure, as well as its management of large estates, was also intensely practical and part of the broader policy of sustaining the internal labour market of the firm: attracting and retaining a skilled workforce in a remote region blighted by emigration and with little in the way of adequate housing or amenities (as well as maintaining sizeable estates as part of the vast water catchment areas needed to collect and supply the hydro-electric installations). Of all groups of workers, a premium was placed on those with families as they would be more likely to put down roots. In addition, in largely single occupational communities such as the BACo villages, they were more likely to be constrained in their negotiation of industrial relations by the threat of destitution for their family. They also provided the potential for another generation of employees, and the semblance of 'order' and 'respectability'. As in AFC's remote Alpine settlements or the dispersed and peripheral company towns of America's Pacific north-west, families were actively sought. However attracting families also required greater emphasis on adequate permanent housing and some amenities (notably schools), as well as for 'order' to be enforced (certain employers even enforced teetotal policies in some company towns).[33] Moreover, the company's engagement in the community was as essential as its literature, pension provision and long service clubs in maintaining a corporate culture and cultivating familiar connections with employees.[34]

British Aluminium's strategy in its Highland communities was, to varying degrees and in more or less similar forms, replicated in settlements at subsidiaries' sites in the British colony of the Gold Coast and in Norway. At Stangfjorden BACo's subsidiary (SEF) planned a company town in a relatively isolated location, building housing for employees, the local school, a public bathhouse, and a local meeting hall, as well as paying the teachers' salaries at the local school and providing the text books. However, much of the credit for the relative harmony in Stangfjorden, aside from the small size of the works (with 70 employees), appears attributable to Maurice Turner.[35] The situation was comparably different at BACo's Gold Coast subsidiary's Awaso works where employees were effectively racially segregated and the communities socially stratified.[36]

In the structure of the Highland communities, BACo's strategies closely resembled those of its French and Canadian counterparts. The social stratification of a village like Kinlochleven was mirrored in the layout of aluminium company villages in the French Alpine departments of Savoie, Haute-Savoie, and Hautes Alpes, of Argentière,

Chedde, Saint-Jean-de-Maurienne, and Salinière, (planned and constructed by AFC), and Arvida in Canada.[37] Moreover the architecture and social code of these settlements bore the imprint of the founders and pursuant senior figures of influence in the companies, as well as the social milieu of these individuals. In British Aluminium's case this was most closely identified with Sir William Murray Morrison, and subsequently cultivated as such. In AFC's case, this 'modelling' of the 'landscape' in their Alpine company villages and towns owed much to Louis Marlio, the company's vice-president and president (1934–40). A *polytechnicien* and former chief of staff at the Ministry of Public Works, Marlio was a social liberal, a paternalist, and an étatist, who was instrumental in planning the company's Alpine garden city of Chedde (designed by the renowned architect Jacques-Henri Le Même), in which the AFC president owned a holiday chalet.[38]

When establishing the major Canadian alumina works and smelter at Ha! Ha! Bay in the Saguenay region of the province of Québec, Alcoa's engineer proposed that the town be called Davis (after Arthur Vining Davis, the company's founder) with the name settled upon, Arvida (incorporating 'Ar', 'Vi' and 'Da' from Davis's name). Davis recruited New York architects Hjalmar Skouger and Gamble Rogers to build a 'company town' with housing and social amenities, which could ultimately 'become an independent city'. While Alcoa's historian acknowledges that the North American giant's housing and welfare measures were intended to 'promote morale and loyalty', he suggests that 'there was little articulation of corporate policy on labor welfare as such beyond some expression of the paternalistic sentiments of its top management'.[39] In marked contrast José Igartua's detailed social history of Arvida, outlines Alcoa, and subsequently Alcan's, attempt to shape the social structures of the town and the layout of the town, like British Aluminium, using an historical narrative, as well as fostering relations with the other major social force in rural Saguenay, the Catholic Church.[40] The Alcan (and previously Alcoa) settlement of Mackenzie-Wismar in Guyana, according to Bradley Cross, was 'an apartheid town, divided along class and race lines', with the largely white Canadian and British ex-patriot management employees set apart in quality housing on the east bank of the Demerara River in Watooka and Richmond Hill some distance from the plant, while the workforce largely composed of 'local people' (those of African or Asian descent) lived on the west bank close to the plant. This division was policed by a company constable who checked passes for those from the latter entering the former, while a marriage bar prohibiting the marriage of Canadian and British staff with 'local girls' operated before 1967.[41]

'Landscaping' the Highlands: 'BA' villages?

Clearly for all the similarities exhibited in these settlements, specific characteristics and distinctions reflecting differing corporate outlooks and national, regional and local conditions within their distinct historical contexts, are evident. As the ensuing examples of Foyers, Kinlochleven, and Inverlochy illustrate, the former differed from the others.

Industrial Scotland has not tended to be synonymous with the Highlands in popular perceptions. As sociologist David McCrone has observed: 'Scotland is dominated by two cultural landscapes. On the one hand, it is a "peopleless place" reflected in its rural, essentially Highland, image of empty spaces as if no one has ever lived there. On the other hand, it is a place of teeming towns, densely populated and dominated by tenements. In the words of George Blake, Scotland appears "overweight with cities".' If this one view of the Highlands has persisted it is partly because too many anthropologists and sociologists have worked from the premise that, as anthropologist Edward Condry put it: 'Too much attention has been paid to the islands and Highlands, and too little to the anthropological study of the Lowlands and the urban areas.'[42] This prevailing view – founded on the pretext that the Highlands is Gaelic and exclusively structured around crofting – ignoring other occupational communities (including industrial) in the region, can be forgiven in light of the prevalence of historical literature that focuses on crofting to the exclusion of other sections of the Highland economy. This oversight on the part of Condry and others says more about a collective synapse in Scottish identity which stemmed from the appropriation by lowland Scots in the late eighteenth century of 'symbols, myths and tartans of the Highlands of Scotland ... to cling on to some distinct culture'. Furthermore it assumes added importance given McCrone's observation that: 'if treating Scotland as a whole as "peripheral" and "underdeveloped" is somewhat problematic, it is the Highlands of Scotland which have attracted the description most often. There is the added irony that the Highlands provide many of the images and meanings for Scotland as a whole in the late twentieth century.'[43] It is also all the more glaring given that Kinlochleven was the subject of a detailed study undertaken by social scientists from the same institution as Condry and McCrone; the book in question – the result of a four-year study by Mary Gregor and Ruth Crichton – *From Croft to Factory*, was published in 1946.

There was, and is, another Highlands and Islands with a long industrial legacy. Economic diversification in the region was not a twentieth-century phenomenon in the Highlands. Aluminium smelting was one of a long lineage of industries that was sited in the region because of natural resources. Others included iron smelting and granite quarrying at Bonawe; slate and granite quarrying at Ballachulish and Easdale; chemical works on the island of Lewis; coal-mining at Brora Machrihanish; lead-mining at Strontian; ship-building at Invergordon; engineering in Inverness; as well as developments from the mid-1950s onwards.[44] Moreover, planned industrial settlements were not alien to the Highlands. As early as the eighteenth century, the Duke of Argyll had planned the 'improved' village of Inverary around a lime kiln and gas works, while the Lorn Furnace Company had constructed tenements for their ironworkers at Bonawe.[45] Communities of industrial workers were already an

Stangfjorden, *c*.1950. Image courtesy of Flykesarkivet i Sogn og Fjordane (Paul Stang collection).

established feature of the Highlands by the nineteenth century. As Neville Kirk has argued in his recent study of industrial conflict in the Ballachulish slate quarries – a community from which a sizeable proportion of British Aluminium's workforce at Kinlochleven was drawn in the early years – 'Ballachulish's relative geographical remoteness did not signify economic "backwardness"', but 'the slate industry tied people with a very strong sense of local place and pride, whether willingly or not, into the wider world of industrial capitalism'.[46] Chris Harvie has famously observed that 'an unlovely "third Scotland" sprawled from South Ayrshire to Fife … old industrial settlements … somewhat isolated, ignored, lacking city facilities or country traditions – even lacking the attentions of sociologists'; while the more pejorative elements of this statement are a question of personal perspective, it does present a model beyond the urban–rural/Highland–Lowland divides that may better provide a more appropriate comparison for Kinlochleven, Inverlochy, and Foyers, than those of anthropological studies of other Highland communities.[47]

What follows is an exploration of the role of British Aluminium (and its successor Alcan) in Foyers, Kinlochleven and Inverlochy, and of everyday life in the west Highland settlements. Like Ballachulish, Kinlochleven and Inverlochy, in particular, were single occupational industrial communities. While sections of the transient workforce at the various Highland reduction works were, in the early years, crofters or crofter-fishermen from outlying areas, the permanent male residents of the two company villages were predominantly occupied in British Aluminium's reduction factories and hydro-electric works with a smattering employed in professional and service jobs, or on the company's estates. The economy of these communities was for much of the twentieth century dependent on the fortunes of aluminium. As such they shared far more in common with the industrial communities of that 'third Scotland'. Even Foyers, characterised by a more diverse local labour market, was still heavily dependent on the industry.[48] Increasingly the income from these communities was a major contributor to the wider west Highland and regional economies. However, the contraction of employment in the works – and eventually the closure of Foyers and Kinlochleven – presented challenges (alongside their remoteness, broader social change, and the draw of urban centres for younger residents) socially and culturally for these communities. For example, between 1939 and 1973 the size of the workforce at BACo Kinlochleven was nearly halved, while the population in the village shrank by around 18 per cent between 1961 and 1966 alone.[49]

Exploring occupational communities

To understand the structures of these west Highland industrial villages better, a fuller airing of the nature and characteristics of communities is necessary. David Lee and Howard Newby have identified three main definitions employed by those using the term 'community': a fixed geographical locale; a set of social interactions which take place within a particular locality; and a common interest or identity group.[50] The most prevalent type among studies of industrial communities has been the latter. The epitome of this was embodied in David Lockwood's typology of 'proletarian traditionalism'. The chief characteristics of this sort of 'occupational community' are that workers tend to socialise with their own workmates, that the workplace features centrally in workers' conversations outside the workplace, and that the occupation is the 'reference group' by which behaviour, status and rank are established. It is these same work groups and communities that bear the hall mark of the 'isolated mass'– workers placed by their 'industrial environment … in the role of members of separate classes distinct from the community at large' – embodying Emile Durkheim's notion of 'mechanical solidarity', a cohesion based on similarities between individuals and common moral sentiments.[51] These insular characteristics (both positive and negative) were reflected in Martin Bulmer's study of Durham mining communities, with one miner observing: 'At one time everybody knew everybody else. Over the last four or five years, a lot of strangers have moved in and a lot of local people moved out. The new people don't seem to be so friendly, so easy to get on with.'[52] Stuart Macintyre's study of the 'Little Moscows' of Maerdy and Lumphinnans in the south

Wales and Scottish coalfields respectively, apparently illustrate the counter-culture of working-class resistance in these two mining towns.[53] Like coal-mining communities, the nature of the work undertaken in the Highland aluminium settlements sharply defined the identities (particularly male) of those who lived in them, and the social and cultural patterns of life. Similar characteristics to those of other 'traditional proletarian' communities studied by sociologists, anthropologists, as well as historians over the years, were identifiable in both Kinlochleven and Inverlochy. However, while acts of resistance were evident (such as the early strike at Kinlochleven in 1910, and that at Lochaber in 1936) questioning the power of 'paternalism', the company did manage to modulate behaviour patterns and mores in Kinlochleven. As chapter three suggests, the 1910 and 1936 strikes may be better characterised as acts of community chastisement of the company for contravening the rules of the 'moral economy'. This was a sentiment visible too in the response to the closures of Foyers and Kinlochleven, where the factories represented for many former employees a community resource, as opposed to an economic unit.[54]

Questions over the fixed nature of 'community' have continued to vex anthropological and sociological studies of 'traditional proletarian' communities in the aftermath of the decline of the very industries with which they were associated.[55] As Bruno Latour observes the use of the word 'social' should not be considered to denote 'a type of material' 'which is already assembled together'. Put differently, 'society' and the 'social' cannot be assumed to be fixed and impervious to change. Joanna Bourke, among others, has observed of working-class identities in Britain between 1890 and 1960, 'working-class individuals constructed and reconstructed their states of desire'.[56] Bourke's work has reflected a growing trend among historians of the regional and local politics of class and of working-class organisation to question overly deterministic accounts. In particular, the work of Gareth Stedman Jones and Patrick Joyce, respectively examining working-class London and Lancashire, were influential in prompting a re-evaluation of the fixed nature of class relations. In the words of E. P. Thompson, 'in the old days, vulgar Political Economy saw men's economic behaviour as being lawed (although workers were obtuse and refractory in obeying these laws), but allowed to the autonomous individual an area of freedom, in his intellectual, aesthetic or moral choices. Today, structuralisms engross this area from every side.'[57] In contrast to Macintyre's Little Moscows, Joyce, Drummond and Catriona Macdonald have identified cross-class alliances in Lancashire, Cheshire (Crewe), and Paisley. Similarly these were evident in the embattled Ballachulish, where as Kirk shows, local professional elites and the slate quarriers formed a united front against the 'outsider' company.[58] In this context the 'local' versus the perceived 'outsider' becomes critical, as the ensuing evidence around all three west Highland settlements illustrates.

In his study of a former mining community in central Scotland, 'Cauldmoss', Daniel Wright – who approached 'community' from the perspective of 'a set of social relationships which take place wholly, or mostly within a locality' – observed many of Durkheim's characteristics of 'organic solidarity', noting that 'unemployment', alongside the village's heritage of mining, had replaced 'work' has the chief characteristic. Under these circumstances, occupational 'status' within the community was replaced by divisions and identification along the following lines: gender; private and public housing tenants; 'belonging' to the village as opposed to being an 'incomer'; religion (in this case Protestant versus Catholic); respectable and non-respectable; and working and not working. Wright observed that long after the disappearance of a mining industry, Cauldmoss residents continued to define themselves in occupational terms. However the most important social distinction in the village was that of 'kinship', whether a resident was 'local' or an 'incomer'.[59] While Sharon Macdonald, in her study of a west Highland crofting community, observed that 'although aspects of life such as crofting, Highland Presbyterianism and Gaelic undoubtedly have an important place in local identity, being a local does not necessarily mean that you have to practise any of them'. Macdonald goes on to note that 'kinship ties and less visible matters, such as knowing the cultural codes of behaviour, are equally important', but that 'identities can change and adapt, and if there is any one particular theme that seems to emerge from this story it is local people's capacity to be resourceful, to appropriate and reshape that which emanates from outside'.[60] Similarly, in his study of Scotland's largest minority ethnic group, the English, Murray Watson reinforced the enduring importance of participation and belonging, as opposed to ethnicity, as being the means by which individuals were accepted into communities; while also recognising the underlying cultural semaphores that can be misinterpreted.[61] All of these are evident in the narratives provided by long-term residents.

With the physical and social transformation of Kinlochleven and Inverlochy – the demolition of familiar landmarks that identified the villages, the disappearance of familiar social networks, and the decline of the proportion of the population with links to the dominant industry – consistent characteristics and competing group and individual identities are both evident in the forthcoming accounts, as are the endurance of BACo's cultural presence in these communities. These are both vividly evoked and carefully observed by former employees and residents of Kinlochleven and Inverlochy in their oral testimony, reflecting competing and, at times, conflicting identities and memories belying how the social experiences have been received by groups and individuals across time.

Foyers

In his entry to the Scottish national survey, *The Third Statistical Account*, in October 1953, the Reverend Angus Macaskill observed of the Parish of Boleskine and Abertarff (including the village of Foyers) that 'probably the biggest change that has taken place in the parish since the time of the *New Statistical Account* [1835] has been the establishment of the aluminium factory at Foyers'. Macaskill went on to describe Foyers as:

> The rather unusual combination of an industrial and rural economy in a beautiful setting and within a reasonable distance of a market town. But, although it has an industry, Foyers has remained essentially a rural village. The people hail from many parts – Inverness, Stratherrick, Moray, Aberdeen, England, Ireland, Wales and the Hebrides – yet with few exceptions they seem to fit perfectly into a compact community and pride themselves on being Foyers folk.[62]

Foyers rises up from eastern shore of Loch-Ness side to Boleskine (meaning 'the summit of the furious cascade', referring to the falls of Foyers). Originally practically all of the estate of Boleskine was owned by the Frasers of Foyers and the Frasers of Lovat. Both families having fought on the Jacobite side in the failed 1745 rising, they managed to retain their estates by handing them to a younger generation or 'redeeming' them, after forfeiting them, through military service in British imperial campaigns in Canada. The last named descendant of the Frasers of Foyers leaving them to his wife's niece in 1842. These were subsequently sold, eventually ending up in the hands of the lowland Scottish iron magnate, John 'Charlie' Cunninghame, in 1873.

The Foyers estate, when it went on sale in 1891, was judged to be 'one of the best sporting estates in the North', with 'all kinds of game on the property' and 'magnificent' scenery. According to the estate records 'Charlie' Cunninghame and his guests had a voracious appetite for shooting, with 9,944 head of wildlife (from deer to woodcocks) killed in the years 1892–94 alone. Alongside the £58,500 paid to Cunninghame for his estate, British Aluminium paid a further £19,510 to various other local landowners (the lion's share going to Lord Lovat) for their holdings to secure the 7,729 acres estates of lower Foyers, Gorthli(e)ck and Wester Aberchalder – incorporating woodlands, arable land and pastures, as well as moorland, as well as the extensive water rights at Loch Garth and the falls, a large mansion house and outbuildings, a farm, and eighty-four households (including one hotel).[63] Despite BACo's ulterior motives for presenting itself as a benefactor to the region, the company's report of its impact on Foyers in a pamphlet of 1908 was not entirely disingenuous:

> At Foyers the Company has built a village which now counts a population of some 600 souls, all of whom are dependent on the new industry for their daily bread. The impoverished crofters and fisherfolk of the Western Highlands acclaim with gladness the advent of this industry into their midst, offering as it

does a thrice-welcome addition to their scanty opportunities of wage-earning. It inspires them with a genuine hope that the devastating tide of emigration may be stayed, and that their beautiful but desolate glens may ere long witness a prosperity hitherto unknown.[64]

Some sixty years before the construction of the Foyers scheme, in 1835, the Presbyterian minister for the Parish of Boleskine and Abertarff painted a dismal picture of his charge. The Reverend William Fraser described a desolate area, with few opportunities beyond those employed in poorly paid yearly agricultural labour, some in trade and cottage industries (under half of the families in the parish), and others working on unrewarding land (other than the low lying ground, of which there was little and the rent for which was 'far too high') in husbandry – with much of the land being 'enclosed' and given over to the 30,000 Cheviot sheep introduced to the area. Fraser continued by venturing that recent depopulation from the parish, 'has been occasioned by the introduction of the sheep-farming system'. Those remaining locals derived much of their 'daily food and raiment' from hart and roe in the woods. He observed that those seeking assistance (around 3 per cent of the Presbyterian population) from poor funds from the Kirk were so destitute that 'instead if being disinclined, they solicit to be received on the poors [sic] roll, notwithstanding of the small pittance in the power of the distributors to bestow'.[65]

Immediately prior to BACo's purchase of the estates, the size of the population of the parish had shrunk further by one-fifth. Thereafter the population rose by 30 per cent between 1891 and 1901, with a further 6 per cent rise experienced between 1901 and 1931; This, despite the 'severe depopulation' suffered to the 'up-country part of Boleskine', and changes to parish boundaries, was attributed to the company's works. At the time of purchasing the Foyers estates, a number of the occupied males in the district were employed in agricultural jobs (labourers, ploughmen and shepherds) or as gamekeepers on the farm and estates. Though few personnel records survive for the Foyers works, it is possible from alternative sources to establish employment patterns. Most of the local adult male population, and some women, went onto to work either in the British Aluminium factory, the hydro works or its vast estates. A petition from the workmen and foremen to the manager of the factory for increased wages in July 1918 reveals that most of those, excepting professionals and traders, who appeared as tenants on the particulars of sale for the estates in 1895 (a number of whom were identified in the latter as being labourers or estate hands) were by this later date factory workers. By the early 1950s British Aluminium employed around 150 men and women in and around Foyers – in the factory, hydro-works, and the estates (as labourers, foresters, and ghillies (game keepers) – although, as Macaskill noted, 'everyone in Foyers, even farmers, is in some way connected with the works'.[66] As late as December 1966, just prior to the closure of the plant, a joint survey by the Scottish Office and the Scottish Industrial Estates Corporation (SIEC) revealed that no less than 51 per

Foyers aluminium works (taken from the western shore of Loch Ness), c.1962. © RTA/GUA.

cent of the working-age population of the village (either directly or indirectly) relied on British Aluminium for employment, although given the seasonal nature of other agricultural work this figure may well have been much higher depending on the time of year. Nevertheless, local businesses continued to derive some income from tourism, while smaller numbers obtained work with the Forestry Commission. During, and immediately after, the construction of the factory and hydro-works at Foyers, British Aluminium had been required to house the incoming elements of the workforce in five newly constructed huts, with the rest in the dilapidated Foyers House and their two farms. From the outset British Aluminium invested in the infrastructure of the area, building roads and an emergency hospital, and constructing a further sixty houses for workers in a crescent in Upper Foyers above their Glenlia farm. These blocks of semi- and detached houses were completed around 1901, symbolically featuring at their centre a small communal garden with an ornamental fountain to mark the diamond jubilee of Queen Victoria. Added to the pre-existing properties, the company's construction of housing at lower and upper Foyers and Glenlia meant that by the 1960s they owned most of the housing in the area. The Scottish Office/ SIEC report of 1966 noted most of these were offered by BACo at 'trivial rents which

Furnace room, Foyers, *c.*1920. © RTA/GUA.

the company would probably wish to sell along with the premises'. All of these houses received their water supply from the company and, until the advent of the NSHEB, their electricity too.[67] Prior to the establishment of the Highlands and Islands Medical Service, BACo had employed the services of a medical officer for the district, and thereafter continued to pay part of the post-holder's wages (along with subscriptions from the workforce themselves) until the establishment of the National Health Service in 1948. The advent of the works saw the expansion of education in the area from a small elementary school established in January 1901 (covering Boleskine and Foyers) to a primary school of 79 pupils by 1905. After reorganisation in 1948 it was renamed as a primary and junior secondary school with a roll of over 90, indicating the growth of the village itself and the importance of the factory. In addition the company constructed a village hall and a workmen's club, and supported and promoted other culture and leisure activities such as local horticulture through a yearly competition for the Murray-Morrison cup.[68] John Blair, a newly appointed BACo chemist from Glasgow, moved to Foyers (before returning to Kinlochleven) in the late 1940s with his wife and found the village to be a vibrant hub of activity centred around the church and the company's social activities.

Furnace room, Foyers, in operation, *c.*1920. © RTA/GUA.

This sense of proximity to the company was further enhanced by the employment of many generations of the same family working in the Foyers factory. In the case of one prominent local family, the Batchens, this amounted to three generations by 1975 with the first William Batchen employed in 1896. There was also a low turnover of managerial staff. Of the four works managers who served between 1901 and 1967, the last manager, A. B. Jones, held the post for the briefest period, six years. E. E. Eccles was manager at Foyers between 1901 and 1913, and was followed by Herbert Ashlin Skelton (formerly manager at Stangfjorden and then Kinlochleven) who served in his role as manager for 31 years. Skelton's successor, D. Menzies Fraser (an Invernessian) managed the plant from 1944 until 1961, having joined BACo at Foyers in 1920. Following stints at Kinlochleven and secondment to the Australian Government, Jones became manager in 1961. In addition senior staff, such as William Murray Morrison, Eccles (who later became BACo's assistant general manager and a director) and George Boex had served in managerial roles at this, the crucible of the company's operations. Thus it had an added significance and symbolism. Moreover, the role of the works manager was not confined to the factory. Both Fraser and Jones served as county councillors respectively for Inverness-shire and Argyll-shire, with Fraser also a Justice of the Peace, a Sheriff substitute and the session clerk for Boleskine and Stratherrick Church of Scotland. Staff from the factory also led the village boys' club and wives of staff the Women's Rural Institute. As in the communities of Kinlochleven and Inverlochy, Foyers was divided along class and gender lines. Eleanor MacDonald, who was brought up in the company village of Kinlochleven and was employed to run the hostel in Foyers also in the 1940s, recalled that the Inverness-shire village had many of the social networks of its larger, and more closely planned sister, as well as the social stratification, observing that they were 'very much the same [...] and even where, well, there were only, sort of, there were two that you could see were in the managerial side in Foyers, and there was *still* [respondent's emphasis] that class distinction [...] It was a sort of smaller scale, you know, but a close community too ...'

In keeping with the company's wish to assimilate and complement existing cultural forms, they also supported Highland sports such as shinty.[69] Similarly, the company's insistence that all foremen at both Foyers and Kinlochleven were bilingual in English and Gaelic was not simply a practical measure to ensure that they might communicate better with employees from areas such as the Western Isles and from parts of the landward Highlands, where Gaelic was still the dominant language, but also symbolised a sensitivity to local culture. This was significant in a climate in which the Gaelic tongue was gradually being eradicated from these areas. The Rev. Fraser in *The New Statistical Account* of 1835 noted that Gaelic, not English, was the predominant language spoken in the area around Foyers historically, but that English had become more common around or just before the turn of the nineteenth century. By 1953 Rev. Macaskill observed that 'those between 60 and 90 years of age can still speak Gaelic ... Gaelic ceased to be the general language of the children about the beginning of the century.'[70] Although this dying out of Gaelic would appear to have coincided with the arrival of the aluminium works, the folklorist and Gaelic speaker Calum Maclean observed the language being spoken in the locale as late as the 1950s, by young people.[71] Thus the company's practice could be viewed as attempting to support Gaelic, as a device to indicate its wish to complement existing structures. The same could also be said of its response to religion in Foyers where the company was careful to be as supportive as possible to all the denominations: the official Kirk, the Catholicism of the Frasers of Lovat, as well as popular support in parts of the Highlands and Islands for the Free Church.[72] As in peacetime duties so in war, the company sought to make those bonds clear, with managers at the Highland works serving alongside the shopfloor, particularly in the Scottish regiments, Menzies Fraser being among those managers awarded the Military Cross during the First World War.[73] The company inculcated its catechism of loyalty to crown, empire, and company, alongside that of community and region.

This proximity and integration laid the foundations of a social contract, which remained intact until the move to a multi-divisional structure was adopted. Though characterised by a high degree of deference, this fealty brought with it obligations.

BACo housing, Foyers, *c.*1967. © RTA/GUA.

When departing Foyers in December 1913 for his post at Head Office, E. E. Eccles and his wife entertained the workforce at the Foyers hall. During the evening's festivities they received gifts from the employees and were pressed to remember their obligations to the locale as well as the Highlands.[74] The air of deference was also clear too. In contrast to disputes settled through the Ministry of Labour tribunals at Kinlochleven in 1918, at Foyers foremen and labourers submitted a 'request' for wage increases by petition.[75] This contract was consummated by the sense of a special bond between the village, the works and the company, which the company, through the pages of the *The B.A. News*, was quick to exploit; Jimmie Batchen – one of the third generation of that family to work for British Aluminium – recalled his father's stories of the heady pioneering days, including working with Morrison: 'I always remember my father telling me about those days. One night Murray Morrison came in very late and he and my father fried a steak on one of the steel shovels.' He continued by observing: 'The outstanding memories are of everyone's honesty.'[76] This was particularly illuminating and relates directly to the closure of Foyers and that posed to the Lochaber smelter. While this declaration of *organic solidarity* – of exchange and reliance – was, to some degree, clearly distinguishable in Foyers, explaining in part why Foyers (like the small Larne works) never adopted a JWC, Batchen's comments in the *B.A. News* in 1975 reflected other undercurrents. Aware of the ongoing threat to all the remaining west

Highland smelters, and having been infinitely aware of the effects of the closure of Foyers (through his family), this reflected a careful reminder of the ties that bound the company to the area. It is also quite possible that individuals within the management at a local level wished to do precisely the same to ensure funding was granted to modernise Lochaber. Equally, at a strategic level, the company was acutely aware of the significance of such stories, and a continuity with the past, to maintaining morale, corporate image and local political capital.[77]

It was the apparent permanence of British Aluminium as a presence in the immediate area, but even more so perhaps the social contract with the local community and the company's narrative and culture, that made the closure of the works, and break with the past, come as so much of a shock. For some in Foyers, this surpassed the bombing of the factory and village by the Luftwaffe in 1941. For many it was viewed as a betrayal. This was the theme pursued by the campaign to save the works and by journalists. To others, the writing was on the wall and the closure was seen as inevitable, a view captured by one journalist in April 1967:

In September 1939, on the outbreak of war, the street lights which guided the footsteps of night workers round the villages and down the hillside to the factory were switched off. It was an ominous portent that they have never been re-lit. After the German capitulation, the prisoners-of-war returned from the stalags, womenfolk returned to the kitchen sink, and by degrees the life of the community returned to normal. Or so it seemed. But Foyers was doomed because its relatively small output made it an uneconomic proposition in competition with newer and much larger plants both in the Highlands and abroad. All credit must go to the British Aluminium Company for a final effort to save Foyers.[78]

Foremen and managers had expressed their gloomy outlook for the works in the years preceding the closure to Board of Trade and Scottish Office civil servants.[79] As at Kinlochleven and Inverlochy, the company had started to offer an 'Assisted House Purchase' scheme – initially to staff to provide some flexibility to families when managerial employees were moved between works, and then to all employees – from the late 1940s, and around the same time sold off property in and around Foyers. This was partly to raise capital and draw back from their social and community commitments and expenditure.[80] In November 1964, the *Press & Journal* (*P & J*) reported on local people's concerns that British Aluminium was no longer expanding its workforce and withdrawing from the community. With the closure of the remaining local schools and twelve company houses lying empty, the 'fear of Foyers' was that their village was 'dying'.[81] When the plant shutdown was announced, the gamut of responses reflected the range of emotions expressed in most industrial shutdowns.[82] Some shopfloor workers expressed little surprise. 42 year-old fitter George Jack, interviewed for the *P & J* just after the press release, observed: 'It does not come as a surprise. The place has not been paying for years. I can always find another job at my trade.' Though unsurprised, others, especially those with a long familial association with the works, company and locale, saw it as a direct assault on their community. Willie Batchen, the powerhouse superintendant and district councillor who would later be one of the leaders of the campaign to save the works, observed: 'There have been closure threats for years. Personally I think it's the greatest tragedy for the whole place.'[83] With 22 company houses in the village lying empty and the prospect of those remaining employees not close to retirement age being transferred to Kinlochleven, Lochaber or one of the BACo's other plants, an HIDB report on meetings held to discuss the possible closure in May 1966 – eight months before the closure was announced – predicted that 'the village will virtually die'.[84] For others at the works, especially young apprentices, female clerical staff, the unskilled and those close to or past retirement age, the closure when it was announced came as more of a shock, reflecting their personal conditions. In a vein that was to characterise public criticisms of Alcan over the closure of Kinlochleven, those seeking to reverse the decision represented this in terms of the breaking of the social contract, engineered by the 'outsider' US parent company Reynolds Metals. As one district councillor, Laurence Hasson, expressed it, 'It's the greatest possible blow to everyone. We knew when the Americans took a controlling interest in the firm that something would happen, since their sympathies did not lie with the people here.'[85]

Like the direct appeal in the *P & J* of October 1964 for intercession by British Aluminium on moral grounds, Hassan's comments reflected the sense of betrayal in a village, attempting to come to terms with the psychological and familial ties being broken. This was to be evident in the tenor of the campaign to save the works. Campaigners against the closure also sought to remind BACo of its moral obligations to the Highlands. In drawing distinctions between the 'BA' and the 'outsider' foreign investors, the English-based TI and US Reynolds Metals, the campaigners were exhibiting both a sense of bereavement (and incomprehension) at the loss and expressing sentiment about foreign takeovers that were expressed by communities across the advanced capitalist world, at this time, coming to terms with the human effects of industrial closure. In a meeting to contest the closure of the works on 14 April 1964, Hasson once again resurrected the spectre of the outsider company, this time TI, 'To say that the British Aluminium Company did their best to keep the factory going is wrong. They did not. When I heard that Tube Investments were buying holdings in the BAC I realised this was the end. At the stroke of a pen they not only dismissed 68 employees, but they killed a community ...'[86] Using a speech by Willie Ross to the Labour Party conference in Dundee eighteen months previously in which he attacked the SNP and the Conservatives on their plans for the Scottish economy, the Foyers Survival Committee (formed at the 14 April meeting, chaired by Willie Batchen and Hasson) argued on the grounds of economic protectionism in a

Table 1.2 *Populations of Foyers (Parish of Boleskine & Abertarff), Kinlochleven and Inverlochy, 1891–2001*

	Location and county		
	Boleskine & Abertarff (including Foyers), Inverness†	*Kinlochleven, Argyll (and Inverness)‡*	*Inverlochy, Inverness*
1891	1,429	–	–
1901	1,843	–	–
1911	1,896	(1,189)	–
1921	1,966	(1,441) 1,356	–
1931	1,976	(1,610) 1,060	1,126
1951	1,478 (Foyers, 365)	896	1,423
1961	1,559 (Foyers, 334)	1,515 (incl. Kinlochmore)	1,262
1971	(Foyers, 276)	1,243	875
1981	1,178	1,046	–
1991	–	1,065	–
2001	–	897	–

Sources: *Censuses for Scotland for 1891–2001*; H. Barron (ed.), *Third Statistical Account for Scotland, County of Inverness*; Gregor and Crichton, *From Croft to Factory*, Table I.

† Figures for Foyers alone are only provided for 1951–71. However given the impact of British Aluminium's factory on the outlying areas, it is entirely appropriate that population figures for the entire parish are given.

‡ Figures in brackets are from the National Register of September 1939 cited in *From Croft to Factory*. All others are taken from the Census. Kinlochleven was in the unusual situation that the two sides of the village were split between two counties: Kinlochbeg was in Argyllshire, and Kinlochmore in Inverness-shire. With the development of the Inverness side, at Kinlochmore, of the village, figures from 1961 include population on both sides of the village.

letter to Scottish MPs, the Prime Minister and the relevant government departments around a fortnight later:

> This closure, which has not been given much publicity, is the result of the take-over movement in Britain which is now being conducted by international corporations, and is an important manifestation of the international spread of American business. In this case it represents a take-over of the British

Aluminium production industry in Britain which is one basic to our economy, and already there are rumours that the two remaining factories could be closed down also, and that the aluminium industry which is U.S. controlled intend moving production out of Europe altogether to such places as Ghana ...[87]

As late as May 1966 BACo had not taken the final decision to close the plant. In advance of an agreement on this at the end of the following month, British Aluminium managers met with officials from Scottish Office, HIDB, and NSHEB in Edinburgh and Foyers to discuss options for other uses for the plant. At the HIDB and Scottish Office's request, BACo held back from a public announcement until January 1967 and opened up access to the Forestry Commission, the British Army, as well as other interested parties to seek other uses for the site. In the end the only option left open was for NSHEB to develop BACo's existing hydro-capacity as a storage pumping station. Curiously, and despite the HIDB's involvement in discussions with BACo about the proposed closure since May 1966, Inverness-shire County Council seems to have been oblivious to these plans. Moreover HIDB and DAFS, whose Permanent Secretary, Sir Matthew Campbell, had apparently been kept informed of plans, had failed to keep the SDD apprised of the NSHEB plans further delaying that option.[88] The public announcement of the closure, on 18 January 1967, indicated that the plant would be run down for closure on 31 March. In the end, of the 61 employees, 41 chose redundancy (of these 15 were close to or over retiral age), with the rest transferring to other BACo plants.[89] While the village continued to attract tourists during the season, the closure of the works removed the major source of employment. Symbolically and psychologically, it was devastating. The profound long term effects were seen in the sense of betrayal at and the backlash over the closure; it was a measure of the loyalty, and the compelling nature of the historical narrative, that the 'BA' name remained relatively unbesmirched in the Highlands, although this may owe more to how collective memory has sought to associate these deeds with 'outsiders'.

Conclusion

BACo adopted a sophisticated political strategy in the Highlands – cultivating alliances with landed elites and development campaigners – placing it at the centre of the region's civic society. This complimented both high politics of national defence and empire, and embraced the tenets of loyalty and order; themes which the board of directors and the managers in place until the late 1950s shared in common with the 'county set'. The west Highlands remained, figuratively speaking, the jewel in their crown, more a symbol of their origins and past glories than a reflection of their current position. While the potency of this was, and remains, evident, the effects could equally be seen in the sense of betrayal keenly felt by communities such as those at Foyers when closure came. The survival of Foyers illustrated the symbolic significance of the site to British Aluminium as the 'crucible' of the British aluminium industry, especially given the importance laid on its 'Highland story'. It was steeped in the company's relationship with the Highlands and significant political players in the region (notably Lord Lovat), and its public profile as a social benefactor to the area. This became all the more important after the RTIA takeover and the move to a multi-divisional structure shifting power to the centre. Concurrently the centripetal forces in the new multi-divisional structure put more distance between British Aluminium and its Highland roots. The company's long tradition of social engagement in the area inured a sense of fealty in the workforce and in the village at large. In closing the plant British Aluminium was perceived by some as severing its social contact with the community. The social organisation within the settlements around BACo's Highland plants was integral to industrial relations within the works, to broader corporate culture and to its public face. Initially British Aluminium proved to be every bit as astute an operator in the politics of the region, as it was nationally. Initially, the senior management of the company lost sense of the significance of the west Highlands at times. Nowhere would this social landscaping and cultural symbolism be more apparent than in the planned villages of Kinlochleven and Inverlochy. For if British Aluminium supported and promoted social organisations and clubs in Foyers, then Kinlochleven, especially after the strike at the new plant in 1910, was to become its laboratory for social engineering.

6

'The city among the hills' and the 'Garden City'[1]: Kinlochleven and Inverlochy

... Perhaps the most remarkable and romantic example of Highland, or even of Scottish, industrial development is that of the British Aluminium Company at Kinlochleven. Here, in a remote and once almost inaccessible spot, has sprung up, as if by magic, in less than twenty years a large and up-to-date factory with the necessary accommodation for the workers and their families. The haunt of the sheep, the deer, and the lonely shieling have given place to a hive of industry and a modern town of about 2000 inhabitants ... This Highland town was planned and built on modern lines, and has benefited from the lively practical interest in it continually shown by the Chairman and Directors of the Aluminium Company. The houses are modern, electrically lighted, and comfortable, and the streets are well laid out and lit all night. There is an excellent water supply, and drainage and scavenging are thorough ... Kinlochleven by night bears an impressive scenic aspect, which makes it worth the visitor's while to tarry until the shades of evening fall. Hosts of brilliant electric lights, every home illuminated, and the twinkling aluminium furnaces in a sombre setting of frowning bens and darkened sea, raise up fancies of fairyland and the magical power of Pluto. The resounding hum of the great power house, dominating a chorus of minor undertones, might pass for music of the Titans, and as we leave the romantic panorama behind, we involuntarily repeat Rossetti's line:– The sighing sounds, the lights around the shore ...

> Lachlan Grant, 'The city among the hills: Present day industrial activities – Kinlochleven', *The Oban Times*, 24 March 1923.

L ACHLAN GRANT's romantic vision of a gem of a utopian industrial settlement set in the Highlands, and overseen by the grand vision and benevolent hand of British Aluminium, was as characteristic of this sort of description of Kinlochleven, as were the periodic c accounts of the village; one Scottish national newspaper describing it in 1936 as the 'Motherwell of the Highlands' (a reference to Scotland's 'Steelopolis').[2] Although the 'Garden City' of Inverlochy village excited far less in the way of adverse publicity – no doubt in part because of its far more carefully planned (and executed) built environment, distance from the Lochaber reduction works, and the way that it was promoted – and certainly attracted some equally verbose and idealistic descriptions, it was still viewed with some derision by residents of the nearby burgh of Fort William.[3] These diverging impressions were, to some degree, like the reaction to the works themselves, symbolic of clashes over the uses of landscape in the Highlands, as well as of British Aluminium's attempts at 'sculpting the "Garden of Eden"'.

The ensuing pages provide a description of the anatomy of these two planned company settlements, showing how British Aluminium, through the built environment, social organisations and networks, and its literature, sought like the deft horticulturalist to 'landscape' the villages, extending the social structures of the factory out into the eco-system of the community. As with other British employers, British Aluminium's planning of the built environment and promotion of social organisations was also part of its broader labour management strategies and in direct response to specific events. In particular this was prompted by the 1910 and 1936 strikes, and more broadly by the 1940s the growth in support for and power of the trade union movement, a more competitive labour market, as well as the expansion of the welfare state.

However, as in the planned railway town of Crewe, strategies such as these cannot be assumed to simply produce a supplicant mass. Similarly residents' behaviour and opinions should not simply be characterised by the nature of their place within work hierarchies. As the preceding discussion illustrates, the long service of some of the BACo managers, and their social firmament, sometimes conflicted with the directives received from head office. They were inextricably bound up in local social and economic networks. Indeed until the 1960s they wielded considerable power locally and showed themselves capable of adopting positions based on moral choices, as independent social actors, that clashed with those of senior managers. This chapter examines responses to the company, through contemporary reports and the narratives of oral history respondents, to explore 'lived' collective, group and individual experiences within Kinlochleven and Inverlochy. How residents experienced life in these communities reflected the various lenses through which village 'living' was perceived, determined by a number of factors, not least that of the company's own 'social landscaping' and historical narrative.[4] In so doing it aims to capture the fabric of everyday life in its full and colourful diversity, alongside broader social movements. Equally it is important to examine the influence of external opinion in forging identities within these communities, as well as on the company's planning and public promotion of them.

Navvy camps at Kinlochleven *c.*1906. Image courtesy of Robert Cairns.

As with BACo's hydro-electric schemes and factories, so Kinlochleven was always to be a 'contested terrain'. To the apocalyptic visions such as those of the 'secluded glens and peaceful lochs … giving place to the guilt and grime, the smoke and squalor, and sin of a busy manufacturing district', supplanting the 'sacred groves' with the 'sordid blackguardism' of the 'mining villages', were to be added fears over unruly navvies who 'come to drink, fight, desecrate the land'.[5] Recognising this latter narrative as an asset, British Aluminium sought to draw a distinction between the 'pioneer years' of Kinlochleven on the one hand, and the settled, planned and respectable peacefulness of the permanent settlements of Kinlochleven and Inverlochy, on the other, once again reinforcing the importance of the literary 'design' of landscapes and their symbolic representation. Over time the rugged stories of hardship and endurance on the scheme, embellished with Patrick MacGill's descriptions, were deployed to illustrate the excitement and pioneering ardour of the company; if the schemes and the navvy camps represented chaos, then the villages represented natural order restored. In part this grew out of the need to provide assurances to regional elites and surrounding locales (as well as to defy critics) that their developments would complement the traditions and environment of the west Highlands. BACo also wished the ideal behind these communities to be replicated in the social relations in the factories. British Aluminium, and supporters of other such schemes in the Highlands, such as Grant, would also have been only too aware that critics would use Kinlochleven as a battleground in debates over industrialisation in the Highlands, as indeed happened after the Cooper Report was published in 1943. Hence it was of the utmost importance that the idea of a wholesome social and moral environment, detracting from the very real pollution in places like Kinlochleven, was sustained.

'Sculpting the "Garden of Eden"': The physical and human geography of Kinlochleven and Inverlochy

As even its critics were willing to concede, Kinlochleven's geographical situation did not immediately endow it with a sunny disposition. The veteran ecologist Frank Fraser Darling, who later referred to the village as 'that going-in-the-face-of-nature example of Kinlochleven', noted of it in 1955 that even accounting for the 'smoke that hangs above the town' it faced an 'immense' 'environmental challenge' sited as it was: 'at the head of this extremely narrow fjord, with some of the higher tops in Scotland rising steep on each side and behind. Possible sunshine cannot be high, actual ones are very low, caused by cloudiness and excessive rainfall …'[6] Kinlochleven – *Ceann Loch Liobhuinn*, the Gaelic meaning 'head or end of the elm water' – is enclosed by *Am Binnein Mor* ('the large pinnacle') to the north with the dark Mamore forest reaching up to it, and *Garbheinn* ('rugged ben') to the south. In the mid-twentieth century, annual rainfall in Kinlochleven frequently averaged 80 inches and the town received no sunshine for around a quarter of the year or more. Until the construction of a road linking the village to the nearby settlement of North Ballachulish (around the south side of Loch Leven) was completed in 1922, access to and from the village was either by means of one of the ships that plied the waters between Ballachulish and Kinlochleven, or the eighteenth century 14 mile road built by military engineers through the glen entrenched in *Binnein Mor* and connected by means of a track from Kinlochleven to Glencoe via the ominously, and appropriately, named 'devil's staircase'. Approaching this meant traversing the expanses of Rannoch Moor and the 'Glen of Weeping'; the latter, the site of the massacre of members of the Clan MacDonald by elements of the Clan Campbell on the orders of Lord Breadalbane in 1692, an event that was to become as infamous in collective memory as it was for the animosity between the two clans and as a symbol of brutal government suppression in the Highlands. Perhaps understandably, as the chronicler for the *Third Statistical Account* noted in the 1950s, 'Newcomers to Kinlochleven are apt to suffer from claustrophobia'.[7] The sense of being cut off from the outside world was progressively eroded first with the dredging of the straits of narrows of the River Leven – allowing for larger vessels to ply the waters between Kinlochleven and Ballachulish – and the completion of the Kinlochleven–North Ballachulish Road (and its widening in 1927),

SS Mountaineer delivering supplies to the jetty at Kinlochleven, 1907.   Courtesy of Robert Cairns.

part of the work being undertaken by German prisoners-of-war. The completion of the Ballachulish Bridge in 1975 – allowing tourists to the area to bypass Kinlochleven – was met with mixed responses in the village, with some feeling that it saved the village the heavy traffic that passed through it during the holiday season, while others predicting that it would 'kill' it. The village that emerged was in the curious position of falling under two separate county councils: with Kinlochbeg under Argyllshire County Council, and Kinlochmore in Inverness-shire. This lent to the village a slightly schizophrenic identity. Combined with the social sculpting of the village and the external dystopian accounts, it is this perhaps that also led Darling to see it as unnatural, a feeling that is redolent in oral history respondent's descriptions of Kinlochbeg, old Kinlochleven, as the 'dark side of the village'. Though within seven and a half miles of the slate quarrying village of Ballachulish, Kinlochleven was truly isolated. During construction work on the scheme much was made of the 'frontier' town feel of Kinlochleven – of brawling, wild navvies and lawlessness, set against the fierce landscape – contrasted against the 'improving' order of British Aluminium's emerging company village.

Navvies at the dam, 1908. © RTA/ GUA.

The navvies engaged on the civil engineering works (at the peak of construction numbering around 3000) were housed in encampments of temporary huts from the pier at the loch-head up to the Blackwater Reservoir, some 1,000 feet up. MacGill provides a vivid description of this temporary settlement and his own accommodation:

A muddle of shacks, roofed with tarred canvas, and built of driven piles, were huddled together in bewildering confusion. These were surrounded by puddles, heaps of disused wood, tins, bottles and all manner of discarded rubbish. Some of the shacks had windows, most of them had none ... Although it was high mid-summer the slush around the dwelling rose over our boots ... the building, which was a large roomy single compartment that served the purpose of bedroom, eating-room, dressing-room, and gambling saloon ... A spring oozed through the earthen floor, which was nothing but a puddle of sticky clay and water.[8]

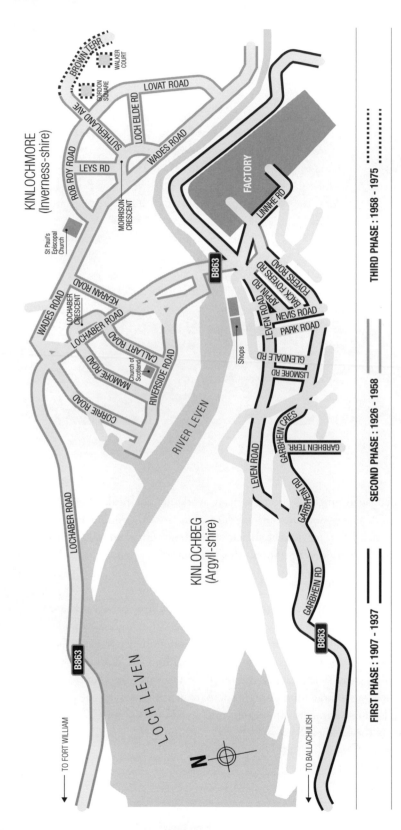

Map of Kinlochleven. Illustrated by Alasdair Robertson.

The Medical Officer for Argyll, Dr Roger McNeill, condemned the 'primitive arrangements' at the camps, while the company's managing director, in a letter to the *Oban Times* in August 1907, confirmed the squalor in the camps but blamed this on 'vagrants' and 'hangers-on'. This, and the dangerous nature of the work on the scheme, in part explains the high turnover and hasty departure of those who came to work on the scheme.[9] Besides, the navvies were the subject of ill-repute, particularly for drunkenness and fighting. Many of the subsequent accounts underplayed the navvies' role in the construction of Kinlochleven, characterising them as feckless, drunken and crude; men drawn from 'the mire and social gutter of human degradation', as one account called them.[10] The most detailed account of the navvy at Kinlochleven comes from MacGill who worked on the construction of the hydro scheme and dam. While no highly detailed account of the origins of the labouring workforce on the scheme is available, it is clear that the navvy population was mixed, with many west Highlanders (from the nearby slate quarries at Ballachulish, at the time still involved in a series of bitter labour disputes), Hebrideans, English and Welsh, as well as Irish (the latter chiefly from the northern counties of Donegal, Antrim, and Fermanagh). Much was made by contemporary commentators of the last group, usually conveying the endemic prejudices towards and discrimination experienced periodically by the Irish in Britain. For example, the migratory patterns of Highland crofters and crofter-fishermen were portrayed as natural and in keeping with long-running patterns of employment in the region, while the Irish, who also migrated in a similar way from the north to work on the harvests in Scotland, and in labouring before returning to help on the land, were described as having 'itchy feet'. As the most recent and detailed research on navvies in Britain has pointed out, the ranks of 'McAlpine's Fusiliers' were swelled by the English, Welsh and Scots at this time too.[11]

If this image of a rough pioneering town later suited British Aluminium, the chief constable of Inverness-shire, Alexander McHardy, attributed civil disturbances and public displays of inebriation in Fort William, such as the incarceration of 250 people on their way to the 'Loch Leven Aluminium Works', to the absence in Kinlochleven of a licensed establishment, a welcoming social venue to escape the mud and squalor of the inadequate provisions of the encampments. When a licensed canteen was provided, prior to the completion of the factory, this did indeed serve to moderate drinking and limit public order offences. Moreover drunkenness and fighting were not limited to the navvy population. In his account of the town, Norman Morrison – a one time policeman, founder of the Scottish Police Federation, and latterly a zoologist – who served as a sergeant in Kinlochleven between November 1913 and February 1916 described the navvies as 'generally speaking ... humane, honourable, conscientious and kind hearted'. Morrison reserved his most critical comments for Belgian refugees employed at the works during the First World War (alongside Norwegians, and Belfast and Dublin dockers) who were 'difficult to handle'.[12]

In contrast to the provision for the navvies, Dr McNeill praised British Aluminium's

Newly constructed housing at Leven Road, Kinlochleven, *c.*1908. © RTA/GUA.

subsidiary, the Loch Leven Water and Electric Power Company, for the 'decent accommodation and other material comforts' for the factory workers in the 'new village'.[13] The themes of both order and chaos were central to retrospective accounts of the development of the industry in the west Highlands, with chaos – whether in the form of the 'Sons of Desolation' (the navvies) or the 'wilderness' tamed for the good of mankind – being deployed to illustrate the credentials of British Aluminium as 'pioneers' and as 'improvers', both morally and socially. One such example is provided by Norman Morrison's accounts. Writing in 1937, Morrison extolled the virtues of the company's 'improving' of the wilderness:

> Fifty years ago, if a stranger took the trouble of walking from Fort William to Kinlochleven along General Wade's old road, skirting the base of Ben Nevis and traveling through lonely mountain passes and gorges and traveling on his way thither, he would, on his arrival, be rewarded with a picture of desolation and savage grandeur ... To-day, if the same visitor were to return, he would find that in the interval a magical transformation had been effected. The lonely glen of fifty years ago is to-day a modern town and a veritable hive of industry ...

Shops in Kinlochleven, *c.*1908. © RTA/GUA.

Loch Leven, dark and somber [*sic*], is seen winding among the everlasting hills, looking like a gigantic sea serpent. The surroundings almost beggar description. They are among the wildest and most savage scenery in all Scotland ... The town was brought into existence by that energetic and far-seeing firm, the British Aluminium Company, Limited, who saw the commercial advantage of utilising one of Nature's most powerful forces for the service of man ... What appeared to be an impossible task yielded reluctantly to the magical wand of modern science. Astounding achievements of this nature force one to the conclusion that the sons of men must be really the sons of the gods.[14]

In the ensuing reflections of his tenure in Kinlochleven, Morrison presents a picture of model order, of a planned utopia in which 'the electricity here is as free as the air we breathe', and 'there are no unemployed and no poor', while his evocation of the 'savage scenery' tamed by the ingenuity of 'modern science' was all very reminiscent of Lord Kelvin's descriptions and the subsequent company narrative.[15] Visitors to the village may have been awed in the early years by lights set out in the hills welcoming them, spelling out 'British Aluminium Company', but as Crichton

British Aluminium employees outside the office at the temporary factory at Kinlochleven, 1907. Standing on the far left and third from right respectively are Edward Shaw Morrison and William Murray Morrison. © RTA/GUA.

and Gregor noted in the 1940s: 'It has been said, with some truth, that the only time Kinlochleven looks really beautiful is after dark on a winter evening, when the light of the village glitter from afar like some jewel set amid the darkness of the hills.'[16]

The Kinlochleven that grew out from the factory would be described in far less favourable terms in the years to come. Construction of the town that flowed out from the factory was at first restricted to the Argyll side of the glen – Kinlochbeg, the 'dark side of the village'. To some extent this restriction accounted for crowded conditions in some of the housing. The initial permanent edifices on this side of the village, constructed between 1906 and 1910, comprised a handful of shops, eighteen blocks of cottages (each comprising four flats) – in Nevis, Appin and Lismore Roads – and six blocks of eight flats (in Foyers Road) bordered by the factory on one side, the electric railway running from the wharf to the factory on another, and the River Leven on the far side. As well as these, the village retained some older, temporary wooden huts besides the pipelines ascending the hillside, and stone caretakers' cottages next to the Penstocks. Until 1921, inhabitants received free electricity, with the village being one of the earliest to have electric street and house lighting in the UK, leading to its other

Foyers and Appin Roads, 1908. © RTA/GUA.

Kinlochbeg from Garbhein Road, 1908. © RTA/GUA.

nomenclature, 'the electric village'. For all the fairy-tale depictions of the early village, as Mary Gregor and Ruth Crichton observed of its outlook, 'The factory dominates Kinlochleven. One cannot but regret its smoking chimneys and unsightly buildings even while one recognizes the many advantages it has brought to the inhabitants.'[17] An even less flattering description was provided by the Scottish Committee of the Association of Scientific Workers in their 1943 publication *Highland Power*:

> Most of the inhabitants live in the most appalling slum conditions. More than half the houses on the Argyllshire side of the river are without hot water systems, bathrooms, internal laundry facilities and larders … the factory emits an almost continuous stream of dirty fumes which hang low in the valley and add to the pall of smoke from a host of domestic chimneys … and even the birds seem to have deserted the locality.[18]

Singled out for particular criticism were the 48 flats in Foyers Road. Built between 1909 and 1910, these three-bedroom flats were cramped, used cheap and inappropriate building materials for the climate (cement rather than bricks) and were generally of a poor standard. Though they had sculleries and indoor water closets, they had no baths. While they were being constructed British Aluminium was undergoing financial restructuring. Although this may partly explain why comparatively little thought appears to have gone into their design other than keeping the costs low, the same economising was not to the forefront where the staff housing was concerned. By 1936, British Aluminium's own factor for the Highland estates, Edward Shaw Morrison, identified these three-bedroom flats (with a total area of 350 square feet) as over-crowded and 'should be pulled down'. Under the prescriptions of the 1935 Overcrowding Act, the size of bedrooms in the Foyers Road flats was deemed inappropriate for anyone above the age of ten. Morrison went on to paint an unflattering picture of the state of housing stock in Kinlochbeg. Of the 181 houses built on the Argyll-side of the village, 176 houses (97 per cent) had no baths and no space for bathrooms to be installed. Like the flats, the hostel for workmen – housing seventy men, sleeping in cubicles of less than fifty square feet – was legally overcrowded and, Morrison judged, should 'cease to be used', and of the houses, 31 were judged to be overcrowded. Indeed his general remarks on the housing stock were not far removed from those in either the Crichton and Gregor account or *Highland Power*:

> The old Kinlochleven Village has now a very drab appearance, the obvious remedy – whitewashing the houses – is useless because of the awful atmosphere. Some of the houses have been cement washed occasionally, this is done to save the fabric and to keep the houses weather-tight, but a few weeks later the cement wash is again as black as ever. The lead sheeting used in roof construction etc. has in some cases been pitted by fumes from the factory and

has had to be renewed. It would be quite feasible to white-wash the houses at the western end, but this would give a piebald village. There is no hope of obtaining houses with a reasonable exterior until dust, dirt and fumes have been eliminated.[19]

Just how disingenuous, in contrast, Lachlan Grant's professions about the state of the Argyll side of the village were – and how much his views were compromised by his political beliefs and the private assurances of William Murray Morrison – is revealed by Grant's evidence to the House of Commons in support of the Lochaber Water Power Bill:

The houses are well finished and well ventilated. All have W.Cs., sculleries, coal cellars, large kitchens, 2 or 3 bedrooms, water supply and electric light introduced. The windows are made to open top and bottom and kept in repair. All the more recent houses have bathrooms, and some of the older houses have had bathrooms put in ... There are four hostels or model lodging houses for the accommodation of single men ... In the men's temporary hostels the accommodation is similar excepting that each resident has a separate cubicle instead of a bedroom. In the hostels there is ample bathroom accommodation with hot and cold water. The places are kept cleanly. From the public health point of view these buildings are constructed on modern lines ... The planning of the village is good, the space at disposal being well laid out. There are no slums or anything approaching such a description. The Health of the community all along has been very satisfactory ...[20]

As one local wryly observed of Grant's recent letter to *The Lancet* in September 1931 – in which Dr Grant once again remarked upon the general health of Kinlochleven's population and of working conditions within the plant – the renowned Highland physician would not know as he rarely spent much time in the village, choosing instead to leave the rounds to his assistants.[21]

Despite the privately acknowledged shortcomings of these flats, provision for BACo's employees housed in the flats or workers' cottages, at the time of their construction, was markedly better than that for many working-class households in Scotland. The terrible state of overcrowding and insanitary conditions in Scotland's cities, burghs and counties were revealed in the minority report of the Royal Commission on Industrial Housing in 1917 (the Ballantyne Commission). In industrial Burghs like Armadale, Coatbridge and Kilsyth respectively 82.8, 76.5 and 74.3 per cent of the population lived in one or two rooms. In the mining counties of Ayrshire, Clackmannanshire, Dunbartonshire, Fifeshire, Lanarkshire, Linlithgowshire, Midlothian, and Stirlingshire, the proportion of the population living in one or two rooms ranged between 44.5 and 67.8 per cent. Commissioners

Staff Road. *Above:* Staff housing on Garbhein Road, Kinlochleven. © RTA/GUA.

Works manager's house, *Edem Mohr*, Garbhein Road. © RTA/GUA.

Staff Road. *Tigh-na-fleasgaach*, Garbhein Road. © RTA/GUA.

visiting the mining areas gave more detailed accounts of the types of conditions that tenants endured. During their inspection of the Rosehall colliery rows in Whiflet, Lanarkshire, in March 1914, the commissioners observed that the one and two bedroom houses had no scullery, water closets or baths, and were sometimes inhabited by seven to eight per room. While those visited at Drongan rows at Old Taigburn, Ayrshire, soon after revealed that there was one toilet for every fifteen households, and in some cases five inmates per room with bare earth floors. Railway employees and their employees in rural districts, the commission discovered, experienced 'inadequate and poor housing', 'overcrowding and discomfort', and were forced to accept any housing whatever the conditions, 'for fear of being turned out and losing their jobs'. Equally, those crofters from the Western Isles employed by British Aluminium may well have found conditions in the village to be better than the 'pretty dire conditions on Harris and Lewis' reported by medical officers in those areas, with certain districts considered to be 'wretchedly bad'.[22] Indeed the knock-on benefit of the employment, in addition to the provision of crofting leave, would have had a profound effect given the Commission's observation that:

Anyone acquainted with the housing conditions in the rural districts of the West Coast and islands twenty-five or thirty years ago, and who revisited

The Dark Side of the Village: Postcard of Kinlochbeg, *c.*1920. © RTA/GUA.

Kinlochleven seen from the new side of the village at Kinlochmore, *c.*1962. © RTA/GUA.

these districts to-day, could scarcely realise the improvement that has taken place. But let it not be supposed that these improvements are effected from the produce of the crofts. The crofter sends his sons and daughters to the large cities of the South and to the Colonies, and if they prosper there they are mindful of, and dutiful to, their parents at home.[23]

Reporting two decades later in their *Report on Rural Housing in Scotland*, the Scottish Housing Advisory Commission reported that 75 per cent of working-class housing in the parishes surveyed (one in Berwickshire, and two more in Angus and Easter Ross respectively) were unfit for human habitation and observed, 'We have no reason to believe that those parishes are in any way exceptional'. Of the 90 per cent of Scotland's farm servants' homes inspected between 1927 and 1932, for example, 53 per cent were deemed 'unfit' (in one county the figure was as high as 95 per cent). In Argyll, of the 47 per cent of the housing stock inspected, 23 per cent were deemed 'unfit' for human habitation and 24 per cent overcrowded.[24] By 1951 31.7 per cent of Scottish residences had only one or two rooms, with more than a quarter of the Scottish population living under these conditions. One third of the population shared a WC, although in many Scottish cities the proportion was much higher (up to 49 per cent in Paisley). As late as 1965 – and in spite of the post-war public housing construction campaigns and demolition of old over-crowded blocks – 6 per cent of the population of Scotland's largest city, Glasgow, lived in overcrowded accommodation.[25]

If the housing conditions in the heart of Kinlochbeg were, at the time of their construction, an improvement on those experienced by the mass of the Scottish proletariat, then they were equally in marked contrast to the houses provided by the company for the managerial staff which were instructed to be 'comfortable and roomy and of different designs'. These elegant, detached Arts and Crafts houses – *Garbhein House, Edenmohr, Tigh-na-Bruich, Tigh-na-fleasgach* and *Inverleven*, designed by the Scottish architect Alexander Alban Scott who had worked on the Glasgow International Exhibition of 1901 and for the Caledonian Railway Company – were set high on the hillside in Garbhein Road overlooking the old village. The Garbhein Road houses symbolised the socially stratified nature of the factory and the village, with the road being referred to more commonly by local residents as 'staff road'. One 90-year-old, lifetime resident of the village, recalled the distinctions in Kinlochleven:

Everybody was the same, but for the managers – what we called the general office workers. There was the manager. There would be the chief electrician and the chief engineer, the chief, eh, factorial man. They were all housed in the bigger houses up what was, was Garbhein Road, but we called it Staff Road, it was called Staff Road because *they* [respondent's emphasis] were staff [...] there was very much a class distinction.[26]

A Highland Village Reborn? Kinlochleven, 2009. © Andrew Perchard.

Asked whether as a young girl she was aware of the differences, Eleanor MacDonald also stated emphatically, 'oh very much, very very much aware of it. It was a very definite class distinction.' The Garbhein Road houses – like the powerhouses at the company's west Highland works, built as monuments to industry and as an affirmation of man's taming of nature – were to reflect the success and primacy of the company, with the staff as its resident representatives. Similarly the French company AFC built resplendent villas for its managers and engineers set in generous grounds.[27] However, if spatial segregation was planned between managers and workmen's housing from the outset, the company's senior managers directed that foremen's houses be integrated into the same rows as that of rank and file workers. This was in contrast to some other employers around this period. The famous Clydebank ship-building firm John Brown's, for example, directed that foremen's cottages be divided from the workers' cottages by the railway line, recognising the significance of supervisors in enforcing discipline and promoting efficiency and wishing to ensure their loyalty.[28] As well as space for housing, land was feued and some support lent to the main religious denominations to establish places of worship. As the ensuing pages show, this was in keeping with British Aluminium's views on social order, and some of the churches came to symbolise the social and ethnic distinctions within Kinlochleven.[29]

With space for housing limited, the company sought to expand housing in the village. With support from the newly established Scottish Housing Commission (formed in 1913), the Kinlochleven Village Improvement Society (KVIS) was formed as a Public Utility Company in the same year and land rented for the purpose of extending the village. Here the protestations of the company that external factors impeded developments were undoubtedly fair. Housing construction was shelved during the First World War. After the cessation of hostilities, despite the backing of the Scottish Board of Health, attempts to secure an extraordinary loan from the government for the £311,380 the company estimated that it needed to construct 200 new houses, was blocked by the Treasury and the Public Works Loan Commissioners. Under the Housing (Financial Provisions) Act of 1919, the company could have expected to receive a lump-sum subsidy of £52,000 (£1.81m), with the company paying the remaining £363,173 (£12.7m). Rather than this they sought a loan of £103,793 (£3.62m). The Treasury and the Public Works Loans Commissioner objected to the plans on principle because they judged that British Aluminium had chosen to locate its industry in Kinlochleven to benefit from cheaper power – as Treasury official, O. E. Niemeyer put it, 'subsidy is meant for abnormal war cost; not for abnormal cost due to building in a desert (in order to get cheap commercial power)' – and that they judged that the company could meet the costs from the recently capitalised reserve funds of £400,000. Revised plans with a more modest proposal for 57 houses were also initially met with suspicion. In fact inhibitions and obstacles to drawing down Treasury subsidies – under the relevant housing legislation of 1919–31 – for housing developments appears to have been widespread in rural Scotland, and especially in the Highlands and Islands, with the Scottish Housing Advisory Committee observing in the mid-1930s that 'The essential fact is that the subsidies were not used and that rural areas were thus deprived of the benefits which these subsidies have conferred upon the rest of Scotland'.[30] Given BACo's expansion plans (due in no small part to government demands) and financial straits, raising this sort of capital, a decade after financial restructuring, would either have left the company exposed or necessitated a further lengthy delay and perhaps even abandonment of the Lochaber scheme.

In addition to the delays in finding the necessary capital – prolonged further by the investment in the construction of the Lochaber schemes and Inverlochy village – British Aluminium struggled to secure sufficient ground for construction of the new houses in Kinlochmore (Inverness-shire side of the River Leven), with the landowner refusing to feu more land unless the company purchased the entire 40,000 acre estate. This was not secured until 1935, and thereafter work started on constructing houses on the Kinlochmore side in phases, with work on the road leading to Fort William and sewage and water pipes in October 1937. In the intervening period 104 houses were ordered and constructed by KVIS on the Argyll side – 24 ordered in June 1923 subsidised under the Wheatley Act of 1919, and a further 80 with diminished subventions under the Housing Act of 1923 – between 1923 and May 1926. At the same time overcrowding and the housing shortage was becoming a considerable problem for British Aluminium, with the company estimating by November 1936 that it needed a further 138 houses to meet the needs of 50 per cent of its workforce, and implementing a progressive programme to construct between 100 and 120 houses in Kinlochmore.[31] Between 1938 and the late 1950s KVIS had ordered and constructed (without government subsidy) a further 130 houses for shopfloor employees on the Inverness side, and four staff houses. The first group of houses in Corrie, Mamore, Riverside, Callart and Lochaber Roads was completed by 1938, and a further twenty in Lochaber Crescent, and Wades and Kearan Road by 1958. In Kinlochmore, larger houses constructed for and occupied by staff – *Eas-na-Ba, Innistore, Taobh-an Allt, Gortem-Nam-Bath, Tigh-an-Rudha, Corrieholm*, 'Greymares', and *Ardbeg* – were set back from Wades Road. In the case of the houses in Wades and Kearan Roads, these were in mixed streets, with the rest of the houses predominantly owned and constructed by Inverness-shire County Council, which had built an additional 146 houses – in Morrison Crescent, Sutherland Avenue, and Wades, Leys, Rob Roy, Lovat and Loch Eilde Roads – in the post-war public housing boom. These were joined by the mid-1970s by the additions of Brown Terrace, Gordon Square, and Walker Court.[32]

Describing developments in Kinlochmore, Gregor and Crichton observed in 1946 that 'The situation on the Inverness side of the river is in many respects a pleasant contrast to that in the old village'. This optimism for pastures new was not confined to the fact that Kinlochmore received more sunlight and was less affected by emissions from the factory, but also because the new houses were far larger, and had bathrooms, hot water systems, and separate gardens for each household.[33] Eleanor MacDonald, born in 1916, was brought up for much of her childhood in a three-bedroom house in Appin Road in Kinlochbeg before moving with her family to the other side. She shared the Appin Road residence with her parents, four sisters and three brothers, with the three girls sharing one room and the boys another. The house had an outside toilet, and, in common with many of the houses in the Argyll side of the village, a scullery in the living room. Eleanor recalled the changing village and the mixture of anticipation, impatience and excitement over the move:

> We moved over to the Kinlochmore side, as we called it. See the river divided us and there was *nothing* on that side of the village that I remember […] but I was ten when we moved over […] I remember the houses being built, and it seemed to take *years* to build them […] my father knew, yes, that we were to get one, and that was great because there was a bathroom, there was hot water, there was a bath, and oh it was wonderful big garden […] it was, it was just great.[34]

Despite the improvements and considerable programme of housebuilding undertaken both by the KVIS and the county council there were still marked housing shortages in Kinlochleven (as well as in Inverlochy), with 65 married couples and 174 single employees living in one of the company's hostels in the village as late as October 1948. In a letter to the Scottish Home Department, commenting on the issue of housing shortages in both Kinlochleven and Inverlochy that same month (and only two years after the publication of *From Croft to Factory*), a Board of Trade official observed that it was 'creating labour difficulties for the firm' and concluded that 'my reason for getting this information was to show how urgent the problem of housing existing in industry in this part of the world really is'.[35]

If in some respects the bricks and mortar of the village of Kinlochleven evolved in a sporadic fashion – not least because of external events stagnating developments – then the planning and execution of construction of the built environment in Inverlochy was more measured. The root of this lay not only in British Aluminium's sensitivity to slights on its public image and credentials as a welfarist employer, but in wider public debates about housing conditions within Scotland among policymakers and planners in the aftermath of the Ballantyne Report. As the social reforms prior to, during, and after the First World War had prompted a strategic re-think among employers, so too did the social and political impetus to reform working-class housing in Scotland, arising from the Ballantyne Commission's revelations. While the increased intervention of the state – as in other areas of welfare provision – undoubtedly also had an effect on employers.[36] Although Scottish housing planners were not in the end to turn to the 'Garden City' movement for solutions – in which the built environment was more closely developed in conjunction with 'nature' – BACo was both amenable to it and recognised the value of it in promoting its welfarist credentials. However it should not be assumed from this that British Aluminium was entirely guided by devising strategies for social control, and protecting its public profile; for much as the company's tenets lent itself to these aims, the progressive nature of the 'Garden City' genuinely appealed to leading lights within the company.[37]

Across the (now disused) train lines to British Aluminium's pier on Loch Linnhe – now cordoned off by the A82, the main road leading from Fort William to Inverness – the landscaped village of Inverlochy grew up half a mile to the west of British Aluminium's Lochaber smelter. To the west, it is bordered by the River Lochy just before it meets with the River Ness to flow into the Linnhe. A mile to the south lies the town of Fort William, and approximately five miles to the south and east the imposing Nevis mountain range (including the towering Ben Nevis). The nascent settlement was built on land previously owned by Lord Abinger and sold by him to British Aluminium in March 1926, with its construction being overseen by another Public Utility Company, the Inverlochy Village Society, formed by NBACo under the chairmanship of Sir John Sutherland in September of that year. Initial plans estimated the costs of the first phase of the village at £45,000 (£2.2m).[38] This sizeable outlay, alongside the spiralling costs of the Lochaber scheme, showed the social commitment of the company, the perennial Highland problem of a shortage of housing for workforces, and the need for the company to be seen as a social benefactor.

Over the next ten years the planned village took shape around the residential streets of Abrach, Lochy and Wade's Road, *Pairc an Dubh* (Parkan Dubh), Montrose Avenue and Montrose Square, as well as sports and leisure facilities (tennis courts, a bowling green, a pavilion) and space for shops and banks (at Battlefield and Lochy Crescents and Montrose Avenue); the 'old village', as it has come to be known. Significantly, the village was planned by the prominent architect Frank (later Sir Frank) Mears (a collaborator with, and son-in-law of, Sir Patrick Geddes). Like Geddes – Scotland's pre-eminent urban planner of the twentieth century and the author of *Cities of Evolution* (1915) – Mears was a civic-minded architect and planner judged to have been 'single-handedly responsible for raising standards in housing design right across the country during and just after the Second World War'.[39] Invested with all the symbolism that British Aluminium was attentive to, one of the first trees in this verdant 'Garden City' had been planted by the Duke of York (later King George VI) when he visited the village. Describing Inverlochy at a ceremony to mark the commencement of the construction of the next phase of the village – for which William Murray Morrison's wife cut the first earth, while Cameron of Lochiel planted a red oak (the symbol of the Clan Cameron) and Murray Morrison the native copper beech (even the choice of trees was symbolic) – *The Scotsman*'s correspondent ruminated:

> If a sacrifice of freedom has been made, the workers enjoy conditions and amenities that would be the envy of toilers in the less salubrious industrial regions of Scotland ... The model village in which the British Aluminium Company's workers are housed has an attractive lay-out, and the dwellings, alike in appearance and convenience, seem to be everything that could be desired in a community scheme ... Every house has its own garden, and the streets through time will become avenues of trees.[40]

These houses – most with three bedrooms, inside toilets, bathrooms, kitchens, as well as their own gardens – were well-proportioned and in marked contrast to the housing conditions not only nationally in Scotland, but also in the nearby burgh of Fort William. Even allowing for a sixteen-year lapse the houses in Inverlochy, built in the first phase, presented a stark alternative to the description provided of working-class districts of Fort William by the provost of the burgh and the medical officer (MO) for the burgh to the select committee considering the Lochaber Water Power Bill. The burgh's MO Dr Alexander Cameron Miller – who also served as the Chief Medical Officer for Inverness and had been on the Dewar Committee – observed of his experience of working-class housing in Fort William:

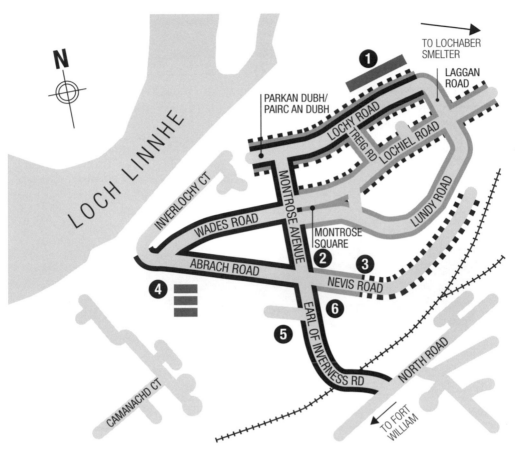

① County Council houses built early 1950s

② New Post WW2 Braxy prefabricated aluminium hall

③ Nevis Road was extended post WW2 for prefabricated housing scheme

④ Site of B.A.C.O. Workers' hostel and canteen

⑤ Inverlochy primary school

⑥ Original Braxy wooden hall with tennis courts and bowling green

FIRST PHASE :	SECOND PHASE :	THIRD PHASE :
1926 - 1937	1937 - 1958	1958 - 1975

Map of Inverlochy village. Illustration by Alasdair Robertson.

The Garden City: Inverlochy Village taking shape, 1926–27. © SCRAN.

Regarding present day conditions in Fort William, housing has till recently, and is even now, deplorable. The death rate in the slum area of this small Burgh is probably double that in better parts of the town. Apart from figures I can substantiate this by my intimate knowledge as Medical Officer of the Burgh. Housing, has, of course, a very serious effect on the health of a community and overcrowding and dilapidated dwellings are still too prevalent in Fort William. There are numbers in this Burgh living at or below the poverty line.[41]

Admittedly, as his comments over health and safety on the construction of the Lochaber scheme illustrated, Miller, like Grant, could be an uncritical advocate of the company. These conditions were certainly a vast improvement also on the conditions experienced by men working on the construction of the Lochaber scheme forced to live in the exposed camps and smaller encampments (adits) that stretched from the former battlefield of Inverlochy to Fersit near Loch Trieg, despite the gloss placed on them by Dr Miller. Yet like Grant, Miller's advocacy of BACo stemmed from his view of them as a force for progress in the region. The village certainly continued to accord British Aluminium fulsome praise in the public sphere locally and nationally.[42] In spite of this, Fort William residents could adopt a disparaging view of Inverlochy.

George Haggart, recounting the recollections of one early resident (now deceased), observed:

> Fort William people looked down on Inverlochy. He's very clear about that and he's very clear that when he mentioned, or they mentioned [...] he didn't need to mention, they mentioned, "oh you're from Inverlochy", you know? And [...] he gives an instance, he gave an instance when that was first said to him and it was a lady who had said it, and then when he found out where she lived in Fort William, if one was talking about slums, that had much more slums than Inverlochy because it was, you know, it was a village built in 1928 and it was a good village. So that was one of the things [...] the people in Fort William were not interested in working in British Aluminium until war broke out and then when it then became a Reserved Occupation then people from Fort William queued up to come in.[43]

This was, to a greater or lesser degree, a common theme amongst some of the other narratives, serving also to distinguish the perception of separate identity and 'otherness' felt by Inverlochians. This extension to the village from 1937 onwards – adding 150 houses in Lochy, Lochiel, Treig, Laggan and Lundy Roads – was complemented by the further programme of construction by Inverness-shire County Council (in Nevis, Lochiel and Lochy Roads) by the late 1950s. The commitment to further housing was much needed with the perennial problem of housing shortages in the Highlands. By 1936, 13 houses in the village were over-crowded, and, with sufficient housing for just over 40 per cent of the Lochaber workforce, John Bullen expressed his concerns about retaining newer employees who 'are forced to find accommodation in the South where conditions are better'. While Edward Morrison expected to have at least 30 of the 150 houses completed by spring 1939, he estimated that the village would require the full complement to house one-third of the Lochaber workforce. Despite this work, housing shortages – caused by low turnover of permanent staff and long-term residents, as well as delays to work caused by the Second World War and immediate post-war shortages of materials and labour – meant that there were still significant numbers of married and single employees at the Lochaber works living in the hostels (189 in October 1948), not aided by the flooding of the village hostel (with a capacity to house 250 men) in the winter of 1947. Over time the problem was alleviated by the expansion of housing in the nearby locales of Banavie, Torlundy, Caol and Corpach – where BACo employees settled into more mixed communities, especially with the arrival of pulp and paper mill – and more disconcertingly the contraction of the workforce at the plant. Even with further additions to Nevis Road by the council, as late as the mid-1970s Inverlochy remained predominantly a company village.[44] While the factory did not dominate the settlement as at Kinlochleven, there was no disguising the presence of British Aluminium (and the Inverlochy Village Society

(IVS) in Inverlochy – from the IVS' offices at the entrance to the village to its involvement in the social fabric of the day-to-day – and its occupational character. Staff at the Lochaber works were housed in the commanding heights of Argyle Road or on Achintore Road, physically separating them from the shopfloor by a few miles from Inverlochy. In contrast to the villages of Foyers and Kinlochleven, residents of Inverlochy worshipped in the mixed congregations in and around Fort William and thereabouts.[45]

Many features emerge from the patterns of development and the evolution of the planned environment in both villages. They illustrate one of the perennial brakes on economic growth in the Highlands and Islands, namely that of sufficient and adequate housing for workforces. They also highlight the conscious attempts by British Aluminium to structure the built environment to reflect the social structures within the factory and the communities at large. Of added importance was the company's commitment to promote its role as a welfarist employer embedded in the local community and equally a genuine commitment to that nebulous of terms, 'social capital' (that investment and commitment to 'social networks' (structures) adds to the value of society and communities).[46] Yet British Aluminium's vision of the utopia of *gemeinschaft* was tinged by its patrician outlook and values. As these motives were embodied in the built environment and the company literature – constructing 'landscapes of the mind' – so too were they reflected in the social structures and rituals of Inverlochy and especially Kinlochleven, with the factory extending out into the villages.

The establishment and expansion of both of these centres – surrounded as they were by areas that continued throughout the twentieth century to experience marked depopulation – contributed to the emergence of the Lochaber area as a major sub-regional 'growth point', and subsequently to its selection, under the Distribution of Industry Act of 1945, as a Development Area. Indeed, as with Foyers, both were responsible, until the arrival of the Wiggins Teape Pulp and Paper Mill at Corpach along the loch from Inverlochy, for reversing the general trend of depopulation in the area. Initial reversal of this trend gathered pace with the arrival of the West Highland Railway in Fort William in 1894 but grew significantly with the opening of British Aluminium's Lochaber works. This is illustrated by an examination of comparative population trends for the parishes of Kilmonivaig, Kilmallie and Lorn (including the two settlements), against those of surrounding areas. Between 1841 and 1961 the population of the parishes of Kilmallie and Kilmonivaig grew by 31 per cent. In contrast the other parishes of the area – such as Arisaig, Moidart, Ardgour, Ardnamurchan, Morvern, Sunart – experienced a 61 per cent outflow of population. The slower rate of decline in Lismore and Appin was attributable to the fact that by 1911 the town of Kinlochleven had grown to 1,186 inhabitants constituting around one-third of the population of that parish. Almost exclusively as a result of the construction of Inverlochy village, the Parish of Kilmonivaig expanded by 64 per cent between 1921 and 1931, bringing it above the peak figures of the mid-1800s. These figures are even more pronounced when looked at from the perspective of diversification of the Highland economy. While the Lochaber area accounted for around 6 per cent of the adult working population of the 'crofting counties', by 1963 nearly 19 per cent of industrial workers in the region – the majority at BACo's Fort William and Kinlochleven works, with smaller numbers employed in the fishing operations at Mallaig – were based in the area.[47] In both cases these communities were transplanted into sites with limited and dispersed populations. After an initial period of expansion in both villages, by the mid part of the twentieth century the Argyll side of Kinlochleven was starting to experience a pronounced outward flow of people, with the population of Inverlochy diminishing and ageing by the early 1970s. In contrast the Kinlochmore side of the village of Kinlochleven experienced growth until the 1970s when this slowed into a decline. This resulted from a number of factors. The contraction of the population of Kinlochbeg started in the 1930s with the re-housing of the Argyll-side residents in the new properties in Kinlochmore. By the 1960s both villages were being affected by the contraction of the workforces at Kinlochleven and Lochaber, off-set to some degree by an influx of council tenants. The loss of jobs at both plants was, unsurprisingly, most acutely felt in Kinlochleven, with a lack of alternative employment opportunities. Inverlochy's population and the occupational composition of the village were also mediated by the increase in BACo employees choosing to find accommodation in the newer and more mixed suburbs of Caol, Corpach, and Torlundy. In Kinlochleven, as well as the reduction of the workforce, and apprenticeships, on the choice of young people to leave was also affected by the increased isolation of the area after the completion of the Ballachulish Bridge. Equally, broader social and cultural changes – and opportunities (pulls) further afield and constraints (pushes) in the villages – also contributed to the outflow of the youngest age groups from the area by the 1970s.[48]

Aside from the spatial distance between the habitations of staff and workers, the social constitution of most streets within the Kinlochleven and Inverlochy was initially fairly mixed, although progressively foremen moved out of the same streets as other grades of workers. Examination of selected streets within Kinlochmore and Inverlochy, using the county valuation rolls, reveals that there was a high degree of stability in the population of the village. Admittedly comparable housing was hardly forthcoming in the area. Long-term residence was a pronounced characteristic of these locations, suggesting a degree of satisfaction and stability in these communities, especially against the context of the outflow of population from the Highlands, although these parts of Lochaber bucked the general Highland trend. Of the five company-dominated, and oldest, streets in Kinlochmore – Corrie, Mamore, Callart, Riverside and Lochaber – between 25 and 50 per cent of the residents were the same between 1937 and 1957, and in Corrie and Mamore Roads 12.5 and 14 per cent respectively of the residential population remained static between the early date and the mid-1970s. In Inverlochy in the original Abrach and Wade's Road and *Pairc an Dubh*, between 26 and 50 per cent of the residents were the same (or members of the same family) in 1957 as those in 1937, with 15 and 23 per cent staying ensconced between 1937 and 1974. A number of those who had moved in both locations had simply migrated to the next street. Moreover these streets remained predominantly inhabited by British Aluminium workers and their families, interspersed with the occasional public servant (police officers and school teachers) and merchants.[49] As one former smelter worker and long-term Inverlochy resident observed, 'it was every Jack in the village worked for the BA'. This should not be read as some simple nostalgia but also as an attempt to make sense of the profound social changes in and the loss of the occupational character in these communities.[50]

Though British Aluminium's repeated statements to affirm the predominance of Scottish, and particularly Highland, workers in the Highland smelters and residents in the company villages were intended to assure leading public figures that the company was providing employment and shelter to Highlanders (and upholding its role as a social benefactor) and assuaging paranoia over the influx of foreign workers (particularly the Irish), they were also accurate. The ethnic make-up of the villages of Kinlochleven and Inverlochy was predominantly Scottish, with a smattering of English, Irish and Welsh workers. There was a noticeable consistency in some of the families who first started out at Foyers, and spread to the winds at Kinlochleven and then Lochaber. Hebridean workers (the largest cohorts from the Isle of Lewis) first came to Kinlochleven as seasonal workers (aided by the company's provision of crofting leave) – working in the factory in early summer and winter, and returning to the Islands for the spring and late summer/autumn harvesting – but over time some laid down their roots in the village. Between the 1930s and 1950s numbers of workers from industrial lowland Scotland – the central belt as well as the eastern cities of Aberdeen and Dundee – laid down roots in both villages. Of the smaller minorities in the villages, English immigrants to Kinlochleven were predominantly over time represented among the staff. As a recent historical study of the largest immigrant group in Scotland, the English, has observed, employment in British Aluminium attracted one of the most visible groups of professional staff from south of the border to Scotland. Many of the Irish immigrants in the villages, and some of the lowland Scots, came to work on the large civil engineering schemes and stayed on. As well as the early minority groups of the English, Irish and Welsh, smaller groups of eastern Europeans (primarily from the Baltic States) took up employment and settled in the company villages immediately after the Second World War, part of the European Voluntary Workers (EVW) scheme. Any distinctions between individuals and groups in these villages were not apparently drawn on ethnic lines (however much labelling suggested otherwise) but upon social lines and more fundamentally between 'local' and 'outsider' (dependent upon time in the village, length of 'service' with the company, and willingness to conform with the regime and rituals of the settlement).

The lines of social distinction were cultivated by British Aluminium, represented by the staff houses on Garbhein Road in Kinlochbeg, or those of Achintore and Argyle Road in Fort William. Equally the tendency of some of the English managers at the Highland smelters until the late 1950s, among the staff at Kinlochleven (and the other Highland smelters), to attend the Scottish Episcopal church of St Paul's on 'staff road', led to it being dubbed the 'English church'. This was a common association in Scotland, not least because of the doctrinal shift within the Scottish Episcopal Church to 'the "high Church wing" of the Church of England'. These early English immigrants were to differ both in social background and religious persuasion from later immigrants from England.[51] However, the nomenclature owed more to social and religious, rather than ethnic, distinctions. Equally evident were the gender distinctions, traversed by class lines. However, this is not to suggest that the separate spheres that women tended to operate within deprived them of their own agency.

'Social landscaping': Social structures and regimen in Kinlochleven and Inverlochy[52]

If there was no ignoring the presence of the company and works at the heart of the community as symbolised by the built environment and the social distinctions that these made, then the routines and rituals of everyday life were, especially in Kinlochleven, equally indivisible from the factory and British Aluminium; as the *Scotsman*'s correspondent had observed at the ground-breaking ceremony in Inverlochy village in 1937, the 'workers' had had made a 'sacrifice of freedom' for better social amenities.

At the most rudimentary level, the factory hooter ordered the pace of life in Kinlochleven, as one long-term resident of the village recalled:

We would hear the hooters going at certain [...] times [...] Well it would blow, quarter to 7, getting them up in the morning. Quarter to 8 you are supposed to have left. You'd be in the gates and started at 8 o' clock. There was 3 hooters in the morning. Then there was another one at 12 o'clock where you would stop for, and all the men came home for their lunch [...] Then it would go at half past 5. That was when they were finished [...] We became used to them. We could always tell the times and that. And I always remember on New Year that the hooter always went off [...] instead of the bells, the church bells, they blew the hooter [...] And they blew it when they had the two minutes silence. It was sort of the centre of the community, the factory [...][53]

When King George V died, it was the factory hooter that signalled the two minutes' silence.[54] Eleanor MacDonald recalls: 'The factory was there, as I say, the hooter controlled your lives [...] but the factory was still very, very much the *centre of everything* [...] the BA seemed to control the village life [...] it was just all *factory* [respondent's emphasis].'[55] As Mary MacPherson and Eleanor MacDonald recalled, the hooter reminded everyone that the factory was there and that their lives were structured around it and dependent upon it.

British Aluminium pursued the maxim that the family that works, plays, prays (and enlists) together, stays together. Like the cover of *The B.A. News* for Christmas 1949 – on which a contented family receive presents from a benign looking father figure – British Aluminium acted as the benevolent parents doling out gifts to their grateful, blissfully content and obedient children.[56] As Gregor and Crichton observed in 1946:

> In Kinlochleven the one Company not only employs the vast majority of the male population but also owns the greater part of the village. True the Kinlochleven Village Improvement Society is the nominal owner of Kinlochmore, but everyone acknowledges that the Company is really at the back of the K.V.I.S. Thus the firm is the foundation of the whole social structure, and is in a position to make or mar any new social enterprise. This could be a dangerous situation, though at Kinlochleven the Company has actually been very generous in its support of local activities, so much so in fact that the people are inclined to take it too much for granted. Some, however, are quite aware of this tendency, and one of them aptly summed up the situation by saying that the village suffered from a 'Company should' complex.[57]

Belying BACo's generous capital outlay was its ambitions to sculpt the loyalty and behaviour of the workforce through the setting up of social organisations, endorsing others and supporting still more, in the company settlements. In Kinlochleven, in particular, life was regulated from the cradle to the grave at school, in church, in the workplace, in the home, and through leisure time. Gregor and Crichton's observation of a form of dependency becoming deep-seated in Kinlochleven as a result of the central role of British Aluminium in the community was evident still to the researchers from CEED in 2003. The company sought to modulate behaviour not alone but in conjunction with the churches, schools, and other social organisations. At the heart of this strategy – and at the root of its success – was the understanding that this had to be exercised through a social contract: the workforce and residents must feel that they owned a share in the undertaking. Equally they needed to complement the existing social structures in the area. The latter was even more pointed in the case of Inverlochy, and the neighbouring burgh of Fort William, where they could not be seen to supplant the established elite and had to gradually increase their influence.

At the centre of British Aluminium's social designs were the KVIS and the IVS. These organisations, formed in 1913 and 1926 respectively, were ostensibly set up by the company – in the case of KVIS, in conjunction with the Co-operative Society

– as Public Utility Companies to own and manage the villages. These continued to be underwritten by British Aluminium until the 1960s. Although the company was heavily represented on the boards of directors of these societies by the senior managers from within the highest echelons of British Aluminium it was also keen to ensure that other figures from the regional elite were reflected in their numbers, such as Sir John Sutherland, who chaired both the KVIS and IVS, the latter from its foundation until his retirement in 1948. He was subsequently replaced by the convenor of Inverness County Council, Sir Francis Walker. This provided a conduit into county and burgh political circles. Even more significant – for their unstated, but evident, aims towards a stake-holding, property-owning working class (albeit one that was supplicant) – was representation of shopfloor workers and foremen as shareholders and directors of the societies, for without this their strategy would have lacked the credibility and social capital to sustain it. As Edward Morrison pointed out to his fellow BACo managers in 1936, the IVS needed 'workmen' on its board.[58] In spite of these appeals for shopfloor participation, both the IVS and KVIS boards were dominated by company managers. Until his retirement in 1947 Edward Morrison represented the BACo board on both the KVIS and IVS from their inception. He was joined in the 1940s by Gordon Chalmers, BACo's Highland factor, and Morrison's place was taken by Commodore Linzee. Moreover voting rights within the societies, exercised through shareholdings, were also heavily weighted in the company's, rather than employee-residents', favour.[59] As well as acting as the conduit between the residents and the company, and between the company and the county councils, these organisations were responsible for overseeing the maintenance of properties (in conjunction with the factor's office) in both villages, providing subventions to local societies and running the cinema in Kinlochleven. A more detailed examination of the exercise of some of these functions by these agents provides some insight into how pervasive British Aluminium's influence and control could be within the communities. As late as the 1950s, when the KVIS was divesting itself (or being relieved) of responsibilities for provision of domestic electricity (taken over by NSHEB), refuse and sanitation and some housing provision (the county councils), it employed a 'welfare officer', trained in the rudiments of 'social welfare', as well as property management, to carry out regular inspections. Tenants who did not maintain the appearance of their houses and gardens were threatened with and could be evicted, while the society used informal social networks to air disapproval of tenants whose behaviour was seen as unbecoming; a legacy visible in the observations of the social dynamics of the village to this day.

In the summer of 1947 Kinlochleven Village Council was formed. According to the summer 1948 edition of *The B.A. News*, this 'owed its inception to the Welfare Department of the British Aluminium Co.'. Though the village council (formed out of the factory JWC, and with trade unions and managers represented on it) was dubbed a 'Local Citizens' organization' by KVIS directors, it did not seek to usurp the village improvement society but simply to work with it to press home demands for improvements to amenities, continuing to use the Society as a conduit for discussions with other organisations.[60] As well as enforcing control over the village, the KVIS also acted as a lobby to ensure that work was undertaken by the county councils.[61] Thus the village improvement societies, and the company, were able to exercise a good deal of power directly over tenants, and indirectly through their funding of and their role as landlord to all of the village leisure societies.

The company's role in the communities was also emphasised through its provision of leisure facilities – with bowling greens, tennis courts, and pitches – at the heart of Inverlochy, and Kinlochmore. Both villages sported a number of football and shinty teams, as well as angling, bowls, and tennis clubs. Moreover in the routine day-to-day life of the villages, the company's ideals and control were permeated throughout a network of organisations representing the twin maxims of loyalty and service. This also further embodied their embrace of 'Muscular Christianity'. Provision of sports facilities – as a means of retaining staff, and as a core labour management strategy – was more widely spread across British industry than has been generally recognised. A nationwide survey for the Industrial Welfare Society (IWS) in 1936 revealed that 80 out of the 88, admittedly large, manufacturing firms surveyed provided either sporting fields or facilities for their workforce; an earlier study by IWS showed that in some locations they were the only providers of leisure facilities. At their Liverpool and London works, Bryant and May also supported leisure and educational clubs, operating a company-wide Bryant and May Athletics Association, while Lever Brothers promoted the activities of no fewer than 29 societies within Port Sunlight by 1909, including the Boys' Brigade and a Mutual Improvement Society.[62] 'BA'-sponsored sporting activities were also a means to promote order and values of loyalty and service – whether to company, or to church, crown and country – reflected in the welter of social organisations which reflected these ideals. In Kinlochleven and around BACo's other Highland sites, these ranged from the provision of boys' camps (often led by company officers), the Boys' Brigade, Girls' Guildry, and Scouts to all the main branches of cadets and territorial military units – some of these overlapping with the role of the Christian churches (particularly the Church of Scotland) in the village, and displaying once again the importance of 'Muscular Christianity'. As well as the company culture, that the military ethos prevailed partly reflected the service backgrounds of some of the managers. Col. F. E. Laughton – who finally retired as Colonel of the 4th Battalion of the Queen's Cameron Highlanders in 1928, after being awarded the Military Cross during the First World War – came from a naval background (his father later became a renowned naval historian, a brother remained in the Royal Navy, and a sister became Director of the Women's Royal Naval Service (WRNS), while his wife's father and uncle were both British Army generals.[63] Prior to studying science tripos at Cambridge, John Bullen had served on the western front as a major in the army. Similarly W. Henkel, works manager at Kinlochleven (1937–1955) had served as a commissioned officer between 1914 and 1919.[64] Unsurprisingly a high number of men among the workforce until the 1960s had also served in the armed forces.

Staff from the works and their spouses frequently held key offices in these organisations, reflecting the hierarchies of workplace and villages as well as gender distinctions. Similarly, managers and their wives were well represented in positions of power in local sporting, debating and horticultural societies, as well as organisations such as the Scottish Women's Rural Institute led by staff wives and those of other members of the rural elite.[65] This extension of the hierarchy of the factory into the 'squirearchy' of the villages was also reflected in the political activities undertaken and civic positions held by company managers. Edward Morrison, for example, was a Justice of the Peace for both Argyll and Inverness-shire and an Argyll county councillor. Henkel was chairman of the local Unionist Association, while A. B. Jones, assistant manager at Kinlochleven and then manager of Foyers, was a county councillor for Kinlochleven from 1951. However, political allegiance also hinged on the self-same social contract, as well as broader voting habits. Similarly those trade unionists represented from British Aluminium's works and the villages, serving on Fort William Burgh and the county councils, while benefiting from their social status in the works, were also subject to the electoral voting habits of the region.[66]

One respondent, recalling the pointed class distinctions in Kinlochleven, observed that in spite of the active participation of staff and their wives in societies, their sense of social elevation was made clear:

> We used to have big whist drives, you know, if they were fundraising you would have big whist drives and it was done on a basis of a woman would take a table and you sold four tickets, and that was your table. And it was very noticeable when, *they* [respondent's emphasis] would, the staff ladies, or those up on Staff Road, they would have their table as well, but they would come down with their bone china and their silver tea service, do you know? And their fancy cloths and that, whereas the other people were just sort of ordinary, you know?[67]

Indeed it was the class, rather than gender, distinctions that underpinned many of the reflections of women's experiences of these groups in the testimonies of residents of Kinlochleven. George Haggart's enduring recollections of social relations in the Inverlochy of the 1930s and 1940s were of little mixing between the staff and shopfloor from the Lochaber works. This was no doubt all the more pronounced because senior staff at that plant lived in large houses in Fort William rather than, as at Kinlochleven, close by (albeit looking down on the shopfloor). The importance of this memory, like that of Eleanor MacDonald, lies in the perception of this division. Recounting etiquette on the Inverlochy tennis courts and encounters with the 'company class', Haggart remembered:

Some of them [the 'company class'] played tennis, for example, at Inverlochy [...] But it was very much a clique, you know. If you were waiting to get onto the court and you were waiting for somebody to play with and somebody else that they the company class come along. They were waiting on their own ones to come along. Now having said that, there were [...] the odd people from the shop floor who managed to get themselves through to the company class and they got to play with them, and they were the type of people that people would suggest were the crawlers or they were: 'Yes sir, no sir. Three bags full, sir' – that type of thing [...] So there wasn't a lot of [...] of contact between staff and shopfloor out of hours.[68]

Although part of the 'county set', some managers, such as Colonel Laughton and his wife, Haggart felt, did make more of an attempt to engage with shopfloor workers outside of the workplace, with this encouraging (or perhaps prompting) other staff to circulate more: 'they were never at ease with people in the way that Mrs Laughton, or the Colonel's wife, was and the Colonel was.'[69] Certainly Laughton appears to have been very involved in community sports and events.[70] Thus while senior managers may have held office in the KVIS and IVS, as well as leading other social activities, the company's 'control' was diluted because some staff and their families were overly keen on reinforcing social distinctions, suggesting once again that the nurturing of 'consent' was critical to loyalty.

Social stratification and order were equally expressed in the community at prayer, particularly in Kinlochleven: the marriage of spiritual needs with the appearance of good physical health. In the late 1950s, the local Church of Scotland Minister approvingly recounted the anecdotal, and possibly apocryphal, observation of an American visitor to Kinlochleven: 'I guess the folk hereabouts work hard, play hard, and worship hard!' Attendance at the three churches of the main religious denominations in Kinlochleven stood at around 41 per cent of the population in 1961, with smaller congregations at the two evangelical missions.[71] As Gregor and Crichton observed, the company was generous to the churches as to other organisations, chiefly recognising them as a font of cohesion and order, as Britain's churches still appear to have been before the *Annus Mirabilis* of 1963, after which growing secularisation saw a decline – or in the case of Catholicism, a levelling off – in attendance at all the main Christian denominations. Although the company was supportive of all denominations in Kinlochleven, the established church in the eyes of British Aluminium was that of the Church of Scotland, although the Episcopalian Church was perceived as being the *de facto* spiritual home of the English staff. The centrality of religion and the company was signified at events. In January 1916, for example, a 'soirée' was held for Sunday School children overseen by the then factory manager, R. P. Tod, supported by the clerics and preachers from all of the main religious denominations as well as the local headmaster. The marriage of company and church was visible too in the new

Kirk in Kinlochmore (completed in 1930), to which British Aluminium donated just under one-third of the construction costs. The foundation stone for the church was laid by William Murray Morrison's wife, while the church incorporated stained-glass windows in the nave of the south wall depicting the patron saints of Scotland and England (Sts Andrew and George); 'symbolising the close association of Scots and English in the growth of the village'. Here too, managers and their wives served as church elders, and as bible studies teachers and guildry leaders.[72]

The original Scottish Episcopalian Church, St Paul's Church, at Kinlochbeg was replaced in 1954 with a permanent brick building in Kinlochmore. If St Paul's continued to have a reputation as the church of the English elite, then details of its office-holders suggest otherwise by the 1950s. Of the four-person church committee, three were shopfloor workers. Yet there was no mistaking how the Episcopalian Church was viewed – partly as a result of more general perceptions within Scotland of it as an extension of Anglicanism – and apparently substantiated to many residents by the fact that a number of the managers, such as John Gris Bullen, were leading figures within the congregation at both St Paul's and St Andrew's (the latter, the Episcopalian parish church in Fort William). The Roman Catholic Church of the Good Shepherd started off, like the other denominations, as a mission, ministering to the navvies moving from the original primitive wooden hut of a chapel (used as a place of worship from 1909) to new premises on the Kinlochmore side in 1961. Though the Catholic presence in the village was mostly associated with the original navvies, the size of the congregation suggests that numbers must have been bolstered by other worshippers. It is quite possible that some of these may have come from among the Hebridean islanders who settled in the village, although most seem to have been from Lewis, a trenchantly Presbyterian island, some may have come from the Catholic islands of Barra or South Uist. Equally, this part of the west Highlands itself had a strong tradition of native Catholicism, with numbers added from among Anglo-Catholics and refugees from Europe after the Second World War. As well as the main denominations, a Salvation Army Hall was established in the village in 1927, and the evangelist Faith Mission established a place for worship in 1917 (with financial support from the company). These evangelical groups apparently found much favour in the Highlands (and further afield) because of the role given to women in them, though the Kirk minister flippantly observed of the Salvation Army's appeal in Kinlochleven that it was hard to resist 'An instrumental band used to parade the streets on a Sunday morning in all weathers, proclaiming a message for all to hear, not least the defaulters from church worship!' While British Aluminium's support for the churches was undoubtedly motivated by its pursuit of social order in its workplaces and the community, as well as the principles and beliefs of leading company figures, then the involvement of staff members in positions within the churches should not be used to over-extrapolate about managers' motivations for engagement in religious or leisure activities, especially given the very central role that religion played in many people's lives before the mid-1960s. Of those Kinlochleven residents interviewed, religion appears to have played a very significant part in the lives of men and women over the age of 70. Most of the female respondents attended the Church of Scotland, and had been active in their church since their childhood and progressed through the Girls' Guildry and Women's Guild. It was clear from their testimony that this was critical as a social outlet, as much as for its religious aspects.[73] If the churches were relied upon to minister to spiritual needs, then encouraging social advancement through approved learning was also encouraged by the company from an early stage, with Kinlochleven's Debating Society holding its first debate in 1909, on whether women should be granted the vote (the affirmative was supported unanimously), in the same year as Lachlan Grant's lecture on the value of reading.[74]

Most of the women interviewed expressed some ambivalence in the testimonies about their experiences of church-related social organisations in Kinlochleven; noting the hierarchy within the church, and other social organisations, alongside a longing for bygone days and the joys of friendship. An insight into how patterns of gender socialisation, as well as class distinctions, were promoted is provided in some of these. As with the boys, order and discipline was impressed on girls from a young age in these organisations, as Eleanor MacDonald recalled of the regime in the Girls' Guildry, 'Oh marching, marching was […] the usual thing; marching to music and all the usual bits and pieces of exercises […] you had your usual housewifery and caring and that, ye had to go to the captain's house and light the fire and things like this […]' These guildry activities (training for housekeeping) undertaken for the leaders of the Girls' Guildry and other social organisations – of whom MacDonald observed, 'in my time they were all off the 'Staff Road people' – also came as a form of cheap domestic labour: 'You'd go up there and maybe she'd give you a job of lighting the fire, or setting the table or something like that, and you'd have your knitting badge.'[75] Eleanor's daily after-school routine included delivering her father's lunchtime 'pieces' to the factory, and going up to the manse to do the daily shop for the Minister's wife. Like many girls of their generation (and social background) growing up in Kinlochleven, Eleanor MacDonald, Mary MacPherson and Margaret Mathieson all ended up working in domestic service for a time.[76] Their adulthood coincided with Gregor and Crichton's social survey, allowing us to place their social experience within the wider context of paid and unpaid female employment patterns in the village, in which the social researchers observed that a far greater proportion of young women left the village in the 1940s than men. Of those that remained, many married. Of the paid employment open to women in the village at the time: 52 per cent of jobs were in domestic service; 26 per cent in retail; and 22 per cent in the factory.[77] As with many Scottish workplaces at the time, women in Kinlochleven relinquished their jobs upon getting married. After she married in her early twenties in 1939, Eleanor MacDonald was resigned to giving up her job primarily as a secretary at the Kinlochleven Road Transport Trust (another BACo subsidiary) but the war intervened and she went to run the company's hostel in Foyers. Similarly, Mary MacPherson worked in domestic service and as a shop assistant before being directed towards wartime work – her mother having denied her permission to join the WRNS – operating a compressor machine in the factory. This she did for seven years, until she and her female companions were forced to leave in 1950. Mary MacPherson was unusual among her contemporaries in that the premature death of her husband in the mid-1960s, with three children between the ages of 4 and 17, precipitated her return to the labour market to work in the school canteen. Margaret Mathieson's job as a head housemaid for a large land-owning family determined her job when she joined the Women's Auxiliary Air Force (with the aspiration to be a driver) in 1942. Instead she ended up keeping house in the officers' quarters. She continued in domestic service, returning to the village in 1962 after her father died to look after her mother. Of her sisters, two worked in the BA laboratories, and the two others in retail work and domestic service before marrying at a young age and becoming full time mothers and housewives.[78]

The enforcement of order and structure was also evident in the corralling of Kinlochleven cinema-goers. By the 1950s the Kinlochleven cinema was directly funded by the KVIS and ran showings on Monday and Thursday nights, and two showings on a Saturday. Seating was strictly monitored, as Cynthia Cassidy recalls:

> You'd go in and the screen would be in front of you and on the left hand side, the girls, the right hand side, the boys, with the big aisle up between [...] Now, well, this is the whole point of it. When you were small, and you started going to the cinema, you sat down the front, right? And the girls' toilet was on the left hand side through the door there [gestures], the boys' toilet was on the right hand side through the door, so I presume that's why the girls sat on the left and the boys sat on the right. As you got older you moved back a couple of seats, and another couple of seats, to let the younger ones sit in front, it was all a process. Then, when you got to teenagers, you did a very daring thing. The girls went in and they sat on the boys' side. So that was a sort of signal to say 'hello boys, we like you', you know? And then sort of further back, in the back half of the cinema.[79]

She observed that the same was true of dances in the village which were closely policed, although as in the case of the cinema as they reached their teenage years these rules were, to some degree, subverted. Yet the enduring theme for Cynthia Cassidy appeared to have been the ordered lines within Kinlocheleven: 'It's not until you look back that you realise it's a society, a society all on its own [...] it's just, there's unwritten rules, and each generation that comes along just did the same.'[80]

The company also encouraged order through its close links with the local schools, by offering prizes particularly for diligence, good behaviour and attendance and by making it clear that favourable reports from the local headmaster would almost certainly (prior to the freezing of apprenticeship schemes) lead to an apprenticeship in the factory for boys and, for the girls, employment in the offices, labs, hostels, or the private homes of the staff. Initially Kinlochleven's children were schooled in a wooden building on the Argyll side of the village (constructed in 1909, and burnt down in 1919), with various buildings being used until the construction of a new school on the Kinlochmore side was completed in 1927 (funded by Argyll County Council, and then Inverness-shire). Even after the Education (Scotland) Act of 1945, schooling was offered only up to leaving age, with those pursuing a route leading to university or training college having to attend Fort William Secondary School (now Lochaber High School) or Oban High School until the latter part of the twentieth century. Inverlochy was served by a primary school with most leavers attending Lochaber High School, either until statutory leaving age or until they progressed to further or higher education. In all cases, although education was the locus of the local authorities, British Aluminium provided equipment and building materials for the schools. Schooling was non-denominational and given the geography of the Highlands most parents of all faiths sent their children to the same school. The school roll at Kinlochleven stood at around 330 pupils between 1933 and 1963, while at Inverlochy student numbers were around 200 by the early 1960s. The full significance of British Aluminium's enticements to achievement is seen when considered alongside school leavers' destinations. Between 1922 and 1933, Oban High School took 10 students from Kinlochleven School (of these 8 were from Kinlochleven itself). Between 1934 and 1943 – admittedly not a wholly representative sample of years – 7 went to Oban High, and 30 to Fort William. Most other male school leavers went directly into the factory (in some cases into apprenticeships) and female students into offices, labs, shops or domestic service prior to marriage. Even among those who moved on to Oban and Lochaber High Schools, many of the male students ended up eventually being employed by the 'BA'.

Order and performance were instilled from a young age both inside and out of the classroom. Margaret Mathieson, who started at the Kinlochleven school in 1927, recalled that each day started with the 'Lord's Prayer' and discipline was drummed into you: '... in the school there was a big placard say "manners is next to Godliness" and then a whole line of, I can't remember them now, but I do remember that one. They were very particular about manners in school.'[81] Eleanor MacDonald described the weekly tests on arithmetic and spelling with pupils being arranged from the back of the class forward on the basis of 'ability' and performance: 'The top was the first, the first desk at the top, at the very top [...] and then it came down, down through the classes. I mean if you were sitting at the front you were the lowest [...] You avoided that, yes. You went by your, by your ability and by your marks for tests, because you had tests every week, every Friday.' Even outside of the classroom, MacDonald recalled that teachers (many of whom lived in the same streets) were treated with the utmost deference. Asked whether they saw teachers outside school, she replied, 'Not other than meeting them in the street, and then you had to bow to your teacher [...] you did not pass your teacher or the headmaster without [...] say they came up, passed you by, you bowed like that to your teacher [gestures].'[82] All of this was maintained by the final sanction of the use of corporal punishment. This preparation for later life – of a culture of deference and order – was maintained outside the school too in both Kinlochleven and Inverlochy through the surveillance of other residents and informal networks feeding back information to parents, teachers and the village improvement societies. Some interviewees looked back wistfully on those days, while others were more conflicted in their memories. Though evoking memories of a 'blissful' childhood in 1940s and 1950s Inverlochy, Sandy Walker and Brian Murphy noted the formal order of the place and the paternalism of British Aluminium; for her part, Eleanor MacDonald balanced very happy memories of her upbringing in Kinlochleven with a recognition that life was very disciplined and strict, and Margaret Mathieson referred approvingly to the discipline in the old days.[83] However young people's experiences of education and social interaction while growing up in Kinlochleven and Inverlochy during the first half of the twentieth century was similar to that of their contemporaries elsewhere in Scotland, and the rest of Britain. As one sociological account of childhood and education in Scotland has observed, 'the introduction of compulsory schooling should not simply be seen as part of a wish to protect children from the dangers of the adult world. It was also intended as a measure of social control, which sought to instil in children the dominant middle-class values of society.' Equally the 'mythology' of a democratic educational tradition in Scotland – associated with the social mobility of the much-lauded 'lad of parts' – 'idealised and simplified the facts'. In a similar vein, one historian of childhood in England during the twentieth century has observed of collections of nostalgic reminiscences of schooling, 'it is more than likely that obedient, attentive, conscientious, cooperative and clever children found school reasonably enjoyable, if only because they rarely incurred the teacher's wrath'. However, if schooling in Kinlochleven appears to have fulfilled an important role in socialising young people so that they were prepared for their role in later life – *Learning to Labour*, the phrase coined by sociologist Paul Willis in his 1977 study of the educational experiences of a group of working-class youth – then in the cinema and dancing, youth did attempt to subvert these norms.[84] Recognition of the promotion of conformity in schooling should not detract from its other benefits, or be given as an indication of explicit complicity on the part of teaching staff as opposed to the implicit import of shared social values.

The social control exercised by the company and the churches over employee-residents in Kinlochleven, though greater than in Inverlochy, loosened gradually from the 1940s and resulted from a variety of specific local and broader social factors. With the vesting of control of utilities (water, electricity) and some housing in the hands of the county councils in both areas, the village improvement societies and the company exercised less power. In February 1963 most of the Kinlochmore housing stock, bar 24 houses in Corrie Road, was transferred to British Aluminium to clear the debts of KVIS. Thereafter BACo conducted its business on a far more limited transactional basis, while the KVIS (with limited powers) had far less influence in the day-to-day social activities of the village. During the last three decades of the twentieth century, the sale of company housing to employees at affordable prices further signalled the disappearance of the company from the life of the villages. Critically, with the organisational changes of the 1960s, after the RTIA takeover, control within the company was centralised removing almost an entire layer of local management. Moreover, although Stedeford had indicated that the new owners were sensitive to any alterations of the social contract, he made it clear he was not keen on espousing the paternalism that had previously characterised British Aluminium. Concurrently BACo was reducing its Highland workforce, with an associated fall in the number of apprenticeships, and, with other employment opportunities opening such as at Corpach paper mill, council housing was rented out to non-BA workers. This was set against the social changes associated with the 'long sixties', the challenges to traditional forms of authority, and advancing secularisation, on British society.[85]

As with the residents of the railway town of Crewe or the cottonopolis of Paisley, the all-absorbing nature of these structures of social control should not be assumed to have been simply accepted by the residents of Kinlochleven and Inverlochy – collective and individual agency independent of the company was evident, as the strikes of 1910 and 1936 showed. E. P. Thompson's observation for an earlier period that, 'deference was often without the least illusion: it could be seen from below as being one part necessary self-preservation, one part the calculated extraction of whatever could be extracted', was equally applicable to the social contract between these smelter communities and British Aluminium.[86]

Everyday life: the diversity of 'lived' experiences

Visitors to Kinlochleven today are greeted now with a sign marking what remains of the factory site, welcoming them to a 'Highland Village Reborn'. Though the social structures of yesterday in Kinlochleven and Inverlochy may now have been replaced by different social networks, and the socially stratified nature of the built environment may have lost its significance for visitors or new residents, the enduring legacy of their past as industrial settlements and of British Aluminium's strategies are visible in the testimonies of long-term residents of these locations.

For some there is a sense of loss that the way of life has been transformed. Sandy Walker's testimony is characteristic of some of these voices. Born in June 1940 in Laggan Road, Inverlochy, he was brought up and still lives in the village (having spent much of his working life as an employee of British Aluminium, and then Alcan).

His account of his working life in the industry, and his upbringing in Inverlochy, was strongly embedded in his family narrative within the collective memory of the region, notably the clearances. This has been stimulated by his interest in the Highland clearances and incorporates a number of recognisable features from the company's narrative. He was unequivocal in his estimation of the industry's benefits for the region:

> I will say this, that if it were not for Lord Kelvin and his compatriots, who initialised the building of the Foyers smelter and started this thing off, where would I have been today? Here I am in a wonderful part of the country, I've got my family, I've got my granddaughter, it's been good. The aluminium industry was a saviour to the Highlands. There is no doubt about that.[87]

Like a number of the respondents, if he expressed loyalty to British Aluminium – tempered with misgivings about the work environment, and his wish to stress his trade union credentials – he was equally clear in his condemnation of Alcan's place in the community:

> British Aluminium took a very strong interest in the social aspects of their employees. They had well, I played tennis as a young boy, they had a wonderful tennis court up there called the Braxi. It was a braxi – it's a sheep's disease [...] But anyway they built this just up the road there. They built the tennis court and bowling green with a wooden building in between that was called the Braxi. They then contributed towards the building of the village hall. It was nicknamed the Braxi as well too [...] There were hundreds of people employed up there [points in the direction of the Lochaber smelter] at one time, hundreds of people. Gradually over time technology, jobs became pretty scarce, and it was the diminution of the workforce I suggested – I suggest that led to the loss of the community spirit as I described [...] the ethos of the Alcan management did not lend itself to a community spirit.[88]

Walker was not alone in this view. Brian Murphy, who grew up in Inverlochy around the same time, and then served as an electrician in the Lochaber works and as a shop steward in the trade unions, acknowledged the 'high-handedness' of British Aluminium at times but looked back wistfully to a time when the village was a hive of social activity and was well maintained.[89] While it is clear that BACo had scaled back its community commitments long before the merger with Alcan, what is critical in both of these accounts is the perception of the 'outsider' company's invisibility in the community, the emotional redolence of the 'BA' version, and an allusion to the sense of loss of the old company, particularly disconnected from the social space of the factory. This same vein was evident in the testimony of others. John Blair moved from a job at the Royal Ordnance Factory at Bishopton, in the heavily industrialised central belt, to employment as a chemist at the Kinlochleven laboratory just after the Second World War. He served as a district councillor for the village and was an elder in the Church of Scotland. Interviewed for a Scottish newspaper in January 1976, one year after the opening of the Ballachulish bridge, councillor John Blair warned: 'I tell you I am worried about the future. If we are not going to slip into oblivion, we must make Kinlochleven known to the tourists and improve the amenities. We must safeguard against the death of this great little place.'[90] Thirty years later, though some circumspection had crept into his reflections, John remained fairly pessimistic about changes in the village:

> Nowhere stays the same for any length of time and I suppose change is progress, but one looks back nostalgically to the old days. It's been an experience to see the way that the village has developed over these years. The factory's gone and lots of people commute to Fort William for work and so on and so forth. There has been virtually nothing come in to replace BA at any level, or whether there is the Ice Factor [the UK's only artificial ice climbing training wall, housed in the old Carbon Factory building] and whether two small businesses that have opened up […] So the village now has become imbalanced in that there are many more pensioners than young people. In fact it's rather depressing. I was sitting at church the other day and out of a congregation of about 50, there was 15 widows, which rather depressed me.[91]

He suggested that his pessimism was to some extent a reflection of his age. However when contrasted against his memories of Kinlochleven in the 1940s, it paints a gloomy picture:

> I found the change coming up here from the city of Glasgow to a small Highland village was quite dramatic, but there was plenty to do in these days. There were lots of organizations that you could participate in and so on and so forth, and there was a community feeling that's a lot here that didn't exist in Glasgow. People worked together and played together […] It's a happy place, a bustling place and there were lots of young, single men living in the hostel which led to a sort of imbalance in the population but they mixed very well with the village people and we used to have, for instance, half a dozen football teams. Each department had a team and every Saturday the main occupation in the village was football and we used to get hundreds down at the field, at the park next to the bowling green and it was quite an occasion […] There were, as I said, lots of things to do particularly with our young people, and there was dancing and the rest of it. The social life was very active.[92]

John Blair went on to further paint the tableau of a bustling, self-reliant community, with everything provided, 'from the cradle to the grave as it were'.[93] Similarly MacPherson, Mathieson and MacDonald picture described Kinlochleven as a lively hub. While some blamed Alcan for the demise of the village as it was, others identified the change as pre-dating them. Margaret Mathieson recalled returning to the village in 1962 and observing what she felt was the social vacuum by then. 'When I came home, and there was nothing much to join for me. I joined the guild with some of my friends and the church and I did flower arranging and there was photography I went to but it fell through after a few weeks after I joined. It was, there was nothing much else to join, so I was quite happy being at home watching television which I never did very much of.'[94] In spite of the protestations of one linchpin of the local Air Training Squadron, and a mechanical engineer at the factory, in 1977 that the village was dying because young people were more mobile and did not value what they had in the village, Mathieson's account – as a woman by then in her forties – suggests that social activity in the village had started to wane by the early 1960s. Certainly the sense of despondency among some young residents interviewed after the opening of the Ballachulish Bridge was clear:

> In this place if you're not going with someone you're snookered. There's only one pub and the *British Aluminium Club and you've got to be 18 to get in* [journalist's emphasis]. The alternative is the disco on a Saturday night, but that's for the 12 to 16 age group ... so if you are between 16 and 18 there's nothing to do ... it's driving me up the wall.[95]

While the diversion of tourist traffic as a result of the Ballachulish Bridge may have added to Kinlochleven's sense of isolation and decline, the social changes in the 1960s and 1970s appear to have stemmed from contraction of the workforce and the changes to the village's social structures. An earlier oral history interview conducted with a long-term Kinlochleven resident reveals a similar nostalgia for a lost past, and a struggle to come to terms with local and wider social change:

> Well, before the war and during the war and for some years after the war, things were really pleasant in the village. We had this neighbourliness and community spirit but sadly that seemed to disappear. A number if years after the war, well, a number of years after the war it seemed to go. I think perhaps the fact that in households both parents go out to work and they haven't got time for anything outwith their household and family duties and that has made a difference to the village. You see nowadays it is very difficult to get voluntary workers – people who are willing to lead the youth in organizations and suchlike. All that went out with the war. Well, a number of years after the war this seemed to change.[96]

Thus long before Alcan entered the scene corporate social engagement in the villages had dissipated. This narrative also reflects redolent collective themes about national unity during wartime as well as the distinction that emerges in the testimony between those who saw themselves as belonging to the villages, and those (usually later arrivals) who were both viewed as 'outsiders' and felt apart. Jimmy Dunlevy – brought up in Dundee, and formerly employed as a marine engineer in the shipyards of the Tay and at Greenock – came to the Lochaber works in the 1950s. Jimmy and his wife (a native of Fort William) settled in the outlying estate of Caol as they could not get a house in Inverlochy. Jimmy suggested that his wife was also adamant that they did not settle in Inverlochy, saying, 'I don't want you to stay in Inverlochy which was largely British Aluminium people and because they would never be off your doorstep'. Dunlevy observed: 'It was largely the earlier people who worked in the smelter stayed in Inverlochy and that developed into the family, the family took over from them in the village [...] a lot of people who came into the area stayed in Caol.'[97] This is certainly born out by the returns in the valuation rolls for both Inverlochy and Kinlochmore. The distinction between newer arrivals and older residents was sometimes also denoted in a different view of what the company's role should be in the community. In contrast to the sense of betrayal that a number of the respondents felt towards Alcan, attributing the loss of community spirit to the company, others were quick to point to the palpable sense of expectation among sections of the communities that the company should provide (mirroring Gregor and Crichton's earlier observations). Another interviewee, who moved to an engineer's job at the Lochaber plant from the central belt of Scotland in 1969, expressed just such a view:

And the big thing was that they assumed that the company would do everything for them, you know? And that's the difference with coming in here from elsewhere where you were [...] you were an employee but that was it. Over here they had err, the attitude that the company will do that. And that was again, I said, I mentioned I was involved in the social club [known locally still as the BA club], but that involvement the company said that was not their responsibility, and I agreed with them. You know but the people said, 'oh the company should do that, the company should do that [...] The company shouldn't do it.' They gave them the premises, they gave them everything but it was up to them to run it, but they wouldn't.[98]

He later became an office-holder of the BA club not long after arriving. His testimony also further illustrates British Aluminium's attempts to reduce its role in the community by the 1960s. Bob Herbert, originally from just outside London, moved to Kinlochleven in the 1980s with his wife, having spent many years in the army, and then in a variety of jobs in the north of England and the west Highlands. He has lived in the village for over twenty years, many of those working for Alcan at the

Kinlochleven and then Lochaber smelters. Asked how he and his wife had integrated into the village, Bob Herbert observed, 'oh like with any small community [...] we're still outsiders', despite having been the chair of the parent teacher association, having put two children through the local school and participated in other aspects of village life. However overall he felt that, 'we slid in nicely, and yes, we fit in, we enjoy ourselves here, and this is our home now ...'[99] Asked about the enduring legacy of the company and the industry in village life in Kinlochleven, he observed:

> You've got the older folk that the BA did everything for them, and I mean when you think the BA used to provide free electricity until people started putting in the hen houses [laughs] to keep their hens warm [British Aluminium in fact abandoned free electricity to Kinlochleven residents in the 1920s], but everything was done for them, and once again not resentment, but people, the older people, couldn't understand why Alcan wasn't doing it.[100]

The prevalence of this sense of dependency was, in Herbert's view, evident in the reaction of some residents in Kinlochleven to the closure of the works, and their sense of Alcan's reneging on the social contract. Herbert felt that the closure had been carried out in a model fashion and was unavoidable: 'There was a bit of sadness the fact that it's [the smelter] been here so long. People couldn't understand why money wasn't being spent on it to bring it up to modern day standards, but you only had to look at the economics of it.' He felt that the effects on the village were minimal:

> This is purely a personal thing, I don't think the economic effects on the village, well I don't think there were any economic effects on the village because everybody else [...] those that wanted a job had got up and gone. Those that had the chance had gone over to Fort William, very little had sort of been made redundant and some moved and stayed, retired, and other people had got jobs so err, you know, the economic effect was minimal really, but a lot of people would take me to task on that because they used it as a lever to get money into the village which I thought was a bit of a waste.[101]

Among those interviewed, these different reactions to Alcan's role in the community varied according, as Herbert's testimony infers, to tenure in these locations, as well as personal circumstances and outlook. What is evident is that the withdrawal of corporate involvement in the community considerably pre-dated the merger with Alcan. Some of these were extraneous to the company – wider social and cultural change – others can be pinpointed to the takeover of British Aluminium by RTIA, and the changes in organisational structure and corporate outlook. Even if BACo had not been taken over by RTIA, experience from other previously paternalistic concerns (such as Lever Brothers and ICI) suggests that it is unlikely that British Aluminium would have sustained its welfarist programme well into the late twentieth and early twenty-first centuries. Overwhelmingly the narratives reflect a profound sense of loss at the disappearance of the industry from Kinlochleven, and the attempts to come to terms with the accompanying social changes in these communities.

Conclusion

British Aluminium's attempts at 'Sculpting the Garden of Eden' in both Kinlochleven and Inverlochy were highly visible, through the built environment and social organisation of the villages. Even the street names in both, such as Lochiel Road and Morrison Crescent, were 'as almanacs registering those personalities and events, mythic or real, which have imprinted themselves on popular consciousness', with the layout of the villages representing 'a powerful social law'.[102] As the French philosopher Maurice Halbwachs observed of the built environment, 'place and group have each received the imprint of the other. Each aspect, each detail of this place has a meaning intelligible only to members of the group, for each portion of its space corresponds to various and different aspects of the structure and life of their society.' Thus, as Spiro Kostof observed, streets take on the form of 'communal registers', rich with collective and individual memories.[103] This 'social landscaping' was a distinct part of the company's labour management strategies evolving over time in response to a mix of internal and external changes. The measure of their impact, as with their broader industrial welfare measures and company culture, has already been examined to some degree through the industrial relations record at BACo's, and later Alcan's, Highland smelters. However, it is also abundantly evident in the preceding pages of this chapter, not least through how residents and former employees perceived and responded to attempts at control in the villages. However the legacy of the 'BA' version, and particularly 'Our Highland Story', is glaringly evident, fashioning the recollections of employees and residents, carried down also in time-honoured fashion through word of mouth.

At its most profound level, British Aluminium's social control appears to have lodged a deep-seated dependency in sections of these communities; visible both in the real sense of bereavement evident after the merger with Alcan, and an expectation that the company would continue to provide. Until the 1940s this was reinforced by the civic vacuum left in the Highlands by the absence of the state, and by BACo's enlisting and wooing of regional elites. Aside from ulterior motives – and despite shortcomings – it was also aided by a genuine commitment on the part of the company to improving living conditions for its residents and employees, set against poor housing infrastructure in the region. This was illustrated by the choice of Frank Mears as the lead architect for Inverlochy, and identification with reformers and more progressive elements within regional elites. For example, aside from being a powerful political figure in the region, Sir Francis Walker had campaigned to improve housing in the region and had backed the formation of the NSHEB.

The hold of the company over these locations was diluted with the profound social and cultural changes that took hold in Britain in the latter half of the twentieth century. Where the state had been largely absent, by the 1950s it was far more evident in these locations. Control and consent were also undermined by the superior attitudes displayed and betrayed by some staff and their spouses at the Highland works. Real change arrived also with the takeover of BACo by RTIA, and the profound cultural shift (although not always visible to the casual observer) within the company signalled by TI's Ivan Stedeford, not least with the complete reorganisation of the management structures at the Highland reduction works and a greater degree of redefined and centralised business objectives. Thus while Alcan may have been the recipient of the adverse publicity, the tactical withdrawal of the company from the level of participation in these communities seen hitherto had started far earlier. Nevertheless British Aluminium continued to be of great importance in local social and economic networks after the Second World War, supporting social and cultural activities, and contributing significantly to economic growth. Even prior to post-war changes the local communities and workforce – such as in 1936 – had reminded the company of its social contract, signalling that even if people in these locations could appear to the visitor as being immensely deferential, when they wished to residents could effect change.

The conflict evident in the voices of the residents and former employees reflects attempts to make sense of these profound changes to a world in which the company had offered certainty. At the same time these testimonies recognise the level of the control exercised by the company, and the socialisation of the young by the social code, in these villages. The demise of those certainties is tinged with sadness among some, and ambivalence by others. BACo's legacy is reflected in the endurance of the company's historical narrative absorbed within residents' testimonies, and the means of regulating behaviour in the village to this day is through the network of residents.

Conclusion

Though the historical provenance of the Old Testament story of the feast of the Babylonian King Belshazzar has long since been rejected, the use of the 'writing on the wall' as a warning to those overlooking foreboding signs has permeated common parlance.[1] Certainly it is a fitting allegory for the native UK aluminium industry and in particular for that of its leading company, British Aluminium, for much of the twentieth century. That an integrated native British aluminium industry has managed to survive into the twenty-first century is remarkable. As the industry's pre-eminent observer Donald Wallace noted of the UK in the late 1930s, it lacked the necessary preconditions to sustain a commercially viable primary aluminium industry (only a handful of global producers did), while economists and policymakers in Edinburgh and London from the closing years of the Second World War onwards periodically questioned the long-term commercial viability of maintaining primary aluminium production in Britain. However the past three decades have wrought dramatic changes on the global industry, with many of the 'first movers' and 'pioneers' either moving into energy markets and divesting themselves of other upstream and downstream assets, or, more commonly, being absorbed into the assets of global conglomerates in the minerals and metals, and power clusters. These were often companies with little feel for the heritage of the industry.

There is also no doubt that the immense political acumen, financial management and strategic outlook of Andrew Wilson Tait – a figure who receives little acclaim in the corporate history, if much recognition of his role as a 'business doctor' in the revival of the fortunes of a number of large British companies – played a significant role in turning the fortunes of British Aluminium around at a pivotal time in the company's history. That he has remained relatively absent from the history of that company, aside from the lack of attention paid to the British industry, owes much to the company narrative, which for reasons of its own focused attentions on the 'heroic' engineers and scientists like Sir William Murray Morrison, and Lord Kelvin. Despite their evident failures in corporate governance, the entrepreneurial drive of Emmanuel Ristori and Roger Wallace – who paid the price in terms of personal bankruptcy by risking everything on an industry they saw an opening for – also deserve their recognition.

That British Aluminium survived its turbulent infancy and early corporate mismanagement, in such a capital-intensive industry, was largely a result of political developments arising from the growing strategic importance of the metal after the First World War, as well as the exponential rise in demand for the metal. The significance of this metal in the conduct of modern warfare for the vital period between the First World War and the late 1950s – from the allied and imperial munitions crisis of 1915 until the hydrogen age – cannot be overstated, despite criticisms that this was driven by the misinformation of the industry, particularly in relation to military aircraft production, in some developed economies. This marriage of convenience with the state, which initially sustained the industry with political support, Treasury loans and orders, gradually soured into a fractious co-existence, in which neither party was satisfied with the other. BACo was increasingly manipulated, while its Canadian counterpart prospered with the aid of the UK government who could not longer rely on the native industry to meet its strategic requirements. The continued, and misplaced, faith in government, despite the changed circumstances, was most evident in the negotiations of wartime prices and Treasury loans, as well as over the Volta River Project, but most brutally exposed during the 'aluminium war'. More profoundly, its effects were to be seen in the 'behavioural lock-in' of the firm, compounded by the recruitment of retired senior military officers and civil servants to the board (bringing with them their values shaped by the social milieu from which they were drawn), organisational learning and corporate culture. The observation of leading historian of empire, John M. Mackenzie, that 1959 proved a watershed for Britain, and what remained of its empire – after which the 'winds of change' metaphorically blew through Whitehall, every bit as much as Africa, shattering the 'cultural illusion' that had sustained the idea of empire, against all the competing evidence in the 1940s and 50s – serves as somewhat of an allegory for British Aluminium, that most patrician and imperial-minded of concerns. Despite a palpable shift in outlook after the RTIA takeover, shortcomings in senior management, and their unhealthy proximity and obeisance to government, were further glaringly revealed over the fateful negotiations over the Invergordon smelter. Like metropolitan Britain's recurring cultural attachment to the nostalgia of empire and potency of imperial rhetoric throughout the late twentieth century, so too BACo's attachment to the state and the tenets of loyalty and order – embodied in the 'service', with its corporate culture and traditions, including the company's historical narrative – endured.[2] The disastrous results in the long term were evident for all to see in the judgments taken during the Invergordon smelter negotiations. Nonetheless, Reynolds and TI's period of stewardship of BACo did oversee a dramatic reorganisation with a move to more fixed multi-divisional structure staffed by professional management, as well as presiding over an improvement of the company's finances, so that the business that merged with Alcan in 1982 was radically altered from the 'service' it had been. As such – and in conjunction with the evidence that has emerged from studies of defence contractors – BACo's relationship with the state casts light on an area of business-government relations in strategic raw materials sectors that are worthy of renewed or new attention, particularly as this subject has become *au courant* once again. Linked to this are the effects of these exogenous relationships on the culture of the firm and corporate governance.

To many within the company, as well as outside observers, the perception was that it remained a quintessentially patrician British institution. This was due in no small part to RTIA's recognition of the desirability and allure of aspects of the 'BA' culture, not least its historical narrative. BACo's public persona was inextricably linked to its portrayal of itself as a 'pioneer', 'social benefactor' and 'key industry'. Yet while elements of this were justified, they were all part of its *lingua franca* deployed to great effect in fostering political alliances and as part of its labour management strategies; like the creation of a national identity, 'crystallised around the notion of a common ancestry, language and history',[3] it aimed to create a 'community of interest' bound by tenets of 'service' and 'loyalty', with Sir William Murray Morrison as the *pater familias*. The changed emphasis in company culture under RTIA, signalled by Ivan Stedeford's declaration in the Spring 1959 edition of *The B.A. News*, recognised that for this to retain its currency as an effective labour management tool, it would have to confer on employees the rights (and responsibilities) of full 'citizens'. And yet, the value of BACo's historical narrative as a tool for promoting consensus and encouraging loyalty was recognised by both RTIA and Alcan. It is also hoped that this book sheds light on the great potential offered by oral history (critically as an interpretive, as well as reconstructive, tool) and broader narrative analysis as a means of enlightening and enriching studies of organisational culture; these are methods much overlooked by within business studies, including the history of the firm, in the UK.[4]

British Aluminium's strategic outlook and strategies at a UK, Scottish, regional and local level, were also forged by the politics of regional development, with the company carefully cultivating regional elites and political campaigners to consolidate its position in the Highlands and counteract criticisms of its activities, such as those of conservationists. This was not only crucial in maintaining support for its Highland presence, but also because the region became the jewel in the crown of the company's historical narrative. It was one decorated with the popular emblems of Highland history, in order to inure 'consent' among their workforce in their smelters. The organisation's culture was also shaped by the feedback of the 1910 and 1936 strikes. It was a lesson that Alcan was forced to relearn after the 1990 strike. Fealty was achieved only through recognition of a social contract, which required nurturing. The results were visible from the generally civil tone of industrial relations at the plants – invaluable for such a capital-intensive industry, and a company so sensitive to its public reception – and, whatever the final outcome, in aiding it to secure Scottish Office and Board of Trade support in the campaign to secure the

Lochaber power house, 2005. © Alex Gillespie/RTA.

Invergordon site. Ultimately, the recent chequered past of the region – suffering the effects of peripherality, and government neglect (including inadequate infrastructure funding) – further aided the company in substantiating its claim to be benefactors to the region. Both before and after the formation of the HIDB, concerned by the potential loss of the industry in a region, which had suffered the effects of widespread migration, unemployment and rural poverty, as well as the importance of the metal as a strategic material, directly determined the response of policy makers, elites and even trade unionists towards health and environmental effects presented by the industry. Ironically, the same arguments over the introduction of industry to this 'contested terrain' have been resurrected periodically.[5] If the duplicity of the BACo senior management's commitment to community was revealed by the 'behind closed door' negotiations over industrial hazards, then the response of local managers at their Highland and Norwegian smelters to threats to human and animal health is testament to their divided loyalties to the communities in which they lived and the company they served. This and their long service, reveal much about the nature of industrial relations at the Highland plants. As over the conduct of industrial relations and the evaluation of health risks by key players, the endurance of the narrative owes much also to the historical context of social and economic conditions in the Highlands, and the sense of injustice felt by Highlanders at the perceived neglect of the region by successive political administrations until the formation of the HIDB. Certainly this does, in part, explain the receptiveness of key figures within the political elite, as well as development campaigners, to the company. It also explains the 'Hobson's choice' facing trade unionists, their members and the surrounding communities over health issues.

While the physical 'sites of memory' – whether the remaining smelter, hydro-electric schemes and the villages of Kinlochleven and Inverlochy – offer a lasting reminder of the prominence of the industry in the Highlands at one time, the enduring legacy of the 'BA' has been the almost religious devotion reserved for it among some local residents and former employees seen in the oral testimony, replicating the company narrative. This is reflected in the catechism of the 'BA' version, and aided by tributes such as these:

> Behind the mining of bauxite, the production of alumina, the reduction to aluminium and the various fabricating processes are the men and women who have made possible this history of industrial achievement. We salute the original pioneers and all those who came after them, secure in the knowledge that future historians will confirm our early appraisal.[6]

As with Morrison's private entreaties to Grant and Lochiel, the powerful potential of this is to be found in the 'cultural circuit' that shaped collective memories and informed personal identity. The perverse effect of this, however, has been seen in the profound impact that the disappearance – whether at Foyers, Invergordon, Kinlochleven, and other former BACo sites – has had psychologically. For while the extension of public utilities and services gradually took over what had previously been provided by the company in the west Highlands, or new industries gradually came into these areas – such as the bio-fuel and fabrication companies on the site of the former smelter at Invergordon – the sense of bereavement or betrayal, compounded by the deeply ingrained traditions and narrative of the BA, among former employees and local residents is often palpable. These localised experiences mirror the experiences of thousands of communities who have experienced the wake of the global movements of capital and industry. These narratives of local residents reflect a 'critical nostalgia', which is both alive to the shortcomings of the workplace and village life while also reflecting the profound loss at the disintegration of the communities and workplace networks and loyalties they also cherished.

Seen from the perspective of the twenty-first century, there is no denying the very

The 'crucible' of the modern British aluminium industry: Foyers factory building, 2009. © Andrew Perchard.

real benefits that the British aluminium industry also brought to the Highlands – if not to other parts of the globe where it placed its flag – and its importance globally, nationally and locally, directly and indirectly. Sir William Murray Morrison was certainly being duplicitous when he declared to Lachlan Grant in 1936 that he was pleased to have been able to effect some 'practical and lasting good' for his 'beloved Highlands'. And yet the lasting legacy of these buildings, as well as the company's narrative and political strategies, are symbolically and materially vested in those words of one of the company's long-service Highland employees, Sandy Walker: 'were it not for Lord Kelvin and his compatriots, who initialised the building of the Foyers smelter and started this thing off, where would I have been today?'[7]

Lochaber smelter from the air, 2005. © Alex Gillespie/RTA.

Notes

Glossary

1   I. Grinberg, *L'aluminium: Un si léger metal* (Gallimard: Paris, 2003).
2   *Ibid.*, p. 58.

Introduction

1   R. S. Tarr, 'The Scottish Highlands', *Bulletin of the American Geographical Society*, vol. 40, no. 12 (1908), pp. 743–4.
2   British Aluminium Company Ltd (BACo), *The History of the British Aluminium Company Limited 1894–1955* (BACo: London, 1955) [hereafter BACo, *History*], pp. 33–4.
3   P. MacGill, *Children of the Dead End*, (Birlinn: Edinburgh, 2001), pp. 221–2, 237.
4   W. M. Morrison, 'Aluminium and Highland water power', *17th Autumn lecture to the Institute of Metals* (1939), pp. 33–4, 466–7; Aluminium-Pechiney, 'Dossier-Grande Bretagne, Collection Historique Pechiney', Institut pour l'histoire d'aluminium (IHA), IHA-502/1-8-51292; I. Grinberg and F. Hachez-Leroy (eds), *Industrialisation et sociétés en Europe occidentale de la fin du XIXe siècle à nos jours* (Armand Colin: Paris, 1997), Table 3; P. L. Payne, *The Hydro: A study of the development of the major hydro-electric schemes undertaken by the North of Scotland Hydro-Electric Board* (Aberdeen University Press (AUP): Aberdeen, 1988), p. 6.
5   BACo, *History*, p. 34.
6   *Royal Commission on the Poor Laws and Relief of Distress, Vol. IX: Minutes of Evidence*, PP, 1910 (c.5068), Q. 37 (Mr Charles Cleveland Ellis, Local Government Board for Scotland, 14 January 1908), Qs 90365–6 (Mr James Ferguson, Indoor Asst. Inspector of Poor for Glasgow Parish Council, 20 January 1908), and appendix no. CXVIII (Statement of evidence by Rev. Duncan Cameron, Minister of the Parish of Bridge of Allan); M. J. F. Gregor and R. M. Crichton, *From Croft to Factory: The evolution of an industrial community in the Highlands* (John Nelson & Co: Edinburgh, 1946), pp. 22–5; N. Kirk, *Custom and Conflict in the 'Land of the Gael': Ballachulish, 1900–1910* (Merlin: Trowbridge, 2007), p. 95; J. E. Handley, *The Navvy in Scotland* (Cork University Press: Cork, 1970), pp. 78–9.
7   'Gigantic enterprise. Electricity form Highland glens', *Otago Witness*, iss. 2844, 16 September 1908, p. 40. For details of Highland settlement in New Zealand see: T. Brooking, '"Tam McCanny and Kitty Clydeside" – The Scots in New Zealand', in R. A. Cage (ed.), *The Scots Abroad: Labour, capital, enterprise, 1750–1914* (Croom Helm Ltd: Beckenham, 1985),

pp. 156–90.

8 *The Engineer*, 25 April and 29 May 1930; Morrison, 'Aluminium and Highland water power'; Payne, *The Hydro*, pp. 6–12.

9 E. Ristori, Notes on the formation of the British Aluminium Company Ltd, 1 May 1894, Rio Tinto Alcan collection, Glasgow University Archives (GUA), UGD 347/21/46/2; *The B.A. News*, vol. 2, no. 2 (March–April 1949), pp. 8–9, UGD 347/21/33/3; E. Storli, 'The Norwegian Aluminium Industry, 1908–1940: Swing producers in the hands of the international oligopoly?', *Cahiers d'histoire de l'aluminium (CHA)*, special issue 2 (2007), pp. 11–28; J. Bocquetin, 'La fabrication de l'aluminium par électrolyse', in P. Morel (ed.), *Histoire technique de la production d'aluminium* (Presses Universitaires de Grenoble: Grenoble, 1992), pp. 21–57; British Market Research Board (BMRB), 'The image of Alcan and aluminium: Report of two surveys', December 1967, UGD 347/6/5/3; Alcan, Primary Metals Europe, *Lochaber Smelter. Environmental Statement 2005 Update* (Alcan: Fort William, 2006), p. 3; World Aluminium, output figures for western Europe, 2003–2005, see: http://www.world-aluminium.org/iai/stats/formServer.asp?form=1 [accessed 3 May 2007].

10 Alexander was misinformed about some of these works' start-up dates, with initial production commencing at Foyers in 1896 and Kinlochleven in 1907: Sir K. Alexander, 'The Highlands and Islands Development Board', in R. Saville (ed.), *The Economic Development of Modern Scotland, 1950–1980* (Edinburgh University Press: Edinburgh, 1985), p. 224; A. Young, 'Industry', in A. Hetherington (ed.), *Highlands and Islands: A generation of progress, 1965–1990* (AUP: Aberdeen, 1990), p. 106.

11 *Report to the Board of Agriculture for Scotland on Home Industries in the Highlands and Islands*, PP, 1914 (c.7564), p. 143.

12 D. I. Mackay and N. K. Buxton, 'The North of Scotland economy: A case for redevelopment?', *Scottish Journal of Political Economy*, vol. 12, no. 4 (1965), p. 23.

13 Quoted in Hetherington, *Highlands and Islands*, p. xv.

14 British Alcan, Pension Data, 1983; *Census*, 1981: http://census.ac.uk/casweb [accessed 12 March 2007]; Highlands and Islands Development Board (HIDB), *15th Annual Report* (1980), Table 3, App. 4; HIDB, *16th Annual Report* (1981), Table 2, App. 4; HIDB, *17th Annual Report* (1982), Table 2, App. 3; HIDB, *18th Annual Report* (1983), Table 3, App. 3.

15 Testimony of Mr Colin Young to the Committee reviewing evidence on the Lochaber Water Power Bill, 1921, UGD 347/21/24/5/11.

16 J. M. Brock, *The Mobile Scot: A study of emigration and migration 1861–1911* (John Donald: Edinburgh, 1999), Tables 2.6, 2.7.

17 M. Harper, *Emigration from Scotland between the Wars: Opportunity or exile?* (Manchester University Press (MUP): Manchester, 1998), pp. 6, 71–108.

18 Scottish Economic Committee (SEC), *The Highlands and Islands of Scotland. A review of the economic conditions with recommendations for improvement* (HMSO: Edinburgh, 1938), p. 132; Gregor and Crichton, *From Croft to Factory*, pp. 25–9; T. M. Devine, 'Temporary migration and the Scottish Highlands in the nineteenth century', *The Economic History Review* [hereafter *EHR*], vol. 32, no. 3 (August 1979), p. 347.

19 SEC, *The Highlands and Islands of Scotland*, p. 131; R. Saville, 'The industrial background to the post-War Scottish economy', in Saville (ed.), *The Economic Development of Modern Scotland*, Table 1(b); A. K. Cairncross (ed.), *The Scottish Economy: A statistical account of Scottish life by members of the staff of Glasgow University* (Cambridge University Press (CUP): Cambridge, 1954), Table 58.

20 D. H. Anderson, *Aluminium for Defense and Prosperity* (Public Affairs Institute: Washington, 1951), p. 3.

21 Grinberg and Hachez-Leroy, *Industrialisation et sociétés*, pp. 18–19, 95–105, 127–42.

22 D. Edgerton, *Warfare State: Britain, 1920–1970* (CUP: Cambridge, 2005); G. C. Peden, *Arms, Economics and British Strategy: From dreadnoughts to hydrogen bombs* (CUP: Cambridge, 2007).

23 For discussions of these points see: M. Kipping, 'Business–government relations: Beyond performance issues', in F. Amatori and G. Jones (eds), *Business History around the World* (CUP: Cambridge, 2003), pp. 391, 372–93; S. J. D. Green and R. C. Whiting (eds), *The Boundaries of the State in Modern Britain* (CUP: Cambridge, 1996).

24 B. Cross, 'White metal: Labour, capital, and the land, under multinational aluminum corporations in Guyana and Jamaica', paper to the Global Economic History of Bauxite Workshop, Fondation Maison des Sciences de l'Homme, 21–24 September 2008.

25 For examples see bibliography and references.

26 BACo, *History*; D. C. Campbell, *Global Mission: The story of Alcan, Volume I to 1950* (Alcan: Ontario, 1985); D. C. Campbell, *Global Mission: The story of Alcan, Volume II* (Alcan: Ontario, 1989); D. C. Campbell, *Global Mission: The story of Alcan, Volume III and Index* (Alcan: Ontario, 1990); For a discussion of developments in company histories, see: D. Coleman, 'The uses and abuses of business history', *Business History*, vol. 39, no. 2 (April 1987), pp. 141–56.

27 L. Cailluet, 'The British aluminium industry, 1945–80s: Chronicles of a death foretold?', *Accounting, Business and Financial History (ABFH)*, vol. 11, iss. 1 (2001), pp. 79–97.

28 *Ibid.*; M. Knauer, 'The "Golden Years": The European Aluminium Industry during the postwar economic boom', CHA, Special Issue 1 (2003), pp. 11–13; I. Grinberg, 'Introduction: L'aluminium, matériau emblématique de la dexième industrialisation', in Grinberg and Hachez-Leroy, *Industrialisation et société*, p. 17; R. Lesclous, *Histoire des sites producteurs d'aluminium: Les choix stratégiques de Pechiney 1892–1992* (École des Mines: Paris, 1999), pp. 160–1.

29 R. Graham, *The Aluminium Industry and the Third World* (Zed Books: London, 1982).

30 E. A. Cameron, 'The Scottish Highlands as a Special Policy Area, 1886 to 1965', *Rural History*, vol. 8, no. 2 (1997), p. 204; G. C. Peden, 'The managed economy: Scotland, 1919–2000', in T. M. Devine, C. H. Lee and G. C. Peden (eds), *The Transformation of Scotland: The economy since 1700* (Edinburgh University Press (EUP): Edinburgh, 2005), p. 245.

31 L. Hannah, *Engineers, Managers and Politicians: The first fifteen years of nationalised electricity supply in Britain* (Macmillan: London, 1982), pp. 149–50.

32 J. Hunter, *Last of the Free: A millennial history of the Highlands and Islands of Scotland* (Mainstream: Edinburgh, 1999), p. 356; See also J. Miller, *The Dam Builders: Power from the glens* (Birlinn: Edinburgh, 2002), pp. 15, 16; J. Macleod, *Highlanders: A history of the Gaels* (Sceptre: London, 1996), pp. 294–5.

33 D. Turnock, *Patterns of Highland Development* (Macmillan: London, 1970);*Idem, Industrial Britain: The New Scotland* (David & Charles: Newton Abbot, 1979), pp. 30, 94–102, 121, 128.

34 Payne, *The Hydro*; L. Hannah, *Electricity before Nationalisation: A study of the development of The Electricity Supply Industry in Britain to 1948* (Macmillan: London, 1979), p. 173; Hannah, *Engineers, Managers and Politicians*, pp. 149–50.

35 For example: A. Perchard, '"Of the highest Imperial importance": British strategic priorities and the politics of colonial bauxite, c.1915–1958', in R. Gendron, M. Ingulstad and E. Storli (eds), *Bauxite, State, and Society in the Twentieth Century* (University of British Columbia Press: Vancouver, forthcoming 2012); A. Perchard, 'A marriage of convenience? The British Government and the UK aluminium industry in the twentieth century', in H. O. Frøland and M. Ingulstad (eds), *From Warfare to Welfare State: Business–Government relations*

in the Aluminium Industry (Tapir Akademisk Forlag: Trondheim, forthcoming, 2012); N. G. MacKenzie, 'Be careful what you wish for: Comparative advantage and the Wilson Smelters Project, 1967–82', in some edited collections.

36 A. D. Chandler, Jr., *Scale and Scope: The dynamics of industrial capitalism* (Belknap: Cambridge, MA, 1990), *passim*; M. E. Porter, *Competitive Advantage: Creating and sustaining superior performance* (Palgrave: London, 1998), pp. 37–40, 69–175, 499–507; J. Zeitlin, 'Productive alternatives: Flexibility, governance, and strategic choice in industrial history', in F. Amatori and G. Jones (eds), *Business History around the World* (CUP: Cambridge, 2003), pp. 62–82.

37 For criticisms of precisely such approaches see: G. M. Hodgson, *How Economics forgot History: The problem of historical specificity in social science* (Routledge: London, 2001).

38 For criticisms of the treatment of these factors traditionally as 'externalities' by economists and business historians see: R. Warren and G. Tweedale, 'Business ethics and business history: Neglected dimensions in management education', *British Journal of Management*, vol. 13 (2002), pp. 209–19; C. M. Rosen, 'The business–environment connection', *Environmental History*, vol. 10, no. 1 (2005), p. 75; P. Nora, *Realms of Memory: The construction of the French past, Vol. 3: Symbols* (Columbia University Press: New York, 1998).

39 *The Observer*, 18 January 2009.

40 A. Portelli, *The Death of Luigi Trastulli and Other Stories: Form and meaning in oral history* (State University of New York (SUNY): New York, 1991), p. 51.

41 *Ibid.*, p. 50.

42 A. Thomson, 'Anzac memories: putting popular memory theory into practice in Australia', in R. Perks and A. Thomson (eds) *The Oral History Reader*, (Routledge: London, 2002), pp. 300–2.

43 Portelli, *The Death of Luigi Trastulli and Other Stories, passim*.

44 J. K. Conway, *When Memory Speaks: Reflections on autobiography* (Knopf: New York, 1998), p. 7.

45 J. G. Bullen, 'Aluminium', in C. A. Oakley (ed.), *Scottish Industry: An account of what Scotland makes and where she makes it* (Scottish Council Development and Industry (SCDI): Edinburgh, 1953), p. 163.

46 B. Marsden and C. Smith, *Engineering Empires: A cultural history of technology in nineteenth-century Britain* (Palgrave Macmillan: Basingstoke, 2005), p. 1.

47 L. Abrams and C. G. Brown, 'Introduction', in L. Abrams and C. G. Brown (eds), *A History of Everyday Life in Twentieth-Century Scotland* (EUP: Edinburgh, 2010), p. 1.

Chapter 1: Aluminium in the UK

1 S. Moos, 'The structure of the British aluminium industry', *The Economic Journal*, vol. 58, no. 232 (December 1948), p. 524.

2 D. H. Wallace, 'Aluminium', in W. Y. Elliott, E. S. May, J. W. F. Roew, A. Skelton and D. H. Wallace (eds), *International Control in the Non-Ferrous Metals* (Macmillan: New York, 1937), p. 229.

3 Chandler, *Scale and Scope*, pp. 231, 242, 600.

4 Cailluet, 'The British aluminium industry, 1945–80s', pp. 94–6; R. E. Utiger, 'The British Aluminium Company, Ltd, 1945 to 1978', lecture notes, 27 April 1981, UGD 347/21/46/24.

5 D. H. Wallace, *Market Control in the Aluminium Industry* (CUP: Cambridge, 1937), pp. 6, 36–68; M. J. Peck, *Competition in the Aluminium Industry 1945–1958* (Harvard University Press (HUP), Cambridge MA, 1961), pp. 1–20; J. A. Stuckey, *Vertical Integration and Joint*

Ventures in the Aluminium Industry (HUP: Cambridge MA, 1983), *passim*; Chandler, *Scale and Scope*, pp. 279–80, 321; A. Heertje, *Schumpeter on the Economics of Innovation and the Development of Capitalism* (Edward Elgar (EE): Cheltenham, 2005), pp. 5–9.

6   Lesclous, *Histoire des sites producteurs d'aluminium*, Tables 24, 82; Stuckey, *Vertical Integration and Joint Ventures*, Table 2.8; R. F. Mikesell and J. W. Whitney, 'An overview of the world mining industry', in C. Schmitz (ed.), *Big Business in Mining and Petroleum* (EE: Cheltenham, 1995), pp. 3–6, 32; C. Schmitz, 'The rise of big business in the world copper industry 1870–1930', *EHR*, second series, vol. 39, no. 3 (1986), pp. 392–410; Peck, *Competition in the Aluminium Industry*, pp. 8–17.

7   Wallace, 'Aluminium', pp. 213–14; F. Hachez-Leroy, *L'Aluminium français: L'invention d'un marché 1911–1983* (CNRS: Paris, 1999); M. Knauer, 'Une industrie née de la guerre. L'aluminium en Allemagne de 1890 à 1950', in Grinberg and Hachez-Leroy, *Industrialisation et sociétés*, pp. 127–238; E. Hexner, *International Cartels* (Pitman: London, 1946), pp. 216–21; Peck, *Competition in the Aluminium Industry*; G. Jones, 'Multinationals from the 1930s to the 1980s', in A. D. Chandler, Jr. and B. Mazlich (eds), *Leviathans: Multinational Corporations and The New Global History* (CUP: Cambridge, 2005), p. 85.

8   Lesclous, *Histoire des sites producteurs d'aluminium*, p. 22 and Table 1; R. Gagni and C. Nappi, 'The cost and technological structure of aluminium smelters worldwide', *Journal of Applied Econometrics*, vol. 15 (2000), p. 419; F. G. Johnson, 'Hydro-electric power in the UK: Past performance and potential for future development', *Institute of Electrical Engineers Proceedings*, vol. 133, no. 3 (April 1986), pp. 110–11.

9   Gagni and Nappi, 'The cost and technological structure of aluminium smelters worldwide', pp. 428–9; Lesclous, *Histoire des sites producteurs d'aluminium*, Figs 14, 15; R. Lesclous, 'Nuclear power and the revival of primary aluminium production in Europe', *CHA*, special issue 1, pp. 29–36.

10 Porter, *Competitive Advantage*, pp. 37–40, 69–175, 499–507; Chandler, *Scale and Scope*, pp. 33–45, 235, 250–2; D. F. Channon, *The Strategy and Structure of British Enterprise* (Macmillan: London, 1973), p. 75; L. Hannah, *The Rise of the Corporate Economy* (Methuen: London, 1976), *passim*; M. Roper, *Masculinity and the British Organisation Man since 1945* (Oxford University Press: Oxford, 1989), pp. 54, 142.

11 Rosen, 'The business–environment connection'; Warren and Tweedale, 'Business ethics and business history'; T. Gourvish 'Introduction: the business–government relationship', in T. Gourvish (ed.), *Business and Politics in Europe 1900–1970: Essays in honour of Alice Teichova* (CUP: Cambridge, 2003), p. 1; N. Rollings, 'British business history: A review of the periodical literature for 2005', *Business History*, vol. 49, no. 3 (2007), p. 278.

12 C. A. Russell and S. A. H. Wilmot, 'Metal Extraction and Refining', in C. A. Russell (ed.), *Chemistry, Society and Environment: A new history of the British Chemical Industry* (The Royal Society of Chemistry: Cambridge, 2000), pp. 311–18; A. Perchard, 'A "Micawber-like" undertaking? Innovation, Intrigue, Entrepreneurship and "Dynamic Capabilities" in the early British aluminium industry', *CHA* 46–7 (2011).

13 Memo and articles of association of the British Aluminium Company Ltd, 5 May 1894, UGD 347/21/1/1; Notes on the formation of the British Aluminium Company Ltd, 1 May 1894; BACo, Register of Directors and Managers, 1894–1948, UGD 347/21/5/1; Register of applicants for membership of the Institution of Civil Engineers, 1888 – Dr Emmanuel Ristori, Institute of Civil Engineers Library; *92nd Annual General Meeting of the Royal Astronomical Society*, February 1912, 251–2; J. T. W. Echewari, 'Aluminium and some of its uses', *Journal of the Institute of Metals* vol. 1, no. I (1909), p. 146; Morrison, 'Aluminium and Highland water power', p. 459; Chandler, *Scale and Scope*, pp. 280–1.

14 Crewdson, Youatt & Howard report to BACo Board of Directors on expenditure on fixed

capital costs at Foyers, Greenock, Larne and Milton, 25 March 1898, UGD 347/21/46/2; BACo, Chairman's report to the first AGM of British Aluminium shareholders, 16 July 1896, UGD 347/21/46/2; Average costs per ton of aluminium and average works costs for Foyers, 1896–1900, UGD 347/21/34/1/6.

15 G. Chappuis, *Le Chemin de Fer Électrique Martiny-Orsières* (no date c.1911–12), UGD 347/21/29/26; Report on Swiss Water Power Scheme by William Murray Morrison, 14 June 1906; Report by P. W. and C. S. Meik on the development of Orsières water power, 26 July 1906, UGD 347/21/46/2; BACo, Directors Report and Accounts for year ending 31 December 1910, UGD 347/21/6/3; BACo, Report of Directors to 9th Ordinary General Meeting (OGM), 5 July 1904, UGD 347/21/6/2; S. Kloumann, 'Pioneers in Norway – attraction of cheap water power', *The Times – Trade & Engineering*, March 1937, p. xxxiv; *The B.A. News*, vol. 7, no. 2 (March–April 1954), p. 2, UGD 347/21/33/6.

16 BACo, Chairman's speech to 3rd OGM, 28 July 1898; Report from William Murray Morrison to BACo Directors, 22 November 1905, UGD 347/21/46/2; Loch Leven Water & Electric Power Company, Minute books 1 and 2, 1906–1911, UGD 347/21/2/3–4; Letter from L. S. F. Charles, BACo, to D. W. F. Hardie, Imperial Chemical Industries Ltd, 21 January 1955, Maison-Alcan Rio Tinto Alcan Information Centre (RTAIC), 00158-08; 'Lochleven Water Power', *The Scotsman*, 6 July 1904; 'The development of the Aluminium Corporation, Ltd', *The Electrochemical and Metallurgical Industry*, vol. 7, no. 1 (January 1909), p. 165; Lesclous, *Histoire des sites producteurs d'aluminium*, graph 16; Hannah, *The Rise of the Corporate Economy*, pp. 19–22.

17 BACo, Chairman's report to 1st AGM, 16 July 1896; BACo, Chairman's report to 3rd OGM, 28 July 1898; D. C. Coleman and C. Macleod, 'Attitudes to new techniques: British businessmen, 1800–1950', *EHR*, second series, vol. 39, no. 4 (1986), pp. 588–611; M. E. Porter, *The Competitive Advantage of Nations* (Free Press: London, 1998), pp. 499–507; Chandler, *Scale and Scope*, pp. 250–2.

18 Departmental Committee on the Non-Ferrous Metals Trades (DC-NFMT), minutes of evidence: William Murray Morrison, 25 May 1917, TNA, BT 55/46; Letter from N. McPherson, Aluminium Corporation Ltd to L. V. Chilton, BACo, 'Dolgarrog Smelter Output', 27 March 1956, Maison-Alcan RTAIC, 00161-08; Letter from Chilton, BACo, to Hardie, ICI, 21 January 1955, Maison-Alcan RTAIC, 00161-08; M. A. Mariage, 'The use of aluminium wire in traction motors', *The Tramway and Railway World*, 4 May 1911, pp. 316–18; *The Engineer*, 13 October 1899; *The Electrician*, 26 October 1900; *Final Report of the Royal Commission on Coal Resources in the United Kingdom, Part X: Evidence* – Qs 23659–67 – Professor G. Forbes, electrical engineer, UK Parliamentary Papers, PP, 1904 (c.1917); Hannah, *Electricity before Nationalisation*; G. D. Smith, *From Monopoly to Competition: The transformations of ALCOA, 1888–1986* (CUP: Cambridge, 1988), pp. 91–3; J. M. Laux, *In First Gear: The French automobile industry to 1914* (Liverpool University Press: Liverpool, 1976), pp. 88–9, 207; R. Church, *The Rise and Decline of the British Motor Industry* (CUP: Cambridge, 1995), pp. 3–7; Hachez-Leroy, *L'Aluminium français*, p. 62.

19 A. Von Zeerleder, 'Harnessing Switzerland's water: Electrolytic method of production', *The Times Trade & Engineering*, March 1937, p. xx; Smith, *From Monopoly to Competition*, pp. 30–2, 49–81, 143, 153, 196–8; D. Cannadine, *Mellon: An American life* (Knopf: New York, 2006), pp. 96–9; M. Le Roux, 'Paul Héroult et son milieu. Des années de formation à «l'aluminium à bon marché»' and I. Grinberg 'Pechiney, pivot de la structuration de l'industrie de l'aluminium en France', in Grinberg and Hachez-Leroy, *Industrialisation et sociétés*, pp. 23–37.

20 Loch Leven Water & Electric Power Company, Minute books 1 and 2, 1904–1911, UGD 347/21/2/3–4; *Royal Commission on the Poor Laws and Relief of Distress, Vol. IX: Minutes of*

Evidence, PP, 1910, Q. 37, Qs 90365–6, Appendix CXVIII.

21 BACo, Directors' Reports and Accounts for 1912–1914, UGD 347/21/6/5–7; BACo, Register of Directors and Managers, 1894–1948; Notes on the British Aluminium Company Ltd, Maison-Alcan RTAIC, 00161-08; McPherson to Chilton, 27 March 1956; Chilton to Hardie, 21 January 1955; Grinberg and Hachez-Leroy, *Industrialisation et sociétés*, Annexes 1.1, 2.1; Storli, 'The Norwegian Aluminium Industry', pp. 11–28; J. Henden, H. O. Frøland and A. Karlsen (eds), *Globalisering gjennom et århundre: Norsk aluminiumindustri 1908–2008* (Fagbokforlaget: Oslo, 2008).

22 *The Times*, 19 July and 6 December 1911.

23 'The Affairs of Mr. Roger Wallace, K.C.', *The Times*, 17 December 1913; 'The Affairs of Mr. Roger Wallace', *The Times*, 15 January 1919.

24 *The Times*, 8 July 1903 and 6 December 1904; *Financial Times* (*FT*), 22 November 1902.

25 D. Matthews, 'The Business Doctors: Accountants in British management from the nineteenth century to the present day', *Business History*, vol. 40, no. 3 (1998), pp. 80, 85; J. R. Edwards, 'Tait, Andrew Wilson (1876–1930)', *Oxford Dictionary of National Biography* (*ODNB*), http://www.oxforddnb.com.ezproxy.webfeat.lib.ed.ac.uk/view/article/ 47710 [accessed 4 March 2008]; J. F. Wilson, *Ferranti and the British Electrical Industry, 1864–1930* (MUP: Manchester, 1988), p. 81.

26 E. Schatzberg, 'Symbolic culture and technological change: The cultural history of aluminium as an industrial material', *Enterprise and Society*, vol. 4, iss. 3 (2003), pp. 236–42.

27 G. Hardach, *The First World War 1914–1918* (Penguin: Harmondsworth, 1987), pp. 11–19, 21, 61; Knauer, 'Une industrie née de la guerre', in Grinberg and Hachez-Leroy, *Industrialisation et sociétés*, pp. 127–32.

28 L. Cailluet, 'L'impact de la Première Guerre mondiale et le rôle de l'État dans l'organisation de la branche et des enterprises', in Grinberg and Hachez-Leroy, *Industrialisation et sociétés*, pp. 95–105; Hardach, *The First World War*, pp. 88, 90.

29 Smith, *From Monopoly to Competition*, pp. 126–7; Campbell, *Global Mission, Vol. I*, p. 72.

30 Al. Corp. Ltd, Internal document – company history, RTAIC, 00031-21; Chilton to Hardie, 21 January 1955, RTAIC, 00158-08.

31 One reason for this may be that figures on the actual discrepancy between native production and consumption may well have been suppressed by the British government for strategic reasons: Grinberg and Hachez-Leroy, *Industrialisation et sociétés*, Annexes 1.1, 2.1.

32 Memo on the national importance of the aluminium industry from D. A. Bremner to Sir L. Llewlyn, Director of Materials, Ministry of Munitions of War, 31 August 1916, TNA, MUN 4/2046; *Report of the War Cabinet for 1918*, PP (c.325), p. 114.

33 BACo, Directors Report and Accounts for 1914–1917, UGD 347/21/6/7–10; Memo from Bremner to Llewelyn, 31 August 1916; Hardach, *The First World War*, Table 9.

34 S. Ritchie, *Industry and Air Power: The expansion of British aircraft production, 1935–1941* (Frank Cass: London, 1997), p. 65; C. McCombe, 'One hundred years of aluminium', *Aluminium: The First 100 Years – A Fuel and Metallurgical Journals Technical Supplement* (March 1986), pp. 4–6; Schatzberg, 'Symbolic culture and technological change', pp. 81–2; Wallace, 'Aluminium', p. 234.

35 BACo, Lochaber Water Power Bill 1921 – proof of Andrew Wilson Tait; C. Trebilcock, '"Spin-Off" in British economic history: Armaments and industry, 1760–1914', *EHR*, new series, vol. 22, no. 3 (December 1969), pp. 474–90.

36 *Statement of receipts in respect of surplus property held by Government Departments and disposed of, together with a statement of sales from 1st April to 30th June 1920*, PP (c.850), Appendix C.

37 Grinberg and Hachez-Leroy, *Industrialisation et sociétés*, Annexes 1.1, 2.1; Wallace,

'Aluminium', pp. 234–7.

38 Letter from A. W. Tait to L. Marlio, 18 November 1918; Letter from L. Marlio to A. W. Tait, undated but reply written around same time, Alcan-Paris 001-0-11335; E. Storli, *Out of Norway Falls Aluminium: The Norwegian aluminium industry in the international economy, 1908–1940* (Norwegian University of Science and Technology doctoral thesis: Trondheim, 2010), pp. 7, 111–15.

39 Wallace, 'Aluminium', p. 241.

40 Alliance Aluminium Company, Terms and conditions, 3 July 1931, Maison Alcan, Montréal RTAIC, 00021-26; British Aluminium Intelligence Report, Note on International Aluminium Cartel – International Cartels, Berlin Congress Publication no. 4 (IAC: Paris, 1937), IHA-00161-08; J. Hurtsfield, 'The control of British raw material supplies, 1919–1939', *EHR*, vol. 14, no. 1 (1944), pp. 10–21; M. Bertilorenzi, 'The International Aluminium Cartels, 1901–1939: The construction of international corporate business', I jordanas de historia empresarial: España y Europa, 11–12 December 2008; Grinberg and Hachez-Leroy, *Industrialisation et sociétés*, Annex 1.1; Wallace, 'Aluminium', pp. 261, 272–6; Hachez-Leroy, *L'Aluminium français*, pp. 218–20; Lesclous, *Histoire des sites producteurs d'aluminium*, figure 8; Campbell, *Global Mission, Vol. I*, pp. 421–2; Storli, *Out of Norway Falls Aluminium*, pp. 202–11 and 274; J. Fear, 'Cartels', in G. Jones and J. Zeitlin (eds), The Oxford Handbook of Business History (Oxford University Press: Oxford, 2007), pp. 268–92.

41 Perchard, 'Of the highest Imperial importance'; J. Henden, 'Stangfjordens Elektrokemiske Fabriker: The First and the Smallest Aluminium Smelter in Norway, *CHA* 41 (2008), pp. 95–121; Storli, 'The Norwegian Aluminium Industry', pp. 11–28.

42 BACo, Directors Reports and Accounts, 1927–1939, UGD 347/21/9/2; The North British Aluminium Company Ltd (NBACo), Minute book no. 1, 1924–1938, UGD 347/21/2/7; Notes on the British Aluminium Company Ltd, Maison-Alcan RTAIC, 00161-08; BACo, Minutes of Managers' Annual Conferences, 26 June 1935 and 23 November 1938, UGD 347/21/2/2; Moos, 'The structure of the British aluminium industry', pp. 530–2; Smith, *From Monopoly to Competition*, pp. 129–31, 171–3.

43 BACo, Proceedings at the 21st OGM, 31 March 1931.

44 Morrison, 'Aluminium and Highland water power', p. 468; Hannah, *Electricity before Nationalisation*, pp. 1–71; Payne, *The Hydro*, p. 9; Storli, *Out of Norway Falls Aluminium*, pp. 156–62.

45 BACo, Memo for consideration by counsel, H. P. Macmillan, K.C., Lochaber Water Power Bill 1921; Lochaber Water Power 1921 – Proof of Andrew Wilson Tait.

46 Lochaber Water Power Bill 1921, Evidence; HM Cabinet, Committee on the Lochaber Water Power Bill and the Grampian Electricity Supply Bill – Meeting between Sir Eric Geddes, Rt Hon Christopher Addison MP and Sir John Snell, 25 April 1921, National Archives (TNA), CAB 27/148.

47 NBACo, Minute Book, no. 1, 20 January 1925 and 16 March 1926; *Trade Facilities Acts, 1921–1924*, PP, 1924 (c.121).

48 NBACo, Minute Book, no. 1, 14 September 1926, 5 June 1928, 12 June 1928 and 25 June 1929; BACo, Extraordinary General Meeting, 21 November 1930; BACo, Proceedings of the 21st OGM, 28 March 1931; Morrison, 'Aluminium and Highland water power', p. 471.

49 *Ibid.*, pp. 474–5; Minutes of Meeting of the Coal Owners of Scotland, 26 December 1935, National Archives of Scotland (NAS), CB7/1/7; Payne, *The Hydro*, pp. 29–35, 292; Lee, *Scotland and the United Kingdom*, p. 156–8; A. F. Mutton, 'Hydro-Electric Power Development in Norway', *Transactions of the Institute of Geographers*, vol. 19 (1953), pp. 123–30.

50 Scottish Economic Committee, *The Highlands and Islands of Scotland. A review of the*

economic conditions for improvement [hereafter the *Hilleary Report*] (HMSO: Edinburgh, 1938), p. 48; *Minutes of evidence to Royal Commission on canals and waterways, Vol. III, 1907*, PP (c.3598), Evidence from: C. P. Hogg, 9 July 1907 (Qs 29610–40), Col. J. Denny, 10 July 1907 (Q. 2998), W. Murray Morrison, 10 July 1907 (Qs 30087–154), J. Macpherson Grant, 16 July 1907, Mackintosh of Mackintosh, 16 July 1907, and testimony of C. J. M. Macintosh, 23 July 1907; *Third report of Royal Commission into canals and inland navigation – minutes of evidence, 1909*, PP (c.4840), evidence of D. H. MacBrayne, 19 November 1907, and H. Duncan, 19 November 1907 (Q. 34900); Notes of evidence received from the Highland Development League, 19 November 1937 to 10 December 1937, Fisheries Board for Scotland, NAS, AF 62/1972/8; J. McGregor, *The West Highland Railway: Plans, politics and people* (John Donald: Edinburgh, 2005), pp. 151–2, 196, 244.

51 *Hilleary Report*, p. 35.

52 BACo, Directors Report and Accounts for 1936 and 1937; Notes of evidence received by the Committee on the Highlands and Islands, 19 November 1937 to 10 December 1937, Fisheries Board for Scotland.

53 Annexe I to cypher from Ministry of Aircraft Production (MAP) to British Air Commission, Washington, 2 September 1944, TNA, SUPP 3/82; BACo, Minutes of Managers Annual Conference, 20 June 1934; Campbell, *Global Mission, vol. I*, p. 161.

54 Memo from Rt Hon Walter Runciman to HM Cabinet, 'Anglo-Norwegian Negotiations', 11 April 1933, CAB 24/240; *Ottawa Agreements 1932*, PP (c.4174), p. 33; *Agreement between the United Kingdom and the Kingdom of Norway in relation to trade and commerce, 1932–33*, PP (c.4254), pp. 2, 22; *59th Statistical Abstract for British Dominions and Protectorates, 1934–35*, PP (c.4819), no. 105b – Exports of aluminium from Canada by markets; *27th Report of Commissioners of Customs and Excise for year ending 31 March 1936*, PP (c.5296), Table 83; *28th Report, Customs and Excise for year ending 31 March 1937*, PP (c.5573), Table 83; *29th Report, Customs and Excise for year ending 31 March 1938*, PP (c.5876), Table 83; P. T. Sandvik and E. Storli, 'Big business, market power and small nations: The Norwegian aluminium and nickel industry 1920–39', paper to the EBHA conference, Geneva, 2007; T. Rooth, *British Protectionism and the International Economy: Overseas commercial policy in the 1930s* (CUP: Cambridge, 1993), pp. 71–143.

55 BACo, Directors Reports and Accounts, 1931–1936; *Import Duties Advisory Committee – additional import duties*, PP, 1934 (c.4582), no. 16; *Import Duties (General Orders)*, PP, 1935–36 (c.5052), p. 34.

56 BACo, Minutes of Annual Managers' Meeting, 23 November 1938; 'Northern Aluminium Company Ltd: An Account of Its Growth, Equipment and Methods of Production', *Modern Metals* (November and December 1953); Campbell, *Global Mission, vol. I*, pp. 103–4; Smith, *From Monopoly to Competition*, p. 145; D. White, 'Competition among Allies: The North American Triangle and Jamaican Bauxite', *CHA*, special issue 2 (2007), pp. 39–52.

57 BACo, Directors Reports and Accounts, 1927–1939; *Scientific and Industrial Research*, PP, *1923–24* (c.2223), pp. 30, 33; *Scientific and Industrial Research, 1930–31*, PP (c.3789), p. 7; *Scientific and Industrial Research*, PP *1933–34* (c.4483), pp. 58, 90; BACo, Minutes of Managers' Annual Conferences, 20 June 1934; Hannah, *Electricity before Nationalisation*, pp. 118–19.

58 BACo, Minutes of Managers' Annual Conferences, 21 June 1932, 19 June 1934 and 25 June 1935, 4–6 November 1936 and 23 November 1938.

59 BACo, Minutes of Managers' Annual Meetings, 25 June 1935; Church, *The Rise and Decline of the British Motor Industry*, pp. 18, 32.

60 G. Boex, *The Aluminium Industry in Scotland* (IME: London, 1933), p. 58, GUA, BACo/Alcan library item 936.

61 *Ibid.*, p. 66.

62 BACo, Minutes of Managers' Annual Conferences, 4–6 November 1936 and 23 November 1938; J. Hurstfield, *The Control of Raw Materials* (HMSO: London, 1953), pp. 100–1.

63 S. Tolliday, *Business, Banking, and Politics: The case of British Steel, 1918–1939* (CUP: Cambridge, 1987), pp. 321, 323.

64 Memo from Sir F. Phillips to Sir R. Hopkins and Mr Barlow, 12 September 1936, SUPP 3/82.

65 Notes from A. Cairncross interview of Geoffrey Cunliffe, 25.6.40, AVIA 10/375.

66 Minutes of the Gold Coast Bauxite Co. Ltd, 30 May 1933 and 4 December 1940, UGD 347/21/2/14; Graham, *The Aluminium Industry and the Third World*, pp. 120–4; Perchard, 'Of the highest Imperial importance'.

67 'Obituary: Lt Col Stephen Pollen', *The Times*, 26 March 1935, 21; 'Funeral and Memorial Services: Lieutenant-Colonel S. H. Pollen', *The Times*, 29 March 1935, 19; R. P. T. Davenport-Hines, 'Pollen, Arthur Joseph Hungerford (1866–1937)' in D. J. Jeremy and C. Shaw (eds), *Dictionary of Business Biography: A Biographical Dictionary of Business Leaders Active in Britain in the Period 1860–1980, Volume 4* (Butterworths: London, 1986), pp. 753–8.

68 *The Times*, 1 July 1930, 26 April 1932, 21 September 1935, 23 December 1970; Wilson, *Ferranti and the British Electrical Industry*, p. 111.

69 Grinberg and Hachez-Leroy, *Industrialisation et sociétés*, Annexes 1.1, 2.1.

70 *Ibid.*, Annex 1.1; Knauer, 'Une industrie née de la guerre', in Grinberg and Hachez-Leroy, *Industrialisation et sociétés*, pp. 134–8; Knauer, 'The "Golden Years"', pp. 11–12; Cailluet, 'L'impact de la Première Guerre mondiale', in Grinberg and Hachez-Leroy, *Industrialisation et sociétés*, p. 100.

71 R. Petri, 'L'industrie italienne de l'aluminium à la veille de la Seconde Guerre Mondiale', in Grinberg and Hachez-Leroy, *Industrialisation et sociétés*, pp. 143–52; Knauer, 'Une industrie née de la guerre', in Grinberg and Hachez-Leroy, *Industrialisation et sociétés*, p. 137; Knauer, 'The "Golden Years"', pp. 11–12; M. Bertilorenzi, 'The Italian Aluminium Industry: Cartels, Multinationals and the Autarkic Phase, 1917–1943', CHA 41 (2008), pp. 42–71.

72 Knauer, 'Une industrie née de la guerre', in Grinberg and Hachez-Leroy, *Industrialisation et sociétés*, p. 138; Grinberg and Hachez-Leroy, *Industrialisation et sociétés*, Annex 1.2.

73 For details of the administration of control see: J. Backman and L. Fishman, 'British war time control of aluminium', *The Quarterly Journal of Economics*, vol. 56, no. 1 (November 1941), pp. 20–4.

74 Hurstfield, *The Control of Raw Materials*, pp. 37, 49, 63, 73, 100–1; M. M. Postan, *History of the Second World War: War production* (HMSO: London, 1952), pp. 38, 89–91; Ritchie, *Industry and Air Power*, pp. 65–6, 221, 232, 263.

75 Minutes of 11th meeting of Lord President's Committee of the War Cabinet, 26 July 1940, TNA CAB 139/15.

76 Cypher from UK High Commissioner (UKHC) in Canada to MAP, 19 August 1940; Telegram from UKHC in Canada to MAP, 26 September 1940, AVIA 46/457; MAP – Light Alloys and Magnesium Control, Report on arrangements for control of aluminium and magnesium and their alloys and the control of fabrication of those metals, 16 June 1941, TNA CAB 139/15; Hurstfield, *The Control of Raw Materials*, pp. 164, 172, 348–9.

77 This alludes to the famous assessment of Britain after the Second World War by US Secretary of State Dean Acheson who remarked that Britain had 'lost an Empire' and 'not yet found a role': A. Thompson, *The Empire Strikes Back? The impact of Imperialism on Britain from the mid-nineteenth century* (Pearson: London, 2005), pp. 205–16.

78 Organisation for Economic Co-operation and Development (OECD), *Problems and*

Prospects of the Primary Aluminium Industry (OECD: Paris, 1973), p. 69; Grinberg and Hachez-Leroy, *Industrialisation et sociétés*, Annexes 1.1, 2.1; Sir A. Cairncross, 'Economic policy and performance, 1945–1964', in R. Floud and D. McCloskey (eds), *The Economic History of Britain since 1700, Vol. 3: 1939–1972*, second edition (CUP: Cambridge, 1994), pp. 36–7; J. Tomlinson, *Democratic Socialism and Economic Policy: The Attlee Years 1945–1951* (CUP: Cambridge, 1997), pp. 31–5, 38; Knauer, 'The "Golden Years"', pp. 11–13.

79 HM Treasury, *Economic Survey for 1950*, PP (c.7915), paragraph 33; *Agreements between the Governments of the United Kingdom of Great Britain and Northern Ireland and the United States of America on Mutual Assistance in the supply of Steel, Aluminium and Tin, PP*, 18 January 1952 (c.8464).

80 Organisation for European Economic Co-operation, Non Ferrous Metals Committee (OEEC-NFMC), *Technical Reports – VI: Non-ferrous metals*, 10 February 1949, Chap. 2.

81 *Ibid.*; OEEC-NFMC, Report on possible reductions in 1952–53 of programmed dollar imports, Paris, 9 October 1949; OEEC, NFMT, Report on study of light metals, Paris, 10 October 1949, TNA, BT 64/3820.

82 BACo, Directors Reports and Accounts, 1946–1953; Ministry of Supply: Light Metals Division, United Kingdom Aluminium Industry: Progress from 1946 to 1953, 1 October 1953, TNA, SUPP 14/217.

83 Graham, *The Aluminium Industry and the Third World*, pp. 160–78; Lesclous, *Histoire des sites producteurs d'aluminium*, pp. 159–98.

84 BACo, Proceedings of the OGM, 29 March 1946; Hannah, *The Rise of the Corporate Economy*, Appendix 3, Table A.6.

85 BACo, Minutes of Managers' Annual Conferences, 15 May 1947; *Housing Return for Scotland*, PP, September 1951 (c.8390), Table F; *Housing Return for England and Wales*, PP, 31 December 1951 (c.8458), Table 9; *Fourth annual report of the British Transport Commission*, PP, 1951–52 (c.218), p. 148; *Seventh annual report of the British Transport Commission*, PP, 1955–56 (c.20-I), p. 35; M. Chick, *Industrial policy in Britain 1945–1951: Economic planning, nationalisation and the Labour governments* (CUP: Cambridge, 1998), pp. 40–4.

86 *Third report of the Select Committee on Estimates: Rearmament*, PP, 1950–51 (c.178), p. ix, and evidence of Sir Archibald Rowlands and Mr A. F. Dobbie-Bateman, 6 December 1950; *Tenth Report of the Select Committee on Estimates: Rearmament*, PP, 1951–52 (c.288), Evidence from Lt Gen. Sir Ronald Weeks; Sir Hew Kelner; and Messrs P. H. Muirhead and F. P. Laurens (all from Vickers Armstrong), 20 February 1952 (Qs 167–74); *Survey on Industry and Employment in Scotland*, PP, 1952 (c.8797), p. 47; BACo, *Aluminium Facts & Figures* (BACo: London, 1959), p. 3; *The B.A. News*, vol. 7, no. 5 (September–October 1955), pp. 16–17, UGD 347 21/33/6; *Noral News*, vol. 1, no. 2 (Spring 1951), p. 2; *Noral News*, vol. 6, no. 3 (Summer 1956), p. 28, UGD 347/10/16/7.

87 *7th Report and Statement of Accounts of the British Electricity Authority, 1954–55*, PP (c.72), pp. 29–30; *1st Report of the United Kingdom Atomic Energy Authority* (hereafter *UKAEA*) *for period from 19 July 1954–31 March 1955*, PP (c.95), pp. 12, 21; *UKAEA, 2nd report, 1 April 1955–31 March 1956*, PP (c.323), pp. 15, 19–20; BACo, Directors Reports and Accounts for 1954–1960; 'A is for Atom', *The B.A. News*, vol. 7, no. 5 (September–October 1955), pp. 7–9; *Noral News*, vol. 7, no. 4 (Autumn 1957), p. 15, UGD 347/10/16/7; Smith, *From Monopoly to Competition*, p. 261; L. Arnold, *Windscale 1957: Anatomy of a nuclear accident* (Palgrave: Hampshire, 2007), pp. 8, 14, 21; H. G. Cordero (ed.), *World's Non-Ferrous Smelters and Refineries* (IMM: London, 1950), p. 236.

88 Telegram from Governor's Deputy for North Borneo to the Secretary of State for the Colonies, 26 November 1951, CO 1022/265; Telegram from Secretary of State for Colonies to Governor of North Borneo, 1 December 1951, CO 1022/265; BACo, Minutes of Managers

Annual Meetings, 1948–1953; E. B. Wolfenden, 'Bauxite in Sarawak', *Economic Geology*, vol. 56, no. 5 (August 1961), pp. 972–81; *Volta River Aluminium Scheme*, PP, 1952 (c.8702); Graham, *The Aluminium Industry and the Third World*, pp. 147–9; Utiger, 'The British Aluminium Company Ltd'; BACo, Directors Report and Account for 1950; Perchard, 'Of the highest Imperial importance'; B. K. Campbell, 'Negotiating the Bauxite/Aluminium Sector under Narrowing Constraints', *Review of African Political Economy*, vol. 51 (July 1991), p. 33.

89 BACo, Directors Reports and Accounts, 1955–1959; Utiger, 'The British Aluminium Company, Ltd'.

90 Board of Trade (BoT), Scottish Development Group: Highlands and Islands Study, Future of the Highland Reduction Works of the British Aluminium Co. Ltd, 22 May 1964; BoT, Office for Scotland, Report of visit to Lochaber by R. S. Forsyth (BoT, Inverness office), 6 August 1964, NAS, SEP2/454/1; BACo, Minutes of Managers' Annual Conferences, 14 May 1947, 26 April 1948, and 25 April 1949; BACo, Directors Reports and Accounts, 1946–1953; Campbell, *Global Mission, Vol. II*, p. 480; BACo, Annual Report and Accounts, 1959.

91 BoT, Office for Scotland, Production & Export Section, Report on visits to Falkirk, 23 April 1956 and 18 March 1958, NAS, SEP2/539.

92 Utiger, 'The British Aluminium Company Ltd'.

93 *Ibid.*; R. Lesclous, 'What bauxite strategy? An overview of the different players and their behaviour from 1890 to the present', *CHA*, vol. 40 (2008), p. 25; Cailluet, 'The British aluminium industry', p. 80.

94 'The Aluminium Battlefield', *Time Magazine*, 19 January 1959; Perchard, 'Of the highest Imperial importance'; Graham, *The Aluminium Industry and the Third World*, pp. 160–78; N. Ferguson, *High Financier: The Lives and Time of Siegmund Warburg* (Penguin: London, 2011), pp. 185–6.

95 'La guerre de l'aluminium', *Nord Littoral (Calais)*, 1 December 1958; 'Kampf um Aluminium mit Dutzenden von Milliarden', *Le Nouveau Rhin Français*, 20 November 1958; F. Lincoln, 'How they took aluminium', *Life Magazine*, 15 July 1959; S. Hatch and M. Fores, 'The Struggle for British Aluminium', *Political Quarterly*, vol. 31, no. 4 (October–December 1960), pp. 477–87.

96 Lincoln, 'How they took aluminium'; Hatch and Fores, 'The Struggle for British Aluminium', Tables 2.b, 3; 'How Reynolds Won the Battle', *Business Week*, 17 January 1959; W. R. Grossman, 'Reynolds Metals Company', in A. Hurst (ed.), *International Directory of Company Histories, Vol. IV* (St James Press: Chicago and London, 1991), pp. 186–8; Hannah, *The Rise of the Corporate Economy*, Table A.6; Graham, *The Aluminium Industry and the Third World*, p. 163; White, 'Competition among Allies', pp. 39–49.

97 Lincoln, 'How they took aluminium'; Graham, *The Aluminium Industry and the Third World*, pp. 128, 138–9, 157, 163.

98 Lex, 'When was the Alcoa agreement signed?', *FT*, 1 December 1958.

99 Lincoln, 'How they took aluminium'; Cailluet, 'The British aluminium industry, 1945–80s', pp. 84–9.

100 D. Kynaston, *The City of London:, A club no more, 1945–2000* (Pimlico: London, 2002), p. 114.

101 *Ibid.*; Lincoln, 'How they took aluminium'; 'How Reynolds Won the Battle', *Business Week*; *The Economist*, 14 March 1959; 'Treasury Decision on British Aluminium Plans Soon', *FT*, 3 December 1958; 'The Aluminium Battlefield', *Time Magazine*, 19 January 1959; BBC Home Service, BBC TV and ITN, 'Third Offer' (1 January 1959, 7 a.m.), 'New Tube Investments Offer' (5 January 1959, 7 a.m.), 'British Aluminium's Decision' (9 January 1959, 6 & 7.25 p.m.), '80%' (9 January 1959, 6 & 7.25 p.m.), UGD 347/21/23/3; Statement from Lord Portal

to British Aluminium Shareholders, 5 December 1958, UGD 347/21/19/2; D. Richards, *Portal of Hungerford. The Life of Marshal of the Royal Air Force Viscount Portal of Hungerford KG, GCB, OM, DSO, MC* (Heinemann: London, 1977), p. 379.

102 *Ibid.*, pp. 374–9.

103 *Ibid.*, pp. 360–8; cf. Ferguson, *High Financier*, p. 187.

104 G. Jones and F. Bostock, 'U.S. Multinationals in British Manufacturing before 1962', *BHR*, vol. 70, no. 2 (Summer, 1996), pp. 207–56; *Hansard*, vol. 554, 20 June 1956, Cols 1431–1512; R. Roberts, 'Regulatory responses to the rise of the market for corporate control in Britain in the 1950s', *BH*, vol. 34, iss. 1 (January 1992), pp. 183–200.

105 P. Thompson, 'The pyrrhic victory of gentlemanly capitalism: The financial elite of the City of London, 1945–1990', *Journal of Contemporary History*, vol. 32, no. 3 (July 1997), p. 287; Ferguson, *High Financier*, pp. 195–9.

106 P. Thompson, 'Snatching defeat from the jaws of victory: The Last Post of the Old City Financial Elite, 1945–95', in A. Kidd and D. Nicholls (eds), *The Making of the British Middle Class? Studies of regional and cultural diversity since the eighteenth century* (Sutton: Stroud, 1998), pp. 231–2; Ferguson, *High Financier*, p. 197.

107 La chronologie historique de la cie Alais, Froges et Camargue devenue en 1950 la cie Pechiney, entry for 19 January 1959, Collection Historique Pechiney, Rio Tinto Alcan-Paris archive, 502/1-8-512292.

108 *The B.A. News*, vol. 9, no. 2 (March–April 1956), pp. 5–6; *The B.A. News*, vol. 4, no. 3 (May–June 1951), p. 3; Aluminium Pechiney (AP), 'Visite des usines d'aluminium de la British Aluminium Company. I – usine de Kinlochleven', 24 July 1951; *idem*, 'Visite des usines d'aluminium de la British Aluminium Company. II – Usine de Lochaber', 1 August 1951, Rio Tinto Alcan – France Archive, IHA-00-15-20-442.

109 Jones and Bostock, 'U.S. Multinationals in British Manufacturing before 1962', p. 209.

110 Smith, *From Monopoly to Competition*, p. 325.

111 Utiger, 'The British Aluminium Company, Ltd'.

112 *Ibid.*; Lesclous, *Histoire des sites producteurs d'aluminium*, p. 244; Lesclous, 'What bauxite strategy?', Tables I–IV.

113 BoT, Scottish Development Group: Highlands and Islands Study, Future of the Highland Reduction Works of the British Aluminium Co. Ltd, 22 May 1964; BoT, Office for Scotland, Production and Export Section, Report of visit to Lochaber by R. S. Forsyth (BoT, Inverness office), 6 August 1964, NAS, SEP2/454/1. BACo, Directors Reports and Accounts, 1959–70; Utiger, 'The British Aluminium Company, Ltd'; Cailluet, 'The British aluminium industry'; Bocquetin, 'La fabrication de l'aluminium par électrolyse', pp. 103–13.

114 The Monopolies Commission, *Report on the Supply of Aluminium Semi-Manufactures*, 20 December 1966, PP (c.263), para. 3; National Board for Prices and Incomes, *Report No. 39: Costs and Prices of Aluminium Semi-Manufactures*, PP, August 1967 (c.3378), paras 53–60; Utiger, 'The British Aluminium Company, Ltd'; Smith, *From Monopoly to Competition*, pp. 325–6.

115 G. M. Le Noan, 'La politique de Reynolds Metals à l'etranger', 15 September 1964, RTA Archive, Paris, 502/1-7-51261; Lesclous, *Histoire des sites producteurs d'aluminium*, pp. 197–8.

116 J. Scott, *Corporation, Classes and Capitalism* (Hutchinson: London, 1985), pp. 59–84.

117 Utiger, 'The British Aluminium Company, Ltd'; Le Noan, 'La politique de Reynolds Metals à l'etranger'; N. Girvan, *Corporate Imperialism: Conflict and Expropriation. Transnational corporations and economic nationalism in the third world* (Myron E. Sharpe: New York, 1976), pp. 106–7; Graham, *The Aluminium Industry and the Third World*, pp. 160–78; Smith, *From Monopoly to Competition*, pp. 287–8.

118 For a sample: BACo, Directors Reports and Accounts for 1956 and 1961; 'Bristol Bloodhound',

The B.A. News, vol. 10, no. 5 (September–October 1957), p. 1; 'Progress in the Air', *The B.A. News*, vol. 15, no. 2 (July–August 1963), p. 6, UGD 347/21/33/11; *Noral News*, vol. 7, no. 4 (Autumn 1957), p. 2, UGD 347/10/16/8.

119 D. A. Pinn evaluation of relative strengths and weaknesses of Alcan and BACo in UK markets, July 1972, UGD 347/10/3/1.

120 BACo, Directors Reports and Accounts for 1963–66; Utiger, 'The British Aluminium Company, Ltd'.

121 Appendix of letter from P. J. Elton, AAUK, to P. E. Thornton, Department of Trade and Industry, 31 July 1972, Table B, UGD 347/10/3/1; J. Tomlinson, 'British industrial policy', p. 171 and C. R. Schenk, 'Britain and the Common Market', pp. 192–211, in R. Coopey and N. Woodward (eds), *Britain in the 1970s: The troubled economy* (UCL: London, 1996).

122 Submission from AAUK to DTI, 27 June 1972, UGD 347/10/3/1.

123 Memo from Rt Hon. John Davies MP, Secretary of State for Trade and Industry, to Rt Hon. Edward Heath, Prime Minister (PM), 3 November 1971, TNA, PREM 15/344.

124 *Ibid.*; Note from Peter Gregson to Eric Wright, Department of Trade and Industry (DTI), 9 November 1971, TNA, PREM 15/344; Memo from the First Secretary, British Embassy, Washington, on commercial visit to Reynolds Metals, 9 July 1968, NAS, SEP2/454/1; Memo from E. J. King to D. J. Hedgecock, Engineering – Primary, 'Lochaber Furnace Room Environmental Problems', 3 April 1975, UGD 347/21/34/5/22.

125 Letter from D. A. Pinn to P. J. Elton, 4 May 1972, UGD 347/10/3/1.

126 Pinn to Elton, 4 May 1972.

127 *Ibid.*

128 Appendix to Elton to Thornton letter, 31 July 1972.

129 Campbell, *Global Mission, Vol. III*, pp. 946, 964, 1408.

130 Letter from Elton to Thornton, 31 July 1972.

131 Lesclous, 'Nuclear power', pp. 29–36; H. Morsel, *Histoire générale de l'électricité, tome troisième. Une œuvre nationale: l' équipement, la croissance de la demande, lenucléaire (1946–1987)* (Fayard: Paris, 1996), p. 891; Lesclous, *Histoire des sites producteurs d'aluminium*, pp. 51, 57, figure 14; Johnson, 'Hydro-electric power in the UK', p. 115.

132 Arnold, *Windscale 1957*, pp. 11–18, 24.

133 R. Utiger, *Never Trust An Expert: Nuclear power, government and the tragedy of the Invergordon Smelter* (London School of Economics: London, 1995), p. 3; MacKenzie, 'Be careful what you wish for'; Cailluet, 'The British aluminium industry', pp. 89–93.

134 'West Highland smelters', *The B.A. News,* vol. 31, no. 1 (January–February 1979), p. 7, UGD 347/21/33/20; 'Progress at Lochaber', *The B.A. News*, vol. 31, no. 1 (January–February 1979), pp. 3–5, UGD 347/21/33/20; 'The new Lochaber', *The B.A. News*, vol. 33, no. 3 (August–September 1981), pp. 3–4, UGD 347/21/33/21.

135 Statement on defence estimates, PP, 1971–72 (c.4891), pp. 41, 43; *Defence Select Committee: The Royal Dockyards & the Dockyard Stud,* PP, 1980–81 (c.362-I), *Minutes of Evidences*, 18 June 1981: Vice Admiral Sir William Pillar, Chief of Fleet Support, Royal Navy (Q. 168).

136 Memo from J. S. Potten, AUK, Mills Products Division, to D. Morton, Managing-Director, AUK, Banbury, 'The British Aluminium Company Ltd.', 25 June 1979, UGD 347/10/3/4; Appendix to Elton to Thornton letter, 31 July 1972; Memo and report from C. E. Scarrett, AUK, to Morton, 'BACO 1980 results', 8 April 1981, UGD 347/10/3/4; P. G. Polsue and I. Eastwood, 'The modernisation of Lochaber aluminium smelter', *Mining Magazine* (May 1982), pp. 399–401.

137 Memo from Potten to Morton, 25 June 1979; Memo and report from Scarrett to Morton, 8 April 1981; Campbell, *Global Mission, Vol. III*, pp. 955–60.

138 Memo from J. S. Potten, AUK, Mills Products Division, to D. Morton, Managing-

Director, AUK, Banbury, 'The British Aluminium Company Ltd.', 25 June 1979; Memo and report from Scarrett to Morton, 8 April 1981; Letter from G. G. Walker to D. C. Campbell, 3 December 1982, RTAIC, 00161-08.

139 Memo and report from Scarrett to Morton, 8 April 1981; Memo from G. Russell, AUK, to R. Wagner, Alcan Aluminiumwerke GmbH, 'Visit to Falkirk', 22 July 1982, UGD 347/10/3/4.

140 Memos about visits to BACo foil operations at Silvertown (5 August 1982) and Glasgow (6 August 1982) from R. Wagner to P. J. J. Rich and G. Russell, 10 August 1982.

141 Letter and report from J. C. [John] Winch and I. Suchoversky, 1 November 1982, UGD 347/1/7/4.

142 Letter from Dr. S. J. Ford, BACo, to G. Russell, AUK, containing revised figures for slides for presentation to boards over merger, 2 July 1982, UGD 347/10/3/4; Campbell, *Global Mission, Vol. III*, pp. 958–9.

143 Memos and agenda for meetings between Ford and Russell, 14 and 20 October 1982; Memo from John Allen, Department of Trade and Industry (DTI), to Mr Caines, DTI, 21 December 1983, NAS, SEP4/4052/1; Campbell, *Global Mission, Vol. III*, pp. 961–3.

144 British Alcan Aluminium Ltd presentation to bankers on post-merger achievements, 11 December 1985, UGD 347/1/7/45; Campbell, *Global Mission, Vol. III*, pp. 961–3.

145 British Alcan Aluminium Ltd, Annual Reports and Accounts, 1982–89, UGD 347/1/1/1–8; *Ministry of Defence: Statement on Defence Estimates 1988*, PP (c.428), p. 41; *MoD: Statement on Defence Estimates 1989*, PP (c.675), p. 32; Campbell, *Global Mission, Vol. III*, pp. 967–9; K. Dahlström, P. Ekins, J. He, J. Davis and R. Clift, 'Iron, steel and aluminium in the UK: Material flows and their economic dimensions', Final project report, Policy Studies Institute and University of Surrey, March 2004; A. Collins and R. I. D. Harris, 'Does plant ownership affect the level of pollution abatement expenditure', *Land Economics*, vol. 78, no. 2 (May 2002), pp. 171–89.

146 Alcan Aluminium UK, *Alcan in the Highlands. 1996 Review: Celebrating one hundred years of aluminium production* (Alcan: Fort William, 1996); Scottish Parliament, *Enterprise and Culture Committee Official Report*, 24 May 2005, Col. 1871.

147 'The Takeover Battle: Mining Mergers Explored', *Mining – Technology*, 11 December 2007; T. Webb and J. Finch, 'Shareholders start fight against Rio Tinto's $20bn Chinese bail-out', *G24*, 13 February 2009; 'BHP's battle for Rio Tinto could run and run', *The Times*, 10 February 2008; 'BHP drops hostile bid for Rio Tinto', *The International Herald Tribune*, 25 November 2008; 'Rio/Chinalco', *FT*, 17 February 2009.

148 *FT*, 21 December 1904; For a recent historical review of 'corporate governance' see: R. Lloyd-Jones, J. Maltby, M. J. Lewis and M. Matthews, 'Corporate governance in a major British holding company: BSA in the interwar years', *ABFH*, vol. 16, no. 1 (March 2006), pp. 69–98.

149 D. A. Levinthal and J. G. March, 'The Myopia of Learning', Strategic Management Journal, vol. 14 (Winter 1993), pp. 95–112; N. Chikudalê, 'Collective hyperopia and dualistic natures of corporate social responsibility', Asia Business and Management, vol. 8 (2009), pp. 169–184; Schatzberg, 'Symbolic culture and technological change', pp. 74–96; W. Allsop, 'Bulk processes in the manufacture of PVC', in R. H. Burgess (ed.), *Manufacture and processing of PVC* (Taylor and Francis: London, 1990) pp. 42–3.

Chapter 2: Aluminium and the British government

1 Ritchie, *Industry and Air Power,* p. 263; Grinberg and Hachez-Leroy, *Industrialisation et sociétés,* pp.18–19; Smith, *From Monopoly to Competition.*

2 G. Federico and J. Foreman-Peck, 'Industrial Policies in Europe' in J. Foreman-Peck and G. Federico (eds), *European Industrial Policy: The twentieth-century experience* (OUP: Oxford, 1999), p. 3; M. J. Bastable, *Arms and the State: Sir William Armstrong and the remaking of British naval power, 1854–1914* (Ashgate: Aldershot, 2004), pp. 161–9.

3 Peden, *Arms, Economics and British Strategy.*

4 W. Barnes, M. Gartland and M. Stack, 'Old habits die hard: Path dependency and behavioral lock-in', *Journal of Economic Issues,* vol. 38, no. 2 (June 2004), p. 372.

5 Porter, *The Competitive Advantage of Nations,* pp. 504–7.

6 N. Poulantzas, *Classes in Contemporary Capitalism* (New Left Review: New York, 1978), *passim*; W. Grant, *Business and Politics in Britain* (Palgrave: London, 1993); For an example of selective and overly deterministic accounts in the case of aluminium see: A. Spackman, 'The role of private companies in the politics of the empire: A case study of bauxite and diamond companies in Guyana in the early 1920s', *Social and Economic Studies,* vol. 24, no. 3 (September 1975), pp. 341–78.

7 Gourvish, 'Introduction', in Gourvish (ed.), *Business and Politics in Europe 1900–1970,* p. 1.

8 Kipping, 'Business–government relations', pp. 391, 372–93.

9 Tolliday, *Business, Banking and Politics,* pp. 281–343; L. Johnman and H. Murphy, 'Subsidy and Treasury: The Trade Facilities Act and the UK Shipbuilding Industry in the 1920s', *Contemporary British History,* vol. 22, no. 1 (2007), pp. 89–110; W. J. Reader, 'Imperial Chemical Industries and the State, 1936–1945', in B. Supple (ed.), *Essays in British Business History* (Clarendon Press: Oxford, 1977), pp. 227–43; T. Boyns, 'Strategic responses to foreign competition: The British coal industry and the 1930 Coal Mines Act', *BH,* vol. 32, no. 3 (1990), pp. 133–45; M. Dintenfass, 'Entrepreneurial Failure Reconsidered: The case of the interwar British Coal Industry', *BH,* vol. 62 (1988), pp. 1–34.

10 J. Turner, 'The Politics of Business', in J. Turner (ed.), *Businessmen and Politics: Studies of business activity in British politics 1900–1945* (Heinemann: London, 1984), p. 3.

11 G. Kennedy, 'The concept of Imperial Defence 1856–1956', in G. Kennedy (ed.), *Imperial Defence: The old world order 1856–1956* (Routledge: London, 2008), pp. 2–3.

12 Edgerton, *Warfare State*; S. Ball, 'Big Guns', H-net book reviews, 4 August 2006.

13 M. Edmonds, 'Government contracting and renegotiation: A comparative analysis', *Public Administration,* vol. 58 (1972), pp. 59–60 and footnote 53.

14 R. Higham, 'Government, companies and national defense: British aeronautical experience, 1918–1945 as the basis for a broad hypothesis', *BHR,* vol. 39, no. 3 (August 1965), pp. 323–47.

15 Bastable, *Arms and the State,* p. 168.

16 L. J. Butler, 'Business and British Decolonisation: Sir Ronald Prain, the mining industry and the Central African Federation', *The Journal of Imperial and Commonwealth History (TJICH),* vol. 35, no. 3 (2007), p. 477; P. J. Cain and A. G. Hopkins, 'Gentlemanly capitalism and British expansion overseas II: New imperialism, 1850–1945', *EHR,* second series, vol. 40 (1987), pp. 1–26; N. J. White, 'The business and the politics of decolonization: The British experience in the twentieth century', *EHR,* vol. 53, no. 3 (2000), pp. 544–64; B. Porter, *The Absent-Minded Imperialists: What the British really thought about empire* (OUP: Oxford, 2004), p. xiii; R. E. Dumett (ed.), *Gentlemanly Capitalism and British Imperialism: The new debate on empire* (Pearson: London, 1999).

17 P. Daniels, 'Industrial Policy', in M. Harrop (ed.), *Power and Policy in Liberal Democracies* (CUP: Cambridge, 1992), pp. 139–40; Kipping, 'Business–government relations', p. 390;

C. Charle, 'Le pantouflage en France (vers1880–vers1980)', *Annales ESC*, 5 (September–October 1987), pp. 1115–37; W. Genieys, 'The sociology of political elites in France: The end of an exception?', *International Political Science Review*, vol. 26 (2005), pp. 413–30.

18   M. Kipping and L. Cailluet, 'Mintzberg's emergent and deliberate strategies: Tracking Alcan's activities in Europe, 1928–2007', *BHR*, vol. 84, no. 1 (Spring 2010), pp. 75–104; Campbell, *Global Mission, Vol. III*, pp. 945–6, 1220–1; H. Pemberton, *Policy Learning and British Governance in the 1960s* (Palgrave: Basingstoke, 2004), p. 8.

19   *Annual accounts of manufacturing establishments under the War Department for year 1862–3*, PP (c.392), p. 47; *Return of annual accounts of ordinance factories* (hereafter *Army Ordinance*), PP, 1890–1 (c.129), pp. 98, 104; *Army Ordinance*, PP, 1892–3 (c.61), pp. 94, 114, 116; *Balance sheets and accounts of shipbuilding and dockyard transactions* (hereafter *Navy dockyard expenses accounts*), PP, 1890–1 (c.147), p. 194; *Royal Commission on scientific instruction and the advancement of science, Vol. II: Minutes of evidence*, PP, 1874 (c.958), Qs 414–15: evidence of Lt Col Alexander Strange F.R.S.; Russell, *Chemistry, Society and Environment*, pp. 313–14; BACo, Chairman's speech to the third OGM; 'Aluminium manufacture', *Cassier's Magazine*, October 1899, pp. 647–59.

20   C. Cooke, 'The advance of aluminium', 1895, UGD 347/21/46/2; 'Obituary: Sir Clement-Kinloch Cooke', *The Times*, 5 September 1944.

21   Schatzberg, 'Symbolic culture and technological change', pp. 226–71; Bastable, *Arms and the State*, p. 163; M. S. Seligmann, *Naval Intelligence from Germany: The reports of British naval attachés in Berlin, 1906–1914* (Ashgate: Aldershot, 2007), p. xxii.

22   BACo, *Aluminium*, 1908, UGD 347/21/29/3.

23   *Army Ordinance*, PP, 1900–1 (c.101), pp. 34, 46; *Army Ordinance*, PP, 1904–5 (c.68), p. 218; *Report of Adjutant-General of Yeomanry on stores for South African campaign*, PP, 1902 (c.803), pp. 121, 134; *Report of Commissioners appointed to enquire into military preparations and other matters connected with the War in South Africa, Vol. II: Minutes of evidence*, PP, 1904 (c.1791), Evidence of Col Forbes Macbean, 18 March 1903; *Army Ordinance*, PP, 1906–7 (c.52), p. 180; *Departmental Committee on the National Physical Laboratory, minutes of evidence with appendices and index*, PP, 1908 (c.3927), Qs 57–65: Evidence of Dr. R. T. Glazebrook; *Statistical report of the health of the Navy*, PP, 1909 (c.302), p. 199; 'Lochleven Water Power', *The Scotsman*, 6 July 1904; *Report of the Advisory Committee on Air for 1909–10* (hereafter *Air Force: Advisory Committee*), PP (c.5282), pp. 9, 90–94, 121, 165, 174; *Air Force: Advisory Committee*, PP, 1910–11 (c.5453), pp. 22–6; *Air Force: Advisory Committee*, PP, 1912–13 (c.6858), p. 16.

24   'Lt Col Stephen Pollen', *The Times*, 26 March 1935; 'Funeral and Memorial Services: Lieutenant-Colonel S. H. Pollen', *The Times*, 29 March 1935; Davenport-Hines, 'Pollen, Arthur Joseph Hungerford (1866–1937)', pp. 753–8; *The Times*, 29 April 1919, 24 June 1932, and 17 June 1935.

25   J. Turner, 'The Rise and Fall of "Business as Usual"', in K. Burk (ed.), *War and the State: The Transformation of British Government, 1914–1919* (Routledge: London, 1982), pp. 7–31; Hardach, *The First World War*, passim; H. Strachan, *Financing the First World War* (OUP: Oxford, 2004), passim; Peden, *Arms, Economics and British Strategy*, pp. 49–97; G. C. Peden, *The Treasury and British Public Policy, 1906–1959* (OUP: Oxford, 2000), pp. 73–127.

26   Ministry of Munitions (MoM), *Official History, Vol. 7: The Control of Materials* (HMSO: London, 1922), pp. 44–71 and part III, chapters I and V.

27   C. J. Wrigley, 'The Ministry of Munitions: An Innovatory Department', in Burk, *War and the State*, pp. 32, 52.

28   *Ibid.*

29 BACo, Directors Reports and Accounts for years ending 31 December 1914–1917, UGD 347/21/6/7–10; R. P. T. Davenport-Hines, *Dudley Docker: The life and times of a trade warrior* (CUP: Cambridge, 1984), pp. 106–8; Cailluet, 'L'impact de la Première Guerre mondiale', in Grinberg and Hachez-Leroy, *Industrialisation et sociétés*, p. 101.

30 Report of US charge d'affaires of visit by E. G. Lowry to German Prisoners of War at Kinlochleven camp, 15 September 1916, TNA, FO 383/164; Report by Dr Schwyzer and A. L. Fischer, Swiss Legation to Kinlochleven camp, 27 June 1917, FO 383/277; MoM, *Official History, Vol. 7*, part III, p. 76.

31 D. A. Bremner, Ministry of Munitions (MoM), to Sir L. W. Llewelyn, Director of Materials, MoM, 31 August 1916, TNA, MUN 4/2046; Strachan, *Financing the First World War*, pp. 16, 21–2.

32 *Ibid.*

33 *Ibid.*; Letter from Edmund Phipps to Under-Secretary of State for India, 14 October 1916; Note from H. A. Hayden, Director of Geological Survey of India, 30 October 1915, MUN 4/2046.

34 Bremner to Llewelyn, 31 August 1916.

35 Bremner to Llewelyn, 31 August 1916; Strachan, *Financing the First World War*, pp. 16, 21–2.

36 Memo from Ministry of Munitions to Inter-Allied Munitions Board (IAMB), 13 July 1917; Memo from R. H. Brand, IAMB, to IAMB Ottawa, 27 October 1916; Memo from Capt. W. Broadbridge to R. H. Brand, 2 January 1917; Brand to Broadbridge, 12 July 1917, TNA, MUN 4/5402.

37 Memo from IAMB to Edmund Phipps, General Secretary, MoM, 1 November 1916, TNA, MUN 4/1170; MoM, Figures of Aluminium Released, December 1918, MUN 4/724; Circular from Edmund Phipps to all Heads of Government Departments, 28 November 1916, MUN 5/207/1830/1; MoM, *Official History, Vol. 7*, part III, p. 8.

38 Memo from IAMB to Phipps, 1 November 1916; Letter from Adjt Col J. Ronneaux to Under-Secretary, Ministry of Munitions, 7 December 1916, TNA, MUN 4/1170.

39 S. Ball, 'The German Octopus: The British Metal Corporation and the Next War, 1914–1939', *Enterprise & Society*, vol. 5, no. 3 (2004), pp. 451–89; D. French, *The Strategy of the Lloyd George Coalition, 1916–1918* (OUP: Oxford, 1992).

40 DC-NFMT, Minutes of Evidence – Captain Walter Broadbridge, 26 June 1917, TNA, BT 55/46

41 Memo from Broadbridge to Wigglesworth (with attached translation of AIAG Neuhausen annual report for 1916), 16 May 1917, MUN 4/795; 'Obituary: Mr E. E. Sawyer', *The Times*, 17 April 1937; Hardach, *The First World War*, p. 61;

42 Memo by Sir L. W. Llewelyn, 21 June 1917; Sir Cecil L. Budd to W. T. Layton, 31 January 1919, MUN 4/724; Ball, 'The German Octopus', p. 459; Cailluet, 'L'impact de la Première Guerre mondiale', pp. 102–3; Storli, *Out of Norway Falls Aluminium*, pp. 113–14.

43 Christopher Addison notes for promotion of the Non-Ferrous Metals Bill, 7 December 1917, Bodleian Library, University of Oxford, MS. Addison dep. c. 114, fols 20–1; Ball, 'The German Octopus', pp. 460–1; H. G. Cordero and L. H. Tarring, *Babylon to Birmingham: An historical survey of the development of the world's non-ferrous metal and iron and steel industries and the commerce in metals since the earliest times* (Quinn Press: London, 1960), pp. 163–6.

44 *Statement with regard to advisory bodies appointed by the Minister of Reconstruction, 1918*, PP, 7 (c.9195); *Report of the Departmental Committee on the Non-Ferrous Metal Trades* (HMSO, 1917).

45 DC-NFMT, Evidence of Andrew Wilson Tait and William Murray Morrison, 25 May 1917, MUN, BT 55/46.

46   DC-NFMT, Evidence of Capt. Walter Broadbridge, Ministry of Munitions, 29 June 1917, BT 55/46.

47   *Report of the Departmental Committee on the Non-Ferrous Metal Trades*, points 98 and 102

48   Report of the Sub-Committee appointed by the Minister of Reconstruction to inquire into the post-war position of aluminium, 17 June 1918, MUN 5/207/1830/2.

49   By this time Sir Cecil Budd was also liquidator for non-ferrous metals: Notes from Budd to Mr W. T. Layton, 24 January 1919, Budd to Layton, 31 January 1919, and Budd to Mrs F. Woods, 18 February 1919, MUN 4/724.

50   Memo from the Minister of Munitions, Imperial Minerals Resources Bureau, 31 August 1917, CAB24/25.

51   Letter from E. C. Darling to Admiral Sir E. J. W. Slade, Admiralty, 25 November 1915; Letter from Darling to Sir R. L. Antrobus, Crown Agents for the Colonies, 15 December 1915; Letter from Darling to Long, Colonial Office, 29 December 1915, TNA, CO 111/603; Colin Newbury, 'Milner, Afred, Viscount Milner (1854–1925)', *ODNB*, http://www. oxforddnb.com/view/article/35037 [accessed 15 Jan 2009]; L. J. Butler, *Britain and Empire: Adjusting to a post-imperial world* (I. B. Tauris: London, 2008), p. 17.

52   Ball, 'The German Octopus', p. 452; O. Lyttleton, *The Memoirs of Lord Chandos* (Bodley Head: London, 1962), pp. 125, 129; Cordero, *World's Non-Ferrous Smelters*, pp. 219–21, 231; S. Ball, *The Guardsmen: Harold Macmillan, three friends, and the world they made* (Harper Collins: London, 2004), *passim*.

53   Register of BACo Directors; P. Richardson, 'Robinson, William Sydney (1876–1963)', *Australian Dictionary of Biography*, http://adbonline.anu.edu.au/biogs/A110438b.htm [accessed 23 June 2009].

54   Sir R. Streat, 'Government consultation with industry', *Public Administration*, vol. 37 (1959), p. 1.

55   *First annual report of the Colonial Research Committee for period ending 31 December 1920*, PP, 1921 (c.1144), Appendix I: dispatch from 10 Downing Street to the Colonies and Protectorates; Perchard, 'Of the highest Imperial importance'.

56   Letter from D. F. Campbell to W. Long, Under Secretary of State, Colonial Office (CO), 20 April 1915; Letters from Campbell to Long (CO), 19 March and 7 April 1915, CO 111/603.

57   Letter from W. M. Morrison to L. S. Amery, Under Secretary of State for the Colonies, 15 March 1920; Letter from Dr J. Evans, Imperial Mineral Resources Bureau (IMRB), to Amery, 23 June 1920, CO 111/634.

58   Perchard, 'Of the highest Imperial importance'.

59   W. M. Morrison to Secretary of the Board of Trade, 7 August 1936, TNA, SUPP 3/82; *Trade Facilities Acts*, PP, 1921–24 (c.121); V. Cerretano, 'The Treasury, Britain's post-war reconstruction and the industrial intervention of the Bank of England, 1921–1929', Economic History Review, vol. 62, Series 1 (2009), pp. 80–100; Johnman and Murphy, 'Subsidy and Treasury'.

60   *Air Force: Advisory Committee*, PP, 1917–18, (c.8629), p. 8; *Air Force: Advisory Committee*, PP, 1917–18 (c.9145), pp. 9–20; *Air Force: Advisory Committee*, PP, 1918–19 (c.488), pp. 16–19, 51–74; *Advisory Committee on Aeronautics*, PP, 1919–20 (c.1120), pp. 12, 35, 50; *Report on Scientific and Industrial Research* (hereafter *Scientific and Industrial Research*), PP, 1923–24 (c.2223), pp. 30, 33; *Scientific and Industrial Research*, PP, 1926–27 (c.3002), p. 4; *Scientific and Industrial Research*, PP, 1930–31 (c.3789), p. 7.

61   *Scientific and Industrial Research*, PP, 1919–20 (c.905), p. 28; Sir H. Melville, *The Department of Scientific and Industrial Research* (DSIR: London, 1962), pp. 19, 102–3.

62   *Proceedings of the Second Air Conference held on 7th and 8th of February 1922*, PP (c.1619), p. 55; *Appropriation Accounts for Air Services*, PP, 1922 (c.44), p. 81; *Scientific and Industrial*

Research, PP, 1921–22 (c.1735), p. 47; *Scientific and Industrial Research*, PP, 1922–23 (c.1937), pp. 54, 75; *Scientific and Industrial Research*, PP, 1924–25 (c.2491), pp. 45, 61, 64; *Scientific and Industrial Research*, PP, 1925–26 (c.2782), pp. 11, 35, 47, 52, 80; *Scientific and Industrial Research*, PP, 1927–28 (c.3258), pp. 24, 88; *Scientific and Industrial Research*, PP, *1931–32* (c.3989); *Scientific and Industrial Research*, PP, 1932–33 (c.4254), pp. 38, 68; *Committee on public accounts with proceedings*, PP, 1933–34 (c.98), Q. 5228 Evidence given by Sir C. Bullock and B. E. Holloway (Holloway later became Director of Contracts at the Air Ministry), 29 May 1934; Statement of Secretary of State for Air in *Air Estimates for 1937–38*, PP (c.5677), p. 8

63   P. Fearon, 'The British Airframe Industry and the State, 1918–35', *EHR*, new series, vol. 27, no. 2 (May 1974), pp. 236–51; Ritchie, *Industry and Air Power*, pp. 64–8; Hurstfield, *The Control of Raw Materials*, pp. 100–1; Boex, *The Aluminium Industry in Scotland*, p. 63.

64   *Scientific and Industrial Research*, PP, 1933–34, (c.4483), pp. 12, 58, 90–1; *Scientific and Industrial Research*, PP, 1934–35 (c.4787), pp. 72, 102; *Scientific and Industrial Research*, PP, 1935–36 (c.5013), p. 6, 59; *Scientific and Industrial Research*, PP, 1936–37 (c.5350), p. 104; Edgerton, *Warfare State, passim*.

65   BACo, Directors' Reports and Accounts, 1927–1939; Hannah, *Electricity before Nationalisation*, pp. 118–19.

66   BACo, Directors' Reports and Accounts, 1931–1936; *Import Duties Advisory Committee – additional import duties*, PP, 1934 (c.4582), no. 16; *Import Duties (General Orders)*, PP, 1935–36 (c.5052), p. 34.

67   *Ottawa Agreements 1932*, PP (c.4174), p. 33; *59th statistical abstract for British Dominions and Protectorates*, PP, 1934–35 (c.4819), no. 105b; *27th Report of Commissioners of Customs and Excise for year ending 31 March 1936*, PP (c.5296), Table 83; *28th Report of Commissioners of Customs and Excise for year ending 31 March 1937*, PP (c.5573), Table 83; *29th Report of Commissioners of Customs and Excise for year ending 31 March 1938*, PP (c.5876), Table 83; Rooth, *British Protectionism and the International Economy*, p. 97; J. Foreman-Peck, 'Industry and industrial organisation in the inter-war years', in Floud and McCloskey, *The Economic History of Britain, Vol. 2, 1860–1939* (CUP: Cambridge, 2004), p. 405.

68   'British Aluminium Company', *The Times*, 28 March 1934.

69   *The Times*, 30 March 1935, 1 April 1936, and 29 March 1939.

70   'Obituary: Mr. G. A. Steel', *The Times*, 16 December 1963.

71   Scottish Office, *Report of the committee on hydro-electric development in Scotland* [hereafter *Cooper Report*], PP, 1942 (c.6406), p. 17; Payne, *The Hydro*, Table 26; R. H. Campbell, 'The Scottish Office and the Special Areas in the 1930s', *Historical Journal*, vol. 22 (1979), pp. 167–83.

72   *Hilleary Report*, pp. 118–19, 130–2 and Table A; Report from Sir William Goodchild on Argyll, Fisheries Board for Scotland, 19 November 1937, NAS, AF62/1972/8; J. Hunter, *The Claim of Crofting: The Scottish Highlands and Islands, 1930–1990* (Mainstream: Edinburgh, 1991), pp. 42–7; C. M. Birnie, 'The Scottish Office and the Highland problem, 1930 to 1965', unpublished Ph.D. thesis (University of Edinburgh, 2008), pp. 17–44.

73   'Caledonian Power Order, 1937. Production of calcium carbide', Memo from Sir Thomas Inskip to HM Cabinet, 9 February 1937, TNA, CAB 24/268.

74   Committee on Imperial Defence, Principal Supply Officers Committee (CID-PSO), Mining of bauxite in British Guiana by foreign companies, P.S.O. 283, December 1930, SUPP 3/74; Peden, *Arms, Economics and British Strategy*, pp. 19–20, 104–5.

75   CID-PSO Committee's 7th Annual Report, 1 August 1930–31 July 1931, and Minutes of Meeting with Canadian representatives during the Imperial Conference, 31 October 1930, SUPP 3/73.

76   H. MacKenzie, '"Arsenal of the British Empire"? British orders for munitions production in Canada, 1936–39', *TJICH*, vol. 31, no. 3 (September 2003), p. 48; Peden, *Arms, Economics and British Strategy*, p. 100; S. Lobell, 'Second image reversed: Britain's choice of freer trade or imperial preferences, 1903–1906, 1917–1923, 1930–1932', *International Studies Quarterly*, vol. 43, no. 4 (December 1999), p. 686.

77   CID-PSO, Progress Report, 11 July 1935, SUPP 3/82; BACo, Directors Reports and Accounts, 1927–1939; 'New Appointments at Head Office', *The B.A. News*, vol. 2, no. 1 (January–February 1949), pp. 5–6.

78   'Obituary: Lt Gen. Sir Ronald Charles', *The Times*, 28 December 1955; My thanks are due to Dr John Bourne of the Centre for WWI Studies, University of Birmingham, for additional information about Lt Gen. Sir Ronald Charles: CID-PSO, Memo from Lt Gen. Sir Ronald E. Charles, K.C.B., C.M.G., D.S.O., to CID-PSO, 29 April 1935; B. Bond, *British Military Policy between the Two World Wars* (OUP: Oxford, 1980), pp. 51, 156, 384–5.

79   'Responsibility for defence: Preserving the chain', *The Times*, 10 January 1936; '"In defence of freedom": New Army League to help recruitment', *The Times*, 18 February 1938; 'Readiness for defence: Registration and service', *The Times*, 1 November 1938.

80   Johnman and Murphy, 'Subsidy and Treasury', p. 94.

81   Letter from W. M. Morrison to the Secretary, Board of Trade, 7 August 1936; Sir W. Palmer, Board of Trade, to E. E. Bridges, Treasury, 11 August 1936; Sir F. Phillips to Sir R. Hopkins and Mr Barlow, Treasury, 12 September 1936; Memo from Bridges to Barlow, 22 October 1936; Memo from Bridges to Mr Wilson Smith along, with minute relating to Treasury Inter Service Committee – Proposed guarantee to British Aluminium Company, 23 October 1936, SUPP 3/82; BACo, Directors Report and Accounts for 1936–1939; G. C. Peden, *British Rearmament and the Treasury: 1932–1939* (Scottish Academic Press: Edinburgh, 1979), pp. 72–9; Johnman and Murphy, 'Subsidy and Treasury'.

82   Hurstfield, *The Control of Raw Materials*, p. 101

83   Letter from Trend to L. T. Little, MAP, 12 June 1944, TNA, SUPP 3/82.

84   Treasury note – The British Aluminium Co. Ltd, Lochaber Loan, 6 March 1947, T 228/639; Treasury note – United Kingdom Government loans to the Aluminium Company of Canada (Alcan), 5 September 1958, TNA, T 228/642

85   W. Ashworth, *Contracts and Finance* (HMSO: London, 1953), p. 223.

86   Treasury note – The British Aluminium Co. Ltd, Lochaber Loan, 6 March 1947; Treasury note – United Kingdom Government loans to the Aluminium Company of Canada (Alcan), 5 September 1958; Letter from Little to Trend, 6 June 1944; Letter Trend to Little, 12 June 1944; Letter from Sir W. Palmer, Board of Trade, to A. Fforde, Treasury, 21 June 1944; Letter from Fforde to Palmer, 7 July 1944, SUPP 3/82; Memo from Trend to Blunt, Treasury, 27 July 1944.

87   Letter from Palmer to A. Fforde, 21 June 1944.

88   Letter from Fforde to Palmer, 7 July 1944.

89   Memo to the Prime Minister from the Sub-Committee on Air Services, 17 May 1940, CAB 127/160; Cypher from UK High Commissioner (UKHC) in Canada to MAP, 19 August 1940; Telegram from UKHC in Canada to MAP, 26 September 1940, AVIA 46/457; *Report from the Committee of Public Accounts – Evidence*, PP, 1943–44 (c.108-I), Qs 4031–8, 4116–17, 4130–64: evidence from Sir Harold Scott, Sir W. Lindsay Scott and Mr H. P. Bruckshaw.

90   Campbell, *Global Mission, Vol. I*, pp. 255–6.

91   C. Muller, 'Aluminium and power control', *The Journal of Land & Public Utility Economics*, vol. 21, no. 2 (May 1945), pp. 119–23.

92   I am grateful to Mats Ingulstad for the following reference and sight of this letter: Letter from W. H. Harrison to Hon. L. B. Johnson, US Senate, US National Archives, Maryland;

see also: M. D. Evenden, *Fish versus Power: An environmental history of the Fraser River* (CUP: Cambridge, 2004), pp. 167–8.

93 R. Bothwell and W. Kilbourn, *C. D. Howe: A biography* (McClelland and Stewart: Toronto, 1980), *passim*; D. J. Savoie, *Visiting Grandchildren: Economic development in the Maritimes* (UT Press: Toronto, 2006), pp. 40, 48–9; J. Douglas Gibson, 'Post-War economic development and policy in Canada', *The Canadian Journal of Economics and Political Science*, vol. 20, no. 4 (November 1954), pp. 439–43.

94 Notes from A. Cairncross interview with Geoffrey Cunliffe, 25 June 1940, AVIA 10/375.

95 Moos, 'The structure of the British aluminium industry', p. 524; S. Moos, 'Price formation and price maintenance on the aluminium market', *The Manchester School* (1948), pp. 66–93.

96 Letter from I. T. Little, Ministry of Aircraft Production (MAP), to A. R. Bull, Treasury, 16 November 1944, TNA, SUPP 3/82.

97 M. Chick, 'Listing potential candidates for nationalisation: Britain, 1948', *Enterprises et Histoire*, no. 37 (December 2004), pp. 167–71; R. Millward, 'Industrial organisation and economic factors in nationalisation' and J. Singleton, 'Labour, the Conservatives and nationalisation', in R. Millward and J. Singleton (eds), *The Political Economy of Nationalisation in Britain 1920–50* (CUP: Cambridge, 1995), pp. 3–33.

98 *The B.A. News*, vol. 5, no. 1 (January–February 1952), p. 5.

99 'United Kingdom aluminium industry: Progress from 1946 to 1953', Memo from H. E. Thatcher, Asst Secretary, Light Metals Division, Ministry of Supply, to Armed Service and Supply Departments, 1 October 1953, SUPP 14/217; Note from L. I. McBeth, BoT, Office for Scotland, 'The British Aluminium Co. Ltd.', 12 July 1962, NAS, SEP2/454/1.

100 E. A. Cameron, 'The Scottish Highlands: From contested district to objective one', in T. M. Devine and R. J. Finlay, *Scotland in the Twentieth Century* (EUP: Edinburgh, 1996), p. 161.

101 Birnie, 'The Scottish Office and the Highland problem', p. 45.

102 Association of Scientific Workers (AScW), Scottish Area Committee, *Highland Power. A Report of the utilisation of the Hydro-Electric Power envisaged in the Hydro-Electric Development (Scotland) Act – 1943* (Glasgow, 1944), p. 78.

103 Hunter, *The Claim of Crofting*, pp. 51–2.

104 *Cooper Report*, pp. iv, 17; *Hilleary Report*, p. 138.

105 *First report of the Committee appointed to enquire into certain aspects of the Scottish valuation and rating system*, PP, 1943–44 (c.6526), points 38 and 39.

106 *Ibid.*, pp. 47–9; *Local Government (Scotland) Act 1929*, PP (c.25); Letter from Col Donald Walter Cameron of Lochiel to Sir Alexander MacEwen, 8 July 1935, Lochaber Archive Centre (LAC), Fort William, CL/3/3/18/4/1; Payne, *The Hydro*, pp. 56–9.

107 I. Levitt, 'The Treasury, public investment and the development of hydro-electricity in the north of Scotland, 1951–64', *Northern Scotland*, 24 (2004), pp. 75–92.

108 'United Kingdom Aluminium Industry: Progress from 1946 to 1953', 1 October 1953, SUPP 14/217; Payne, *The Hydro*, Table 28 (b).

109 BoT, Office for Scotland, Production and Export Section, Report by W. H. B. Smith on visit to Lochaber works, 22 February 1961; Notes on the British Aluminium Co. Ltd, Lochaber Works, for the visit of the Parliamentary Secretary on 15 October 1963, prepared by E. B. Templeman, BoT, Inverness Office, 25 September 1963; BoT, report of visit to Lochaber by R. Forsyth, 6 August 1964, NAS, SEP2/454/1; For press accounts see: 'Aluminium firm to get more power.' *The Scotsman*, 7 November 1961; 'Electricity for Lochaber Works', *Press & Journal (P&J)*, 7 November 1961; 'Power stand-by for B.A. works', *The Oban Times*, 11 November 1961.

110 Evenden, *Fish versus Power*, p. 162.

111   I. G. C. Hutchison, 'Government', in Devine and Finlay, *Scotland in the Twentieth Century*, pp. 49–50.

112   R. Saville, 'The industrial background to the post-war Scottish economy' and G. McCrone and J. N. Randall, 'The Scottish Development Agency', in Saville (ed.), *The Economic Development of Modern Scotland*, pp. 22–3 and 241; C. H. Lee, *Scotland and the United Kingdom: The economy and the union in the twentieth century* (MUP: Manchester, 1995), pp. 106–7; J. S. Gibson, *The Thistle and The Crown: A history of the Scottish Office* (HMSO: Edinburgh, 1985), pp. 78–9.

113   Peden, 'The managed economy', p. 236.

114   Birnie, 'The Scottish Office and the Highland problem', pp. 52–98; Cameron, 'The Scottish Highlands', pp. 160–3; N. G. MacKenzie, '"Chucking Buns across the Fence?" Government-Sponsored Industry Development in the Scottish Highlands, 1945–1982', *Business and Economic History On-Line*, 4 (2006) http://www.thebhc.org/publications/BEHonline/2006/mackenzie.pdf.

115   Saville, 'The industrial background to the post-war Scottish economy' and N. Buxton, 'The Scottish economy, 1945–79: performance, structure and problems', in Saville (ed.), *The Economic Development of Modern Scotland*, Table 1(b) and p. 67; Cairncross, *The Scottish Economy*, Table 58; Lee, *Scotland and the United Kingdom*, Table 3.

116   Thatcher to Workman, Ministry of Supply, 21 July 1949, T 228/640; Discussion between Minister of Supply and Lord Privy Seal and Aluminium Industry Council, 1 June 1951, BT 172/5.

117   Note on the Volta River Aluminium Scheme and the British Aluminium Company, 6 January 1956, BT 258/128.

118   D. Richards, 'Charles Frederick Algernon Portal', *ODNB*, http://www.oxforddnb.com [accessed 21 March 2008]; K. Harris, *Attlee* (Weidenfeld and Nicolson: London, 1995), p. 289; E. Plowden, *An Industrialist in the Treasury: The Post-War Years* (Andre Deutsch: London, 1989); R. Armstrong, 'Obituaries: Lord Plowden', *The Independent*, 19 February 2001.

119   *Report of Select Committee on civil estimates*, PP, 1945–46 (c.158), Evidence: Qs 172, 236 – Mr O. S. Franks and A. C. Gordon, 3 April 1946, and Mr E. F. Muir, 30 April 1946; *Fifth Report of Select Committee on estimates*, PP, 1945–46, (c.191-I), Evidence: Q. 304 – Boddis, 23 July 1946; BACo, Directors Reports and Accounts, PP, 1945–1958; British Electricity Authority, *Second Report and Accounts for the year ended 31 March*, PP, 1950–51 (c.267), pp. 34, 38, 42; UK Atomic Energy Authority (UKAEA), *Second Report for the period 1 April 1955–31 March 1956*, PP (c.323), p. 19.

120   *Third Report of the Committee of Public Accounts with Proceedings, Evidence, Appendices, and Index*, PP, 1955–56 (c.124-I), Evidence from Sir John Lang, Permanent Secretary, Admiralty, 3 May 1955 (Qs 3416–23); *Scientific and Industrial Research*, PP, 1956–57 (c.213), pp. 172–3; *Second Report with Evidence taken before Sub-Committee E of the Committee of Session, 1955–56: Supply of Military Aircraft*, PP (c.34), Evidence of Sir Roy Fedden, 12 June 1956; L. Rotherham, 'The Research Branch of the Industrial Group of the United Kingdom Atomic Energy Authority', *Proceedings of the Royal Society of London, Series A, Mathematical and Physical Sciences*, vol. 249, no. 1256 (1 January 1956), pp. 1–15. Rotherham was formerly director of the research branch of UKAEA (Industrial Group).

121   N. Tiratsoo and J. Tomlinson, *The Conservatives and Industrial Efficiency, 1951–64: Thirteen wasted years?* (Routledge: London, 1998), p. 158.

122   *Volta River Aluminium Scheme*, PP, 1952 (c.8702); Telegram from Governor's Deputy for North Borneo to the Secretary of State for the Colonies, 26 November 1951, CO 1022/265; Telegram from Secretary of State for Colonies to Governor of North Borneo, 1 December

1951, CO 1022/265; Graham, *The Aluminium Industry and the Third World*, pp. 160–78.

123 The Volta River Aluminium Scheme and the British Aluminium Company – note prepared by G. T. Field, Board of Trade, 6 January 1956, BT 258/128; Campbell, 'Negotiating the Bauxite/Aluminium Sector', p. 33.

124 Briefing notes for meeting of 11 January 1956 between Lord Portal and the Permanent Secretary, Board of Trade, 9 January 1956, BT 258/128.

125 Memo from A. C. Hill to Mr Reid, 12 January 1956, BT 258/128.

126 The Volta River Aluminium Scheme and the British Aluminium Company – note prepared by G. T. Field, Board of Trade, 6 January 1956, BT 258/128.

127 Graham, *The Aluminium Industry and the Third World*, pp. 180–8.

128 Hatch and Fores, 'The Struggle for British Aluminium', pp. 30–47; Note from Chancellor of the Exchequer to Prime Minister, 31 December 1958, PREM 11/2670; Note from President of Board of Trade to Prime Minister, 1 January 1959, PREM 11/2670; Minutes of Cabinet meeting to discuss British Aluminium Company, 8 January 1959, CAB 130/158.

129 Tiratsoo and Tomlinson, *The Conservatives and Industrial Efficiency*, p. 107.

130 Background note for Cabinet discussion on British Aluminium, 8 January 1959, CAB 130/158.

131 Tiratsoo and Tomlinson, *The Conservatives and Industrial Efficiency*, p. 32; *Hansard* – HC Debs, vol. 554, cc.1431–512, 20 June 1956; Roberts, 'Regulatory responses', pp. 183–200.

132 Memo from Rt Hon. D. Heathcoat-Amory, Chancellor of the Exchequer, to Rt Hon. H. Macmillan, Prime Minister (PM), 2 November 1958, PREM 11/2670; Background note for Cabinet discussion on British Aluminium, 8 January 1959.

133 Memo from Heathcoat-Amory to PM, 24 November 1958, PREM 11/2670.

134 Memo from PM to Heathcoat-Amory, 15 December 1958, PREM 11/2670; Minute on shipping of aluminium, 8 December 1958, PREM 11/2670.

135 Memo from Rt Hon. Frank Erroll to PM, 1 January 1959, PREM 11/2670; Richards, *Portal of Hungerford*, pp. 376–9.

136 *Ibid.*, pp. 376–9.

137 Memo from John Simon, Financial Secretary to the Treasury, to PM, 3 January 1959, PREM 11/2670.

138 Letter from Viscount Portal of Hungerford, Chairman of the British Aluminium Company, to PM, 6 January 1959, TNA, PREM 11/2670.

139 Letter from Sir Ivan Stedeford, TI, to J. E. S. Simon, HMT, 2 January 1959, PREM 11/2670.

140 Note for the record, Harold Macmillan, 9 January 1959, PREM 11/2670

141 Kynaston, *The City of London*, pp. 108–15; Richards, *Portal of Hungerford*, pp. 27, 369–79.

142 Lord Chandos to Eden, 14 October 1971 quoted in Ball, *The Guardsmen*, p. 377.

143 M. Francis, 'Tears, tantrums and bared teeth: the eomotional economy of three conservative prime ministers, 1951–1963', *Journal of British Studies*, vol. 41, no. 3 (2002), pp. 354–5.

144 *Hansard* – HC Debs, vol. 608, cc.34–174, 29 June 1959; *Hansard* – HC Debs, vol. 606, c.22, 2 June 1959.

145 *TUC, Report, 1959*, pp. 356, 471.

146 J. Tomlinson, '"Liberty with Order": Conservative economic policy, 1951–1964', in M. Francis and I. Zweiniger-Bargielowska (eds), *The Conservatives and British Society 1880–1990* (University of Wales Press: Cardiff, 1996), p. 278.

147 Board of Trade (BoT), Report of visit by W. H. B. Smith, BoT, Office for Scotland, Production & Export Section, to British Aluminium, Falkirk, 3 July 1963, NAS, SEP2/539.

148 Arnold, *Windscale 1957*, pp. 20–1; L. Arnold, *Britain and the H-Bomb* (Palgrave: London, 2001), p. 112; BACo, *Annual Report and Accounts for 1946*.

149 Hannah, *Engineers, Managers and Politicians*, pp. 161–241; BACo, *Annual Report and Accounts for 1960 and 1961*; W. C. Patterson, *Going Critical: An unofficial history of British Nuclear Power* (Paladin: London, 1985), p. 38.

150 G. Dudley and J. Richardson, *Why Does Policy Change? Lessons from British Transport Policy* (Routledge: London, 2000), p. 51.

151 Utiger, *Never Trust an Expert*, pp. 11, 56.

152 Hannah, *Engineers, Managers and Politicians*, pp. 236–44.

153 *Ibid.*, pp. 284–5; Arnold, *Windscale 1957*, pp. 24–5; D. Edgerton, *The Shock of the Old: Technology and Global History since 1900* (Profile: London, 2006), p. 21.

154 *Report of the Select Committee on Science and Technology: UK Nuclear Reactor Programme*, PP, 1966–67 (c.381-XVII), p. xxxvi.

155 Edgerton, *Warfare State*, pp. 256–66; S. Schrafstetter and S. Twigge, 'Spinning into Europe: Britain, West Germany and the Netherlands. Uranium enrichment and the development of the gas centrifuge, 1964–70', *Contemporary European History*, vol. 11 (2002), pp. 253–72; S. Twigge, 'A baffling experience: Technology transfer, Anglo-American nuclear relations, and the development of the gas centrifuge 1964–70', *History and Technology*, vol. 19, iss. 2 (June 2003), pp. 151–63.

156 J. Tomlinson, *The Labour Governments 1964–1970, Vol. 3: Economic policy* (MUP: Manchester, 2004), p. 87.

157 G. O'Hara, *From Dreams to Disillusionment: Economic and social planning in 1960s Britain* (Palgrave: Basingstoke, 2007), p. 117; D. Tanner, 'Richard Crossman, Harold Wilson and Devolution, 1966–70: The making of government policy', *Twentieth Century British History*, vol. 17, no. 4 (2006), pp. 545–78.

158 Scottish Council Development and Industry (SCDI), *Inquiry into the Scottish economy 1960–1961. Report of a Committee appointed by the Scottish Council (Development and Industry) under the Chairmanship of J. N. Toothill, Esq., C.B.E.* (SCDI: Edinburgh, 1961), pp. 181–92; I. G. C. Hutchison, 'Government', in Devine and Finlay (eds), *Scotland in the Twentieth Century*, p. 48; Gibson, *The Thistle and the Crown*, p. 134.

159 BoT, Scottish Development Group: Highlands and Islands Study, 'Future of the Highland Reduction Works of the British Aluminium Co. Ltd.', 22 May 1964, NAS, SEP2/454/1.

160 Submission from Scottish Development Department (SDD) to Lord Hughes and Willie Ross, 7 April 1967; Memo from T. R. H. Godden, Scottish Office, Regional Development Division 2, SDD, to Scott Whyte, SDD, 30 March 1967, NAS, SEP21/5747.

161 SDD to Hughes and Ross, 7 April 1967.

162 HIDB, *1st Annual Report*, 1965–1966, pp. 1–5; Cameron, 'The Scottish Highlands', pp. 153–69; W. Hughes, 'Ross, William, Baron Ross of Marnock (1911–1988)', *ODNB*, http://www.oxforddnb.com.ezproxy.webfeat.lib.ed.ac.uk/view/article/39856?docPos=7 [accessed 15 July 2008].

163 F. Gillanders, 'The Economic Life of Gaelic Scotland Today', in D. S. Thomson and I. Grimble (eds), *The Future of the Highlands* (Routledge and Keegan Paul: London, 1968), pp. 126–46; J. Grassie, *Highland Experiment: The story of the Highlands and Islands Development Board* (AUP: Aberdeen, 1983), pp. 56–64.

164 Minutes of meeting between Willie Ross, Dr Jesse Dickson Mabon (Minister of State), Sir Matthew Campbell (Secretary of the Department of Agriculture and Fisheries), Professor Robert Grieve (HIDB), and Mr Prophet Smith (HIDB), House of Commons, 15 March 1967, NAS, SEP12/557; D. Torrance, *The Scottish Secretaries* (Birlinn: Edinburgh, 2006), p. 248.

165 Minute from SDD to Ross, 12 April 1967, NAS, SEP12/557.

166 Letter from P. J. Elton to N. V. Davis, 23 June 1967, RTAIC, 00161-08.

167 Minute from C. J. A. Whitehouse, BoT, to Sir Douglas Haddow, 'Alcan (U.K.) Limited', 4 May 1967, NAS, SEP4/3444.

168 'Proposal for power leasing for special industrial development', Minute from J. F. Robertson, on behalf of the Secretary of State for Scotland, to P. J. Elton, Alcan, 6 June 1967, RTAIC 000161-08; Letter from Elton to Davis, 23 June 1967; Grassie, *Highland Experiment*, pp. 59–61; A. Hetherington, 'Northern Scotland – Real Lives', in Hetherington, *Highlands and Islands*, pp. 9–10.

169 BACo, Annual Report and Accounts, 1947; BoT, Office for Scotland, reports of visits by J. Solis to Foyers on 7 March and 19 June 1963, NAS, SEP2/454/1; '"Only new industry and new life will save dying community": The fear of Foyers. Villagers worried by apathy and depopulation', *P&J*, 1 October 1964; Minutes of meetings of the HIDB for (1966), 6 and 19 May, 23 June, 22 September, 20 October, 3 November, and (1967) 24 and 25 January; Letter from Sir W. Strath, BACo, to Sir M. Campbell, 22 December 1966; Letter from John Rollo, HIDB, to William Russell, 31 January 1967; Letter from L. Hasson, Inverness County Councillor, and W. Batchen, District Councillor, to Prime Minister, 17 April 1967; Letter from R. W. Wallace, Inverness County Council County Clerk, to Permanent Secretary, SDD, 15 March 1967, NAS, SEP12/574.

170 'Millions invested in new aluminium project', *The Scotsman*, 24 March 1966; J. Phillips, *The industrial politics of devolution: Scotland in the 1960s and 1970s* (MUP: Manchester, 2008), *passim*.

171 *Ibid.*; T. Dickson (ed.), *Scottish Capitalism: Class, state and nation from before the Union to the present* (Lawrence and Wishart: London, 1980), pp. 245–320; Buxton, 'The Scottish economy, 1945–79', in Saville (ed.), *The Economic Development of Modern Scotland*, p. 57; D. McCrone, *Understanding Scotland: The sociology of a stateless nation* (EUP: Edinburgh, 1992), pp. 34–54, 121–45; W. W. Knox, *Industrial Nation: Work, culture and society in Scotland, 1800–present* (EUP: Edinburgh, 1999), pp. 254–64; W. W. Knox and A. McKinlay, 'Working for the Yankee Dollar: American inward investment and Scottish labour, 1945–70', *Historical Studies in Industrial Relations (HSIR)*, vol. 7 (1999), pp. 1–26.

172 Letter from P. J. Elton to N. V. Davis, 22 August 1967, Maison-Alcan RTAIC, 00161-08.

173 Letter from Elton to Davis, 22 August 1967.

174 *Ibid.*; 'Highlights of Alcan smelter events', *News from Alcan*, 19 January 1968.

175 Grassie, *Highland Experiment*, p. 62.

176 *News from Alcan*, 19 January 1968.

177 BBC Scottish Television – News and Magazine, 'Campaign to Reopen Colliery', 22 January 1968, 5.55 p.m.; BBC Scottish Home Service "Newsreel", 'Alcan's Proposed Smelting Plant', 24 January 1968, 6.25 p.m.; Grampian Television – News, 'Coal Supply Plan Attacked', 24 January 1968, 6.05 p.m.; Note from J. T. Hyland, 4 October 1967, all Alcan-Montreal RTAIC, 00161-08; A. Perchard, *The Mine Management Professions in the Twentieth-Century Scottish Coal Mining Industry* (The Edwin Mellen Press: Lampeter, 2007), pp. 220–3.

178 Letter from J. T. Hyland to Elton, 19 July 1968, Alcan-Montreal RTAIC, 00161-08.

179 Letter from Elton to Whitehouse, 2 May 1967; Minute from Whitehouse to Sir Douglas Haddow, Scottish Office, 4 May 1967, NAS, SEP4/3444; Utiger, *Never Trust an Expert*, pp. 6–8; G. G. Drummond, *The Invergordon Smelter: A case study in management* (Hutchinson: London, 1997), pp. 11–29.

180 MacKenzie, 'Be careful what you wish for'; Utiger, *Never Trust an Expert*, p. 5.

181 Utiger, *Never Trust an Expert*, pp. 9–28; MacKenzie, 'Be careful what you wish for'; E. Dell, *Political Responsibility and Industry* (Allen and Unwin: London, 1973), p. 106.

182 O' Hara, *From Dreams to Disillusionment*, pp. 2, 53.

183 Memo and position paper from W. S. Ryrie, HMT, to PS/Paymaster General, 9 December

1974, TNA, T319/2540.

184 *Ibid.*

185 Letter from A. M. Cochran (Office of the Chief Engineer of the NSHEB) to H. F. G. Kelly, SDD, 19 March 1973, NAS, SEP14/1868; See also MacKenzie's observations about this in 'Be careful what you wish for?'

186 DTI, *Rolls-Royce Ltd and the RB211 Aero-Engine*, PP, 1972 (c.4860), p. 24.

187 DTI note from Miss M. M. Deyes to Mr Mountfield, 11 July 1973, T319/2090

188 Treasury minute from C. J. Carey to Mrs Percy-Davis, 24 May 1973; DTI note from Miss M. M. Deyes to Mr Mountfield, 11 July 1973, T319/2090.

189 DTI note from Miss M. M. Deyes to Mr Mountfield, 11 July 1973; Letter from H. F. G. Kelly, SDD, to G. Corti, HMT, 5 February 1973; DTI memo from H. S. Tovey to Deyes, 16 April 1973, T319/2090.

190 Letter from D. C. Clark, DTI, to W. S. Ryrie, HMT, 19 July 1973, T319/2090.

191 Letter from K. R. Vernon, NSHEB, to J. B. Beaumont, SDD, 2 February 1973, NAS, SEP14/1868.

192 Letter from W. Ross to E. Dell, 10 April 1974, T319/2090.

193 Letter from E. Dell to A. W. Benn, 29 April 1974, T319/2090.

194 Letter from Dell to Benn, 9 December 1974; Letter from Benn to Dell, 17 December 1974; Letter from E. Varley to Dell, 18 December 1974; Letter from P. Shore to Dell, 6 January 1975, T319/2090.

195 Letter from D. C. Clark to W. S. Ryrie, 23 January 1975, T319/2090.

196 Letter from J. A. Scott, SEPD, to D. C. Clark, HMT, 5 February 1975; Letter from Scott to M. D. C. Johnson, Department of Industry, 10 March 1975; Letter from Scott to Ryrie, 8 April 1975, T319/2090.

197 Treasury briefing from F. H. Orr to Mr Norton and PS/Paymaster General, 4 March 1975, T319/2090.

198 Memo from J. S. Beastall to Norton, 5 March 1975; Letter from Scott to M. D. C. Johnson, Department of Industry, 10 March 1975, T319/2090

199 Treasury briefing, Orr to Norton and PS/Paymaster General, 4 March 1975; Utiger, *Never Trust an Expert*, p. 26; MacKenzie, 'Be careful what you wish for?'

200 MacKenzie, 'Be careful what you wish for?'; Utiger, *Never Trust an Expert*.

201 Edgerton, *Warfare State*, p. 265.

202 J. Tomlinson, 'Mrs Thatcher's macroeconomic adventurism, 1979–1981, and its political consequences', *British Politics*, vol. 2 (2007), pp. 3–19.

203 J. Mitchell, *Conservatives and the Union: A study of conservative attitudes towards Scotland* (EUP: Edinburgh, 1990), pp. 98–9.

204 J. Mitchell, 'Scotland in the Union, 1945–95: The changing nature of the union state' in Devine and Finlay, *Scotland in the Twentieth Century*, pp. 97–9.

205 Secure MUFAX, from A. Muir Russell, PS/Secretary of State, to PS/SEPD, Cc'd to PS/Minister of State; PS/US of S, 'Invergordon Smelter', 10 December 1981, NAS, SEP12/663; R. Finlay, 'Scottish Conservatism and Unionism since 1918', in Francis and Zweiniger-Bargielowska, *The Conservatives and British Society*, pp. 122–3.

206 J. Tomlinson, 'British economic policy since 1945', in Floud and McCloskey, *The Economic History of Britain since 1700, Vol. 3*, p. 261.

207 E. J. Evans, *Thatcher and Thatcherism*, second edition (Routledge: London, 2004), pp. 22–4.

208 Mitchell, *Conservatives and the Union*, p. 99; D. Stewart, 'Fighting for survival: The 1980s campaign to save Ravenscraig steelworks', *Journal of Scottish Historical Studies (JSHS)*, vol. 25, no. 1 (2005), p. 49.

209 C. Wrigley, 'After the Great Coal Strike: The government, unions and strikes, 1985–92',

paper to the (UK) Economic History Society conference, 29 March 2008.

210   Memo from Rear Admiral D. A. Dunbar-Naismith to Rt Hon. G. Younger, 4 September 1981, NAS, SEP12/663.

211   Minute from Mrs J. M. Spence, PS/SEPD, to PS/Mr Fletcher, PS/Secretary of State, and PS/Under Secretary of State, 19 October 1981, NAS, SEP12/663.

212   Minute and draft paper from Dr. G. McCrone to Secretary of State for Scotland, 10 December 1981, NAS, SEP12/663.

213   Minute from D. Harrison, SEPD, to PS/Secretary of State, 'British Aluminium Company: Invergordon Smelter', 3 December 1981, NAS, SEP12/663.

214   Letter from George Younger, Secretary of State for Scotland, to Margaret Thatcher, Prime Minister, 12 December 1981; Letter from Younger to Thatcher, 14 December 1981; Letter from R. G. L. McCrone, SEPD, to Younger, 15 December 1981, NAS, SEP4/4055; MacKenzie, 'Be careful what you wish for'; Finlay, 'Scottish Conservatism and Unionism since 1918', in Francis and Zweiniger-Bargielowska, *The Conservatives and British Society*, pp. 122–3; Mitchell, 'Scotland in the Union, 1945–95', in Devine and Finlay, *Scotland in the Twentieth Century*, pp. 97–9.

215   Letter from J. F. Laing, SEPD, to G. Russell, AUK, 19 May 1982, UGD 347/1/2/3; Letter from B. Sawyer, Managing Director, AUK, to Laing, 11 June 1982; Note about comparative power costs written by R. T. V. Martin, AUK, 26 August 1982, UGD 347/10/18/3.

216   Letter from Rt Hon. John W. W. Peyton to Patrick Jenkin, Secretary of State for Industry, 18 May 1982; Letter from Rt Hon. Patrick Jenkin, Secretary of State for Industry, to Rt Hon. John W. W. Peyton, 20 May 1982, UGD 347/1/2/4; C. Tighe, 'Coal price rise may kill Alcan smelter', *The Sunday Times*, 15 August 1982.

217   Jenkin to Peyton, 20 May 1982.

218   'Obituaries: Lord Gray of Contin: Popular Conservative Minister', *The Independent*, 18 March 2006.

219   HIDB, *Area Profile of East Ross, Statistical area 7*, November 1985, p. 7; HIDB, *Report, 1983*, Appendix 4; A. Young, 'Industry', in Hetherington, *Highlands and Islands*, p. 105; 'Obituary: Lord Gray of Contin', *The Daily Telegraph*, 17 March 2006.

220   Letter from B. Sawyer, British Alcan, to I. Laing, Secretary of State for Scotland, 11 June 1982, NAS, SEP12/668.

221   Grassie, *Highland Experiment*, pp. 118–23.

222   Armstrong, 'Obituaries: Lord Plowden', *The Independent*, 19 February 2001.

223   E. Dell, *A Strange and Eventful History: Democratic socialism in Britain* (Harper Collins: London, 2001), p. 374; R. Sheldon, 'Dell, Edmund Emmanuel (1921–1999)', *ODNB*, http://www.oxforddnb.com.ezproxy.webfeat.lib.ed.ac.uk/view/article/73166 [accessed 3 June 2008].

224   M. Kipping, 'Strategizing in a complex environment: Business, government and the Lynemouth aluminium smelter, 1965–1973', Paper to the Economic and Social History Department, University of Glasgow, 15 April 2010.

225   MacKenzie, 'Be careful what you wish for'.

226   Dell, *A strange and eventful history*, pp. 371–5.

227   O'Hara, *From Dreams to Disillusionment*, p. 71; R. Millward, 'Industrial and commercial performance since 1950', in Floud and McCloskey, *The Economic History of Britain since 1700, Vol. 3*, pp. 123–67; P. L. Payne, 'The Economy', in Devine and Finlay, *Scotland in the Twentieth Century*, pp. 22–3; Perchard, *The Mine Management Professions*, pp. 252–8.

228   O'Hara, *From Dreams to Disillusionment*, p. 205–19.

229   J. Sillars, *Scotland: The case for optimism* (Polygon: London, 1986), p. 1.

230   A. W. Coats, 'The changing role of economists in Scottish Government since 1960', *Public Administration*, vol. 56 (1978), pp. 399–424.

231 Kipping, 'Strategizing in a complex environment'.

232 Memos of meetings between Ford and Russell, 14 and 20 October 1982; Letter from P. J. Elton to G. Younger, NAS, SEP12/668; Evenden, *Fish versus Power*.

233 Memo from Rt Hon. John Davies MP, Secretary of State for Trade and Industry, to Rt Hon. Edward Heath, Prime Minister, 3 November 1971, TNA, PREM 15/344.

234 AAUK submission to DTI, 27 June 1972, UGD 347 10/3/1; Letter from Elton to Thornton, 31 July 1972.

235 Memorandum on proposed merger between Alcan Aluminium (UK) Limited and British Aluminium Company Limited accompanying letter from Elton to Thornton, 31 July 1972.

236 J. Foster and C. Woolfson, *The Politics of the UCS Work-IN: Class alliances and the right to work* (Lawrence and Wishart: London, 1986); Phillips, *The industrial politics of devolution*, pp. 79–116.

237 T. Gourvish, '"Beyond the merger mania": merger and de-merger activity', in Coopey and Woodward, *Britain in the 1970s*, pp. 240–3.

238 Memo from Allen to Caines, DTI, 21 December 1983, NAS, SEP4/4052/1.

239 *Ibid.*

240 *Ibid.*; British Alcan Aluminium Ltd presentation to bankers on post-merger achievements, 11 December 1985; 'British Alcan (Redundancies)' *Hansard*, 8 February 1983; 'Human disaster' for Falkirk', 'Scots Ministers accused of negligence' and 'Falkirk workers 'duped', *The Scotsman*, 9 February 1983; 'A painful blow', 'Fight on for Alcan jobs' and 'Younger accused of negligence over Alcan', *The Glasgow Herald*, 9 February 1983; 'Falkirk and the fight against despair', 'Alcan axe 700 despite top-level plea' and 'Jobs and handouts', *Daily Express*, 9 February 1983; I. Gazeley and A. Newell, 'Unemployment', in N. Crafts, I. Gazeley and A. Newell (eds), *Work and Pay in Twentieth-Century Britain* (OUP: Oxford, 2007), Table 10.3; A. Booth, *The British Economy in The Twentieth Century* (Palgrave: London, 2001), Tables 5.2, 5.3; Knox, *Industrial Nation*, p. 254.

241 Letter from G. W. Budd to R. Forder, 2 June 1983, UGD 347 21/26/14; Letter from Budd to Aluminium Federation Press Office, 1 June 1983, UGD 347/10/17/3; Aluminium Federation, *Aluminium Federation Statement on Fire in Ships*, 28 May 1982, UGD 347 10/17/3; 'Ships Design, Aluminium, and Reports to the MoD', *FT*, 7 December 1982; *Statement on the Defence Estimates*, PP, 1972 (c.4891), pp. 41, 43; *Defence Select Committee: The Royal Dockyards & the Dockyard Study*, PP, 1980–81 (c.362-I), Evidence from Vice Admiral Sir William Pillar, Chief of Fleet Support, Royal Navy, 18 June 1981 (Q. 168); *Defence Select Committee: Defence White Paper*, PP, 1981–82 (c.428), Evidence from Rt Hon. John Nott MP, 23 June 1982 (Q. 75); *Ministry of Defence (MoD): Statement on Defence Estimates*, PP, 1987–88 (c.344), p. 41; *Trade and Industry Select Committee: Exports to Iraq*, PP, 1991–92 (c.86-iv), Evidence from Mr Christopher Cowley, 15 January 1992 (Q. 1088); *Defence Select Committee: Acquisition of support vehicles and related equipment and related equipment*, PP, 1995–96 (c.89-I) Evidence from Sir Robert Walmsley, Chief of Defence Procurement, MoD, 6 December 1995 (Q. 1971); *Arms to Iraq Enquiry: Report of the Inquiry into the Export of Defence Equipment and Dual-Use Goods to Iraq and Related Prosecutions*, PP, 1995–96 (c.115), p. 891; *National Audit Office: Ministry of Defence – initiatives to manage technical risk on defence equipment programmes. Report by the Comptroller and Auditor General*, PP, 1995–96 (c.361), p. 2223.

242 Scottish Development Department – Central Research Unit, *Review of the Highlands and Islands Development Board: Economic and Social Change in the Highlands and Islands*, July 1987; Cameron, 'The Scottish Highlands'; S. Black, 'Economic Change and Challenges in the Highlands and Islands' in D. Newlands, M. Danson, J. McCarthy (eds), *Divided Scotland? The Nature, Causes and Consequences of Economic Disparities within Scotland*

(Ashgate: Aldershot, 2004), pp. 60–9; D. Newlands, 'The Regional Economies of Scotland' in Devine, et al., *The Transformation of Scotland*, pp. 159–83.

243 Alcan Aluminium UK, *Alcan in the Highlands*; Scottish Parliament, *Enterprise and Culture Committee Official Report*, 24 May 2005, Col. 1871; BBC, 'Aluminium firm slashes 200 jobs', 4 December 2001; 'Alcan to axe 85 jobs as it closes Falkirk mill', *The Scotsman*, 20 August 2004; BBC, 'Chemical Plant closure "a tragedy"', 5 September 2005; Rio Tinto Plc, '£45 million investment secures future of Scottish Highlands aluminium industry', 8 January 2008.

Chapter 3: Manufacturing Consent: From BACo's 'Service' to Alcan's 'good corporate citizens'

1   M. Burawoy, *Manufacturing Consent: Changes in the labor process under monopoly capitalism* (University of Chicago Press: Chicago, 1982); Elton to Thornton, 31 July 1972; Aspects of this have been discussed in an earlier article: A. Perchard, 'Sculpting the "Garden of Eden": Patronage, community and the British Aluminium Company in the Scottish Highlands, 1895–1982', *Scottish Labour History*, vol. 42 (2007), pp. 49–69.

2   My thanks to Dr Meg Bateman and Dr Gillian Munro of Sabhal Mòr Ostaig for the translation of this Gaelic inscription on the coin.

3   I am grateful to Alexander Fraser's grandson, Alistair McDougall, for providing me with a copy of this letter: Letter from William Murray Morrison to Alexander Fraser, 5 February 1920; For details of Fraser's career: *British Aluminium's Highland News, Christmas Number* (December 1947), p. 3, UGD 347/21/33/1; *The B.A. News, Highlands Edition*, vol. 1, no. 1 (July–August 1948), p. 3, UGD 347/21/33/2.

4   'The late Sir Murray Morrison', *The B.A. News*, vol. 1, no. 1 (July–August 1948), p. 7.

5   The Royal Technical College became the University of Strathclyde in 1964: L. Stott, 'Morrison, Sir (William) Murray, (1873–1948), metallurgist and electrical engineer', *ODNB*, www.oxforddnb.com.ezproxy.webfeat.lib.ed.ac.uk/view/article/40348 [accessed 21 September 2006].

6   BACo, *Annual Report and Accounts*, 1934, UGD 347/21/19/2; *The Times*, 28 March 1934.

7   *The B.A. News*, vol. 12, no. 1 (January–February 1959), p. 3, UGD 347/21/33/8.

8   Elton to Thornton, 31 July 1972.

9   Kipping and Cailluet, 'Mintzberg's emergent and deliberate strategies', pp. 79–104.

10 For what is still surely one of the best studies of organisational culture in a not too dissimilar, but larger and ultimately far more successful and enduring, company, see A. M. Pettigrew, *The Awakening Giant: Continuity and change in ICI* (Basil Blackwell: Oxford, 1986); and also: Roper, *Masculinity and the British Organization Man*.

11 I am grateful to Professor Mike Rowlinson for allowing me an early sight of this article: M. Rowlinson, C. Booth, P. Clark, A. Delahaye, and S. Procter, 'Social Remembering and Organisational Memory', *Organization Studies: Special Section on Organizational Memory: The Dynamics of Organizational Remembering and Forgetting* vol. 31, no. 1 (2010), pp. 69–87.

12 E. H. Schein, *Organizational Culture and Leadership* (third edition, Jossey Bass: San Francisco, 2004), pp. 15–17.

13 *Ibid.*

14 C. Dellheim, 'Business in Time: The Historian and Corporate Culture', *Public Historian*, vol. 8 (Spring 1986), pp. 9–22 cited in J. Griffiths, '"Give my Regards to Uncle Billy …": The rites and rituals of company life at Lever Brothers, c.1900–c.1990', *BH*, vol. 37, no. 4 (1995), pp. 25–45.

15 Schein, *Organizational Culture and Leadership*, p. 254; A. M. Pettigrew, 'On Studying Organisational Cultures', *Administrative Science Quarterly*, vol. 24, iss. 4 (December 1979), pp. 570–81.

16 Pettigrew, 'On Studying Organisational Cultures', pp. 570–1; Griffiths, '"Give my Regards to Uncle Billy …"', p. 28; Schein, *Organizational Culture and Leadership*, p. 307.

17 Barnes *et al.*, 'Old habits die hard', p. 372; D. C. North, *Institutions, Institutional Change and Economic Performance* (CUP: Cambridge, 1990), p. 7.

18 E. P. Thompson, 'The moral economy of the English crowd in the eighteenth century', *Past and Present*, vol. 50 (1971), pp. 76–136; Andrew Sayer, *Why Things Matter to People: Social Science, Values and Ethical Life* (CUP: Cambridge, 2011).

19 J. Boswell, 'The informal social control of business in Britain: 1880–1939', *BHR*, vol. 57, no. 2 (Summer, 1983), p. 237.

20 Burawoy, *Manufacturing Consent*, *passim* especially pp. xii, 132–5, 201; See the special edition of *Contemporary Sociology*, vol. 30, no. 5 (September 2001), pp. 446–8; See also, M. Korczynski, 'Consumer Capitalism and Industrial Relations' and P. Edwards, 'The Future of Industrial Relations', in P. Ackers and A. Wilkinson (eds), *Understanding Work and Employment: Industrial relations in transition* (OUP: Oxford, 2003), pp. 266–7, 349; H. Braverman, *Labor and Monopoly Capital* (Monthly Review Press: New York, 1974); A. L. Friedman, *Industry and Labour: Class struggle at work and monopoly capitalism* (Macmillan: London, 1977); C. Goodrich, *The Frontier of Control: A study of British workshop politics* (Pluto: London, 1975).

21 G. Vindt, *Les hommes de l'aluminium: Histoire sociale de Pechiney 1921–1973* (Les editions de l'atelier: Paris, 2006), *passim*; Charle, 'Le pantouflage en France', pp. 1118–19; A. Picon, 'French engineers and social thought, 18–20th centuries: An archeology of technocratic ideals', *History and Technology*, vol. 23, iss. 3 (2007), pp. 197–208.

22 *The Times*, 1 April 1916, 26 and 29 March 1935; D. Cannadine, *The Decline and Fall of the British Aristocracy* (Picador: London, 1992), pp. 77, 265, 270, 278.

23 *The Times*, 4 July 1912, 1 April 1916, 29 April 1919, 26 April 1932, 17 June 1935, 23 December 1970; R. McKibbin, *Classes and Cultures in England 1918–1951* (OUP: Oxford, 1998), p. 35.

24 C. Smith and M. Norton Wise, *Energy and Empire: A biographical study of Lord Kelvin* (CUP: Cambridge, 1989), pp. 802–10; P. J. Cain and A. G. Hopkins, *British Imperialism, 1688–2000* (Longman: London, 2001), p. 675; Butler, *Britain and Empire*, pp. 5–10, 148–59.

25 *The Times*, 1 April 1916.

26 *The Times*, 5 March 1943 and 28 December 1955; S. Robbins, *British Generalship on the Western Front 1914–18: Defeat into victory* (Frank Cass: London, 2005), p. 31, fn. 143; C. G. Brown, *The Death of Christian Britain: Understanding secularisation 1800–2000* (Routledge: London, 2001), pp. 88, 96–114; N. J. Watson, S. Weir and S. Friend, 'The development of muscular Christianity in Victorian Britain and beyond', *Journal of Religion and Society*, vol. 7 (2005), pp. 1–21.

27 *The Times*, 16 December 1963.

28 'Works Managers: Reduction Works', *The B. A. News*, vol. 5, no. 4 (July–August 1952), pp. 10–11, UGD 347/21/33/5; 'Works Managers: Rolling Mills & Latchford', *The B. A. News*, vol. 5, no. 5 (September–October 1952), pp. 20–1; 'The man at the wheel', *The B. A. News*, vol. 16, no. 3 (May–June 1964), pp. 15–17.

29 R. V. Clements, *Managers: A study of their careers in industry* (Allen & Unwin: London, 1958), Table 18; Pettigrew, *The Awakening Giant*, p. 128; W. J. Reader, *Imperial Chemical Industries: A History, Volume II: The First Quarter Century 1926–1952* (Clarendon: Oxford, 1975) pp. 70–2; J. M. Quail, 'From personal patronage to public school privilege: Social closure in the recruitment of managers in the United Kingdom from the late nineteenth

century to 1930' in Kidd and Nicholls, *The Making of the British Middle Class?*, pp. 169–85; Perchard, *The Mine Management Professions.*

30 J. F. Wilson and A. Thomson, *The Making of Modern Management: British management in historical perspective* (OUP: Oxford, 2006); F. Fauri, 'British and Italian management education before the Second World War: A comparative analysis' and N. Tiratsoo, 'Management education in postwar Britain', in L. Engwall and V. Zamagni (eds), *Management Education in Historical Perspective* (MUP: Manchester, 1998), pp. 34–45, 111–25.

31 R. Trainor, 'Neither Metropolitan nor Provincial: the Interwar Middle Class' in Kidd and Nicholls, *The Making of the British Middle Class?*, pp. 208–10.

32 McKibbin, *Classes and Cultures*, pp. 104–5.

33 D. McCrone, 'Towards a Principled Society: Scottish Elites in the Twentieth Century', in A. Dickson and J. H. Treble (eds), *People and Society in Scotland, Volume III: 1914–1990* (John Donald: Edinburgh, 1992), pp. 174–200.

34 R. Coopey and A. McKinlay, 'Stealing the Souls of Men': Employers, supervisors and work organization (c.1890–1939)', in P. Van den Eeckhout (ed.), *Supervision and Authority in Industry: Western European experiences, 1830–1939* (Berghahn: New York, 2009), pp. 182–3.

35 A. Fox, *History and Heritage: The social origins of the British Industrial Relations system* (Allen & Unwin: London, 1985), p. 3; R. Fitzgerald, *British Labour Management and Industrial Welfare 1846–1939* (Croom Helm: London, 1988), pp. 9–26; P. Ackers, 'On paternalism: Seven observations on the uses and abuses of the concept in industrial relations, past and present', *HSIR*, no. 5 (Spring 1998), pp. 173–93; H. Mintzberg and J. A. Waters, 'Of strategies, deliberate and emergent', *Strategic Management Journal*, vol. 6 (1985), pp. 257–72.

36 Vindt, *Les hommes de l'aluminium*; J. E. Igartua, *Arvida ou Saguenay: Naissance d'une ville industrielle* (McGill-Queen's University Press: Montréal and Kingston, ON, 1996); Griffiths, '"Give my Regards to Uncle Billy …"'.

37 'The Aluminium Works at Kinlochleven: The Men's Grievances', *Forward*, 22 October 1910.

38 Reports from William Murray Morrison to the directors of the British Aluminium Company about the strike at the Company's Kinlochleven works, 29 August and 3 September 1910, UGD 347/21/34/4/24.

39 Report by the Chief Constable of Argyllshire, 12 October 1910, Argyll and Bute County Archives. Courtesy of Neville Kirk; Reports from William Murray Morrison to the British Aluminium's directors on the Kinlochleven Strike, 29 August 1910–3 September 1910.

40 Letters from Morrison to Directors, 29 August 1910 and 3 September 1910; *Forward*, 22 October 1910, pp. 3, 7.

41 *Departmental Committee on the employment of women and young persons on the two-shift system*, PP, 1920 (c.1038), Evidence – Miss Gilmore, Miss Owen, and Miss Edwards (BACo employees, Warrington), 15 October 1920; Ministry of Labour, Industrial Commissioners Department, Arbitration between the Workers' Union and the British Aluminium Company Ltd, 20 September and 5 November 1918, TNA, LAB 2/188/IC4775/1918; *Report for 1921 on conciliation and arbitration*, PP (c.185), p. 90.

42 NBACo, Minute book, no. 1, 16 June 1936; 'Inverlochy strikers', *The Scotsman*, 16 June 1936; 'Inverlochy strikers decision', *The Scotsman*, 27 July 1936.

43 BACo, Minutes of Annual Managers' Conferences, 22 June 1932 and 19 June 1934.

44 *The Scotsman*, 16 June 1936; 'Board of Trade and Inverlochy Strike', *The Scotsman*, 3 July 1936; Scottish Trades Union Congress (STUC), 'Lochaber gassing accidents', *29th Annual Report* (1926), STUC Archive, Glasgow Caledonian University (GCU); *British Medical Journal*, 10 July 1948, p. 80; R. Cooter, 'The rise and decline of the medical member: Doctors and parliament in Edwardian and interwar Britain', *Bulletin of the History of Medicine*, vol. 78, no. 1 (Spring 2004), p. 88; J. McGregor, 'Labour relations on the West

Highland Railway, 1894–1924', *Scottish Labour History*, vol. 43 (2008), pp. 30–46; Gregor and Crichton, *From Croft to Factory*; Knox, *Industrial Nation*, parts III–V.

45 Letter from the Duke of Atholl to Mackintosh of Mackintosh, 9 December 1920, Cameron of Lochiel estate papers, LAC, CL/A/3/2/45/2; 'Inverlochy strike', *The Scotsman*, 9 July 1936.

46 'Lochiel and the Aluminium Strike', *Oban Times*, 11 July 1936; *The Scotsman*, 27 and 30 July 1936; NBACo, Minutes, 7 August 1937; BACo, Minutes of Managers' Annual Conferences, 24 November 1937.

47 BACo, *Annual Report and Accounts, 1936*.

48 *Ibid.*

49 NBACo, Minutes, 22 December 1936; BACo, Minutes of Annual Managers' Conference, 24 November 1937; J. Zeitlin, 'The internal politics of employer organization: The Engineering Employers' Federation 1896–1939', in J. Zeitlin and S. Tolliday (eds), *The Power to Manage? Employers and industrial relations in comparative-historical perspectives* (Routledge: London, 1991), p. 73.

50 A. J. McIvor, *A History of Work in Britain, 1880–1950* (Palgrave: Basingstoke, 2001), pp. 130–44, 158–70.

51 J. Hinton, *Shop Floor Citizens: Engineering democracy in 1940s Britain* (EE: Aldershot, 1994), *passim*; A. Campbell, N. Fishman and J. McIlroy, 'The Post-War compromise: Mapping industrial politics, 1945–64', in A. Campbell, N. Fishman and J. McIlroy (eds), *British Trade Unions and Industrial Politics: The Post-War Compromise, 1945–64* (Ashgate: Aldershot, 1999), pp. 69–116.

52 J. A. Schumpeter, *Capitalism, Socialism and Democracy* (Unwin: New York, 1976), pp. 219–20.

53 A. Calder, *The People's War: Britain, 1939–1945* (Random House: London, 1969).

54 *Ibid.*; BACo, Minutes of Managers' Annual Conferences, 14 May 1947 and 28 April 1948; A. J. McIvor, *Organised Capital: Employers' associations and industrial relations in northern England 1880–1939* (CUP: Cambridge, 1996), p. 22; Zeitlin, 'The internal politics of employer organization', pp. 52–80; J. Phillips, 'Business and the limited reconstruction of industrial relations in the UK in the 1970s', *Business History*, vol. 51, no. 6 (2009), p. 803.

55 *The B.A. News*, vol. 5, no. 4 (July–August 1952), p. 3; BACo, Annual Report and Accounts, 1968; H. Ramsay, 'Cycles of control: Worker participation in sociological and historical perspective', *Sociology*, no. 11 (1977), pp. 481–506.

56 J. Melling, 'Welfare capitalism and the origins of welfare states: British industry, workplace welfare and social reform, c.1870–1914', *Social History*, vol. 17, no. 3 (October 1992), pp. 454, 477–8.

57 P. Nora, *Realms of Memory: The construction of the French past, Vol. 3: Symbols* (New York: Columbia University Press, 1998); Conway, *When memory speaks*, p. 7.

58 BACo, Minutes of Managers' Annual Conference, 28 April 1948; W. J. Reader, *Fifty Years of Unilever 1930–1980* (Clarendon: Oxford, 1980), pp. 22–3, 52; *idem, ICI*, p. 23.

59 M. E. Dimock, 'The Administrative Staff College: Executive Development in Government and Industry', *The American Political Science Review*, vol. 50, no. 1 (March 1956), pp. 167–8; N. Tiratsoo, 'Management education in post-war Britain', in Engwall and Zamagni, *Management Education in Historical Perspective*, pp. 111–26.

60 *The Times*, 7 November 1945; 'Sir Hector James Wright Hetherington (1888–1965)', *ODNB*, www.oxforddnb.com.ezproxy.webfeat.lib.ed.ac.uk/view/article/33845?docPos=2 [accessed 24 March 2008].

61 BACo, Minutes of Annual Managers' Conference, 25 April 1949.

62 Wilson and Thomson, *The Making of Modern Management*, pp. 165, 167, 206; N. Tiratsoo and J. Tomlinson, *Industrial Efficiency and State Intervention: Labour 1939–51* (Routledge:

London, 1993), pp. 110, 114–16.

63 'British Aluminium appointment Invergordon top man. Dundee man is smelter manager', *P&J*, 11 December 1968.

64 Roper, *Masculinity and the British Organisation Man*; Perchard, *The Mine Management Professions*, pp. 141–206.

65 Griffiths, '"Give my Regards to Uncle Billy …"', pp. 38–40; Tiratsoo and Tomlinson, *Industrial Efficiency and State Intervention*, p. 120.

66 R. Taylor, 'Trade Unions since 1945: Scapegoats of economic decline?', *Contemporary British History*, vol. 1, no. 2 (1987), p. 7.

67 BACo, Minutes of Annual Managers' Conference, 24 April 1948.

68 *Ibid.*

69 *Ibid.*

70 Tiratsoo and Tomlinson, *The Conservatives and Industrial Efficiency*, p. 21.

71 BACo, Minutes of Annual Managers' Conference, 24 April 1948.

72 *Ibid.*

73 *HC Debs.,* vol. 358, Cols 833–4, 11 March 1940; *TUC Reports,* 1944, p. 301.

74 BACo, Minutes of Managers' Meetings, 14 May 1947.

75 A. McKinlay, 'Management and workplace trade unionism: Clydeside engineering, 1945–1957', in J. Melling and A. McKinlay (eds), *Management, Labour and Industrial Politics in Modern Europe: The quest for productivity growth during the twentieth century* (EE: Cheltenham, 1996), pp. 174–86.

76 BACo, Minutes of Managers' Annual Conference, 14 May 1947.

77 I. Gazeley, 'The levelling of pay in Britain during the Second World War', *European Review of Economic History*, vol. 10, no. 2 (2006), pp. 174–204; *idem,* 'Manual work and pay, 1900–70', in Crafts, Gazeley and Newell, *Work and Pay in Twentieth-Century Britain*, p. 74; Campbell, *et al.*, 'The Post-War compromise', in Campbell *et al.*, *British Trade Unions and Industrial Politics*, pp. 69–116.

78 BACo, Minutes of Managers' Conferences, 26 April 1948.

79 *Ibid.*, 28 April 1948.

80 *Ibid.*

81 Campbell *et al.*, 'The Post-War compromise', in Campbell *et al.*, *British Trade Unions and Industrial Politics,* p. 78; See also: J. Phillips, *The Great Alliance: Economic recovery and the problems of power 1945–1951* (Pluto Press: London, 1996), pp. 1–26.

82 BACo, Minutes of Annual Managers' Conferences, 28 April 1948.

83 *Ibid.*, 14 May 1947 and 28 April 1948; 'A Red that May be Missed', *The B.A. News*, vol. 7, no. 2 (March–April 1954), p. 20; Hinton, *Shop Floor Citizens*, *passim*; R. Stevens, 'Cold War Politics: Communism and Anti-Communism in the Trade Unions' in Campbell *et al.*, *British Trade Unions and Industrial Politics*, pp. 168–91, as well as Table 3.3.

84 Tiratsoo and Tomlinson, *Industrial Efficiency and State Intervention*, pp. 90–1.

85 *The B.A. News*, vol. 2, no. 3 (May–June 1949), p. 5.

86 *The B.A. News*, vol. 2, no. 4 (July–August 1949), pp. 2–3.

87 *The B.A. News, Highland Edition*, vol. 1, no. 1 (July–August 1948), p. 15.

88 Campbell *et al.*, 'The Post-War compromise', p. 78; Tiratsoo and Tomlinson, *Industrial Efficiency and State Intervention*, *passim*; Hinton, *Shop Floor Citizens*, pp. 150–205; C. J. Wrigley, *British Trade Unions Since 1933* (CUP: Cambridge, 2002), pp. 56–7.

89 BACo, Minutes of Managers' Annual Conference, 28 April 1948; *The B.A. News, Highland Edition*, vol. 1, no. 1 (July–August 1948), p. 15.

90 BACo, Minutes of Managers' Conferences, 25 April 1949.

91 Letter from G. Chalmers to Board of Trade, Office for Scotland, 5 July 1948, NAS,

SEP2/454/1.

92 French producers AFC had introduced method study in 1924: BACo, Minutes of Managers' Conferences, 24 April 1950; Vindt, *Les hommes de l'aluminium*, pp. 40–1.

93 BACo, Minutes of Managers' Conferences, 25 April 1949.

94 *The B.A. News,* vol. 3, no. 2 (March–April 1950), p. 3.

95 BACo, Minutes of Managers' Conferences, 28 April 1948, 24 April 1949, 24 April 1950.

96 *Ibid.,* 24 and 25 April 1950.

97 Wrigley, *British Trade Unions Since 1933*, pp. 56–7; Campbell *et al.*, 'The Post-War compromise', pp. 78–9; A. Taylor, 'The Conservative Party and the Trade Unions', in J. McIlroy, N. Fishman and A. Campbell (eds), *The High Tide of British Trade Unionism: Trade Unions and industrial politics, 1964–79* (Merlin: Monmouth, 2007), p. 151.

98 'Joint Works Councils', *The B.A. News*, vol. 6, no. 1 (January–February 1953), pp. 6–9, UGD 347/21/33/5.

99 *Ibid.*

100 Ramsay, 'Cycles of control', p. 482.

101 'What productivity really means', *The B.A. News*, vol. 7, no. 2 (March–April 1954), p. 3.

102 BACo, *A Plan for your Retirement* (BACo: London, 1956), p. 4.

103 BACo, Minutes of Managers' Annual Conferences, 28 April 1948 and 25 April 1949.

104 BACo, Minutes of Managers' Conference, 28 April 1948.

105 *Ibid.*, 14 May 1948, 24 April 1950; Vindt, *Les hommes de l'aluminium*, pp. 40–1.

106 Interview with George Haggart, 16 August 2006.

107 Report of the Royal Commission on Trade Unions and Employers' Associations 1965–1968, PP, June 1968 (c.3623), pp. 36–7.

108 'The History of the Company', *The B.A. News,* vol. 1, no. 2 (September–October 1948), p. 3; 'History of the Company, Part II', *The B.A. News*, vol. 1, no. 3 (November–December 1948), p. 3; 'History of the Company, Part III', *The B.A. News*, vol. 2, no. 1 (January–February 1949), p. 3; 'History of the Company, Part IV', *The B.A. News*, vol. 2, no. 2 (March–April 1949), p. 5; *The B.A. News*, vol. 2, no. 3 (May–June 1949), p. 5; 'Establishment Division', *The B.A. News*, vol. 2, no. 5 (September–October 1949), pp. 8–9, UGD 347/21/33/3; 'Our Highland Story', *The B.A. News*, vol. 5, no. 4 (July–August 1952), pp. 8–9; BACo, *History*; BACo, *Employees Handbook* (BACo: London, 1948), UGD 347/21/32/18; BACo, Minutes of Annual Managers' Conferences, 28 April 1948; R. G. H. Linzee, Royal Navy service record, TNA, ADM 196/123/0/256.

109 'The city among the hills: Present day industrial activities – Kinlochleven', *The Oban Times*, 24 March 1923; Boex, *The Aluminium Industry in Scotland*, pp. 18, 54.

110 M. Foucault, *Psychiatric Power: Lectures at the Collège de France 1973–1974* (Palgrave: Basingstoke, 2006), pp. 38–46.

111 Schein, *Organizational Culture and Leadership*.

112 Vindt, *Les hommes de l'aluminium*, pp. 6, 132.

113 Perchard, 'Sculpting the "Garden of Eden"'.

114 BACo, *Employees Handbook*, June 1948.

115 C. Bloom, *Bestsellers: Popular fiction since 1900* (Palgrave: Basingstoke, 2002), Appendix 4; J. Richards, *Films and British National Identity: From Dickens to Dad's Army* (MUP: Manchester, 1997), pp. 52–6, 175–211; A. Calder, *The Myth of the Blitz* (Pimlico: London, 1991); M. Connelly, *We Can Take It! Britain and the memory of the Second World War* (Longman: London, 2004).

116 *The B.A. News*, vol. 1, no. 3 (1948), p. 2.

117 *The B.A. News*, vol. 1, no. 3 (1948), p. 3.

118 *Ibid.*, p. 19.

119 *The B.A. News*, vol. 2, no. 3 (1949), p. 5.

120 *Ibid.*

121 For example: James Grant's story in 'People We Meet', *The B.A. News*, vol. 7, no. 3 (May–June 1954), p. 16.

122 *The B.A. News*, vol. 5, no. 4 (1952), pp. 8–9.

123 BACo, *History*, p. 24

124 *The B.A. News*, vol. 5, no. 4 (1952), pp. 8–9.

125 *Ibid.*

126 BACo, *History*, pp. 5, 18.

127 *The BA News*, vol. 1, no. 2 (1948), p. 19.

128 'We Visit Lochaber', *The B.A. News*, vol. 2, no. 5 (1949), pp. 3, 18–20.

129 *The B.A. News*, vol. 4, no. 1 (January–February 1951), p. 3.

130 *The Times*, 10 January 1936, 18 February 1938, 5 March 1943, 28 December 1955.

131 *The BA News*, vol. 3, no. 2 (March–April 1950), pp. 4–5; *The B.A. News*, vol. 2, no. 2 (March–April 1949), p. 3.

132 BACo, Minutes of Annual Managers' Conferences, 28 April 1948; *The B.A. News*, vol. 2, no. 4, (1949), p. 21; *The B.A. News*, vol. 3, no. 4 (1950), p. 2.

133 *The B.A. News*, vol. 1, no. 2 (1948), p. 4; vol. 2, no. 1 (1949), pp. 5–6; vol. 2, no. 2, (1949), p. 4; vol. 2, no. 3 (1949), p. 4; vol. 4, no. 6 (November–December 1951); vol. 8, no. 5 (September–October 1955), pp. 1–2, 16–17; *Highland News, Christmas Edition*, no. 18 (December 1947), p. 1.

134 *The B.A. News*, vol. 10, no. 5 (September–October 1957), p. 1, UGD 347/21/33/7; In contrast to BACo's comparatively restrained features about its defence contracts see Northern's frequent pieces: *Noral News*, vol. 1, no. 2 (Spring 1951), front cover, UGD 347/10/16/7; vol. 2, no. 4, (Autumn 1952), p. 8; vol. 3, no. 1 (Winter 1952–3), pp. 3, 9; vol. 3, no. 4, (Autumn 1953), pp. 9–10; vol. 5, no. 4, (Autumn 1955), pp. 2–6; vol. 6, no. 3, (Summer 1956), p. 28; vol. 6, no. 4, (Autumn 1956), p. 32; vol. 7, no. 4, (Autumn 1957), p. 2, UGD 347/10/16/8.

135 'The Company on the Gold Coast', *The B.A. News*, vol. 1, no. 1 (1948), pp. 10–11.

136 *The B.A. News*, vol. 2, no. 1 (1949), p. 10.

137 'The Company in India', *The B.A. News*, vol. 2, no. 2 (1949), pp. 8–9.

138 White, 'The business and politics of decolonization', pp. 547–9.

139 *The B.A. News, Highlands Edition*, vol. 1, no. 1 (1948), p. 12; *The B.A. News*, vol. 2, no. 1 (1949), p. 4; *The B.A. News*, vol. 2, no. 2 (1949), pp. 10–16; *The B.A. News*, vol. 2, no. 4 (1949), pp. 8–9; *The B.A. News*, vol. 2, no. 5 (1949), p. 4; McIvor, *A History of Work in Britain*, p. 191; E. Roberts, *A Woman's Place: An oral history of working class women, 1890–1940* (OUP: Oxford, 1995).

140 *The B.A. News*, vol. 2, no. 1 (1949), p. 4.

141 For example: *The B.A. News*, vol. 1, no. 2 (1948), p. 4; *The B.A. News*, vol. 2, no. 2 (1949), p. 4.

142 Roper, *Masculinity and the British Organisation Man*, pp. 161–88; *The B.A. News*, vol. 2, no. 4 (1949), pp. 8–9; *The B.A. News*, vol. 2, no. 1 (1949), p. 4; *The B.A. News*, vol. 5, no. 1 (January–February 1952), p. 11; *The B.A. News*, vol. 3, no. 6 (November–December 1950), pp. 3, 8, 9.

143 M. Carver, 'Guingand, Sir Francis Wilfred [Freddie] de (1900–1979)', *ODNB*, www.oxforddnb.com.ezproxy.webfeat.lib.ed.ac.uk/view/article/31022 [accessed 23 March 2008]; R. Mead, *Churchill's Lions: A biographical guide to the key British generals of World War II* (Barnes & Noble: Stroud, 2007), pp. 112–16.

144 Lt Col J. K. Stanford, 'Essays of a Non-soldier', c.1968, Imperial War Museum, DS/MISC/75, details: http://www.nationalarchives.gov.uk/A2A/records.aspx?cat=062-jks&cid=–

1&Gsm=2008–06–18#–1, [accessed 21 September 2008].

145 J. Hatch, 'African Assignment', International Affairs, vol. 30, no. 2 (April 1954), p. 254.

146 'This is TI today', The B.A. News, vol. 12, no. 2 (March–April 1959), pp. 3–7.

147 The B.A. News, vol. 16, no. 4 (September–November 1963); 'Two sides of the coin', The B.A. News, vol. 21, no. 4 (July–August 1969), pp. 2–3, UGD 347/21/33/15.

148 Ibid., pp. 2–3, 6–7; The B.A. News, vol. 21, no. 6 (November–December 1969), p. 5; The B.A. News, vol. 22, no. 5 (May–June 1970), p. 5; UGD 347/21/33/15; The B.A. News, vol. 27, no. 1 (January–February 1975), p. 13, UGD 347/21/33/18; The Scotsman, 15 October 1966.

149 Interview with George Haggart conducted by A. Perchard, as well as questionnaire and CV; The B.A. News, vol. 31, no. 1 (January–February 1979), p. 7, UGD 347/21/33/20; Campbell, Global Mission, Vol. III, pp. 968–9.

150 Interview with George Haggart.

151 Interviews with George Haggart, Douglas McDiarmid, Rev. Iain Grainger, and John Blair; Surveys provided by the aforementioned as well as Adrian Hope, William Aitken, Angus Christie, David Flett, Peter Preston, James Ramsay, and Michael Rowbottom.

152 J. McIlroy and A. Campbell, 'The high tide of Trade Unionism: Mapping industrial politics, 1964–79', in McIlroy et al., The High Tide of British Trade Unionism, pp. 94–9.

153 See for example: NBACo, Introducing... The North British Aluminium Company (London, no date but c. 1962–64).

154 The B.A. News, vol. 5, no. 4 (July–August 1952), p. 10 and vol. 11, no. 4 (July 1958), pp. 7–9.

155 'President George', The B.A. News, vol. 29 (1977), p. 9.

156 Interview with Alexander (Sandy) Walker.

157 Interview with James (Jimmy) Dunlevy.

158 Interviews with Jimmy Dunlevy and Douglas MacDiarmid.

159 The B.A. News, vol. 5, no. 4 (1952), p. 10; The B.A. News, vol. 23, no. 2 (March–April 1971), p. 5; BoT, Notes on British Aluminium Co. Ltd, Lochaber works, Fort William, for visit of Parliamentary Secretary of State's visit of 15 October 1963, prepared by E. B. Templeman, BoT, Inverness Office, 25 September 1963.

160 'End of an era', The B.A. News, vol. 11, no. 4 (July–August 1958), pp. 7–9, UGD 347/21/33/8; 'Change in B.A. managership. August retiral of Mr S. H. Weston', Oban Times, 28 March 1963.

161 BACo, Minutes of Managers' Annual Conference, 24 November 1938; The B.A. News, vol. 21, no. 1 (January–February 1969), p. 8, UGD 347/21/33/15; T. Strangleman, Work Identity at the End of the Line: Privatisation and Culture Change in the UK Rail Industry (Basingstoke, 2004), p. 59.

162 BoT, Scottish Development Group: Highlands and Islands Study, 'Future of the Highland Reduction Works of the British Aluminium Co. Ltd', 22 May 1964; Minutes from L. I. McBeth and W. H. B. Smith, BoT, 12 and 30 July 1962; Memo from Smith to C. J. A. Whitehouse, BoT, 30 July 1962; Whitehouse to T. Lister, Scottish Home and Health Department, 27 July 1962; Notes on the British Aluminium Company, Lochaber Works, for the visit of the Parliamentary Secretary's visit to Scotland, 25 September 1963, NAS, SEP2/454/1.

163 'Major Falkirk Project Likely: British Aluminium Ltd', The Scotsman, 22 December 1959; 'The Aluminium men are ready for a new battle', Evening Citizen, 17 March 1960; '£10m. Expansion Programme for British Aluminium', FT, 18 May 1961; 'Brit. Aluminium short-time: four-day week at Falkirk', FT, 31 January 1962; '150 workers given notice', Glasgow Herald, 9 February 1962; BoT, note of visit by C. J. A Whitehouse to British Aluminium Co. Ltd, Falkirk, 6 June 1961, NAS, SEP2/539; 'British Aluminium closing stoke-on-trent plant', FT, 17 September 1961; '1500 in Falkirk walk-out: Factory at standstill',

The Scotsman, 2 February 1966; 'Falkirk Strikers return to work: Negotiations proceeding', *The Scotsman*, 3 February 1966.

164 Report of visit by R. Forsyth, BoT, to BACo, Lochaber, 6 August 1964; BoT, 'Future of the Highland Reduction Works of the British Aluminium Co. Ltd', 22 May 1964.

165 BoT, 'Future of the Highland Reduction Works of the British Aluminium Co. Ltd', 22 May 1964; BoT, Production & Export Section, Office for Scotland, Report of W. H. B Smith of visit to Foyers, Fort William, and Kinlochleven, 27 November 1958; BoT, Production & Export Section, Office for Scotland, Report of R. Forsyth of visit to Lochaber, 19 February 1959; BoT, Production & Export Section, Office for Scotland, Report of Forysth's visit to Lochaber, 29 December 1959; 'The British Aluminium Co. Ltd.', Board of Trade minute no.7 prepared by L. I. McBeth,12 July 1962; Letter from W. H. B. Smith, BoT, Office for Scotland, to C. J. A. Whitehouse, BoT, 3330 July 1962; BoT, Notes on British Aluminium Co. Ltd. for visit of Parliamentary Secretary of State's visit, 25 September 1963; '500 to lose jobs at Renfrew and Falkirk', *The Scotsman*, 18 November 1971.

166 Buxton, 'The Scottish economy, 1945–79', in Saville (ed.), *The Economic Development of Modern Scotland*, p. 61.

167 Notes on the British Aluminium Company, Lochaber works, for the visit of the Parliamentary Secretary's visit to Scotland, 25 September 1963, NAS, SEP2/454/1.

168 'HIDB should be more open', *The Fort William Free Press*, 19 September 1975: Letter from W. M. Wood, LTC, to J. Jack, STUC, 19 September 1975, GCAL, STUC Archive, Lochaber Trades Council (LTC) (formerly Fort William & District Trades Council), File 1: 1975–78.

169 *Fort William Free Press*, 19 September 1975; LTC, Minutes for 26 June 1975.

170 Letter from D. F. Hunter, LTC, to J. Milne, STUC, 7 November 1977.

171 Letter from Milne to Hunter, 30 November 1977.

172 LTC, minutes for meeting, 13 May 1981, GCAL, STUC, LTC, File 2, 1978–82.

173 Drummond, *The Invergordon Smelter*.

174 SEPD, Letter from Baillie, Highlands and Islands Development Board (HIDB), to Sir Douglas Haddow, 3 April 1967, NAS, SEP12/557; 'Steel erectors walk out at Invergordon', *The Scotsman*, 10 January 1970.

175 Utiger, *Never Trust an Expert*, p. 21; M. Ash, J. Macaulay and M. A. Mackay, *This Noble Harbour: A history of the Cromarty Firth* (John Donald: Edinburgh, 1991), p. 257.

176 *Ibid.*, p. 22; *The B.A. News*, vol. 27, no. 1 (January–February 1975), p. 10.

177 Interview with George Haggart.

178 Ash *et al.*, *This Noble Harbour*, pp. 255–67; Interviews with Sandy Walker and Bob Herbert.

179 BoT, 'Future of the Highland Reduction Works of the British Aluminium Company Ltd', 22 May 1964; Interviews with Jimmy Dunlevy and George Haggart; *The B.A. News*, vol. 31, no. 1 (January–February 1979), pp. 3–5, UGD 347/21/33/20; *The B.A. News*, vol. 33, no. 3 (August–September 1981), pp. 3–4; British Alcan, RILA Plan: Working party recommendations on representative structure, November 1983; Interviews with Jimmy Dunlevy and George Haggart; Turnock, *Industrial Britain*, Table 7.

180 Lesclous, *Histoire des sites producteurs d'aluminium*, p. 23.

181 G. B. Margraf, 'Millions invested in new aluminium project', *The Scotsman*, 24 March 1966; See also W. H. Smith report of visit to BACo Falkirk, 3 July 1963, NAS, SEP2/539.

182 *The B.A. News*, vol. 21, no. 3 (May–June 1969), p. 2.

183 *The B.A. News*, vol. 27, no. 3 (May–June 1975), p. 8, UGD 347/21/33/18.

184 *The B.A. News*, vol. 29, no. 5 (October–November 1977), p. 9, UGD 347/21/33/19; BACo, *Aluminium in the Highlands* (Raithby, Lawrence & Co: London, 1978).

185 *Metal in Harmony*, colour, Anglo-Scottish Film Company (1962); *The Invergordon Smelter*,

colour (1972), Scottish Screen Archive.

186   *The B.A. News*, vol. 21, no. 3 (May–June 1969), p. 3.

187   A. Marwick, *The Sixties: Cultural revolution in Britain, France, Italy, and the United States, c.1958–c.1974* (OUP: Oxford, 1998), p. 13.

188   For example: J. Bourke, *Dismembering the Male: Men's bodies, Britain and the Great War* (Reaktion: London, 1996); M. Roper, *The Secret Battle: Emotional survival in the Great War* (MUP: Manchester, 2010); A. Allport, *Demobbed: Coming Home after the Second World War* (Yale UP: Yale, 2010).

189   *The B.A. News*, vol. 15, no. 1 (May–June 1963), front page, UGD 347/21/33/11; *The B.A. News*, vol. 22, no. 6 (November–December 1970), front page.

190   *The B.A. News*, vol. 24, no. 4 (August–September 1972), p. 24, UGD/347/21/33/16; *The B.A. News*, vol. 28, no. 1 (January–February 1976), pp. 6–7, UGD 347/21/33/18.

191   'Race Relations in employment', *The B.A. News*, vol. 22, no. 1 (January–February 1970), pp. 3–4; D. Smith Wilson, 'Gender: Change and continuity', in P. Addison and H. Jones (eds), *A Companion to Contemporary Britain 1939–2000* (Blackwell: Oxford, 2009), pp. 245–62; Roper, *Masculinity and the British Organisation Man*, pp. 162–213.

192   For example: *Topical* (in-house journal for Alcan rolling mills), 91, (January 1974), p. 3; *Topical*, 93 (March 1974), p. 4; *Topical*, 97 (July 1974), p. 1; *Topical*, 100 (October 1974), p. 1; *Topical*, 101 (November 1974), p. 3; *Topical*, 102 (December 1974), *passim*, UGD 347/10/16/4; *Topical*, 103–114 (January–December 1975), *passim*, UGD 347/10/16/5; *Newspak*, no. 3 (February 1978), p. 2; *Newspak*, no. 7 (October/November 1978), p. 6, UGD 347/10/16/6.

193   Letter from unidentified former senior sales manager at Aluminium Union Ltd. to T. Brock, Secretary, Alcan Canada, 24 July 1971, Maison-Alcan, RTAIC, 00026-41; Campbell, *Global Mission, Vol. II* and *Vol. III*, pp. 404, 433, 741–2.

194   *The B.A. News*, vol. 33, no. 1 (January–April 1981), p. 7 and vol. 34, no. 1 (January–April 1982), p. 3, UGD 347/21/33/20. For comparison with British Rail, see Strangleman, *Work Identity at the End of the Line*, p. 73.

195   Memo from Russell to Wagner, 'Visit to Falkirk', 22 July 1982; BMRB, 'The image of Alcan and Aluminium: Report on two surveys'.

196   J. Peyton, *Without Benefit of Laundry: The autobiography of John Peyton* (Bloomsbury: London, 1997), p. 177.

197   Letter from McCrone to PS/Secretary of State for Scotland, 25 October 1982; Letter from G. Drummond, HIDB, to J. S. B. Martin, Asst. Secretary, SEPD, 25 October 1982, NAS, SEP12/663.

198   'Smelter job cuts expected', *Glasgow Herald*, 28 February 1991; Figures supplied by Rio Tinto Alcan of numbers of Lochaber workforce.

199   Letter from G. G. Walker, AUK, to D. C. Campbell, Alcan Aluminium Ltd, Montreal, 3 December 1982, Maison-Alcan, RTAIC, 00161-08.

200   Interview with George Haggart.

201   Interview with Douglas McDiarmid, Fort William, 13 October 2008.

202   *Ibid.*; For examples of this literature see: M. Weiner, *English Culture and the Decline of the Industrial Spirit 1850–1980* (CUP: Cambridge, 1981); C. Barnett, *The Audit of War: The illusion and reality of Britain as a Great Nation* (Macmillan: London, 1986); For an overview and rebuttal of declinism, see: J. Tomlinson, *The Politics of Decline: Understanding Post-War Britain* (Pearson: London, 2001)

203   Minute from John Allen, DTI-IDU, to Mr Caines, 21 December 1983, NAS, SEP4/4052/1; Letter from John Peyton MP to Rt Hon George Younger MP, 9 January 1985, NAS, SEP12/663.

204   Interview with Douglas McDiarmid; Tomlinson, *The Politics of Decline*.

205 Interviews with Sandy Walker, and with Brian Murphy and Jack Silver.

206 See Alcan's advert in: *The Times – Trade & Engineering*, March 1937

207 Kipping and Cailluet, 'Mintzberg's emergent and deliberate strategies'; D. Hunt, 'Alexander, Harold Rupert Leofric George, first Earl Alexander of Tunis (1891–1969)', *ODNB*, http://www.oxforddnb.com/view/article/30371 [accessed 8 September 2009].

208 Letter from John Aitchison, British Alcan, to Dr Gordon W. Lodge, HM Industrial Pollution Inspectorate, 4 April 1990, NAS, DD9/498.

209 P. Musgrave, *British Alcan Lynemouth Limited* (Alcan: London, 1986); P. Edwards, J. Bélanger and M. Wright, 'The social relations of productivity: A longitudinal and comparative study of aluminium smelters', *Industrial Relations*, vol. 57 (2002), pp. 322, 324.

210 D. Gallie, M. Rose and R. Penn, 'The British debate on Trade Unionism: Crisis and continuity' in D. Gallie, M. Rose and R. Penn (eds), *Trade Unionism in Recession* (OUP: Oxford, 1996), pp. 1–32; Knox, *Industrial Nation*, p. 254; Peden, 'The managed economy', pp. 233–64.

211 Interview with Bob Herbert, Kinlochleven, 3 April 2007.

212 For a restating of elements of the 'BA' version, see: Alcan UK, *Aluminium in the Scottish Highlands* (Alcan: London, 1996); For discussion of the notion of 'trust' in industrial relations literature, see: C. Crouch, *Industrial Relations and European State Traditions* (OUP: Oxford, 1993), pp. 26, 46.

213 Edwards *et al.*, 'The social relations of productivity', p. 324.

214 Centre d'economie et d'ethique pour l'environnment et le development (CEEED), *Implementation of a system of indicators for social responsibility reporting* (Guyancourt, 2003), p. 6.

215 R. Sennett, *The Corrosion of Character: The Personal Consequences of Work in the New Capitalism* (W. W. Norton and Co.: New York, 1998); R. Sennett, *The Craftsman* (Allen Lane: London, 2008).

Chapter 4: Health and environment: 'contested' terrain

1 'Lord Kelvin and the Falls of Foyers works', *The Scotsman*, 5 August 1897; Smith and Norton Wise, *Energy and Empire*, pp. 721–2.

2 R. Burns, 'Written with a Pencil, standing by the Fall of Fyers [sic], near Loch-Ness', in J. Kinsley (ed.) *Burns – Poems and Songs* (OUP: Oxford, 1969), p. 285.

3 'The Falls of Foyers – Mr. Ruskin's Opinion', *The Times*, 16 September 1895.

4 *The Bristol Mercury*, 27 December 1851.

5 T. C. Smout, *Nature Contested: Environmental history in Scotland and Northern England since 1600* (EUP: Edinburgh, 2000), pp. 112–13, 154–5; Payne, *The Hydro*, p. 5; I. G. Simmons, *An Environmental History of Great Britain: From 10,000 years ago to the present* (EUP: Edinburgh, 2001), pp. 182–3.

6 *The Times*, 14, 17 and 23 August 1895.

7 'The Falls of Foyers', *The Scotsman*, 4 March 1895; 'The Falls of Foyers', *The Scotsman*, 18 February 1895.

8 BACo, short account of the proposed works at Foyers for the personal information of the members of the County Council of Inverness-shire, 24 April 1895, GUA, UGD 347/21/34/1/1; 'Water power in the watershed of the River Foyers, Loch Ness', Report submitted to British Aluminium Company by A. W. Peregrine Birch, 15 November 1894; Letter from the Swiss Department of Foreign Affairs, Bern, to the British Aluminium Company, attaching reports by the Swiss Factory Inspector for IIIth Division for 1892–1894 about the Neuhausen

aluminium factory in accordance with Police Regulations in Schaffhausen, 26 July 1895; Letter from C. F. Jones, Secretary of the of the British Aluminium Company, to the Duke of Westminster, 19 and 30 September 1895; Letter from A. Lawley, Secretary to the Duke of Westminster, to BACo, 3 October 1895, UGD 347/21/46/2; *The Times,* 20 and 30 September 1895; Payne, *The Hydro,* p. 5.

9   BACo, account of the proposed work at Foyers for the ICC, 24 April 1895.

10 'On the sanitary provision of a new industry at Foyers in Inverness-shire', *Second Annual Report of the Local Government Board for Scotland,* PP, 1895–96 (c.8219), p. 75.

11 'The Foyers Question', *The Northern Chronicle,* 27 March 1895.

12 *Ibid.*; E. A. Cameron, 'Conservatism and Radicalism in the Highland Press: the Strange Cases of the *Highlander* and the *Northern Chronicle*', *Northern Scotland,* vol. 27 (2007), pp. 117–29.

13 *The Times,* 10 August 1895.

14 'Inverness County Council and the Falls of Foyers', *The Scotsman,* 18 October 1895.

15 'The Falls of Foyers', *The Times,* 15 October 1895.

16 Smith and Norton Wise, *Energy & Empire,* p. 722; Smout, *Nature Contested,* pp. 19–26.

17 'Lord Kelvin and the Falls of Foyers works', *The Scotsman,* 5 August 1897.

18 Smout, *Nature Contested,* p. 20.

19 T. Carlyle, *Works* (London, 1829), vol. 2, pp. 59–60 cited in *ibid.*

20 For example: 'Highland Water Schemes', *The Scotsman,* 21 April 1919; 'Highland Hydro-Electric Board Scheme', *The Scotsman,* 16 December 1935.

21 C. T. Reid, A. Pillai and A. R. Black, 'The emergence of environmental concerns: Hydroelectric schemes in Scotland', *Journal of Environmental Law,* vol. 17, no. 3 (2005), pp. 361–82.

22 R. J. Moore-Colyer, 'Sir George Stapledon (1882–1960) and the Landscape of Britain', *Environment and History,* vol. 5 (1999), pp. 221–2.

23 J. R. Payne, 'Land-use and landscape: Hydro-electricity and landscape protection in the Highlands of Scotland, 1919–1980', unpublished Ph.D. Thesis (University of St Andrews, 2008), pp. 38–86.

24 D. Ross and A. Munro, 'Contested energy: A long-term perspective on opposition to renewable power developments in Scotland', paper to EBHA conference, Glasgow 2010; For an example, see: E. Douglas, 'Beauly–Denny power line is vandalism', *The Guardian,* 7 January 2010.

25 Russell, *Chemistry, Society and Environment,* p. 316. Simmons, *An Environmental History of Great Britain,* p. 185; Payne, 'Land-use and landscape', pp. 38–86, 142; 'Lochaber Housing Development: Extension of Aluminium Works', *The Scotsman,* 8 September 1937.

26 'Highland Hydro-Electric Power Scheme', *The Scotsman,* 12 December 1935.

27 Minutes of the Loch Leven Water & Electric Power Company, Minute books 1 (1904–1907) and 2 (1907–1911), 5 and 19 December 1905, 15 May and 14 August 1906, 9 July 1907, 14 and 28 January and 27 March 1908, UGD 347 21/2/3–4; 'Society small talk by Upper-Crust Gossipers', *Hampshire Telegraph and Sussex Chronicle,* 18 April 1891.

28 Political and Economic Planning (PEP), *The State of the Highlands,* broadsheet no. 81, 8 September 1936, pp. 2–3, NLS, LG collection, Acc 12187/10.

29 H. Quigley, *A Plan for the Highlands: Proposals for a Highland Development Board* (Highland Development League: London, 1936), p. 20.

30 *Cooper Report,* p. 34; See also Smout, *Nature Contested,* p. 113.

31 Smout, *Nature Contested* p. 166; J. R. McNeill, *Something new under the sun: An environmental history of the twentieth-century world* (Norton: New York, 2000), pp. 336–9; J. Sheail, '*Torrey Canyon*: The political dimension', *Journal of Contemporary History,* vol. 42,

no. 3 (2007), pp. 485–504.

32   P. Dorman, *Markets and Mortality: Economics, dangerous work, and the value of human life* (CUP: Cambridge, 1997), p. 103.

33   A. Sen, *Rationality and Freedom* (OUP: Oxford, 2002), pp. 46, 66, 86–9.

34   I. Levitt, 'Regenerating the Scottish Highlands: Whitehall and the Fort William Pulp Mill, 1945–63', *Journal of Scottish Historical Studies*, vol. 25, no. 1 (2005), p. 34.

35   For a discussion of 'lay epidemiology': M. Bloor, 'The South Wales Miners' Federation, miners' lung and the instrumental use of expertise, 1900–1950', *Social Studies in Science*, vol. 30, no. 1 (2000), pp. 125–40.

36   J. Reason, *Human Error* (CUP: Cambridge, 1990), pp. 37–9, 57, 167; For a few examples of a growing literature: D. Michaels, *Doubt is their Product: How industry's assault on science threatens your health* (OUP: Oxford, 2008); J. McCulloch and G. Tweedale, *Defending the Indefensible: The global asbestos industry and its fight for survival* (OUP: Oxford, 2008); R. Johnston and A. McIvor, *Lethal Work: A history of asbestos tragedy in Scotland* (Tuckwell: East Linton, 2000).

37   A. Ross and J. Rowan-Robinson, 'Behind closed doors: The use of agreements in the UK to protect the environment', *Environmental Law Review*, iss. 1 (1999), pp. 82–94.

38   R. Johnston and A. McIvor, 'Whatever Happened to the *Occupational* Health Service? The NHS, the OHS and the asbestos tragedy on Clydeside', in C. Nottingham (ed.), *The NHS in Scotland: The legacy of the past and the prospect of the future* (Ashgate: Aldershot, 2000), p. 80.

39   McIvor, *A History of Work in Britain*, pp. 112, 135, 147.

40   Johnston and McIvor, 'Whatever Happened to the *Occupational* Health Service?', p. 83.

41   W. G. Carson, 'White-Collar Crime and the Enforcement of Factory Legislation', *British Journal of Criminology*, 10 (1970), pp. 383–98 cross-referenced in A. Higgison, 'Asbestos and British Trade Unions, 1960s and 1970s', *Scottish Labour History*, vol. 40 (2005), pp. 72–3; A. McIvor and R. Johnston, *Miners' Lung: A history of dust disease in British coal mining* (Ashgate: Aldershot, 2007), in Nottingham, *The NHS in Scotland*, p. 210.

42   Johnston and McIvor, 'Whatever Happened to the *Occupational* Health Service?', pp. 86–93.

43   Scottish Home and Health Department, *General Medical Services in the Highlands and Islands*, PP, June 1967 (c.3257), Table 5 and pp. 14–15, 24; J. Jenkinson, 'Scottish Health Policy 1918–1948' in Nottingham, *The NHS in Scotland*, pp. 1–19.

44   A. Kessel, *Air, the Environment and Public Health* (CUP: Cambridge, 2006), pp. 51–97.

45   Smout, *Nature Contested*, p. 139.

46   N. D. Priest and T. V. O' Donnell, 'Preface: Health issues within the aluminium industry', in N. D. Priest and T. V. O'Donnell (eds), *Health in the Aluminium Industry: Managing health issues in the aluminium industry* (Middlesex University: London, 1998), p. i.

47   Russell, *Chemistry, Society and Environment*, p. 318.

48   A selection of examples includes: J. Spofforth, 'Case of aluminium poisoning', *The Lancet*, CC: I (18 June 1921), p. 1301; J. Mitchell, 'Pulmonary fibrosis in an aluminium worker', *British Journal of Industrial Medicine (BJIM)*, vol. 16 (1959), pp. 123–5; G. W. Gibbs and I. Horowitz, 'Lung cancer mortality in aluminium reduction plant workers', *Journal of Occupational Medicine (J. Occ. Med.)*, 21:5 (May 1979), pp. 347–53; G. W. Gibbs, 'Mortality of aluminium reduction plant workers, 1950 through 1977', *J. Occ. Med.*, 27 (1985), pp. 761–70; J. J. Spinelli, P. R. Band, L. M. Svirchev, R. P. Gallagher, 'Mortality and cancer incidence in aluminium reduction plant workers', *J. Occ. Med.*, vol. 33, no. 11 (1991), pp. 1150–5.

49   G. Markowitz and D. Rosner, *Deceit and Denial: The deadly politics of industrial pollution* (UCP: Berkeley, 2002), pp. 141, 146.

50 Payne, *The Hydro*, pp. 6–7.
51 MacGill, *Children of the Dead End*; *Royal Commission on the Poor Laws and Relief of Distress, Vol. IX: Minutes of Evidence*, 1910, Qs 37, 90365–6, and Appendix no. CXVIII; Handley, *The Navvy in Scotland*, pp. 78–9.
52 Scottish Trades Union Congress (STUC), 'Lochaber gassing accidents', *29th Annual Report* (1926).
53 P. Howat, *The Lochaber Narrow Gauge Railway* (Narrow Gauge Railway Society: Alexandria, 1980), pp. 22–3; I am grateful to Dr Chris Robinson for these figures from files that are not accessible to the public.
54 A. C. Miller, 'Medical work on the Lochaber water-power scheme', *Caledonian Medical Journal (CMJ)*, vol. 13, no. 3 (July 1926), p. 108; See also: *CMJ*, vol. 13, no. 2 (April 1926), pp. 63–70 and no. 5 (January 1927), pp. 183–8, and 'editorial', *CMJ*, vol. 14, no. 8 (October 1930), pp. 257–9.
55 Miller, 'Medical work on the Lochaber water-power scheme', *CMJ*, vol. 13, no. 2 (April 1926), p. 63.
56 Melling, 'Welfare capitalism and the origins of welfare states', pp. 453–78; T. Albarn, 'Senses of belonging: The politics of working-class insurance in Britain, 1880–1914', *The Journal of Modern History*, vol. 73, no. 3 (September 2001), pp. 561–602.
57 *Report of the Committee on the Highlands and Islands Medical Service*, 1913, PP (c.6920), Evidence: Dr Ronald Cadell Macdonald, 19 August 1912 (Qs 1808–1908, 1942); Dr Lachlan Grant, 28 October 1912 (Q. 19,719); Rev. Malcolm McCallum, 30 October 1912, (Q. 21,180).
58 Miller, 'Medical work on the Lochaber water-power scheme', *CMJ*, vol. 13, no. 2 (April 1926), p. 66.
59 For example: *Annual Report of the Chief Inspector for Factories and Workshops for 1930*, PP (c.3927), Tables A and B; *Annual Report of the Chief Inspector for Factories and Workshops for 1937*, PP (c.5802), Tables A and B; *Annual Report of the Chief Inspector for Factories and Workshops for 1950*, PP (c.8445), pp. 60–1 and Appendix III; *Annual Report of the Chief Inspector for Factories and Workshops for 1952*, PP (c.9154), p. 82; *Annual Report of the Chief Inspector for Factories and Workshops for 1955*, PP (c.8), Figure 7; *Annual Report of the Chief Inspector for Factories and Workshops for 1957*, PP (c.521), Table 6; *Annual Report of the Chief Inspector for Factories and Workshops for 1967*, PP (c.3745), pp. 118–19; *Annual Report of the Chief Inspector for Factories and Workshops for 1971*, PP (c.5098), Appendix 7; *Annual Report of the Chief Inspector for Factories and Workshops for 1974*, PP (c.6322), Appendix 5.
60 *The B.A. News*, vol. 3, no. 5 (September–October 1950), p. 3; *The B.A. News*, vol. 2, no. 1 (January–February 1949), p. 2.
61 BACo, Minutes of Managers' Meetings, 26 April 1948.
62 'Pot' was also the technical term used to describe aluminium reduction furnaces in North America: H. W. Keen, *Death in the Pot* (n.p. London, 1937), see: M. Clement, *Aluminium: A Menace to Health* (London, n.d. but around 1942), *passim*, BACo/Alcan library.
63 BACo, Proceedings of the 22nd OGM, 31 March 1932.
64 *British Medical Journal*, 9 April 1932.
65 J. Spofforth, 'Case of aluminium poisoning', *The Lancet*, vol. 200, no. 1 (18 June 1921), p. 1301.
66 Letter from Swiss Department of Foreign Affairs, Bern, attaching Reports by Swiss Factory Inspectors for 111th Division for 1892, 1893 and 1894 about Neuhausen aluminium factory in accordance with Police Regulations for Schaffhausen, to the British Aluminium Company Ltd, 26 July, 1895, GUA Alcan/BACo collection; Letter from C. F. Jones, Secretary of the British Aluminium Company Ltd, to Duke of Westminster, 19 September 1895, UGD 347/21/46/2.

67 Interview with Sandy Walker.

68 *Hansard*, HC Deb, 28 November 1950, vol. 481, cc.922–3.

69 *The Lancet*, 14 March 1953, p. 543.

70 *Hansard*, HC Debs, 14 May 1953, vol. 515, cc.1556–664.

71 *Annual Report of the Chief Inspector for Factories and Workshops for 1969*, PP (c.4461), p. 63.

72 K. Sogner, 'Constructive power: Elkem, 1904–2004' in S. Fellman, M. J. Iversen, H. Sjögren and L. Thue (eds), *Creating Nordic Capitalism: The business history of a competitive periphery* (Palgrave Macmillan: Basingstoke, 2008), pp. 494–527.

73 Vindt, *Les hommes de l'aluminium*, p. 29.

74 Bocquetin, 'La fabrication de l'aluminium par électrolyse', pp. 71–110; Sogner, 'Constructive power', p. 505.

75 D. C. Ménégoz, 'Protection de l'environnement autour des usines d'électrolyse' in Morel, *Histoire Technique de la production d'aluminium*, p. 135.

76 W. Taylor, 'Manufacturing processes: Aluminium manufacture', *Journal of the Society for Occupational Medicine*, vol. 28 (1978), pp. 25–6; International Agency for Research on Cancer (IARC), *Polynuclear aromatic compounds: Part 3, Industrial exposures* (IARC: Lyon, 1984).

77 T. V. O'Donnell, 'Asthma and respiratory problems – a review', *The Science of the Total Environment*, vol. 163 (1995), pp. 137–45.

78 *The Lancet*, 14 March 1953, p. 543; *Occupational Medicine*, vol. 3, no. 4 (1954), p. 321; D. J. Gawkroger, 'Occupational skin cancers', *Occupational Medicine*, vol. 54 (2004), pp. 458–63; F. J. Jongeneelen, 'Biological Monitoring of PAH: Review and Update' in Priest and O'Donnell, *Health in the Aluminium Industry*.

79 *Royal Commission on Civil Liability and Compensation for Personal Injury, Vol. 1: Report*, PP, 1977–78 (c.7054), Annex 7.

80 *Industrial Injuries Advisory Council: a review of the schedule*, PP, 1980–81 (c.8393), p. 53.

81 C. McDonald and R. Saracci, 'Metals and Chemicals', in J. Corbett MacDonald (ed.), *Epidemiology of work related diseases* (BMJ: London, 1995), pp. 8, Table 2.2.

82 F. J. Jongeneelen, 'Biological Monitoring of PAH: Review and Update', pp. 90–104.

83 Department of Social Security, Industrial Injuries Advisory Council, *Bladder and Lung Cancer in Relation to Work in Aluminium Smelting*, PP, December 1992 (c.2104).

84 B. Dinman, 'A Case of Lymphatic Leukaemia in a Söderberg Aluminium Smelter Preportedly (sic) Caused by Static Electromagnetic Field Exposures: Analysis and Implications' in Priest and O'Donnell, *Health in the Aluminium Industry*, pp. 56–67.

85 *Ibid.*, p. 26.

86 P. Sherwood Bruge, 'Occupational asthma' and D. J. Hendrick, 'Toxic lung injury: Inhaled agents', in R. A. L. Brewis, G. J. Gibson, and D. M. Geddes (eds), *Respiratory Medicine* (Ballière Tindall: London, 1990), pp. 717, 1485; Kessel, *Air, the Environment and Public Health*, pp. 107, 119.

87 D. A. Christie and E. M. Tansey, 'Environmental Toxicology: The legacy of *Silent Spring*', The Transcript of a Witness Seminar held by the Wellcome Trust Centre for the History of Medicine, UCL, London, 12 March 2002, pp. viii, 47–8, 66–70.

88 Industrial Pulmonary Diseases Committee (IPDC), *Report on a clinical and radiological examination of workers exposed to alumina dust* (IPDC: London, 1936); *The Lancet*, 19 December 1936, pp. 1478–80.

89 *Ibid.*, p. 1479.

90 M. W. Bufton and J. Melling, 'Coming up for air: Experts, employers, and workers in campaigns to compensate silicosis sufferers in Britain, 1918–1939', *Social History of Medicine*, vol. 18, no. 1 (2005), pp. 63–86; McIvor and Johnston, *Miners' Lung*.

91 Cf. K. A. Perry, 'Pulmonary disease in relation to metallic oxides', *The Lancet*, 3 September 1955, pp. 463–9.

92 *Ibid.*; 'Aluminium and Silicosis', *The Lancet*, 8 September 1956, pp. 500–1; Mitchell, 'Pulmonary fibrosis in an aluminium worker', pp. 123–5; C. L. Sutherland, 'Pneumoconiosis – its Effects and Complications – The Wyers Memorial Lecture, 1959', *Transactions of the Association of Industrial Medical Officers*, 10 (1960), p. 11; 'Aluminium and Pulmonary Fibrosis', *The Lancet*, 7 May 1960, p. 1009; G. Nagelschmidt, 'The relation between lung dust and long pathology in pneumoconiosis', *BJIM*, 17 (1960), pp. 247–59; J. Mitchell, G. B. Manning, M. Molyneux and R. E. Lane, 'Pulmonary fibrosis in workers exposed to finely powdered aluminium', *BJIM*, vol. 18 (1961), pp. 10–20.

93 Medical Research Council IPDC, Goodall evidence.

94 Minutes of the Industrial Pulmonary Diseases Committee (IPDC), 23 October 1936, TNA, FD 1/2883.

95 Dr Bradford A. Hill, 'Appendix 1: Sickness among workers in alumina' and MRC-IPDC, 'Report on the clinical and radiological examination of workers exposed to dust of alumina – results of the clinical and radiological examinations', 23 October 1936, TNA, FD 1/2883.

96 BACo, Minutes of Managers' Meetings, 24 November 1937.

97 BACo, Minutes of Managers' Meetings, 26 June 1934; Opinion of Lord Birnam in the case of Ben Nevis Distillery (Fort William) against the North British Aluminium Co. Ltd, 11 March 1949, TNA, F18/363.

98 Memo from King to Hedgecock, 'Lochaber Furnace Room Environmental Problems', 3 April 1975; BACo, Directors' Reports and Accounts for year ending 31 December 1947 and 31 December 1948; Aluminium Pechiney (AP), 'Visite des usines d'aluminium de la British Aluminium Company. II – Usine de Lochaber', 1 August 1951, p. 3; AP, 'Visite des usines d'aluminium de la British Aluminium Company. I – usine de Kinlochleven', 24 July 1951, p. 3; Medical Research Council (MRC), *Industrial Fluorosis: A study of the hazard to man and animals near Fort William, Scotland. A report to the Fluorosis Committee by John N. Agate, G. H. Bell, G. F. Boddie, R. G. Bowler, Monamy Buckell, E. A. Cheeseman, T. H. J. Douglas, H. A. Druett, Jessie Garrad, Donald Hunter, K. M. A. Perry, J. D. Richardson, and J. B. de V. Weir* (HMSO: London, 1949), p. 15.

99 R. G. Bowler, M Buckell, H. Druett and J. D. Richardson, 'Studies of the contamination produced in the Fort William area by fluorine compounds', in MRC, *Industrial Fluorosis*, p. 20.

100 AP, 'Usine de Lochaber', 1 August 1951, p. 7.

101 Bowler *et al.*, 'Studies of the contamination produced in the Fort William area by fluorine compounds' in MRC, *Industrial Fluorosis*, p. 11, 20.

102 *Ibid.*, p. 15.

103 AP, 'Usine de Kinlochleven', 24 July 1951; *idem*, 'Usine de Lochaber', 1 August 1951; United Nations (UN), *Environmental aspects of aluminium smelting: A technical review UN Environment Programme (UNEP) – Industry & Environment Technical Series, Volume 3*, (UN: Paris, 1981), p. 19.

104 AP, 'Usine de Kinlochleven'.

105 *Ibid.*; AP, 'Usine de Lochaber', p. 4.

106 *Ibid.*; AP, 'Usine de Kinlochleven', p. 3; BACo, Minutes of Managers' Meetings, 26 June 1936.

107 BACo, Minutes of Managers' Meetings, 25 April 1950.

108 Interviews with Brian Murphy, Fort William, 16 August 2006, and Sandy Walker; BoT, Report from Forsyth, 29 December 1959; Igartua, *Arvida au Saguenay*, p. 93; Revd's A. Robertson, A. J. Maclean, M. A. MacCorquodale, J. M. Annand and Neilston

McCarthy Ltd, 'The parish of Kilmallie' in H. Barron (ed.), *The Third Statistical Account for Scotland. The County of Inverness* (Scottish Academic Press: Edinburgh, 1985), p. 401.

109   UN, *Environmental aspects of aluminium smelting*, p. 6, Institut pour l'histoire d'aluminium (IHA) Archive, Gennevilliers, 5MEN01.

110   BACo, Minutes of Managers' Annual Meetings, 30 November 1936 and 23 November 1938 – reports of John Gris Bullen and Edward Shaw Morrison; Gregor and Crichton, *From Croft to Factory*, p. 70.

111   *Ibid.*, p. 48.

112   'Report on a clinical and radiological examination of workers exposed to alumina dust', *The Lancet*, 19 December 1936, pp. 1478–80; BACo, Minutes of Managers' Meetings, 24 November 1937; Interview with Duncan Haggart, Inverlochy, by A. Perchard, 16 August 2007.

113   Court of Session papers, Case 4586 vs. British Alcan Aluminium, Kinlochleven, NAS, CS258/1987/4586.

114   *The B.A. News*, vol. 4, no. 1 (January–February 1951), p. 23, UGD 347/21/33/4; 'Fort-William factory blaze', *P&J*, 11 January 1962.

115   I am grateful to Johan Henden of the National Library of Norway for copies of this correspondence (held in Norway) and an English translation of his own work on A/S Stangfjordens Elektrokemiske Fabriker: Telegram from G. A. Steel to M. R. Turner, 10 October 1932; Telegram from Turner to Steel, 24 October 1932; Telegram and report from Turner to Steel, 2 February 1933; Telegram from Steel to Turner, 10 February 1933.

116   Telegram from Turner to Steel, 16 March and 18 April 1933; L. Thue, 'Norway: a resource-based and democratic capitalism' in Fellman, *et al.*, *Creating Nordic Capitalism*, pp. 430–1.

117   Telegram from Steel to Turner, 28 April 1933.

118   Telegrams from Turner to Steel, 4 January, 23 March and 3 October 1934; Telegram from Steel to Turner, 14 March 1934.

119   Henden, 'Stangfjordens Elektrokemiske Fabriker', pp. 33–67.

120   *Ibid.*, p. 110; BACo, Minutes of Managers' Annual Conferences, 24 November 1937.

121   Forestry Commission note from March 1949; Letter from G. A. Steel, BACo, to Sir R. L. Robinson, Forestry Commission, 31 July 1939, TNA, F18/363; BACo, Minutes of Managers' Meetings, 23 June 1932; BACo, Minutes of Managers' Meetings, 4, 5 and 6 November 1936.

122   G. F. Boddie, 'Effects of fluorine compounds on animals in the Fort William area' in MRC, *Industrial Fluorosis*, pp. 31–5; Opinion of Lord Birnam in the case of Ben Nevis Distillery (Fort William) against the North British Aluminium Co. Ltd, 11 March 1949, TNA, F18/363.

123   C. I. Maclean, *The Highlands* (Birlinn: Edinburgh, 2006), p. 75.

124   Gregor and Crichton, *From Croft to Factory*, pp. 2, 55.

125   For example: AScW, *Highland Power*, p. 57.

126   *Ibid.*, pp. 69–70; *The Lancet*, 9 April 1949, pp. 632–3.

127   C. L. Sutherland, 'The world outside the factory: Bones and Teeth', *Transactions of the Association of Industrial Medical Officers* (1960), p. 62.

128   MRC, *Industrial Fluorosis*, pp. 128–9; 'Public Health: Fluorosis at Fort William', *The Lancet*, 9 April 1949, pp. 632–3.

129   J. N. Agate, D. Hunter and K. M. A. Perry, assisted by J. Garrard and E. A. Cheeseman, 'Clinical, radiological, haematological and biochemical findings in selected groups of individuals from the districts of Fort William and Kinlochleven' and T. H. J. Douglas, 'The dental condition of adults and school-children in the Fort William Area' in MRC, *Industrial Fluorosis*, pp. 47–84; *The Lancet*, 9 April 1949, pp. 632–3.

130 *The Lancet*, 9 April 1949, pp. 632–3.

131 MRC, *Industrial Fluorosis*, p. 95; MRC, Note on fluorine hazard at Fort William, March 1947, TNA, F18/363.

132 L. H. Weinstein and A. Davison, *Fluorides in the Environment: Effects on animals and plants* (HUP: Cambridge MA, 2004), p. 127.

133 Opinion of Lord Birnam, 11 March 1949; French figures from: Ménégoz, 'Protection de l'environnement autour des usines d'électrolyse', in Morel, *Histoire Technique de la production d'aluminium*, pp. 142–3.

134 Opinion of Lord Birnam; Kessel, *Air, the Environment and Public Health*, Table 5.2.

135 Quoted in Kessel, *ibid.*

136 *Ibid.*

137 BACo, Minutes of Managers' Meetings, 28 April 19482.

138 Opinion of Lord Birnam; *The Scotsman*, 12 March 1949.

139 BACo, Minutes of Managers' Annual Conferences, 28 April 1948.

140 *The Scotsman*, 12 January 1950.

141 BACo, Minutes of Managers' Meetings, 25 April 1950.

142 Evenden, *Fish versus Power*, pp. 149–78.

143 AP, 'Usine de Lochaber', p. 4.

144 I. Glover, 'British management and British history: Assessing the responsibility of individuals for economic difficulties', *Contemporary British History*, vol. 13, no. 3 (Autumn 1999), p. 143.

145 Ménégoz, 'Protection de l'environnement autour des usines d'électrolyse', in Morel, *Histoire Technique de la production d'aluminium*, p. 131; G. De Luigi, E. Meyer and A. F. Saba, 'La *Società italiana dell'alluminio* et son impact sur l'environnement dans la province de Trente (1928–1938)', *CHA*, vol. 14 (1994), pp. 38–53; D. Boullet, 'Pechiney et l'environnement (1960–1980) Précocité et diversité d'une expérience', *CHA*, vol. 26 (2000), pp. 11–37.

146 Letter from Dr E. Sweeney to the Medical Research Council, 18 December 1963; Reply from Dr P. J. Chapman, MRC, to Sweeney, 24 December 1963; MRC notes, 24 December 1963 and 7 January 1964; Letter from Chapman to Sweeney, 7 January 1964; Letter from Chapman to Professor C. R. Lowe, 7 January 1964, TNA, FD23/990.

147 'Health check at Fort William', *The B.A. News*, vol. 28, no. 2 (March–April 1976), pp. 10–11; Taylor, 'Manufacturing processes: Aluminium manufacture', pp. 25–6.

148 SOHC – SOHS – 2. Dundee, 25 September 2001.

149 Interview with Dr Chris Robinson.

150 Letter from Dr James Douglas, Lochaber Smelter Medical Adviser, to Andrew Perchard, 24 July 2008.

151 Letter from W. McCamley, Deputy Senior Inspector HMIPI Scotland, to G S Murray, SEPD, and Dr H. McNeil, Scottish Health Department (SHD), 20 March 1975; Letter from Murray to Lister, Department of Agriculture and Fisheries, Scotland (DAFS), 24 March 1975; Letter from H. D. Wylie, SEPD, to McCamley, 1 April 1975; Minute from McCamley to Lister, Murray and McNeil, 28 April 1975; Minute from H. Robertson, SEPD, to J. A. Scott, SEPD, 19 June 1978, NAS, SEP12/663.

152 Memo from King to Hedgecock, 3 April 1975.

153 Letter from McCamley to Murray and McNeil, 20 March 1975, NAS, SEP12/663.

154 Letter from McCamley to Murray and McNeil, 20 March 1975; Minute from McCamley to Lister, Murray and McNeil, 28 April 1975; Minute from H. Robertson, SEPD, to J. A. Scott, SEPD, 19 June 1978, NAS, SEP12/663.

155 Memo from Scottish Office-Development Department to Chief Inspector of HM Industrial Pollution Inspectorate (HMIPI) and Animal Health Branch, Department of Agriculture

and Fisheries for Scotland (DAFS), 10 January 1977, NAS, AF72/451; S. Early, 'British Aluminium in Scotland', *Metal Bulletin Monthly* (September 1981), pp. 6–9.

156   *The Ross-shire Journal*, 6 and 13 October and 17 November 1967, 9 February and 8 March 1968.

157   *The Ross-shire Journal*, 13 January 1967, 15 September 1967, 26 April 1968.

158   Invergordon Smelter – fluorosis compensation agreement between the National Farmers Union of Scotland (Easter Ross Branch) and the British Aluminium Company Ltd, 18 May 1970, NAS, AF72/451; Memo and agenda for confidential meeting between Russell and Ford, 18 October 1982.

159   Memo from N. G. Campbell, Scottish Development Department (SDD), to D. Wilkinson, Department for Agriculture and Fisheries Scotland (DAFS) and W. McCamley, Chief Inspector, HM Inspectorate of Industrial Pollution (HMIPI), 10 January 1977, NAS, AF72/451.

160   Council Council of Ross and Cromarty, Planning permission – decision V/09/D/8457, 8 November 1967, AF72/459.

161   Evenden, *Fish versus Power*, p. 170.

162   Memo from J. S. Nicol, Scottish Office Development Department (SO-DD), to W. McCamley, Chief Inspector of Industrial Pollution, and D. Wilkinson, DAFS, 20 October 1978; Letter from J. K. Forsyth, SO-DD, to Solicitor to the Secretary of State for Scotland, copied to Hon. Hamish Gray MP, 27 September 1978; Memo from N. G. Campbell, SO-DD, to Wilkinson and McCamley, 10 January 1977, NAS, AF72/451; P. Durham, *Highland Whistle Blower: The true story of the Phil Durham Affair* (Northern Books: Edinburgh, 1997), pp. 56–60.

163   Minute from Wilkinson to SDD (Mackay, McCamley and Nicol), Solicitor's Office (Angus) and DAFS (Drummond, Marshall and Brownlie), 10 November 1978; Letter from Professor Lewis Littlejohn of NOSCA to G. S. Murray, DAFS, 18 January 1979, NAS, AF72/451.

164   Letter from D. G. Mackay, SDD, to Miss J. E. Forsyth, 22 November 1978, AF72/451.

165   Letter from Professor L. Littlejohn, NOSCA, to G. S. Murray, DAFS, 18 January 1979, AF72/451.

166   Minute from P. M. Marshall to G. Drummond, DAFS, 3 April 1979, AF72/451.

167   Minute from Ian Wright, HMIPI, to D. Bownlie, Senior Inspector of Pollution, about complaint from Robert Trotter, Delny, 24 January 1980, AF72/451.

168   DAFS, *Fisheries of Scotland report for 1979*, PP (c.7947), p. 26.

169   Minutes of meetings at BACo Invergordon, 4 March and 7 October 1980, AF72/451; Early, 'British Aluminium in Scotland', p. 8.

170   'Public Inquiry at Dingwall', *The Ross-shire Journal*, 8 March 1968; 'Easter Ross: Further 1,100 acres to be re-zoned', *Farming* News,1 August 1969.

171   McNeill, *Something new under the sun*, pp. xxiii, 3, 296–323.

172   Ménégoz, 'Protection de l'environnement autour des usines d'électrolyse', in Morel, *Histoire Technique de la production d'aluminium*, p. 145.

173   Memos from Wagner to Rich and Russell, 10 August 1982; Memo from J. S. Potten to Morton, 25 June 1979.

174   Interview with G. A. Haggart, Fort William, conducted by A. Perchard, 16 August 2006.

175   Interview Industrial Medicine, Scottish Oral History Centre, SOHS/2.

176   P. G. Polsue and I. Eastwood, 'The modernization of Lochaber aluminium smelter', *Mining Magazine*, (May 1982), pp. 399–401; Interviews with G. A. Haggart, J. Dunlevy, J. Ross (Inverlochy, 16 August 2006), and D. Haggart (Inverlochy, 17 August 2006).

177   Memo and Report from Scarrett to Morton, 8 April 1981.

178   Evenden, *Fish versus Power*; Igartua, *Arvida au Saguenay*, pp. 93, 96; B. Christensen, *Too*

Good to be True: Alcan's Kemano Project (Talonbooks: Vancouver, 1995).

179 British Alcan, presentation by Rich to bankers on post-merger achievements, 11 December 1985.

180 'Recycling: The Alcan initiative at Warrington', *Aluminium Industry*, vol. 17, no. 1 (February/March 1992), pp. 10–13; 'Alcan seeks UK can collection boom', *Metal Bulletin Monthly* (February 1992), pp. 84–7; Department of the Environment, *This Common Inheritance: First Year Report*, PP, 1990/91 (c.1655), pp. 148, 150, 188.

181 *Environment Select Committee: Recycling. Minutes of Evidence*, PP, 1993–94 (c.63-I), Evidence from Aluminium Federation, pp. xxI and xxx; *Environmental Audit Select Committee fifth report in 2 volumes with proceedings, evidence* [hereafter *Environmental Audit Select Committee: Waste: an audit*], PP, 2002–03, PP, Evidence from Confederation of British Industry citing DEFRA figures, 15 January 2003.

182 Trade and Industry Select Committee: *The impact on industry of the climate change levy*, PP, 1998–99 (c.678), Appendix 45: Aluminium Federation.

183 *Key Scottish Environment Statistics 2005*, http://www.scotland.gov.uk/Publications/2005/08/15135632/56477 [accessed 15 March 2007]; DEFRA, *Municipal Waste Management Statistics*, 1999–2005, http://www.defra.gov.uk/environment/statistics/wastats/archive.htm [accessed 15 March 2007]; Eurostat, *Municipal waste by treatment:* http://epp.eurostat.ec.europa.eu/portal/page?_pageid=1996,39140985&_dad=portal&_schema=PORTAL&screen=detailref&language=en&product=REF_TB_environment&root=REF_TB_environment/t_env/t_env_was/ten00045 [accessed 15 March 2007]; Simmons, *An Environmental History of Great Britain*, Table 8.7.

184 *Environmental Audit Select Committee: Waste: an audit*, 2002–03, Evidence 208.

185 Dept of the Environment, *Climate change: the UK programme*, PP, 1993–94 (c.2427), p. 52.

186 I am grateful to Mary Malcolm at Health and Safety Executive (HSE), Aberdeen, for copies of these reports: HSE, Lochaber inspection by C. F. Woodrow and A. MacNab (client number 0800003544; location 0039570), 4 June 1998; *idem*, HSE Kinlochleven – inspection by C. F. Woodrow (client number 0800003544; location 0039581), 5 June 1998.

187 Idem, HSE Reports on provision and use of Personal Protective Equipment, power station, health surveillance, cell rooms, and health and safety management at Kinlochleven by C. F. Woodrow, 5 June 1998; Alcan Aluminium UK, *Alcan in the Highlands*, p. 10.

188 Interview with Bob Herbert.

189 HSE, Kinlochleven: Cell Rooms: Aluminium Electrolysis – inspection by C. F. Woodrow (client number 0800003544; location 0039581), 5 June 1998.

190 McIvor and Johnston, *Miners' Lung*, p. 180.

191 Case 3529 vs. British Alcan Aluminium Primary & Recycling Ltd, NAS, CS258/1994/3529.

192 See articles from conferences held in Bergen in June 1994 and funded by the Norwegian National Institute of Occupational Health and the Nordic Aluminium Industry's Secretariat for Health, Environment and Safety and that held in Montreal three years later: *The Science of the Total Environment*, vol. 163, iss. 1–2, (1995); Priest and O'Donnell, *Health in the Aluminium Industry*.

193 HSE, Lochaber: Health and Safety Management – report by A. Macnab, 4 June 1999.

194 HMPI, British Alcan Primary and Recycling: Lochaber Smelters – report by J. A. Hetherington, Deputy Chief Inspector, HMPI, 31 August 1993, NAS, DD9/498.

195 HSE, Lochaber: Rodding Room, Cell Rooms, and Health and Safety Management – report by D. A. Conner, 26 August 2004.

196 Idem, HSE Lochaber: Cell Rooms: Aluminium Electrolysis, Casting Shop, and services – report by C. F. Woodrow (client number 0800003544; location 0039570), 4 June 1998.

197 HSE, Lochaber: Noise vibration – report by G. Chisholm of visit by Chisholm and Dr

S. Doherty, 14 August 1998.

198   Idem, HSE Lochaber: Casting Shop – report by C. F. Woodrow, 15 July 1999; *idem,*
Lochaber: Health and Safety Management – report by J. Blackburn, 18 May 2000.

199   Alcan, Primary Metals Europe, *Lochaber Smelter,* pp. 3–5; Scottish Environmental Protection
Agency (SEPA), *SEPA National Air Quality Report 2007,* Table 2.

200   A. D. McIntosh, C. F. Moffat, G. Packer and L. Webster, 'Polycyclic aromatic hydrocarbon
(PAH) concentration and composition in farmed blue mussels (*Mytilus edulis*) in a sea loch
pre- and post-closure of an aluminium smelter', *Journal of Environmental Monitoring,* vol. 6
(2004), p. 216; L. Webster, R. J. Fryer, C. Megginson, E. J. Dalgarno, A. D. McIntosh and
C. F. Moffat, 'Polycyclic aromatic hydrocarbon and geochemical biomarker composition
of sediments from sea lochs on the west coast of Scotland', *ibid.,* pp. 219–28; CEEED,
Implementation of a system of indicators for social responsibility reporting, pp. 4–11.

201   *Environment Transport and Regional Affairs Select Committee: UK climate change programme.
Minutes of Evidence,* PP, 1998–99 (c.171-IV), Evidence from Mr. Ian Blakey, Chairman of
International Federation of Industrial Energy Users (IFIEU), 13 March 1999 (Qs 447–67),
and supplementary memo by Ms. Lisa Waters, Economic Adviser to IFIEU, 28 April
1999, p. 110; *Environment Transport and Regional Affairs Select Committee: UK climate
change programme. Minutes of Evidence,* PP, 1998–99 (c.171-VIII), Evidence from Mr
Simon Virley, Head of Environmental Tax Branch, HM Inland Revenue, 26 May 1999
(Q. 1048); *Environmental Audit Select Committee: The budget 1999. Environmental Audit
Select Committee eighth report with proceedings, evidence and appendices,* PP, 1998–99
(c.326), Evidence from Chris Hewitt, Institute of Public Policy Research, (Qs 45–8), and
Dr Dominic Hogg, Economic and Social Consultancy (ECOTEC), (Q. 200); *Trade and
Industry Select Committee: The impact on industry of the climate change levy. Trade and
Industry Select Committee ninth report with proceedings, evidence and appendices,* PP, 1998–99
(c.678), p. xx and Appendix 45, 2 July 1999; *Environment Transport and Regional Affairs Select
Committee: UK climate change programme. Fifth Report,* PP, 1999–2000 (c.194), Evidence
from Dr. David A. Harris, Al. Fed., 16 November 1999, p. 91.

202   Collins and Harris, 'Does plant ownership affect the level of pollution abatement
expenditure?', pp. 171–89.

203   1979 *The B.A. News*; Death certificates (anonymised) for Stubber, Kinlochleven (d. 26
January 1951); Furnaceman, Kinlochleven (d. 23 December 1970); Furnaceroom foreman,
Kinlochleven (d. 5 September 1976); Furnaceman, Kinlochleven, (d. 29 August 1976);
Shift foreman, cell room, Kinlochleven (d. 5 December 1981); Factory foreman, cell room,
Kinlochleven (d. 4 October 1981).

204   I am grateful to Roger Black of the Cancer Surveillance Unit for allowing me a copy of
this report. For reasons of confidentiality, the observed and expected numbers of cases
have been suppressed: Cancer Surveillance Unit, 'Incidence of cancer in Kinlochleven and
Invergordon, 1975–1996', *Cancer Surveillance,* January 1999, pp. iii, iv.

205   'Aluminium and Health', *The Lancet,* 14 September 1931, p. 622, Acc.12187/6.

206   L. Grant, *Aluminium Throat Swabs* (Lachlan Grant: London, 1922); Letter from J. Ramsay
MacDonald to Lachlan Grant, 26 December 1933, NLS, Acc.12187/7.

207   STUC, *29th Annual Report* (1926), Motion 17; STUC, *46th Annual Report* (1943), p. 46;
STUC, *54th Annual Report* (1951), p. 46; STUC, *57th Annual Report* (1954); Lochaber and
District Trades Council records, GCAL, Files 1 & 2: 1975–1982.

208   CS258/1994/1701;   CS258/1994/3553;   CS258/1994/3308;   CS348/1996/903;   CS348/1996/1868;
CS348/1998/2292;   CS348/1998/2700;   CS348/1999/234;   CS348/1999/709;   CS348/1999/2012,
NAS.

209   Interviews ALC6 (Inverlochy, 5 December 2006); ALC16 (Fort William, 16 August 2006),

ALC18 (Inverlochy, 16 August 2006); and ALC24 (Inverlochy, 17 August 2006).

210 McNeill, *Something under the sun*, p. 3.

211 Payne, 'Land-use and landscape', p. 13; See also: Cameron, 'The Scottish Highlands', p. 158; J. Hunter, 'The Scottish Highlands: A contested country', in National Museums of Scotland, *Fonn's Duthchas: Land and legacy* (National Museums of Scotland: Edinburgh, 2006), pp. 7–8; Simmons, *An Environmental History of Great Britain*, pp. 1–22.

212 J. Melling, 'The risks of working and the risks of not working: Trade unions, employers and responses to the risk of occupational illness in British industry, c.1890–1940s', Discussion paper 12, ESRC Centre for Analysis of Risk and Regulation, London School of Economics (December 2003).

Chapter 5: 'Practical and Lasting Good': Aluminium and community in the Highlands

1 Letter from Morrison to Grant, 1 January 1935.

2 In view of the fact that the figures for 1920 salaries were supplied to the House of Commons select committee by British Aluminium, I use them with a degree of caution. The Grand Hotel operated as a subsidiary concern taking in tourists during the season as well as accommodating "BA" staff. Inverlochy Castle was the site of two significant battles, in 1431 and 1645 in Scottish History: 'Water Power Resources: Effect of development in Scotland. Committee's conclusions', *The Scotsman*, 15 December 1921; Book of particulars for estates of Lower Foyers, Gorthlick and Wester Aberchalder, and Upper Foyers and Glenmarkie, UGD 347/21/34/1/4; *The B.A. News*, vol. 2, no. 2 (1949), p. 8; *The B.A. News*, vol. 5, no. 4 (1952); Report from Goodchild on Argyll, Fisheries Board for Scotland, 19 November 1937; J. McEwen, *Who Owns Scotland: A study in land ownership*, second edition (Mainstream: Edinburgh, 1981), pp. 10, 22, 26; A. Crab, *Who Owns Scotland Now: The use and abuse of private land* (Polygon: Edinburgh, 2001), p. 26; Rev. A. Macaskill, 'The Parish of Boleskine and Abertarff', in Barron, *The County of Inverness*, pp. 14–26.

3 John Lewis and Helen Smith inaccurately stated that BACo purchased Inverlochy Castle and the surrounding area in 1920, when in fact this took place in 1945. Their confusion may have stemmed from their assumption that its purchase occurred around the time that the company were building the factory complex and Inverlochy Village: J. Lewis and H. Smith, 'Excavations at Inverlochy Castle, Inverness-shire, 1983–95', *Proceedings of the Society of Antiquities for Scotland*, 128 (1998), p. 622; For entry about the purchase of Inverlochy Castle see: North British Aluminium Company (NBACo), Minute books 1 (1924–1938) and 2 (1938–1961).

4 The concept of the 'panoptican' was originally devised by the English philosopher Jeremy Bentham as a prison in which prisoners would discipline themselves in the knowledge that they were under surveillance. This was revived by the French social scientist and philosopher Michel Foucault who saw the 'panoptican' as the epitome of the transition in modern society to 'disciplinary power', 'an exhaustive capture of the individual's body, actions, time, and behavior': Foucault, *Psychiatric Power*, pp. 38–46; For an exploration of the application of these ideas to the workplace, see: C. Carter, A. McKinlay and M. Rawlinson, 'Introduction: Foucault, Management and History', *Organization*, vol. 9, no. 4 (2002), pp. 515–24; Perchard, 'Sculpting the "Garden of Eden"', pp. 16–17; McCrone, *Understanding Scotland*, pp. 16–33.

5 P. Joyce, *Work, Society and Politics: The culture of the factory town in Late Victorian England* (Taylor & Francis: London, 1980), p. xiv.

6 A. F. McEvoy, 'Working environments: An ecological approach to industrial health and safety', in R. Cooter and B. Luckin (eds), *Accidents in History: Injuries, fatalities and social relations* (Rodopi: Amsterdam, 1997), p. 62 cf. R. Johnston and A. McIvor, 'Narratives from the urban workplace: Oral testimonies and the reconstruction of men's work in the heavy industries in Glasgow', in R. Rodger and J. Herbert (eds), *Testimonies of the City: Identity, community and change in a contemporary urban world* (Ashgate: Aldershot, 2007), p. 25.

7 D. K. Drummond, *Crewe: Railway town, company and people, 1840–1914* (Scolar: Aldershot, 1995), p. 210.

8 Igartua, *Arvida au Saguenay*, pp. 7, 113.

9 Macaskill, 'The Parish of Boleskine and Abertarff' and Revs. A. Robertson, A. J. Maclean, M. A. MacCorquodale and J. M. Annand, 'The Parish of Kilmallie', in Barron, *The County of Inverness*, pp. 25, 381–407.

10 Carter's use of Barrington-Moore Jr's typology was heavily influenced by his focus on black cattle and kelp. As such this particularly applies to the north and western Highlands with its patterns of temporary migration as opposed to the permanent migration of the south and east of the region, as differentiated by Malcolm Gray and Tom Devine: I. Carter, 'The Highlands of Scotland as an underdeveloped region', in E. DeKadt and G. Williams (eds), *Sociology and Underdevelopment* (Tavistock: London, 1974), p. 301 cited in McCrone, *Understanding Scotland*, pp. 51–4; Devine, 'Temporary migration and the Scottish Highlands', pp. 344–59; L. Leneman, *Fit for Heroes? Land settlement in Scotland after World War I* (AUP: Aberdeen, 1989) pp. 3–4.

11 Letter from Sir Donald Walter Cameron of Lochiel to G. Erskine Jackson, 17 September 1937, Scottish Land and Property Federation collection, NAS, GD325/1/315; Leneman, *Fit for Heroes?, passim.*

12 A. I. Macinnes, 'Landownership, Land Use and Elite Enterprise in Scottish Gaeldom: from Clanship to Clearance in Argyllshire, 1688–1858', in T. M. Devine (ed.), *Scottish Elites: Proceedings of the Scottish Historical Studies Seminar University of Strathclyde 1991–1992* (John Donald: Edinburgh, 1994), p. 3; Harper, *Emigration from Scotland between the Wars*, p. 74.

13 Lochiel had opposed the original scheme on the grounds that it intended taking the water from Inverness-shire and diverting it to Argyll-shire. However he wholeheartedly endorsed the amended Bill: Petition to the Scottish Office from Col D. W. Cameron of Lochiel against the Lochaber Water Power Bill, January 1918, Lochaber Archives Centre (LAC), CL/A/3/2/45/1; Letter from William Murray Morrison to Col D. W. Cameron of Lochiel, 12 May 1921; See also: Morrison to Lochiel, 29 December 1920, 24 February 1921, 18 May 1921, and 15 and 22 June 1921, LAC, CL/A/3/2/45/2; *Royal Commission on Canals and Waterways, Minutes of Evidence and Appendices, Vol. III*, 1907, PP (c.3718), Q. 30154, W. Murray Morrison, British Aluminium Company, 10 July 1907.

14 Lochaber Water Power Bill, Minutes of Evidence, 6 May 1921 – Col. D. W. Cameron of Lochiel, CMG., ADC; The Rt Hon. Lord Lovat, KT, KCMG, KCVO, CB, DSO; 'Highland problem: Lord Lovat on agricultural employment', *The Scotsman*, 2 October 1920; 'Lochaber Housing Development: Extension of Aluminium Works', *The Scotsman*, 8 September 1937.

15 Hunter, *The Claim of Crofting*, p. 45; Gibson, *The Thistle and The Crown*, p. 81.

16 *Caledonian Medical Journal*, vol. XII, no. 5 (February 1924), p. 1.

17 Letter from Col. D. W. Cameron of Lochiel to Sir Alexander MacEwen, 8 and 12 July 1935, LAC, CL/3/3/18/4/1.

18 Rev. A. Macaskill, 'The Parish of Boleskine and Abertarff', and Revds. A. Robertson, A. J. Maclean, M. A. MacCorquodale, and J. M. Annand, 'The Parish of Kilmallie', pp. 18–19, 369–78; Cameron, 'Conservatism and Radicalism in the Highland Press',

pp. 117–29; Stott, 'Morrison, (Sir William) Murray (1873–1948)', *ODNB*; Cameron, *Land for the People?*, *passim*.

19   J. Martin, 'Fraser, Simon Joseph, fourteenth Lord Lovat and third Baron Lovat (1871–1933)', *ODNB*, http://www.oxforddnb.com.ezproxy.webfeat.lib.ed.ac.uk/view/article/33254?docPos=5 [accessed 5 October 2007].

20   Letter from Col A. D. Gardayne to Erskine Jackson, 18 July 1939, NAS, GD325/1/315.

21   T. Dalyell, 'Obituaries: Col Sir Donald Cameron of Lochiel, 26th Chief of the Clan Cameron', *The Independent*, 15 June 2004, http://www.independent.co.uk/news/obituaries/col-sir-donald-cameron-of-lochiel-730576.html [accessed 5 January 2008].

22   Leneman, *Fit for Heroes?*, p. 71; For examples of 'influence politics' see: Joyce, *Work, Society and Politics*; and D. C. Moore, *The Politics of Deference: A Study of the mid-nineteenth century political system* (Harvester: Hassocks, 1976).

23   Letter from Atholl to the Mackintosh, 9 December 1920.

24   Dr Lachlan Grant, 'Work and leisure', *CMJ*, vol. 14, no. 5 (January 1930), p. 160.

25   *The Oban Times and Argyllshire Advertiser*, 6 March 1909.

26   Gardayne to Jackson, 18 July 1939.

27   Letter from 'Another West Highlander' (notes in the Grant collection indicate that Grant was the correspondent), *The Scotsman*, 5 October 1936, NLS, Grant Collection, vol. 10, Acc.12187/10.

28   *Oban Times*, 16 and 23 February 1918, and 5 February 1921; *Highland News*, 29 May 1921; 'Aluminium and Health', *The Lancet*, 14 September 1931; *SDE*, 20 April 1934.

29   Letter from Morrison to Grant, 1 January 1935.

30   Grant, 'Highland Life, Its Past and its Future', *CMJ*, vol. 15, no. 13 (July–October 1935), Grant Collection, vol. 8, Acc.12187/8.

31   Letter from Morrison to Grant, 18 December 1936, Acc.12187/10.

32   Payne, 'Land-use and landscape', pp. 83, 232; Cameron, 'Conservatism and Radicalism in the Highland Press'; I. G. C. Hutchison, 'The Nobility and Politics in Scotland, c.1880–1939' in Devine, *Scottish Elites*, pp. 131–51; Martin, 'Fraser, Simon Joseph, fourteenth Lord Lovat and third Baron Lovat (1871–1933)'; P. Warner, 'Fraser, Simon Christopher Joseph, fifteenth Lord Lovat and fourth Baron Lovat (1911–1995)', *ODNB*, http://www.oxforddnb.com.ezproxy.webfeat.lib.ed.ac.uk/view/article/58071?docPos=4 [accessed 5 March 2007]; For details of the political engagement of Sir Donald Walter Cameron, 25th Chief, see Cameron and Payne: 'Obituaries: Col Sir Donald Cameron of Lochiel, 26th Chief of the Clan Cameron', *The Independent*, 15 June 2004; Lochaber Water Power Bill, Minutes of Evidence, 6 May 1921 – Mr Charles Sievewright, Chairman of the National Union of Railwaymen, Fort William Branch; Letter from Hon. J. H. Thomas MP, General Secretary NUR.

33   Vindt, *Les hommes de l'aluminium*, pp. 48–9; L. Carlson, *Company Towns of the Pacific Northwest* (University of Washington Press: Seattle, 2003), *passim*.

34   H. Gospel, *Markets, Firms and the Management of Labour in Modern Britain* (CUP: Cambridge, 1992); Fitzgerald, *British Labour Management*; M. Heller, 'Sport, bureaucracies and London clerks 1880–1939', *The International Journal of the History of Sport*, vol. 25, no. 5 (2008), pp. 579–614.

35   Henden, 'Stangfjordens Elektrokemiske Fabriker', pp. 95–119.

36   *The B.A. News, Highlands Edition*, (1948), pp. 10–11; *The B.A. News*, (1949), p. 10.

37   Vindt, *Les hommes de l'aluminium*, pp. 50–2, 132; H. Frouard, *Du coron au HLM: Patronat et logement social (1894–1953)* (Presses Universitaires de Rennes: Rennes, 2008); Igartua, *Arvida au Saguenay*.

38   H. Morsel, 'Louis Marlio, position idéologique et comportement politique. Un dirigeant

d'une grande enterprise dans la première moitié du XXe siècle', in Grinberg and Hachez-Leroy, *Industrialisation et sociétés*, pp. 106–24; Vindt, *Les hommes de l'aluminium*, p. 132; Frouard, *Du coron au HLM*, pp. 154–5.

39 Smith, *From Monopoly to Competition*, pp. 72, 144, 147; Campbell, *Global Mission, Vol. I*, pp. 115, 125–7.

40 Igartua, *Arvida au Saguenay*, *passim*.

41 Cross, 'White Metal'.

42 D. McCrone 'Bidin' in the Toon: Life in Urban Scotland' in J. Beech, O. Hand, M. A. Mulhern and J. Weston (eds) *Scottish Life and Society, A compendium of Scottish ethnology: Vol. 9, The Individual and Community Life* (Tuckwell Press: Edinburgh, 2005), p. 358; E. Condry, *Scottish Ethnography* (EUP: Edinburgh, 1983), p. 133; D. Wight, *Workers not Wasters: Masculine respectability, consumption and employment in Central Scotland* (EUP: Edinburgh, 1993), p. 2; For a critique of precisely these sorts of assumptions see the work of S. Macdonald, *Reimagining Culture: Histories, identities and the Gaelic Renaissance* (Berg: Oxford, 1997), pp. 67–95.

43 McCrone, *Understanding Scotland*, pp. 17, 48.

44 J. Butt, I. L. Donnachie and J. R. Hume, *Industrial History in Pictures: Scotland* (David & Charles: Newton Abbot, 1968); C. A. Oakley, *Scottish Industry To-day: A survey of recent developments undertaken for The Scottish Development Council* (SDCI: Edinburgh, 1937), pp. 50–1; Turnock, *Patterns of Highland Development*, pp. 149–87; J. M. Lindsay, 'Charcoal iron smelting and its fuel supply: The example of Lorn Furnace, Argyllshire, 1753–1876', *Journal of Historical Geography*, 1 (1975), pp. 283–98; D. Morrison, 'The beginning and end of the Lewis chemical works, 1857–1874', in Scottish History Society, *Scottish Industrial History: A miscellany* (Scottish Academic Press: Edinburgh, 1978), pp. 181–212; Macinnes, 'Landownership, Land Use and Elite Enterprise in Scottish Gaeldom', in Devine (ed.), *Scottish Elites*; Smout, *Nature Contested*, p. 56.

45 J. Butt, *The Industrial Archeology of Scotland* (David & Charles: Newton Abbot, 1967), pp. 106–7, 213.

46 Kirk, *Custom and Conflict in the 'Land of the Gael'*, p. 19.

47 C. Harvie, *No Gods and Precious Few Heroes: Scotland 1914–1980* (Blackwell: London, 1981), p. 66.

48 *Census for Scotland, 1951*; Rev. A. Macaskill, 'The Parish of Boleskine and Abertarff', p. 24.

49 Gregor and Crichton, *From Croft to Factory*, Table 3; Turnock, *Industrial Britain*, Table 7; D. Turnock, 'Population studies and regional development in West Highland Scotland', *Geografiska Annaler. Series B, Human Geography*, vol. 49, no. 1 (1967), Table 2.

50 D. Lee and H. Newby, *The Problem of Sociology: An introduction to the discipline* (Unwin Hyman: London, 1983), p. 57.

51 D. Lockwood, 'Sources of variation in working class images of society', *Sociological Review*, vol. 14, iss. 3 (1966), p. 263; C. Kerr and A. Siegel, 'The Interindustry Propensity to Strike – an International Comparison' in A. Kornhauser, R. Dubin and A. Ross (eds), *Industrial conflict* (McGraw Hill: New York, 1954), p. 193; See also; N. Dennis, F. Henriques and C. Slaughter, *Coal is our life: An analysis of a Yorkshire mining community* (Eyre & Spottiswoode: London, 1956).

52 M. Bulmer, *Mining and Social Change: Durham County in the twentieth century* (Croom Helm: London, 1978), p. 15.

53 S. Macintyre, *Little Moscows: Communism and working-class militancy in Inter-war Britain* (Croom Helm: London, 1980)

54 For an erudite discussion of workplaces as social and community resources, see: J. Phillips, 'Collieries and Communities: The Miners' Strike in Scotland, 1984–1985', *Scottish Labour*

History, vol. 46 (2010), pp. 18–36.

55 For example: Wright, *Workers not wasters*; I. Roberts, *Craft, Class and Control: The sociology of a shipbuilding community* (EUP, Edinburgh, 1993).

56 B. Latour, *Reassembling the Social: An introduction to Actor-Network-Theory* (OUP: Oxford, 2005), pp. 2, 3; J. Bourke, *Working-Class Cultures in Britain 1890–1960: Gender, class and ethnicity* (Routledge: London, 1994), pp. 1–26; See also: G. Stedman Jones, *Languages of Class: Studies in English working class history 1832–1982* (CUP: Cambridge, 1983), pp. 179–238.

57 Stedman Jones, *Languages of Class*; G. Stedman Jones, *Outcast London: A Study in the Relationship between Classes in Victorian Society* (OUP: Oxford, 1971); Joyce, *Work, Society and Politics*; For a Scottish example, see: C. M. M. Macdonald, *The Radical Thread: Political change in Scotland, Paisley Politics, 1885–1924* (Tuckwell: East Linton, 2000), pp. 1–35.

58 *Ibid.*; Drummond, *Crewe*; Kirk, *Custom and Conflict in the 'Land of the Gael'*; N. Kirk, 'A State of War in the Valley of Glencoe: The Ballachulish Quarries Disputes, 1902–1905', *Scottish Labour History*, vol. 38 (2003), pp. 14–36.

59 Wright, *Workers not wasters*, pp. 3, 23, 28–58.

60 S. Macdonald, 'Locality and community: A West Highland Parish', in Beech *et al.*, *Scottish Life and Society, A compendium of Scottish ethnology: Vol. 9, The Individual and Community Life*, pp. 415–16.

61 M. Watson, *Being English in Scotland* (EUP: Edinburgh, 2003), *passim*.

62 Macaskill, 'The Parish of Boleskine and Abertarff, p. 24.

63 *Ibid.*, pp. 18–19; 'Society Small-Talk by Upper-Crust Gossipers', *The Hampshire Telegraph and Sussex Chronicle*, 18 April 1891; T. J. Byres, 'Entrepreneurship in the Scottish Heavy Industries, 1870–1900' in P. L. Payne (ed.), *Studies in Scottish Business History* (Cass: London, 1967), pp. 272–3; Book of particulars for Foyers, 31 January 1895.

64 Quoted in BACo, *History*, p. 19.

65 Rev. W. Fraser, 'United Parishes of Boleskine and Abertarff. Presbtery of Abertarff, Synod of Glenelg', *The New Statistical Account of Scotland, Vol. XIV: Inverness, Ross, Cromarty* (W. Creech: Edinburgh, 1835), pp. 51–63.

66 Macaskill, 'The Parish of Boleskine and Abertarff, pp. 19–24.

67 *Local Government Board for Scotland, Second Annual Report*, PP, 1895–96 (c.8219), 'Report on the Sanitary Supervision of a New Industry at Foyers in Inverness-shire', Ogilvie Grant, MD, DPH, County Medical Officer, p. 75; Petition from foremen and labourers at Foyers for an increase in wages, 31 July 1918, UGD 347/21/34/1/17; Macaskill, 'The Parish of Boleskine and Abertarff', pp. 23–4; Note of visit by J. K. Adams, SEPD, to Foyers, 29 November 1966, NAS, SEP2/454/1; BACo, *History*, pp. 70–73.

68 Macaskill, pp. 19–26.

69 'Water Power and the Cost', *The Scotsman*, 3 December 1913; *The B.A. News*, vol. 5, no. 4 (1952), p. 11; *The B.A. News*, vol. 16, no. 4 (1964), p. 15; *The B.A. News*, vol. 27, no. 3 (1975), pp. 8–9 ; Henden, 'Stangfjordens Elektrokemiske Fabriker', pp. 33–67; Macaskill, pp. 19–26; Interviews with John Blair, Kinlochleven, undertaken by A. Perchard, and with Eleanor MacDonald, Kinlochleven, undertaken by A. Bartie.

70 Fraser, 'United Parishes of Boleskine and Abertarff', pp. 57–8; Book of particulars for Foyers, 31 January 1895; Macaskill, pp. 16–17.

71 Maclean, *The Highlands*, pp. 168–9.

72 Fraser, 'United Parishes of Boleskine and Abertarff', pp. 61–2; Macaskill, pp. 19–21.

73 'British Aluminium Company's Roll of Honour', *The Scotsman*, 27 January 1915; *The B.A. News*, vol. 5, no. 4 (1952), p. 10.

74 'Water Power and the Cost', *The Scotsman*, 3 December 1913.

75 Petition from foremen and labourers at Foyers for an increase in wages, 31 July 1918.

76 'The day they BOMBED Lochaber', *The B.A. News*, vol. 27, no. 5 (September–October 1975), pp. 8–9.

77 *The B.A. News*, vol. 3, no. 4, (March–April 1950), p. 3; The concept of 'organic solidarity' was developed by US sociologist Talcott Parsons, who identified it as a relationship of exchange and reliance: B. A. Turner, *Industrialism* (Prentice Hall: London, 1975), pp. 41–6.

78 'Between the wars – better conditions but bitter years: The community that died', *P&J*, 14 April 1967.

79 Report of visits by J. Solis, BoT, Office for Scotland, to Foyers, 7 March and 19 June 1963; Note of visit by J. K. Adams, SEPD, to Foyers, 29 November 1966.

80 BACo, Minutes of Managers' Annual Conferences, 14 May 1947 and 28 April 1948.

81 'Only new industry and new life will save dying community', *P&J*, 1 November 1964.

82 For example: S. L. Linkon and J. Russo, *Steeltown USA: Work and memory in Youngstown* (University of Kansas Press: Lawrence, 2002), p. 145; S. High and D. W. Lewis, *Corporate Wasteland: The Landscape and Memory of Deindustrialization* (ILR Press: Ithaca, 2007); T. A. K'Meyer and J. L. Hart, *I Saw it Coming: Worker narratives of plant closings and job loss* (Palgrave Macmillan: New York, 2010).

83 'Foyers bombshell', *P&J*, 18 January 1967.

84 Minutes of HIDB meetings at Edinburgh, 6 May 1966, and Foyers, 19 May 1966, 'Proposed Closure of Foyers Factory', NAS, SEP12/574.

85 'Foyers bombshell', *P&J*, 18 January 1967.

86 'A meeting on the future of Foyers', *Evening Express*, 15 April 1967; 'Hope is fading at Foyers', *Evening Express*, 14 April 1967; High and Lewis, *Corporate Wasteland*.

87 'Eleventh-hour bid to save Foyers', *Evening Express*, 29 April 1967.

88 Minutes of HIDB meetings at Edinburgh, 6 May 1966, and Foyers, 19 May 1966, 'Proposed Closure of Foyers Factory'; Extracts of minutes of HIDB plenary meetings, 23 June 1966, 21 July 1966, 22 September 1966, 3 November 1966, and 24 and 25 January 1967; Letter from Sir William Strath, BACo, to Sir Matthew Campbell, DAFS, 22 December 1966; Minute from T. R. H. Godden, Regional Development Division 2, DAFS, to Mr Hughes (cc. Gillett and Russell), 17 March 1967; Minute from Gillett to Hughes, 28 March 1967; Drafts of Minutes from Godden, SDD, to Lord Hughes, Dr Mabon and Secretary of State viz. valuation, 30 March and 6 April 1967; Letter from R. W. Wallace, County Clerk, ICC, to Permanent Secretary SDD, 'Closure of Factory, Foyers: Unemployment Position', 15 March 1967; Reply from Cowell, DD, to Wallace, 18 April 1967, NAS, SEP12/574; 'Foyers Shut-Down', *The Scotsman*, 18 January 1967.

89 Note of visit by J. K. Adams, SEPD, to Foyers, 29 November 1966, NAS, SEP2/454/1; 'End of an era at Foyers', *P&J*, 1 April 1967.

Chapter 6: 'The city among the hills' and the 'Garden City': Kinlochleven and Inverlochy

1 L. Grant, 'The city among the hills', *The Oban Times*, 24 March 1923

2 BACo, Minutes of Managers' Annual Meeting, 30 November 1936 – Report by John Gris Bullen; R. Duncan, *Steelopolis: The making of Motherwell, c.1750–1939* (John Donald: Edinburgh, 1991).

3 For an example of a very enthusiastic description of British Aluminium's developments at Fort William, see: W. M. T. Gilmour, 'The Lochaber Hydro-Electric Scheme', *Scots Magazine*, vol. II, no. 5 (February 1925), pp. 342–6;

4 The distinction between perceptions of the world we encounter, the 'lived' experience, as conscious beings and the reductionist behavioural and natural approaches of 'living' are explored in: M. Merleau-Ponty, *The Phenomonology of Perception: An introduction* (Routledge: London, 2002).

5 *The Scotsman*, 22 February 1895; *The Scotsman*, 4 March 1895.

6 F. F. Darling, 'Ecology of land use in the Highlands and Islands', in D. S. Thomson and I. Grimble (eds), *The Future of the Highlands* (Routledge and Keegan Paul: London, 1968), p. 50; F. F. Darling, *West Highland Survey: An essay in human ecology* (OUP: Oxford, 1955), pp. 58–9.

7 Rev. Alexander Robertson *et al.*, 'The parish of Kilmallie', p. 381; Gregor and Crichton, *From Croft to Factory*, pp. 1–9; For two very contrasting accounts of the massacre at Glencoe see: J. Prebble, *Glencoe* (Penguin: London, 1973); M. Lynch, *Scotland: A New History* (Pimlico: London, 1992).

8 MacGill, *Children of the Dead End*, pp. 175–7; Kirk, *Custom and Conflict in the 'Land of the Gael'*, pp. 15–19; A. H. Roberts, 'The Loch Leven Water-Power Works', *Proceedings of the Institute of Civil Engineers*, vol. 188, Pt. I (1912), pp. 3–48 cited in Gregor and Crichton, *From Croft to Factory*, p. 8.

9 *RC, Poor Laws and Relief of Distress*, 1910, Q. 37, Qs 90365–6, Appendix. CXVIII; *Oban Times*, 10 August 1907 cited in Gregor and Crichton, *From Croft to Factory*, pp. 8–10.

10 N. Morrison, *My Story* (Highland News: Inverness, 1937), pp. 51–66.

11 *Ibid.*; Gregor and Crichton, *From Croft to Factory*, pp. 8–10; Handley, *The Navvy in Scotland* pp. 78–9, 130–1, 243, 251, 332–3, 350–4; H. Holmes, 'Employment and Employment Conditions of Irish Migratory Potato Workers (Achill Workers) in Scotland From the Late Nineteenth Century to the Early 1970s', *The Journal of the Scottish Labour History Society* (subsequently *Scottish Labour History*), pp. 8–22; U. Cowley, 'The Irish in British construction industry', *British Association for Irish Studies Newsletter*, no. 30 (April 2002), http://ics.leeds.ac.uk/papers/vp01.cfm?outfit=ids&folder=15&paper=108 [accessed 22 March 2008].

12 *My Story; First Report of the Departmental Committee on questions arising in connection with the reception and employment of Belgian Refugees in this country*, PP, 1914–1916 (c.7779), evidence of Mr J. Sutherland, 14 November 1914 (Qs 2977–3016); Request from British Aluminium Company to bring Norwegian workers to Kinlochleven, 1915, TNA, FO 383/34.

13 Kirk, *Custom and Conflict in the 'Land of the Gael'*, pp. 15–19; *Report of the Departmental Committee on the Operation, in Scotland, of the Law relating to Inebriates and their detention in Reformatories and Retreats, Evidence and Appendices*, PP, 1909 (c.4767), Qs 5183, 5215, Evidence of Alexander McHardy, Chief Constable of Invernesshire, 27 February 1909.

14 Morrison, *My Story*, pp. 51–2.

15 *Ibid.*

16 Gregor and Crichton, *From Croft to Factory*, p. 50

17 Loch Leven Water & Power Company Ltd, Minute books 1 & 2; Gregor and Crichton, *From Croft to Factory*, pp. 2, 50–5; Interview with Eleanor MacDonald, Kinlochleven, September 2008, conducted by Angela Bartie.

18 AScW, *Highland Power*, pp. 56–7.

19 BACo, Minutes of Managers Annual Meetings, 30 November 1936 – report of E. S. Morrison; AScW, *Highland Power*, pp. 56–7; Gregor and Crichton, *From Croft to Factory*, pp. 50–62.

20 Minutes of evidence to the select committee on private bills: Lochaber Water Power Bill, Dr Lachlan Grant, 6 May 1921.

21 His two assistants were Drs Murdie and Falconer: *ibid.*; *The Lancet*, 14 September 1931; *The Lancet*, 23 April 1932.

22 *Royal Commission on the Housing of the Industrial Population of Scotland, Rural and Urban* (hereafter the *Ballantyne Report*) Minority Report, PP, 1917 (c.8731), pp. 109–10, 146, 158–9, 180, 209–11; J. Butt, 'Working-class housing in the Scottish cities 1900–1950', in G. Gordon and B. Dicks (eds), *Scottish Urban History* (AUP: Aberdeen, 1983), pp. 233–67; M. Glendinning, 'The Ballantyne Report: A "1917 Revolution" in Scottish housing', in D. Mays (ed.), *The Architecture of Scottish Cities* (Tuckwell: East Linton, 1997), pp. 161–70.

23 *Ballantyne Report*, p. 204.

24 Scottish Housing Advisory Committee, *Report on Rural Housing in Scotland*, PP, 1936–37 (c.5462), pp. 11–12, Appendix III.

25 J. B. Cullingworth, *A profile of Glasgow housing 1965* (University of Glasgow: Glasgow, 1967), Table 23; M. Anderson, 'Population and Family Life', in Dickson and Treble, *People and Society in Scotland, Volume III*, pp. 40–1.

26 A. Alban Scott, *Concrete and Constructional Engineer*, vol. IV (1909), pp. 585–9 in the *Dictionary of Scottish Architects*, http://www.scottisharchitects.org.uk/architects [accessed 14 December 2008]; Interviews with Mary MacPherson, Kinlochleven, 3 April 2007, and Eleanor MacDonald, 5 April 2007.

27 Frouard, *Du coron au HLM*, pp. 16–17; Vindt, *Les hommes de l'aluminium*, p. 52.

28 Loch Leven Water & Power Company, Minute book 1, 27 November 1906; Gregor and Crichton, *From Croft to Factory*, pp. 50–62; J. Melling, '"Non-commissioned officers": British employers and their supervisory workers, 1880–1920', *Social History*, vol. 5, no. 2 (May 1980), pp. 209–11.

29 Leven Water & Power Company Ltd, Minute books 1 & 2.

30 Otto Niemeyer gained notoriety later on in his career for advising Churchill to return to the Gold Standard: Letter from G. A. Calder, Secretary, Scottish Board of Health, to the Public Works Loan Board, 3 December 1920; Letter from Calder to Secretary, HM Treasury, 11 December 1920; Memo on the Kinlochleven Village Improvement Society, Public Works Loan Board, 20 December 1920; Letter from O. F. Niemeyer, HMT, to Calder, 5 January 1921; Letter from Sir George McCrae, Housing Secretary, SBH, to Niemeyer, 14 January 1921; Letter from B. P. Blackett, PWLB, to McCrae, 8 February 1921; Letter from Niemeyer to McCrae, 9 February 1921; Letters from J. Brough, on behalf of McCrae, to Niemeyer and PWLB, 9 August 1921; Letter from H. G. H. Barnes, Secretary, PWLB, to McCrae, 10 August 1921, TNA, T160/71; *Second Annual Report of the Scottish Board of Health*, PP, 1920 (c.1319), p. 184; *Report on Rural Housing in Scotland, 1936–37*, PP (c.5462), p. 9, see also p. 21.

31 BACo, Minutes of Annual Managers' Meetings – reports by Edward Shaw Morrison, 30 November 1936 and 23 November 1938; Gregor and Crichton, *From Croft to Factory*, pp. 55–7.

32 *Valuation Rolls for the County of Inverness – Years of 1937–1938 – Parish of Kilmallie*, pp. 231–6, LAC, CI/L/4/2/64; *Valuation Rolls for the County of Inverness – Years of 1957–1958 – Parish of Kilmallie*, pp. 282–96, CI/L/4/2/84; *Valuation Rolls for the County of Inverness – Years of 1974–1975 – Parish of Kilmallie*, pp. 397–405, CI/L/4/2/101; *The B.A. News*, vol. 23, no. 2 (March–April 1971), p. 5, UGD 347/21/33/16; *The B.A. News*, vol. 29, no. 1 (January–February 1977), pp. 12–13, UGD 347/21/33/19.

33 Gregor and Crichton, *From Croft to Factory*, pp. 55–9.

34 Interview with Eleanor MacDonald.

35 Chalmers to Renfrew, 26 October 1948; Renfrew to Johnston, 28 October 1948, NAS, SEP2/454/1.

36 Melling, 'Welfare capitalism and the origins of welfare states'; R. Fitzgerald, 'Employment relations and industrial welfare in Britain: Business ethics versus labor markets', *Business*

and Economic History, vol. 28, no. 2 (Fall 1999), pp. 167–79.

37 Glendinning, 'The Ballantyne Report: A "1917 Revolution" in Scottish housing', pp. 167–9; Butt, 'Working-class housing in the Scottish cities 1900–1950', pp. 239–44; H. Jones, 'Employers' welfare schemes and industrial relations in inter-war Britain', *Business History*, vol. 25, iss. 1 (1983) pp. 61–75; Boswell, 'The informal social control of business in Britain', pp. 237–57.

38 NBACo, Minute book, no. 1, 14 September, 12 October and 4 December 1926, 14 June 1927 and 10 January 1928; Petition of behalf of the Rt Hon. Hugh Richard Scarlett, DSO, Baron Abinger (of county of Surrey and City of Norwich, and of Inverlochy Castle) to Lords of Council and Session, 31 December 1930, Lochiel estate papers, LAC, CL/A/3/2/27/3/1 (2), items 131–3.

39 *Valuation Rolls for the County of Inverness, Years of 1923–1924 and 1937–1938 – Parish of Kilmonivaig*; NBACo, Minute book, no. 1, 9 April 1935; Dictionary of Scottish Architects – (Sir) Frank Charles Mears, b.1880 (Tynemouth), k. 1946, d.1953 (New Zealand), http://www.scottisharchitects.org.uk/architect_full.php?id=202402 [accessed 12 December 2008]; 'Mears (Sir Frank Mears 1880–1953)', http://www.scran.ac.uk [accessed 17 December 2008]; For details for Geddes see: Mays (ed.), *The Architecture of Scottish Cities*, pp. 48, 53–5, 166, 171–2.

40 'A crofting and industrial contrast: Factory Workers in a Model Village in Lochaber', *The Scotsman*, 8 September 1937.

41 Minutes of evidence to the select committee on private bills: Lochaber Water Power Bill, Dr Alexander Cameron Miller, Mr. Donald Shaw and Provost Andrew Stewart, 6 May 1921.

42 Dr A. C. Miller, b.1861, d.1927. See the serialised: Dr A. C. Miller, 'Medical work on the Lochaber water-power scheme', *CMJ*, vol. 13, no. 2 (April 1926), pp. 63–70; *idem, CMJ*, vol. 13, no. 3 (July 1926), pp. 102–8; *idem, CMJ*, vol. 13, no. 5 (January 1927), pp. 183–8; *CMJ*, vol. 14, no. 8 (October 1930), pp. 257–8; *The Engineer*, 9 May 1930, p. 512; *The Evening Standard*, 9 May 1934; *The Scotsman*, 8 September 1937.

43 Interview with George Haggart, Fort William, 16 August 2006, conducted by A. Perchard; see also interviews with Sandy Walker, Duncan Haggart and Brian Murphy.

44 BACo, Minutes of Managers' Annual Conferences, 30 November 1936 and 23 November 1938; Letter from A. G. Chalmers to W. H. Renfrew, 26 October 1948, NAS, SEP2/454/1; *Valuation Rolls for the County of Inverness, Years of 1937–1938 and 1957–1958 – Parish of Kilmonivaig*; BACo's *Highland News, Christmas Number*, no. 18 (December 1947), p. 3; Turnock, 'Population studies and regional development in West Highland Scotland', pp. 55–68; G. Munro and K. Hart, '"The Highland Problem": State and community in local development', *Arkleton Research Papers No. 1* (Arkleton Research Centre: Aberdeen, 2000), p. 37; MacKenzie, '"Chucking buns across the fence?"'; S. Black, 'Economic Change and Challenges in the Highlands and Islands', pp. 60–9.

45 *Valuation Rolls for the County of Inverness, Years of 1957–1958 – Parish of Kilmonivaig*, p. 296; Rev. A. Mackinnon, with Rev. I. Montgomery, Rev. J. W. Moore and Rev. R. Tuton, 'The Parish of Kilmonivaig', in Barron, *The County of Inverness*, pp. 422–6.

46 D. Halpearn, *Social Capital* (Polity: London, 2005); For a critique of the inconsistencies endemic in the use of the term, see: B. Fine, *Theories of Social Capital: Researchers Behaving Badly* (Pluto: London, 2010).

47 *Census returns 1911–1961*; Rev. I. Carmichael, 'Lorn: The Parish of Lismore and Appin', in C. M. MacDonald (ed.), *Third Statistical Account of Scotland: County of Argyll* (SAC: Glasgow, 1961), p. 161; D. Turnock, 'Lochaber: West Highland growth point', *Scottish Geographical Magazine*, vol. 82 (1966), p. 17.

48 *Ibid.*, pp. 17–28; *idem*, 'Fort William, Scotland: Problems of urban expansion in a Highland area', *Tijdschrift voor Econmiske en Social Geografie*, vol. 59, (September/October 1968), pp. 260–70; 'The Ghost Town: Forgotten Kinlochleven fights for its survival', *Evening Times*, 30 January 1976.

49 *Valuation Rolls for the County of Inverness, Years of 1937/38, 1957/58, and 1974/75 – Parish of Kilmonivaig; Valuation Rolls for the County of Inverness – Years of 1937/38, 1957/58, and 1974/75 – Parish of Kilmallie.*

50 Interview with Sandy (Alexander) Walker, Inverlochy, 16 August 2006; for similar narratives in their occupational communities, see: Wight, *Workers not Wasters*.

51 *The Scotsman*, 8 September 1937; Rev. A. Mackinnon *et al.*, 'The Parish of Kilmonivaig' and Rev. A. Robertson *et al.*, 'The Parish of Kilmallie', in Barron, *The County of Inverness*, pp. 365–407 and 407–31; Rev. I. Carmichael, 'Lorn: The Parish of Lismore and Appin', in MacDonald, *Third Statistical Account of Scotland: County of Argyll*, pp. 160–8; *The B.A. News*, vol. 3, no. 4 (July–August 1950), pp. 6–8; *The B.A. News*, vol. 4, no. 2 (March–April 1951), p. 13; *The B.A. News*, vol. 7, no. 4 (July–August 1954), p. 4; *The B.A. News*, vol. 11, no. 4 (July–August 1958), pp. 7–9; *The B.A. News*, vol. 27, no. 1 (January–February 1975), pp. 22–3; A. G. MacKenzie, *Church of Scotland, Kinlochleven: Golden Jubilee 1930–1980* (CoS: Kinlochleven, 1980), p. 24; Watson, *Being English in Scotland*, pp. 51, 53, 87–90; Gregor and Crichton, *From Croft to Factory*, pp. 23–29.

52 Vindt, *Les hommes de l'aluminium*

53 Interview with Mary MacPherson, Kinlochleven, 3 April 2007, conducted by Angela Bartie; See also interview with Margaret Mathieson, Kinlochleven, conducted by Bartie.

54 *Oban Times*, 1 February 1936.

55 Interview with Eleanor MacDonald.

56 *The B.A. News*, vol. 2, no. 6 (November–December 1949), front cover.

57 Gregor and Crichton, *From Croft to Factory*, p. 139.

58 The KVIS was formed in 1913, as Gregor and Crichton correctly identify, not in 1907 as one account claimed (*The B.A. News*, vol. 3, no. 5 (September–October 1950), p. 16). Similarly the same account incorrectly states the IVS as being formed in 1927. In fact the IVS was formed between September and October 1926, and registered on 12 October 1926: *ibid.*, pp. 16–17; Loch Leven Water & Power Company, Minute books 1 (1904–1907) and 2 (1907–1911); NBACo, Minute book no. 1, 14 September and 12 October 1926; BACo, Minutes of Managers' Annual Conference, 30 November 1936 – report from Edward Shaw Morrison; Minutes of the Kinlochleven Village Improvement Society (KVIS), 1946–1963, UGD 347/34/14/1; *The Scotsman*, 8 September 1937; For detail on Sir Francis Walker: http://www.historic-scotland.gov.uk/gardens_search_results/gardenssearchmoreinfo.htm?s=&r=&bool=0&PageID=2302&more_info=Site [accessed 15 June 2007].

59 The records of the IVS were not forthcoming, and only minutes for the years 1946–63 were available in the Company archive: *The B.A. News*, vol. 2, no. 5 (September–October 1949), pp. 8–9; *The B.A. News*, vol. 3, no. 5 (September–October 1950), p. 16; KVIS, minutes, 1946–1963.

60 KVIS, minutes, 16 July 1947, 31 March 1948 and 9 February 1950; *The B.A. News, Highlands Edition*, vol. 1, no. 1 (July–August 1948), p. 9; *The B.A. News*, vol. 3, no. 3 (May–June 1950), p. 8.

61 KVIS minute book.

62 Brown, *The Death of Christian Britain*, pp. 88, 96–114; Heller, 'Sports, bureaucracies and London clerks 1880–1939', pp. 559–60; R. Fitzgerald, 'Employers' labour strategies, industrial welfare, and the response to New Unionism at Bryant and May, 1888–1930', *BH*, vol. 31 (April 1989), p. 60; Griffiths, '"Give my Regards to Uncle Billy …"', p. 27.

63 *The Times*, 1 April 1916, 4 March 1921, 24 December 1924, 4 January 1928, 16 January 1946, 1 April 1952; G. A. R. Callender, 'Laughton, Sir John Knox (1830–1915)', rev. Andrew Lambert, *Oxford Dictionary of National Biography*, Oxford University Press, 2004; online edn, Oct 2007 [http://www.oxforddnb.com/view/article/34420, accessed 17 Sept 2010].

64 *The B.A. News*, vol. 5, no. 4 (1952), p. 10.

65 'The New Great War', *The B.A. News*, vol. 1, no. 2 (September–October 1948), p. 16; 'Spare Time for Britain' *The B.A. News*, vol. 2, no. 2 (March–April 1949), p. 3; 'Highland wives are busy', *The B.A. News*, vol. 5, no. 1 (January–February 1952), p. 11, and 'Works Managers: Reduction Works', no. 4 (May–June 1952), pp. 10–11; 'People we meet', *The B.A. News*, vol. 7, no. 3 (May–June 1954), pp. 14–16; *The B.A. News*, vol. 12, no. 1 (January–February 1959), p. 3; '50 years of village life for Ian', *The B.A. News*, vol. 29, no. 1 (January–February 1977), pp. 12–13; Brown, *The Death of Christian Britain*, pp. 88, 96–114; G. I. T. Machin, *Churches and Social Issues in Twentieth-Century Britain* (OUP: Oxford, 1998), *passim*; N. Garnham, 'Both praying and playing: "Muscular Christianity" and the YMCA in the North-East County of Durham', *Journal of Social History*, vol. 35, no. 2 (2001), pp. 397–407.

66 Garnham, 'Both praying and playing'; *The B.A. News*, vol. 3, no. 3 (May–June 1950), p. 8, and no. 5 (September–October 1950), p. 16; *The B.A. News*, vol. 5, no. 4 (May–June 1952), pp. 10–11; 'The man at the wheel', *The B.A. News*, vol. 16, no. 3 (May–June 1963), pp. 15–16; Gregor and Crichton, *From Croft to Factory*, pp. 105–7.

67 Eleanor MacDonald

68 Interview with George Haggart.

69 *Ibid.*; 'Northern meeting ball at Inverness', *The Times*, 23 September 1938

70 *The B.A. News*, vol. 1, no. 3 (1948), p. 16.

71 A. Robertson *et al.*, 'The Parish of Kilmallie', in Barron, *The County of Inverness*, p. 395.

72 *Oban Times*, 8 January 1916; MacKenzie, *Church of Scotland, Kinlochleven*, pp. 21–4.

73 Interviews with Eleanor MacDonald, Margaret Mathieson and Mary MacPherson; For reflections on women's religious participation in Scotland see: C. G. Brown and J. Stephenson, '"Sprouting Wings"?: Women and religion in Scotland c.1890–1950', in E. Breitenbach and E. Gordon (eds), *Out of Bounds: Women in Scottish Society 1800–1945* (EUP: Edinburgh, 1992), pp. 95–120.

74 *Ibid.*; C. G. Brown, 'Religion and secularisation', in Dickson and Treble, *People and Society in Scotland, Volume III*, pp. 56–59; *Oban Times*, 2 January 1909.

75 Interview with Eleanor MacDonald; For reflections on socialisation of women in Scotland see: L. Moore, 'Educating for the "Women's Sphere": Domestic training versus intellectual discipline', in Breitenbach and Gordon, *Out of Bounds*, pp. 10–41.

76 Interviews with MacDonald, MacPherson and Mathieson.

77 Gregor and Crichton, *From Croft to Factory*, pp. 38–43.

78 Interviews with MacDonald, MacPherson and Mathieson.

79 Interview with Cynthia Cassidy, Ardgour, 25 April 2007, conducted by A. Bartie; KVIS minutes, 1950–59.

80 KVIS minutes, 1950–59.

81 Interview with Margaret Mathieson, Kinlochleven, conducted by A. Bartie; Rev. A. Mackinnon *et al.*, 'The Parish of Kilmonivaig' and A. Robertson *et al.*, 'The Parish of Kilmallie', in Barron, *The County of Inverness*, pp. 397–9 and 326–428; Gregor and Crichton, *From Croft to Factory*, pp. 73–91.

82 Interview with Eleanor MacDonald.

83 Sandy Walker; Eleanor MacDonald; Margaret Mathieson; Interview with Brian Murphy, Fort William, 16 August 2006, conducted by A. Perchard.

84 P. Willis, *Learning to Labour: How working class kids get working class jobs* (Saxon House:

Farnborough, 1977); R. Anderson, 'In search of the "Lad of Parts": the mythical history of Scottish education', *History Workshop Journal*, no. 19 (Spring 1985), pp. 82–3; J. Annetts, 'The Family and Childhood in Scotland' in Beech et al. (eds), *Scottish Life and Society, A compendium of Scottish ethnology: Vol. 9, The Individual and Community Life*, p. 31; H. Hendrick, *Children, Childhood and English Society 1880–1990* (CUP: Cambridge, 1997), p. 77.

85 KVIS, minutes, 2 February 1963; Marwick, *The Sixties*; Brown, *The Death of Christian Britain, passim.*

86 E. P. Thompson, *Customs in Common* (Penguin: London, 1993) p. 85.

87 Interview with Sandy Walker.

88 *Ibid.*

89 Interview with Brian Murphy.

90 'The Ghost Town', *Evening Times*, 30 January 1976.

91 Interview with John Blair.

92 *Ibid.*

93 *Ibid.*

94 Interview with Margaret Mathieson.

95 'The Ghost Town', *Evening Times*, 30 January 1976; '50 years of village life for Ian', *The B.A. News*, vol. 29, no. 1 (January–February 1977), pp. 12–13.

96 Provided by: Interview with Mary Donald by Audrey Tod, c.1987.

97 Interview with Jimmy Dunlevy, Caol, 5 April 2007, conducted by A. Perchard.

98 Interview with Bill Maxwell, Fort William, 6 April 2007, conducted by A. Perchard.

99 Interview with Bob Herbert, Kinlochleven, 3 April 2007.

100 *Ibid.*

101 *Ibid.*

102 R. Samuel, *Theatres of Memory Volume 2: Island Stories, Unravelling Britain* (Verso: London, 1998), p. 34, quoted in M. Hebbert, 'The street as locus of collective memory', *Environment and Planning D: Society and Space*, vol. 23 (2005), p. 583.

103 Quoted in *ibid*, pp. 583–4.

Conclusion

1 S. Gandz, 'Mene Mene Tekel Upharsin, a chapter in Babylonian mathematics', *Isis*, vol. 26, no. 1 (December 1936), pp. 82–94.

2 J. M. MacKenzie, 'The persistence of empire in metropolitan culture', in S. Ward (ed.), *British Culture and the End of Empire* (MUP: Manchester, 2001), pp. 32–3.

3 J. Habermas and C. Cronin, 'The European Nation-State: On the past and future of sovereignty and citizenship', *Public Culture*, vol. 10, iss. 2 (1998), p. 404.

4 For example of recent criticisms of this: R. Perks, 'The roots of oral history: Exploring contrasting attitudes to elite, corporate, and business oral history in Britain and the U.S.', *Oral History Review*, vol. 37, iss. 2 (2010), pp. 215–54.

5 Ross and Munro, 'Contested energy'.

6 *The B.A. News*, vol. 2, no. 3 (May–June 1949), p. 5.

7 Interview with Sandy Walker.

Bibliography

Primary sources

Interviews, questionnaires and correspondence:
The following former employees and residents in the west Highlands kindly gave of their time, and hospitality, to speak of their experiences. For access to these interviews, please contact the Scottish Oral History Centre:

John Blair
Cynthia Cassidy
Jimmy Dunlevy
Iain Grainger
Duncan Haggart
George Haggart, OBE
Bob Herbert
Margaret Mathieson
Bill Maxwell
Douglas MacDiarmid
Eleanor MacDonald
Mary MacPherson
Brian Murphy
Jack Silver
Alexander (Sandy) Walker

Bodleian Library, University of Oxford
Papers of Christopher Addison, 1st Viscount Addison (1869 – 1951)

British Alcan/ British Aluminium Company Archive, Glasgow University Business Archives (GUA)
This large collection of papers for BACo, British Alcan and its subsidiaries, contains everything from annual reports to company employee publications, like *The B.A. News* and *Noral News* (catalogue number UGD 347). That these records were saved is only due to the foresight of Douglas MacDiarmid and Mairi MacKay. For further details contact the Duty Archivist at: enquiries@archives.gla.ac.uk

Highland Council, Lochaber Archive (LAC), Fort William
Cameron of Lochiel correspondence and papers
Valuation rolls, County of Inverness-shire

Institut pour l'histoire de l'aluminium (IHA)/ Rio Tinto Alcan France, Gennevilliers, France
Collection Historique Pechiney
Collection IHA

National Archives (TNA), Kew
The records of the following government departments and other public bodies were consulted. As
    with other collections specific references are to be found in the end notes:
Admiralty
Board of Trade
Colonial Office
Department of Trade and Industry
Department of Industry
HM Cabinet papers
Medical Research Council papers
Ministry of Aircraft Production
Ministry of Labour
Ministry of Munitions
Ministry of Supply

National Archives of Scotland (NAS)/ National Registers Scotland, Edinburgh
Court of Session papers
Death certificates
Department of Agriculture and Fisheries Scotland
Scottish Development Department
Scottish Economic Planning Department

National Library of Scotland (NLS), Edinburgh
Dr Lachlan Grant Collection

Rio Tinto Alcan archive, Montreal
Records of Alcan Inc

Scottish Trades Union Congress (STUC) Library, Glasgow Caledonian University
Reports of the Scottish Trades Union Congress
Records of Lochaber Trades Council, 1975–82

Parliamentary sources and agency reports, and other online sources:
Hansard accessed through: http://hansard.millbanksystems.com/
All House of Commons Select Committee Reports, published departmental reports and those
    of Royal Commissions, accessed through House of Commons Parliamentary Papers: http://
    parlipapers.chadwyck.co.uk/marketing/index.jsp
Highland and Islands Development Board, Annual Reports, 1965 – 1990

Newspapers/ journals
Except where indicated this were generally sourced through institutional subscription to online
    catalogues, or were found in other archive collections:
British Journal of Industrial Medicine
British Medical Journal
Caledonian Medical Journal (Royal College of Physicians of Glasgow Library)
Evening Express

Evening Times
Farming News
Glasgow Herald
Glasgow Forward
Guardian
Highland News
Journal of Occupational Medicine
Metal Bulletin Monthly
Mining Magazine
Northern Times
Oban Times (and Argyllshire Advertiser) (Highland Libraries, Fort William)
Observer
Occupational Medicine
Otago Witness
Press & Journal
Proceedings of the Institute of Civil Engineers
The Engineer
The Lancet
The Ross-shire Journal (Alness Heritage Centre)
The Scotsman
The Scots Magazine
The Times

Published books and articles

Abrams, L. and Brown, C. G. (eds) (2010), *A History of Everyday Life in Twentieth-Century Scotland*, EUP, Edinburgh.

Ackers, P. (1998), 'On paternalism: Seven observations on the uses and abuses of the concept in industrial relations, past and present', *Historical Studies in Industrial Relations*, no. 5, pp. 173–93.

Ackers, P. and Wilkinson, A. (eds) (2003), *Understanding Work and Employment: Industrial relations in transition*, OUP, Oxford.

Addison, P. and Jones, H. (eds) (2009), *A Companion to Contemporary Britain 1939–2000*, Blackwell, Oxford.

Alcan Aluminium UK (1996), *Alcan in the Highlands. 1996 Review: Celebrating one hundred years of aluminium production*, Alcan, Fort William.

Alcan, Primary Metals Europe (2006), *Lochaber Smelter. Environmental Statement 2005 Update*, Alcan, Fort William.

Albarn, T. (2001), 'Senses of belonging: The politics of working-class insurance in Britain, 1880–1914', *The Journal of Modern History*, vol. 73, no. 3, pp. 561–602.

Alexander, Sir K. (1985), 'The Highlands and Islands Development Board', in R. Saville (ed.), *The Economic Development of Modern Scotland 1950–1980*, Edinburgh University Press, Edinburgh, pp. 214–32.

Allport, A. (2010), *Demobbed: Coming Home after the Second World War*, Yale University Press, Yale.

Anderson, D. H. (1951), *Aluminum for Defense and Prosperity*, Public Affairs Institute, Washington.

Anderson, R. (1985), 'In search of the "Lad of Parts": The mythical history of Scottish education', *History Workshop Journal*, no. 19, pp. 82–104.

Arnold, L. (2001), *Britain and the H-Bomb*, Palgrave, London.

—— (2007), *Windscale 1957: Anatomy of a nuclear accident*, Palgrave, Hampshire.

Ash, M., Macaulay, J. and Mackay, M. A. (1991), *This Noble Harbour: A history of the Cromarty Firth*, John Donald, Edinburgh.

Ashworth, W. (1953), *Contracts and Finance*, HMSO, London.

Association of Scientific Workers, Scottish Area Committee (1944), *Highland Power. A Report of the utilisation of the Hydro-Electric Power envisaged in the Hydro-Electric Development (Scotland) Act – 1943*, AScW, Glasgow.

Backman, J. and Fishman, L. (1941), 'British war time control of aluminium', *The Quarterly Journal of Economics*, vol. 56, no. 1, pp. 18–36.

Ball, S. (2004), 'The German Octopus: The British Metal Corporation and the Next War, 1914–1939', *Enterprise & Society*, vol. 5, no. 3, pp. 451–89.

—— (2004), *The Guardsmen: Harold Macmillan, Three Friends, and the World they Made*, Harper Collins, London.

Barnes, W., Gartland, M. and Stack, M. (2004), 'Old habits die hard: Path dependency and behavioral lock-in', *Journal of Economic Issues*, vol. 38, no. 2, pp. 371–7.

Barnett, C. (1986), *The Audit of War: The illusion and reality of Britain as a Great Nation*, Macmillan, London.

Barron, H. (ed.) (1985), *The Third Statistical Account of Scotland, The County of Inverness*, Scottish Academic Press, Edinburgh.

Bastable, M. J. (2004), *Arms and the State: Sir William Armstrong and the remaking of British naval power, 1854–1914*, Ashgate, Aldershot.

Beech, J., Hand, O., Mulhern, M. A. and Weston, J. (eds) (2005), *Scottish Life and Society, A compendium of Scottish ethnology: Vol. 9, The Individual and Community Life*, Tuckwell Press, Edinburgh.

Bertilorenzi, M. (2008), 'The International Aluminium Cartels, 1901–1939: The construction of international corporate business', I jordanas de historia empresarial: España y Europa.

—— (2008) 'The Italian Aluminium Industry: Cartels, Multinationals and the Autarkic Phase, 1917–1943', *Cahiers d'histoire de l'aluminium*, vol. 41, pp. 42–71.

Birnie, C. M. (2008), 'The Scottish Office and the Highland problem, 1930 to 1965', unpublished Ph.D. thesis, University of Edinburgh.

Bloom, C. (2002), *Bestsellers: Popular fiction since 1900*, Palgrave, Basingstoke.

Bloor, M. (2000), 'The South Wales Miners' Federation, miners' lung and the instrumental use of expertise, 1900–1950', *Social Studies in Science*, vol. 30, no. 1, pp. 125–40.

Bocquetin, J. (1992) 'La fabrication de l'aluminium par électrolyse', in P. Morel (ed.), *Histoire technique de la production d'aluminium*, Presses Universitaires de Provence, Grenoble, pp. 21–57.

Bond, B. (1980), *British Military Policy between the Two World Wars*, OUP, Oxford.

Booth, A. (2001), *The British Economy in The Twentieth Century*, Palgrave, London.

Boswell, J. (1983), 'The informal social control of business in Britain: 1880–1939', *Business History Review*, vol. 57, no. 2, pp. 237–257.

Bothwell, R. and Kilbourn, W. (1980), *C. D. Howe: A biography*, McClelland and Stewart, Toronto.

Boullet, D. (2000), 'Pechiney et l'environnement (1960–1980) Précocité et diversité d'une expérience', *Cahiers d'histoire de l'aluminium*, vol. 26, pp. 11–37.

Bourke, J. (1994), *Working-Class Cultures in Britain 1890–1960. Gender, Class and Ethnicity*, Routledge, London.

—— (1996), *Dismembering the Male: Men's Bodies, Britain and the Great War*, Reaktion, London.

Boyns, T. (1990), 'Strategic responses to foreign competition: the British coal industry and the 1930 Coal Mines Act', *Business History*, vol. 32, no. 3, pp. 133–45.

Braverman, H. (1974), *Labor and Monopoly Capital*, Monthly Review Press, New York.

Breitenbach, E. and Gordon, E. (eds) (1992), *Out of Bounds: Women in Scottish Society 1800–1945*, EUP, Edinburgh.

Brewis, R. A. L., Gibson, G. J. and Geddes, D. M. (eds) (1990), *Respiratory Medicine*, Ballière Tindall, London.

British Aluminium Company Ltd (1956), *The History of the British Aluminium Company Limited 1894–1955*, BACo, London.

—— (1959), *Aluminium Facts & Figures*, BACo, London.

—— (1978), *Aluminium in the Highlands*, Raithby, Lawrence & Co, London.

Brock, J. M. (1999), *The Mobile Scot: A study of emigration and migration 1861–1911*, John Donald, Edinburgh.

Brooking, T. (1985), '"Tam McCanny and Kitty Clydeside" – the Scots in New Zealand' in Cage, R. A. (ed.), *The Scots Abroad: Labour, capital, enterprise, 1750 – 1914*, Croom Helm, Beckenham, pp. 156–90.

Brown, C. G. (2001), *The Death of Christian Britain: Understanding secularisation 1800–2000*, Routledge, London.

Bufton, M. W. and Melling, J. (2005), 'Coming up for air: Experts, employers, and workers in campaigns to compensate silicosis sufferers in Britain, 1918–1939', *Social History of Medicine*, vol. 18, no. 1, pp. 63–86.

Bullen, J. G. (1953) 'Aluminium' in Oakley, C. A. (ed.) *Scottish Industry. An account of what Scotland makes and where she makes it*, SCDI, Edinburgh, pp. 161–4.

Bulmer, M. (1978), *Mining and Social Change: Durham County in the twentieth century*, Croom Helm, London.

Burawoy, M. (1982), *Manufacturing Consent: Changes in the labor process under monopoly capitalism*, University of Chicago Press, Chicago.

Burgess, R. H. (ed.) (1990), *Manufacture and processing of PVC*, Taylor and Francis, London.

Burk, K. (ed.) (1982), *War and the State: The Transformation of British Government, 1914–1919*, Routledge, London.

Butler, L. J. (2007), 'Business and British Decolonisation: Sir Ronald Prain, the Mining Industry and the Central African Federation', *The Journal of Imperial and Commonwealth History*, vol. 35, no. 3, pp. 459–84.

—— (2008), *Britain and Empire: Adjusting to a Post-Imperial World*, I. B. Tauris, London.

Butt, J. (1967), *The Industrial Archeology of Scotland*, David & Charles, Newton Abbot.

—— (1983), 'Working-class housing in the Scottish cities 1900–1950', in Gordon, G. and Dicks, B. (eds), *Scottish Urban History*, AUP, Aberdeen, pp. 233–67.

Butt, J., Donnachie, I. L. and Hume, J. R. (1968), *Industrial History in Pictures: Scotland*, David & Charles, Newton Abbot.

Cailluet, L. (2001), 'The British aluminium industry, 1945–80s: Chronicles of a death foretold?', *Accounting, Business and Financial History*, vol. 11, iss. 1, pp. 79–97.

Cain, P. J. and Hopkins, A. G. (1987), 'Gentlemanly capitalism and British expansion overseas II: New imperialism, 1850–1945', *Economic History Review*, second series, vol. 40, pp. 1–26.

—— (2001), *British Imperialism, 1688–2000*, Longman, London.

Cairncross, A. K. (ed.) (1954), *The Scottish Economy: A statistical account of Scottish life by members of the staff of Glasgow University*, CUP, Cambridge.

Calder, A. (1969), *The People's War: Britain, 1939–1945*, Random House, London.

—— (1991), *The Myth of the Blitz*, Pimlico, London.

Cameron, E. A. (1996), 'The Scottish Highlands: From congested district to objective one', in Devine, T. M. and Finlay, R. J. (eds), *Scotland in the Twentieth Century*, EUP, Edinburgh, pp. 153–69.

—— (1997), 'The Scottish Highlands as a Special Policy Area, 1886 to 1965', *Rural History*, vol. 8, no. 2, pp. 195–216.

—— (2007), 'Conservatism and Radicalism in the Highland Press: the Strange Cases of the *Highlander* and the *Northern Chronicle*', *Northern Scotland*, vol. 27, pp. 117–29.

Campbell, A., Fishman, N. and McIlroy, J. (eds) (1999), *British Trade Unions and Industrial Politics: The Post-War Compromise, 1945–64*, Ashgate, Aldershot.

Campbell, B. K. (1991), 'Negotiating the Bauxite/Aluminium Sector under Narrowing Constraints', *Review of African Political Economy*, vol. 51, pp. 27–49.

Campbell, D. C. (1985), *Global Mission: The story of Alcan, Volume I to 1950*, Alcan, Ontario.

—— (1989), *Global Mission. The story of Alcan, Volume II*, Alcan, Ontario

—— (1990), *Global Mission. The story of Alcan, Volume III and Index*, Alcan, Ontario.

Campbell, R. H. (1979), 'The Scottish Office and the Special Areas in the 1930s', *Historical Journal*, vol. 22, pp. 167–83.

Cannadine, D. (1992), *The Decline and Fall of the British Aristocracy*, Picador, London.

—— (2006), *Mellon: An American life*, Knopf, New York.

Carter, C., McKinlay, A. and Rawlinson, M. (2002), 'Introduction: Foucault, Management and History', *Organization*, vol. 9, no. 4, pp. 515–24.

Carver, M. (2008), 'Guingand, Sir Francis Wilfred [Freddie] de (1900–1979)', *ODNB*, www.oxforddnb.com.ezproxy.webfeat.lib.ed.ac.uk/view/article/31022 [accessed 23 March 2008].

Centre d'economie et d'ethique pour l'environnment et le development (2003), *Implementation of a system of indicators for social responsibility reporting*, CEEED, Guyancourt.

Cerretano, V. (2009), 'The Treasury, Britain's post-war reconstruction and the industrial intervention of the Bank of England, 1921–1929', EHR, vol. 62, Series 1, pp. 80–100.

Chandler Jr., A. D. (1990), *Scale and Scope: The dynamics of industrial capitalism*, Belknap Press, Cambridge MA.

Channon, D. F. (1973), *The Strategy and Structure of British Enterprise*, Macmillan, London.

Charle, C. (1987), 'Le pantouflage en France (vers1880–vers1980)', *Annales ESC*, 5, pp. 1115–37.

Chick, M. (1998), *Industrial policy in Britain 1945–1951: Economic planning, nationalisation and the Labour governments*, CUP, Cambridge.

—— (2004), 'Listing potential candidates for nationalisation: Britain, 1948', *Enterprises et Histoire*, no. 37, pp. 167–71.

Christensen, B. (1995), *Too Good to be True: Alcan's Kemano Project*, Talonbooks, Vancouver.

Christie, D. A. and Tansey, E. M. (2002), 'Environmental Toxicology: The legacy of *Silent Spring*', The Transcript of a Witness Seminar held by the Wellcome Trust Centre for the History of Medicine, UCL, London.

Church, R. (1995), *The Rise and Decline of the British Motor Industry*, CUP, Cambridge.

Clements, R. V. (1958), *Managers: A study of their careers in industry*, Allen & Unwin, London.

Coats, A. W. (1978), 'The changing role of economists in Scottish Government since 1960', *Public Administration*, vol. 56, pp. 399–424.

Coleman, D. (1987) 'The uses and abuses of business history', *Business History*, vol. 39, no. 2, pp. 141–56.

Coleman, D. C. and Macleod, C. (1986), 'Attitudes to new techniques: British businessmen, 1800–1950', *Economic History Review*, second series, vol. 39, no. 4, pp. 588–611.

Collins, A. and Harris, R. I. D. (2002), 'Does plant ownership affect the level of pollution abatement expenditure', *Land Economics*, vol. 78, no. 2, pp. 171–89.

Cooter, R. and Luckin, B. (eds) (1997), *Accidents in History: Injuries, fatalities and social relations*, Rodopi, Amsterdam.

Condry, E. (1983), *Scottish Ethnography*, EUP, Edinburgh.

Connelly, M. (2004), *We Can Take It! Britain and the memory of the Second World War*, Longman, London.

Conway, J. K. (1998), *When Memory Speaks: Reflections on Autobiography*, Knopf, New York.

Coopey, R. and Woodward, N. (eds) (1996), *Britain in the 1970s: The Troubled Economy*, UCL, London.

Cooter, R. (2004), 'The Rise and Decline of the Medical Member: Doctors and Parliament in Edwardian and Interwar Britain', *Bulletin of the History of Medicine*, vol. 78, no. 1, pp. 59–107.

Corbett MacDonald, J. (ed.) (1995), *Epidemiology of work related diseases*, BMJ, London.

Cordero, H. G. (ed.) (1950), *World's Non-Ferrous Smelters and Refineries*, IMM, London.

Cordero, H. G. and Tarring, L. H. (1960), *Babylon to Birmingham: An Historical Survey of the Development of the World's Non-Ferrous Metal and Iron and Steel Industries and the Commerce in Metals since the Earliest Times*, Quinn Press, London.

Cowley, U. (2002), 'The Irish in British construction industry', *British Association for Irish Studies Newsletter*, no. 30, http://ics.leeds.ac.uk/papers/vp01.cfm?outfit=ids&folder=15&paper=108 [accessed 22 March 2008].

Crab, A. (2001), *Who Owns Scotland Now: The use and abuse of private land*, Polygon, Edinburgh.

Crafts, N., Gazeley, I. and Newell, A. (eds) (2007), *Work and Pay in Twentieth-Century Britain*, OUP, Oxford.

Cross, B. (2008), 'White Metal: Labour, Capital, and the Land, under multinational aluminum corporations in Guyana and Jamaica', unpublished paper to the Global Economic History of Bauxite Workshop, Fondation Maison des Sciences de l'Homme, 21–24 September.

Crouch, C. (1993), *Industrial Relations and European State Traditions*, OUP, Oxford.

Cullingworth, J. B. (1967), *A profile of Glasgow housing 1965*, University of Glasgow, Glasgow.

Dahlström, K., Elkins, P., He, J., Davis, J. and Clift, R. (2004), 'Iron, steel and aluminium in the UK: Material flows and their economic dimensions', Final project report, Policy Studies Institute and University of Surrey, March 2004.

Darling, F. F. (1968) 'Ecology of land use in the Highlands and Islands', in D. S. Thomson and I. Grimble (eds), *The Future of the Highlands* (Routledge and Keegan Paul, London.

Darling, F. F. (1955), *West Highland Survey: An essay in human ecology*, OUP, Oxford.

Davenport-Hines, R. P. T. (1984), *Dudley Docker: The life and times of a trade warrior*, CUP, Cambridge.

—— (1986), 'Pollen, Arthur Joseph Hungerford (1866–1937)', in Jeremy, D. J. and Shaw, C. (eds), *Dictionary of Business Biography: A Biographical Dictionary of Business Leaders Active in Britain in the Period 1860–1980, Volume 4*, Butterworths, London, pp. 753–8.

David, P. A. (2001) 'Path Dependence, its critics and the quest for 'historical economics' in P. Garrouste and S. Ioannides (eds), *Evolution and Path Dependence in Economic Ideas: Past and Present*, Edward Elgar, Cheltenham, pp. 15–40.

DeKadt, E. and Williams, G. (eds) (1974), *Sociology and Underdevelopment*, Tavistock, London.

De Luigi, G., Meyer, E. and Saba, A. F. (1994), 'La *Società italiana dell'alluminio* et son impact sur l'environnement dans la province de Trente (1928–1938)', *Cahiers d'histoire de l'aluminium*, vol. 14, pp. 38–53.

Dell, E. (1973), *Political Responsibility and Industry*, Allen and Unwin, London.

—— (2001), *A Strange Eventful History: Democratic socialism in Britain*, Harper Collins, London.

Devine, T. M. (1979), 'Temporary migration and the Scottish Highlands in the nineteenth century', *Economic History Review*, vol. 32, no. 3, pp. 344–359.

—— (ed.) (1994), *Scottish Elites: Proceedings of the Scottish Historical Studies Seminar University of Strathclyde 1991–1992*, John Donald, Edinburgh.

Dickson, A. (ed.) (1980), *Scottish Capitalism: Class, state and nation from before the Union to the present*, Lawrence and Wishart, London.

Dickson, A. and Treble, J. H. (eds) (1992), *People and Society in Scotland, Volume III: 1914–1990*, John Donald, Edinburgh.

Dimock, M. E. (1956), 'The Administrative Staff College: Executive development in government and industry', *The American Political Science Review*, vol. 50, no. 1, pp. 167–70.

Dintenfass, M. (1988), 'Entrepreneurial Failure Reconsidered: The case of the interwar British Coal Industry', *Business History*, vol. 62, pp. 1–34.

Dorman, P. (1997), *Markets and Mortality: Economics, dangerous work, and the value of human life*, CUP, Cambridge.

Douglas Gibson, J. (1954), 'Post-War economic development and policy in Canada', *The Canadian Journal of Economics and Political Science*, vol. 20, no. 4, pp. 439–443.

Drummond, D. K. (1995), *Crewe: Railway town, company and people, 1840–1914*, Scolar, Aldershot.

Drummond, G. G. (1977), *The Invergordon Smelter: A case study in management*, Hutchison, London.

Dudley, G. and Richardson J. (2000), *Why Does Policy Change? Lessons from British Transport Policy*, Routledge, London.

Durham, P. (1997), *Highland Whistle Blower: The true story of the Phil Durham Affair*, Northern Books, Edinburgh.

Dumett, R. E. (ed.) (1999), *Gentlemanly Capitalism and British Imperialism: The new debate on empire*, Pearson, London.

Dunne, P. (1990), 'The political economy of military expenditure: An introduction', *Cambridge Journal of Economics*, vol. 14, no. 4, pp. 395–404.

Echewari, J. T. W. (1909), 'Aluminium and some of its uses', *Journal of the Institute of Metals*, vol. 1, no. I, pp. 146–149.

Edgerton, D. (2005), *Warfare State: Britain, 1920–1970*, CUP, Cambridge.

—— (2006), *The Shock of the Old: Technology and Global History since 1900*, Profile, London.

Edmonds, M. (1972), 'Government Contracting and Renegotiation: A comparative analysis', *Public Administration*, vol. 58, pp. 59–65.

Edwards, J. R. (2008), 'Tait, Andrew Wilson (1876–1930)', *Oxford Dictionary of National Biography (ODNB)*, http://www.oxforddnb.com.ezproxy.webfeat.lib.ed.ac.uk/view/article/47710 [accessed 4 March 2008].

Edwards, P., Bélanger, J. and Wright, M. (2002), 'The Social Relations of Productivity: A longitudinal and comparative study of aluminium smelters', *Industrial Relations*, 57, pp. 309–30.

Engwall, L. and Zamagni, V. (eds) (1998), *Management education in historical perspective*, MUP, Manchester.

Evans, E. J. (2004), *Thatcher and Thatcherism*, Routledge, London.

Evenden, M. D. (2004), *Fish versus Power: An environmental history of the Fraser River*, CUP, Cambridge.

Fagerberg, J., Maney, D. and Verspagen, B. (eds) (2009), *Innovation, Path Dependence, and Policy: The Norwegian Case*, OUP, Oxford.

Fear, J. (2007) 'Cartels' in Jones, G. and Zeitlin, J. (eds), *The Oxford Handbook of Business History*, OUP, Oxford.

Fearon, P. (1974), 'The British airframe industry and the state, 1918–35', *EHR*, new series, vol. 27, no. 2, pp. 236–51.

Fellman, S., Iversen, M. J., Sjögren, H. and Thue, L. (eds) (2008), *Creating Nordic Capitalism: The business history of a competitive periphery*, Palgrave Macmillan, Basingstoke.

Fitzgerald, R. (1988), *British Labour Management and Industrial Welfare 1846–1939*, Croom Helm, London.

—— (1989), 'Employers' labour strategies, industrial welfare, and the response to New Unionism at Bryant and May, 1888–1930', *Business History*, vol. 31, pp. 48–65.

—— (1999), 'Employment relations and industrial welfare in Britain: Business ethics versus labor markets', *Business and Economic History*, vol. 28, no. 2, pp. 167–79.

Floud, R. and McCloskey, D. (eds) (1994), *The Economic History of Britain since 1700, Vol. 2: 1860–1939*, CUP, Cambridge.

—— (1994), *The Economic History of Britain since 1700, Vol. 3: 1939–1972*, CUP, Cambridge.

Foreman-Peck, J. and Federico, G. (eds) (1999), *European Industrial Policy: The twentieth-century experience*, OUP, Oxford.

Foster, J. and Woolfson C. (1986), *The Politics of the UCS Work-IN: Class alliances and the right to work*, Lawrence and Wishart, London.

Foucault, M. (2006), *Psychiatric Power: Lectures at the Collège de France 1973–1974*, Palgrave, Basingstoke.

Fox, A. (1985), *History and Heritage: The Social Origins of the British Industrial Relations System*, Allen & Unwin, London.

Francis, M. (2002), 'Tears, tantrums and bared teeth: The emotional economy of three conservative prime ministers, 1951–1963', *Journal of British Studies*, vol. 41, no. 3, pp. 354–65.

Francis, M. and Zweiniger-Bargielowska, I. (eds) (1996), *The Conservatives and British Society 1880–1990*, University of Wales Press, Cardiff.

Fraser, W. (1835), 'United Parishes of Boleskine and Abertarff. Presbtery of Abertarff, Synod of Glenelg', *The New Statistical Account of Scotland. Vol. XIV Inverness, Ross, Cromarty*, W. Creech, Edinburgh, pp. 51–63.

French, D. (1992), *The Strategy of the Lloyd George Coalition, 1916–1918*, OUP, Oxford.

Friedman, A. L. (1977), *Industry and Labour: Class struggle at work and monopoly capitalism*, Macmillan, London.

Frouard, H. (2008), *Du coron au HLM: Patronat et logement social (1894–1953)*, Presses Universitaires de Rennes, Rennes.

Gagni, R., and Nappi, C. (2000), 'The cost and technological structure of aluminium smelters worldwide', *Journal of Applied Econometrics*, vol. 15, pp. 417–32.

Gallie, D., Rose, M. and Penn, R. (eds) (1996), *Trade Unionism in Recession*, OUP, Oxford.

Gandz, S. (1936), 'Mene Mene Tekel Upharsin, a chapter in Babylonian mathematics', *Isis*, vol. 26, no. 1, pp. 82–94.

Garnham, N. (2001), 'Both praying and playing: "Muscular Christianity" and the YMCA in the north-east County of Durham', *Journal of Social History*, vol. 35, no. 2, pp. 397–407.

Gawkroger, D. J. (2004), 'Occupational skin cancers', *Occupational Medicine*, vol. 54, pp. 458–63.

Gazeley, I. (2006), 'The levelling of pay in Britain during the Second World War', *European Review of Economic History*, vol. 10, no. 2, pp. 174–204.

Genieys, W. (2005), 'The sociology of political elites in France: The end of an exception?', *International Political Science Review*, vol. 26, pp. 413–30.

Gibson, J. S. (1985), *The Thistle and The Crown: A history of the Scottish Office*, HMSO, Edinburgh.

Girvan, N. (1976), *Corporate Imperialism: Conflict and Expropriation. Transnational corporations and economic nationalism in the third world*, Myron E. Sharpe, New York.

Glendinning, M. (1997), 'The Ballantyne Report: A "1917 Revolution" in Scottish housing', in D. Mays (ed.), *The Architecture of Scottish Cities*, Tuckwell, East Linton, pp. 161–70.

Glover, I. (1999), 'British management and British history: Assessing the responsibility of individuals for economic difficulties', *Contemporary British History*, vol. 13, no. 3, pp. 121–47.

Goodrich, C. (1975), *The Frontier of Control: A study of British workshop politics*, Pluto Press, London.

Gospel, H. (1992), *Markets, Firms and the Management of Labour in Modern Britain*, CUP, Cambridge.

Gourvish, T. (ed.) (2003), *Business and Politics in Europe 1900–1970: Essays in honour of Alice Teichova*, CUP, Cambridge.

Graham, R. (1982) *The Aluminium Industry and the Third World*, Zed Books, London.

Grant, W. (1993), *Business and Politics in Britain*, Palgrave, London.

Grassie, J. (1983), *Highland Experiment: The story of the Highlands and Islands Development Board*, AUP, Aberdeen.

Green, S. J. D., and Whiting, R. C. (eds) (1996), *The Boundaries of the State in Modern Britain*, CUP, Cambridge.

Gregor, M. J. F. and Crichton, R. M. (1946), *From Croft to Factory: The evolution of an industrial community in the Highlands*, John Nelson & Co., Edinburgh.

Griffiths, J. (1995), "Give my Regards to Uncle Billy...": The rites and rituals of company life at Lever Brothers, c.1900–c.1990', *Business History*, vol. 37, no. 4, pp. 25–45.

Grinberg, I. (2003), *L'aluminium: Un si léger metal*, Gallimard, Paris.

Grinberg, I. and Hachez-Leroy, F. (eds) (1997), *Industrialisation et sociétés en Europe occidentale de la fin du XIXe siècle à nos jours*, Armand Colin, Paris.

Grossman, W. R. (1991), 'Reynolds Metals Company', in Hurst, A. (ed.), *International Directory of Company Histories, Vol. IV*, St James Press, Chicago and London, pp. 186–8.

Habermas, J. and Cronin, C. (1998), 'The European Nation-State: On the past and future of sovereignty and citizenship', *Public Culture*, vol. 10, iss. 2, pp. 403–10.

Hachez-Leroy, F. (1999), *L'Aluminium français: L'invention d'un marché 1911–1983*, CNRS, Paris.

Handley, J. E. (1970), *The Navvy in Scotland*, Cork University Press, Cork.

Hannah, L. (1976), *The Rise of the Corporate Economy*, Methuen, London.

—— (1979), *Electricity before Nationalisation: A study of the development of the electricity supply industry in Britain to 1948*, Macmillan, London.

—— (1986), *Engineers, Managers and Politicians: The first fifteen years of nationalised electricity supply in Britain*, Macmillan, London.

Hardach, G. (1987), *The First World War 1914–1918*, Penguin, Harmondsworth.

Harris, K. (1995), *Attlee*, Weidenfeld and Nicolson, London.

Harper, M. (1998), *Emigration from Scotland between the Wars: Opportunity or exile?*, Manchester University Press (MUP), Manchester.

Harrop, M. (ed.) (1992), *Power and Policy in Liberal Democracies*, CUP, Cambridge.

Harvie, C. (1981), *No Gods and Precious Few Heroes: Scotland 1914–1980*, Blackwell, London.

Hatch, J. (1954), 'African Assignment', *International Affairs*, vol. 30, no. 2, pp. 254–56.

Hatch S. and Fores, M. (1960), 'The Struggle for British Aluminium', *Political Quarterly*, vol. 31, no. 4, pp. 477–87.

Hebbert, M. (2005), 'The street as locus of collective memory', *Environment and Planning D: Society and Space*, vol. 23, pp. 581–96.

Heertje, A. (2005), *Schumpeter on the Economics of Innovation and the Development of Capitalism*, Edward Elgar, Cheltenham.

Heller, M. (2008), 'Sport, bureaucracies and London clerks 1880–1939', *The International Journal of the History of Sport*, vol. 25, no. 5, pp. 579–614.

Henden, J. (2008), 'Stangfjordens Elektrokemiske Fabriker: The First and the Smallest Aluminium Smelter in Norway', *Cahiers d'histoire de l'aluminium*, vol. 41, pp. 95–131.

Henden, J., Frøland, H. O. and Karlsen, A. (2008), *Globalisering gjennom et århundre; Norsk aluminiumindustri 1908–2008*, Fagbokforlaget, Oslo.

Hendrick, H. (1997), *Children, childhood and English society 1880–1990*, CUP, Cambridge.

Hetherington, A. (ed.) (1990), *Highlands and Islands: A generation of progress, 1965–1990*, AUP, Aberdeen.

Hexner, E. (1946), *International Cartels*, Pitman, London.

Higgison, A. (2005), 'Asbestos and British Trade Unions, 1960s and 1970s', *Scottish Labour History*, vol. 40, pp. 70–86.

High, S. (2003), *Industrial Sunset: The making of North America's Rust Belt, 1969–1984*, University of Toronto Press, Toronto.

Higham, R. (1965), 'Government, companies, and national defense: British aeronautical experience, 1918–1945 as the basis for a broad hypothesis', *Business History Review*, vol. 39, no. 3, pp. 323–47.

Hinton, J. (1994), *Shop Floor Citizens: Engineering democracy in 1940s Britain*, Edward Elgar, Aldershot.

Hodgson, G. M. (2001), *How Economics forgot History: The problem of historical specificity in social science*, Routledge, London.

Holmes, H. (1997), 'Employment and Employment Conditions of Irish Migratory Potato Workers (Achill Workers) in Scotland From the Late Nineteenth Century to the Early 1970s', *The Journal of the Scottish Labour History Society* (subsequently *Scottish Labour History*), no. 32, pp. 8–22.

Hornby, W. (1958) *Factories and Plants*, HMSO, London.

Hughes, W. (2008), 'Ross, William, Baron Ross of Marnock (1911–1988)', *ODNB*, http://www.oxforddnb.com.ezproxy.webfeat.lib.ed.ac.uk/view/article/39856?docPos=7 [accessed 15 July 2008].

Hunt, D. (2008), 'Alexander, Harold Rupert Leofric George, first Earl Alexander of Tunis (1891–1969)', *ODNB*, http://www.oxforddnb.com/view/article/30371 [accessed 8 September 2009]

Hunter, J. (1991), *The Claim of Crofting: The Scottish Highlands and Islands, 1930–1990*, Mainstream Publishing, Edinburgh.

—— (1999), *Last of the Free: A millennial history of the Highlands and Islands of Scotland*, Mainstream, Edinburgh.

—— (2006),'The Scottish Highlands: A contested country', in National Museums of Scotland, *Fonn's Duthchas: Land and legacy*, National Museums of Scotland, Edinburgh.

Hurtsfield, J. (1944), 'The control of British raw material supplies, 1919–1939', *EHR*, vol. 14, no. 1, pp. 10–21.

—— (1953), *The Control of Raw Materials*, HMSO, London.

Igartua, J. E. (1996), *Arvida ou Saguenay: Naissance d'une ville industrielle*, McGill-Queen's University Press, Montréal and Kingston, ON.

Industrial Pulmonary Diseases Committee (1936), *Report on a clinical and radiological examination of workers exposed to alumina dust*, IPDC, London.

International Agency for Research on Cancer (1984), *Polynuclear aromatic compounds: Part 3, Industrial exposures*, IARC, Lyon.

Johnman, L. and Murphy, H. (2007), 'Subsidy and Treasury: The trade facilities act and the UK shipbuilding industry in the 1920s', *Contemporary British History*, vol. 22, no. 1, pp. 89–110.

Johnson, F. G. (1986), 'Hydro-electric power in the UK: Past performance and potential for future development', *Institute of Electrical Engineers Proceedings*, vol. 133, no. 3, pp. 110–20.

Johnston, R. and McIvor, A. (2000), *Lethal Work: A history of asbestos tragedy in Scotland*, Tuckwell, East Linton.

Jones, G. (2004), *Multinationals and Global Capitalism from the Nineteenth to the Twenty-First Centuries*, OUP, Oxford.

—— (2005), 'Multinationals from the 1930s to the 1980s', in Chandler, A. D. Jr., and Mazlich, B. (eds), *Leviathans: Multinational Corporations and The New Global History*, CUP, Cambridge.

Jones, H. (1983), 'Employers' welfare schemes and industrial relations in inter-war Britain', *Business History*, vol. 25, iss. 1, pp. 61–75

Jones, G. and Bostock, F. (1996), 'U.S. Multinationals in British Manufacturing before 1962', *Business History Review*, vol. 70, no. 2, pp. 207–56.

Joyce, P. (1980), *Work, Society and Politics: The culture of the factory town in Late Victorian England*, Taylor & Francis, London.

Kaldor, M. (1983), *The Baroque Arsenal*, Pluto Press, London.

Kennedy, G. (ed.) (2008), *Imperial Defence: The old world order 1856–1956*, Routledge, London.

Kessel, A. (2000), *Air, the Environment and Public Health*, CUP, Cambridge.

Kidd, A. and Nicholls, D. (eds) (1998), *The Making of the British Middle Class? Studies of regional and cultural diversity since the eighteenth century*, Sutton, Stroud.

Kinsley, J. (ed.) (1969), *Burns – Poems and Songs*, OUP, Oxford.

Kipping, M. (2003), 'Business–government relations: Beyond performance issues' in Amatori, F. and Jones, G. (eds), *Business History around the World*, CUP, Cambridge, pp. 372–93.

—— (2010), 'Strategizing in a complex environment: Business, government and the Lynemouth aluminium smelter, 1965–1973', Paper to the Economic and Social History Department, University of Glasgow.

Kipping, M. and Cailluet, L. (2010), 'Mintzberg's emergent and deliberate strategies: Tracking Alcan's activities in Europe, 1928–2007', *Business History Review*, vol. 84, no. 1, pp. 75–104.

Kirk, N. (2003), 'A State of War in the Valley of Glencoe: The Ballachulish Quarries disputes, 1902–1905', *Scottish Labour History*, vol. 38, pp. 14–36.

—— (2007), *Custom and Conflict in the 'Land of the Gael': Ballachulish, 1900–1910*, Merlin Press, Trowbridge.

K'Meyer, T. A. and Hart, J. L. (2010), *I saw it coming: worker narratives of plant closings and job loss*, Palgrave Macmillan, New York.

Knauer, M. (2003) 'The "Golden Years": The European Aluminium Industry during the postwar economic boom', *Cahiers d'histoire de l'aluminium*, special issue 1, pp. 11–13.

Knox, W. W. (1999), *Industrial Nation: Work, culture and society in Scotland, 1800–present*, EUP, Edinburgh.

Knox, W. W. and McKinlay, A. (1999), 'Working for the Yankee Dollar: American inward investment and Scottish labour, 1945–70', *Historical Studies in Industrial Relations*, vol. 7, pp. 1–26.

Kornhauser, A., Dubin, R. and Ross, A. (eds) (1954), *Industrial conflict*, McGraw Hill, New York.

Kynaston, D. (2002), *The City of London: A club no more, 1945–2000*, Pimlico, London.

Latour, B. (2005), *Reassembling the Social: An introduction to Actor-Network-Theory*, OUP, Oxford.

Laux, J. M. (1976), *In First Gear: The French automobile industry to 1914*, Liverpool University Press, Liverpool.

Lee, C. H. (1995), *Scotland and the United Kingdom: The economy and the union in the twentieth century*, MUP, Manchester.

Lee, D. and Newby, H. (1983), *The Problem of Sociology: An introduction to the discipline*, Unwin Hyman, London.

Leneman, L. (1989) *Fit for Heroes? Land settlement in Scotland after World War I*, AUP, Abderdeen.

Lesclous, R. (1999), *Histoire des sites producteurs d'aluminium: Les choix stratégiques de Pechiney 1892–1992*, École des Mines, Paris.

—— (2005), 'Nuclear power and the revival of primary aluminium production in Europe', *Cahiers d'histoire de l'aluminium*, special issue 1, pp. 29–36.

—— (2008), 'What bauxite strategy? An overview of the different players and their behaviour from 1890 to the present', *Cahiers d'histoire de l'aluminium*, vol. 40, pp. 11–33.

Levitt, I. (1999), 'The creation of the Highlands and Islands Development Board, 1939–65', *NS*, vol. 19, pp. 85–105

—— (2004), 'The Treasury, public investment and the development of hydro-electricity in the north of Scotland, 1951–64', *Northern Scotland*, vol. 24, pp. 75–92

—— (2005), 'Regenerating the Scottish Highlands: Whitehall and the Fort William Pulp Mill, 1945–63', *Journal of Scottish Historical Studies*, vol. 25, no. 1, pp. 21–39.

Lewis, J. and Smith, H. (1998), 'Excavations at Inverlochy Castle, Inverness-shire, 1983–95', *Proceedings of the Society of Antiquities for Scotland*, vol. 128, pp. 619–644.

Lindsay, J. M. (1975), 'Charcoal iron smelting and its fuel supply: The example of Lorn Furnace, Argyllshire, 1753–1876', *Journal of Historical Geography*, vol. 1, pp. 283–98.

Linkon, S. L. and Russo, J. (2002), *Steeltown USA: Work and memory in Youngstown*, University of Kansas Press, Lawrence.

Lloyd-Jones, R., Maltby, J., Lewis, M. J., and Matthews, M. (2006), 'Corporate governance in a major British holding company: BSA in the interwar years', *Accounting, Business and Financial History*, vol. 16, no. 1, pp. 69–98.

Lobell, S. (1999), 'Second image reversed: Britain's choice of freer trade or imperial preferences, 1903–1906, 1917–1923, 1930–1932', *International Studies Quarterly*, vol. 43, no. 4, pp. 671–93.

Lockwood, D. (1966), 'Sources of variation in working class images of society', *The Sociological Review*, vol. 14, iss. 3, pp. 249–267.

Lyttleton, O. (1962), *The Memoirs of Lord Chandos*, Bodley Head, London.

MacDonald, C. M. (ed.) (1961), *Third Statistical Account of Scotland: County of Argyll*, SAC, Glasgow.

Macdonald, C. M. M. (2000), *The Radical Thread: Political Change in Scotland, Paisley Politics, 1885–1924*, Tuckwell, East Linton.

MacDonald, S. (1997), *Reimagining Culture: Histories, Identities and the Gaelic Renaissance*, Berg, Oxford.

—— (2005), 'Locality and Community: A West Highland Parish', in Beech, J., Hand, O., Mulhern, M. A. and Weston, J. (eds), *Scottish Life and Society, A Compendium of Scottish Ethnology: Volume 9, The individual and community life*, Tuckwell Press, Edinburgh, pp. 403–19.

MacGill, P. (2001), *Children of the Dead End*, Birlinn, Edinburgh.

Machin, G. I. T. (1998), *Churches and Social Issues in Twentieth-Century Britain*, OUP, Oxford.

Macintyre, S. (1980), *Little Moscows: Communism and working-class militancy in Inter-war Britain*, Croom Helm, London.

Mackay, D. I. and Buxton, N. K. (1965), 'The North of Scotland economy: A case for redevelopment?', *Scottish Journal of Political Economy*, vol. 12, no. 4, pp. 18–26.

MacKenzie, A. G. (1980), *Church of Scotland, Kinlochleven: Golden Jubilee 1930–1980*, Church of Scotland, Kinlochleven.

MacKenzie, H. (2003), '"Arsenal of the British Empire"? British orders for munitions production in Canada, 1936–39', *The Journal of Imperial and Commonwealth History*, vol. 31, no. 3, pp. 36–53.

MacKenzie, N. G. (2006), '"Chucking Buns across the Fence?" Government-Sponsored Industry Development in the Scottish Highlands, 1945–1982', *Business and Economic History On-Line*, 4, http://www.thebhc.org/publications/BEHonline/2006/mackenzie.pdf.

—— (2008), 'Be Careful What You Wish For: Comparative Advantage and the Wilson Smelters Project, 1967–82', Unpublished paper to European Business History Association conference, Bergen, 12–14 August.

Maclean, C. I. (2006), *The Highlands*, Birlinn, Edinburgh.

Macleod, J. (1996), *Highlanders: A history of the Gaels*, Sceptre, London.

McGregor, J. (2005), *The West Highland Railway: Plans, politics and people*, John Donald, Edinburgh.

—— (2008), 'Labour relations on the West Highland Railway, 1894–1924', *Scottish Labour History*, vol. 43, pp. 30–46.

Mariage, M. A. (1911), 'The use of aluminium wire in traction motors', *The Tramway and Railway World*, 4 May, pp. 316–18.

Markowitz, G. and Rosner, D. (2002), *Deceit and Denial: The deadly politics of industrial pollution*, University of California Press, Berkeley.

Marsden, B. and Smith, C. (2005), *Engineering Empires: A cultural history of technology in nineteenth-century Britain*, Palgrave Macmillan, Basingstoke.

Martin, J. (2004), 'Fraser, Simon Joseph, fourteenth Lord Lovat and third Baron Lovat (1871–1933)', *ODNB*, http://www.oxforddnb.com.ezproxy.webfeat.lib.ed.ac.uk/view/article/33254?docPos=5 [accessed 5 October 2007].

Marwick, A. (1998), *The Sixties: Cultural revolution in Britain, France, Italy, and the United States, c.1958–c.1974*, OUP, Oxford.

Matthews, D. (1998), 'The Business Doctors: Accountants in British management from the nineteenth century to the present day', *Business History*, vol. 40, no. 3, pp. 75–93.

McCombe, C. (1986), 'One hundred years of aluminium', *Aluminium: The First 100 Years – A Fuel and Metallurgical Journals Technical Supplement*.

McCrone, D. (1992), *Understanding Scotland: The sociology of a stateless nation*, EUP, Edinburgh.

McCulloch, J. and Tweedale, G. (2008), *Defending the Indefensible: The global asbestos industry and its fight for survival*, OUP, Oxford.

McEwen, J. (1981), *Who Owns Scotland: A study in land ownership*, Mainstream, Edinburgh.

McIlroy, J., Fishman, N. and Campbell, A. (eds) (2007), *The High Tide of British Trade Unionism: Trade Unions and industrial politics, 1964–79*, Merlin, Monmouth.

McIvor, A. J. (1996), *Organised Capital: Employers' associations and industrial relations in northern England 1880–1939*, CUP, Cambridge.

—— (2001), *A History of Work in Britain, 1880–1950*, Palgrave, Basingstoke.

McIvor, A. and Johnston, R. (2007), *Miners' Lung: A history of dust disease in British coal mining*, Ashgate, Aldershot.

McKibbin, R. (1998), *Classes and Cultures in England 1918–1951*, OUP, Oxford.

McNeill, J. R. (2000), *Something New Under the Sun: An environmental history of the twentieth-century world*, Norton, New York.

Medical Research Council (1949), *Industrial Fluorosis: A study of the hazard to man and animals near Fort William, Scotland. A report to the Fluorosis Committee by John N. Agate, G.H. Bell, G.F. Boddie, R.G. Bowler, Monamy Buckell, E.A. Cheeseman, T.H.J. Douglas, H.A. Druett, Jessie Garrad, Donald Hunter, K.M.A. Perry, J.D. Richardson, and J.B. de V. Weir*, HMSO, London.

Melling, J. (1980) '"Non-commissioned officers": British employers and their supervisory workers, 1880–1920', *Social History*, vol. 5, no. 2, pp. 183–221.

—— (1992), 'Welfare capitalism and the origins of welfare states: British industry, workplace welfare and social reform, c.1870–1914', *Social History*, vol. 17, no. 3, pp. 561–602.

—— (2003), 'The risks of working and the risks of not working: Trade Unions, employers and responses to the risk of occupational illness in British industry, c.1890–1940s', Discussion paper 12, ESRC Centre for Analysis of Risk and Regulation, London School of Economics.

Melling, J. and McKinlay, A. (eds) (1996), *Management, Labour and Industrial Politics in Modern Europe: The quest for productivity growth during the twentieth century*, EE, Cheltenham.

Melville, Sir H. (1962), *The Department of Scientific and Industrial Research*, DSIR, London.

Merleau-Ponty, M. (2002), *The Phenomonology of Perception: An introduction*, Routledge, London.

Michaels, D. (2008), *Doubt is their Product: How industry's assault on science threatens your health*, OUP, Oxford.

Mikesell, R. F. and Whitney, J. W. (1995), 'An overview of the world mining industry', in C. Schmitz (ed.), *Big Business in Mining and Petroleum*, EE, Aldershot.

Miller, J. (2002), *The Dam Builders: Power from the glens*, Birlinn, Edinburgh.

Millward, R. and Singleton, J. (eds) (1995), *The Political Economy of Nationalisation in Britain 1920–50*, CUP, Cambridge.

Ministry of Munitions (1922), *Official History: Vol. 7, The Control of Materials*, HMSO, London.

Mintzberg, H. and Waters, J. A. (1985), 'Of strategies, deliberate and emergent', *Strategic Management Journal*, vol. 6, pp. 257–72.

Mitchell, J. (1990), *Conservatives and the Union: A study of Conservative attitudes towards Scotland*, EUP, Edinburgh.

Mitchell, J. (1959), 'Pulmonary fibrosis in an aluminium worker', *British Journal of Industrial Medicine*, vol. 16, pp. 123–5.

Moore, D. C. (1976), *The Politics of Deference: A Study of the mid-nineteenth century political system*, Harvester, Hassocks.

Moore-Colyer, R. J. (1999) 'Sir George Stapledon (1882–1960) and the Landscape of Britain', *Environment and History*, vol. 5, pp. 221–36.

Moos, S. (1948), 'The structure of the British aluminium industry', *The Economic Journal*, vol. 58, no. 232, pp. 522–37.

—— (1948), 'Price formation and price maintenance on the aluminium market', *The Manchester School*, pp. 66–93.

Morel, P. (ed.) (1992), *Histoire technique de la production d'aluminium*, Presses Universitaires de Grenoble, Grenoble.

Morrison, D. (1978), 'The beginning and end of the Lewis chemical works, 1857–1874', in Scottish History Society, *Scottish Industrial History: A miscellany*, Scottish Academic Press, Edinburgh, pp. 181–212.

Morrison, N. (1937), *My Story*, Highland News, Inverness.

Morrison, W. M. (1939) 'Aluminium and Highland water power', *17th Autumn Lecture to the Institute of Metals*, pp. 33–467.

Morsel, H. (1996), *Histoire génerale de l'électricité, tome troisième. Une œuvre nationale: l'équipement, la croissance de la demande, l nucléaire (1946–1987)*, Fayard, Paris.

Muller, C. (1945), 'Aluminium and power control', *The Journal of Land & Public Utility Economics*, vol. 21, no. 2, pp. 119–23.

Munro, G. and Hart, K. (2000), '"The Highland Problem": State and community in local development', *Arkleton Research Papers No. 1*, Arkleton Research Centre, Aberdeen.

Mutton, A. F. (1953), 'Hydro-Electric Power Development in Norway', *Transactions of the Institute of Geographers*, vol. 19, pp. 123–30.

Musgrave, P. (1986), *British Alcan Lynemouth Limited*, Alcan, London.

Newbury, C. (2008), 'Milner, Afred, Viscount Milner (1854–1925)', *ODNB*, http://www.oxforddnb.com/view/article/35037 [accessed 15 January 2009].

Newlands, D., Danson, M., McCarthy, J. (eds) (2004), *Divided Scotland? The Nature, Causes and Consequences of Economic Disparities within Scotland*, Ashgate, Aldershot.

Nora, P. (1998), *Realms of Memory: The construction of the French past, Vol. 3: Symbols*, Columbia University Press, New York.

North, D. C. (1990), *Institutions, Institutional Change and Economic Performance*, CUP, Cambridge.

Nottingham, C. (ed.) (2000), *The NHS in Scotland: the legacy of the past and the prospect of the future*, Ashgate, Aldershot.

Oakley, C. A. (ed.) (1937), *Scottish Industry To-day: A survey of recent developments undertaken for The Scottish Development Council*, SDCI, Edinburgh.

O'Donnell, T. V. (1995), 'Asthma and respiratory problems – a review', *The Science of the Total Environment*, vol. 163, pp. 137–45.

O'Hara, G. (2007), *From Dreams to Disillusionment: Economic and social planning in 1960s Britain*, Palgrave, Basingstoke.

Organisation for Economic Co-operation and Development (OECD) (1973), *Problems and Prospects of the Primary Aluminium Industry*, OECD, Paris.

Patterson, W. C. (1985), *Going Critical: An unofficial history of British Nuclear Power*, Paladin, London.

Payne, J. R. (2008), 'Land-use and landscape: Hydro-electricity and landscape protection in the Highlands of Scotland, 1919–1980', unpublished PhD. Thesis, University of St Andrews.

Payne, P. L. (ed.) (1967), *Studies in Scottish Business History*, Cass, London.

—— (1988), *The Hydro: A study of the development of the major hydro-electric schemes undertaken by the North of Scotland Hydro-Electric Board*, AUP, Aberdeen.

Peck, M. J. (1961), *Competition in the Aluminium Industry 1945–1958*, Harvard University Press (HUP), Cambridge, MA.

Peden, G. C. (1979), *British Rearmament and the Treasury: 1932–1939*, Scottish Academic Press, Edinburgh.

—— (2000), *The Treasury and British Public Policy, 1906–1959*, OUP, Oxford.

—— (2005), 'The Managed Economy: Scotland, 1919–2000' in Devine, T. M., Lee, C. H. and Peden, G. C. (eds), *The Transformation of Scotland: The economy since 1700*, EUP, Edinburgh, pp. 233–265.

—— (2007), *Arms, Economics and British Strategy: From dreadnoughts to hydrogen bombs*, CUP, Cambridge.

Pemberton, H. (2004), *Policy Learning and British Governance in the 1960s*, Palgrave, Basingstoke.

Perchard, A. (2007), *The Mine Management Professions in the Twentieth-Century Scottish Coal Mining Industry*, The Edwin Mellen Press, Lampeter.

—— (2007), 'Sculpting the "Garden of Eden": Patronage, community and the British Aluminium Company in the Scottish Highlands, 1895–1982', *Scottish Labour History*, vol. 42, pp. 49–69.

—— (2008), 'A marriage of mutual convenience? The British Government and the UK aluminium industry in the twentieth century', unpublished paper to the EBHA conference, Bergen, 12–14 August.

—— (2010), '"Of the highest Imperial importance": British strategic priorities and the politics of colonial bauxite, c.1915–1958', in Gendron, R., Ingulstad, M., and Storli, E. (eds), *Bauxite, State, and Society in the Twentieth Century*, University of British Columbia Press, forthcoming.

Perks, R. (2010), 'The roots of oral history: Exploring contrasting attitudes to elite, corporate, and business oral history in Britain and the U.S.', *Oral History Review*, vol. 37, iss. 2, pp. 215–54.

Pettigrew, A. M. (1979) 'On Studying Organisational Cultures', *Administrative Science Quarterly*, vol. 24, iss. 4, pp. 570–81.

—— (1986), *The Awakening Giant: Continuity and change in ICI*, Basil Blackwell, Oxford.

Peyton, J. (1997), *Without Benefit of Laundry: The autobiography of John Peyton*, Bloomsbury, London.

Phillips, J. (1996), *The Great Alliance: Economic recovery and the problems of power 1945–1951*, Pluto Press, London.

—— (2008), *The Industrial Politics of Devolution: Scotland in the 1960s and 1970s*, MUP, Manchester.

—— (2009), 'Business and the limited reconstruction of industrial relations in the UK in the 1970s', *Business History*, vol. 51, no. 6, pp. 801–16.

—— (2010), 'Collieries and Communities: The Miners' Strike in Scotland, 1984–1985', *Scottish Labour History*, vol. 46, pp. 18–36.

Picon, A. (2007), 'French engineers and social thought, 18–20th centuries: An archeology of techno-cratic ideals', *History and Technology*, vol. 23, iss. 3, pp. 197–208.

Plowden, E. (1989), *An Industrialist in the Treasury: The Post-War Years*, Andre Deutsch, London.

Polsue, P. G. and Eastwood, I. (1982), 'The modernisation of Lochaber aluminium smelter', *Mining Magazine*, pp. 399–401.

Portelli, A. (1991), *The Death of Luigi Trastulli and Other Stories: Form and meaning in oral history*, State University of New York, New York.

Porter, B. (2004), *The Absent-Minded Imperialists: What the British really thought about empire*, OUP, Oxford.

Porter, M. E. (1998), *Competitive Advantage: Creating and sustaining superior performance*, Palgrave, London.

Porter, M. E (1998), *The Competitive Advantage of Nations*, Free Press, London.

Postan, M. M. (1952), *History of the Second World War: War production*, HMSO, London.

Poulantzas, N. (1978), *Classes in Contemporary Capitalism*, New Left Review, New York.

Priest, N. D. and O'Donnell, T. V. (eds) (1998), *Health in the Aluminium Industry: Managing health issues in the aluminium industry*, Middlesex University, London.

Quigley, H. (1936), *A Plan for the Highlands: Proposals for a Highland Development Board*, Highland Development League, London.

Ramsay, H. (1977), 'Cycles of control: Worker participation in sociological and historical perspective', *Sociology*, no. 11, pp. 481–506.

Reader, W. J. (1975), *Imperial Chemical Industries: A History, Volume II: The First Quarter Century 1926–1952*, Clarendon, Oxford.

—— (1977), 'Imperial Chemical Industries and the State, 1936–1945', in B. Supple (ed.), *Essays in British Business History*, Clarendon Press, Oxford, pp. 227–43.

—— (1980), *Fifty Years of Unilever 1930–1980*, Clarendon, Oxford.

Reason, J. (1990), *Human Error*, CUP, Cambridge.

Reid, C. T., Pillai, A. and Black, A. R. (2005), 'The emergence of environmental concerns: hydroelectric schemes in Scotland', *Journal of Environmental Law*, vol. 17, no. 3, pp. 361–382.

Richards, D. (1977), *Portal of Hungerford. The Life of Marshal of the Royal Air Force Viscount Portal of Hungerford KG, GCB, OM, DSO, MC*, Heinemann, London.

—— (2008), 'Charles Frederick Algernon Portal', *ODNB*, http://www.oxforddnb.com [accessed 21 March 2008].

Richards, J. (1997) *Films and British National Identity: From Dickens to Dad's Army*, MUP, Manchester.

Richardson, P. (2006), 'Robinson, William Sydney (1876–1963)', *Australian Dictionary of Biography*, http://adbonline.anu.edu.au/biogs/A110438b.htm [accessed 23 June 2009].

Ritchie, S. (1997), *Industry and Air Power: The expansion of British aircraft production, 1935–1941*, Frank Cass, London.

Robbins, S. (2005), *British Generalship on the Western Front 1914–18: Defeat into victory*, Frank Cass, London.

Roberts, E. (1995), *A Woman's Place: An oral history of working class women, 1890–1940*, OUP, Oxford.

Roberts, I. (1993), *Craft, Class and Control: The sociology of a shipbuilding community*, Edinburgh University Press, Edinburgh.

Roberts, R. (1992), 'Regulatory responses to the rise of the market for corporate control in Britain in the 1950s', *Business History*, vol. 34, iss. 1, pp. 183–200.

Rodger, R. and Herbert, J. (eds) (2007), *Testimonies of the City: Identity, Community and Change in a Contemporary Urban World*, Ashgate, Aldershot.

Rollings, N. (2007), 'British business history: A review of the periodical literature for 2005', *Business History*, vol. 49, no. 3, pp. 271–92.

Rooth, T. (1993), *British Protectionism and the International Economy: Overseas commercial policy in the 1930s*, CUP, Cambridge.

Roper, M. (1989), *Masculinity and the British Organisation Man since 1945*, OUP, Oxford.

—— (2010), *The Secret Battle: Emotional survival in the Great War*, MUP, Manchester.

Rosen, C. M. (2005), 'The Business–environment connection', *Environmental History*, vol. 10, no. 1, pp. 75–9.

Ross, A. and Rowan-Robinson, J. (1999), 'Behind closed doors: The use of agreements in the UK to protect the environment', *Environmental Law Review*, iss. 1, pp. 82–94.

Ross, D. and Munro, A. (2010), 'Contested Energy: A long-term perspective on renewable power developments in Scotland', Paper to European Business History Association Conference, Glasgow.

Rotherham, L. (1956), 'The research branch of the industrial group of the United Kingdom Atomic Energy Authority', *Proceedings of the Royal Society of London, Series A, Mathematical and Physical Sciences*, vol. 249, no. 1256, pp. 1–15.

Rowlinson, M., Booth, C., Clark, P., Delahaye, A. and Procter, S. (2010), 'Social Remembering and Organisational Memory', *Organization Studies: Special Section on Organizational Memory: The Dynamics of Organizational Remembering and Forgetting* vol. 31, no. 1, pp. 69–87.

Russell, C. A. and Wilmot, S. A. H. (2000), 'Metal extraction and refining', in C. A. Russell (ed.), *Chemistry, Society and Environment: A new history of the British Chemical Industry*, The Royal Society of Chemistry, Cambridge, pp. 311–18.

Russell, C. A. (ed.) (2000), *Chemistry, Society and Environment: A new history of the British Chemical Industry*, The Royal Society of Chemistry, Cambridge.

Sandvik, P. T. and Storli, E. (2007), 'Big business, market power and small nations: The Norwegian aluminium and nickel industry 1920–39', paper to the European Business History Association conference, Geneva.

Saville, R. (ed.) (1985), *The Economic Development of Modern Scotland, 1950–1980*, Edinburgh University Press, Edinburgh.

Savoie, D. J. (2006), *Visiting Grandchildren: Economic development in the Maritimes*, UTP, Toronto.

Sayer, A. (2011), *Why Things Matter to People: Social Science, Values and Ethical Life*, CUP, Cambridge.

Schatzberg, E. (2003), 'Symbolic culture and technological change: The cultural history of aluminium as an industrial material', *Enterprise and Society*, vol. 4, iss. 3, pp. 236–42.

Schein, E. H. (2004), *Organizational Culture and Leadership*, Jossey Bass, San Francisco.

Schmitz, C. (1986), 'The rise of big business in the world copper industry 1870–1930', *Economic History Review (EHR)*, second series, vol. 39, no. 3, pp. 392–410.

Schrafstetter, S. and Twigge, S. (2002), 'Spinning into Europe: Britain, West Germany and the Netherlands. Uranium enrichment and the development of the gas centrifuge, 1964–70', *Contemporary European History*, vol. 11, pp. 253–72.

Schumpeter, J. A. (1976), *Capitalism, Socialism and Democracy*, Unwin, New York.

Scott, J. (1985), *Corporation, Classes and Capitalism*, Hutchinson, London.

Scottish Council (Development and Industry) (1961), *Inquiry into the Scottish economy 1960–1961. Report of a Committee appointed by the Scottish Council (Development and Industry) under the Chairmanship of J. N. Toothill, Esq., C.B.E.*, SCDI, Edinburgh.

Scottish Economic Committee (1938), *The Highlands and Islands of Scotland. A review of the economic conditions with recommendations for improvement*, HMSO, Edinburgh. [*Hilleary Report*]

Seligmann, M. S. (2007), *Naval Intelligence from Germany: The reports of British naval attachés in Berlin, 1906–1914*, Ashgate, Aldershot.

Sen, A. (2002) *Rationality and Freedom*, OUP, Oxford.

Sennett, R. (1998), *The Corrosion of Character: The Personal Consequences of Work in the New Capitalism*, W. W. Norton and Co., New York.

—— (2008), *The Craftsman*, Allen Lane, London.

Sheail, J. (2007), '*Torrey Canyon*: The political dimension', *Journal of Contemporary History*, vol. 42, no. 3, pp. 485–504.

Sheldon R. (2008), 'Dell, Edmund Emmanuel (1921–1999)', *ODNB*, http://www.oxforddnb.com.ezproxy.webfeat.lib.ed.ac.uk/view/article/73166 [accessed 3 June 2008].

Sillars, J. (1986), *Scotland: The case for optimism*, Polygon, London.

Simmons, I. G. (2001), *An Environmental History of Great Britain: From 10,000 years ago to the present*, EUP, Edinburgh.

Smith, C. and Norton Wise, M. (1989), *Energy and Empire. A biographical study of Lord Kelvin*, CUP, Cambridge.

Smith, G. D. (1988), *From Monopoly to Competition: The transformations of ALCOA, 1888–1986*, CUP, Cambridge.

Smout, T. C. (2000), *Nature Contested: Environmental history in Scotland and Northern England since 1600*, EUP, Edinburgh.

Sogner, K. (2008), 'Constructive power: Elkem, 1904–2004', in Fellman, S., Iversen, M. J., Sjögren, H. and Thue, L. (eds), *Creating Nordic Capitalism: The business history of a competitive periphery*, Palgrave Macmillan, Basingstoke, pp. 494–527.

Spackman, A. (1975), 'The role of private companies in the politics of the empire: A case study of bauxite and diamond companies in Guyana in the early 1920s', *Social and Economic Studies*, vol. 24, no. 3, pp. 341–78.

Stedman Jones, G. (1983), *Languages of Class: Studies in English working class history 1832–1982*, CUP, Cambridge.

Stewart, D. (2005), 'Fighting for survival: The 1980s campaign to save Ravenscraig steelworks', *Journal of Scottish Historical Studies (JSHS)*, vol. 25, no. 1, pp. 40–57.

Storli, E. (2007), 'The Norwegian Aluminium Industry, 1908–1940: Swing producers in the hands of the international oligopoly?', *CHA*, special issue 2, pp. 11–28.

—— (2010), *Out of Norway Falls Aluminium: The Norwegian Aluminium Industry in the international economy, 1908–1940*, Norwegian University of Science and Technology doctoral thesis, Trondheim.

Stott, L. (2008), 'Morrison, Sir (William) Murray, (1873–1948), metallurgist and electrical engineer', *ODNB*, www.oxforddnb.com.ezproxy.webfeat.lib.ed.ac.uk/view/article/40348 [accessed 21 September 2008].

Strachan, H. (2004), *Financing the First World War*, OUP, Oxford.

Strangleman, T. (2004), *Work Identity at the End of the Line: Privatisation and Culture Change in the UK Rail Industry*, Palgrave, Basingstoke, p. 59.

Streat, R. (1959), 'Government consultation with industry', *Public Administration*, vol. 37, pp. 1–10.

Stuckey, J. A. (1983), *Vertical Integration and Joint Ventures in the Aluminium Industry*, Harvard University Press (HUP), Cambridge, MA.

Sutherland, C. L. (1960), 'The world outside the factory: Bones and Teeth', *Transactions of the Association of Industrial Medical Officers*, pp. 61–65.

Tanner, D. (2006), 'Richard Crossman, Harold Wilson and Devolution, 1966–70: The making of government policy', *Twentieth Century British History*, vol. 17, no. 4, pp. 545–78.

Tarr, R. S. (1908), 'The Scottish Highlands', *Bulletin of the American Geographical Society*, vol. 40, no. 12, pp. 743–4.

Taylor, R. (1987), 'Trade Unions since 1945: Scapegoats of Economic Decline?', *Contemporary British History*, vol. 1, no. 2, pp. 61–95.

Taylor, W. (1978), 'Manufacturing processes: Aluminium manufacture', *Journal of the Society for Occupational Medicine*, vol. 28, pp. 25–8.

Thomson, A. (2002), 'Anzac memories: putting popular memory theory into practice in Australia' in Perks, R. and Thomson, A. (eds), *The Oral History Reader*, this edition, Routledge, London, pp. 300–10.

Thomson, D. S. and Grimble, I. (eds) (1968), *The Future of the Highlands*, Routledge and Keegan Paul, London.

Thompson, A. (2005), *The Empire Strikes Back? The impact of imperialism on Britain from the mid-nineteenth century*, Pearson, London.

Thompson, E. P. (1971), 'The moral economy of the English crowd in the eighteenth century', *Past and Present*, vol. 50, pp. 76–136.

—— (1993), *Customs in Common*, Penguin, London, p. 85.

Thompson, P. (1997), 'The pyrrhic victory of gentlemanly capitalism: The financial elite of the City of London, 1945–1990', *Journal of Contemporary History*, vol. 32, no. 3, pp. 427–440.

Tiratsoo, N. and Tomlinson, J. (1993), *Industrial Efficiency and State Intervention: Labour 1939–51*, Routledge, London.

—— (1998), *The Conservatives and Industrial Efficiency, 1951–64: Thirteen wasted years?*, Routledge, London.

Tolliday, S. (1987), *Business, Banking, and Politics: The Case of British Steel, 1918–1939*, CUP, Cambridge.

Tomlinson, J. (1997), *Democratic Socialism and Economic Policy: The Attlee Years 1945–1951*, CUP, Cambridge.

—— (2001), *The Politics of Decline: Understanding post-war Britain*, Pearson, London.

—— (2004), *The Labour Governments 1964–1970: Vol. 3, Economic policy*, MUP, Manchester.

—— (2007), 'Mrs Thatcher's macroeconomic adventurism, 1979–1981, and its political consequences', *British Politics*, vol. 2, pp. 3–19.

Torrance, D. (2006), *The Scottish Secretaries*, Birlinn, Edinburgh.

Trebilcock, C. (1969), '"Spin-Off" in British economic history: Armaments and industry, 1760–1914', *EHR*, new series, vol. 22, no. 3, pp. 474–90.

Turner, B. A. (1975), *Industrialism*, Prentice Hall, London, pp. 41–6.

Turner, J. (ed.) (1984), *Businessmen and Politics: Studies of business activity in British politics 1900–1945*, Heinemann, London.

Turnock, D. (1966), 'Lochaber: West Highland growth point', *Scottish Geographical Magazine*, vol. 82, pp. 17–28.

—— (1967), 'Population studies and regional development in West Highland Scotland', *Geografiska Annaler. Series B, Human Geography*, vol. 49, no. 1, pp. 55–68.

—— (1968), 'Fort William, Scotland: Problems of urban expansion in a Highland area', *Tijdschrift voor Econmiske en Social Geografie*, vol. 59, pp. 260–70.

—— (1970), *Patterns of Highland Development*, Macmillan, London.

—— (1979), *Industrial Britain: The New Scotland*, David & Charles, Newton Abbot.

Twigge, S. (2003), 'A baffling experience: Technology transfer, Anglo–American nuclear relations, and the development of the gas centrifuge 1964–70', *History and Technology*, vol. 19, iss. 2, pp. 151–63.

Utiger, R. (1995), *Never Trust an Expert: Nuclear power, government and the tragedy of the Invergordon Smelter*, London School of Economics, London.

Van den Eeckhout, P. (ed.) (2009), *Supervision and Authority in Industry: Western European experiences, 1830–1939*, Berghahn, New York.

Vindt, G. (2006), *Les hommes de l'aluminium: Histoire sociale de Pechiney 1921–1973*, Les editions de l'atelier, Paris.

Wallace, D. H. (1937), *Market Control in the Aluminium Industry*, CUP, Cambridge.

—— (1937), 'Aluminium' in Elliott, W. Y., May, E. S., Rowe, J. W. F., Skelton, A., and Wallace, D. H. (eds), *International Control in the Non-Ferrous Metals*, Macmillan, New York.

Ward, S. (ed.) (2001), *British Culture and the End of Empire*, MUP, Manchester.

Warren R. and Tweedale G. (2002), 'Business ethics and business history: Neglected dimensions in management education', *British Journal of Management*, vol. 13, pp. 209–19.

Watson, M. (2003), *Being English in Scotland*, Edinburgh University Press, Edinburgh.

Watson, N., Weir, S. and Friend, S. (2005), 'The development of muscular christianity in Victorian Britain and beyond', *Journal of Religion and Society*, vol. 7, pp. 1–21.

Weiner, M. (1981), *English Culture and the Decline of the Industrial Spirit 1850–1980*, CUP, Cambridge.

Weinstein, L. H. and Davison, A. (2004), *Fluorides in the Environment: Effects on animals and plants*, HUP, Cambridge, MA.

White, D. (2007), 'Competition among Allies: The North American Triangle and Jamaican Bauxite', *Cahiers d'histoire de l'aluminium*, special issue 2, pp. 39–52.

White, N. J. (2000), 'The business and the politics of decolonization: the British Experience in the twentieth century', *EHR*, vol. 53, no. 3, pp. 544–64.

Wight, D. (1993), *Workers not Wasters: Masculine respectability, consumption and employment in central Scotland*, EUP, Edinburgh.

Willis, P. (1977), *Learning to Labour: How working class kids get working class jobs*, Saxon House, Farnborough.

Wilson, J. F. (1988), *Ferranti and the British Electrical Industry, 1864–1930*, MUP, Manchester.

Wilson, J. F. and Thomson, A. (2006), *The Making of Modern Management: British management in historical perspective*, OUP, Oxford.

Wolfenden, E. B. (1961), 'Bauxite in Sarawak', *Economic Geology*, vol. 56, no. 5, pp. 972–81.

Wrigley, C. J. (2002) *British Trade Unions Since 1933*, CUP, Cambridge.

Wrigley C. (2008), 'After the Great Coal Strike: The government, unions and strikes, 1985–92', paper to the (UK) Economic History Society conference.

Zeitlin, J. (1991), 'The internal politics of employer organization: The Engineering Employers' Federation 1896–1939' in Zeitlin, J. and Tolliday, S. (eds), *The Power to Manage? Employers and industrial relations in comparative-historical perspectives*, Routledge, London, pp. 52–80.

—— (2003), 'Productive alternatives: Flexibility, governnnance, and strategic choice in industrial history' in Amatori, F. and Jones, G. (eds), *Business History around the World*, CUP, Cambridge, pp. 62–82.

Index